NEW KEYNESIAN ECONOMICS/POST KEYNESIAN ALTERNATIVES

This collection of original essays by the world's most prominent Post Keynesian Economists offers a critique of what has come to be known as New Keynesian Economics and provides alternative conceptions to each of its principal areas:

- price and quantity adjustments
- the labour market
- the capital market
- coordination failures
- public policy

The volume is a response to Mankiw and Romer's *New Keynesian Economics*, and to the claim that New Keynesian Economics has provided a unique micro-economic foundation for so-called Keynesian features and Keynesian results.

John Maynard Keynes wrote that any theory based on such foundations was theoretically flawed, did not represent the world in which we lived and would entail disastrous consequences if used as the basis of public policy. Adhering to this position of Keynes, Post Keynesians reject any neoclassical foundation for Keynesian economics. Instead, they provide a richer theoretical foundation – which does not rely on the classical dichotomy embraced by all neo-classical economists – consistent with Keynes' monetary theory of production.

Roy J. Rotheim is Professor of Economics at Skidmore College, Saratoga Springs, New York. He was previously Executive Editor of *Challenge – The Magazine of Economic Affairs* and Associate Editor of the *Eastern Economic Journal.* His principal publications have been in the areas of Keynesian uncertainty, economic theory, and the history of economic thought.

ROUTLEDGE FRONTIERS OF POLITICAL ECONOMY

1 Equilibrium Versus Understanding: Towards the Rehumanization of Economics within Social Theory – Mark Addleson
2 Evolution, Order and Complexity – Edited by Elias L. Khalil and Kenneth E. Boulding
3 Interactions in Political Economy: Malvern After Ten Years – Edited by Steven Prassman
4 The End of Economics – Michael Perelman
5 Probability in Economics – Omar F. Hamouda and Robin Rowley
6 Capital Controversy, Post Keynesian Economics and the History of Economic Theory: Essays in Honour of Geoff Harcourt, Volume One – Edited by Philip Arestis, Gabriel Palma and Malcolm Sawyer
7 Markets, Unemployment and Economics Policy: Essays in Honour of Geoff Harcourt, Volume Two – Edited by Philip Arestis, Gabriel Palma and Malcolm Sawyer
8 Social Economy: The Logic of Capitalist Development – Clark Everling
9 New Keynesian Economics/Post Keynesian Alternatives – Edited by Roy J. Rotheim
10 The Representative Agent in Macroeconomics – James E. Hartley
11 Borderlands of Economics: Essays in Honour of Daniel R. Fusfeld – Edited by Nahid Aslanbeigui and Young Back Choi
12 Value Distribution and Capital – Edited by Gary Mongiovi and Fabio Petri
13 The Economics of Science – James R. Wible
14 Competitiveness, Localised Learning and Regional Development: Specialization and Prosperity in Small Open Economies – Peter Maskell, Heikki Eskelinen, Ingjaldur Hannibalsson, Anders Malmberg and Eirik Vatne
15 Labour Market Theory: A Critical Assessment – Ben J. Fine
16 Women and European Employment – Jill Rubery, Mark Smith, Damian Grimshaw
17 Explorations in Economic Methodology: From Lakatos to Empirical Philosophy of Science – Roger Backhouse
18 Wanting and Choosing: Essays on Subjectivity in Political Economy – David P. Levine

NEW KEYNESIAN ECONOMICS/POST KEYNESIAN ALTERNATIVES

Edited by Roy J. Rotheim

ROUTLEDGE

London and New York

First published 1998
by Routledge
11 New Fetter Lane, London EC4P 4EE

Simultaneously published in the USA and Canada
by Routledge
29 West 35th Street, New York, NY 10001

Typeset in Garamond by Pure Tech India Ltd, Pondicherry
Printed and bound in Great Britain by
TJ International Ltd, Padstow Cornwall

British Library Cataloguing in Publication Data
A catalogue record for this book is available from the British Library

Library of Congress Cataloguing in Publication Data
A catalogue record for this book has been requested
ISBN 0–415–12388–7

CONTENTS

List of contributors viii

Foreword ix
G. C. HARCOURT

Introduction 1
ROY J. ROTHEIM

PART I
Prices, outputs and markets

1 **Setting the record straight** 15
PAUL DAVIDSON

2 **Keynes and the New Keynesians on market competition** 39
J. A. KREGEL

3 **New Keynesian macroeconomics and markets** 51
ROY J. ROTHEIM

4 **Price theory and macroeconomics: stylized facts and New Keynesian fantasies** 71
EDWARD J. NELL

PART II
The labour market

5 **Wages and employment: a Keynesian model** 106
CLAUDIO SARDONI

6 **New Keynesian macroeconomics and the determination of employment and wages** 118
MALCOLM SAWYER

7 **Some questions for New Keynesians** 134
SERGIO NISTICÓ
FABIO D'ORLANDO
Appendix by BENEDETTO SCOPPOLA

8 **Social norms as rational choices** 153
MURRAY MILGATE
CHERYL B. WELCH

9 **New Keynesians, Post Keynesians and history** 168
JOHN B. DAVIS

10 **Elements of conflict in UK wage determination** 182
PHILIP ARESTIS
IRIS BIEFANG-FRISANCHO MARISCAL

PART III
Money, credit rationing and asymmetric information

11 **Menu costs and the nature of money** 205
MALCOLM SAWYER

12 **Knowledge, information and credit creation** 214
SHEILA DOW

13 **Post and New Keynesians: the role of asymmetric information and uncertainty in the construction of financial institutions and policy** 227
DORENE ISENBERG

14 **Disembodied risk or the social construction of creditworthiness?** 241
GARY A. DYMSKI

15 **A Kaleckian view of New Keynesian macroeconomics** 262
TRACY MOTT

PART IV
Post Walrasian macroeconomics

16 **Beyond New Keynesian economics: towards a post Walrasion macroeconomics** 277
DAVID COLANDER

17 **Complex dynamics in New Keynesian and Post Keynesian models** 288
J. BARKLEY ROSSER, JR.

18 **Post Keynesian and strong New Keynesian macroeconomics: compatible bedfellows?** 303
COLIN ROGERS

PART V
Public policy

19 **On a recent change in the notion of incomes policy** 328
GIOVANNI CARAVALE

20 **Money and interest rates in a monetary theory of production** 339
BASIL J. MOORE

21 **Macroeconomic policy for the long haul** 356
HERBERT GINTIS

Bibliography 370
Index 396

CONTRIBUTORS

Philip Arestis, University of East London, England.
Iris Biefang-Frisancho Mariscal, University of East London, England.
Giovanni Caravale, formerly University of Rome, 'La Sapienza', Italy.
David Colander, Middlebury College, USA.
Paul Davidson, University of Tennessee, Knoxville, USA.
John B. Davis, Marquette University, USA.
Fabio D'Orlando, University of Rome, 'La Sapienza', Italy.
Sheila Dow, University of Stirling, Scotland.
Gary A. Dymski, University of California–Riverside, USA.
Herbert Gintis, University of Massachusetts–Amherst, USA.
G. C. Harcourt, University of Cambridge, England.
Dorene Isenberg, Drew University, USA.
J. A. Kregel, University of Bologna, Italy.
Murray Milgate, University of Cambridge, England.
Basil J. Moore, Wesleyan University, USA.
Tracy Mott, University of Denver, USA.
Edward J. Nell, New School for Social Research, USA.
Sergio Nisticó, University of Rome, 'La Sapienza', Italy.
Colin Rogers, University of Adelaide, Australia.
J. Barkley Rosser, Jr., James Madison University, USA.
Roy J. Rotheim, Skidmore College, USA.
Claudio Sardoni, University of Rome, 'La Sapienza', Italy.
Malcolm Sawyer, University of Leeds, England.
Cheryl B. Welch, Simmons College, USA.

FOREWORD

It is a pleasure and a privilege to write a Foreword to Roy Rotheim's volume on *New Keynesian Economics/Post Keynesian Alternatives*. I have known Roy since he was a graduate student and have noted with sustained admiration his range of scholarship, sound judgement and fine analytical abilities. I also know personally most of the contributors to the volume, and their writings, and for them too I have much respect. What inspires them all is their thorough understanding of both the economy and Keynes's interpretation of it. So the contributors are not expressing mere piety sixty years on from the publication of *The General Theory* and fifty years on from the death of Keynes; rather, it is that they recognize deep insights when they see them and want to build on the basis of those insights. To do so not only means making the positive contributions to theory and policy which characterize this volume but also requires the need to criticize error, no matter how well intentioned the perpetrators of it.

Thus, the New Keynesian theories are criticized because they are a thorough misnomer. They are based on a misinterpretation of Keynes which has disastrous consequences for understanding and policy. That Keynes-type results in the economy emanate from price-stickiness is a howler in two senses: it is a false reading of *The General Theory* and, more importantly, of how the economy actually works. If we are ever to get a just, equitable and efficient society, policies which try to increase the flexibility of markets are exactly the wrong ones to propose – that way lies greater instability, crisis and ultimately chaos. The essays in this collection are therefore greatly to be welcomed as an offset to this highly influential but misleading school of thought. The essays show the value of knowing what the really great in the profession actually said and, even more important, what the economy itself is able to tell us.

Now read on.

G. C. Harcourt
Cambridge
March 1997

INTRODUCTION*

Roy J. Rotheim

This collection began with a paper given at the Post Keynesian Study Group, University College London, in the Fall of 1993, called 'On Butterflies' Wings and Hurricanes: A Post Keynesian Critique of New Keynesian Economics' (Rotheim, 1993). I wrote that paper, a very early version of the one contained in the current volume, to come to grips with the publication of a 'Symposium on Keynesian Economics Today' in the Winter 1993 issue of the *Journal of Economic Perspectives* (as well as the then recently published two-volume collection of essays on *New Keynesian Economics* (Mankiw and Romer, 1991a)). The essays in that symposium were primarily written by New and Neo-Keynesians and New Classicals, to the complete exclusion of anyone professing to be Post Keynesian. The total disregard of Post Keynesian economics as a viable programme capable of having something meaningful to say about 'Keynesian economics today', caused me to address and assess, from a Post Keynesian perspective, the Keynesian foundations of New Keynesian economics.[1]

A few nights after that presentation, following a meeting of Tony Lawson's Realism and Economics Group at Cambridge, I found myself lamenting about this unfortunate turn of events to Alan Jarvis, Economics Editor at Routledge. I said something to the effect that 'Post Keynesians should come out with a response to the Mankiw/Romer volume'; to which he replied: 'So do it!'

Upon returning to the States, I began the process by contacting those whom I considered to be the leading Post Keynesians, asking them what they thought of the idea of a volume of Post Keynesian alternatives to New Keynesian economics, and whether they would be willing to contribute to such a project. Some were busy, while some had other agendas which caused them not to be represented. Fortunately, however, most agreed to sign on. What follows, then, is the result of the four-and-a-half-year process to provide some clear alternatives to New Keynesian economics.

This book bears the title 'Post Keynesian Alternatives', emphasizing the plural of that term. Authors were chosen based on their stature in the discipline with the charge to write a piece in response to New Keynesian economics. Broad areas were suggested by me, but that was the extent of the instructions. Still, unanimity among those assessments was not to emerge. Most saw little redeeming value in any variant of New Keynesian economics. Some, however, recognized elements of merit in certain aspects of the overall programme. These differences will be clearly evident to the reader. However, because of this diversity of views and assessments, it seemed appropriate to call this book Post Keynesian *alternatives* to New Keynesian economics.

Should one be concerned about this lack of a single vision amongst Post Keynesians? Bill Gerrard suggests that '[d]efining the nature of Keynesian economics is no easy task. It is a diverse and continuing research effort, characterised at times more by its fragmentation and internal division than by any unity of purpose' (1995, p. 445). Surely he has a point, especially when considering such a discursive text as Keynes's *General Theory*. Still, I think there is more to the matter. To the extent that Post Keynesian economics envisions the economic process as an open system (in the spirit of Keynes), it should come as no surprise that individuals, all calling themselves Post Keynesians, might choose to emphasize different aspects of the overall programme. In fact, this broader and diverse interpretation of Post Keynesian economics should not be seen as a defect of the programme, but rather it should be considered as one of its merits. For it is orthodoxy in which we find the greatest amount of unanimity, differences only occurring when speaking of matters of degree. Unanimity is what one would expect from any theoretical system whose laws rely on a closed system reflecting a constant conjunction of events (see Lawson, 1996). As Paul Wells once wrote in his assessment of Paul Davidson's *Money and the Real World* (1972), it is better to be roughly right as in Davidson's Post Keynesian approach, than to be precisely wrong, as is to be found in the closed economic system of orthodoxy (Wells, 1973).[2]

As one reads through this volume, one will notice what appears at times to be an excessive amount of repetition of defining principles of New Keynesian and Post Keynesian economics, references and even quotations. However, because of the different perspectives held by the individual authors, I chose not to ask them to make what would have seemed to be necessary excisions. Eliminating those redundancies under the guise of enhancing the overall form of the volume would have taken too great a toll, in my opinion, on the content of those individual contributions.

Diversity of opinion is not the sole terrain of Post Keynesians, as one finds an equal amount of differences among New Keynesians about what fits into the parameters of their own programme. Still, with this caveat in mind, I think it is appropriate that there be provided for the general reader brief introductions to these two perspectives to highlight some of the unifying principles of each.

First, what is the nature of this New Keynesian view which has gained so much acclaim amongst such a diversity of esteemed economists and which has equally caused so much dismay amongst Post Keynesians? The long answer to this question can be found in the previously mentioned two-volume collection by Mankiw and Romer (1991a) and in the commendable text by Shaun Hargreaves-Heap (1992). Shorter introductions can be found in Gordon (1990), Mankiw (1990) or the previously mentioned 'Symposium on Keynesian Economics Today' in the

Journal of Economic Perspectives (Mankiw 1993). A brief, although I hope not terribly inaccurate, version might be the following.[3]

New Keynesian economics seeks a distinctively microeconomic foundation to what have previously been accepted as Keynesian macroeconomic conclusions. It focuses on a representative agent's reactions to changes in nominal variables observed in output, capital and labour markets as the sources of fluctuations in output and employment. Weak New Keynesian economics, as defined by Barkley Rosser (in this volume), holds that fluctuations in output and employment in the aggregate are caused by market failures or coordination problems, uniquely focused on the supply side, which either result in wages and prices being relatively sticky in a downward direction or settle at sub-optimal equilibria in response to aggregate demand shocks. Strong New Keynesian economics (also defined by Rosser; see in addition the essay in this volume by Colin Rogers) lays great emphasis on questions of interdependencies, spillovers and strategic complementarities in the context of such coordination failures of the market (see Cooper and John, 1988).

New Keynesian economists, by and large, support the belief that in the long run one would expect sufficient wage and price flexibility to cause any random exogenous nominal shock to be totally borne by other nominal rather than real variables. In the short run, however, there might be small costs perceived by firms which would inhibit them from lowering prices in the face of nominal demand shifts which, as New Keynesian economists contend, have large external aggregate effects on output and welfare loss (see Mankiw, 1985; Akerlof and Yellen, 1985). In the labour market, this perspective seeks explanations as to why nominal as well as real wages do not fall in light of downward fluctuations in demand for output and therefore for labour. Plausible interpretations can be found in the theories of shirking (Shapiro and Stiglitz, 1984), implicit contracts (Azariadis and Stiglitz, 1983), efficiency wages (Yellen, 1984), insider/outsider relationships (Lindbeck and Snower, 1986b) and hysteresis (Blanchard and Summers, 1986). In the capital market, nominal real interest rates are sticky downward, preventing market clearing leading to credit rationing, as a result of asymmetric information between lenders and borrowers over the prospective yields on capital assets (see Stiglitz and Weiss, 1981; Jaffee and Stiglitz, 1990).

Since there is no Walrasian auctioneer to orchestrate the internalization of these externalities, fluctuations in nominal variables will be disproportionately borne by fluctuations in real output and employment, rather than in nominal prices and wages. Thus, the classical dichotomy is violated as nominal changes affect real outcomes and the economy experiences so-called Keynesian features, i.e. secondary effects on employment and output (a form of multiplier mechanism) and Keynesian-type involuntary unemployment as these secondary falls in demand for output coupled with firms' unwillingness to offer lower wages in response to these demand failures cause the full impact to be borne by unemployment rather than downward real wage flexibility.

New Keynesian models that rely on questions of spillover (actions affecting payoffs) and strategic complementarities (actions affecting strategies) indicate that multiple symmetric Nash equilibria may occur which are sub-optimal but stable, in the sense that a series of individual actions will cause outcomes which do not necessarily improve economic welfare. Low-level equilibria can occur because firms do not have the incentive to lower their price or change output. However, any change in output benefits consumers through a spillover effect or demand externality which, in turn, allows for strategic complementarities and movements to higher-level equilibria through multiplier effects (Cooper and John, 1988). The potential richness of this approach is reflected in the extent to which multiplier effects brought about by strategic complementarities cause income to change, affecting the underlying circumstances facing each individual.

How this programme perceives the necessity of policy intervention differs among adherents. Intervention may be warranted to the extent that the market is unable to extricate itself from coordination failures (see Mankiw and Romer, 1991b, p. 3). Still, the overriding concern centres on questions relating to a natural rate of unemployment and a non-accelerating inflation rate of unemployment. Thus, DeLong and Summers 'raise questions about the validity of the natural rate hypothesis and argue that demand management policies can and do affect not just the variance, but also the mean, of output and unemployment' (1988, p. 433). At the other extreme, Ball and Mankiw observe that their

> model exhibits a strong form of the natural rate hypothesis: the average level of (log) output is invariant to the distribution of aggregate demand. We thus provide a counterexample to the claim that asymmetric (price) rigidity provides a rationale for demand stabilisation.
>
> (1994, p. 248).

As a basis for comparison, and despite the previous disclaimer about the potential richness in the diversity of interpretations about what is Post Keynesian economics, I offer the following. The interested reader who seeks a fuller exposition should consult the volumes by Philip Arestis (1992), Paul Davidson (1994b), Marc Lavoie (1992) and Victoria Chick (1983). Shorter introductions can be found in Harcourt (1985), Harcourt and Homouda (1988), Dow (1991), Chick (1995), Sawyer (1995) and Arestis (1996a).

Post Keynesian economics carries on in the tradition of classical political economy, especially with regard to Smith, Malthus, Ricardo (to a lesser degree), Marx, Kalecki and Keynes. It accepts Keynes's notion of a monetary theory of production in which interactions between nominal and real variables are not seen as *violations* of the Classical Dichotomy. In fact, Keynes rejected the validity of that dichotomy at any point other than at full employment equilibrium. The appropriate dichotomy, according to Keynes, occurred between the individual firm or industry, and industry as a whole (see 1936, ch. 21). Unlike the Orthodox approach, in which firm behaviour and market phenomena determine *relative prices*, while *nominal prices* occur in the aggregate,[4] a Post Keynesian perspective recognizes the significance of nominal contracting at the level of the individual (for both output and input pricing decisions). Labour is seen to negotiate for a *money* wage, no matter how much real wages are kept in mind, firms seek *money* profits, and savers hold financial assets in search of *monetary* returns. The validity of this *monetary theory of production* does not follow because of the imperfectionist assumption of money illusion on the part of firms or suppliers of labour or capital. Instead, it bears credibility because in a world of fundamental uncertainty, bargaining in money terms denotes *rational* behaviour (see Davidson, 1991, 1994b; Lawson, 1985, 1991; Rotheim, 1988, 1995a). Uncertainty, in this case, is not seen as an imperfection in an otherwise perfect configuration of economic reality (implying a closed system based on constant conjunctions of events), but rather as a logical extension of viewing an economy in terms of an open system. Any form of methodological individualism or crude holism is thereby rejected, as agency and structure presuppose the existence of the other (see Lawson, 1988, 1997; Rotheim, 1988). As a result, questions pertaining to the level as well as fluctuations in the absolute price level emanate from circumstances occurring at the level of the firm and industry, in the context of economy-wide interactions of the consequences of those behaviours, rather than from exogenous monetary shocks to pre-existing equilibrium positions (as is the customary approach of New Keynesianism). Thus, it is not of interest to Post Keynesians to enquire as to the extent to which changes in the money supply violate real sector equilibria (see Moore, in this volume).

By and large, Post Keynesian theory holds as unacceptable the transition *in thought* from individual markets to markets in the aggregate (a weak form of methodological individualism). It was to this contention that Keynes directed his accusation that the postulates of orthodoxy did not characterize the world in which we lived, and that to use such logic to make policy prescriptions would have disastrous effects on employment and output as a whole (see 1936, ch. 1). Because the Post Keynesian approach disavows the metaphor of individual markets when considering employment and output as a whole, questions which are important to New Keynesian economics, which stand at the heart of what they believe to be Keynesian economics – that being the speeds of reaction between prices and quantities – lose all relevance in a Post Keynesian world (see Part I in this volume).

Moreover, because rational decision making occurs in light of fundamental uncertainty, money matters in a way that is profoundly richer and more general in comparison to the interpretation offered by orthodoxy in which it serves, at best, as a neutral means of circulation (which can be temporarily upset as a result of short-run imperfections in otherwise smoothly functioning markets). To the extent that monetary considerations bear directly on individual rational decision making, it is possible for money to be demanded for its purposes as liquidity *par excellence*, causing it to remain, at times, primarily in financial rather than industrial circulation. The demand for money, itself, as a store of wealth and the subsequent demand revealed in a means of payment (distinct from means of purchase), can be the signal for, as well as the result of, effective demand failures that cannot be explained by imperfections in the markets for goods, labour or capital. The imperative for sustaining the Classical Dichotomy forces Orthodox economists (including New Keynesians) to posit an exogenous nominal money stock which can be controlled by the monetary authorities to observe the extent to which money neutrality is or is not violated. By integrating monetary factors into real decision making processes, Post Keyensian economists are not shackled by this unrealistic assumption regarding the stock of money, but rather are freer to articulate a more general perspective by which the money stock can change either exogenously (through policy actions) or endogenously (by virtue of a modern credit-money-based banking system).

From a Post Keynesian perspective, cyclical fluctuations do not occur because markets fail, in the traditional sense of the term – especially as a result of imperfections in those markets – but rather because the organic interdependencies among all agents, in terms of industry as a whole, cause the relationship among the variables of income, output and spending, in an open sense, to yield contracting or expanding concentric results. Such normal tendencies in capitalist economies have nothing to do with traditional market conceptualizations and cannot, therefore, be mitigated by any form of manipulation of factors involved in the internal natures of those markets; sticky prices, sticky wages and sticky interest rates simply do not matter. In this regard, Post Keynesians would find troublesome the statement by Alan Blinder that sticky wages and prices explain 'why recessions cure themselves only slowly' (1991, p. 89). Whether recessions *cure* themselves has nothing to do with sticky wages or prices. Recessions do not occur or worsen because prices somehow become artificially high; nor do they abate to the extent that those prices fall. Market clearing is not the appropriate metaphor when speaking of employment and output as a whole. Rather, recessions occur, from a Post Keynesian perspective, on account of an implosive concentricity among income, output and spending. The extent to which things are relatively cheaper does not expedite a recovery if the income to purchase those goods and services is not sufficient to support those purchases – *at any reasonable price.*

A Post Keynesian interpretation of and proposals for ameliorating such occurrences involves a dual focus on relations occurring within firms as well as on factors beyond the language of the individual firm, in favour of language unique to industry as a whole. Assessing the nature of these processes and intervening when necessary is a logical outgrowth of such an interpretation of economic phenomena. Intervention is not intended to rectify imperfections in markets, but rather to reverse those processes that result from those organic interdependencies endemic to market economies.

ACKNOWLEDGEMENTS

This volume owes many debts. Philip Arestis and Victoria Chick provided the initial invitation for me to speak at the Post Keynesian Study Group. Adrian Winnett was instrumental in allowing four of the papers in this volume to be presented at a subsequent meeting of the PKSG in October of 1994. Alan Jarvis was the catalyst to getting this project off the ground and the stable force behind my continued attempts to shepherd this flock of cats to the pen. Many thanks, also, to Neville Hankins and Sally Carter at Routledge. John Hillard provided immeasurable moral and technical support from beginning to end; I tapped, probably too often, his wide knowledge and editorial expertise. Kate Asmuth and Thanuja Lintotawela served as tireless and trustworthy assistants throughout the editorial process. Geoff Harcourt was extremely gracious in agreeing to write the Foreword to this volume. It is with deep sadness that I must report the premature death of Giovanni Caravale in May of 1997. Giovanni's friendship and mentoring to so many Post Keynesian economists throughout the world will be profoundly missed. And Paul Davidson fitted me with the initial set of spectacles without which I would never have bothered to think about Keynes or Post Keynesian economics in the first place. The greatest debt, however, goes to all of the authors who, despite their busy schedules and sometimes divergent opinions, saw enough of a common purpose to commit themselves to this project of providing some Post Keynesian alternatives to New Keyensian economics.

NOTES

* Thanks to Victoria Chick, Geoff Harcourt, John Hillard, Tim Koechliln and Malcolm Sawyer for reading an earlier version of this introduction.

1 By then, there were only two critical pieces written by Post Keynesians. See Davidson (1992) and Lawler (1993).

2 Referring to Major Douglas, Mandeville, Malthus, Gesell and Hobson, Keynes notes that 'following their intuitions, [they] have preferred to see the truth obscurely and imperfectly rather than to maintain error, reached indeed with clearness and consistency and by easy logic but on hypotheses inappropriate to the facts' (1936, p. 371).

3 This section relies, in part, on Rotheim (1997).

4 Orthodoxy focuses on explaining *fluctuations* in the absolute price level through changes in the money supply given real sector equilibrium. It is incapable of explaining the *existence* of the absolute price level, for it is incapable of proving the existence of money (see Hahn, 1965).

Part I

PRICES, OUTPUTS AND MARKETS

Part I

PRICES, OUTPUTS AND MARKETS

The first part of this book contains chapters which consider the broader theoretical issues underlying New Keynesian economics. As was pointed out in the Introduction, there are so many ways that economists have used the name *Keynesian*, that it is hard to know which writer is falling into which frame of reference. For example, New Keynesians admonish New Classical economists for their assumption of instantaneous market adjustment, despite the fact that they share a heuristical framework of thinking in terms of markets and factors underlying market phenomena. Still, on which side of the market clearing fence they fall determines their particular acceptance of government intervention as a device for smoothing business cycles, confirming their self-assigned terminological distinction between New *Keynesian* and New *Classical* economics.

New Keynesians and Post Keynesians share the *Keynesian* mantle, along with, alas, Neo-Keynesians, as well. Neo-Keynesians share the importance of policy activism with New Keynesians, and play down (although do not abandon) market metaphors when thinking in terms of aggregate structures. However, both of these latter types of Keynesians embrace notions of a future outlined by probability distributions (risk) which force their thinking about economic phenomena into conjunctions of events yielding relatively determinate solutions (see Lawson, 1994).

The next four chapters consider these myriad incarnations of the phrase *Keynesian* from a *Post* Keynesian perspective. Together, they attempt to set the tone by which the remainder of the chapters in this book may be appreciated. The common foci of these chapters are the extents to which thinking in terms of markets to understand employment and output as a whole are methodologically and theoretically tenable. The reader is asked to think, as he or she works through this first part, about Keynes's critical point in the *Preface* to *the General Theory*, that theories based on market metaphors can explain shifts in employment and output between and among firms and industries in an economy, but that such frameworks are not capable of analysing situations in which employment and output change for *industry as a whole.*

Appropriately, the story gets off the ground with a contribution by Paul Davidson. In his 'Setting the Record Straight', Davidson takes on both the Neo-Keynesians and the New Keynesians as he attempts to clarify what he believes to be among the salient issues which distinguish their *Keynesian* views from his own Post Keynesian programme. Davidson investigates how James Tobin has attempted to distinguish between what he believes is Keynes's framework of economic analysis and that provided by New Keynesians. Tobin insists that Keynes's *General Theory* logic is still the appropriate analytical system for solving today's major macroproblems. In this regard he finds the New Keynesian perspective to be a *caricature* of Keynes and therefore not very useful for policy purposes. Consistent with a proper Keynesian perspective, Tobin asserts that the correct focus should be on the principle of effective demand and not price rigidity in the face of nominal shocks. However, Davidson asserts that in presenting what he believes to be this proper Keynesian analysis, Tobin insists that he will not 'defend the literal text of *The General Theory*'. Such a dismissal, according to Davidson, has given Tobin a licence to promulgate an updated version of the *old* (neoclassical synthesis) Keynesianism, focusing on a partial view of Keynes, maintaining too many of those limiting assumptions that Keynes, himself, was attempting to overthrow.

Thus, Davidson attempts to set the record straight on what Keynes believed to be his revolutionary analysis. By comparing Keynes's literal text with the analyses of Tobin and those of the New Keynesians, this chapter demonstrates that both Tobin's Old Keynesian as well as New Keynesian models require restrictive analytical foundations which were explicitly rejected by Keynes as necessary conditions for his *General Theory*. Davidson's identification of Tobin's asserting that 'all Keynesian macroeconomics really requires that product prices and money wages are not perfectly flexible', becomes an admission that New *and* Old Keynesian models are merely *special cases* requiring, for logical consistency, additional restrictive classical axioms that are not necessary for a general theory. Here it is evident that Tobin has not rejected the traditional market metaphor of orthodoxy in favour of Keynes's theory of effective demand.

At the heart of much of the New *and* Old Keynesian logic are still questions pertaining to speeds of adjustment of prices and quantities in market-based logical frameworks. Among the many contributions one finds in this chapter by Davidson is the identification of a correct interpretation of Keynes's theory of effective demand in which the very question of the speeds of adjustment between prices and quantities is inappropriate and meaningless. One cannot have it both ways: a theory of effective demand deals with the interdependent natures of aggregate demand *and* aggregate supply regardless of the degree of competition, and therefore regardless of the existence of constraints on individual behaviour which cause the analysis to slip back into traditional modes of reasoning.

To repeat, what needs to be considered, then, is the possibility that any programme which calls itself *Keynesian* must reject market metaphors along with all of the heuristical implications that such metaphors require. This conjecture runs like a thread through all of the chapters contained in the first part of this book, as well as in many if not most of the chapters in subsequent parts.

Next, Jan Kregel takes up some of the points addressed by Davidson, in the second chapter entitled 'Keynes and the New Keynesians on Market Competition'.

Kregel asserts that interpretations of the 1930s' Depression, including the rather interesting ones put forth by Irving Fisher, were not consistent with Keynes's. Any attempt to understand those events in terms of 'a pathological malfunctioning of the competitive price mechanism' was misguided. Keynes's interpretation, that there could exist an excess supply of goods and labour, had no grounding in a market-based framework and thus questions surrounding the degree of competition as an explanation for such excess supplies were immaterial. Whether wages and prices were flexible or not made no difference whatsoever to the framework being proposed by Keynes to understand the problem.

As Kregel points out, such a warning was not heeded by the host of economists during and following Keynes's lifetime who continued to think in terms of market metaphors, enquiring about the extent to which wages were or were not rigid and markets were or were not perfect, all in attempting to understand the causes of economy-wide unemployment. Questions at the heart of Keynes's own framework, centring on money and uncertainty, were relegated to secondary status.

Kregel explores the ideas of Joan Robinson, G. B. Richardson and Ronald Coase on market process and price adjustment in an attempt to show that, like Keynes, their analyses lead to the conclusion that the extent to which free market economies adjust does not rely on the flexibility of wages or prices: 'The real problem', we see Kregel saying, 'concerns the impact of imperfect information and the ways individuals respond to uncertainty over the future implication of currently available information, including prices.'

From here Kregel focuses his attack on the New Keynesian theories of wage and interest rate rigidities, having a common lineage in Akerlof's writings on asymmetric information.

Then, the goal of my own contribution to this volume, 'New Keynesian Macroeconomics and Markets', is to identify Keynes's own criticisms of market-based interpretations of economic fluctuations. From a New Keynesian perspective, economic downturns, unemployment and sluggish capital accumulation emanate from imperfections in output, labour and capital markets, respectively. Keynes rejected any methodological individualist interpretation of market failure as the basis for economic disequilibria, contending that such heuristical frameworks could only be considered if output and employment in the aggregate were not capable of changing. As such, one can only wonder, as Keynes did about A. C. Pigou's understanding of the situation over sixty years ago, how it is possible to enquire into the causes of fluctuations in output and employment in the aggregate, when the method underlying such an investigation only has validity when neither of those variables may change. Continued adherence to a New Keynesian perspective after it is shown to have no consistent theoretical foundation can only be explained by an equally suspicious adherence to the crudest form of positivism, another element of coherence between New Keynesian and New Classical (neoclassical) perspectives.

The second half of this essay addresses newer incarnations of New Keynesian economics, what Barkley Rosser has referred to as 'Strong New Keynesianism', in which irregularities in market-based scenarios can cause strategic complementarities, spillovers and multipliers, which allows for the possibility of cumulatively caused changes in aggregate output and employment. What I indicate in this section is that such innovations come a long way to considering the organic interdependencies that were on Keynes's mind as he formulated his theory of effective demand. However, it was these organic interdependencies that also laid the foundation for Keynes's rejection of market-based metaphors in macroeconomic analysis. As such, in their effort to push outward and beyond the limits of the weak New Keynesian analysis, i.e. with their acceptance of many of the salient thrusts of Keynes's perspective, they have unwittingly rejected the very foundation of the weak New Keynesianism that provided their initial impetus into considering such questions.

The final chapter in this first part of the book, 'Price Theory and Macroeconomics: Stylized Facts and New Keynesian Fantasies', is written by Edward J. Nell. In light of the development of New Keynesian economics, Nell wants us to think about whether economic relationships are timeless (as seems to be the case underlying all neoclassically based theories of rational choice) or whether they should be considered to be '*historical*, in the sense that they hold for particular periods of history'? He observes that general equilibrium theories of price (included in which is New Keyensian economics) are abstracted from time or historical context, such that many of the rich institutional factors which originally provided the impetus for such theories have been lost. What Nell contends is that the stylized facts which provided for the foundation of price theories and macroeconomics (and which are implicitly retained) do not reflect the world in which we now live and function. In an earlier period, Nell believes that markets were more akin to the representations depicted by orthodoxy, whereas now 'the stabilizing aspects of market adjustment appear to have vanished . . . market responses appear to exacerbate fluctuations, as would be expected from Keynesian theory and from early Keynesian accounts of the business cycle'. In the former, output was more inflexible over sectors, such that prices might have been considered as stabilizing factors. However, with new and modern technologies, the ability of output and employment to be more liable to change causes the focus of stabilization and destabilization to switch from prices to output and employment.

Put succinctly, Nell's aim in this chapter is to indicate that *history matters*, that the conditions which underlaid what he calls the *Old Trade Cycle of the Nineteenth Century*, which still appear to permeate neoclassical thinking (small business units, inflexible methods of production, flexible prices and money wages, a functioning price system which helped indicate cyclical changes), are profoundly different from conditions that have been evident in the era after World War II.

1

SETTING THE RECORD STRAIGHT

Paul Davidson

On page IX of the Preface to the printed German language edition of *The General Theory of Employment, Interest and Money*, published by Duncher and Humblot in 1936, the following sentences appear:

> This is one of the reasons which justify my calling my theory a *General* [emphasis in the original] Theory. Since it is based on *fewer restrictive assumptions* [*weniger enge Voraussetzungen stutz*] than the orthodox theory, it is also more easily adopted to a large area of different circumstances.[1]

These sentences echo Keynes's insistent theme that a general theory required fewer restrictive axioms. For example, Keynes declared classical economists

> resemble Euclidean geometers in a nonEuclidean world who, discovering that in experience straight lines apparently parallel often meet, rebuke the lines for not keeping straight.... Yet, in truth, there is no remedy except *to throw over the axiom of parallels and to work out a non-Euclidean geometry. Something similar is required in economics today.*
>
> (1936, p. 16, emphasis added).

In any logical argument, it is for those who adopt highly special assumptions to justify them, rather than for those who dispense with such axioms to prove a general negative. Thus, by declaring that his analysis was a general theory that required fewer restrictive axioms, Keynes placed the onus on the classical economists to justify their assumptions that an economic system required the axioms of gross substitution (i.e. everything is a substitute for everything else), neutral money and an ergodic economic processes so that the future was not uncertain – rather future outcomes were controlled by immutable objective probability distributions.[2]

Galbraith (1994) has noted the relationship between the 'first three words' of Keynes's book (i.e. 'The General Theory') and Einstein's General Theory of Relativity. Galbraith demonstrates that 'The parallels between Keynes's economics and Einstein's relativity theory are deep enough, and evidently intentional enough, to provide a useful framework for thinking about what Keynes meant to do with his scientific revolution' (ibid., p. 62).

Tobin, on the other hand, provides a different interpretation of what Keynes meant by calling his analysis 'The General Theory'. Tobin does declare that 'the crucial issue of macroeconomic theory today is the same as it was sixty years ago when John Maynard Keynes revolted against what he called the 'classical' orthodoxy of his day' (1992, p. 387). Moreover, Tobin claims to be an 'unreconstructed old Keynesian' who believes that macroeconomic models based on Keynes's chapter 3 principle of effective demand are more useful than either 'old or new classical macroeconomics', or even New Keynesian models (1993, pp. 45–6).

In discussing 'the issues of theory, Keynesian versus Classical, both then and now' (Tobin, 1992, p. 387), however, Tobin insists that 'the word "General" in the title was used to distinguish his [Keynes's] theory of a demand-constrained regime *vis-à-vis* the 'classical' supply-constrained market-clearing model' (ibid., p. 392). For Tobin, therefore, the term general does not mean that Keynes's principle of effective demand analytical framework can apply to both less than full employment and over full employment systems without requiring the restrictive axioms of classical theory. Instead Tobin suggests that Keynes's 'principle of effective demand' applies *only* to the case where 'aggregate economic activity is constrained by demand but not supply' (ibid., p. 387). Classical theory rather than Keynes's principle of effective demand then would be applicable to 'a second regime' where 'extra demand could not be satisfied at the economy's existing capacity to produce'[3] (ibid.).

This dichotomization between a Keynes demand-constrained regime and a classical supply-constrained regime is part of mainstream folklore. It is, however, in direct conflict with Keynes's argument that the principle of effective demand is a general theory applicable to *all* economic regimes, while the classical case was not applicable to any real world economy. The classical theory is merely

> a special case only and not the general case . . . the characteristics of the special case assumed by the classical theory happen not to be those of the economic society in which we actually live, with the result that its teaching is misleading and disastrous if we attempt to apply it to the facts of experience.[4]
>
> (Keynes, 1936, p. 3).

In other words, the classical analysis is obtained by adding additional special axioms to Keynes's general theory (similar to adding the axiom of parallels to the general geometry situation where space–time is curved (Galbraith, 1994, p. 65)). But Keynes warns that the policy implications of applying the classical case to real world economic problems is misguided and calamitous.

Despite Tobin's claim that Keynes's principle of effective demand does not apply to a supply-constrained regime, in writing *How To Pay For The War* Keynes (1940) used his principle of effective demand to explain how his 'General' theory is applicable even to the full employment supply-constrained war years. The classical analysis simply would not do. The fact that Keynes wrote *How To Pay For The War* illustrates there is a conflict between Tobin's restrictive claim that Keynes's general theory is not applicable to real world supply-constrained regimes and Keynes's claim of universal applicability of his general theory to the world in which we live. This difference can be traced to analytical incompatibilities between Tobin's brand of (Old) Keynesianism and Keynes's own explicit development of the principle of effective demand in *The General Theory*.

Tobin (1993, p. 46) does not 'defend the literal text of *The General Theory*' in putting forth what he claims is the substance of Keynes's *general* theory. As a debating device, this caveat is impeccable for it allows Tobin to defend whatever he thinks is 'Keynesian' without having to demonstrate that his model is based on the explicit properties and axioms that Keynes identified as *essential* to the *substance* of his principle of effective demand. Nevertheless, anyone claiming to put forth an explanation that reflects the *substance* of Keynes's *General Theory* must be required, at a minimum, to present nothing that is explicitly in disagreement with Keynes's own words.

Tobin rebukes New Keynesians for developing 'a caricature of the true thing' (Tobin, 1992, p. 395) when they argue that output and employment fluctuations result solely from exogenous changes in *nominal* demand in the face of *rigid* nominal wages and prices. Tobin argues that the 'central Keynesian proposition is *not* nominal price *rigidity* but the principle of effective demand' (Tobin, 1993, p. 46, emphasis added). If, however, Tobin has misinterpreted what Keynes meant by his 'General' theory, then, as we will demonstrate, his Old Keynesianism is also a travesty of the real thing.

This chapter will demonstrate that Tobin's interpretation of Keynes is in expositional and logical conflict with Keynes's own writings on what is *essential* to and the *substance* of the general theory of employment. In the hope that the Old and New Keynesians' incorrect representations of Keynes's *General Theory* will not continue to be perpetuated in the literature, this chapter will set the record straight by demonstrating:

1 Keynes recognized that his *general* theory of employment required the jettisoning of some restrictive axioms of classical theory, while retaining the possibility of instantaneously flexible prices. This permitted Keynes to demonstrate that in the general case (a) the determinants of the aggregate demand function were not identical with the determinants of aggregate supply (i.e. supply did not create its own demand), and (b) it is in the aggregate demand determinants and the demand for liquidity, and *not* in imperfect market price (supply) conditions, that a general theory of unemployment equilibrium for a market-oriented, *laissez-faire* economy is nested.
2 Keynes's principle of effective demand produces different *long-run*, *permanent* policy implications for the role of government compared to the policy implications of Old Keynesian, New Keynesian, Old Classical or New Classical models.

TOBIN VS. KEYNES ON EFFECTIVE DEMAND AND SUPPLY IMPERFECTIONS

To begin with an obvious, albeit not the most important, expositional inconsistency, Tobin states: 'aggregate spending in dollars on goods and services . . . is not what Keynes meant by "effective demand". He [Keynes] was referring to demands for quantities of goods and services, *measured in constant prices, not dollars*' (1992, pp. 394–5, emphasis added). When analysing the question of whether perfectly flexible wages and prices assure full employment, however, Keynes explicitly states:

> the precise question at issue is whether the reduction in money-wages will or will not be accompanied by the same *aggregate effective demand as before measured in money*, or, at any rate, by an aggregate effective demand which is not reduced in full proportion to the reduction in money-wages.
>
> (1936, p. 259–60, emphasis added).[5]

More importantly, however, Tobin insists that the *absence* of 'perfectly and instantaneously flexible prices' is *a necessary condition* for Keynes's unemployment equilibrium; and that '[c]omplete price flexibility means instantaneous adjustment, so that prices are always clearing markets, jumping sufficiently to all demand and supply shocks' (1992, p. 394). This is in direct conflict with Keynes's claim that his general theory was applicable to 'any degree of competition' and therefore unemployment equilibrium can occur even with perfectly competitive flexible prices (1936, p. 245). This view merely perpetuates the modern fable that Keynes' underemployment analysis requires a reversing of the Marshallian speed of adjustment of prices and quantities.

In Keynes's 'General' theory, *complete price flexibility is neither a necessary nor a sufficient condition for full employment equilibrium.*[6] Since Old and New 'Keynesians' typically start their analysis of Keynesian unemployment with an economy initially in full employment equilibrium (with less than perfect price flexibility),[7] there is a 'Keynesian' presumption that instantaneous flexibility is not a necessary condition for the existence of full employment equilibrium.

Is complete flexibility a sufficient condition for full employment in Keynes's general theory? Tobin's insistence that 'Keynesian' unemployment requires less than instantaneous price flexibility means that it is an *aggregate supply imperfection(s)* in market price adjustments that prevents a market system from establishing full employment after any demand shock. If this is true, then as a matter of logic and despite Keynes's claim in chapter 3 (1936, pp. 24–6), unemployment cannot be attributed *solely* to the determinants of the aggregate demand function independent of aggregate supply conditions.

If Tobin is correct, this would be an amazing *volte face* for Keynesianism. Keynes would be a charlatan theorist who was really only pretending he has produced a theoretical revolution. In Tobin's own words, '*Keynes pretended to be assuming pure competition in all markets*' (1993, p. 56, emphasis added). Fortunately for Keynes's reputation as a theorist, Tobin's claim of what the substance of Keynes's general theory is, is in direct conflict with what Keynes wrote. Tobin's brand of Keynesianism is as much a travesty of Keynes's principle of effective demand as is New Keynesianism.

TOBIN'S OLD KEYNESIAN *IGNORATIO ELENCHI*

Tobin declares that 'the absence of instantaneous and complete market clearing' causes an uncleared labour market; unemployment is *solely* due to the 'failure of prices' to adjust instantaneously to any exogenous change in demand (1993, p. 46; also see Tobin, 1992, p. 394). Tobin justifies this belief by arguing that 'In standard Walrasian/Arrow-Debreu theory, perfect flexibility of all wages and prices present and future would maintain full employment equilibrium' (1993, p. 53).[8] Hahn, however, demonstrated that 'the view that with "flexible" money wages there would be no unemployment has no convincing argument to recommend it.... Even in a pure *tatonnement* in traditional models convergence to equilibrium cannot be generally proved' (1977, p. 37).

It will be demonstrated below that Keynes's *explicit* rejection of a classical axiom assured that, in a general theory of employment, all existence proofs of a full employment equilibrium are jeopardized. Keynes's general principle of effective demand recognizes the possible existence of a stable unemployment equilibrium even with perfect price flexibility.

Tobin does not acknowledge that the word 'general' in Keynes's general theory refers to a logical framework that requires fewer axioms than the classical case.[9] The only difference between Keynes's effective demand analysis and the classical theory, Tobin insists, is a pragmatic one (1992, p. 391; also see pp. 394–5, and Tobin, 1993, pp. 55–6). Tobin claims that the 'essence of the Keynesian (and Keynes?) – new Classical dispute' involves the real world fact that changing product prices require some finite period of *real time*, no matter how small, to be operational. 'Complete flexibility means instantaneous adjustment, so that prices are always clearing markets' (Tobin, 1992, p. 394) and '*All Keynesian macroeconomics really requires is that product prices and money wages are not perfectly flexible*' (Tobin, 1993, p. 56, emphasis added).[10]

If this *real time* lag is an essential operational characteristic of *every* real world economy, while the classical case requires instantaneous price flexibility, then how can Tobin assert that the classical model is applicable to any supply-constrained real world of full employment (1992, p. 387)? If Tobin's *real time* argument is correct, even at full employment, instantaneous price flexibility is a pragmatic impossibility and the classical supply-constrained model is not applicable.

Using a Marshallian cross diagram[11] 'for a *single* commodity and its market' (ibid., p. 391, emphasis added) and hypothesizing an exogenous decline in the nominal demand curve, Tobin illustrates how textbooks explain how an instantaneous price adjustment to any exogenous shift in Marshallian demand will always 'clear' the market. *Keynes, however, explicitly rejected this single industry Marshallian cross-type analysis as the basis for the claim of classical economists that instantaneous flexible prices provided a 'self-adjusting' mechanism that assured full employment.* Keynes wrote:

> For the demand schedules for particular industries can only be constructed on *some fixed assumption* as to the nature of demand and supply schedules of other industries and *to the amount of [nominal] aggregate demand. It is invalid, therefore, to transfer the argument to industry as a whole* [i.e. Tobin's 'whole economy' argument (1992, p. 391)] *unless we transfer our assumption that aggregate effective demand is fixed.* Yet this assumption reduces the argument to an *ignoratio elenchi.* For whilst no one would wish to deny the proposition that a reduction of money-wages accompanied by the same aggregate effective demand as before will be associated with an increase in employment, *the precise question at issue is whether the reduction in money-wages will or will not be accompanied by the same effective demand as before measured in money*, or, at any rate, by an aggregate effective demand which is not reduced in full proportion to the reduction in money wages (i.e. which is somewhat greater measured in wage-units). But *if the classical theory is not allowed to extend its conclusions in respect to a particular industry to industry as a whole, it is wholly unable to answer the question what effect on employment a reduction in money wages will have. For it has no method of analysis wherewith to tackle the problem.*
>
> (1936, pp. 259–60, emphasis added).

Tobin's textbook example of a 'Marshallian single commodity market analysis' (1992, p. 391) to analyse the effect of an exogenous decrease in aggregate demand involves the same classical *ignoratio elenchi*, i.e. the fallacy of offering a proof that is irrelevant to the proposition in question. For Keynes, the use of a single-commodity market Marshallian cross for macroeconomic analysis is not *logically* permissible for answering the question of whether an instantaneously flexible price system is a sufficient condition for a full employment equilibrium. Tobin, on the other hand, argues that this Marshallian analysis is not applicable because in a decentralized economy 'how do workers and employers engineer an economy wide reduction in real wages?' (1993, p. 58). Thus Tobin relies on pragmatism rather than logic to reject the classical special assumption of universal instantaneously flexible prices.

Tobin cannot have captured the *central proposition* of Keynes if he insists on using what Keynes labelled an *ignoratio elenchi* as representative of what would happen if all prices were instantaneously flexible. Whenever the economy is modelled (using *either* Marshall's geometric cross or general equilibrium algebra) the analyst is presuming, rather than proving, that with perfectly flexible prices, the market system operates 'as if all markets, labor as well as product markets, are cleared by price adjustments at every moment of time' (Tobin, 1992, p. 391). Keynes, however, insisted that such modelling techniques were incapable of explaining why it is proper to 'assume that aggregate effective demand is fixed' in terms of employment level if, *as a matter of logic*, all prices and wages (and therefore factors' aggregate nominal incomes) instantaneously fall after the initial exogenous decline in aggregate demand. Instead, a different analysis is required (see below).

WILL FLEXIBLE PRICES ALWAYS CONTINUOUSLY CLEAR ALL MARKETS?

Keynes claimed that the 'precise question' on which his *General Theory* could focus, one that the classical case was incapable of analysing, was whether any possible change in wages and prices induced by an exogenous decline in aggregate demand would automatically restore full employment. This 'precise question' required a 'difference of analysis' (1936, p. 257) than classical theory (whether in the form of a Marshallian cross or a Walrasian algebraic system) could provide.

Keynes's 'method of analysis to answering the problem falls into two parts' (ibid., p. 260). First, would a decline in money wages (and prices) in response to an exogenous fall in nominal aggregate demand increase employment given the propensity to consume, invest, and the interest rate? Second, would a *pari passu* decline in all nominal prices affect employment through 'repercussions on these three factors'?

'The first question we [Keynes] have already answered in the negative in the preceding chapters' (ibid.) of Books I–IV of *The General Theory*. Keynes's answer to the second question involved tracing the repercussions of flexible prices and wages on the various components of aggregate demand including, *in an open economy*, the foreign sector (1936, pp. 262–9). At the end of this discussion of repercussions, Keynes warned: 'To suppose that a (completely) flexible wage policy is a right and proper adjunct of a system which on the whole is one of *laissez-faire*, is the opposite of the truth' (1936, p. 269).

Tobin does recognize ultimately the relevance of Keynes's second question regarding repercussions of flexible wages on the propensity to consume, invest, and the interest rate when he writes 'the question boils down to whether proportionate deflation of all nominal prices, both money wages and product prices, will or will not increase aggregate real effective demand' (1992, p. 395). At this critical juncture, Tobin ducks this question when he continues: 'This is *a complicated matter*, and I cannot do it justice here' (ibid., emphasis added). (The unwary reader is left with the impression that the answer must lie in Tobin's earlier assertion that perfectly flexible prices assure full employment despite this undiscussed 'complicated matter'.)

An attempt to answer this 'complicated matter' is provided by Tobin when he utilizes the equivalent of Marshall's single commodity demand curve by imposing the 'assumption that demand is related negatively to the price level' (ibid., p. 397). This negative relationship is justified by invoking a 'Keynes effect' which assumes an exogenous money supply so that a flexible price level affects the interest rate and not the marginal efficiency of investment.[12]

Keynes, on the other hand, did not put much hope in a 'Keynes effect' to restore full employment in a flexible price system. In his analysis of the repercussions of flexible prices on the rate of interest, Keynes warned '[i]f the quantity of money is itself a function of the wage-and price-level [i.e. an endogenous money], there is indeed, nothing to hope in this direction' (1936, p. 266). By doing *justice* to

Tobin's *complicated matter* of how a reduction in the price level can impact on the supply of money in a bank credit economy, Keynes was able to show that instantaneously flexible prices do not necessarily assure full employment in a *laissez-faire* market system.

KEYNESIAN UNEMPLOYMENT: SHORT-RUN DISEQUILIBRIUM OR LONG-PERIOD EQUILIBRIUM?

Keynes anchored his argument for the possibility of a *stable long-period underemployment equilibrium* in his 'essential properties' of money chapter (Keynes, 1936, pp. 257–309). Only by ignoring this chapter can Tobin assert that 'all Keynesian macroeconomics really requires is that product prices and money wages are not perfectly flexible. *Keynes pretended to be assuming pure competition in all markets*' (1993, p. 56, emphasis added).

In his 1939 response to Dunlop and Tarshis, however, Keynes indicated that he was not merely pretending to assume perfect competition. Rather as *a matter of logical argument*, Keynes was 'conceding a little to the other view' (Keynes, 1939, p. 441). Keynes was convinced that the fatal flaw of the classical analysis did not reside in price inflexibilities. As early as 1935, Keynes stated that 'we must not regard conditions of supply... as being the fundamental source of our troubles' (1973b, p. 486).

Despite this evidence, Tobin insists that the lack of instantaneous price flexibility is the essence of Keynesian economics (1993, pp. 55–8). In a letter to me (dated 5 May 1993) in response to an earlier draft of this chapter, Tobin explains his position when he writes:

> I regard 'perfect flexibility' as a condition that never exists, never can exist. As I define it, it means that never for any finite period of time, however short, do supplies and demands at existing prices diverge. This means that any shocks to supply and demand are absorbed by 'jumps' in prices, so that there is no period of real time during which prices are adjusting, but have not yet fully adjusted, to the shock.

Tobin is arguing that, *as a pragmatic matter rather than one of theoretical logic*, even with computer bar code pricing techniques and other computer control processes, it will take some period of *real time* (at least a nanosecond) for prices to adjust. Unemployment is therefore inevitable after any reduction in aggregate demand. But, it also takes some *real time* to discharge workers and stop production flows. Consequently Tobin's *real time* argument implies that entrepreneurs can reduce employment and outputflows quicker (i.e. in less than a nanosecond) than the brief real time necessary to adjust computer-controlled prices.

Relying on a mainstream reader's Walrasian reflex, Tobin conflates the notion of equilibrium with that of market clearing. For example, Tobin writes that when involuntary unemployment occurs 'the economy is not in equilibrium in any sense. It is not in a position of rest, markets are not clearing' (1993, p. 59).

The equilibrium concept, however, was brought into economics by Marshall who borrowed it from physics where equilibrium means a balancing of endogenous forces so that the body under study is 'at rest". Keynes, a student of Marshall, insisted that in an involuntary unemployment equilibrium there are no endogenous free market forces that would automatically alter the existing balance of market forces to change the unemployment equilibrium position even if prices are perfectly flexible. The concept of clearing is not necessary for a body-at-rest economic equilibrium.

Leijonhufvud indicates that mainstream theory has neglected these 'differences between Marshallian and Walrasian thought.... But Keynes was, of course, a price-theoretical Marshallian, and in the present context, ignoring this fact will simply not do' (1974, pp. 164–5). Even Patinkin ultimately recognizes that equilibrium means in 'the usual sense of the term that nothing tends to change in the system' (1965, p. 643), even though throughout most of his book Patinkin conflates clearing with equilibrium.

As a matter of taxonomy and logic *market clearing may be a sufficient, but it is not a necessary, condition for equilibrium* (see Davidson, 1967). Only if one posits classical well-behaved (i.e. substitution-effects-without income-effects-dominated) demand and supply curves *and* flexible prices in the Marshallian single commodity case can the analyst be sure that clearing and equilibrium occur simultaneously.

In Keynes's general theory an 'essential property' of all liquid assets (including money) is that the elasticity of substitution between liquid assets and producible goods is 'equal to, or nearly equal to, zero' (Keynes, 1936, p. 231, also see p. 241, n. 1). This 'essential property' meant that Keynes had to discard the classical ubiquitous gross substitution axiom just as the mathematician had 'to throw over the axiom of parallels... to work out a non-Euclidean geometry' (ibid., p. 16). Arrow and Hahn (1971, pp. 105, 126–7, 215, 305) have demonstrated that the removal of the gross substitution axiom jeopardizes all existence proofs. There need not exist any vector of prices that assures a full employment equilibrium.

If all markets clear simultaneously, then, *by definition*, there is a full employment equilibrium. Keynes's involuntary unemployment equilibrium involves cleared markets for the products of industry in tandem with an uncleared labour market that has no endogenous forces propelling the latter towards a clearing solution. In any economy where money has the 'essential properties' explicitly described by Keynes, *Tobin cannot demonstrate the existence of a full employment equilibrium even with instantaneously flexible prices.* When Keynes threw over some classical axioms (see Keynes, 1936, p. 16), including the axiom of gross substitution, to develop a *logical* more 'general theory of employment, interest and money' than the classical analysis, Keynes was not relying on a pragmatic fact that any price change requires *real time.*

Tobin finally concedes that Keynes did not require imperfect competition for his *general* theory, '[b]ut Keynes certainly would have done better to assume imperfect or monopolistic competition throughout the economy' (Tobin, 1993, p. 48). By 1939, however, Keynes had already admitted that his task of explaining unemployment could have been easier had he assumed imperfect competition (1973a, p. 400). If, however, unemployment depends solely on any fixity of prices, then as Hahn notes:

> there is not much left of the '[Keynesian] revolution'. For Keynes's contemporaries were all agreed that the lack of 'price flexibility' was responsible for the trouble.... there is a good deal more to Keynesian economics than that.
> (1977, p. 32).

Keynes defended not making imperfect competition the necessary basis for explaining unemployment by indicating the need 'for conceding a little' to the classical argument while using the principle of effective demand to locate the fatal classical flaw. In so doing, Keynes developed a *general* theory applicable to all degrees of price flexibility.

ARE DIFFERING SPEEDS OF ADJUSTMENT OF PRICES VS. QUANTITIES RELEVANT?

The major difference between Old and New Keynesians involves the former's concept of nominal *stickiness* and the latter's notion of nominal *rigidities* (Tobin, 1993, pp. 47–8). New Keynesians see *rigidities*, i.e. unchanging nominal values for long periods of calendar time, as an essential aspect of Keynesianism, while Old Keynesians are willing to make a 'much less restrictive assumption' (ibid., p. 46) regarding the time duration before prices adjust. This latter assumption 'leaves plenty of room for flexibility in any common sense meaning of the word' (ibid.). Old and New Classical models envision perfectly flexible market prices.

For Tobin (1992, p. 391), 'the essence' of the Keynesian vs. Classical dispute is only the question 'How fast?' do prices adjust. Between classical immediate flexibility and the New Keynesian long-term rigidity there are 'various speeds of price adjustment... during which markets are not clearing' (1992, p. 394). Tobin claims that Old Keynesianism is the embodiment of reasonableness, since it 'owns the middle ground' between the polar New Classical and New Keynesian views on price flexibility (ibid., p. 394).[13]

Is all the fussing amongst Classical and mainstream Keynesian theories of employment a tempest in a teapot involving different assumptions about the speed of adjustment of prices vs. output compared to Marshall? (In Marshall, any exogenous change in demand results in an instantaneous change in (spot) market period prices. Only in a short period, whose duration is longer than the market period, could output adjust.)

According to Tobin, both Old and New Keynesians assume a slower price speed of adjustment than the instantaneous adjustment presumption of classical theorists such as Marshall and Walras. The only fundamental distinction between Old Keynesians and New Keynesians is that the latter presume an even slower speed of price adjustment than the former.

Was Keynes's entire anti-classical argument based solely on reversing Marshall's speed of adjustment argument? Keynes did not concede this, nor have other renowned scholars (e.g. Leijonhufvud 1994, p. 169, Hahn) who have studied Keynes, Marshall, and the Walrasian system.

Leijonhufvud (1968) was the first to attribute to Keynes this reversal of Marshall's speed of adjustment argument. Six years later, however, Leijonhufvud recanted by stating:

> It is *not* correct to attribute to Keynes a general reversion of the Marshallian ranking of relative price and quantity adjustment velocities. In the 'shortest run' for which the system behaviour can be defined in Keynes' model, output-prices *must* be treated as perfectly flexible.
>
> (1994, p. 169).

Leijonhufvud's recantation is a belated recognition that in numerous places in *The General Theory*, Keynes specifically accepted the notion that any change in market demand will instantaneously alter all current (spot[14]) market prices. For example, Keynes wrote:

> There is no escape from the dilemma that if it [a change] is not foreseen there will be no effect on current affairs, while if it is foreseen, the [spot] price of existing goods will be forthwith so adjusted.
>
> (1936, p. 142).[15]

Hahn has also argued that

> Keynes did not posit fix prices. Rather the reverse. Nor did he seem to argue that prices change more slowly than quantities, as can be verified in the chapter which tells us why labour cannot control its real wage.
>
> (1977, p. 35).

Old Keynesians such as Tobin, however, have always seen Keynes as providing a 'theory of nominal wage *stickiness*' (Tobin, 1993, p. 48, emphasis added), while New Keynesians see wage and/or price *rigidities* as the essence of Keynes (ibid., p. 47; Gordon, 1990, p. 1135; Mankiw, 1990, p. 1654). Both Old and New *Keynesians* ignore the chapter in *The General Theory* entitled 'Changes in Money-Wages' that Hahn refers to where Keynes specifically rejected nominal inflexibilities as the fundamental and sole cause of unemployment. Keynes states:

> the classical theory has been accustomed to rest the supposedly self-adjusting character of the economic system on the assumed fluidity of money wages; and, *when there is a rigidity*, to lay this rigidity the blame of maladjustment.... My difference from this theory is primarily a difference of analysis.
>
> (1936, p. 257, emphasis added)

The claim that less than perfect price flexibility was the cause of unemployment was, of course, widely recognized by classical economists long before Keynes wrote *The General Theory*. In distinguishing between those classical economists (Ricardo) who presumed the clearing of all markets, and other ('weaker spirits') classical economists who, observing unemployment in the real world, tried to develop non-market-clearing classical model by *presuming some price inflexibility*, Keynes wrote:

> Ricardo offers us the supreme intellectual achievement, unattainable by weaker spirits, of adopting a hypothetical world remote from experience as though [as if?] it were the world of experience and then living in it consistently. With most of his successors common sense cannot help breaking in – with injury to their logical consistency.
>
> (1936, p. 192).

Old *and* New Keynesians have resurrected hi-tech variations of the 'weaker spirits' analysis that Keynes was arguing against. Old and New Keynesians accept the classical axiomatic value theory of Walrasian systems as a universal truth and a necessary prerequisite for producing a scientific discipline for economics.[16] By accepting all the classical microfoundation axioms, in contradistinction to Keynes, Old and New Keynesians are presuming that their models are special cases of the general theory of classical economics.

When their common sense gets in the way of their New Classical axiomatic-based logic, these 'weaker spirits' Classical Synthesis Keynesians impose *ad hoc* short-run nominal stickiness or rigidity assumptions to explain unemployment. For example, in a personal letter to me (dated 5 May 1993) Tobin wrote:

> the essential debate . . . concerns the efficacy of natural market adjustment mechanisms in eliminating any involuntary unemployment (excess supply of labor in a non-cleared market) that occurs. This debate cannot occur at all if one assumes, as New Classicals do and New Keynesians do also for competitive markets, that no involuntary unemployment or any other excess supply ever exists.

Keynes, on the other hand, insisted that no automatic market mechanism (including completely flexible prices) exists that assures a full employment equilibrium in a monetary economy. Despite Tobin's protest, neither Old nor New Keynesians are able to engage classical theorists in any consistent logical discussion in support of Keynes's principle of effective demand as described in his chapter 3. Mankiw, at least, recognized this inability when he wrote 'If new Keynesian economics is not a true representation of Keynes's views, then so much the worse for Keynes' (1992, p. 561).[17]

KEYNES'S PRINCIPLE OF EFFECTIVE DEMAND

Keynes wrote to D. H. Robertson that his aggregate supply function 'is simply the age-old supply function . . . it is only a re-concoction of our old friend the supply function' (1973b, p. 513). Keynes's aggregate supply conditions were derived from Marshallian micro-supply functions (1936, pp. 44–5). The properties of this aggregate supply function 'involved few considerations which are not already familiar' (ibid., p. 89). Keynes insisted that 'it was the part played by the aggregate demand function which has been overlooked' (ibid., p. 89) and *not imperfections in supply conditions* that underlay the general case of unemployment equilibrium.

In his chapter 3 Keynes argued that the classical analysis of Say's Law did not provide 'the true law relating the aggregate demand and supply functions' because it presumed that aggregate demand involved the identical determinants as the aggregate supply function so that 'Supply creates its own Demand' (1936). Say's Law specifies that all expenditure (aggregate demand) on the products of industry is always exactly equal to the total costs of aggregate production (aggregate supply) including gross profits. Letting D^w symbolize aggregate demand and Z^w aggregate supply (both measured in wage units, i.e. nominal values deflated by the money wage rate), then

$$D^w = f_d(N) \tag{1}$$

and

$$Z^w = f_z(N) \tag{2}$$

Since Keynes used the 'age-old' classical supply function of perfect competition as a microbasis for the aggregate supply function,[18] completely flexible market prices are consistent with equation (2). The existence of inflexibilities, therefore, is not a necessary condition for Keynes's effective demand analysis.

According to Keynes, Say's Law asserts that

$$f_d = f_z(N) \tag{3}$$

> "for *all* values of N, i.e. for all values of output and employment... effective demand, instead of having a unique equilibrium value, is an infinite range of value all equally admissible... (and) there is no obstacle to full employment."
>
> (Keynes, 1936, pp. 25–6).

In an economy subject to Say's Law, the aggregate demand and aggregate supply curves coincide (see Figure 1.1). There can never be a lack of effective demand no matter what the degree of price flexibility. The total costs (including profits and rents) of the aggregate production of firms (whether in perfect competition or not) are recouped by the sale of output.

Keynes insisted that Say's Law was not the 'true law' relating aggregate demand and supply functions (equations (1) and (2)) (1936, p. 26). Thus 'there is a vitally important chapter of economic theory which remains to be written and *without which all discussions concerning the volume of aggregate employment are futile*' (ibid., emphasis added).

A general theory incorporating this 'true law' required a model where the aggregate demand and aggregate supply functions, $f_d(N)$ and $f_z(N)$, *need not be coincident* (see Figure 1.2). The general theory would result in a unique equilibrium 'point of the aggregate demand function, where it is intersected by the aggregate

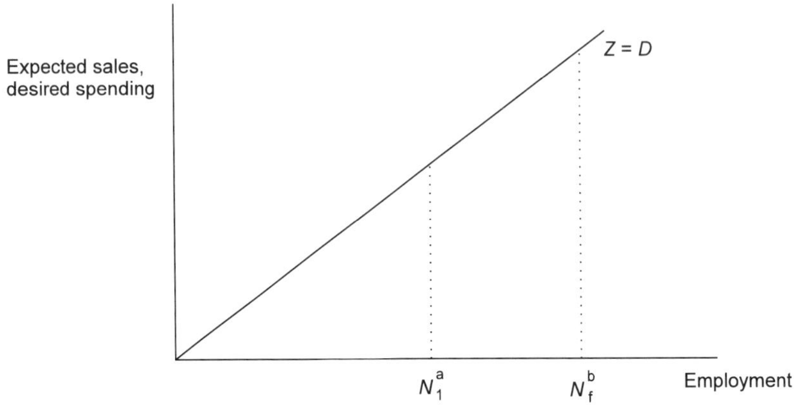

Figure 1.1

supply function, [that] will be called *the effective demand.... this is the substance of the General Theory of Employment*' (Keynes, 1936, p. 25, emphasis added). This principle is what Tobin (1993, p. 46) calls the 'central Keynesian proposition'.

When classicists impose the condition that supply always creates its own demand, the classical case can be seen to be a special case where 'effective demand, instead of having a unique equilibrium value, is an infinite range of values'. The more general theory, where there is no necessity for the determinants of the aggregate demand function to be identical with the determinants of aggregate supply, required Keynes to develop a taxonomic expansion of the classical demand classification system.[19]

Equation (1) indicates that the classical case reduced all expenditures into a single category, D^w, aggregate demand (which is controlled entirely by the deter-

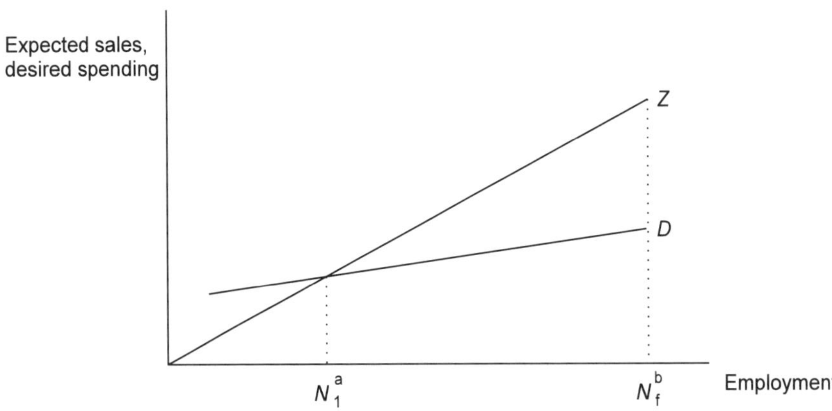

Figure 1.2

minants of aggregate supply conditions). Keynes indicated that 'the essence of the General Theory of Employment' (1936, pp. 28–9) involved dividing all types of expenditures into two demand classes, i.e.,

$$D^w = D_1^w + D_2^w \tag{4}$$

where D_1^w represented *all* expenditures which 'depend on the level of (current) aggregate income and, therefore, on the level of employment N' (ibid., p. 28), i.e.,

$$D_1^w = f_1(N) \tag{5}$$

and D_2^w which represents *all* expenditures *not* related to current income and employment,

$$D_2^w \neq f_2(N) \tag{6}$$

Classical theory then becomes a *special case* of Keynes's taxonomy where additional axioms are imposed to force the determinants of aggregate demand to be the same as aggregate supply so that the aggregate demand function consists entirely of expenditures *equal* to current income at all levels of N. Classical theory requires that there be zero expenditures that are not related to current income and employment, i.e. *classical theory is the case where*

$$D_2^W = 0 \tag{7}$$

and therefore

$$D_1^w = f_1(N) = f_z(N) = Z \tag{8}$$

for all values of N.

But even if D_2^w is not an empty category, Keynes still had to demonstrate that this type of spending was not related to current income and employment by being equal to 'planned' savings (defined as $f_z(N) - D_1^w$)[20]. *If* D_2^w *is equal to planned savings*, then

$$D_2^w = f_z(N) - D_1^w \tag{9}$$

and

$$D^w = D_1^w + D_2^w = D_1^w + f_z(N) - D_1^w = f_z(N) \tag{10}$$

Comparing equation (10) and equation (2) shows that if D_2^w equals planned savings, then aggregate demand and supply are identical at all levels of N.

To assure that equations (9) and (10) are not the general case, Keynes argued that the economic future was uncertain in the sense that it cannot be either foreknown or statistically predicted by analysing past and current market price signals. In terms of today's terminology, *an uncertain world is one where the classical ergodic axiom is not applicable.* In a non-ergodic environment, current and past market signals do not provide statistically reliable information about future events. In a (non-ergodic) uncertain world, future profits, the basis for current D_2^w investment spending, can neither be reliably forecasted from existing market information nor endogenously determined from today's 'planned' savings function $f_z(N) - D_1^w$ (Keynes, 1936, p. 210). Rather, investment expenditures depend on the exogenous (and therefore, by definition, sensible) but not rational (ergodic-axiom-based) expectations of entrepreneurs. Non-ergodic expectations are what Keynes called 'animal spirits'. Thus

$$D_2^w \neq f(N) \tag{11}$$

in both the short and long run.

NON-PRODUCIBLE ASSETS – HEDGES AGAINST AN UNPREDICTABLE FUTURE

The next logical task for Keynes was to demonstrate that 'the characteristics of the special case assumed by classical theory happen not to be those of the economic society in which we actually live' (ibid., p. 3). In other words, Keynes had to demonstrate that even if $D_2^w = 0$, any D_1^w function describing demand in a money using entrepreneurial economy would not be coincident with his macroanalogue of the age-old supply function. To do this Keynes had 'to throw over' the classical axioms of (1) *neutral money* (i.e. the possession of money *per se* provides no utility), (2) *gross substitution* and (3) *ergodicity*. Keynes (ibid., ch. 17) introduced the 'essential properties' of money (and all other liquid assets) that distinguish buying (and holding) liquid assets from buying the products of industry.

> Money (and all other liquid) assets possess two essential properties. These are:
> [1] the elasticity of production of money is zero. In essence, all liquid assets are non-producible by the use of labour in the private sector. In other words, *Money does not grow on trees*. Money (and all liquid assets) therefore cannot be produced by hiring otherwise unemployed workers to harvest money trees whenever people demand to hold additional liquid assets as a store of value[21] instead of spending all their current income on the products of industry.
> [2] the elasticity of substitution between all liquid assets (including money) with respect to producible goods is zero. This means there is no significant gross substitution between non-producible liquid assets and the products of industry.
>
> (ibid., pp. 230–1).

Keynes insisted 'the attribute of "liquidity" is by no means independent of these two (elasticity) characteristics' (ibid., p. 241). The products of industry do not possess these peculiar properties and therefore are illiquid assets. Producibles, therefore, can never provide any utility for liquidity purposes no matter how much prices of liquid assets rise relative to prices of producible assets.

Accordingly, any increase in demand for liquidity (i.e. for non-producibles to be held as a liquid store of value) that induces an increase in the price of non-producible liquid assets will not divert the demand for liquidity into a demand for goods and services. As long as wealth owners want to store value in liquid assets whose 'elasticities of production and substitution may be very low', unemployment equilibrium is possible independent of the degree of price flexibility in the system.

Since classical theory assumes that only producibles provide utility, then, in the long run, only a lunatic would engage in the disutility of working to earn income merely to hold some income in non-producible liquid assets such as money no matter how expensive money becomes relative to producible goods. Keynes used the concept of a non-probabilistic uncertain future to explained why, even in the long run, people would reveal a preference to hold non-producibles such as money as a store of value no matter how high its relative price rose *vis-à-vis* the products of industry (1936, ch. 12; see also 1973c, pp. 112–5).

If non-producibility is an *essential* characteristic of anything that possesses liquidity in a non-ergodic environment while the products of industry never posses a liquidity premium which exceeds their carrying costs (Keynes, 1936, p. 239), then the holding of liquid assets can provide a long-run security blanket against a non-predictable future. Liquid assets provide utility against uncertainty in a way that producibles cannot.

Hahn has demonstrated that, even in a perfectly competitive economy, unemployment equilibrium can occur, when 'there are in this economy resting places for savings other than reproducible assets' (1977, p. 31). This holds because the existence of 'any non-reproducible asset allows for a choice between employment-inducing and non-employment-inducing demand' (Hahn, 1977, p. 39).

By jettisoning classical axioms, Keynes could demonstrate that, as a more general case applicable to the facts of experience, money is never neutral and a stable unemployment equilibrium could exist. The necessary classical postulates that must be added to change this *General Theory* of a unique point of effective demand to a case where 'competition between entrepreneurs would always lead to an expansion' up to full employment (Keynes, 1936, p. 26) are: [1] the *axiom of ergodicity* which asserts that the future is calculable from past and present market data (in Old Classical theory ergodicity was usually subsumed when it claimed that decision makers possessed foreknowledge of the future; in New Classical theory, it is presumed that agents have rational expectations about a statistically reliable predictable future)[22]; [2] *the axiom of gross substitution*[23]; and [3] *the axiom of neutral money*, at least in the long run.

The axiomatic value theory underlying a classical general equilibrium system had not yet been explicitly developed in 1936. Keynes, therefore, could not precisely label the classical theory equivalents of the 'axiom of parallels' that had to be thrown over to produce his general theory. Nevertheless, by 1933, Keynes recognized that in any 'monetary theory of production', the axiom of the neutrality of money was not applicable in either the shortrun or the longrun (1973a, pp. 408–9).

Today Blanchard still proclaims that *all* mainstream macroeconomic models 'impose the long-run neutrality of money as a maintained assumption. This is very much a matter of faith, based on theoretical considerations [i.e. axiom based], rather than on empirical science' (1990, p. 828). If Blanchard is correct, then all mainstream macroeconomists including Tobin have still failed to grasp the logical underpinnings of Keynes's revolutionary analysis.

The 'hard-headed' axiomatic microfoundations of orthodox macroeconomic theory require the classical axioms Keynes discarded. These axioms assure that money is a veil, as all the income earned by utility maximizing agents will, in the long run, always be spent on the products of industry.[24] In the simplest one-period case, all expenditures are equal to income as utility maximizers are constrained by income (the budget line constraint) in their choice among good A and all other producible goods in this period. To spend less than one's income on the products of industry is to reveal a preference below the budget line and thereby to engage in non-utility-maximizing behaviour.[25] The aggregate of all this microfoundation spending behaviour should be classified as D_1^w in Keynes's taxonomy. The marginal propensity to spend out of current income is unity and any additional supply (the microequivalent is an upward shift in budget constraint lines) creates its own additional demand.

In an intertemporal multiperiod setting with gross substitutability over time, agents plan to spend lifetime income on the products of industry over their life cycle. The long-run marginal propensity to spend is unity. Consequently, in the longrun, $f_d(N) = f_z(N)$ for all values of N and Figure 1.1 is relevant.[26]

If the essential properties of money described by Keynes are relevant, then the restrictive axioms of gross substitution, ergodicity and neutral money must be jettisoned. Consequently, some portion of a utility maximizing agent's income might be withheld from the purchase of producible goods – even in the long run. The utility maximizing long-run marginal propensity to spend out of income on the products of industry can be less than unity.[27]

In sum, Keynes's principle of effective demand is a general theory of employment applicable to both a classical (perfectly certain or actuarially certain – rational expectations – world) and a non-ergodic uncertain (non-ergodic) environment. In the classical case, money is neutral – a *numeraire* – and 'there is no asset for which the liquidity premium is always in excess of the carrying costs . . . the best definition I can give of a so-called "non-monetary" economy' (Keynes, 1936, p. 239). The existence of a money that is neutral require the assumption of an ergodic system where everything is known to be a good substitute for everything else. There are no obstacles to endogenous market forces restoring full employment any time the system experiences an exogenous shock to aggregate demand.[28]

Once the ergodic axiom is thrown away, then the future is uncertain; agents cannot reliably predict the future from analysing past data. If agents then adopt a moneyusing entrepreneurial system to solve their economic problems, then, Keynes argues, all liquid assets (including money) possess certain essential properties so that their liquidity premium will always exceed their carrying costs. Agents can obtain utility (by being free of fear of possible future unpredictable insolvency or even bankruptcy) only by holding a portion of their income in the form of non-producible liquid assets. If the gross substitutability between all liquid assets and producible goods is approximately zero (ibid., ch. 17; Davidson, 1984), then when agents want to save (in the form of non-producible liquid assets) out of income, money is not neutral, even with perfectly flexible prices. Thus, the general case underlying the principle of effective demand is:

$$D_1^w = f_1(N) \neq f_z(N) \tag{12}$$

for all values of N. The propensity to save or planned savings $(f_z(N) - D_1^w)$ is equal to the amount out of current income that utility maximizing agents plan to increase their holdings of non-producible liquid assets. The decision to save today means 'a decision not to have dinner today. But it does not necessitate a decision to have dinner or to buy a pair of boots a week hence or a year hence or to consume any specified (producible) thing at any specified date' (Keynes, 1936, p. 210).

By proclaiming this 'fundamental psychological law' associated with 'the detailed facts of experience' where the marginal propensity to consume *out of current income* is always less than unity, Keynes finessed the possibility that equation (8) would ever apply to the real world – even in a supply-constrained full employment environment (ibid., p. 96). If the marginal propensity to consume is always less than unity, then $f_1(N)$ would never coincide with $f_z(N)$, even if $D_2^w = 0$, and the special classical case is not applicable to 'the economic society in which we actually live' (ibid., p. 3).

HOW TO ANSWER KEYNES'S *PRECISE QUESTION*

The answer to Keynes's *precise question* of whether complete price flexibility assures the simultaneous clearing of all markets can be understood with the help of Figure 1.3. Assume a discrete one-time exogenous decline in the aggregate demand function from D_a^{w1} to D_b^{w1}. If nothing else occurred, employment would fall

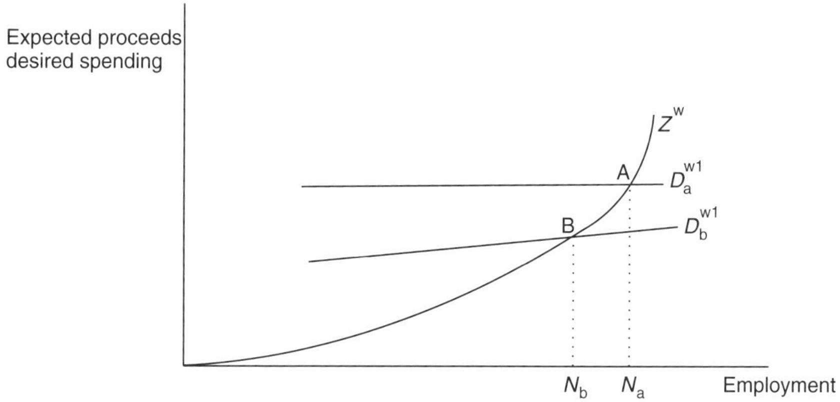

Figure 1.3

from N_a to N_b as the point of effective demand declines from point A to point B. Even if money wages and product prices instantaneously fall *pari passu*, however, the aggregate supply function, Z^w in Figure 1.3, will be unchanged, since it is deflated by the money wage. By fixing the position of the aggregate supply function, Keynes can insist that if anyone (including Tobin) is to claim that instantaneous price flexibility maintains a full employment equilibrium, then he or she must demonstrate what effects any degree of flexibility has on the various components of the aggregate demand function. Will the *pari passu* fall in all prices and wages increase the propensity to consume and/or the inducement to invest (*both measured in wage units*) or lower the interest rate sufficiently so that the aggregate demand function is sufficiently 'greater measured in wage units' (Keynes, 1936, p. 260) to shift the point of effective demand completely back from B to A in Figure 1.3? Until Tobin explicitly responds to this query with an explanation using Figure 1.3 to affirm his position, his claim that his analysis is a true representation of Keynes's principle of effective demand is unproven.

CONCLUSION

Keynes's principle of effective demand demonstrates that, in a non-ergodic world, it is the existence of non-producible assets that are held for liquidity purposes and for which the products of industry are not gross substitutes that is the fundamental cause of involuntary unemployment. The lack of perfect flexibility is neither a necessary nor a sufficient condition for demonstrating the existence of unemployment equilibrium.

The policy implication that evolves from Keynes's general theory is different from those logically derived from mainstream Keynesianism. One major implication of both Old and New Keynesianism is that long-term full employment policies should be aimed at creating more competitive price flexibility by (a) deregulation,(b) promoting the dissemination of market information and the removal of entrepreneurial coordination failures,[29] and (c) in an open economy, promoting global competition with freely flexible spot exchange rates (so that, in a global context, relative product prices and money wages between nations can instantaneously change).

A government budget deficit fiscal policy might be justified by mainstream Keynesians in the shortrun, but cannot be recommended as a permanent long-run solution to the unemployment problem. In other words, Old and New Keynesian perspectives may justify government deficit spending on infrastructure (i.e. D_2^w) as, at best, a short-run palliative to solve a temporary problem. A balanced federal budget over the cycle remains the long-run fiscal objective of Old and New Keynesians. This fiscal goal in combination with an unfettered global competitive market economy with freely flexible exchange rates will not only be more 'efficient' in determining the volume of D_2^w spending, but will lead to the best of all possible economic worlds.

Logical consistency with their microfoundation's axiomatic framework requires Old and New Keynesians to permit only short-run ('putting out fires') government tinkering with the global economy. In the long run, there is no economic role for government.

Keynes, however, argued that there was a need for a *permanent* role for government in the socialisation of D_2^W investment spending as 'the only means of securing an approximation to full employment' (Keynes, 1936, p. 378). Keynes argued for a separation of government expenditures into a current expenditures budget and a capital budget. He argued that government should not deficit-finance current expenditures, but might be required to deficit-finance capital budget expenditures permanently and that the borrowing for the capital budget to finance public investments be done by the federal government rather than the local government (Keynes, 1980, pp. 277–80, 321–2, 352; also see Brown-Collier and Collier, 1995). Keynes also recommended a fixed, but adjustable, exchange rate system with permanent government policies on capital flight controls embedded in an international payments system which pressured nations that ran persistent current account surpluses to bear the major onus for making trade adjustments (see Keynes, 1980, esp. pp. 27, 168. 176; Davidson, 1994b, pp. 231–9, 262–72).

Until we get our general theory of what is the fundamental cause of unemployment correct for the money-using entrepreneurial world in which we live, we are unlikely to get our policies right. The insistence of Old and New Keynesians that unemployment is entirely nested in the quantity adjustment speed being greater than the price adjustment speed eviscerates Keynes's essential message: it is liquidity problems and not price inflexibilities that are the basic cause of a persistent unemployment state that can destroy the capitalist system. For policy purposes as well as for a correct history of economic thought, this chapter has attempted to set the record straight on Keynes's principle of effective demand.

NOTES

1 Second emphasis added. These sentences do not appear in the preface to the German edition in the *Collected Works of John Maynard Keynes* (1973a, pp. xxv–viii). Schefold (1980) has called attention to the fact that these sentences do not appear in *The Collected Works.*

2 Keynes clearly rejects the assumption of gross substitution when he asserts that an essential property of money is that elasticity of substitution between money (i.e. all liquid assets) and producible goods is zero (1936, p. 231). In his *Monetary Theory of Production* Keynes specifically rejects the classical long-run neutrality of money assumption (1973b, pp. 408–10). In his emphasis on uncertainty and his rejection of both probabilistic expectations (Keynes, 1936, pp. 161–2) and Tinbergen's econometric methodology for predicting the economic future (Keynes, 1973c, p. 308), Keynes rejected the ergodic axiom of classical theory.

3 Tobin insists that a different type of analysis is required for each of two regimes: a 'Keynesian regime where aggregate economic activity is constrained by demand... (and) a classical... supply-constrained (regime).... Keynesians believe the economy is sometimes in one regime, sometimes in the other' (Tobin, 1992, p. 388–9).

4 The classical case is reached by adding restrictive axioms to Keynes's 'general' theory of employment. See Keynes's comment that classical economists are Euclidean geometers in a non-Euclidean world and what is 'required in economics' today is to 'throw over' some

restrictive classical axioms to 'work out' a more general theory equivalent to non-Euclidean geometry (1936, p. 16).

5 Despite Tobin's claim, Keynes specifically argued against deflating nominal values by the price level of products to obtain a measure of aggregate real output. Keynes spent a whole chapter in *The General Theory* (1936, ch. 4, especially p. 40) to explain why any attempt to use such a measure of real output is an exercise in futility. Instead, on occasion, Keynes deflates nominal output by the wage unit (the money wage). Some have argued that deflating by the money-wage unit rather than a goods-price index is an unimportant secondary matter. *It is not.* As explained *infra*, deflating by the wage unit permitted Keynes to freeze the position of the aggregate supply function (one blade of Marshall's proverbial scissors) in order to focus full attention on changes in aggregate demand. Deflating by a goods price index will not permit such a single moving blade analysis.

6 Keynes insists that, as a theoretical matter, unemployment equilibrium is possible for 'any degree of competition' including perfect competition (1936, p. 245).

7 Tobin, in fact, insists that 'Keynesian theory regards recessions as lapses from full employment' (Tobin, 1992, p. 387). This implies that either (a) the real world is always in a 'lapse' and can never achieve full employment, or (b) the real world does achieve full employment even in the absence of instantaneously flexible prices. In the former case, if full employment is an unattainable state, why develop full employment policy prescriptions for a state that cannot be reached? In the latter case, instantaneous price flexibility is not a necessary condition for full employment. (Of course, there is plenty of empirical evidence of real world economies that have achieved full employment without flexible prices.)

8 If only *all* agents (including workers) could instantaneously adjust prices downwards, then all markets would clear (Tobin, 1993, p. 46–7). In Tobin's terminology, this would occur in the case of 'continuously price-cleared competitive markets' (ibid., p. 47).

9 The fewer axioms a theory requires, the more general (by definition) a theory is.

10 Tobin therefore must be assuming that Keynes accepted all the classical axioms (which are currently the basis for modern axiomatic value theory) despite the evidence suggested in note 2 and discussed further *infra* that Keynes specifically rejected three classical axioms.

Surprisingly, neither Old Keynesians nor New Keynesians think it is important to consider what Keynes claimed are 'The Essential Properties of Interest and Money' in their explanation of Keynes's theory of the operations of a monetary economy (1936, pp. 222–44). Post Keynesians, on the other hand, have incorporated Keynes's 'essential properties' into the necessary conditions for a general theory of employment.

11 Tobin calls this the 'economists' favorite diagram for beginning students and ... the unquestioned assumption of Ph.Ds' (1992, pp. 390–1).

12 Tobin could have reached this same negative relationship by invoking a real balance effect in a system with an exogenous (outside) money supply. But, as the next paragraph indicates, Keynes suggested that there was not much hope for such effects if the money supply is endogenous – as it is in a bank-credit monetary system.

13 Tobin apparently believes that the 'middle ground' is always the virtuous position. For example, see Tobin's earlier debate with Friedman where he suggests the absence of 'extreme' assumptions is somehow *per se* virtuous (1974, p. 80). Yet, does obtaining the middle ground often require waffling on the essential logical issues?

14 Spot prices are, of course, the only market prices existing for goods available for delivery today!

15 For additional statements regarding the possibility of perfectly flexible prices in his analysis, see Keynes (1936, pp. 227, 231–2).

16 For example, see Blanchard's statement in *infra*. Also see Samuelson where he made the 'ergodic hypothesis' the *sina qua non* of the scientific method in economics (1969, p. 184).

Lucas and Sargent have also insisted that endogenous expectations without persistent errors (rational expectations which require the ergodic axiom) are a necessity for developing economics as an 'empirically based science' (1981, pp. xi–ii).

17 Mankiw continues '*The General Theory* is an obscure book. I am not sure that even Keynes himself knew completely what he really meant.... *The General Theory* is an outdated book.... We are in a much better position than Keynes was to figure out how the economy works.... The long run is not so far away that one can cavalierly claim, as Keynes did, "that in the long run we're all dead"' (1992, pp. 560–1).

18 The *New Palgrave* provides a derivation of Keynes's aggregate supply function from Marshallian microsupply foundations (see Davidson, 1987).

19 'Classification in economics, as in biology, is crucial to scientific structure.... It was Keynes' extraordinarily powerful intuitive sense of what was important that convinced him that the old classification was inadequate. It was his highly developed logical capacity that enabled him to construct a new classification of his own' (Harrod, 1951, pp. 463–4).

20 'Thus – except on the special assumptions of the classical theory according to which there is some force in operation which, when employment increases, always causes D_2 to increase sufficiently to fill the widening gap between Z and D_1 – the economic system may find itself in stable equilibrium with N at a level below full employment, namely at the level given by the intersection of the aggregate demand function with the aggregate supply function' (Keynes, 1936, p. 30).

21 If money does not grow on trees (is not reproducible), then involuntarily unemployed workers canned be hired by the private sector to harvest money, even if the marginal productivity of picking fruit from the money tree exceeds the marginal disutility of reaching for the fruit.

22 Classical theory deals with a system in which 'relevant facts were known more or less for certain... facts and expectations were assumed to be given in a definite and calculable form; and risks, of which, though admitted, not much notice was taken, were supposed to be capable of an exact actuarial computation. The calculus of probabilities, though mention of it was kept in the background, was supposed to be capable of reducing uncertainty to the same calculable status as that of certainty itself... (whereas) the fact that our knowledge of the future is fluctuating, vague and uncertain, renders wealth a peculiarly unsuitable subject for the methods of the classical economic theory.... By "uncertain" let me explain I do not mean merely to distinguish what is known for certain from what is probable.... About these matters there is no scientific basis to form any calculable probability whatever. *We simply do not know*' (Keynes, 1973c, pp. 112–14, emphasis added).

23 In the absence of ubiquitous gross substitution, all existence proofs are jeopardized (see Arrow and Hahn, 1971, pp. 15, 127, 215, 305).

24 Classical microfoundations assume that the earning of income always involves disutility, while the products of industry are the *only* scarce things which generate utility. It therefore follows that if future outcomes are knowable (i.e. ergodic), then utility maximizers will bear the irksomeness of engaging in income producing activities only to the point where the marginal disutility of earning income equals the expected marginal utility of the products of industry that the agents 'know' they want to buy. All utility maximizing agents are on their budget constraint line, allocating *all* their income on purchasing producible goods and services. A demand to hold a non-producible money or other assets solely for liquidity purposes is irrational, given the special assumptions of the classical case. Money is therefore merely a neutral veil!

25 Holding savings in the form of money or other liquid non-producibles provides zero utility.

26 Only the introduction of overlapping generations *and* a growing population of younger agents relative to retirees can assure that, in the short run, each period's aggregate marginal propensity to consume will be less than unity. In equilibrium with

an unchanging population (i.e. the long run) even the overlapping generation model will exhibit a short-run marginal propensity to spend equal to unity.

27 Cf. Keynes: 'Unemployment develops, that is to say, because people want the moon; – men cannot be employed when the object of desire (i.e., money) is something which cannot be produced and the demand for which cannot be readily choked off' (1936, p. 235).

28 Alternatively, if an economic system never uses money in its production and exchange activities, but instead organizes its economic activities on either a cooperative basis or by rule of a central authority, then there need never be any involuntary unemployment (cf. Keynes, 1973b, pp. 408–10).

29 In the Spring of 1982, President Reagan suggested that unemployment could be ended if each business firm in the nation immediately hired one more worker. Since there are more firms than workers, the solution is obviously statistically accurate – but unless the employment by each of these additional workers created a demand for the additional output at a profitable price (additional supply creating *pari passu* additional demand), it will not be profitable for entrepreneurs to hire additional workers.

New Keynesians who believe that unemployment is the result of a coordination failure should have applauded Reagan's clarion call for firms to coordinate increased hiring. If each firm does hire an additional worker so that full employment is (at least momentarily) achieved, then actual income flows earned would be equal to notional income and therefore aggregate demand would not be constrained short of full employment. There is no coordination failure – and no short-side rule limits job opportunities.

2

KEYNES AND THE NEW KEYNESIANS ON MARKET COMPETITION

J. A. Kregel

Although many economists were quick to adopt Keynes's policy conclusions concerning the best way to emerge from the 1930s' Depression, there was widespread resistance to the implications of the underlying theory. One of the basic reasons for the relative success of Keynes's policy proposals for public works spending was that they had already been repeatedly recommended by economists from a wide range of backgrounds during the 1920s and 1930s. Even Herbert Hoover, while Secretary of Commerce during the 1920s, had taken action to formulate specific public expenditure packages which could be introduced in the event of cyclical downswings. He was later to implement these policies as President of the United States in the period after the 1929 stock market crash.

Most economists believed that the events of the 1930s were due to impediments to the self-adjusting competitive price mechanism. There was division amongst economists as to whether these impediments simply acted to slow the process of adjustment to equilibrium or whether they were structural imperfections which had been slowly building since the turn of the century. In either case, the economic situation was sufficiently serious, and the downturn had proved sufficiently durable, to recommend emergency action to attempt to *jump-start* the autonomous adjustment process. Thus, public works expenditures were looked upon as *pump priming* devices which would restore the operation of the perfectly competitive, automatically adjusting price mechanism. The structural imperfections, such as might occur when monopoly becomes extensive in product markets, could be eliminated by means of anti-trust legislation and reducing the power of trade unions to fix wages at excessively high levels.

An important corollary to this view was Irving Fisher's idea that under certain specific conditions the automatic adjustment mechanism of the competitive price system might operate perversely. Just as an economy which operates by allowing economic agents to become indebted on the basis of future expected incomes could experience a self-reinforcing inflationary boom due to excessive money or credit creation, it might also experience a self-reinforcing deflationary slump due to the destruction of money and credit. Falling prices mean that debts cannot be repaid, leading to default and the inability of even solvent agents to meet their commitments. As agents are forced to sell assets to meet debt payments this creates additional market supplies and further downward pressure on prices in a cumulative collapse.

The basic difference in this collateral view was that it recommended measures to prevent the forces of competition from driving prices when they were moving perversely by blocking the fall through price controls. Recovery could only come about when prices were reinflated back to their original levels. Fisher thus provided the theoretical justification of much of the New Deal legislation which promoted measures to stabilize prices through direct intervention and control of competition. But these were to be considered as only temporary measures which should be removed once the normal operation of the price mechanism had been restored. Public expenditure policy could be compatible with this approach because it would stabilize incomes and reverse the dynamic of the fall of asset prices by creating artificial demand to meet the ever rising attempts to sell. Fisher accepted that there was some normal range in which the price mechanism operated to restore equilibrium, but that if prices moved outside this normal range the mechanism became pathological. This is very similar to the corridor hypothesis proposed by Leijonhufvud in his interpretation of Keynes.

Keynes knew Fisher's work well and admired it. However, he disagreed that the conditions of the Depression were due to a pathological malfunctioning of the competitive price mechanism. The revolutionary aspect of Keynes's theory was that he considered that the absolutely normal operation of the competitive price mechanism could produce an equilibrium position in which there were excess supplies of goods and excess supplies of labour. He thus expressly noted that his theory was independent of the 'degree of competition' and would be equally valid under perfectly competitive prices and wages as under conditions of imperfectly competitive fixed prices and wages. Indeed, despite the fact that the 'imperfect competition' revolution was taking place at the same time as he was writing his book, and some of his closest collaborators were instrumental in developing the theory of imperfect competition, Keynes never made any reference to it and did not introduce it into his theory even though he recognized that it might increase its force.

It is this reversal of the traditional position on the operation of the price mechanism that provides the basic reason for economists' hesitancy to accept Keynes's theoretical framework, since it rejects the idea that the competitive price adjustment mechanism through which equilibrium is attained by falling prices, reducing excess supply, can move the system back to equilibrium. From this view economists could accept Keynes's proposition that unemployment could be an equilibrium condition which required public expenditure to shift the equilibrium closer to full employment as a policy recommendation, but not the theoretical premiss that such a condition could be produced by the normal operation of the price mechanism. Excess supply of labour represented by unemployment could only be indicative of a disequilibrium in which the price mechanism was prevented from exercising influence to return the market to the full employment equilibrium wage.

It thus became commonplace for economists who accepted Keynes's policy recommendation to assume that his theory assumed either rigid wages or market imperfections which prevented the return to full employment. This is the thrust of Modigliani's (1944) response to Hicks's (1937) famous interpretation of the general theory. Hicks had suggested that money and uncertainty, rather than the income multiplier, represented the distinguishing features of Keynes's *General Theory*. He followed Keynes and used the wage unit as a *numeraire*. From this emerged the now well-known classification of the novelty of Keynes's theory in the horizontal stretch of the LM curve exhibiting a constant rate of interest produced by a *liquidity trap*. Hicks went on to suggest his own, 'more general', theory represented by a positively sloped LM curve, the result of assuming a constant quantity of money. All this is set out in his 'Mr Keynes and the Classics: A Suggested Interpretation' which soon came to represent *Keynesian* economics in the textbooks. In his 1944 article Modigliani criticized Hicks's interpretation, and argued that it was the assumption of rigid wages, not money and uncertainty, that explained Keynes's result of unemployment equilibrium. It was thus clearly a case of market disequilibrium caused by impediments blocking the operation of the price mechanism. This directed attention away from money and uncertainty, and back to structural impediments in competition in labour markets.

Given the popularity of this fix price interpretation of Keynes's theoretical apparatus in making the case for active government expenditure policy, many economists thus adopted the formal, aggregate structure of the model but attempted to introduce some modicum of the automatic price adjustment process. They argued that in conditions of excess supplies of labour, downwardly flexible wages would reduce production costs and goods prices. Given the quantity of money, this would bring about an increase in the real quantity of money and a reduction in the interest rate. The fall in the interest rate would then cause an increase in investment spending and, via the multiplier and the propensity to consume, an increase in consumption spending. The higher level of aggregate demand would thus increase the demand for output and for labour to produce it. After Leijonhufvud, this is now known as the *Keynes effect*, in contrast to the *Pigou effect*, which results from a simple excess supply of goods reducing the price level and increasing the purchasing power of a given quantity of money.

Joan Robinson notes that Keynes is criticized for not having admitted this automatic adjustment process within his own framework of aggregate demand because he eliminated it by the assumption

> that money-wage rates are rigid – more accurately, that the supply of liquidity is very much more flexible upwards than money-wage rates are downwards. Of course he did. The contemporary world, inhabited by bankers and financiers (who do not depend on a fixed physical quantity of gold or cowrie shells to carry out monetary transactions) and managers and trade unionists

> (or for that matter mistresses and charwomen) is not reflected in the model in which money-wage rates can fall indefinitely, or in which the quantity of money remains constant when they are rising.
>
> (Robinson, 1965, p. 101)

This version of the theory is what Joan Robinson called *bastard Keynesianism* because it relied on 'arguments which are purely Keynesian (though formalistic and silly), showing how the effect upon prices of changes in money-wage rates reacts upon liquidity preference and the propensity to consume' (ibid., p. 100).

She also notes that there is a corollary to this bastard Keynesian argument in the theories of economic growth which were developed in the 1950s (she cites the work by Hicks and Meade as well as Harry Johnson). These theories assumed that at any point in time a given quantity of capital is capable of providing full employment, if only real wages are permitted to fall to their equilibrium level, i.e. where the supply and demand for labour are equal.

In fact, the two arguments are identical. The automatic adjustment of the economy to full employment produced by flexible wages and prices requires that the fixed quantity of capital and a fixed quantity of money are sufficiently *malleable* to provide full employment at the appropriate level of wages. Both positions thus accept the traditional operation of the price mechanism that Keynes had tried to overturn. Recall Keynes's admonition that his theory was to be a *dynamic* theory which took account of the fact that 'changing views about the future are capable of influencing the quantity of employment and not merely its direction'. (Keynes, 1936, p. xxii)

Joan Robinson noted that the bastard Keynesian argument that

> [a]ny arbitrarily fixed quantity of money . . . is compatible with full employment, in conditions of short-period equilibrium at some level of money-wage rates, the level being lower the smaller the postulated quantity of money, and the larger the labour force to be employed

does not provide any support for the 'contention that falling wages and prices are good for trade' (Robinson, 1965, p. 101), and that the same argument applies to the fixed quantity of capital. Even if there were to exist a level of real wages at which a capital stock appropriate to the existing quantity and quality of labour might have been constructed so as to produce full employment, it would be impossible for the economy to reach that equilibrium state by means of a reduction in money wages. The reasoning was very similar to Fisher's – a fall in wages would reduce rather than increase the demand for labour, but the causes are different. It is no longer the inability to meet interest commitments, but now the inability of labour to spend on consumption goods leading to lower sales and firms' profits and lower national income. The basic difference is the recognition of the impact of falling prices on the level of income, rather than on the destruction of wealth.

A similar criticism of the possibility of automatic dynamic operation of the price mechanism was made in a slightly different way by G. B. Richardson in an *Economic*

Journal article in 1959 and a book in 1960. He argued that if prices in a competitive market were to produce signals leading to the elimination of excess supplies and the optimal allocation of resources, then changes in prices must reflect changes in prospective rates of return to investment across sectors. But if a rise in the prospective return from one sector is signalled by a rise in the price of its output, this signal will also be received by other producers in other sectors, who will also shift their investment towards the higher return sector. If all investors interpret the price signal as a change in relative rates of return, the resulting increase in resources in the sector with rising relative prices will lead to excess investment and output, causing actual returns on investment to be lower than that which had been signalled by the initial rise in price.

Richardson argues that in order for producers to make rational production decisions so as to eliminate excess demands and produce equilibrium, the investment and production intentions of all other agents must be known to all agents. However, if prices were to reflect fully the intended future actions of agents to increase their investment and output, then prices would not rise. But if prices do not rise, there would be no price signals to be perceived by agents, and no actions would be taken to adjust investment and output. If all producers have perfect information, none of them will undertake adjustments of their position for fear of loss, and the new equilibrium can never be achieved. If price changes are perfect predictors of future resource commitments in the sector, then they should not rise, for they should reflect the new flow of resources to the sector which will cause a rise in output which reduces prices. Hence the paradox: if prices do not change then no new investment will take place; if prices do change and investment is reallocated across sectors, there is no guarantee that it will be of precisely the amount which will restore global equilibrium.

To resolve the paradox a market coordinator or auctioneer would have to provide the information necessary in order for the competitive process to operate; since it is not in the interest of any single producer to provide information concerning his or her own intentions, he or she cannot be relied upon to do so without remuneration. But the information concerning intended actions is only useful if no one else possesses it, so each agent will be led to conceal intentions. Imperfect information will be the rule, rather than the exception, in competitive markets.

A similar argument, made by Ronald Coase, has been awarded a Nobel Prize. Amongst the many interpretations of Coase's ideas is one which says that the *auctioneer* of Walrasian theory cannot remain exogenous to the analysis of the process by which price changes produce adjustment to equilibrium. Real, live market makers in the form of auctioneers or dealers will be required to operate the adjustment process. Since they will be expected to receive remuneration for their time and effort, and to earn the market rate of return on the capital they invest in their activities, they should be considered under the category of what are now called *transactions costs*. They thus provide an alternative explanation of the impact of impediments to the operation of the markets, but produce the same sorts of anomalies when introduced into efficient, perfect market theories. Coase has distanced himself from this interpretation of his theory.

However interpreted, one of the implications of this approach is that in perfectly competitive conditions, the transactions costs associated with the organization of the market by means of an auctioneer may be greater than the benefits of multilateral exchange. If this is the case, competitive equilibrium cannot be achieved by the adjustment of prices in a free market. Coase's major insight is that the theoretical analysis of market organization cannot be undertaken by means of the theory of competitive price formation, since the theory presumes the existence of the market makers whose actions it is supposed to explain.

For example, in *competitive* conditions, if returns to organizing markets as an intermediary or market maker are sufficiently high, new entrants should bring down intermediation or transactions costs; alternatively, new transactions technologies or organizational forms may be developed and introduced in order to reduce transactions costs. This may lead either to the disappearance of market makers as returns to organizing markets fall below the market makers' supply price, or to the dominance of a small number of market makers and a breakdown of competitive conditions.

Coase also suggests that there may be competing forms of organization of economic exchange besides the *competitive* market. One would be to internalize transactions under a central coordinating authority which replaces the auctioneer. This is commonly called a firm. Coase also notes that there is virtually no explanation of the methods of organization within firms in the theory of perfect competition.

If the costs of using the market are excessive, this will lead to its substitution with an alternative form of internal organization. Coase suggested that it would be the *firm*. This change would reduce the number of transactions which would remain in the market, which might then cause an increase in the transactions costs of using the market. This could create a vicious circle in which eventually no economic transactions take place via the market. The introduction of the traditional competitive process into the analysis of the provision of the transactions services of the market leads to the paradox that without intermediaries, markets cannot function; but when the intermediation services of market makers are relatively too costly, the market may not be the optimal solution to the problem of economic exchange. It clearly cannot then provide for an automatic adjustment to equilibrium with the full utilization of resources.

It is important to remember that Coase defined those forces, now generally denominated as transactions costs, which produce the impetus to introduce cost saving innovation in market organization such as firms as arising from the *uncertainty* associated with using the free, competitive market to organize transactions. It must be presumed that these uncertainties are the same as those noted by Richardson and are represented by the impossibility for price signals to produce the information required for adjustment to equilibrium except in the case of perfect information concerning the reaction of all agents to price signals.

It is interesting that both the Coase and Richardson arguments, which might be called competitive market *impossibility* theorems, have been well known for some time. It is also interesting that both rely on the idea that it is the operation of the competitive market mechanism itself which produces uncertainty in market transactions. This is what has been called endogenous, rather than exogenous, disequilibrium or instability. They are arguments of the *beauty contest* variety cited by Keynes in chapter 12 of the *General Theory* and as such are compatible with Keynes's approach to a monetary production economy which, as noted above, considers uncertainty as arising from the very operation of the perfectly competitive market in conditions of capitalistic production – conditions which make the use of money a response to that uncertainty, and in which money itself can then introduce endogenous elements of disturbance.

Thus, the arguments of Keynes, Robinson, Richardson and Coase all lead to the same result. The ability of the free competitive market to adjust automatically so as to produce equilibrium is not a question of whether wages and prices are fixed by some authority such as a firm, or flexible via an auction in the market. Exactly the same problems would occur under either assumption. The real problem concerns the impact of imperfect information and the ways individuals respond to uncertainty over the future implication of currently available information, including prices.

Despite the continuous existence of this type of analysis, traditional theorists continued to consider only bastard Keynesian theory grounded in rigid prices. Since it supplied no explanation of why this should be so it was considered to be an *ad hoc* assumption which was possible only because there was no microeconomic foundation for Keynesian theory. The introduction of general equilibrium theory to fill this presumed gap in Keynesian theory took on the name of *the microeconomic foundation of macroeconomics*. It was certainly no surprise that once perfectly competitive equilibrium theory was introduced into the bastard Keynesian theory, the result was the New Classical Economics (NCE) which restored the traditional orthodoxy. Indeed, the NCE went one step further and argued that economic theory outside of equilibrium was impossible; this meant that economic theory was restricted to the discussion of cases of risk, represented by a subjective frequency distribution which corresponds to the objective distribution, rather than to non-probabilistic uncertainty such as might emerge from the process described by Richardson. The result was that not only did the possibility of an unemployment *equilibrium* disappear, but the analysis of money and uncertainty were also expunged from theoretical discourse.

In response to the success of the market clearing, perfectly competitive equilibrium assumptions of the rational expectations hypothesis, there have been a number of attempts in the 1980s to formulate a criticism of the self-regulating nature of the competitive market economy. These are now known as *New Keynesian* approaches. Most of these build on the idea of incomplete information or incomplete markets produced by externalities or moral hazard problems. The basic idea of this approach is to reverse the implicit assumption of competitive price flexibility and investigate the implications of the existence of competitive price rigidity. This is a line which started with the fix price equilibria of Hicks, as extended by Clower, and then Barro and Grossman and others to fixed price equilibria. However, the price rigidities remained *ad hoc*, and thus stimulated attempts to justify them as the outcome of the competitive process and thus explainable by means of general equilibrium theory.

This is an improvement over the traditional analysis of competition by means of general equilibrium theory because it recognizes a 'world [which] is peopled with types . . . who have different roles to play . . . each with his own characteristic motives and problems' (Robinson, 1973, p. 101) in the form of the analysis of the motives of firms, bankers and workers. Thus, while it recognizes the real-world fact that prices are not in reality perfectly flexible, it still attempts to justify Keynes's results by the existence of these rationally based price rigidities in opposition to price flexibility when, in Keynes's view, this should make no difference.

There are two basic approaches to the explanation of rigidities, one criticizing the possibility of flexible wages in the labour market, and one for the role of the rate of interest in producing a level of investment sufficient to absorb full employment savings. Both represent the extension of a line of research initiated by George Akerlof's (1984a) elaboration of the *lemon principle*, or the breakdown of the assumption of product homogeneity in second-hand markets. The example is the market for second-hand, used cars; buyers have little idea of the actual condition of the car, while sellers have *perfect* information. The theory is based on this idea of *asymmetry* of information available to buyers and sellers.

This approach can be applied to the labour market by assuming that employers have imperfect monitoring ability concerning the marginal productivity of new relative to already-employed workers. In the absence of better information, employers are assumed to act on the belief that their workers equate real wages with the marginal disutility of work. In the presence of an excess supply of labour there would then be no incentive for an employer to hire an unemployed labourer who offered to work for a wage lower than that currently prevailing because this must mean that the worker's marginal productivity will be lower than that of the existing workers. Further, if the employer did hire the new labourer at the lower wage, with competition now forcing down the general level of wages, this would lead to a fall in average productivity as all other workers adjusted their work effort to the lower wages. This reduced productivity would offset the change in wages and leave profitability more or less unchanged. Thus, there is no incentive for the employer to change present offers of employment. A similar argument works for an increase in wages.

The result is that it is possible to argue that it is rational for employers not to reduce wages in the face of excess labour supply, even if workers are willing to work at those wages. Workers who are unemployed and (irrationally) are willing to offer greater than average effort for the current wage thus cannot manage to get themselves hired even by offering to work for real wages below the average productivity of the employed labour force, because employers cannot verify the disutility functions of the individual unemployed (or employed) workers. In Clower's language there is a mutually beneficial exchange which is blocked because it cannot be arbitraged. This is supposed to offer an improvement over Keynes's observation that workers resisted wage reductions because they could not be sure that wage relativities would be preserved, by providing a *theoretical* explanation.

For the New Keynesian approach to the flexibility of the interest rates, 'Keynes's analysis of investment was, however, basically a neoclassical analysis: it was failure of the real interest rate (the long-term bond rate) to fall sufficiently that was the source of the problem' (Greenwald *et al.* 1984, p. 194). They argued that a more *Keynesian* approach would rely on rigidities of prices and the existence of imperfections such as credit rationing which would limit the ability of entrepreneurs to finance that level of investment which would bring about full employment saving.

Their argument starts by assuming that bankers have imperfect information concerning the disutility functions of entrepreneurs, or, more realistically, concerning the production function and the real rate of return of investment projects which entrepreneurs want to borrow to finance. In the absence of better information, it is assumed that the banker believes that there is an inverse relation between investment and the rate of return on projects (or, alternatively, that projects offering higher rates of return have higher risk). In the presence of an excess demand to finance investment there is no incentive for the banker to raise interest rates, since the expected return on the project is thought to be below the current lending rate. An entrepreneur who believes in a project with a rate of return greater than the bank's lending rate cannot get a loan even if the entrepreneur offers to pay a higher rate of interest. Better to leave interest rates unchanged, even in the presence of excess demand for loans.

Thus supply and demand may not operate to produce market clearing equilibrium: wages do not fall to eliminate an excess supply of labour (the marginal disutility is below the marginal productivity of labour), and interest rates do not rise to eliminate the excess demand for loans (marginal productivity of capital is above the interest rate). This produces the New Keynesian explanation of equilibrium in conditions of imperfect (asymmetric) information in which there is excess supply of labour and excess supply of investment and no market forces which can operate to match the unemployed labourers with the unfilled jobs in the unfinanced investment projects.

However, it still remains true that perfect information should lead to full utilization of resources. What happens if employers or bankers are not satisfied with making the broad brush assumptions concerning the behaviour of workers and entrepreneurs and attempt to improve the quality of their information?

The New Keynesian argument can be extended to show that even if agents attempt to improve their information, perfect information and thus full utilization is impossible in a competitive market system. Assume that there are a few individuals who decide to improve their information and become better informed. Further, assume that this allows them to make better employment or lending decisions, and as a result it increases their profits. Attracted by the higher returns, this should induce more individuals to become informed until all are equally well informed. If the profits of being informed come at the expense of the uninformed, then the marginal return to information falls until there is no longer any advantage to seeking better information. This leads to the paradoxical result, similar to that outlined by Richardson and Coase, that it is no longer profitable to seek information and no one continues to be fully informed. Since full information of all agents is not a stable equilibrium state, the system will exhibit persistent fluctuation in the imperfections of information; an increase in the quality of information cannot lead to a permanent increase in investment or employment.

Again, this argument differs from that put forward by Keynes, Robinson and Richardson. First, all the information in these models is known by someone – the absence of equilibrium is an information coordination problem. Second, the kind of information that is assumed to be knowable, in general cannot be known: entrepreneurs know the mean and the distribution of the real marginal product of their investment projects, borrowers know their probability of paying off a loan, workers know the mean and distribution of their real marginal product. But the arguments of Coase and Richardson imply that in a market economy these values cannot be known, *ex ante*. The capital theory controversies imply that these values cannot be unambiguously defined without assuming the type of operation of the perfectly competitive market that the New Keynesians are trying to argue cannot exist (the knowledge of the real marginal products which the theory requires can only exist on the basis of conditions which it shows cannot exist).

Note that in all these cases the *normal* laws of supply and demand are inoperative: wages do not fall when there is excess supply of labour (marginal productivity of labour is below the wage), interest rates do not rise when there is excess demand for loans (marginal productivity of capital is above the interest rate). This produces the conclusion of the New Keynesian economics that employment will settle at an equilibrium level in which there is excess supply (excess demand for capital) with perfect competition. We thus have the traditional fixed wage and fixed interest rate model, but now explained in terms of incomplete markets produced by imperfect information. If there were an omnipotent economist who could produce perfect information, the system would naturally produce full employment.

Further, it still remains true that in a New Keynesian world, if real wages could be lowered, employment would be higher, and if the real rate of interest were higher, more investment would be undertaken. Imperfect information just conceals the fact that these models still rely on the rigidity of prices and wages in whose absence the traditional bastard Keynesian approach becomes operative.

In the simplest version of incomplete information in the banker's decision on lending, it still remains true that the interest rate which is charged does not have any impact on the mean rate of return to the investment project, so that the separation theory of traditional capital theory, which makes the behaviour of real variables independent of monetary variables, still holds. Nor does credit rationing have any role in explaining unemployment similar to that of the *fringe of unsatisfied borrowers*, since an increase in the rate of interest which reduces rationing also decreases the supply of loans; total investment falls as the interest rate rises, just as in traditional Keynesian theory. The New Keynesian credit rationing caused by incomplete information concerning borrowers' intentions turns out to be precisely equivalent to that which would have been imposed by the price mechanism. The argument then returns to the interest rate being *too high* relative to full employment marginal efficiency, and the assumption of a fixed supply of money is still required to explain why the interest rate is too high.

This means that to the extent that these models take monetary factors into account, they are purely exogenous money models. No bank with Basil Moore (e.g. 1988) as its loan officer would ever run into such conditions, for it would lend to all comers at the prevailing rate established by the central bank which would then have to come up with the reserves to support it – if there are dishonest borrowers the bankers can always get the central bank (or the deposit insurance fund) to lend to them as a last resort.

But this is not the most important impact of the absence of the discussion of monetary factors in this approach. In the tradition of the Modigliani–Samuelson neoclassical synthesis, it excludes monetary factors from a role in generating instability. Although the New Keynesian tradition appears to be asking the right *Keynes-type* questions and producing *Keynes-type* answers, as all traditional theorists who accept Keynes's policy proposals, it rejects Keynes's theory of monetary production. It is not compatible with the argument that in the presence of a perfectly functioning competitive price mechanism, there was no necessity for full employment to result. A decrease in wages in the face of excess labour supply would not bring about full employment, and an increase in interest rates certainly could not, although a decrease might, depending on how expectations responded. It is the recognition of the monetary nature of production which produces the explanation of these natural but unsatisfactory results in any real economy. It is not that information is incomplete, but that the information that the market requires simply does not exist, or could not be discovered, even by hiring a firm of consultants, nor by waiting or by 'using' cars. Entrepreneurs have to form expectations about values of variables at future dates about which there is no currently existing *objective* information. As a result the economy would be prone to fluctuate as expectations fluctuate, although usually not violently, around a level of output below potential and below full employment. Since expectations are formed in part on the basis of the functioning of the economy and in part on the *imagination* of entrepreneurs, they will have both endogenous and exogenous elements.

Aside from any discussion of whether borrowers misrepresent the probability of successful outcomes or the proportion of shirkers and slackers due to moral hazard, it is necessary to explain this expectations formation process and the uncertainty which makes it necessary. This is what Keynes attempted to do in the monetary theory of production, an aspect of Keynes's work that has gone unnoticed by most of the profession. This information is available only in static equilibrium with full information of resources. But, as Richordson reminds us, it cannot exist in the cases that are being discussed with dynamic adjustment.

Recently Stiglitz (1992) and Greenwald and Stiglitz (1993a) have distanced themselves from these attempts to produce a *rational* explanation of price rigidities. They have proposed an alternative approach in which *risk*, rather than knowledge imperfections, plays a crucial role; price flexibility may itself be a cause of instability. But, Joan Robinson would have argued, in this approach they are only disputing Keynes's *bastard progeny*. Ironically, the analysis recalls aspects of Hicks' presentation of portfolio decisions in the terms of shifts in portfolio composition leading to changes in investment and producing cycles. It is as if the wheel has come round, in which case, this variety of New Keynesian belongs in the category Joan Robinson defined as *pre-Keynesian theory* after Keynes.

3

NEW KEYNESIAN MACROECONOMICS AND MARKETS*

Roy J. Rotheim

INTRODUCTION

Fluctuations in economic activity with real consequences are a common feature of market economies. Understanding such occurrences is another matter. The lament of Frank Hahn that 'General equilibrium is strong on its existence but weak on how it comes about' reminds us that mainstream economists are hard pressed to explain events and processes falling outside of those equilibria, including fluctuations in economic activity. Orthodox neoclassical equilibrium economists, i.e. New Classical economists, dismiss such fluctuations as reflecting *aberrations* from prescribed equilibrium paths occurring as a result of informational misperceptions in prices that will be self-correcting over time. Keynesian neoclassical equilibrium economists, i.e. New Keynesian economists, are less quick to admit to the instantaneous nature of this adjustment mechanism contending, instead, that equilibria are not immediately restored when shocks to the system occur, even when behaviour is rational (or near rational), because relative prices, at the individual level and in the aggregate, can remain sticky owing to a multitude of systemic imperfections.

The element of imperfection is critical, here, because without the assumption that imperfections occur, individual volition, in the context of an aggregative structure, would be non-existent. In a *competitive* model with complete knowledge, the firm is both an output and input price taker. None of its purchases in either market can affect those prices; prices in general are strictly exogenous. The same is true for the supplier of resources and the purchaser of output. Prices are external data to all market participants, implying that price rigidities caused by an individual's ability to influence price or asymmetries in information cannot exist. In such models, price flexibility assures market clearing, because there can be no obstacles preventing prices from becoming flexible. If real time were allowed to enter such models (a stretch of the imagination) then adjustments in prices and quantities might take time and proceed at different speeds, but no individual would be able to affect the overall magnitude of those quantities. Then it is just a matter of time, so to speak, before all markets have cleared and equilibrium has been restored.

New Keynesians have retained the general framework in which such resource allocation questions are posed, as well as the methodological individualist predisposition of orthodoxy. What differs for them is the assumption that individuals may possess some degree of power over market prices. Competition is now perceived as imperfect and information is either elusive to some individuals (uncertainty about future prices) or asymmetrically distributed amongst all individuals. Prices are envisioned as possibly not clearing in the *short run* (there seems to be this underlying belief that sticky prices are not persistent). Thus we hear Mankiw assert: '[t]he conflict between modern neoclassical and traditional Keynesian theories of the business cycle centres upon the pricing mechanism' (1985, p. 529). More specifically, Blanchard and Kiyotaki point out that 'deviations from the competitive equilibrium paradigm are central to a full understanding of macroeconomic fluctuations' (1987, p. xii).

So convinced are New Keynesians that this modification in the ability to set prices is the route to understanding changes in employment and output as a whole that they, as we just observed, choose to identify the *traditional* Keynesian theory as one which centres on imperfections in the pricing mechanism: '[a] key assumption of the Keynesian approach is that wages and prices are sticky' (ibid., p. 372).[1]

This chapter will enquire into the essential nature of market imperfections in the research programmes of Keynes and the New Keynesians. Even *unreconstructed* Keynesians like James Tobin assert that 'Keynes certainly would have done better to assume imperfect or Monopolistic Competition throughout the economy' (1993, p. 48). This current chapter will follow a Post Keynesian perspective contending that the price rigidity New Keynesian programme is of no help in understanding a *Keynesian* view on fluctuations in macroeconomic employment and output. Keynes rejected approaches which relied on methodological individualist perspectives focusing on output, labour and capital markets, because he believed they were inapplicable to analyses which attempt to understand movements in employment and output *as a whole*. Such heuristical devices would only have theoretical significance if it were assumed that output and employment in the aggregate *did not change* (see Keynes, 1936, ch. 19; Rotheim, 1988, 1994). The important conclusion to be reached in this regard is that the framework cast in terms of markets is itself inappropriate for understanding such questions.

A more recent version of New Keynesian economics, which focuses on questions of coordination failure, what Barkley Rosser has called 'Strong New Keynesian Economics' (see this volume), does offer some interesting possibilities in terms of a truly Keynesian perspective on economic fluctuations, in that the essence of this variant considers changes in income, output and employment *as a whole* occurring by means of spillover effects and strategic complementarities. Unfortunately, the dominant mechanism for introducing this approach has been the New Keynesian convention of assuming monopolistic competition and price rigidities. However, as will be seen below, these restrictive assumptions are not necessary to retain many of the salient insights this approach provides.

In the next three sections, I will briefly outline the New Keynesian theories of output, labour and capital, based on imperfections in each of those respective markets. From there, I indicate how Keynes's criticism of such theoretical approaches invalidates the generalizations of what are, in some instances, interesting insights into the workings of individual markets. This I will follow with a description of the New Keynesian coordination failure literature, which continues to rely on the imperfectionist perspective. The chapters ends with some concluding remarks on the nature of market metaphors and methodological perspectives in macroeconomic thought.

PRICE RIGIDITY IN THE OUTPUT MARKET

For the most part, New Keynesian economists support the belief that in the long run one would expect sufficient wage and price flexibility to cause any anticipated exogenous nominal shocks to be totally borne by nominal, rather than real, variables. This predilection follows from the theoretical conclusions of the *Classical Dichotomy*: real things are affected in markets with independent supply and demand relations mediated by relative prices; nominal things do not affect these real relationships, rather revealing themselves in terms of nominal absolute values. Money, in this instance, falls within the latter half of the dichotomy, strictly neutral with regard to real elements of the economy.[2]

In the short run, however, New Keynesian economists contend that in the market for goods there might be small costs of price changes perceived by firms (e.g. changing the prices on menus or published price lists) which might inhibit them from lowering prices in the face of nominal demand shifts. Rational firms find it inopportune to change their prices frequently. Models of these types generally employ an assumption of imperfect competition so that firms are seen to have control over their product prices frequently. In most menu-cost models (see Mankiw, 1985; Ball and Mankiw, 1994), such firms have committed certain fixed costs and thus have established prices prior to the actual occurrence of product sales. In certain instances, monopolistically competitive firms, i.e. firms which *can* control their pricing policies, may not have much incentive to cut prices when the cost of implementing those price changes exceeds the benefits that might accrue to the firm from the increased output that could be sold with the lower price. This despite the fact that the benefit to society of a price cut might be large (first order) even when the benefit to the firm is small (second order). Then, given the pre-existing distortion of monopoly pricing, if firms face even a small menu cost, they are liable to maintain their old prices, despite the substantial social loss from this unusually high price (Mankiw, 1990, p. 1657). In light of a nominal demand shock, these price rigidities can have large aggregate effects on output and welfare loss:

> Specifically, we ask whether movements in demand produce output fluctuations with large welfare costs, even though it would be inexpensive for price setters to reduce these fluctuations through greater nominal flexibility. An

> affirmative answer requires that nominal price rigidity have large negative externalities.
>
> (Ball and Romer, 1989, p. 520)

Since there is no extra-market mechanism to orchestrate the internalization of these externalities, fluctuations in nominal variables will be disproportionately borne by fluctuations in real output and employment, rather than in nominal prices and wages alone. Thus, the classical dichotomy is violated as nominal changes affect real outcomes and the economy experiences so-called *Keynesian features*, i.e. secondary effects on employment and output (what Blanchard and Kyotaki call *aggregate demand externalities*), and *Keynesian-type* involuntary unemployment as these secondary falls in demand for output coupled with firms' unwillingness to offer lower wages in response to these demand failures cause the full impact to be borne by unemployment rather than downward real wage flexibility.

What should be observed, in what New Keynesians refer to as 'the microfoundations of the real impact of aggregate demand disturbances' (Romer, 1993, p. 8), is the template-like form taken by the delineation of the question set: first is the acceptance of the Classical Dichotomy as the heuristic which defines the key language in these arguments, being the distinction between nominal and real changes in the economy.[3] From this positive heuristic, there follows the logical question as to why an exogenous change in some nominal variable, such as the nominal money supply, would affect real output, when traditional theory dictates that changes in the nominal money supply should only affect *absolute* prices, leaving relative prices, and therefore levels of output and employment, unaffected:

> Any microeconomic basis for failure of the classical dichotomy requires some kind of nominal imperfection; otherwise, a purely nominal disturbance leaves the real equilibrium (or the set of real equilibria) unchanged.
>
> (ibid., p. 7)

Moreover, by employing the methodology of the representative firm as the basis for making inferences about firms *en masse*, there is an explicit recognition of a *weak* methodological individualism, in the sense that we can employ the same language in the case of individual firms or workers or in the case of output and employment as a whole.[4] In this view, nominal concepts mean little to individuals and firms – they are ultimately concerned with *real* variables. Conflating these two ideas, the New Keynesian conclusion follows that

> if failure of the classical dichotomy is important to fluctuations in aggregate activity, it must be that nominal frictions that appear small at the level of individual households and firms – like the fact that prices are posted in nominal units, or that obtaining accurate information about the aggregate price level involves a cost – somehow has a large effect on the macroeconomy.
>
> (ibid., pp. 7–8)[5]

WAGE RIGIDITY AND INVOLUNTARY UNEMPLOYMENT IN THE LABOUR MARKET

Continuing its search for a rationally based microfoundation for macroeconomic-behaviour (i.e. the reduction of heuristical propositions to markets where independent supply and demand relations are mediated by some relative price), New Keynesian theory depicts *Keynesian features* with regard to what it calls involuntary unemployment by assessing the extent to which real wages are reluctant to fall in light of a nominal demand shock (remember the importance of addressing the questions about providing explanations for the violation of the classical dichotomy). In other words, they are interested in why the *labour market* does not work, as well as why the price of labour does not fall, measured in both nominal and real terms, to clear that market. Thus we hear Bruce Greenwald and Joseph Stiglitz state:

> One peculiar aspect of old Keynesian analysis was that while its main concern was unemployment, it offered little discussion of the labour market. However, a consensus is growing that an understanding of the labour market must be at the centre of any macroeconomic theory.
>
> (1993b, p. 33)

This admission acknowledges the importance of *real* wage inflexibility as an explanation for involuntary unemployment occurring in some economy-wide market for labour in the same sense that an individual labour market is characterized by an excess supply as some real wage that is reluctant to fall. Thus it is possible for Azariadis and Stiglitz to observe that '[t]he sluggishness of money wage rates, notably in periods of relatively stable inflation, and the strong contribution of layoffs to cyclical unemployment in North America have long been two of the best-documented Stylized facts in economics' (1983, p. 2).

For their *theoretical* foundation to explain sticky wages, New Keynesian economists have appealed to a myriad of institutional idiosyncrasies occurring at the level of the firm, including efficiency wages (Yellin, 1984, Katz 1986), insider–outsider theory (Lindbeck and Snower, 1986a), shirking (Shapiro and Stiglitz, 1984), and hysteresis (see Blanchard and Summers, 1986). Here, behaviours of rational suppliers and demanders at the individual level are generalized to explain real wage rigidity in an aggregate labour market. So, for example, in one demand-side story, it is assumed that labour productivity is not independent of the wage paid: low-paid workers will shirk, whereas higher-paid workers will work harder. As a result '[i]n the face of unemployment, wages may not fall, for firms will recognise that if they lower wages, productivity will decrease, turnover may increase, and profits will fall' (Greenwald and Stiglitz, 1987, p. 124). Another story on the labour supply side goes like this:

> a rational . . . individual [may] reject a low wage now, if he believes that a better paying job will become available in the near future. These have to do with asymmetric information, with the information conveyed by the

> individual's willingness to accept a low wage job as well as with the fact that once someone is unemployed, he becomes 'used labour' with adverse effects on future wages
>
> (ibid.)

And what is the relationship between the *labour market* and the *product market* from a New Keynesian perspective? The answer to this question is provided by the assertion that 'in product markets, prices will tend to be more rigid than output levels as long as uncertainties concerning the impact of prices on demand are greater than uncertainties concerning the impact of output on cost' (Greenwald and Stiglitz, 1988a). Or as Mankiw describes the conclusions of Ball and Romer (1990):

> Nominal rigidities caused by menu costs are enhanced by real rigidities such as efficiency wages. Menu costs prevent prices from falling in response to a reduction in aggregate demand. Rigidity in real wages prevents wages from falling in response to the resulting unemployment. The failure of wages to fall keeps firms' costs high and thus ensures that they have little incentive to cut prices. Hence, although real wage rigidity alone is little help in understanding economic fluctuations because it leads only to classical unemployment and gives no role to aggregate demand, real wage rigidity together with menu costs provide a new and powerful explanation for Keynesian disequilibrium.
>
> (Mankiw, 1990, p. 1658)

So, again, what we see is the programme's methodology of positing a real wage/labour relationship at the firm level, then to be generalized in terms of industry as a whole, yielding some notion of an *aggregate* labour market with independent demand and supply curves in real wage/labour space. Given this framework, unemployment can *only* be perceived in terms of a price – in this case the real wage – not falling sufficiently to *clear* that market. No other heuristic is possible once the framework has been appropriately delimited.

INTEREST RATE RIGIDITY IN THE IMPERFECT CAPITAL MARKET MODEL

New Keynesian economists share the accepted Keynesian assertion that fluctuations in investment are a key ingredient towards our understanding of cyclical activity. However, given their unique and singular interpretation of Keynes, which observes problems occurring as a result of market imperfections, they find fault in what they perceive to be his theory of fluctuations in investment based on an emphasis on questions of expectations and animal spirits. In this sense they find his analysis ephemeral and incomplete, wanting for some theoretical structure/foundation to serve as a framework for *systematically* comprehending fluctuations in investment. Systematic thinking, in this case, leads them to the conventional question as to how some price offered and/or paid by a rational individual is or is not apt to clear some market. And in this particular case their attention is directed towards enquiring as to why a real rate of interest fails to adjust so as to clear the aggregate *credit market*, where the supply of savings should be efficiently transferred to producers to be borrowed to purchase additional capital assets. As would be expected, the model by which this heuristic is explicated is referred to as the 'imperfect capital market model' (see Flemming, 1973; Greenwald and Stiglitz, 1987).

The mechanism by which savings and investment are equated in such a capital market focuses on the nature of 'funds within the firm, and the funds at the disposal of the household' (Greenwald and Stiglitz, 1987, p. 122). In a perfect capital market, it is held, there should be no problem filtering either to the other with appropriate adjustments in real interest rates. However, if capital markets are imperfect, then the market gets clogged and fluctuations in investment may occur. From the New Keynesian perspective, these imperfections arise from asymmetric information in capital markets 'between managers of firms and potential investors, asymmetries which can give rise to what one can call equity rationing' (ibid, p. 125). For example, whereas in a perfect market when credit becomes scarce, real interest rates will rise to clear the market, with market imperfections, lenders may not lower their bidding price for assets (i.e. demand a higher real rate of interest):

> The reasons that suppliers of capital do not raise interest rates in the presence of an excess demand for capital are analogous to the reasons that firms do not lower wages in the presence of an excess supply of labour: increasing interest rates may lower the expected return to the supplier of capital, either because of selection effects (the mix of applicants changes adversely) or because of incentive effects (borrowers are induced to undertake riskier actions).
>
> (ibid., p. 126; see also Stiglitz and Weiss, 1987)

Asymmetries in information have been seen to affect quantity constraints, as well. Greenwald and Stiglitz (1988c) create a framework whereby the inability of suppliers of credit to know the potential profitability of firms (borrowers) causes the former to restrict their lending behaviour: 'Many firms face credit constraints; thus it is the availability of credit, not the interest that firms have to pay, which restricts their investment' (p. 144).

MARKETS AND COMPETITION IN A NEW KEYNESIAN FRAMEWORK: A KEYNESIAN PERSPECTIVE

What I wish to indicate in this section is that from Keynes's perspective, the mode by which we understand and explain business fluctuations had virtually nothing to do with market phenomena or language based on such a market. Unemployment, in the aggregate, should be seen as a phenomenon which affected the demand and supply of labour as a whole, and yet *it was not to have been considered in the context of a labour market.* Fluctuations in effective demand occurred primarily because of fluctuations in investment demand *but not in a capital market setting.* Keynes disavowed the theoretical possibility of an aggregate labour market except at the point of full employment equilibrium, and totally rejected the notion of an aggregate capital market where some real rate of interest mediated independent savings and investment schedules, at any rate of interest – real or otherwise. And finally, sticky prices are an integral part of Keynes's monetary theory of production, and yet they were not the factor that explained fluctuations in economic activity.

To the extent that this reading of Keynes is correct, the entire methodological foundation upon which New Keynesian economics is cast must be considered to be fallacious, despite the apparently plausible nature of their stories and the Keynesian features their models yield. In addition, their relaxation of the assumptions of perfect competition, perfect foresight and perfect knowledge becomes a subterfuge concealing the reality that there is, in fact, no *theoretical* basis for thinking in terms of goods, labour or capital markets as determining the levels of employment and output as a whole. In this regard, Keynes's fundamental criticism of orthodoxy was directed at the inappropriate methodological basis for considering changes in employment and output as a whole. The most important conclusion to come from these statements, in regard to the New Keynesian perspective, is that it really makes no difference as to the degree of competition when understanding fluctuations in employment and output. As Davidson emphatically indicates, Keynes's *general* theory was applicable to any degree of competition (this volume; see also Keynes, 1936, p. 245).

The labour market

Keynes's criticism of the orthodox theory was methodological.[6] He agreed with orthodox theory that it was possible to envision an individual firm where workers and producers could bargain in money terms, which would have virtually no effect on the price of wage goods or demand for that product. Thus, the money-wage bargain directly determined the real wage outcome. However, such logic for the individual firm could not be expanded to industry as a whole *unless certain restrictive assumptions were added.* In particular, to consider an aggregate labour market mediated by a real wage, it was necessary to assume that the wage bargain had no effect on either aggregate demand (and therefore supply and income) or the aggregate price level (see 1936, chs 19 and 20). Then changes in money wages or the price level (in this case as an independent variable considered in terms of the denominator of an aggregate real wage) would not cause a change in the *aggregate* demand for labour (as opposed to the quantity of labour demanded) or in the price level (in an endogenous sense). Such logic did not describe an aggregate labour market, according to Keynes, but only a market in which a given quantity of labour flowed among alternative employments. Unemployment could only occur in a *particular* sector to the extent that there was an excess demand for labour in another sector. Orthodox, including New Keynesian economic, models give the *appearance* of describing changes in employment as a whole – in their use of the language of aggregate demand and supply curves for labour – when, in fact, their market-based framework precludes any concept of *aggregate* unemployment. By means of the orthodox metaphor one could only consider, in Keynes's words, 'the direction of employment but not its quantity' (ibid., p. vii).

Then we find New Keynesian economists speaking of economic fluctuations in terms of the extent to which the Classical Dichotomy is or is not violated when there is some exogenous change in a nominal variable. Keynes rejected any notion of a Classical Dichotomy *other than at the point of full employment equilibrium.* There, increases in the stock of money would affect the general price level because aggregate output was at a maximum. Moreover, for a given level of prices there would be a corresponding real wage, given money wages. General equilibrium would also imply market clearing for labour for each individual firm, also stated in terms of a real wage. It is in this sense that Keynes, in a 1933 draft of *The General Theory*, referred to such a configuration as a *real wage* economy because it was the real wage which was the operative (although not causal) phrase in the equation linking the parts and the whole of the economy (see Rotheim, 1981, 1991). However, if it is the general equilibrium solution which defines the unique real wage which links all individuals, then following this logic leads to the false belief that it is the individual markets which are the sole explanatory elements in the general equilibrium solution. This reflects a methodological individualist approach to the macroeconomic problem: we can add up from individual markets where the real wage is determined by independent supply and demand curves to achieve the aggregate labour market solution in real wage/employment space.

The real wage economy defined for Keynes a structure *at* the point of full employment equilibrium. However, no causal statements could safely be made were the system to be *out* of equilibrium. The real wage could be seen as a compound phrase associated with a *position* of full employment equilibrium. But no operational significance should be assigned to that phrase in any other circumstances. Speaking in terms of a real wage economy was only possible, Keynes held, *if the level of aggregate income did not change* (see 1936, ch. 19). Given this restrictive assumption, changes in the money wage would have no effect on the aggregate level of output or output prices, and workers would be in control of the real wage by means of their money-wage bargain (an aggregate labour supply schedule in realwage/labour space). Moreover, an aggregate demand schedule for labour could be defined in that space, according to the following logic:

> In any given industry we have a demand schedule for the product relating the quantities which can be sold to the prices asked; we have a series of supply schedules relating the prices which will be asked for the sale of different quantities on various bases of cost; and these schedules between them lead up to a further schedule which, on the assumption that other costs are unchanged (except as a result of the change in output), gives us the demand schedule for labour in the industry relating the quantity of

> employment to different levels of wages, the shape of the curve at any point furnishing the elasticity of demand for labour. This conception is transferred without substantial modification to the industry as a whole; and it is supposed, by a parity of reasoning, that we have a demand schedule for labour in industry as a whole relating the quantity of employment to different levels of wages. It is held that it makes no material difference to this argument whether it is in terms of money-wages or real wages. If we are thinking in terms of money-wages, we must, of course, correct for changes in the value of money; but this leaves the general tendency of the argument unchanged, since prices certainly do not change in exact proportion to changes in money-wages.

Given this framework, Keynes immediately recognized that it was 'fallacious':

> For the demand schedules for particular industries can only be constructed on some fixed assumption as to the nature of the demand and supply schedules of other industries and as to the amount of the aggregate effective demand. It is invalid, therefore, to transfer the argument to industry as a whole unless we also transfer our assumption that the aggregate effective demand is fixed. Yet this assumption reduces the argument to an *ignoratio elenchi*. For, whilst no one would wish to deny the proposition that a reduction in money-wages *accompanied by the same aggregate effective demand as before* will be associated with an increase in employment, the precise question at issue is whether the reduction in money-wages will or will not be accompanied by the same aggregate effective demand as before measured in money, or at any rate, by an aggregate effective demand which is not reduced in full proportion to the reduction in money-wages (i.e. which is somewhat greater measured in wage-units). But if the classical theory is not allowed to extend by analogy its conclusions in respect of a particular industry to industry as a whole, it is wholly unable to answer the question what effect on employment a reduction in money-wages will have. For it has no method of analysis wherewith to tackle the problem.
>
> (1936, pp. 258–60)

However, if the assumption of fixed aggregate levels of output and prices were to be dropped, then it becomes impossible to apply the *language* of the individual to that of industry as a whole (see Rotheim, 1988). Here the laws of supply and demand for labour in the aggregate have no meaningful relationship to those laws at the level of the individual firm. There is no longer any unique relationship between changes in money wages or the price of wage goods and well-defined, unique aggregate labour supply and demand curves. Keynes saw the breakdown of this framework occurring because the factors which underlie the aggregate demand and supply curves for labour were not independent of one another. Thus a change in money wages or the price of wage goods would, out of necessity, have an indeterminate effect on the aggregate level of employment. In other words, there is an interdependence among the factors underlying the conditions of supply and demand which precludes the unique definition of an aggregate labour market by which employment in the aggregate can be made comprehensible.[7]

The capital market

Turning to the New Keynesian theory of capital markets, we find the issue couched in terms of an aggregate capital market where some real rate of interest defines that price which equates the supply of loanable funds (savings) with the demand for capital assets. Unlike the orthodox theory of the level of aggregate employment which Keynes believed was consistent with his own theory, although limited only to the point of full employment, he dismissed the orthodox theory of the rate of interest as simply wrong, in that it 'involves a formal error' (1936, p. 179; see also Milgate, 1977; Panico, 1987).[8] One of the independent variables of the orthodox system is the level of aggregate income, while the quantities of savings and investment are the dependent variables for any given rate of interest. Should there be a shift in either the demand curve for capital or the supply curve for savings (the obverse of the demand curve for consumption), then the rate of interest must adjust to change the level of consumption or the quantity of capital demanded; that is, there will be an appropriate movement along the independent supply and demand curves. But, as Keynes observed:

> the assumption that income is constant is inconsistent with the assumption that these two curves can shift independently of one another. If either of them shift, then, in general, income will change; with the result that the whole schematism based on the assumption of a given income breaks down.
> (1936, p. 179)

Keynes's criticism is again based on the degree to which interdependence among the conditions underlying the supply of savings and the demand for capital precludes the possibility of a unique equilibrium for any real rate of interest. Any individual may change his or her savings or purchases of capital goods out of a given amount of income and it may be possible to construct a supply of savings or demand for capital schedule for that individual which is independent of the level of income. In the aggregate, however, a change in either schedule will alter the level of income and thus upset the position of either or both curves. Moreover, since any flow of investment generates its equivalent flow of savings, it is impossible to conceive of an aggregate capital market along orthodox lines:

> The analogy with the demand and supply for a commodity at a given price is a false analogy. For whereas it is perfectly easy to name a price at which the supply and the demand for a commodity would be unequal, it is impossible to name a rate of interest at which the amount of saving and the amount of investment could be unequal.
> (1973c, p. 476)

The goods market in a monetary theory of production

New Keynesian economists claim that they have revived an interest and 'emphasis on microeconomic foundations... attempting to build macroeconomic theory from new developments in the microeconomics of goods, labour, and capital markets' (Mankiw, 1993, p. 4). Again, no one would quibble with their earnest attempt to return a role for the individual decision maker into aggregate models. Indeed, one cold argue that among the deficiencies characterizing aggregate Keynesian models, such as the ISLM framework, is the fact that individuals and individual decisions are nowhere to be found, except in attenuated form (see Rotheim, 1989, 1995b). But the search for such a theory of value and distribution should not be expected to be found from within the heuristic which is orthodox neoclassical economics, especially its Walrasian variant. For it is not a movement in the direction of progress, as New Keynesians admit, to condemn the assumption made by New Classical macroeconomics of continuous market clearing as unrealistic when considering fluctuations in effective demand, especially if the criticism embodies the same theory of value and distribution as the one being contested. Progress can only come when we discard the traditional theory of value and distribution separate from the theory of money and prices, along with the heuristic which emanated from this bifurcated theory. In its place there needs to be established what Keynes called a *monetary theory of production* or what might also be called a *monetary theory of value* in which the separation, which only has ontological significance at the point of full employment equilibrium, is melded so as to embrace *all* levels of aggregate output and employment. For, indeed, it was Keynes's aim both to reject the traditional theory of value which separated questions of money and prices from value and distribution, and to replace it by a monetary theory of value which distinguished between questions relating to firms and to industry as a whole (see Keynes, 1936, ch. 21), but not where there was a methodological individualism which legitimized the use of the language of individual optimizing behaviour when characterizing and discussing the latter.

Appearances can be deceiving, however, because Keynes *did* assume that money wages and money rates of interest were sticky, especially in a downward direction. What, then, is the relevance of these assumptions if they do not fall within the heuristic dictated by the New Keynesian programme? The first thing to recall, from Keynes's perspective, is that money is that durable asset which, among all assets, has those essential properties which keep its value stable relative to all other assets. It has no *market-determined* flow supply price, while possessing the highest liquidity premium relative to its carrying cost. These properties of money translate into relative stickiness in money rates of interest as a result of confidence in the relative stability in the value of that unit over time. The stickiness in money rates of interest occurs because money prices (the things that money buys) are relatively sticky as money wages (the things in which workers conventionally bargain) are relatively sticky. So, unlike the orthodox metaphor where it is sticky wages and prices which cause markets not to clear, in Keynes's system, it is sticky wages and prices which provide for the stability of prices (forward relative to spot), consequently giving individuals confidence in the relationship between the present and future. It allows them to rely on certain modes of convention (rationality), which gives them the confidence to commit resources for a longer period of time rather than in liquid assets (see Lawson, 1991); it keeps the economy growing within ranges of stability. Sticky money wages and prices, then, are not the microeconomic explanation for low-level equilibria in the aggregate, but rather are the precondition to the growth of output, itself. Moreover, for Keynes it was *flexible* wages and prices which caused the economic fluctuations that those flexible variables were expected to mitigate (see 1936, ch. 18).

In this light, involuntary unemployment should not be seen as the result of real wages being sticky downward, as is viewed by New Keynesian economics. Instead, from a Keynesian perspective, involuntary unemployment is a situation where, if every worker were to accept a lower wage, not only would they not get a job, there might even be fewer jobs available than in the initial instance. David Champernowne assess the issue in this way:

> The argument on which Keynes himself relied most was that money wage flexibility, far from allowing an orderly return to full employment would result in the economy being driven either to a state of reckless inflation with money wages, prices, effective demand, and [initially] employment all shooting up, or else to a state of panic with money wages, prices, employment, and effective demand plunging into a bottomless sink. He regarded the relative stability actually found in the economic system as being due to the stickiness of money wages.
>
> (1963, pp. 190–1)

Here unemployment is not a market phenomenon, but rather a manifestation of non-price actions within the context of the relationship among those who receive income, produce output (the supply side), and spend in the aggregate (the demand side). The perspective is not a methodologically individualist reduction to rational, a priori agents whose actions are neither affected by nor affect the actions of other agents.[9]

Keynes's critique of the orthodox macroeconomic approach was focused directly at its fallacious theory of value and distribution. He observed that the questions underlying this approach in terms of the flexibility of relative prices in aggregate market settings suffered, as we saw, from the fallacy of *ignoratio elenchi*, i.e. employing the logic of one system to validate the logic of another. What was true for any individual, in any market, could not be generalized for industry as a whole. As such, the language of the individual or firm, based on factors unique to those individuals and firms, could not be the basis for understanding macroeconomic questions. Moreover, the very nature of beings at the individual level, which could be defined in terms of things *internal* to themselves, i.e. in terms of utility and technology, took on different forms as the nature of individuals bore meaning only as they existed in the social context of the economy, itself. For just as Keynes found it necessary to reject the possibility of markets at the aggregate level characterized by independent supply and demand relations mediated by some price, a corollary of this observation was that such interdependencies implied that the nature of supply and demand decisions could not be reduced to and therefore analysed with respect to matters such as the productivity of labour or capital, or the marginal disutility of labour or marginal time preference. The very foundations of traditional theory were called into question by Keynes's attacks.

COORDINATION FAILURES: SPILLOVERS AND STRATEGIC COMPLEMENTARITIES

What we have seen, so far, is that the programme of New Keynesian economics has been broadly enough defined so as to have given researchers a fairly wide berth in which to operate. And thus, stories abound. And in each of those stories, the mode of behaviour assumed a given core (theory of markets, Classical Dichotomy, representative agent, etc.), devised stories that helped explain the particular violations of the ideal core, and then formalized those stories to adhere to acceptable modes of discourse: small menu costs and near rationality cause prices to be sticky and output to adjust; efficiency wages etc. cause both nominal and real wages to be sticky and employment to bear the impact of changes in nominal demand; investment fluctuates because real interest rates tend to be sticky in light of capital market imperfections.

Recently, there has been a new set of stories created, with a common theme – that being a failure of the market to coordinate individual actions. This new set of examples has the potential of undermining the very foundation of any neoclassical macroeconomic theory, including the New Keynesian variant illustrated above. What all of these stories have in common is the notion that there is a recognized *interdependence* among payoffs and actions such that an individual cannot know the consequences of his or her actions independent of the actions other individuals may be undertaking. Objective functions are no longer a priori sets, but rather affect and are affected by the actions of agents. The foundations of the market metaphors no longer possess any sense of stability or independence, and therefore the structures, themselves, become inappropriate for discussing changes in employment and output in the aggregate. This variant of New Keynesianism may have created the circumstances invalidating most of the conventional New Keynesian programme.

The seminal work in this area has been done by Russell Cooper and Andrew John (1988). Interestingly enough, Cooper and John introduce their paper by citing 'a number of authors [who] have recently constructed examples of economies that exhibit underemployment equilibria, but where the results do not derive from the usual Keynesian assumptions' (ibid., p. 441). Now of course what they mean by Keynesian assumptions are that wages and prices fail to adjust with nominal demand shocks. Instead they construct a general model exhibiting 'Keynesian features' side-stepping Keynesian assumptions, by showing how 'agents are unable to co-ordinate their actions successfully in a many-person, decentralised economy' (ibid.). The two heuristical devices they employ are what are called *spillovers* and *strategic complementarities*:

> The former refers to the interaction between agents at the level of payoffs, while the latter refers to interactions at the level of strategies. Suppose that in a game there are two players who select single-dimensional strategies. Spillovers arise if an increase in one player's strategy affects the *payoffs* of the other players... [whereas] strategic complementarities arise if an increase in one player's strategy increases the *optimal strategy* of the other player.
>
> (ibid., p. 442)

First, consider a simple two-person game where payoffs differ depending upon the collective outcomes of individual actions. Mankiw (1992, p. 315) gives the New Keynesian example where an exogenous reduction in the nominal money stock will have differing consequences on the economy depending upon individual firms' willingness to reduce their prices. If they both lower their prices, then real balances will increase sufficiently causing a restoration of spending and neutrality in the real sector – the impact of the money stock reduction being borne solely on nominal prices. The following payoff matrix could describe what might occur:

		Firm 2: lower price	Firm 2: do not lower price
Firm 1	lower price	30, 30	5, 15
	do not lower price	15, 5	15, 15

If in reaction to a fall in demand both firms lower their price, then the equilibrium payoff will be the best for both involved. However, if one lowers its price while the other does not, then the other gets the larger payoff with significantly less to the firm which lowers its price. The possibility of such a contingency may lead both firms to assume that the other will not lower its price, causing both not to lower price. In this case there is a sub-optimal or low-level Nash equilibrium in which price does not fall, but output falls farther then the original fall: 'When this occurs, a *coordination failure* is present: mutual gains from an all-around change in strategies may not be realised, because no individual player has an incentive to deviate from the initial equilibrium' (Cooper and John, 1988, p. 442). Ball and Romer (1991) have taken this simple idea and expanded on it to show that strategic complementarities can result in a spectrum of equilibria, some optimal, others sub-optimal.

Clearly, the more interesting of the two devices (although they should not be seen as mutually exclusive) are models which exhibit strategic complementarity. For in these cases, the very basis on which individuals can conduct optimizing behaviour is dependent upon the strategies chosen by other players. This story is then formalized by Cooper and John, but their basic message rings through:

> Strategic complementarity...implies that an increase in the action of all agents except agent *i* increases the marginal return to agent *i*'s action... which lead to so-called Keynesian features: with an external shock, multiplier effects are present when the aggregate response exceeds the individual response.
>
> (Cooper and John, 1988, p. 442..)

However, under such circumstances they go on to show that the existence of strategic complementarities gives rise to multiple symmetric Nash equilibria, which are sub-optimal but stable, in the sense that a series of individual actions will cause outcomes which do not necessarily improve social welfare. Low-level equilibria can occur because no individual has the incentive to lower the price or change output. However, any change in output not only affects consumers but also benefits them through a spillover effect or demand externality which, in turn, allows for strategic complementarities and movements to higher-level equilibria through multiplier effects. Such multiplier effects brought about by strategic complementarities cause *income* to change, affecting the underlying data facing each individual. This last assertion has very important implications from a strictly Keynesian perspective.

Moreover, these insights lead them to identify possible sources of economic fluctuations as having their origins in *sectors* of the economy: 'aggregate movements need not be consequences of aggregate shocks but may instead be the result of sector-specific shocks coupled with demand spillovers' (ibid., p. 456).

This coordination failure literature has opened up a plethora of ideas that have the potentiality for transcending the narrow and restrictive theoretically questionable confines of neoclassical price-theoretic macroeconomics. Statements such as those made by Cooper and John, 'One can view this approach as arguing for the importance of macroeconomic quantities in microeconomic choice function.... [A]n individual's optimal strategy depended on an aggregate measure of the actions selected by others in the economy' (ibid., p. 461), are quite reassuring. Still, such writers have not broken completely from the neoclassical mold, in that their initial *entrée* into such questions generally begins with the traditional sticky price and imperfectly competitive premises. Take, for example, this citation to the seminal Blanchard and Kiyotaki paper:

> If starting from the monopolistically competitive equilibrium, a firm decreased its price, this would lead to a small decrease in the price level and thus to a small increase in aggregate demand. While the other firms and households would benefit from this increase in aggregate demand, the original firm cannot capture all of these benefits and thus has no incentive to decrease its price.... Suppose however that all price setters decrease their prices simultaneously; this increases real money balances and aggregate

> demand. The increase in output reduces the initial distortion of underproduction and underemployment and increases social welfare.
> (Blanchard and Kiyotaki, 1987, p. 653; see also Ball and Romer, 1991)

However, while the questions this view raises are interesting, they are still couched in the traditional New Keynesian framework of sticky prices. There is still the accepted view that if firms were to lower their prices, then none of these Keynesian features and Keynesian results would occur; we are still in a Keynesian imperfectionist world where employment and output must be fixed in order for the market heuristic to be a viable mode of discourse. But the Cooper and John framework stands independent of the market metaphor; in fact, given the theoretical flaws in the market metaphor, it would be a marked improvement if that metaphor were discarded altogether.

Two things should be apparent. First, this variant of New Keynesian economics, but without the specific reliance on price rigidities to make its point, has potential as providing a framework into which some of the salient points of Keynes's theory of effective demand and involuntary unemployment might be expounded. And second, what also should be clear is that this framework has value *independent of assumptions made about the degree of competition in particular industries.* Spillovers and strategic complementarities occur to all participating firms regardless of their relative size or their ability to control their pricing and hiring decisions. Davidson (1996) has recently observed that Keynes's theory bears credibility for *any* degree of competition. In this regard he refers to the fact that Keynes explicitly states that he takes as given the degree of competition, but that '[t]his does not mean that we assume these factors to be constant; but merely that, in this place and context, we are not considering or taking into account the effects and consequences of change in them' (1936, p. 245).[10]

Multiplier and other effects occurring on account of meaningful interdependencies do not require any statement regarding the degree of competition or price stickiness. To the extent that nominal demand shocks affect the circle of output, income and employment, either viciously or virtuously, fluctuations in relative prices do not appear to play significant roles, especially if rational behaviour is predicated on socially contextual knowledge or organic uncertainty, depending upon which way the circle is spinning.[11]

CONCLUDING REMARKS

In this chapter we have seen that New Keynesian economics relies on either (a) rigid prices caused by small costs leading to large changes in demand or (b) coordination failures. The former is theoretically inept. It is based on a heuristical construct wholly inappropriate for understanding fluctuations in economic activity in the case of industry as a whole. The latter, once the price-theoretic framework is discarded, opens an entirely new perspective to the extent that interactions of individuals can change the circumstances which underlie individual decisions. In this case what of the notion of equilibrium and the laws of economics that emanate from such equilibrium conditions? What happens to the atomistic individual whose decision set is presumably independent of the actions of others? And, most importantly, what happens to the orthodox theory of value and distribution which stands at the heart of the New Keynesian project?[12]

Towards this end, Murray Milgate, in his critique of efficiency wage theories, makes the most perspicacious point when he says that nothing in the New Keynesian programme threatens the theory of value and distribution:

> I contend that the overwhelming majority of modern controversies in the theory of employment are about whether the existence of imperfections ought to temper the application of our most basic vision of the market mechanism to everyday situations. If this is correct, then there is no ultimate theoretical principle at stake in most of the debates which have occupied the pages of our professional journals and the columns of our newspapers over the past decade or so. It all becomes a matter of degree. I further contend that among those who feel that it is impossible to ignore imperfections, controversy in the theory of employment is exclusively over the question of exactly which of the many possible imperfections is, practically speaking, the most important.
>
> (1988, p. 80)

It is the unbending adherence to orthodoxy which ultimately renders insignificant any macroeconomic theory based on the traditional orthodox microeconomic theories of value and distribution. In fact, I think it is clear that such a conclusion was on Keynes's mind when he found classical economics to be on an errant path. Keynes's own theory of effective demand (as opposed to the New Keynesian elaboration of aggregate supply) embodied some of the very same observations perceived by New Keynesians (especially sticky wages and prices) but in his case these observations dictated the conditions by which a capitalist economy remained *within* a range of stability and determinacy (including the possibility of full employment) rather than as creating the barriers to the achievement of the full employment equilibrium solution. For, at the end of the day, Keynes left us with a revised theory of value and distribution which included the roles of money and prices, in the form of a monetary theory of production. One cannot speak of a Keynesian model without the explicit foundation provided by that alternative theory of value. By leaving intact the basic heuristic of the traditional theory of value, New Keynesian macroeconomists have come no closer to an understanding or articulation of what can safely be called *Keynesian* economics.

At the heart of Keynes's economics is a theoretical critique of both the theories of value and distribution underlying the traditional macroeconomic programme – the language of markets is theoretically invalid at the macroeconomic level. Keynes, instead, attempted to replace that inappropriate macroeconomic theory with a monetary theory of production and value, one that disavows the Classical Dichotomy as the heuristical foundation of discourse so that thinking in terms of real variables, separate from nominal variables, has no methodological justification. Monetary variables become the operationally significant concepts in terms of individuals' decision-making processes as these monetary variables reflect the organically interdependent and temporal nature of a decentralized market process. Assumptions of sticky wages and prices, which contain no validity when there are no theoretical foundations for aggregate labour and product markets as compositions of individual firm activities, such as in the New Keynesian system, become the cornerstone for a Keynesian monetary theory of value in which those institutional assumptions help explain not the disequilibria that permeate a decentralized economy, but rather the existence of a range of stability and determinacy that such an economy appears to have achieved. Sticky wages and prices are not reflective of market failure, but rather are indicative of market health.

NOTES

* The author wishes to thank Victoria Chick, Paul Davidson, Gary Dymski, G. C. Harcourt, Hubert Kempf, Laurence Moss and Fieke van der Lecq for comments on earlier versions of this chapter.

1 This authoritative *imprimatur* can be found in almost every article professing to be New Keynesian in nature. For example, Alan Blinder writes: 'Everyone knows that nominal price or wage rigidities are central to Keynesian theory. Indeed, some critics refuse to consider Keynesianism a full-fledged theory because it lacks a theoretical rationale for the nominal rigidities it assumes' (1989, p. xi). Or we observe Greenwald and Stiglitz saying: 'It has been widely noted of business cycles that, while quantities vary dramatically, prices vary only slightly, if at all. Applied to the labour market, this observation, that employment is far more variable over the cycle than wages, is one of the cornerstones of Keynesian theory' (1989, p. 364). See also Blinder (1991, p. 89) and Mankiw (1993, pp. 312–13).

2 Davidson cites Blanchard as believing that all mainstream macroeconomic models 'impose the long-run neutrality of money as a maintained assumption. This is very much a matter of faith, based on theoretical considerations rather than on empirical science (Blanchard, 1990, p. 828)' cited in Davidson (this volume).

3 It is quite interesting that change only occurs from the New Keynesian perspective (as is also true of all neoclassical approaches) by means of *exogenous* shocks to established equilibria. In other words, the starting-point being equilibrium necessitates the existence of the Classical Dichotomy from the outset. This is essential to these approaches, because at any other point than the point of general equilibrium, the dichotomy would not hold and the set of questions that constitutes the positive heuristic of neoclassical approaches would also be invalidated. Moreover, such approaches conform to what critical realists refer to as the necessity of there being constant conjunctions of events, i.e. the systems must be closed (see Lawson, 1995, 1997). Change never occurs as a part of the system itself being open and therefore in the process of unfolding, so to speak. For in these cases, there need be no exogenous shocks as impetus for change.

4 I am grateful to Laurence Moss for this insight. Clearly New Keynesian economics does not take a strong methodological individualist perspective because the consequent demand externalities brought about by sticky prices preclude a simple addition over all firms to reach aggregate results. Still, using the language of the individual to characterize aggregate mechanisms signifies that a weaker form of methodological individualism is operational.

5 Some empirical confirmations of the menu-cost-based approach to sticky prices can be found in Ball, *et al.* (1991) and Blinder (1991). A recent study of UK firms by Hall, *et al.* (1996) found little direct evidence for the menu-cost-based approach, however.

6 Portions of this section are developed in Rotheim (1992).

7 The origins of these ideas come from Marshall in the *Principles*, where he questions the possibility of drawing a unique supply of labour schedule, since he believed that the schedule *shifted* every time the wage changed, because the marginal utility of income was not insignificant – a requirement for the derivation of such schedules – in the case of labour. Based on these signals, as well as those provided by Sraffa (1925, 1926), Maurice Dobb (1929) elaborated on this theme, proving that wages in the aggregate could not be determined in an aggregate labour market, because the two elements of such a market – independent supply and demand schedules – did not logically exist. On the development of this idea and the influence it had on Keynes, especially in the case of Dobb, see Rotheim (1992).

8 It is rather odd that Greenwald and Stiglitz accuse Keynes of being 'too much a neoclassical economist... [in that] he wanted to rely on adjustments in the rate of interest as the equilibrating mechanism' (1988b).

9 The search for unique *micro*foundations is itself a heuristical manifestation of orthodoxy. The methodological individual of this approach forces a conformity with outcomes as the aggregation (usually linear) of all of these individuals. As an ideology, methodological individualism reinforces a social psychology that one need only look at things *inherent* to one's immediate environment, as opposed to perceiving oneself as a single element in a wider, complex and interdependent social nexus. Granted, no individual is, in most cases, powerful enough to affect the outcome of all socially based activity. Still, the unique social psychology of this paradigm asserts that social elements have *no* bearing or influential force on individual actions.

10 This chapter will not address the question of the relationship between decreasing costs and the degree of competition in *The General Theory*. It was the result of Sraffa's seminal work (1925, especially Section III; see Kahn, 1984, pp. 24–5) that we learn of the incompatibility between the theory of competition and the decrease in individual cost. This factor does not really arise in *The General Theory*, but is raised by Keynes in his reply to Dunlop and Tarshis (1939), when he considers the effects of economic expansion on the real wage (which he originally posited to move counter-cyclically). For a discussion of this topic, see Sardoni (1992).

11 The problem with assuming that things go awry because people take their income and put it in money instead of real assets, is that it assumes that the income already exists. This seems to beg the question, since the theory of effective demand tries to see things in terms of decisions made today based on *expected* income. One may borrow today (and that may be from banks implying that saving out of current income need not occur) to make these purchases.

12 Thus we hear Murray Milgate's assessment of one class of New Keynesian models, the efficiency wage contract: '[T]he traditional conception of labour markets remains in place under the efficiency-wage hypothesis. As in the old debates, two things are simultaneously established by labour contracts – the (real) wage rate and the amount of employment.... [T]his conception is simply an extension to the market for labour services of the vision of price-quantity determination in commodity markets that is at the hearts of the works of Marshall and Walras' (1988, p. 77).

4

PRICE THEORY AND MACROECONOMICS

Stylized facts and New Keynesian fantasies

Edward J. Nell

Macroeconomics makes an occasional bow to history and institutions, noting their importance in understanding policy, particularly in connection with exogenous *shocks*. But the models advanced in most mainstream work, as well as those in contemporary *alternative* schools of thought, tend to be perfectly general. They are not considered specific to any one historical period. Economic behaviour and the working of markets are treated as universal, essentially the same, aside from *imperfections*, in all times and places. Economics is grounded in rational choice, expressed most fully in general equilibrium price theory. Macroeconomics can then be derived from this by specifying any of a large number of imperfections or institutional barriers to the smooth adjustment of markets.

General equilibrium theory is abstract and non-empirical. But price theory does not have to take this form.[1] Ordinary textbook microeconomics – supply and demand – offers a strikingly detailed picture of the way markets work, from which a number of plausible empirical propositions can be derived. For example, this picture suggests that when demand fluctuates, prices will fluctuate in the same direction, and the fluctuations will be greater the more inelastic the supply is. Movements in prices will therefore be positively correlated with movements in output. Real wages will be inversely related to employment and output. Increases in productivity will lead to lower prices. The picture has institutional implications as well: firms will grow to an optimal size and operate at that level indefinitely.

These empirical implications of ordinary price theory are seldom stressed, perhaps because they do not appear to be true of today's economy. Instead, price theory tends to be developed axiomatically, and is presented as an offshoot of a more general theory of rational choice. But this is to do microeconomics a disservice. It was originally formulated as a theory of the working of markets, and it deserves to be taken seriously as just that.

Old-fashioned macroeconomics, as presented in the textbooks of the 1950s, like the simplest models today, took prices as fixed, and examined quantity adjustments. These reflected the multiplier and the accelerator, or 'capital stock adjustment' principle, and provided an account of market adjustment, which could be and was examined empirically in extensive studies.[2] These models also yielded policy implications.

Macroeconomic data suggests a great difference between the working of the economy in the era in which price theory was founded and its behaviour later. In the late nineteenth century when price theory developed, production was organized largely through family firms and family farms, and steam power was used to operate processes that still reflected traditional crafts. In the Keynesian era, production came to be organized by giant modern corporations running modern technologies on electric power and internal combustion (Tylecote, 1991; Perez, 1983, 1985; Solomou, 1986). The technologies are different and so are the institutions. As a result, it will be argued, so is the way the market works.

In the earlier period the market appeared to function in some respects, as would be expected from neoclassical theory, at least in Marshallian form. In the later period aspects of its working appear to be Keynesian, and the neoclassical elements have largely disappeared. In the earlier period there is some evidence to suggest that the market and the price mechanism responded in a stabilizing manner. Financial markets and the monetary system, however, tended to be unstable. The turning points of the business cycle appear to have been endogenous. In the later period, however, the stabilizing aspects of market adjustment appear to have vanished, Indeed, market responses appear to exacerbate fluctuations, as would be expected from Keynesian theory and from early Keynesian accounts of the business cycle. The government, however, perhaps in conjunction with the financial system, has tended to provide a stabilizing influence.

An explanation for the differences between the eras can be suggested, which is supported by the record, namely that the prevalent technology in the earlier period prevented easy adjustment of output and employment. This, in effect, imposed a form of price flexibility, which can be shown to have had a moderately stabilizing influence. But technological innovation greatly increased the adaptability of production processes, so that by the later period, output and employment could be adjusted easily, and the resulting system can be shown to be unstable in a Keynesian sense.

STYLIZED FACTS

Many extraneous influences affect economic variables. So it is difficult to make general claims about the economy – there will always be exceptions. Moreover, few relationships in economics are fully stable; they tend to be affected by external and arguably irrelevant forces. To deal with this Kaldor suggested the use of '*stylized facts*'.[3] These pick out central and defining features and present them with the rough edges smoothed over, highlighted, so they can be seen with clarity.

Stylized facts are stated in general propositions; they present observable, repeatable relationships between measurable variables. They state that two or more variables move together in some definite pattern; or that two or more variables are independent of one another, or that certain relationships, e.g. ratios, can be expressed by constants (Klein and Kosobud, 1952). These facts are said to be valid over some considerable range of times and places, and can be verified or supported by different bodies of data.

'Stylizing' facts means to remove noise, to remove the influence of irrelevant variables, to cut away random or extraneous factors, so as to present the central relationship in pure – and often, in simplified – form. If the relationship is complex or awkward, it may be 'rounded off', or reduced to a more manageable format. What is irrelevant, or extraneous, however, may not be obvious. It will always call for judgement; it may also be a matter of theory.

In particular, many relationships involve variations that take place in the context of a *trend*, so that the relationship cannot be seen, or seen clearly, until the trend has been removed. De-trending, however, requires identifying the trend, not a simple or unambiguous matter. Depending on circumstances, this may require deciding which factors determine the trend, and which the variations around it, a separation that reflects basic assumptions. So de-trending is not innocent; different procedures are likely to yield different patterns of fluctuation around the trend (Canova, 1991).

Stylized facts can be considered at two levels. There are the individual facts, each of which tells us something about a particular area of the economy, and then there is the pattern or configuration that can be seen in a group of such facts. If the stylized facts encompass the main features of the economy this will give us a picture of the system as a whole. To make that judgement, of course, requires a theory that defines the main features of the economy.

A different kind of judgement is needed to determine the range of times and places for which these facts should be expected to hold. Are economic relationships timeless, i.e. expected to hold always and everywhere? If they are derived from rational choice, perhaps they should. But if such a notion of rationality is unrealistic, or inconsistent with other aspects of human thought and culture, as philosophers have suggested (Hollis, 1995), economic relationships may be *historical*, in the sense that they hold for particular periods of history, and not otherwise.

This is the perspective adopted here. A number of general propositions have been established about the trade cycle at different times. These will be grouped under five headings, with representative sources cited. The claims will be presented separately, under the same headings, for an earlier and a later historical period. In each case, taken together the propositions provide an approximately accurate picture over most of the period. The two pictures present a striking contrast. Moreover, the subject-matter is central to economic analysis; prices, money wages, employment, productivity, expenditure and money are at issue. Institutions – government and the firm – are also portrayed. Sources and brief explanations will be given, but no attempt will be made here to justify the claims in detail. Nor is it claimed that the list of proposed 'facts' is complete – only that it is sufficient to suggest two different coherent pictures. The first group of propositions presents a portrait of the old trade cycle of the nineteenth century, running roughly from the Napoleonic Wars to World War I, although respectable data only exists after about

1860 – and even then much is questionable. The second covers the era after World War II.

THE OLD TRADE CYCLE

Business units tended to be small, operating relatively inflexible methods of production, meaning that the factory or shop could be either operated or shut down, but could not easily be adjusted to variable levels of output. Prices, on the other hand, were flexible in both directions, as were money wages. The price mechanism appeared to operate. The cycle could be seen in price data.

Prices and money wages

1 The trend of prices was downwards over the whole period. By contrast, the trend of money wages was more or less flat in the first half century, then moderately rising.[4] (*Sources:* Sylos-Labini, 1989, esp. Tables I, II; 1993, esp. Table I, Appendix I; Pigou, 1929, esp. Charts 3, 11, 14, 15, 16; Phelps Brown and Hopkins, 1981, chs. 7, 8; Phelps Brown and Hopkins, in Carus-Wilson, 1954a, esp. Fig. 1, p. 183.) There was an upturn in prices in the 1860s, and a smaller one just before World War I, but the trend is dominant. The latter half of the nineteenth century shows a slight upward trend in money wages, becoming more pronounced after 1900.[5]

2 Both prices and money wages changed in both directions. Changes in raw material prices (deviations from the trend) were greater in both directions than changes in manufacturing prices, which in turn were grea ter than changes in money wages.[6] (*Sources:* as above, plus Pedersen and Pedersen (1938), who focus on the contrast between flexible and relatively inflexible prices. Most of their most flexible prices were raw materials. It is noticeable, however, that even their 'inflexible' prices (prices that remain unchanged for more than one year, a number of times over the century) exhibit a downward trend, p. 222.)

Employment, output and real wages

3 Changes in unemployment (proxy for output) were less than the changes in prices; changes in unemployment were 'small'. Although direct measurements of output are hard to come by, output and employment varied together, with output variations being larger. Prices and output varied together, with prices being somewhat more variable than output. Changes in investment and net exports are often associated with opposite variations in consumption; they certainly do not lead to variations in the same direction, as the multiplier would require. (*Sources:* as above. Double-digit unemployment was rare, cf. Pigou, 1929, Charts 18, 19. Hoffmann provides an output index based on forty-three series, which Phelps Brown adapts for 1861–1913. Pigou uses unemployment as a proxy for output. Sylos-Labini (1989), compares changes in prices,

wages and output. Nell and Phillips found evidence inconsistent with a multiplier in Canadian data for 1870–1914. Block (1997) and Kucera (1997) have confirmed the correlation between prices and output for Germany and Japan, respectively.

4 Putting these together, it can be seen that real wages, or more particularly product wages, moved counter-cyclically. That is to say, real wages varied directly with unemployment. (*Sources:* Pigou, 1929., esp. Charts 16, 18, 20; Michie, 1987). Michie recalculates the work of Dunlop and Tarshis, and finds that product wages moved counter-cyclically before World War I (ch. 8). US figures are problematical, but a weak counter-cyclical pattern is evident in the late nineteenth century.[7] (This will be a major point of contrast with the post-war era, although Michie contends that international comparisons are so difficult that it is hard to generalize. But in the later period, some patterns of pro-cyclical movement can be detected.) Nell and Phillips find evidence tending to confirm an inverse relationship between real wages and employment in Canadian data; Block and Kucera, respectively, confirm the inverse relationship for Germany and Japan.)

Productivity and output

5 Output as a function of labour, both for individual plants and for the economy as a whole, was believed by virtually all contemporary – and later – economists to exhibit diminishing returns. Actual evidence, however, is weak, although, as will be explained later, a good case can be made for a version of diminishing returns. Productivity, however, is closely correlated with short-run variations in output in many industries, and positively correlated in general, and varies in both directions more than employment. (*Sources:* Pigou, 1929, ch 1, pp. 9–10; Aftalion, 1913. Calculations made from Hoffmann's data on nineteenth-century Germany show the strong correlations between productivity and output in the short run, and the greater variation of productivity compared to employment.[8])

6 Long-run productivity growth (measured in moving averages) was irregular and unpredictable, and lower than in later periods, although significant. It was transmitted to the economy through falling prices, with stable money wages. The rise in long-run real wages is closely correlated to productivity growth. (*Sources:* Pigou, 1929; Phelps Brown and Hopkins, op. cit.; Sylos-Labini, 1989)

Money and interest

7 The (nominal) quantity of money was correlated with both output and prices. Income velocity fluctuated somewhat, but showed no trend. In some respects the system behaved as if money were fixed exogenously. This requires some explanation. (*Sources:* Pigou, 1929, p. 132, *et passim.*, pp. 166–72; Snyder, 1924. By mid-century the economies of Europe had shifted to the gold standard, prior to which they had operated on bi-metallist principles. It is generally agreed that the

gold standard behaved as if the economy relied on 'outside' money, i.e. an exogenous money supply (Patinkin, 1965). To be sure bank checking deposits were beginning, and note issue by country banks was not closely bound by reserves, either in the United States or the UK. But in a loosely organized banking system, without clearly defined policies governing the lender of last resort, prudent financial management required tightening reserves and raising the discount rate in the face of expansion and rising prices, and vice versa in times of falling prices. Central banks followed the 'rules of the game' (Pigou, 1929, p. 279; Eichengreen, 1985).[9] Money may not have been strictly exogenous, but prudent management required the banking system to behave as if it were.

8 Investment booms were accompanied by overeager financial expansion, leading to crises and crashes; these precipitated investment slumps and financial contraction. Variations in employment and prices closely matched expansions and contractions of credit. (*Sources:* Hicks, 1989, ch. 11; Mill, 1844, Book III, ch. 12; Pigou, 1929; Kindleberger, 1978, esp. 3, 4, 6, 8, and Appendix. Interest rates and prices rose together in the upswing and fell together in the downswing. The financial crash was usually the signal for the expansion to collapse.)

9 The average level of the long-term rate of interest was fairly stable, from the mid-nineteenth century until World War I, and after the war continued to be moderately stable until the 1930s. What Keynes termed 'Gibson's Paradox' held during more than a century – levels and changes in the nominal interest rate were closely correlated with levels and changes of the wholesale price index, and the long rate was more closely correlated than the short rate. (Hence the nominal interest rate and the nominal quantity of money were correlated.) Both contrast markedly with the post-war era. (*Sources:* Kalecki (1971) calculates deviations from a nine-year (cycle-long) moving average of UK consols, and shows that they are very small (Osiatinski, 1990, p. 297, Table 16). Kalecki considers this sufficient justification to treat the long rate as a constant in developing models of the business cycle. Keynes (1930, vol. 2), discusses 'Gibson's Paradox'.)

Besides these strictly economic trends and relationships there are a number of important institutional facts that have changed dramatically. These, of course, are more difficult to substantiate with hard data. Nevertheless the historical record seems to support a set of generalizations – with the caveat that there may be many exceptions.

Business organisation, finance and the state

10 Business was organized and operated by family firms. Firms invested to achieve an optimum size, at which they would then remain, varying their output around the least cost level. (*Sources:* Pigou, 1929. Chandler (1977, 1990) examines the rise of large-scale corporations, beginning in the late nineteenth century. These early corporations are clearly the exceptions. Firms grew to their optimum size

and remained at that level thereafter (Robinson, 1931). Nell and Phillips, drawing on Urquhart, found marked changes in firm size and organization for Canada.)

11 Once firms reached their optimum size, they did not retain earnings for investment; profits were distributed, saved (or spent) and then loaned for investment by new firms. Finance for investment was thus predominantly external, raised through issuing bonds. (*Sources:* As above. The bulk of investment represented borrowed savings, and was carried out by new firms (J. B. Clark, 1895). Urquhart, 1986 on Canada.)

12 Governments tended to play a passive role in economic affairs; the 'Night Watchman State' intervened little and planned less. Most intervention took the form of subsidizing development. Government spending and transfers together normally amounted to less than 10 per cent of GNP, in some cases near 5 per cent, and showed no trend until just before World War I. (*Sources:* Maddison, 1984, esp. Table 1, 1991; Hoffman, 1965; Urquhart, 1986.)

Now consider the same categories in the era after World War II.

THE NEW TRADE CYCLE

The family firm has been superseded by the modern corporation, operating mass production technology, in which it is able to lay off labour and adapt output and employment easily to changing sales.[10] The price mechanism is no longer in evidence. The cycle is more evident in relations between quantities than in price data.[11] The growth rate of output is much higher, on average, at least in the first part of the period.

Prices and money wages

1 The trend of prices was upward the whole period, and the trend of money wages rose even more steeply, at least to the 1980s. Neither prices nor money wages (as measured by general indices) turned down, though rates of inflation slowed in recessions. (*Sources:* As above. Also, for comparisons of prices and outputs with the earlier period, Taylor, in Gordon, 1986. For wages and prices, Gordon, in Tobin, 1983. For a brief discussion of '*stylized facts*' regarding wholesale and retail prices, the price level, monetary aggregates, short and long interest rates, investment, and the timing of indicators, Zarnowitz, 1985.)

2 Raw material prices fluctuated more than manufacturing prices, and occasionally fell, though less (in proportion) than in the old trade cycle. Money-wage changes were proportionally greater than price changes. Real prices showed great stability, changing only with changes in productivity. (*Sources:* As above, plus Nield, 1980, and Coutts *et al.* 1978. Ochoa, 1986, 1984, demonstrated the strong stability of real prices using 86 × 86 input–output tables. See also Leontief, 1931.)

Employment, output and real wages

3 Changes in unemployment and output were greater proportionally than changes in prices or money wages; changes in unemployment were large.[12] Output varied in both directions, while prices only rose; the correlation between the two was weak, although price rates of change – inflation – correlate with output. Output variations exhibit a multiplier relationship: autonomous fluctuations in investment and net exports are magnified by a factor estimated at a little less than 2. (*Sources:* As above, esp. Sylos-Labini, 1989. Evans, 1969, surveys the estimates of the value of the multiplier as of that date.)

4 Changes in real wages (product wages) tended either to be mildly pro-cyclical, or not to exhibit a distinct pattern. For the United States a weak pro-cyclical pattern has been 'largely confirmed' (Blanchard and Fischer, 1989, p. 17). (*Sources:* Michie, 1987, chs 4, 5, 6; Blanchard and Fischer, 1989, ch. 1, pp. 17–19.)

Productivity and output

5 Output as a function of employment tends to exhibit constant or increasing returns, according to Okun's Law, supported by Kaldor's Laws. (*Sources:* Lowe, 1970, esp. ch 10.)

6 Productivity growth is transmitted to households through money wages rising more rapidly than prices. It tends to move pro-cyclically and is the major source of increasing per capita income; the trend over the cycle was stable until the 1970s; its decline since then has led to stagnant real incomes. (*Sources:* Michie, 1987; Okun, 1981.)

Money and Interest

7 The supply of money is endogenous, responding to demand pressures. The quantity of money for transactions (M_1) is correlated with *nominal* income, but is not closely related to either output or prices. Income velocity for M_1 shows a strong upward trend. (*Sources:* Moore, 1988; Wray, 1990; Nell, in Halevi *et al.* 1992. 'Endogenous money' has many meanings, but the point is that the money supply is not a constraint on real expansion.)

8 Financial booms and crises became more loosely linked with the movement of prices, unemployment and output. Real booms generated financial expansion, but this proved able to continue in sluggish and even slumping conditions. Credit crunches sometimes but not always appeared to slow inflation, and sometimes but not always slowed expansion. Crashes no longer led to immediate slumps. (*Sources:* Hicks, 1989, ch. 11; Wolfson, 1986; Wray, 1990.)

9 The long-term rate of interest varied substantially in the post-war era. From the early 1950s to the early 1960s, the real long-term rate rose from near zero in both the United States and the UK; it then fell to nearly zero in 1975, then rose steeply to over 7.5 per cent in 1985, and fell again thereafter. Thus it fell during

the inflation of the 1970s, and rose during the early 1980s, as inflation declined. But the *nominal* long-term rate closely tracked the rate of inflation, with interest close to inflation in the 1950s, lying above it in the 1960s, then falling below in the mid–1970s, and rising above again in the 1980s. The correlation is high, and the turning points match closely. (*Sources:* calculated from Citibase. The long rate was calculated as a five-year moving average (the average length of the post-War cycle) from 1950–1990 and then plotted. The prime rate, and triple A bond rates were regressed on the GNP deflator. For a similar relation between nominal short rates and inflation, see Mishkin, 1981, 1992.)

Business Organization, finance and the State

10 The modern multidivisional corporation has replaced the family firm as the organizing institution through which most of GNP is created. Growth is carried out largely by existing firms. Under conditions of mass production there are economies of scale and technological progress accompanies investment. Firms must invest continually just to keep up. It is no longer possible to define an optimal size for firms; the question has become their optimal rate of growth. (*Sources:* Eichner, 1976; Wood, 1976; Penrose, 1954, 1974; Herman, 1981; Williamson, 1980.)

11 Finance for investment has come to be largely internal, raised through retained earnings, for expansion projects carried out by existing firms. (*Sources:* As above. In the 1960s the ratio of corporate debt to assets rose, then fell in the 1970s, but rose again very steeply in the 1980s (Semmler and Franke, 1996). Gross investment is largely financed by retained earnings, but it could be argued that a large part of net investment is financed by borrowing. Gross investment is the relevant figure for growth, however, since replacements incorporate technical innovations. Moreover, much of the growth of corporate debt in the 1980s is connected with takeovers and mergers (Caskey and Fazzari, in Papadimitriou, 1992).)

12 Government intervention and planning became a regular feature of the post-war economic scene. Government expenditures plus transfers had risen to over a third of GNP after the war, and continued to rise as a percentage of GNP throughout the period, faltering only in the 1980s.[13] (*Sources:* OECD, 1986; Nell, 1988)

To summarize the 'stylized' differences between the two periods:

- markets have changed their pattern of adjustments, from one in which prices move pro-cyclically and real wages counter-cyclically, to one in which prices only rise, and real wages move erratically or pro-cyclically;
- a macro economy in which consumption varies inversely to investment and net exports changes to one in which the multiplier is prominent (variations in investment and net exports set off similar variations in consumption);
- the system in which productivity increases are transmitted through falling prices changes to one in which the transmission comes through rising money wages;

- a financial system in which interest rates are pro-cyclical changes to one in which they appear to behave erratically;
- nominal interest rates have changed from being correlated with the level of prices to being correlated with the rate of inflation;
- a money supply that was, or behaved as if it were, exogenous, has changed to one that is endogenous;
- the agents have changed in size and character, from family firms to modern corporations;
- and, finally, a non-intervening 'Night Watchman' state changes to an interventionist Keynesian state.

STRUCTURAL DIFFERENCES

The preceding points concern the nature of firms and the way markets work. Besides these differences there are others which describe the changes in the structure of the economy between the two eras. Two are particularly noticeable: the size relationships between sectors changed, and so did the character of costs.

All through the period of the 'old trade cycle' labour flowed out of agriculture and primary products into manufacturing and services. Output in the latter two grew more rapidly. As labour moved out of the primary sector it settled in large towns and cities, which grew rapidly. In the period of the 'new trade cycle' labour continued to leave agriculture, but manufacturing ceased to grow, while services changed character and became the fastest expanding sector. Urbanization ceased, the cities stagnated, and even declined. But the suburbs expanded, as did the large metropolitan areas. Table 4.1 shows the approximate range of sizes of sectors as proportions of GDP in the two periods:[14]

Table 4.1

Sectors	*Craft-based factories*	*Mass production*
Agriculture	40–50%	5–10%
Services	35–50%	40–60%
	Mostly personal	Mostly business
	Low-tech, unproductive	Increasingly hi-tech
Manufacturing	10–15%	35–50%
	Increasing	Stable or decreasing

Table 4.1 includes government under services. Separating it out is revealing:

Government	10%	40–55%
	Included in services	Services and mfg
	Stable	Rising

Labour costs have fallen in all sectors as a proportion of total costs; they were higher in the earlier era in every sector, but they have fallen as fast in agriculture as in manufacturing:

Agriculture	2/3–3/4	1/5–1/4
Services	3/4	1/3–2/3
Manufacturing	2/3	1/5–1/4

In the earlier period blue-collar labour costs made up between half and two-thirds of all labour costs. In the era of mass production blue-collar work had fallen to much less than half of total labour costs.

In the earlier period plant was designed to produce a certain level of output; varying production was costly and difficult. In the later period, employment and output could be varied more easily, so that average variable cost curves contained a long, flat stretch (Hansen, 1949; Mansfield, 1978; Lavoie, 1992, pp. 118–28).

PRICE VS. QUANTITY ADJUSTMENTS

In the earlier era markets evidently adjusted through price changes; in the later, however, prices no longer seem to be changing in relevant ways. Instead, employment and output are adjusted when demand fluctuates. These two patterns of market response are significantly different. The first is broadly stabilizing, the second, however, is not.[15]

Market adjustment in the era before World War I

In the earlier era, when production was carried out with an inflexible technology, a decline in autonomous components of aggregate demand – investment or net exports – would lead prices to decline; since output could not easily be adjusted, it would have to be thrown on the market for whatever it would fetch. For similar reasons employment could not easily be cut back; hence there would be little or no downward pressure on money wages in the short run. As a consequence, when the current levels of the autonomous components of aggregate demand fall, real wages rise, in conditions in which employment remains generally unchanged. Hence – to summarize – when investment declines, consumption spending rises. Investment and consumption move inversely to one another.

For *relatively small* variations in autonomous demand this is a stabilizing pattern of market adjustment. For *large* – and prolonged – collapses of demand, however, the relative inflexibility of output and employment can lead to disaster. Unable to cut current costs, or unable to cut them in proportion, and facing declining prices, firms will eventually have to shut down. When prices fall to the break-even point, all their employees will be out of work. With no revenue, the firm will have to meet its fixed charges out of reserves, and when these are exhausted, it will face bankruptcy. Shutdowns, of course, reduce consumption and are destabilizing.

Similarly, a rise in the autonomous components of demand lead to a bidding up of prices, but not, initially, of money-wage rates. Hence the real wage falls. With employment fixed, consumption declines in real terms. Again, consumption and investment spending move inversely. In addition, the fall in the real wage makes it possible for employers to absorb the costs of reorganizing work, and thus, in the longer term, to hire additional employees. But so long as the proportional increase in employment is less than the proportion decline in the real wage, consumption will fall.

Such a fall in consumption following a rise in investment can be expected to exert a dampening influence on investment. Similarly the rise in consumption following a decline in investment activity can be expected to provide a stimulus.

These stabilizing influences are reinforced by the behaviour of interest rates. When demand falls, prices fall, and interest rates follow suit. We saw that according to 'Gibson's Paradox' interest rates were highly correlated with the wholesale price index. Hence a decline in investment will be followed by a fall in interest rates, just as consumption spending picks up. The effect will be to provide a stimulus. By contrast, in a boom, interest rates will rise, just as consumption spending turns down.

Of course, the impact of these countervailing tendencies will be reduced by bankruptcies and capacity shrinkage in the slump and by the formation of new firms and the expansion of capacity in the boom. When demand falls sharply and closures and bankruptcies reduce the number of firms, output shrinks, and the pressure on prices might seem to be reduced. But bankruptcies and closures reduce employment, and therefore consumption demand. So demand declines further, and prices continue their downward course, pulling interest rates down with them. Falling prices and low interest rates make replacement investment attractive. At some point it will be worthwhile shifting replacement forward in time. This could then start an upswing. In the same way, capacity expansion will tend to inhibit the rise in prices in the boom – but building new capacity itself increases demand, which will feed the pressure on prices. Interest rates will continue to rise; at some point interest and prices will be sufficiently above normal that it will seem worthwhile to postpone replacement. This could then prove the start of the downturn.

In short, the pattern of market adjustment provides endogenous mechanisms that could bring a boom to a close, and lead to recovery from a slump. The system is self-adjusting, and capable of generating an endogenous cycle around a normal trend. The three internal processes just described contribute to this – real wages, and therefore consumption, move counter-cyclically, replacement investment moves counter-cyclically, while the interest rate moves pro-cyclically. These combine to provide pressure on net new investment to turn eventually against the cycle, perhaps – or probably – with a variable lag that depends on circumstances. Whether such a cycle actually manifests itself, and what its characteristics, amplitude, etc., will be, of course, will depend on the current parameters of the system, and on historical conditions.

Market adjustment in the era after World War II

The mechanism of market adjustment in the earlier era rested on the counter-cyclical movement of real wages, coupled with the pro-cyclical movement of interest rates. Neither of these patterns are observable in the post-war era. The mechanism just does not exist.[16]

In this period prices no longer vary with demand; instead prices are driven by inflationary pressures, partly generated by the new process of transmitting productivity gains through increases in money-wage rates. This tends to upset socially important income relativities. If these are restored as a result of social pressures, costs will be increased without corresponding gains in productivity, thereby leading to price rises, setting off a wage–price spiral.

But the system does respond to variations in autonomous demand. Mass production processes can easily be adjusted to changes in the level of sales. Employment and output will vary directly with sales. Hence when investment rises or falls, employment (including extra shifts and overtime for those already on the job) will also rise or fall, while prices and money wages remain unchanged. In the simplest case, consumption depends on the real wage and employment; as a result consumption will vary directly, rather than inversely, with investment. This is a version of the multiplier (Nell, 1976, 1992).

Multiplier expansions and contractions of demand, if substantial and/or prolonged, will tend to induce further variations in investment in the same direction. This is the accelerator, or capital stock adjustment principle.[17]

Early in the post-war era many Keynesian trade cycle theorists argued that the endogenous processes of the modern economy were fundamentally unstable.[18] The plausible range of values for the multiplier and accelerator seemed to imply either exponential expansion and contraction, or, if a lag were introduced, anti-damped cycles. To develop a theory of the business cycle, it was necessary to postulate 'floors' and 'ceilings', which these movements run up against. The floor was set by gross investment; it could not fall below zero, and arguably it could not fall to zero, since existing capital had to be maintained, which required replacement. Full employment and supply bottlenecks of all kinds provided ceilings. Once the explosive movement was halted, various factors were supposed to lead to turnarounds (which might be endogenous in the case where the multiplier–accelerator generates anti-damped movements). Thus the business cycle was seen to be made up of three parts – an unstable endogenous mechanism, which runs up against external buffers, slowing movement down or bringing it to a halt, at which point various *ad hoc* factors come into play, leading to a turnaround and unstable movement again but in the opposite direction. In short, a mixture of endogenous and exogenous.

The floors and ceilings, however, in practice have seemed too elastic to explain the turning points; depressions could keep sinking, and full employment did not reliably stop booms.[19] Nor was it clear why, when an expansion or contraction hit a ceiling or floor, it should turn around. Even at full employment, demand in monetary terms could keep rising; even when net investment hits zero, replacements could be postponed – and even when replacements have fallen off, consumption might be curtailed. Moreover, even if expansion or contraction stops, will the accelerator actually turn the movement around? The argument is more plausible for the upper turning point. But in fact, in the post-war era most upper turning points appear to have occurred before the economy pressed against full capacity or full employment, while the economy has normally turned up before net investment had settled definitively at zero. Many suggestions have been offered to account for these anomalies, yet no single explanation, or combination of accounts, has generally appeared convincing. Some authors even contended that different cycles might rest on different factors (Duesenberry, 1958). Yet, however unsatisfactory the theory as a whole might have been, the argument that the endogenous mechanism had become unstable appears to be sound.

However, it has been argued that the financial system might stabilize an otherwise unstable economy. A multiplier–accelerator boom would raise incomes, increasing the transactions demand for money. Such a rise in demand for money will increase interest rates, which, in turn, will act as a drag on investment, bringing the boom to a halt. The multiplier–accelerator then goes into reverse, throwing the economy into a downswing, but the falling level of income will bring down the transactions demand, thereby pulling interest rates down. The lower interest rates will then stimulate investment, starting the upswing, setting off the multiplier–accelerator.

Recent estimates of the 'multiplier' (Bryant 1988) take these relationships into account. Most econometric models try to introduce and estimate all relevant factors (Fair, 1984), and hence likewise include interest rate effects, and perhaps other factors as well.[20] This may be a mistake. Both the simple multiplier and the capital stock adjustment principle are based on solid relationships, which are structurally based and economically motivated. When spending in one sector increases, it sets off repercussions in other sectors, leading to further increases in spending. When demand increases, pushing producers against capacity, it makes economic sense for them to increase their capacity. By contrast, when income increases, while the need for a circulating medium increases, it is not at all obvious that an 'increased demand for money' pushes up against a given supply, driving up interest rates. Quite the contrary, as I argue elsewhere Nell (1997a, 1997b), in such cases credit expands, near monies arise, and/or velocity increases – all without any effect on interest rates. The chief determinant of interest rates in the post-war era appears to be central bank monetary policy. Moreover, even when interest increases, its effect on investment is unreliable. It may take a very steep rise in interest, kept in place for a long period, to bring a boom to a halt. As is evident from the early 1990s, a fall in interest rates by no means leads to expansion.

Rather than floors and ceilings, or the working of the financial system, it can be argued that politics has chiefly provided the turning points. Booms led to balance of payments crises or to inflationary wage–price spirals. Pressure from business interests would lead to an induced recession. Full employment also threatened – or was perceived to threaten – work discipline. On the other hand, slumps threatened governments at the ballot box. The actual business cycle of the post-war era has had an irregular and distinctly political character – although the ability to control the economy may well have eroded over time.

However, the turning points do not coincide that neatly with political interests, and in several cases, it is evident that policy did not produce the desired effects. Yet the cycle is still apparent, suggesting that there is room for an endogenous theory.

Changes in technology

There are no doubt many ways to approach explaining the variance between the two periods. However, the technological contrasts between the two eras are so marked that it seems reasonable to turn to the economic implications of such differences for a possible explanation (Nell, 1992, chs 16, 17; 1993).[21] The main features of the old trade cycle are all related, directly or indirectly, to the characteristics of the technology of the period. As we saw earlier, until comparatively recently technology was developed by and for small-scale operations, run largely by households or groups of households. These evolved into family firms. The First Industrial Revolution brought the shift from small craft operations to factories, which, however, were based on essentially the same technologies. Even though, at the end of the nineteenth century, great advances were made as steam power and steel were brought into widespread use, enabling substantial expansions in the size of plants, reaping economies of scale, the technologies still largely operated on the principles of 'batch' production, rather than continuous throughput. In many cases the use of steam power simply permitted a large number of workstations, each organized according to older principles, to run at the same time off a central power source. The power, in turn, ran essentially the same tools that had previously been operated by hand. Operatives had to be present at all work stations in order for any production to take place. Even where continuous throughput developed, start-up and shut-down costs were high.

These limitations had economic consequences. The economy faces continuous shocks from the outside world. Of particular importance are exogenous fluctuations in sales. Firms could not easily vary output to match changes in sales – a firm could either produce or shut down. Craft technologies were inflexible in terms of adapting output and employment (and so costs) to changes in the rate of sales. As a consequence, when demand rose (fell) output could only be increased (decreased) by varying productivity, i.e. work effort. The technology required team effort among workers, generally performing on a small scale, so that changes in output could only come with changes in effort – or by reorganizing the work team. But neither labour nor capital were willing to change work norms, except temporarily. Hence the level of employment would have to change, but this in turn would be costly in terms of disruption, and would take place only if compensated by higher prices, at least for a time. Thus a rise in demand would drive up prices, lowering the real wage, thereby leading to an expansion of employment. Inflexibility thus can help to explain the characteristic patterns of variations in prices, output, wages and employment (Hicks, 1989; Nell, 1992).

Family firms operating craft technologies do not require extensive government oversight or intervention. A private enterprise financial system will serve this kind of economy well, except in hard times, when it will prove unstable.

By contrast, mass production technology permits easy adaptation of employment and output to changes in sales, while leaving productivity unaffected. Variable costs will thus be constant over a large range (Hansen, 1949; Lavoie, 1992). Prices will therefore tend not to vary with changes in demand. Mass production technology also permits expansion to reap economies of scale, leading to larger firms, differently organized, and motivated to grow. Under mass production productivity will tend to grow regularly, and will be reflected in wage bargains. Rising wages for production workers will create tensions with other social groups, leading to pressure to raise their incomes, creating inflationary pressures. Large, growing corporations cannot tolerate a financial system prone to crisis; mass production requires government oversight and intervention in many related dimensions. As a consequence the new trade cycle differs in every one of the above respects.[22]

How can this be reflected in elementary economic theory? The production function has traditionally been the basic analytic tool of neoclassical theory in regard to pricing, employment and output. High theory interprets each point on the production function as representing a different choice of technique – but this was not how Marshall and Pigou understood it (Marshall, 1961, p. 374; Pigou, 1944, pp. 51–2). For them the production function showed output as a function of current employment and the available plant and equipment. This discussion suggests that changes in technology are a primary cause of the changes in the behaviour of economic variables from the old to the new trade cycle. Such a shift in technology can perhaps be represented as a change in a Marshallian production function from one with a pronounced curvature, so that the slope declines as employment increases, to one that is a straight line with a constant slope (Nell, 1992).[23]

SOME IMPLICATIONS FOR CURRENT DEBATES

As between the two eras, the pattern of the cycle is different, the structure of the economy has changed, and the state has developed from a 'Night Watchman' to the guarantor of welfare. Given the different patterns of wage, price, output and productivity movements, it may seem unlikely that the same models will apply to both. Yet many contemporary discussions appear to be predicated on the belief that the basic explanatory models should be universal, implying that the market mechanism, apart from imperfections, would be the same in the two periods. Different results will be the consequence of institutions, interventions or imperfections.

New Keynesians, for example, try to explain the emergence of Keynesian relationships by appealing to imperfections, asymmetric information, risk aversion, and institutional factors. When sufficiently pronounced these can be shown to create price and/or wage rigidity, leading to Keynesian-type relationships. Yet all of these were more strongly present in the earlier period, when the economy still appeared to exhibit neoclassical features. Technological innovations have surely improved communications, transportation, data banks, information processing, the calculation and analysis of risk, and have created more institutional awareness, if not flexibility. The historical record is exactly the reverse of what the New Keynesian approach would lead one to expect. The same can also be shown to apply to aspects of Post Keynesian, New Classical and Neo-Ricardian thought.

First, consider two groups that stress 'microfoundations', and hold that macro phenomena are to be explained by theories of rational choice under constraints, where these constraints may include various kinds of imperfections, and interferences by government or other institutions, and where rationality itself may be limited. In each case we will see that the way markets and the cycle have developed is the opposite of what might be expected from the theory.

The New Keynesians

Keynesian theory was developed at the beginning of the second period, in which output adjustment is comparatively rapid, while price fluctuations are slight. But Keynesian theory is not consistent with full neoclassical equilibrium. To justify Keynesian theory, while still accepting the basic premises of the neoclassical approach, 'New Keynesians' have proposed a variety of mechanisms that purport to explain why real or nominal prices and/or wages, are rigid. Being rigid, they do not adjust to clear the corresponding markets, and this failure is then shown to result in Keynesian consequences.

Many ingenious suggestions have been offered: nominal wages may be rigid because actual or implicit labour contracts are cast in nominal terms, (Gordon, 1990). Such contracts, however, are often clearly sub-optimal; moreover, if prices are flexible, they imply a counter-cyclical movement of the real wage. Recent work has instead focused on rigidities in nominal prices, attributed to 'menu costs' (Mankiw, 1990). Such nominal rigidities may interact with real rigidities – it may cost more to change prices than the expected gain, because of difficulties in disseminating information. Real wages may be sticky because of fears that a variable, market-driven real wage will result in productivity losses. (The 'efficiency' wage, first noted by Adam Smith (Michl, 1992).) Or there may be 'coordination failures', resulting from the resistance of firms to lowering prices. In such cases there may be multiple positions of 'normal' output. Capital and labour markets may fail to adjust readily because of asymmetric information and/or risk aversion (Greenwald and Stiglitz, 1989). Similarly, small effects may be magnified, because of risk aversion. Firms may take decisions in these circumstances in the light of 'near rationality', rather than full rationality (Akerlof and Yellen, 1985). That is, they may decide it is not worth the trouble to recalculate continually (Romer, 1993; Greenwald and Stiglitz, 1989; Mankiw, 1985; Gordon, 1990).

Broadly speaking, the 'New Keynesians' focus on one or another realistic aspect of market imperfection, which would be ruled out by assumption in a world of 'perfect markets', and then develop models of maximizing behaviour showing how such 'imperfections' prevent prices and/or wages from adjusting to clear the relevant markets. There is thus no single dominant explanation for 'Keynesian' results; rather there is a whole class of possible explanations, each applicable to appropriate circumstances.[24]

Almost without exception, however, the imperfections cited in these models were more serious in the period of the old trade cycle, when prices and money wages were flexible, than in the post-war era, when they were not. The costs of changing prices, for example, were greater when printing costs were larger, mail slower and faxes non-existent. Asymmetric information must have been more serious before the existence of data banks and computers. Informational problems must have been greater in the days before telecommunications. (If information costs were not greater then, it would not have been worthwhile to invent and introduce the new methods of communication.) Insider–outsider relations must have been more important before the development of standardized tools and equipment, for then training had to be done on the job, and workers had to learn to cooperate together under unique circumstances. No shop would be exactly like any other. And so on. The conditions that the New Keynesians have identified as causing prices to fail to adjust were more prominent in the period when prices did adjust.

In the same way, the claim that small 'shocks' can have large effects, either because of the risk aversion of firms (Greenwald and Stiglitz, 1989) or because of limited rationality and real rigidities (Mankiw, 1985; Akerlof and Yellen, 1985), also appears likely to be more true of the older period, in which, in fact, prices and wages, both nominal and real, were relatively more flexible. Surely risk aversion would be greater when uncertainty was greater, communication poorer and information harder to come by. Full rationality would be less likely under these conditions, and there would both be more 'frictions' and the real costs of each would be larger, since adjustment would be slower.

It may be objected that conventional theory attributes price flexibility to markets in which there are large numbers of small firms, whereas in the new period markets are characterized by large modern corporations. But while the firms are bigger, so are the markets. In the nineteenth century firms chiefly competed in *local* markets. The railroad, clipper ships and the steamship permitted long-distance trade, but only in some products and only for a minority of firms. By contrast, modern corporations routinely compete in national and world markets. Air transport, air freight, modern communications, refrigeration, container technology, tanker technology, all combine to permit worldwide sourcing and marketing. The effects of world competition are readily apparent, and can be measured in the rising degree of import penetration.

In short, while the new Keynesian approach directs attention to important aspects of markets, it cannot explain the change from relatively flexible money prices and wages, with an inverse relationship between real wages and employment, to downwardly inflexible, upwardly drifting nominal wages and prices, exhibiting a mildly pro-cyclical real-wage–employment pattern.

The New Classicals

New Classicals consider that the price mechanism works to bring about market clearing in all sectors, impeded only by market imperfections or government interference. The latter works only when market agents do not expect it, or during the time it takes for them to learn how to adapt their behaviour to compensate. Since market imperfections prevent optimality, it will pay those in sub-optimal positions to remove the imperfections, and it will be in no one's long-run interest to preserve them – the gains from a change would outweigh the losses, so the losers could be compensated. Hence over time imperfections will be eliminated. We should expect, therefore, to see market processes improve their operation over time; market clearing and market adjustments should be more efficient as time goes on (Hoover, 1990).

Price flexibility appears only in the first period, at a time when market imperfections must be considered more serious than later. Communications were less developed, transportation was slower and more costly, credit was more difficult to check, and calculation was harder and slower. Yet in this period, in spite of the imperfections, the price mechanism appeared to play a role, and the real wage behaved in accordance with marginal productivity theory. But it is only in this period that we see evidence in time series statistics of the price mechanism at work. Market adjustment through prices and market clearing is less in evidence as time passes (of course, the market did not always clear in the early period, but crises and periods of unemployment went with *falling*, never with stable or rising, prices and money wages, as happened later).

Rational expectations, at least when combined with market clearing, imply results that also fit the earlier period better, although the formation of such expectations only makes sense in the later. It is relatively plausible to assume rational expectations in the modern period, when firms have computers, modern telecommunications, access to extensive data banks, and employ trained statisticians and economists – although it must also be assumed that agents know what the relevant variables are, something economists cannot agree on! But having 'rational expectations', as the phrase is usually understood, does not make much sense in an era of family firms, little education, pencil-and-paper calculation, poor communications – and when economic theory was so little developed that it would not be possible to identify the relevant variables in many situations. Yet it is in the earlier era that we see evidence of price movements that suggest a tendency towards market clearing, and where market adjustments appear to accord with marginal productivity theory.

Next consider two groups that explain macro phenomena by reference to institutions, including competition, economic and technological structure and the conditions of the world.[25] Both are therefore much closer to the perspective suggested here, but both nevertheless overlook important historical changes in the economy, and as a result place unwarranted emphasis on certain aspects of market behaviour.

The Post Keynesians

Rather than adapt Keynes to neoclassical microfoundations, Post Keynesians have sought to defend and develop Keynesian thinking, building foundations on a realistic account of institutions (Davidson, 1978, 1994b). Lexicographical and need-based theories of household choice, together with mark-up accounts of corporate pricing, provide an appropriate setting for the theory of effective demand (Nell, 1992; Lavoie, 1992; Eichner, 1989). Labour markets respond chiefly to demand pressures (Nell, 1976, 1988; Lavoie, 1992). Money is seen as adapting endogenously to demand (Moore, 1988). Financial institutions are treated as simply another form of profit-seeking firm responding to market incentives (Minsky, 1986). Uncertainty is ubiquitous, and money and monetary contracts are seen as institutions designed to provide a way of managing practical affairs in the face of our inability to predict the future (Davidson, 1994b). Uncertainty is so pervasive that the economy cannot be expected to gravitate towards equilibrium; as Keynes remarked, 'equilibrium is blither'. Not all Post Keynesians agree; Davidson (1994b) holds that the concept may be useful at times for organizing our thoughts. But many Post Keynesians would argue that it can play no practical role, and should be replaced with the study of dynamics. Investment, in particular, will be volatile, and through the multiplier this will cause fluctuations throughout the economy. These will be exacerbated by financial markets, in which instability is endemic, since financial fragility tends to grow during boom periods (Minsky, 1975, 1986). Conflicting claims during booms give rise to built-in inflation, which is not corrected during the slump, since money wages are not flexible downwards (Rowthorn, 1982; Lavoie, 1992).

Uncertainty, however, must have been much more serious and pervasive in the economic conditions prior to World War I. Communications were poorer, data bases were less developed, calculation was slower, and the basic economic relationships were less understood.[26] There was far less control over the natural environment, and methods of storage and preservation were still backward. Yet in this period talk of equilibrium was not altogether blither; the economy had built-in stabilizing influences. Conflicts, especially class conflict, were more intense and less civilized in this period; but there was no inflation at all. Prior to World War I financial and real crises were strongly linked. Each, it seemed, was capable of precipitating the other, and certainly each exacerbated the other. But in the post-war world, for the developed economies, the linkage is much weaker. A financial crisis, as in 1987, may do no significant damage to the real economy. A serious recession, as in the early 1990s, may do no harm to the stock and bond markets. The characteristics of the post-war world cannot be understood adequately in terms of post Keynesian uncertainty and its effects on financial markets (This does not imply criticism of other aspects of Post Keynesian thinking).

The Neo-Ricardians

Taking its cue from Sraffa (1960), Neo-Ricardian theory builds on given technology, given size and composition of output and a given real wage. From these givens the set of relative prices that will support a uniform rate of profit in a 'long-period position' can be found (Garegnani, 1976). Alternative real wages will be associated with different rates of profit and prices; the wage–profit rate tradeoff can be defined, and its properties examined. Choices of technique can be analysed. A devastating critique of the marginal productivity theory of distribution follows from this, while Walrasian general equilibrium theory can be shown to be characteristically overdetermined, or unable to accommodate a uniform rate of profit (Pasinetti, 1977, 1981). The 'dual' consumption–growth rate tradeoff can be examined in relation to the relative sizes of sectors. Paths of steady growth can be examined, and the effect of alternative wages or techniques explored (Kurz, 1991).

The Neo-Ricardian method is to compare alternative 'long-period positions'. The economy is assumed to gravitate towards those positions, or revolve around them. Actual positions of the economy will not normally, perhaps not ever, be fully adjusted long-period positions. The latter refers to a *theoretical ideal.* But although an ideal, it is considered to be the goal towards which the economy is moving, under the pressure of competitive forces. Capital will be shifted about until prices and industry sizes are correct. (This same perspective is taken by many who work in the newly developing fields of non-linear dynamic analysis and chaos theory.)

But in the modern era, technological change is regular and widespread; it *results* from economic activity – from 'learning by doing', and from organized research and development. Innovation is a part of competitive investment strategy. The coefficients are changing continually, and investment plans are subject to constant revision. Movement towards a long-period position – or, for that matter, in any direction – is quite likely to change the data on which that position is based. The positions towards which the system tends are path-dependent.

In addition, for many purposes Neo-Ricardian theory takes the size and composition of output to be given; but in the modern era the composition of output, and the structure of the economy generally, are continually changing.

Moreover, in the modern world market forces are often destabilizing, which means that there is no process of gravitation. Even if a long-period position could be defined, the forces of competition would not direct the economy towards it.

By contrast, in the era of craft-based production, it may well have made sense to approach the economy on the assumption that at any time it was tending towards a long-period position. Technological change was irregular, firms distributed profits, and entrepreneurs borrowed them to invest. Market forces were stabilizing. Processes of structural change were slower. Under these conditions the 'long-period method' could provide insights. But it is not an appropriate method for studying the post-war economies of mass production.[27] (This does not imply that the Neo-Ricardian equations cannot be used to study mass production; they can, but the interpretation must be different, cf. Nell, 1994, 1996.)

Finally, consider the implications for a recent debate over the amplitude of business cycles.

Cyclical Amplitudes

In a different vein a dispute has arisen over the relative amplitude of fluctuations prior to World War I compared to after World War II. Christina Romer (1986,

1987) has argued, in a series of papers, that the fluctuations in unemployment (and in output) in the economy before World War I have been overstated. Her argument begins with a critique of Lebergott, on whose painstaking work most estimates rely. She notes that he had to interpolate extensively to construct his series, but argues that in doing so, he relied on assumptions that magnified the actual fluctuations. She advances similar objections to Kuznets' series. Her recalculations reduce the fluctuations considerably (though they are still greater than those of the post-war era); but her methodology requires assuming that relationships, such as Okun's law, which characterize the post-war economy, also apply to the economy before World War I. This is unlikely; moreover, she ignores the extensive contemporary commentaries on economic events which Lebergott, especially, used to corroborate his work (Sheffrin, 1989). Other writers, e.g. Balke and Gordon (1989) and (Altman) 1992, re-examining the question, find much larger differences than she did. Taylor, in Gordon (1986), found that wages and prices were more flexible in the earlier period, but that fluctuations were also more severe. But if fluctuations before World War I turn out to be smaller than hitherto believed, the distinctive patterns outlined above will only be enhanced.

From the perspective suggested here, then, the debate over business cycle volatility is on the wrong track. The issue appears to be whether Keynesian policies after World War II helped to stabilize the economy, with Keynesian supporters arguing that such policies made a difference, while critics hold that little or no benefit is evident.[28] The method has been to compare the amplitude of post-war fluctuations with those of an era in which there was no government intervention, i.e. the period prior to World War I. But the character of the cycle in the two periods is not comparable – prices, wages and employment behaved differently. So did money and interest. And the size and nature of government spending differed dramatically. Focusing on the amplitude of fluctuations in employment and output simply misses the more significant changes, which occur, for example, in the relations between the fluctuations in prices, wages and employment. Instead of comparing the time series of a variable from one period directly with that from the other, more would be revealed by comparing the patterns made by the relationships between the time series variables in one period, with the patterns revealed among those relationships in the other.

CONCLUSIONS

A review of *stylized facts* reveals dramatic differences between periods, as regards both the structure and institutions of the economy and the way markets work. A plausible explanation for the changes can be found in the development of technology, as it evolved from what can be termed 'craft-based factory production' to mass production. The reason is that this change affects the nature of costs, turning fixed current costs into variable costs, which, in turn, affects the way markets adjust.

In the earlier period markets adjusted through stabilizing price and real-wage changes, where real wages and employment varied inversely. But these stabilizing movements were often upset by unstable financial markets, resulting in noticeable volatility. By contrast, in the later period, the market mechanism, working through output and employment adjustments, is unstable, and wages tend to move directly with employment and output. Financial markets, although also tending to instability, no longer so directly destabilize the system. Floors and ceilings help to prevent excessive fluctuation, but a larger and more active government holds the key to stabilizing the economy's behaviour. There may be an endogenous cyclical mechanism, but the cycles are damped and controlled. The volatility in the two periods is roughly comparable, but the factors shaping it are quite different.

Between the two periods considered here lie the interwar years. In this period mass production had not yet developed fully, and governments had not learned to cope with the evolving instability of markets. From the perspective suggested here we should expect this period to be the most unstable of all, as indeed it was.

The implication for applied economic analysis is that no 'microfoundations' for 'macro' are possible or relevant. 'Micro' concerns adjustment through flexible prices and applies to the earlier period – and to developing countries with a large sector of craft-based production – while 'macro' applies to mass production economies. Each describes a distinct pattern of adjustment and neither is more fundamental than the other.

NOTES

1 Indeed, it can be argued that the theory of flexible price adjustment *should not* be cast in such a mold. Neoclassical general equilibrium theory, based on rational choice, provides few, if any, empirically testable insights, while at the same time generating serious theoretical difficulties. It cannot rule out multiple equilibria, some or all of which may be unstable (Ingrao and Israel, 1990). It cannot find a plausible rationale for the use of money (Hahn, 1973). It cannot make room for capital, earning a rate of return which competitively tends to uniformity (Garegnani, 1978). A sensible price theory should give us plausible criteria for uniqueness and stability, a reasonable account of the usefulness of money, and a coherent understanding of the rate of return on capital. Early neoclassical theory, as developed by Wicksell, Walras, Clark, Marshall and Pigou, for example, aimed to supply all of these. Their constructions were defective, as later studies have shown, but the answer is surely not to abandon their goals, in order to preserve their approach, but to adjust the approach in order to achieve the goals. Applied economics needs a plausible account of flex-price adjustment.

2 Macroeconomics is often presented as aggregate supply and demand, a sibling to microeconomic theory, expressed in the same format, with downward sloping demand and rising supply curves. The general price *level* functions analogously to the microeconomic price variable. The analogy is flawed. Micro prices are paid and received; no one pays or receives the price *level.* Micro quantities are measurable in their own units; the macro analogues are revenues, price × quantity. Worst of all, in many formulations movements along the aggregate supply curve will cause the aggregate demand curve to shift – the two functions are not independent of one another (Nell, 1992, ch. 25; 1996b, Appendix ch. 1).

3 Kaldor observes, 'in the social sciences, unlike the natural sciences, it is impossible to establish facts that are precise and at the same time suggestive and intriguing in their implications, and that admit to no exceptions ... we do not imply that any of these "facts" are invariably true in every conceivable instance but that they are true in the broad

majority of observed cases – in a sufficient number of cases to call for an explanation' (Kaldor, 1985, pp. 8–9).

4 Measuring trends presents notorious problems. In most of the earlier discussions variations were calculated by simple differencing. In more recent work segmented linear trends have been fitted. In the work done at the New School many approaches have been tried; the results reported have survived different methods of de-trending (Canova, 1991; Nell, 1997b).

5 These trends are consistent with the patterns of the previous centuries. In the latter part of the eighteenth century prices rose dramatically as a result of the French Revolution and the Napoleonic Wars. From 1600 to 1775, however, prices of consumables in southern England were more or less flat, with a slight downward trend from 1650 on, broken only by sudden upturns due to wars. Builder's wages rose very moderately, staying flat for long periods, from 1600 to 1775, then rose steeply up to 1815, then went flat until the last quarter of the nineteenth century. (Phelps Brown and Hopkins, in Carus-Wilson, 1954a, p. 170).

6 Since money wages are less flexible than money prices, it is implied that real wages are flexible. Since primary products are more flexible than manufacturing goods, it is implied that the real price of primaries in terms of manufactures changes. Other real price variations can be calculated from the data.

7 Ray Majewski has examined these figures in a dissertation, using the *Shipping and Commercial List,* and the *Aldrich Report* for pre-1890 prices, as a check on Warren and Pearson's wholesale price index. The BLS provides a historic index of wages per hour, and Angus Maddison has developed (1982) an index of real GNP, based on Gallman's (1966) study, which in turn is based on Kuznets (1961). Kuznets has been criticized by Romer (1989) and defended/revised by Balke and Gordon. Neither the Romer nor the Balke and Gordon data change the result that there is a counter-cyclical pattern evident in the US data.

8 If the relationship between output and employment were described by a well-behaved neoclassical production function, then output and productivity should be related *inversely*, rather than directly. The widespread evidence of a positive relationship makes it clear that the counter-cyclical movement of product wages does not 'confirm' traditional marginal productivity theory. Nevertheless, the traditional theory appears to have been 'on to something', and the object here is to find out what that was.

9 Some studies, notably Nurkse (1944), for the interwar years and Bloomfield (1959) for 1880–1914, have shown that central banks widely violated the rules. It is now generally recognized that central banks had considerable discretion, and that the stability of the gold standard system (which held only for the countries at the centre – the periphery suffered frequent convertibility crises, devaluations and internal credit crunches) reflected successful management (Sayers, 1957), especially by the Bank of England. It was as much a sterling reserve system as a gold standard system.

10 Several studies of the contrasts between the 'old' and the 'new' business cycle are now available. Nell and Phillips (1995), studying Canada, find good evidence for an inverse relationship between product wages and employment in the old period, and a direct relationship in the new. They also find significant differences in the sizes and characteristics of firms, and in the nature of government between the periods. There is little evidence of a multiplier in the earlier period. Kucera (1997), studying Japan, found similar results for product wages and output – with certain qualifications – and also found a weakly negative relationship between consumption and investment in the earlier period, in contrast to a strongly positive relationship in the later. Block (1997), studying Germany, found strongly contrasting relationships between product wages and output in the two periods.

11 The period from World War II to the present breaks somewhere in the early 1970s. The first part has been termed the 'Golden Age' of modern capitalism: growth rates of output

and productivity were high, inflation and unemployment low, and the amplitude of the cycle was moderate. By contrast in the later period, the growth of output and productivity became erratic and fell, inflation and unemployment became severe, and the cycle intensified. However, examining this change is not our purpose here. The era prior to World War I can also be subdivided into periods.

12 That is, even *with* counter-cyclical government intervention, the variations in employment are large in the post-war cycle. They would be far greater in the absence of such policies.

13 In addition, it should be noted that state expenditure in relation to GNP was high and rising during the period, in both military and civilian categories. It rose and/or remained high, in spite of explicit and politically inspired attempts to cut it back.

14 Because these are ranges the percentages do not add up.

15 This discussion concerns the 'normal' behaviour of 'stylized' actual market agents, e.g. family firms or modern corporations, working-class or middle-class households. It is not concerned with the 'idealized rational agents', conceived independently of social context, that populate the models of much contemporary economic theory. The normal behaviour of stylized actual agents may well involve maximizing subject to constraints, and will generally be 'rational' in some sense. But it is shaped and determined by context and institutions (Nell and Semmler, 1991, 'Introduction').

16 The shift to reduced stability was remarked by Duesenberry (1958, p. 285): 'the historical changes in the structure of the American economy which occurred during the first quarter of the twentieth century tended to reduce the stability of the system'. However, Duesenberry did not offer a clear explanation. He suggested that there was a tendency for changes in investment to be offset by opposite changes in consumption in the era between the Civil War and World War I (p. 287) and he developed a multiplier–accelerator model, which, however, was defective (Pasinetti, 1960). But his approach outlined a loose general framework that would apply universally, allowing for changes in parameters that would allow each cycle to be different. He did not suggest a systematic change from a stabilizing market mechanism to an essentially unstable one.

17 Evans (1969, chs 19 and 20), calculates a variety of multipliers, including 'multipliers' with induced investment, on various assumptions, and presents numerical estimates for the post-war United States.

18 Hicks (1950), examined the plausible ranges of values of the multiplier and capital–output ratios, and concluded that, empirically, the system had to be either unstable or generate anti-damped cycles. Matthews (1959), reviews the literature, and appears to regard models with an unstable endogenous mechanism, running up against buffers, as the most reasonable. A related school of thought argued that advanced capitalist economies had an inbuilt propensity to stagnate, which would have to be offset by government expenditure (Kalecki, 1971; Steindl, 1976), possibly abetted by various kinds of private 'unproductive' expenditure (Baran and Sweezy, 1966). In this case, the instability is seen to hold in one direction only – or chiefly – namely, downwards. But it is denied that there are any 'self-correcting' adjustment mechanisms.

19 Duesenberry (1958), judges that ceiling theories cannot explain the upper turning point (p. 278).

20 Fair (1984), for example, holds that the 'word 'multiplier' should be interpreted in a very general way . . . (as showing) . . . how the predicted values of the endogenous variables change when one or more exogenous variables are changed' (p. 301). First the model is estimated, then the initial value(s) of the exogenous parameters are set, and the value(s) of the endogenous variables are calculated. The exogenous parameters are then changed, and the new value(s) of the endogenous variables are found. The difference between the two sets of values shows the impact of the change; if only a single parameter is changed, then the value of a single endogenous variable can be divided by that change to calculate a 'multiplier'. The advantage of this approach is its generality; the

disadvantage is that it incorporates into the same calculation of the impact of a change, processes that rest on foundations that differ greatly in reliability. The 'passing along' of expenditure and of costs is measurable and reliable, but the response of financial variables to other changes is less so, and the response of real variables to financial variables is notoriously unstable.

21 These technological changes did not just happen; they were themselves the product of market incentives and pressures, brought about by the problems and opportunities faced by firms in their everyday business. This is the subject of the theory of *transformational growth*, but the issues are separate from those under discussion here (Nell, 1992; Nell, in Thomson, 1993).

22 For further elaboration, cf. Nell (1992, chs 16, 17), and Nell (in Thomson, 1993), and the references cited there. Argyrous (1991), provides a case study of the aircraft industry. Howell (1993), proposes a similar classification.

23 Assuming for simplicity that all and only wages are consumed, the crucial dividing line occurs when the curvature of the production function is such as to give rise to a marginal product curve of unitary elasticity. At this point the proportional decline in the real wage is exactly offset by the proportional rise in employment. If the curvature were greater, the rise in employment would not offset the fall in the real wage – so that consumption would *decline* as a result of a rise in investment demand that led to a bidding up of prices. If the curvature were less, then a rise in investment, bidding up prices, would lead to such a large rise in employment that consumption would *increase*. This is the multiplier relationship.

24 'The challenge is to choose between the myriad of ways in which markets can be imperfect, and to decide on the central questions and puzzles to be explained' (Greenwald and Stiglitz, 1993a, p. 25; 1993b).

25 It is not implied that these models eschew maximizing behaviour; on the contrary, virtually all draw on some form of maximizing, or profit seeking, behaviour, under some circumstances. But both the goals and the means are shaped by the institutions and social conditions. What both deny is that there could exist an abstract individual with well-ordered preferences, endowments, etc., able to act in a similarly abstract market. Agents in the market, if persons, are themselves *products* of training and education. That is how they acquired their skills and knowledge. Agents which are institutions – corporations – have to be modelled as institutions, since such agents typically make decisions in different ways than individuals.

26 At least two senses of 'uncertainty' can usefully be distinguished – 'natural uncertainty' meaning that the world is non-ergodic and that in general the future cannot be predicted from study of the past, and 'market uncertainty' which arises from the fact that agents do not know each other's intentions, and/or how the various strategies will work out when played. Neither can be reduced to calculable risk. Davidson, for example, stresses the former; Graziani, Nell and Cartelier the latter. The former is compatible with endogenous stability, the latter is not.

27 This does not imply that the Sraffa equations and related models (Von Neumann, Morishima, Pasinetti) are inapplicable; only that they cannot be applied by way of the 'long-period approach'. But if the coefficients are interpreted as weighted averages of the vintages in use (rather than as 'best practice') the equations will exhibit a picture of the position of the economy at a particular moment. This will change only slowly, as the capital stock changes, and it represents the starting point of dynamic adjustment processes (Roncaglia, 1988; Nell, 1993).

28 Since the late 1970s Western governments have adopted austerity policies, and have tried to cut back on the growth of state expenditure. These efforts have tended to slow growth and raise unemployment. In addition world trade has grown faster than world output, without a corresponding development of credit to ease balance of payments problems. Keynesians tend to argue that many of the economic difficulties of the last

two decades stem from mistaken policies. However, the perspective here would suggest looking at developments in technology as well. Are new technologies leading to changes in patterns of cost, and in methods of organizing production? If so – and surely they are – what effects are they having on the responsiveness of markets to policy?

Part II

THE LABOUR MARKET

Part II

THE LABOUR MARKET

This part of the book, comprising six chapters, focuses on the New Keynesian perception of unemployment as occurring as a result of imperfections in what has come to be called *the labour market*. Topics such as efficiency wages theory, insider–outsider analysis, hysteresis, all point to some imperfection in the traditional framework of what A. C. Pigou called, over eighty years ago, *wages policies*. Typical of all New Keynesian models, these explanations rely on the methodological perspective that unemployment in the aggregate can be considered in the same way that it can be done for an individual firm or market. Thus the relevant questions posed by New Keynesians all centre on the extent to which nominal and real wages are or are not flexible in light of exogenous shocks in nominal aggregate demand.

Moreover, the New Keynesian analysis couched in the concept of an aggregate labour market leads them also to embrace the theoretical proposition that there is some natural rate of unemployment, existing because market and governmental policies prevent the real wage from falling to the extent necessary for the labour market to clear. And from the natural rate of unemployment (with all of its theoretical and policy baggage) comes, all too easily, an adherence to some notion of a non-accelerating inflation rate of unemployment (NAIRU). In both cases, any commitments by New Keynesians to public policies which might mitigate unemployment in the aggregate come almost begrudgingly, and, in most cases, find their origins in their political, rather than in their economic, leanings.

Keynes, as we are aware, pointed out the logical fallacy of making the leap from the individual firm or industry to industry as a whole. The main problem, he observed, was that the latter could only be articulated if it was assumed that no changes in aggregate output *or employment* occurred when there were any changes in wages. The traditional approach was capable of describing situations of excess supplies or demands for labour for a particular firm or industry, but could say nothing about unemployment in the economy as a whole. As a result of the logical fallacy of such an approach, Keynes observed that what he called 'classical theory' – into which New Keynesian economics falls quite comfortably – had no basis for understanding the problem. This criticism was pointed out in Chapter 3, and receives further articulation in this second part of the book.

Based on this and other criticisms, to be described in the ensuing chapters, a Post Keynesian perspective on labour and unemployment finds little room for questions addressed at the extent to which wages do or do not fall. Rather, the Post Keynesian approach to unemployment holds true to Keynes's criticisms. And with the attempts, below, to call into question the New Keynesian programme both in its parts and in general, comes a commitment to understanding unemployment in the aggregate in terms of the economy-wide relationship among the factors of income (and its distribution), output and spending – that is, a theory of effective demand.

In the opening chapter, entitled 'Wages and Employment' Claudio Sardoni reminds us of the nature of a Keynesian theory of employment in the aggregate. He reminds us of a common observation made by Post Keynesians that for Keynes unemployment for industry as a whole occurred because of fluctuations in effective demand, and not based on the extent to which wages were either sticky or flexible. Keynes did not ignore the effect that changes in wages could have on employment, but his frame of reference was always the theory of effective demand rather than the traditional labour market analysis of neoclassical theory. Thus, the New Keynesian belief that *Keynesian unemployment* occurs because of rigid or sticky wages had no relevance to Keynes. What Sardoni does in this chapter is to develop what he calls 'a simple model based on some essential elements of Keynes's theory in order to outline the basic aspects of Keynes's position concerning the effects of changes in the money-wage rate on the aggregate level of employment'. Keynes argued in chapter 19 of *The General Theory* that a theory of effective demand requires an understanding of changes in wages through their effects on the conditions that underlie both aggregate demand and supply. Using this framework, Sardoni shows how a change in wages can affect aggregate employment to the extent that it impacts on the distribution of labour between the consumer and capital goods industries as well as 'to the elasticities of labour to output in the two industries'.

He concludes by reaffirming Keynes's important theoretical and methodological point that industry as a whole cannot improve its overall profitability position by asking labour to accept a cut in money wages, a point 'which those nurtured in the classical theory [including New Keynesians] find most difficult to understand'.

In the next chapter, 'New Keynesian Macroeconomics and the Determination of Employment and Wages', Malcolm Sawyer considers the New Keynesian approach to the determination of wages, their consequences for unemployment, and their empirical relevance. He argues that the concepts associated with the new Keynesian approach, such as insider–outsider models, efficiency wage, etc., do not aid in understanding the generally higher levels of unemployment since the mid–1970s (as compared with the 1950s and 1960s) and that the empirical relevance of the New Keynesian approaches to wage setting appears to be declining.

Sawyer then takes on the concept of the NAIRU, asserting that it imposes a severe constraint on thinking about the causes of and cures for high levels of unemployment. Moreover, he contends that adhering to the existence of a NAIRU can be seen as a contributory factor to the prevailing levels of unemployment.

Finally he reasserts a recurrent theme of this book that New Keynesian macroeconomics pays no attention to aggregate demand (nor indeed to the roles of investment and pervasive uncertainty), and hence does not deserve the name Keynesian.

Then, Sergio Nisticó and Fabio D'Orlando raise what they call 'Some Questions for New Keynesians'. Their aim, in this chapter, is to emphasize some drawbacks of New Keynesian macroeconomics, both on methodological and on analytical grounds. From the methodological viewpoint, they argue that the New Keynesian programme is far from constituting a homogeneous paradigm. The reasons they offer for this conclusion rest on their contention that there is an absence of an agreement about the nature of unemployment, and that there is a widespread use of *ad hoc* assumptions, which end up conflicting with one another when the attempt is made to merge the various models in one theoretical scheme.

With regard to the analytical aspects, Nisticó and D'Orlando highlight some logical inconsistencies surrounding the so-called *shirking models* of New Keynesianism. It is shown that the typical results of the efficiency wage theory are crucially linked to the highly restrictive hypothesis that below a given wage workers' effort becomes nil. It is, moreover, shown that the significance and the stability of an unemployment equilibrium can hardly be derived from the hypothesis that firms pay 'efficiency wages'.

Sometimes too much focus can be placed on the traditional frameworks defined by those whom one sets out to criticize. The next two chapters propose to move beyond those narrow strictures defined by the orthodox New Keynesian metaphors exploring questions of society, culture, institutions and psychology. An important distinction between New Keynesian and Post Keynesian approaches can be seen in terms of the breadth of questions that fit within the positive heuristic of each perspective. By virtue of the fact that New Keynesian models rely on the closed, deductive neoclassical framework, anything admitting to considering ideas beyond those factors which affect conditions of supply and demand in particular markets is either ignored or considered to be exogenously given to the model. Thus any attempts at realism, such as thinking in terms of efficiency wages, near-rationality, psychology, etc., do not get very far without calling into question the models into which they are awkwardly fit.

In their chapter on 'Social Norms as Rational Choices', Murray Milgate and Cheryl B. Welch consider that in a given society, at a given stage in its historical development, the idea that wage rates are established as much by the influence of social, cultural and institutional factors as by 'market forces' is as old as the study of economics itself. Such features were featured prominently in the work of the classical economists and, particularly, Marx; and they were only barely submerged even after the rise to dominance of the more individualistic, contractarian approach to economic transactions associated with the marginal revolution. This could be seen in Marshall's treatment of wages, especially in his celebrated discussion of the so-called 'evil paradox'. The same ideas were also present in Keynes's *General Theory*. Now, in the last decade or so, New Keynesian economics has returned to this old theme in its attempts to model the social dimension of wage contracts as the being essentially the result of individual rational choices.

By a comparative analysis of three episodes in which this strategy has been deployed by social philosophers, Milgate and Welch argue that such exercises in modelling social norms as rational choices do not (and cannot) yield the degree of explanatory precision their authors intend. Such approaches not only reduce the designation *social* to thin description, but divert attention away from those crucial institutional, historical and political factors that are central to a proper understanding of social phenomena.

John Davis, in his chapter 'New Keynesians, Post Keyensians and History', continues along the lines opened up by Milgate and Welch, by recognizing that though Post Keynesians are not unsympathetic to New Keynesians' emphasis on asymmetric information, imperfect competition, increasing returns, etc., they strongly reject their use of the standard subjective probability framework. Instead, Davis argues that Keynes's emphasis on true uncertainty about the future undermines much of the New Keynesian project of finding microfoundations for macroeconomics.

Pursuing this line of reasoning, Davis goes on to raise the most salient observation that Post Keynesians find serious problems to exist in New Keynesian thinking about the influence of the past and our ignorance of it on the present. Davis's take-off point considers the recent work of Donald Katzner, who argues that a Post Keynesian understanding rejects hysteresis when thinking of an economy moving in historical time. Davis, then, pursues this view of an economy whose history is created period by period, by looking at the decision-making behaviour of individuals according to recent experimental evidence from psychology. He concludes that Keynes's interest in conventions would support making use of recent experimental evidence, and that Post Keynesians do operate with a fundamentally different view of choice and behaviour compared to that employed by New Keynesians.

The final chapter in this section, 'Elements of Conflict in UK Wage Determination', by Philip Arestis and Iris Biefang-Frisancho Mariscal, asserts that wage determination should be seen as the outcome of a decentralized bargaining process where distributional conflict arises over relative income shares. Conflict, however, does not only arise between workers and capitalists: there is, furthermore, the influence of wage relativities on wage formation. What Arestis and Biefand-Frisancho Mariscal find is that such wage relativities can play an important role in explaining wage stickiness. Wage efficiency theories as well as hysteresis models may also be embedded into this framework as complementary theories, providing further reasons for why wages do not fall. These theories are compatible with the framework proposed in this chapter, although their approach differs from most other contributions because of their emphasis on the importance of wage relativities and the existence of conflict over the functional distribution of income. Clearly, there are differences between the Post Keynesian *real wage resistance* hypothesis, the very Keynesian *wage relativities* hypothesis and the more labour-market-orientated New Keynesian models of *wage efficiency* and *hysteresis*. This chapter, however, demonstrates that so long as conflict elements are the focus of the analysis, the three theories can sit comfortably in a model which is validated by the UK experience.

5

WAGES AND EMPLOYMENT*

A Keynesian model

Claudio Sardoni

INTRODUCTION

In the introduction to a symposium on New Keynesian economics, Mankiw describes the tasks that this strand of economics sets for itself in the following terms: 'Like Keynes, new Keynesians begin with the premise that persistent unemployment and economic fluctuations are central and continuing problems: recessions and depressions represent market-failure on a grand scale' (Mankiw, 1993, p. 3). Whether fluctuations were a central concern for Keynes in *The General Theory* is arguable, but he certainly was deeply interested in unemployment and the ways to cure such a malady.

However, beyond this shared concern for unemployment, it is hard to find significant analytical elements in common between Keynes and New Keynesians. The differences are much more significant. With respect to the problem of unemployment, in particular, New Keynesian economics, differently from Keynes, generally holds that its basic cause is wage rigidity, which prevents the labour market from clearing.

In this respect, New Keynesians are closer to the 'neoclassical synthesis' rather than to Keynes. In fact, they essentially refer to this 'traditional exposition' of Keynes's economics and aim at providing it with more rigorous microfoundations. Mankiw argues: 'Traditional expositions of Keynesian economics emphasised the role of rigidities in nominal wages and prices. It is natural, then, that one strand of new Keynesian economics seeks to explain price rigidities' (ibid., p. 4; see also Mankiw, 1992). Also Romer, in the same symposium, refers to unemployment and fluctuations and observes:

> The famous 'neoclassical synthesis'... postulated a single explanation of both phenomena: that prices in money units adjusted only slowly to imbalances between supply and demand. The most important of these sluggish money prices was the money price of labour – the nominal wage.
>
> (Romer, 1993, p. 5)

Mankiw and Romer still draw a distinction between Keynes himself and the type of Keynesian economics which developed later. The explanation of unemployment by wage rigidity is not attributed to the author of *The General Theory* but to the 'neoclassical synthesis'. However, in the recent literature on wage rigidity, the view that Keynes explained unemployment with wage rigidities is widely held. For example, Akerlof and Yellen put Keynes and Pigou together and attribute to them the view that the labour market does not clear because of sticky wages (Akerlof and Yellen, 1986, p. 1). For Lindbeck (1993, pp. 27–8), there is no doubt that Keynes tried to explain unemployment with wage rigidity and he (along with Old Classical macroeconomists from Hume to Pigou) is blamed for not having provided a satisfactory justification for such a rigidity.

Many Post Keynesians have convincingly argued that Keynes's explanation of unemployment is not contingent on price rigidity and, in particular, on wage rigidity.[1] It is true that, in the first four books of *The General Theory*, Keynes assumed constant money wages but this was a simplification to be dispensed with later on (Book V). In any case, for Keynes, 'the essential character of the argument is precisely the same whether or not money-wages, etc. are liable to change' (Keynes, 1936, p. 27).

This chapter does not aim to present a detailed exposition of Keynes's point of view and then contrast it with either the neoclassical synthesis or the New Keynesian views. Instead, the main object of this chapter is to present a simple model based on some essential elements of Keynes's theory in order to outline the basic aspects of Keynes's position concerning the effects of changes in the money wage rate on the aggregate level of employment.

KEYNES ON CHANGES IN MONEY WAGES

As early as 1932–3 Keynes had already outlined a basic element of his general theory, that is to say the need for a theory of aggregate demand which had been neglected by classical economics. It is the level of aggregate demand which determines the level of aggregate income and employment. From this point of view, changes in the prices of the factors of production, namely changes in wages, can have an effect on the aggregate level of production and employment only to the extent that they affect aggregate demand.

Keynes did not deny that changes in wages can affect the aggregate level of employment, i.e. that a decrease in money wages can have a positive effect on employment, but his position was different from the classical one from the analytical point of view: 'A reduction in money-wages is quite capable in certain circumstances of affording a stimulus to output, as the classical theory supposes. My difference from this theory is primarily a difference of analysis' (Keynes, 1936, p. 257).

In Keynes's analytical approach, a change in wages is able to affect the level of employment if it affects the community's propensity to consume, the marginal efficiency of capital or the rate of interest. If these variables – which together determine aggregate output and employment – are left untouched by a change in wages, entrepreneurs would behave irrationally by increasing employment when the money-wage rate decreases (ibid., pp. 260–1).[2]

A reduction in the money-wage rate, for Keynes, is likely to reduce the community's marginal propensity to consume and, hence, to have a negative effect on employment. He argued that the reduction in wages determines a redistribution of income in favour of the sections of society with a lower marginal propensity to consume (ibid., p. 262).

As to the effects of a wage reduction on the marginal efficiency of capital, Keynes distinguished between two cases: the reduction in the money-wage rate is expected to be a reduction with respect to future money wages; the current reduction in the money-wage rate leads to expectations of further reductions in the future. In the first case, the decline in wages raises the marginal efficiency of capital and has a positive effect on investment; in the second case, the effect is negative (ibid., p. 263). If wages are expected to rise again in the future, firms are more willing to invest now in order to benefit from the current lower costs; if wages are expected to decrease further, firms are induced to postpone investment in order to benefit from future lower costs.

Finally, with some provisos, a decrease in money wages has a positive effect on aggregate demand in that, through the induced reduction in prices and the demand for money for the transactions motive, it lowers the rate of interest and favours investment (ibid., pp. 263–4).[3]

The model of the next section is an attempt to present some of Keynes's basic ideas in a more formal way than in *The General Theory*. In particular, the model focuses on the relation between changes in the money-wage rate and investment as both the marginal propensity to consume and the rate of interest are taken as exogenously given.

A SIMPLE MODEL[4]

In the present model, like in *The General Theory*, firms are assumed to produce under short-period decreasing returns and investment is assumed to depend on long-term expectations, the rate of interest and prices of capital goods. The model differs from Keynes's analysis in that aggregates are measured in prices rather than in wage units and long-term expectations do not depend on the volume of investment as they do in *The General Theory*. As to the effects of a change in the money-wage rate, they are studied by explicitly considering a two-industry economy rather than in aggregate terms like in *The General Theory*. Finally, while Keynes concentrated on the effects of a change in wages on long-term expectations, in the model long-term expectations are initially taken as exogenously given in order to isolate the effects on employment produced by changes in the conditions of supply and prices. Later on, following Keynes, long-term expectations are considered also as a function of changes in money wages.

Let us consider a two-industry closed economy in which a consumer good, C, and a capital good, I, are produced by n and m firms respectively. Let us assume that there is free competition, so that firms maximize expected profits by pushing production to the point at which marginal cost equals expected price. The money-wage rate, w, is uniform throughout the economy.

INDUSTRY SUPPLY AND DEMAND FUNCTIONS

The production decisions of firms depend on costs and expected prices. Costs, in turn, depend on (the given) technology, the produced quantity and wages. Price expectations (i.e. short-term expectations) are taken as given. Let p_i^e be the price expected by the ith firm producing the consumer good C. The firm's supply function is obtained by solving

$$\text{Max }(\pi_i) = p_i^e C_i - q_i(C_i, w)$$

(where $q_i = q_i(C_i, w)$ denotes the ith firm's total cost function) and it is

$$C_{Si} = f_i(p_i^e, w) \quad (i = 1, 2, \ldots, n)$$

If, for simplicity, it is assumed that firms have uniform price expectations $(p_1^e = p_2^e = \ldots = p_n^e = p^e)$, the aggregate supply function of C is

$$C_S = F(p^e, w) \quad \text{with} \quad \frac{dC_S}{dp^e} > 0, \quad \frac{dC_S}{dw} < 0 \tag{1}$$

The individual supply functions and the total supply function of the capital good I are obtained in an analogous way, so that

$$I_S = G(r^e, w) \quad \text{with} \quad \frac{dI_S}{dr^e} > 0, \quad \frac{dI_S}{dw} < 0 \tag{2}$$

where r^e is the expected price of the capital good.

As to the demand functions, the demand for the capital good is essentially based on Keynes's marginal efficiency of capital. The jth firm's demand for the capital good I is

$$I_{Dj} = h_j(r, i, E_j) \quad (j = 1, 2, \ldots, n + m)$$

where r is the price of the capital good, i is the rate of interest and E_j is the jth firm's long-term expectations.

If it is also assumed that $E_1 = E_2 = \ldots = E_{n+m} = E$ (firms have uniform long-term expectations), the total demand for the capital good is

$$I_D = H(r, i, E) \quad \text{with} \quad \frac{dI_D}{dr} < 0, \quad \frac{dI_D}{di} < 0, \quad \frac{dI_D}{dE} > 0 \tag{3}$$

As to the demand function for C, here it is sufficient to hypothesize that income is not entirely spent on the consumer good, so that, if c is the given overall marginal propensity to consume, and $rI_S + pC_S$ is total nominal income, the total demand function for C is

$$C_D = c\left(\frac{rI_S}{p} + C_S\right) = M(c, p, r, p^e, r^e, w) \tag{4}$$

where p is the price of the consumer good.

Employment is an increasing function of output in both industries. Therefore,

$$L_C = L_C(C_S) \quad \text{and} \quad L_I = L_I(I_S) \quad \text{with} \quad \frac{dL_C}{dC_S} > 0, \ \frac{d^2L_C}{dC_S^2} > 0 \quad \text{and} \quad \frac{dL_I}{dI_S} > 0, \ \frac{d^2L_I}{dI_S^2} > 0 \tag{5}$$

since decreasing returns are assumed in both industries.

Total employment is

$$L = L(C_S, I_S) \tag{6}$$

The equilibrium conditions

For equilibrium to obtain, demand and supply must be equal in both industries:

$$C_S = C_D \qquad I_S = I_D$$

In equilibrium $p^e = p$ and $r^e = r$. From (1), (2), (3) and (4) we thus obtain

$$F(p, w) = M(c, p, r, w) \tag{7}$$

$$G(r, w) = H(r, i, E) \tag{8}$$

w, i and E being exogenously given, (7) and (8) together yield the equilibrium prices for C and I.

From inspection of (7) and (8) it emerges that r, the price of the capital good, is independent of p, the price of the consumer good; p, on the contrary, depends on r. Once r is determined the equilibrium quantity of I is determined as well. Thus, the equilibrium price and output of the capital-good industry are independent of the consumer-good industry, whereas the reverse does not hold: both equilibrium price and quantity in the consumer-good industry depend on r and I.

More precisely, we have

$$r^* = \phi(w, i, E) \tag{9}$$

$$p^* = \tau(r^*, w, i, E) \tag{10}$$

where r^* and p^* denote the equilibrium values of the price of the capital good and the consumer good respectively.

As to employment, from (5) and (6), and by denoting the equilibrium outputs in the two industries by C^* and I^*, we obtain

$$L^* = L(C^*, I^*) = I_C(C^*) + L_I(I^*) \tag{11}$$

where L^* is total employment in equilibrium, which is not necessarily equal to full employment.

Changes in money wages

The hypothesis of a fixed money-wage rate is now removed in order to see how wage flexibility affects the equilibrium level of output and employment. The model does not establish a precise relationship between the money-wage rate and the rate of unemployment. The money-wage rate is made to change exogenously in order to inspect the effects on the equilibrium levels of output and employment.

As to the effects of a change in the money-wage rate on the equilibrium prices of the capital good and the consumer good, it is easy to demonstrate that, at $r = r^*$ and $p = p^*$,

$$\frac{d_r}{d_w} > 0 \quad \text{and} \quad \frac{dp}{dw} > 0 \qquad (12)^5$$

In other words, a variation in the money-wage rate determines a change in the same direction of both equilibrium prices.

In order to study the effects of a change in wages on output and employment, it is sufficient to look at the signs of the derivatives of the three following functions at their equilibrium points:

$$\frac{\delta I}{\delta w}, \quad \frac{\delta (rI)}{\delta w}, \quad \frac{\delta C}{\delta w}$$

i.e. the derivatives with respect to w of the physical output of the capital good, the value of the output of the capital good, the physical output of the consumer good respectively.[6] A positive effect of a decrease in the money-wage rate on output and, hence, on employment is denoted by negative derivatives.

The sign of $\delta I/\delta w$ at the equilibrium point $r = r^*$, is determined from (8). It is

$$\frac{\delta G}{\delta w} = \frac{\delta H}{\delta w}$$

i.e.

$$\frac{dG}{dw} + \frac{dG}{dr}\frac{dr}{dw} = \frac{dH}{dr}\frac{dr}{dw}$$

Since

$$\frac{dH}{dr} < 0 \quad \text{and} \quad \frac{dr}{dw} > 0$$

it necessarily is

$$\frac{\delta G}{\delta w} < 0$$

But, at $r = r^*$,

$$G(r^*, w) = I^*$$

so that

$$\frac{\delta I^*}{\delta w} < 0 \qquad (13)$$

A decrease in money wages is unambiguously associated with an increase in the equilibrium output of the capital good.

However, the effect of the same decrease in money wages on the *value* of the equilibrium output is ambiguous. For a decrease in the money-wage rate to have a positive effect on the equilibrium value of the capital good output, then

$$\frac{\delta}{\delta w}(rI) = \frac{\mathrm{d}r}{\mathrm{d}w}I + r\frac{\mathrm{d}I}{\mathrm{d}w} < 0$$

After rearrangement, we obtain that the condition above is fulfilled if (at $r = r^*$ and $I = I^*$)

$$\varepsilon_{I,w} > \varepsilon_{r,w} \qquad (14)$$

where $\varepsilon_{I,w}$ and $\varepsilon_{r,w}$ respectively denote the elasticity of the capital good output and the elasticity of the capital good price to the money-wage rate.

A decrease in the money-wage rate and, hence, in costs causes a fall in the equilibrium price of the capital good; in order to have an increase in the equilibrium value of the output, it is necessary that the physical production grows more than proportionally to the fall in price.

As to the consumer good industry, we can see from (4) above that the equilibrium output of the consumer good is positively affected by a decrease in w if, at $p = p^*$,

$$p\left(\frac{\mathrm{d}r}{\mathrm{d}w}I + \frac{\mathrm{d}I}{\mathrm{d}w}r\right) - (rI)\frac{\mathrm{d}p}{\mathrm{d}w} < 0$$

After rearrangement, it can be shown that the condition above is satisfied if

$$\varepsilon_{I,w} > \varepsilon_{r,w} - \varepsilon_{p,w} \qquad (15)$$

$\varepsilon_{I,w}$ and $\varepsilon_{r,w}$ are the same as in (14) and $\varepsilon_{p,w}$ denotes the elasticity of the consumer good price to w.

Condition (15) can be contrasted with condition (14): the condition for a positive increase in the equilibrium output of the consumer good is less restrictive than the one relative to the volume of the capital good. In fact, it is sufficient to have an elasticity of I to w whose absolute value is larger than $(\varepsilon_{r,w} - \varepsilon_{p,w}) < \varepsilon_{r,w}$. A lower elasticity of I to w is required because a decrease in wages also causes a decrease in p and this can compensate for a possible negative effect on rI. Suppose, for example, that $\varepsilon_{I,w} < \varepsilon_{r,w}$ so that when wages fall the *value* of the equilibrium output of the capital good industry decreases and the monetary *value* of its demand for the consumer good, $c(r^*I^*)$, decreases as well. This, however, is not sufficient to cause a fall in the demand for the consumer good in *real terms*. In fact, the decrease in the equilibrium price of the consumer good can be such as to determine an increase in the *real* purchasing power of the industry I. In other words, the decrease in wages has both an *income* and a *price effect* on the demand for the consumer good by the capital good industry. The *price effect* can be strong enough to compensate for a possible negative *income effect*.

On the other hand, it may well be that $\varepsilon_{I,w} < \varepsilon_{r,w} - \varepsilon_{p,w}$ and, in such a case, there would be a decrease in output and employment of the consumer good industry. The decrease in employment in the consumer good industry can be larger than the increase in the capital good industry, so that a decline in the aggregate level of employment occurs as a consequence of a reduction in the money-wage rate.

In general, in order that a reduction in the money-wage rate give rise to an increase in aggregate employment, it must be

$$\frac{\delta}{\delta w}[L_c(C) + L_I(I)] < 0$$

which is fulfilled if

$$L_C\, \varepsilon_{L_C,C}\, \varepsilon_{C,w} + L_I\, \varepsilon_{L_I,I}\, \varepsilon_{I,w} < 0 \qquad (16)$$

The direction of the change in aggregate employment depends on the elasticity of labour to changes in output (caused by a change in wages) in the two industries and on the distribution of labour between the two industries.

The results achieved so far show that a change in wages can affect employment through its effect on investment. If there were no changes in I^* or r^*I^* there would be no changes in the aggregate levels of output and employment. In the model, Keynes's view that changes in the money-wage rate can produce effects on aggregate employment to the extent that the three crucial variables are affected (the overall propensity to consume, the marginal efficiency of capital and the rate of interest) is confirmed though in a specific form: changes in wages can only affect the marginal efficiency of capital through changes in the price of the capital good because long-term expectations are taken as exogenously given.

Long-term expectations as a function of changes in wages

In this section, we remove the hypothesis of exogenous long-term expectations, which now become a function of changes in the money-wage rate. Following Keynes, we consider both the case in which a decrease in wages positively affects expectations and the opposite case.

A reduction in wages positively affects long-term expectations

In this case

$$\frac{dE}{dw} < 0$$

and it is easy to see that there is no significant change with respect to the results of the previous section. Now the equality $\delta G/\delta w = \delta H/\delta w$ at $r = r^*$ becomes

$$\frac{dG}{dw} + \frac{dG}{dr}\frac{dr}{dw} = \frac{dH}{dr}\frac{dr}{dw} + \frac{dH}{dE}\frac{dE}{dw}$$

$dH/dr < 0$, $dr/dw > 0$, dH/dE and, by hypothesis, $dE/dw < 0$, so that necessarily

$$\frac{\delta G}{\delta w} < 0 \quad \text{i.e.} \frac{\delta I^*}{\delta w} < 0$$

The signs of the two other derivatives depend on the same conditions as in (14) and (15).

A reduction in wages negatively affects long-term expectations.

Now since

$$\frac{dE}{dw} > 0$$

a decrease in wages gives rise to more pessimistic long-term expectations.

In order that $\delta I^*/\delta w < 0$ it must be

$$\frac{dH}{dr}\frac{dr}{dw} + \frac{dH}{dE}\frac{dE}{dw} < 0$$

but now $dE/dw > 0$. After rearrangement, it can be shown that the inequality above is fulfilled if

$$\varepsilon_{H,E}\, \varepsilon_{E,w} < \varepsilon_{H,r}\, \varepsilon_{r,w} \tag{17}$$

where the left-hand member of the inequality denotes the elasticity of the demand for the capital good to a change in expectations due to a change in w, while the right-hand member denotes the elasticity of the demand for the capital good to a change in its price because of a change in w.

In order that a fall in money wages produce an increase in the output of the capital good, the positive effect of a decrease in wages and prices on the demand for the capital good must be stronger than the negative effect owing to the worsening of expectations.

As to the effect of the decrease in wages on the value of the output of the capital good, if (17) is fulfilled the same results of the previous section hold. If (17) is not fulfilled, it is evident that the value of the output necessarily decreases: both the physical production and the price of the capital good decrease as a consequence of the decrease in wages.

Finally, looking at the effect of a decrease in money wages on the output of the consumer good, we have to consider two different cases. First, if (17) above is fulfilled the output of the consumer good increases with a fall in wages if the same condition (15) above is satisfied. If, instead, (17) is not fulfilled, the condition (15) becomes

$$\varepsilon_{p,w} > \varepsilon_{r,w} + \varepsilon_{I,w} \tag{18}$$ [7]

In order that the consumer good output increase, the decrease in the equilibrium price of the consumer good must be such as to offset more than the decrease in the value of the output of the capital good due to the decrease in r^* and I^*. In such a way the real purchasing power of the capital good industry increases.

CONCLUSION

Changes in the money-wage rate can affect the level of employment to the extent that they give rise to changes in the three fundamental variables that, in Keynes's theory, determine the aggregate level of income (the marginal propensity to consume, the marginal efficiency of capital and the rate of interest). Keynes's considerations concerning the relation between a reduction in the money-wage rate and the aggregate level of employment are rather complex as they take into account a large number of interdependencies among the variables. The present model considers only a limited number of these relations; in particular, both the marginal propensity to consume and the rate of interest are taken as exogenously given. Therefore, changes in the money-wage rate can affect employment only through their effect on the marginal efficiency of capital.

The marginal efficiency of capital depends on both the prices of capital goods and long-term expectations. In so far as long-term expectations are taken as exogenously given, a reduction in wages affects the marginal efficiency of capital only through a reduction in the cost of production and the supply price of the capital good. In this context we have arrived at the following results.

A decrease in w causes an unambiguous increase in the level of output and employment in the capital good industry.

The change in the level of output and employment in the consumer good industry is not unambiguous. It depends on the elasticities of the capital good output and of both prices, r and p, with respect to w. More precisely, the lower the elasticity of r to w and the higher the elasticity of p to w, the more likely the output and employment of the consumer good industry will increase.

The effect of a decrease in the money-wage rate on the aggregate level of employment also depends on the elasticities of labour to I and C respectively and on the distribution of labour between the two industries. In particular, condition (15) could not be fulfilled and the decrease in wages gives rise to an increase in employment if the elasticity of labour to I is sufficiently higher than the elasticity of labour to C, so that the increase in employment in the first industry more than compensates for the decrease in the second. On the other hand, employment could increase in the capital good industry and decrease in the consumer good industry to such an extent that aggregate employment declines despite the reduction in money-wage rate.

When the hypothesis of exogenous long-term expectations is removed and they also depend on changes in the money-wage rate, the results, are as follows.

If a reduction in *w* affects *E* positively, there is still an unambiguous increase in the level of output and employment in the capital good industry. As a consequence, the behaviour of employment in the consumer good industry and at the aggregate level is contingent on the same factors as in the case of exogenous expectations.

If a reduction in *w* affects *E* negatively, the response of output and employment in the capital good industry is no longer unambiguous. In order that output and employment increase, the positive effect of the decrease in the price of the capital good must be stronger than the negative effect of the worsening of expectations. When output and employment in the capital good industry decrease, output and employment in the consumer good industry can still increase provided that the decrease in the price of the consumer good is so large as to ensure an increase in the real purchasing power of the capital good industry. Aggregate employment can rise or decline according to the distribution of labour between the two industries and to the elasticities of labour to output in the two industries.

In Keynes's analysis the existence of unemployment does not depend on wagerigidity. The money-wage rate can be fully flexible and unemployment still persists. If changes in the price of labour do not have any effect on aggregate expenditure, then unemployment cannot be cured by recontracting in the labour market.

> The firms, taken as a whole, cannot protect themselves from loss by making revised (i.e. more favourable) money bargains with the factors of production. This is the point which those nurtured in the classical theory find most difficult to understand. They suppose that, if the factors of production are prepared to accept a sufficiently low money wage, this will be reflected in lower real wages and will, therefore, serve to redress the balance in favour of the entrepreneur firms. But, in arguing thus, they forget that it is the earnings paid out to the factors of production which constitute the demand for the output of production. So long as their outgoings are not returning to the firms in full, there is no conceivable money bargain between the firms and their factors of production which will protect them, taken as a whole, from loss.
>
> (Keynes, 1979 pp. 97–8).

Apparently, the economists who came after Keynes remain extraordinarily deaf to his message. They keep analysing aggregate employment as if it could be studied in the same terms as employment in a single industry, an analytical procedure that Keynes had decisively and repeatedly regarded as logically flawed and, hence, unable to provide significant insights for the explanation and cure of unemployment.[8]

NOTES

* I wish to thank A. Roncaglia and G. Harcourt for their comments and suggestions. The essay is part of the work of the research group on 'Non-competitive market forms and economic dynamics' funded by the Italian Ministry for Universities and Scientific Research.

1 See, in particular, Chick (1983, pp. 132–58).

2 Keynes's analysis was carried out under the hypothesis of a marginal propensity to consume of less than 1. If the marginal propensity to consume were equal to 1, a decrease in wages would give rise to an increase in employment (Keynes, 1936, p. 261).

3 Keynes also considered the possible effects of lower wages on the entrepreneurs' state of confidence and on debts (Keynes, 1936, p. 264). His analysis was mainly carried out under the hypothesis of a closed economy. In an open economy, the change in domestic wages has to be considered also relative to changes in wages abroad (ibid., p. 262).

4 A different version of this model has been used in Sardoni (1992).

5 The sign of $\mathrm{d}r/\mathrm{d}w$ can be easily determined from (8). Let us consider the implicit function

$$R(r, w, i, E) = G(r, w) - H(r, i, E) = 0$$

Then

$$\frac{\mathrm{d}r}{\mathrm{d}w} = -\left(\frac{\mathrm{d}R/\mathrm{d}w}{\mathrm{d}R/\mathrm{d}r}\right) = -\frac{\mathrm{d}G/\mathrm{d}w - \mathrm{d}H/\mathrm{d}w}{\mathrm{d}G/\mathrm{d}r - \mathrm{d}H/\mathrm{d}r} = -\frac{\mathrm{d}G/\mathrm{d}w}{\mathrm{d}G/\mathrm{d}r - \mathrm{d}H/\mathrm{d}r}$$

with $\mathrm{d}G/\mathrm{d}w < 0$, $\mathrm{d}H/\mathrm{d}w = 0$, and $\mathrm{d}G/\mathrm{d}r > 0$, $\mathrm{d}H/\mathrm{d}r < 0$.
Therefore,

$$\frac{\mathrm{d}r}{\mathrm{d}w} > 0$$

In order to determine the sign of $\mathrm{d}p/\mathrm{d}w$ let us first consider, from (7), the implicit function

$$p(c, p, r, w) = F(p, w) - M(c, p, r, w) = 0$$

Then

$$\frac{\mathrm{d}p}{\mathrm{d}r} = -\frac{\mathrm{d}P/\mathrm{d}r}{\mathrm{d}P/\mathrm{d}p} = -\left(\frac{\mathrm{d}F/\mathrm{d}r) - (\mathrm{d}M/\mathrm{d}r)}{(\mathrm{d}F/\mathrm{d}p) - (\mathrm{d}M/\mathrm{d}p)}\right)$$

Since $\mathrm{d}F/\mathrm{d}r = 0$, $\mathrm{d}M/\mathrm{d}r > 0$, $\mathrm{d}F/\mathrm{d}p > 0$, $\mathrm{d}M/\mathrm{d}p < 0$,

$$\frac{\mathrm{d}p}{\mathrm{d}r} > 0$$

Given that $\mathrm{d}r/\mathrm{d}w > 0$, then also $\mathrm{d}p/\mathrm{d}w > 0$.

6 The sign of the derivative $\delta(pC)/\delta w$, i.e. the effect of a change in wages on the *value* of the output of the consumer good industry, is not interesting in that, under the hypothesis of $c < 1$, it does not have any implications for real output and employment.

7 This follows because now $\delta I^*/\delta w > 0$.

8 '[T]he demand schedules for particular industries can only be constructed on some fixed assumption as to the nature of the demand and supply schedules of other industries and as to the amount of the aggregate effective demand. It is invalid, therefore, to transfer the argument to the industry as a whole unless we also transfer our assumption that the aggregate effective demand is fixed.... [I]f the classical theory is not allowed to extend by analogy its conclusions in respect of a particular industry to industry as a whole, it is wholly unable to answer the question what effect on employment a reduction in money-wages will have' (Keynes, 1936, pp. 259–60). On this see also Rotheim (1992).

6

NEW KEYNESIAN MACROECONOMICS AND THE DETERMINATION OF EMPLOYMENT AND WAGES

Malcolm Sawyer

INTRODUCTION

This chapter begins by considering the New Keynesian approaches to the determination of wages and the consequences of that for unemployment, and then seeks to evaluate the empirical relevance of that approach. It is argued that the concepts associated with the New Keynesian approach, such as insider–outsider models, efficiency wage, etc., do not aid in understanding the generally higher levels of unemployment since the mid–1970s (as compared with the 1950s and 1960s) and that the empirical relevance of the New Keynesian approaches to wage setting appears to be declining. The second purpose is to argue that a related strand of the New Keynesian approach, namely the non-accelerating inflation rate of unemployment (hereafter NAIRU) imposes a severe constraint on thinking about the causes of and cures for high levels of unemployment, and could be seen as a contributory factor to the prevailing levels of unemployment. Third, it is argued that New Keynesian macroeconomics pays no attention to aggregate demand (nor indeed to the roles of investment and pervasive uncertainty), and hence does not deserve the name Keynesian.

THE NEW KEYNESIAN ANALYSIS OF THE LABOUR MARKET

A major element of the New Keynesian approach is the construction of a wide variety of models in which markets (particularly the labour market) do not clear at levels which are consistent with full employment.[1] The labour market is no longer regarded as akin to a perfectly competitive market with parametric wages but rather wages are set by employers and/or employees in pursuit of their own interests. In a similar vein, employment is offered on a long-term basis and hence does not respond to fluctuations in output demand (or at least employment does not fluctuate to the same degree as demand). It is useful to distinguish three broad (though not completely separable) approaches. First, there are models which involve some bargaining between employers and employees, whether through formal trade union bargaining models or reflected in insider–outsider models (for an introduction see Hargreaves Heap, 1992, pp. 133–46; Lindbeck and Snower, 1988a; Weiss, 1990; and for a general discussion Lindbeck, 1992). The equilibrium outcome is a real wage, employment position which will not usually be a full employment one but one which leaves the parties to the wage, employment agreement with no incentives to seek changes.

The second approch is, the set of ideas which can be described as the efficiency wage approach, in which the setting of wages reflects a positive impact which higher wages have on productivity and labour efficiency. The employers choose the real wage, employment position which is in their best interests, given the impact which the real wage has on productivity. A variant of this is the Shapiro and Stiglitz (1984) model in which the equilibrium is set by the interaction of the aggregate labour demand function (of the real wage) and the aggregate 'no shirking constraint' from which a situation of unemployment is necessarily generated. The third approach is a NAIRU derived from the interaction of price and wage decisions to provide a constant inflation position (e.g. Layard and Nickell, 1986). Since the price, output decision of a firm can be readily translated into real product wage and employment decisions, this third approach has similarities with the first approach, though it differs in the sense that the first approach is constructed at the level of the bargaining unit and then by aggregation to the macro level, whereas the third approach leads to a macro equilibrium. This third approach is essentially a macro (rather than micro) approach in the sense that the equilibrium is not derived from the equilibrium of individuals but rather from the imposition of the condition that inflation is not accelerating.

A central item on the New Keynesian agenda is to answer the question '[i]s it possible for the labour market to be in equilibrium when some individuals wish to work at the prevailing wage but cannot do so? (Mankiw and Romer, 1991, p. 10) in the affirmative by seeking to develop models in which there is, in some sense, equilibrium unemployment. The non-Walrasian equilibrium approach clearly suggests a supply-side equilibrium level of unemployment which will not usually be that of full employment. This is particularly evident in Shapiro and Stiglitz (1984) where the 'no shirking' condition requires unemployment. An equilibrium level of unemployment can be fashioned which could be labelled a NAIRU (though there is no theory of inflation directly associated with these approaches). In these equilibrium models, the explanation of changes in the level of unemployment over time (or differences between countries) would come from changes (or differences) in the underlying parameters of the model (e.g. the effort–productivity schedule).

The question arises as to how to evaluate these ideas. At one level, the underlying ideas (in a sense the assumptions of the models) have a degree of realism in that they do reflect some aspects of the real world which we can readily recognize. For example, we would not wish to deny that there are efficiency-wage-type considerations in the real world in the sense that some firms appear to pay wages above the minimum required and do allow for the effect which wages have on labour productivity. In that way, the New Keynesian macroeconomics has some grounding in the real world in the way in which the New Classical macroeconomics, with continuous price adjustment, clearing markets and rational expectations, does not. Thus we would expect that if the ideas of efficiency wages are empirically evaluated at the level of the firm, they would quite often be broadly (though not universally) confirmed. There may be questions as to how important the ideas are: for example, how far are wages set by efficiency wage considerations and how far by other influences?

There are, of course, numerous obstacles in the empirical evaluation of any set of theoretical ideas, and the New Keynesian models are no exception. Here mention is made of two obstacles which we see as arising particularly in the context of New Keynesian models. First, whilst this is an equilibrium approach, there is little to suggest that any equilibrium is unique. If there are multiple equilibria or if there are significant hysteresis effects, then movements in actual unemployment cannot be predicted from movements in the underlying parameters of the model. The economy may be jumping from one equilibrium to another (under the impetus of exogenous shocks) or the equilibrium positions themselves evolve over time. Colander (1992c) argues that the traditional neoclassical production function can be expanded to include

> a new term *coordination* in the production function ... [where] $X = f(K, L, C)$. The coordination variable, *C*, can cause the production function to shift around; it makes it technically possible for the same inputs to be associated with different levels of output. The New Keynesian research agenda is to examine and understand that coordination function and how it relates with markets.
>
> (p. 446).[2]

Hence, there may be multiple equilibria. Whilst they have not been centre stage in the non-Walrasian literature, both multiple equilibria and hysteresis make honourable mentions in the New Keynesian macroeconomics literature. Indeed, Ees and Garretsen (1992) see multiple equilibria as central when they write that '[i]n comparison with the New Classical framework, New Keynesian economics essentially challenges the hypothesis of a unique rate of production' (p. 465).

The second difficulty is that there are many different models which are brought under the one general heading, and each model will focus on different key parameters. Thus it would be a major project to investigate each of the models within New Keynesian macroeconomics. Further, each model focuses on what may be described as an ideal type (or extreme form), e.g. the model of efficiency wages is cast as though all wages are determined in that fashion. The prediction is that an economy with efficiency wages would display higher wages and higher unemployment than a corresponding one with parametric wages set in anonymous markets. But there appears to be have been no discussion as to whether an economy with a higher proportion of wages set with reference to notions of efficiency wages would be expected to display more unemployment. For example, the existence of a secondary sector in which wages are set as in a competitive labour market alongside a primary sector in which efficiency wage considerations operate could mean that whilst lower wages are paid in the secondary sector, it acts to absorb the labour in effect displaced from the primary sector with no resultant unemployment. In other words, the theory provides a dichotomous view of the world but does not purport to tell us what would happen as the degree of efficiency wages varies continuously.

UNEMPLOYMENT AND THE NEW KEYNESIAN ANALYSIS

Unemployment has been substantially higher in the past two decades than during the 1950s and 1960s with the rise much more pronounced in Europe than in the United States.[3] We take as a broad stylized fact that unemployment in most advanced industrialized economies has been much higher since around 1980 than it was before 1973, and that whilst there have been fluctuations in the rates of unemployment there does not appear to be a downward trend since the early 1980s. Does the New Keynesian macroeconomics shed any light on these experiences of unemployment?. We argue that it does not: the basis of the argument is that the changes which have been observed, especially during the 1980s and 1990s, would, if anything, have led to falls in unemployment according to the New Keynesian macroeconomics.

Although it is not generally explicitly stated, the New Keynesian economists would accept that if the world were characterized by perfect competition (here meaning only that economic agents face parametric prices) then full employment would result. For example, '[w]ithout such [nominal price] rigidities...flexible prices would allow the economy to adjust quickly to whatever shocks it experiences, maintaining all the while full employment and economic efficiency' (Greenwald and Stiglitz, 1993a, p. 25) and New Keynesian economics 'tries to identify more precisely the market imperfections that make wages and prices sticky and that cause the economy to return only slowly to the natural rate' (Mankiw, 1994, p. 313). However, the world is not so characterized, and the identified 'imperfections' lead to unemployment. Some of the 'imperfections' (e.g. trade union power) could be modified or removed by legislation, whilst others (e.g. payment of efficiency wages) could not. Further, some of the 'imperfections' could be seen as having a beneficial purpose (again efficiency wages, and for some of us trade unions). In the discussion below, it is implicitly assumed that more 'imperfections' in an economy would be predicted to lead to more unemployment. It may be acknowledged that there is a dualistic economy in the sense that wages in some parts may be set according to, say, efficiency wage considerations whilst in other parts wages are set in a competitive labour market.

The evidence to which reference is made below can be read in one of two ways. It may first be read to suggest that the scope of efficiency wage (and similar) considerations has been reduced. This would call into some question the relevance of the New Keynesian approach to labour markets. A second reading would suggest that the evidence does not support the view that higher levels of unemployment have arisen through larger degrees of market 'imperfections'. In the main, the generally higher levels of unemployment since 1980 have been accompanied by a decline in the extent of trade union power, of the use of internal labour markets (associated with the payment of efficiency wages). It is not possible to match exactly the timing of the trends in unemployment with those in trade union power, internal labour markets, etc. And, of course, it may be the case that there are other forces which swamp the effects of changing trade union power and internal labour markets. This is a problem which arises with any model which presents a mono-causal explanation of some phenomenon in which factor X alone determines outcome Y: is the model to be literally interpreted as saying that only factor X matters and the theory can be tested by investigation of the relationship between X and Y alone? Or is it rather a *ceteris paribus* prediction which is involved? The role of aggregate demand is of particular significance here in that the higher levels of unemployment since about 1980 could be ascribed to lower levels of aggregate demand but the New Keynesian approach dismisses the role of aggregate demand with its implicit acceptance of Say's Law.

TRADE UNION POWER AND UNEMPLOYMENT

The variant of New Keynesian macroeconomics involving insider–outsider models and specifically the role of trade unions and bargaining would suggest that stronger trade unions (which could mean greater strength in a given bargaining situation or increased coverage of trade unions and collective bargaining) would lead to higher real wages and in general lower levels of employment, though it is well known that the arrival of a trade union in a monopsony situation does not necessarily reduce employment though it is predicted to raise real wages. The decline in trade union power during the 1980s and 1990s in the UK and the United States is well known with falls in trade union membership and the passage of legislation designed to reduce trade union influence. A more general picture is available from OECD (1994a, Table 5.7) which provides statistics for trade union membership in twenty-four countries and in twenty-one of these trade union membership declined during the 1980s (a similar, though rather less pronounced, trend is shown in ibid., Table 5.8 for coverage of collective bargaining). Similarly, for the UK, high levels of unemployment in the interwar period were associated with sharp declines in union membership (along with some major defeats for the trade unions such as the General Strike in 1926). It is difficult to think that greater trade union power has contributed to the experience of higher levels of unemployment (even if one were thinking that such links were possible).

EFFICIENCY WAGES

Efficiency wage models are a second major component of the New Keynesian approach. In this section we seek to investigate whether the use of efficiency wages and related notions has generally increased or decreased in the past fifteen years or so, in view of the generally higher levels of unemployment observed since 1980. There are two clear difficulties here: first, there are many lines of argument used to suggest some (positive) links between wages and productivity and the examination of each of them would be very difficult and time consuming. Second, firms do not use terms such as efficiency wages so that teasing out whether their wage and employment policies conform in some way to efficiency wage notions may be difficult.

It would be expected that there would be some links between the use of internal labour markets and efficiency wage notions. At least, it could be said that the use of external labour markets with the acceptance by employers of the going market wage (if such exists) would not be compatible with efficiency wages. So, at a minimum, efficiency wages require that firms use wages as part of their overall strategies, though that clearly does not necessarily imply that those firms use the other aspects of internal labour markets (such as extensive internal promotion, limited 'ports of entry').

One recent review on labour markets in the UK concludes that:

> Most large British companies, especially in manufacturing and the public sector, formerly provided internal labour markets in which promotion ladders were both 'broad' and 'long'. In some industries and location these employers dominated the local labour markets.... These were typically dominated by employers with 'Fordist' ILMs [Internal Labour Markets].
>
> (Lever, 1979)

While there is room for debate over the degree to which this 'Fordist' employment pattern described the UK labour market as a whole or played a hegemonic role nationally, *there can be little doubt it has declined in terms of employment provided.* 'The ILM [Internal Labour Market] has also been in decline in service industries. Rajan estimates that the number of employees working in ILMs fell from 68% to 52% in banks, 50% to 40% in building societies and 68% to 63% in insurance companies (Savage *et al.* 1988, p. 462)' (Lovering, 1990, p. 14, emphasis added).

He continues by arguing that

> although there are signs that new internal labour markets are emerging, the indications are that they will not be comparable in length or breadth to those which are manifestly disappearing within large manufacturing companies and the public sector. The emergent ILM is characteristically a 'truncated' one.... External labour markets appear to have increased in importance. A number of case studies of employers have identified the significance of external labour markets, especially in the better-paid professions. At the same time, they have shown that many employers also rely on external labour markets for supplies of routine labour.... The growth of self-employment has created another form of 'external labour market'
>
> (ibid., p. 16)

The picture for the United State is not so clear-cut, where one author has recently concluded that

> [t]aken as a whole, these data [relating to the United State for 1979 and 1988] show that long-term employment relationships retain their centrality for men and, indeed, are of increasing importance for men. The more extreme statements about the demise of ILMs or the substantial restructuring of career patterns are not true. However, for men there is a deterioration, with a clear and nontrivial drop in the fraction of middle-age workers in stable employment relationships. Furthermore, this decline occurred in the 1980s, a period of sustained growth in jobs and declining unemployment rates.
>
> (Osterman, 1992, pp. 279–80)

However,

> [i]n the end we are left with a substantial dollop of speculation. We know there is a slight deterioration in the extent of long-term employment relationships among middle-aged men, and we also know there is an increase in various forms of contingent employment relationships. However, only guesswork connects these two developments.
>
> (ibid., p. 282)

Beatson (1995b) reports on the incidence of temporary work (which is self-defined by respondents to the Labour Force Surveys) in the UK over the past ten years. For men temporary work gradually rose from 3.8 per cent of employees in 1984 to 5.5 per cent in 1994 with most of the increase attributable to a rise in fixed period contracts (rather than in seasonal and casual jobs). For women, no trend is detectable though seasonal and casual jobs decline from near 6 per cent to under 4 per cent of employees whilst fixed period contracts rise from around 1.5 per cent to well over 3 per cent.

> Traditionally, the typical European job has been full-time and of indefinite duration. However, such a job is not as prevalent as it used to be. So-called *atypical* employment forms have been growing in importance. This includes part-time and temporary employment, as well as employment for home production, self-employment, and even the underground economy.
>
> (Bertolila and Dolado, 1994, p. 58)

'Temporary employment is gaining ground in Europe. While in 1983 only 4% of employees in the EC held temporary jobs, in 1991 19% did' (ibid., p. 53). For temporary employment (which here includes employment through a temporary work agency and direct fixed term contracts), these authors conclude that it

> has increased [from 1983 to 1991] sharply in France and Spain, and moderately in Ireland, Luxembourg, and the Netherlands, while it has been stable or slightly declining in the remaining EC countries shown [in their table]. Outside the EC, it has increased slightly in Finland and Japan, and declined in Australia and Turkey. (ibid., p. 53)

The authors note, though, that temporary employment displays some cyclical variability and the choice of end points affects the sign of change in several countries. Nätti (1993) states: '[h]owever, most EC countries display a rising trend [in scope of temporary work], although the growth has been uneven . . . : in 1989, the proportion of temporary employees in EC countries varied between 3 and 27%'. The sometimes high levels of temporary employment and the tendency for it to rise rather than fall suggest significant areas of the labour market where the relevance of long-term contracts does not apply.

There would now seem to be a general belief that there has been a decline of 'jobs for life' and an increase in the degree to which people now and in the future will have to change jobs and occupations. The decreased job tenure is confirmed by Gregg and Wadsworth (1995) when they conclude that 'median job tenure has fallen by around 20 per cent since 1975 (14 per cent for employees). This underestimates the increased churning in very short-term positions'. Further, 'labour turnover is rising markedly for older workers and less skilled men' and 'the British labour market can increasingly be categorised as having primary and secondary sectors. The secondary sector is characterised by higher labour turnover among the least skilled, young, and old, and those in atypical employment'. A more general conclusion is given by the statement for the UK that '[a]t the macro-economic level, employment levels now respond more quickly to changing economic conditions' (Beatson, 1995a), which is again suggestive of a decline in the role of internal labour markets and long-term contracts.

On the basis of this rather limited evidence it could be tentatively concluded that the extent of internal labour markets and the use of efficiency wage notions have not risen over the past ten to twenty years. Indeed it is rather ironic: whilst early writers on the internal labour markets (e.g. Doeringer and Piore, 1973, and earlier Kerr, 1954) wrote when such institutional arrangements were of increasing importance, New Keynesian macroeconomists discovered them when they were in some decline.

SHIRKING AND UNEMPLOYMENT

A third variant of the New Keynesian approach, associated with Shapiro and Stiglitz (1984), involves 'equilibrium unemployment as a worker discipline device'. In that approach, the demand for labour is a function of the real wage. The key relationship is the 'no shirking condition' which would shift upwards (thereby reducing equilibrium employment and raising unemployment) with '(a) the smaller the detection probability; (b) the larger the effort; (c) the higher the quit rate; (d) the higher the interest rate; (e) the higher the unemployment benefit; (f) the higher the flows out of unemployment' (ibid., 1984, p. 438). In that model, workers are assumed to choose between zero effort and a particular positive level of effort to which point (b) refers and this makes any comparisons with actual experience difficult to make. On point (a), whilst I could discover no evidence, casual observation would suggest that surveillance and detection rates may have tended to rise. On point (d) interest rates have been generally higher in recent years (notably since 1980) than hitherto, and hence according to this model may have supported higher levels of unemployment. Point (e) can be readily measured, and the figures given in Blöndel and Pearson (1995) suggest a mixed picture across a range of countries on the trends in unemployment benefits relative to earnings (though with a rather pronounced fall in some countries including the UK). The figures for the UK given in Beatson (1995a) on change of employer do not suggest any particular trend in quit rate. Whilst I have not been able to find any direct evidence, it is difficult to believe that the probability of the detection of shirking has fallen rather than risen.

THE NAIRU CONCEPT AS A CONSTRAINT ON THOUGHT

Any mode of economic analysis places a range of constraints on thinking about economic policy, and New Keynesian macroeconomics is no exception. Since the New Keynesian construct has come to be considered as some form of 'conventional wisdom' (to use Galbraith's phrase), it is appropriate to trace the constraints which it imposes.

The current orthodoxy is that the supply side (particularly that relating to wage and price determination) of the economy generates a NAIRU which serves to constrain the employment level in the economy. The estimates of the NAIRU appear to be relatively high (i.e. of the order of 10 per cent or more) and also, as Worswick (1985) noted, have a tendency to track the actual level of unemployment (cf. Jenkinson, 1987, Figure 1). Nickell (1990b) estimates the equilibrium rate of unemployment (equivalent to the NAIRU) in the UK (with actual rates of unemployment given in parenthesis) as follows: 1956–9: 2.2 per cent (2.24 per cent); 1960–8: 2.5 per cent (2.62 per cent); 1969–73: 3.6 per cent (3.39 per cent); 1974–80: 7.3 per cent (5.23 per cent); 1981–7: 8.7 per cent (11.11 per cent); 1988–90: 8.7 per cent (7.27 per cent).

Layard *et al.* (1991, p. 436, Table 14) provide estimates of the 'equilibrium unemployment in 19 industrialised economies for three separate decades with which actual unemployment can be contrasted'. Lombard (1995) reports three estimates for the NAIRU in France for the early 1980s (when the actual unemployment rate averaged 8.3 per cent) of 9.0 per cent, 7.7 per cent and 6.9 per cent which suggest a high level of NAIRU and some sensitivity to methods of estimation. Some further estimates covering a wide range of countries are given in Table 6.1, where the NAWRU is the non-accelerating wage inflation rate of unemployment which is clearly closely related to the NAIRU. The tendency of the NAWRU to mimic the actual level of unemployment over time is clear from that table. A similar picture is given in figures reported in ECE (1992, Table 5.7) and summarized in UNCTAD (1995, p. 170).

The general movement together of NAIRU and actual unemployment could be used to suggest that the former is generally driving the latter, though some explanation of why the NAIRU has changed is required. The alternative view is

Table 6.1 Unemployment rates and NAWRU averages

	1970–9	*1980–9*	*1990–3*	*1994*
Non-European countries:				
Unemployment rates	4.6	5.9	5.6	5.7
NAWRU	4.8	5.8	5.4	5.5
Four major European countries:				
Unemployment rates	4.3	8.7	8.8	10.2
NAWRU	4.3	8.4	9.0	9.4
Small EC countries:				
Unemployment rates	4.7	13.4	12.9	16.7
NAWRU	4.6	12.5	14.1	15.0
Other European countries:				
Unemployment rates	1.3	2.1	3.8	5.8
NAWRU	1.3	2.1	3.5	5.1

Source: OECD (1994, p. 22)
Note: NAWRU is non-accelerating wage inflation rate of unemployment

that there are reasons why the estimates of NAIRU mimic actual unemployment. Most macroeconometric models contain within them the equivalent of the NAIRU, essentially arising from the interaction of price and wage determination. The NAIRU thereby calculated will generally depend on other variables, such as the effective exchange rate. But, typically, the NAIRU does not depend on the level of demand, and can be considered a supply-side phenomenon. The NAIRU is an estimate of the level of unemployment at which inflation would not accelerate; this can be alternatively expressed as saying it is the level of unemployment at which the rate of change of wages minus the rate of increase of prices is equal to the rate of increase of (labour) productivity[4] for otherwise inflation will be tending to accelerate or decelerate. This would mean that real wages rise in line with labour productivity, and hence the distribution of income between wages and profits remains unchanged. It is well known that the share of wages in national income is fairly stable even if it is not the constant which was sometimes claimed. It is perhaps not surprising if a level of unemployment can be found for which the distribution of income would remain unchanged (and inflation be non-accelerating); it will lie in the middle of the range of unemployment observed. The calculation of a NAIRU may then merely reflect that the distribution of income is fairly stable (and specifically the shares of wages and of profits do not exhibit any strong trend), rather than confirming the existence of a NAIRU as portrayed in the underlying theory.

It can be further observed that the price and wage relationships which interact to determine the NAIRU have often proved unstable and subject to shifts, which makes any estimate of the NAIRU also unstable. The findings of Setterfield *et al.* (1992) are also relevant when they

> suggest that estimates of the NAIRU [for Canada] are extremely sensitive to model specification, the definition of variables and the sample period used.

> [Further] . . . the final range of all NAIRU estimates . . . is about 5.5 percentage points. Indeed, the size of this range is so great that it covers virtually the entire range of male unemployment rates in Canada since 1956.

The Directorate-General for Economic and Financial Affairs of the European Commission concluded that the concept of the NAIRU is 'unusable operationally' because

> empirical studies on both sides of the Atlantic have shown that large variations in NAIRU may be caused by apparently small differences in sample, retained explanatory variables and analytical formulation. Furthermore, the confidence interval around these estimates is so large that it generally contains the whole historical range of unemployment rates observed in the last 15 to 20 years.[5]

But as UNCTAD observes 'natural rate estimates are still used to assess and guide macroeconomic policy, thereby contributing to rising unemployment' (1995, p. 172).

Theoretical constructs in economics are unlikely to be neutral in their policy implications or more generally in guiding the way in which economists think about policy issues. As Isaac (1994) notes, the natural rate doctrine (a term which he unfortunately uses to include the NAIRU) is seen 'as inhibiting the conduct of sensible macroeconomic policy: belief in a natural rate encourages resignation in the face of persistent high unemployment' (see also Isaac, 1993). The policy issues arising from the NAIRU are clear: the economy appears condemned to suffer that level of unemployment unless people are prepared to accept accelerating inflation; demand reflation can only have short-term stimulating effects. It also suggests a form of the Classical Dichotomy whereby the level of economic activity is set on the supply side of the economy, leaving the demand side (notably the stock of money) to determine the price level. This approach to modelling plays down (to the point of invisibility) the influence of demand factors, and does not allow for any impact of demand on the supply side.

To produce estimates of *the* NAIRU and to talk as though there is a single supply-side equilibrium flies in the face of much recent theoretical work, some within the New Keynesian approach (as noted above), which suggests that the conditions for a unique equilibrium are strong. Since we do not know whether the conditions for there to be a unique equilibrium hold (indeed we may not know what the conditions are since they depend on the way the economy is modelled), it would be better to operate on the basis that there are multiple equilibria rather than to operate of the basis that there is a unique one. For if we proceed on the basis of a unique equilibrium when there are several we would be unnecessarily condemning people to suffer from an inferior (probably) equilibrium when something better is available. Manning (1992), for example, provides a model of price and wage setting which has two equilibrium positions for which he provides some empirical support.[6]

EFFICIENCY WAGES AND AGGREGATE DEMAND

New Keynesian macroeconomics is not Keynesian (or at least sharply deviates from Keynes) in two related ways.[7,8] First, the modelling of the demand for labour is generally as a function of the real wage without specific reference to the level of aggregate demand.[9] Whilst Keynes postulated a negative relationship between the volume of employment and the real wage, movements from one level of employment to another came about through variations in the level of effective demand with consequent movements in the real wage. When perfect competition is assumed, the effect at the level of the firm of a variation in the level of aggregate demand can only be represented by a shift in the (parametric) expected price which is indistinguishable from a change in relative price at the level of the firm. When a firm operates under imperfect competition, then the demand curve which it faces needs to be located by reference to the level of aggregate demand and the (perceived) actions of competitors.[10] The inclusion of a term reflecting the level of aggregate demand in the demand for labour means, of course, that any resulting equilibrium is conditional on the level of aggregate demand, and hence as that level varies, so does the apparently supply-side equilibrium.

Second, there is no reason to think that the real wage, employment position which is generated for a New Keynesian equilibrium based on supply-side considerations will be aggregate demand sustainable (and that arises whether or not aggregate demand has been allowed for in the modelling of the demand for labour). By this we mean simply that there is no reason to believe that the wages and profits which arise in equilibrium will lead to a level of expenditure sufficient to buy up willingly the output which is produced at the equilibrium level of employment. This can alternatively be expressed by saying that there is no reason for the resulting level of expenditure to equal the expected level of expenditure on which the firms based their employment and output decisions. To assume or assert that the equilibrium outcome will be aggregate demand sustainable is the equivalent of assuming or asserting Say's Law.

The introduction of aggregate demand into the New Keynesian macroeconomics will usually lead to a problem of overdetermination (see Sawyer, 1995, ch. 5, for a similar discussion in relation to Post Keynesian economics). This would arise if, for example, the level of employment (and more generally that of economic activity) is determined on the supply side (e.g. as a NAIRU). Essentially, as will be seen below, the introduction of aggregate demand brings a further relationship between real wages and employment: as the model already has sufficient equations to determine the equilibrium position (involving real wages and employment) then this additional relationship must overdetermine the model. The implicit New Keynesian macroeconomics assumption must be that aggregate demand can (say, through changes in the price level) adjust to the level of employment set by supply-side considerations.

The case of efficiency wages appears as an exception to this (or at least we can set up that model in such a way that it is). The simple efficiency wage model (based on perfect competition in the product market) leads to two first-order conditions (based on profit maximization) relating to the decisions on employment and real wage. To illustrate this point we take a simple monopoly model in which the firm can set price and output level but which allows for the impact of real wages on productivity. This simple model is designed to give the flavour of the argument. The problem facing the monopolist would be modelled as maximizing profits:

$$\Pi = p(Q, D)Q - wL \tag{1}$$

where $Q = Q(Lq(w/w_u))$ to reflect the influence of wage (relative to the level of unemployment benefits w_u on productivity of labour, with Q the level of output, p price and w money wage, L employment, q a measure of labour effectiveness and D an index of the state of demand (for the individual firm this would include prices set by other firms). It is assumed here that there is some given minimum wage (e.g. as set by unemployment benefit levels) and that it is wages relative to that minimum level which influence the effectiveness of labour. For a particular level of D, the monopolist would arrive at a desired L and w (relative to w_u). The first-order conditions yield the well-known result:

$$q/q' = w/w_u \tag{2}$$

Price is a mark-up over marginal cost where the mark-up depends on the elasticity of demand in the usual manner. This can be interpreted in terms of a real product wage (w/p). Variations in D map out a relationship between L and w/p, which may over some range have a positive sign and over others a negative sign.[11] At one level, this model is rather similar to the model of imperfect competition with the addition that the real wage here reflects the productivity-enhancing effects of the real wage as well as the (negative) effect which the real wage has on a firm's demand for labour. For any specific level of aggregate demand, the monopolist would decide upon a particular level of employment and of real wages (and as a result of output as well). But as the level of aggregate demand varies, those decisions would also vary. It is, though, significant to note that the level of aggregate demand is introduced to position the demand function facing the monopolist. Further, it is necessary to consider whether the employment, real wage combination by the monopolist is compatible with the level of aggregate demand which the monopolist faces, and for this it is necessary to model aggregate demand.

The components of private sector demand in a closed economy are consumer expenditure and investment. The propensity to spend on consumer goods out of labour income is taken to be much greater than the corresponding propensity out of profits. Investment expenditure relative to capacity output is taken to depend on the level of capacity utilization and the rate of profitability. This is written as $g(u, P(u)/v)$, where u is the level of capacity utilization, $P(u)$ the ratio of profits to full capacity output, v the capital–output ratio.

The condition for equality between investment and savings (both expressed here relative to capacity output) is

$$g(u, P(u)/v) = s_1 P(u) + s_2 lu \qquad (3)$$

where l is labour share in gross (of depreciation) output (and hence gross profits share is $(1 - l)$), d is the rate of depreciation and v the capital–output ratio. The share of post-tax profits (net of depreciation) can be written as a function of capacity utilization as $P(u) = [(1 - l)u - vd]$.

The relationship between labour share and capacity utilization embedded in equation (3) may be positive or negative. If it is assumed that the marginal effect of a difference in capacity utilization on savings is greater than the effect on investment, then it can be shown that the relationship between u and l will be positive initially and then negative. The first-order condition for the maximum value of u with respect to l is given by the following equation:

$$g_2/v = s_1 - s_2 \qquad (4)$$

The share of labour income, l, is equal to wL/pQ, and hence the u,l relationship can be translated into a $u,w/p$ relationship which will retain the same basic shape. This can be written as

$$g(u, P(u)/v) = s_1 P(u) + s_2(w/p)(L/Q) \qquad (5)$$

and u and Q will be related to L. Hence equation (5) can be viewed as a relationship between real wage and employment.

In Figure 6.1, the relationship between real wage and employment arising from equation (2) is drawn as the ecurve whereas that arising from equation (5) is drawn as the AD curve.

It can be readily seen from Figure 6.1 that an increase in aggregate demand (an outward shift in the AD curve) would raise employment with the effect on real wages depending on which part of the wage curve was relevant, whilst an increase

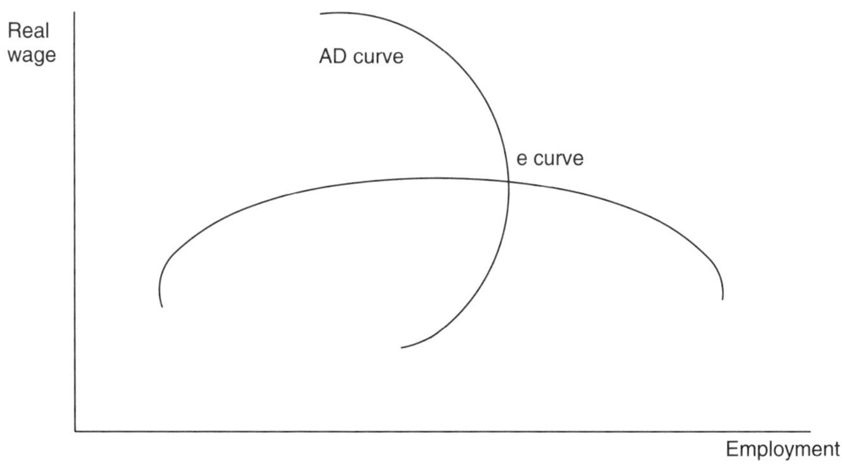

Figure 6.1 Interaction of aggregate demand and efficiency wage determination

in the effectiveness of labour (an upward shift in the wage curve) would raise real wages with the effect on employment depending on which part of the aggregate demand curve was relevant.

The simple point which this model illustrates is that efficiency wage considerations are not sufficient to locate the level of employment and real wage. It is perhaps not surprising that the traditional Keynesian result is reaffirmed by this model, i.e. an increase in aggregate demand (through, for example, an increase in investment expenditure) would be predicted to lead to an increase in the level of economic activity and employment.

CONCLUSIONS

In this chapter, we have sought to evaluate the New Keynesian contribution to the analysis of the labour market and unemployment. It is accepted that efficiency wages and similar notions have reflections in reality and would not question their realism in that sense. It has been argued that efficiency wages would seem to be of declining importance, and cannot explain the rise in unemployment at least as far as the UK is concerned. The concept of the NAIRU is viewed as unduly constraining thinking about the macro economy. Finally attention has been drawn to the absence of any treatment of aggregate demand in New Keynesian macroeconomics.

ACKNOWLEDGEMENTS

I am grateful to Philp Arestis, Bill Gerrard, Geoff Harcourt, Man-Seop Park, Roy Rotheim and Nina Shapiro for comments on the first draft. The usual disclaimer applies.

NOTES

1 In our discussion we continue to use the term 'labour market'. However, elsewhere (Sawyer, 1992) we have questioned the meaning of the term market when applied outside a perfectly competitive framework.

2 Colander does not define coordination and coordination failure, though presumably he is using the term in the sense of Cooper and John (1988) who describe models with multiple, welfare-ranked equilibrium as coordination failure models rather than in the sense of Clower (1965) and others in the reappraisal of the Keynesian economics literature.

3 It should be noted, though, that the employment rate amongst men aged 25–54 is much the same in Europe as in the United States. There are 'missing' men who are not recorded as unemployed or employed (including self-employed), which is presumably explicable in terms of those who are in prison, involved in crime, wealthy, etc.: see, for example, Balls (1994).

4 It would also be necessary to make some assumptions about the rate of change of foreign prices, the exchange rate and indirect taxation.

5 Quote is from *European Economy*, Supplement A, January 1995, p. 2, as reported in UNCTAD (1995, p. 172).

6 For my own approach see Sawyer (1982) which suggests the possibility of multiple equilibria arising from the interaction of price and wage determination.

7 Davidson (1992) is a particularly strong statement of this general view: see also Tobin (1993).

8 'With new Keynesians looking so much like old classicals, perhaps we should conclude that the term "Keynesian" has out-lived its usefulness' (Mankiw, 1992).

9 There are many examples of this: one which is readily to hand is Lindbeck (1992) in which the level of employment and real wages are determined by the interaction of a wage setting equation and a demand for labour equation. The inverse of the former makes employment as a function of wages, unemployment benefit and productivity whilst the latter has the demand for labour as a function of wages, unemployment benefit and the degree of monopoly.

10 For further discussion on these points see Sawyer (1995, ch. 6 and 7).

11 This arises since the relationship between output and employment is not necessarily one involving a diminishing marginal product of labour. A higher level of demand, leading to higher levels of output and employment, may involve a higher marginal productivity of labour (for given real wage), and hence a higher real wage.

7

SOME QUESTIONS FOR NEW KEYNESIANS

Sergio Nisticó and Fabio D'Orlando with an Appendix by Benedetto Scoppola

PURPOSE AND STRUCTURE OF THE WORK

The past fifteen years have witnessed an impressive growth of contributions whose authors have been seen, and have seen themselves, as developing a novel research programme – New Keynesian economics. They claim to have supplied a new approach to macroeconomic theory capable of rescuing Keynesian analysis from the oblivion to which the success and diffusion of New Classical macroeconomics had condemned it; and to have done so through the specification of the previously lacking microeconomic foundations for two of Keynes's crucial results: unemployment equilibrium and the existence of real effects of changes in the quantity of money.

The purpose of the present work is to discuss some aspects of this approach and to show that its methodological and analytical foundations are weak. The argument is developed as follows. In the first part (the second section) we point out the methodological difficulties arising within the New Keynesian approach when the attempt is made to merge into a single theoretical scheme models based on deeply different hypotheses. In the second part (the third section) we focus our attention on the analytical limits of the so-called 'efficiency wage theory' – the core of New Keynesian economics according to its 'manifesto' (Greenwald and Stiglitz, 1987) – and in particular on the difficulties of proving the existence and stability of underemployment equilibria for sufficiently general cases and models. The argument seems to have important implications for the claim of New Keynesian economics to represent a significant point of reference for contemporary macroeconomic theory.

NEW KEYNESIAN ECONOMICS: A NEW THEORETICAL PARADIGM?

The common aim of the New Keynesian literature is to explain those 'imperfections' (notably wage and price rigidity) to which the neoclassical synthesis of Keynes's theory had attributed certain instances of market failure, as the outcome of the rational behaviour of agents. Notwithstanding this common characteristic,

New Keynesian economists seem to be far from constituting an homogeneous theoretical reference point for modern macroeconomics. In this section we try to go beyond the simple acknowledgement of this generally recognized eclecticism[1] and offer two possible explanations for this lack of coherence: the first one relates to the absence of an agreement as to the 'nature' of unemployment and as to the meaning of microfoundations, while the second is linked to the highly inappropriate use of the assumptions sustaining the various New Keynesian models.

First of all, New Keynesian economists seem to diverge on the more typical Keynesian field, namely that of isolating the forces determining the amount of production and therefore the level of employment. On this ground, one should in fact draw a distinction between: (a) the 'labour market' models, which, in accordance with the neoclassical idea that the downward flexibility of the real wage would ensure the full employment of the available labour supply, aim at identifying the microeconomic causes of wage rigidity; and (b) the 'commodity market' models, which, more in line with Keynes's approach, tend on the contrary to identify the causes of a lack of effective demand.

The New Keynesian labour market models mainly explain the existence of wage rigidity and thus of unemployment in terms of insider–outsider relations (Lindbeck and Snower, 1986a, 1988a), of implicit contracts (Azariadis, 1975), wage bargaining (McDonald and Solow, 1981; Nickell and Andrews, 1983; Blanchard and Summers, 1986), or asymmetric information (models founded on the hypothesis of efficiency wages enter this latter group). The commodity market models comprise instead all those formulations that place less emphasis on the role of wage rigidity in explaining unemployment, and develop the analysis mainly by excluding from the Walrasian paradigm, to which they nevertheless refer, the hypothesis of perfect competition in the goods market. In this group we place, for instance, Weitzman's formulation (1982) wherein, on the one hand, the existence of increasing returns keeps the unemployed from employing themselves and, on the other, the absence of perfect coordination induces each firm not to raise labour demand, since nothing ensures that other firms will follow this decision, and that therefore an adequate increase of demand will come out for its outputs. Such a mechanism prevents firms from knowing the increase of demand that could result from their decision to raise employment. The idea of coordination failure is also present in other models of this second group that explain how nominal rigidities (inducing real effects through variations in quantity of money) can derive from the application, on the part of the agents, of the maximizing behaviour (Akerlof and Yellen, 1985; Blanchard and Kiyotaki, 1987).[2]

The need for such a distinction between the labour and the commodity market models[3] is linked to the very *raison d'être* of New Keynesian economics, namely the search for microfoundations to macroeconomics. It is in fact useful to recall that in a lucid anticipation of the problems discussed in later debates on macroeconomics, Keynes, on the one hand, criticized the idea that the existence of unemployment could be linked to wage rigidity and, on the other hand, raised a fundamental objection to the idea of getting meaningful macroeconomic results simply by extending, through aggregation, microeconomic magnitudes to the economic system as a whole.[4] In Keynes's words:

> the demand schedules for particular industries can only be constructed on some fixed assumption as to the nature of the demand and supply schedules of other industries and as to the amount of the aggregate effective demand. It is invalid, therefore, to transfer the argument to industry as a whole unless we also transfer our assumption that the aggregate effective demand is fixed. Yet this assumption reduces the argument to an *ignoratio elenchi*.... But if the classical theory is not allowed to extend by analogy its conclusion in respect of a particular industry to industry as a whole, it is wholly unable to answer the question what effect on employment a reduction in money wage will have. For it has no method of analysis wherewith to tackle the problem.
>
> (Keynes, 1973a, p. 260)

Keynes, emphasizing the limits of microeconomic theory, refuses the analytical validity of the inverse relation between wage and aggregate labour demand. This is the ground on which the main differences between the two groups of models emerge. While the whole New Keynesian literature suffers from the shortages connected with the use of essentially micro tools, the two groups of models express in fact two different ways of understanding the same search for microfoundations. The models of the second group, starting from a Keynesian perspective, try to explain why rational agents persist in actions which do not generate an amount of global demand sufficient to sustain the full employment level of production. The models of the first group, starting instead from the un-Keynesian presupposition that unemployment can be explained by extending to the system as a whole the use of a labour demand schedule, try to explain why agents persist in actions which do not generate downward wage flexibility. The absence of an agreement on such a subtle issue – surely troublesome from the perspective of constituting a New Keynesian paradigm – is epitomized by Weitzman himself:

> Even if it could be done, an all round reduction of real wages cannot cure unemployment. Firms would find it cheaper to hire labour, but this effect is outweighed by a simultaneous decline in the demand for their products... a successful attempt to depress real wages would actually increase the equilibrium level of unemployment.... Under such circumstances, wage stickiness may actually be a blessing.
>
> (Weitzman, 1982, pp. 800–1)

It is, moreover, interesting to observe that focusing on wage stickiness as the true cause of unemployment evidently derives from the supposed equality (in equilibrium) between the wage and marginal product of labour. The emphasis that the second group of models places on the role of demand in determining the single firm's activity level, is instead, in principle, compatible with an alternative determination of equilibrium wage and level of employment. It is not by accident in fact that Weitzman's model contains the assumption that the wage rate is given – an assumption which is incompatible with the marginalist theory of distribution and has instead a classical and Post Keynesian flavour.[5]

In other words, in the New Keynesian literature there coexist, on the one hand, models which assume that firms' rational behaviour ultimately tends to realize the equality between the wage rate and the marginal product of labour; and, on the other, models which are built for instance upon the assumption that the money wage is given and that money prices are directly set by firms at a level that covers the full cost, so that the real wage depends on firms' (and trade unions') bargaining power. Both assumptions are in principle legitimate, but they cannot clearly coexist within the same theoretical paradigm. The former derives in fact from the application of a strict methodological individualism to a perfectly competitive context characterized by atomism, full information and so forth. The latter represents on the contrary the most fitting assumption for models aiming at describing the functioning of 'monetary' or 'entrepreneurial' economies, as Keynes has termed modern economic systems (Keynes, 1979a). Whether the institutional context chosen by New Keynesian economists as their reference point is a 'cooperative' or a 'monetary' economy is, by now, far from being clear.

Another consideration that might help to explain the difficulty that New Keynesian economics is facing in its attempt to originate a new theoretical reference point for macroeconomics, is the absence of an unambiguous indication of the fundamental hypotheses concerning agents' rational behaviour that should be encompassed within their paradigm. The decision not to choose a definite set of fundamental behavioural hypotheses has revealed itself to be a successful short-run strategy. By resorting to special (*ad hoc*) assumptions, often quite suggestive, most New Keynesian models are able to yield the expected results. However, we shall argue that this opportunistic use of such theoretical assumptions seems to have a long-run drawback capable of constituting one further explanation for the lack of consistency within the New Keynesian literature.

Asymmetric information is, for instance, a fundamental assumption frequently used by the New Keynesians to point out possible instances of market failure. Although the assumption of asymmetric information regarding the quality of the goods or services exchanged on the market is the main ingredient of the 'principal–agent' literature, the real impact of this kind of model has, however, been obtained by adding a further fundamental ingredient: the symmetry of the agents. The New Keynesian world is thus made up of an infinity of *identical* 'principals' not trusting the infinity of *identical* 'agents' exchanging goods or services which often show the extraordinary property of being at the same time *single* and of *different* quality. Though strange, the composition of this world is in principle acceptable. What appears instead to be logically unacceptable is the main analytical structure of the models when compared with the fundamental premiss that information is not perfectly distributed among the individuals. The maximizing behaviour of the firms is in fact supposed always to be leaning to the mere application of the traditional neoclassical rule – logically admissible within a context characterized by perfect information – of equality between marginal cost and marginal revenue. But the question of how it is possible for a firm operating in a context characterized by imperfect information to enforce this rule is left unanswered by New Keynesians.[6] Moreover, the heavy reliance on game theory (and in particular on Nash equilibria) by New Keynesians requires, besides the knowledge of demand functions, marginal revenue, reaction curves, etc., the additional assumption 'that beliefs must be consistently aligned' – all this meaning that, agents should have a common knowledge of rationality, i.e. believe that 'there is a uniquely rational way to play the game' (Hargreaves Heap and Varoufakis, 1995, p. 58). All this should be coupled with the main assumption that information is asymmetric.

An example of inappropriate use of the assumptions is offered by those formulations arguing that the existence of sub-optimal equilibria can be explained by reference to monopolistic competition and coordination failures, while the non-neutrality of money can be ascertained once a rationale is provided for monetary rigidities.

The basic idea in these models (e.g. Blanchard and Kiyotaki, 1987) is that the presence of menu costs, however small, can prevent firms from changing their prices in response to demand variations. Second-order losses resulting from the failure to adjust their prices can generate, according to this theory, first-order effects on aggregate supply and therefore on the social welfare.[7] The validity of this way of reasoning is crucially linked to the hypothesis that equilibrium conditions are derived from functions that are homogeneous of degree zero in monetary variables and thus to the hypothesis that, in the absence of adjustment costs, an increase in the quantity of money would have no effect on real quantities. The theorem of the neutrality of money requires, however, two conditions: (a) that increases in the money stock have no distributive effects; (b) that, in response to a monetary shock involving a distortion in relative prices, there is an adjustment mechanism that can bring relative prices back to the prices that existed prior to the variation in the quantity of money. Even admitting, against common sense, that the first condition is met, it does not appear to be obvious within the theoretical context of Blanchard and Kiyotaki's analysis that the second can be met. Generally, in fact, 'if the initial quantity of money is increased, there is no reason, if prices remain unchanged, to expect that the increase of excess demand for any good is proportional to the increase in the quantity of money' (Patinkin, 1956). But if an increase in the quantity of money available to each individual does not necessarily cause an instantaneous equiproportional shift of all demand curves and all cost curves, it must be proved that there are adjustments in the market leading, in the long run, to a situation where all prices and money wages have increased in the same proportion as the quantity of money. Such an outcome is decreed to encounter stability problems and, in the monopolistic competition context with asymmetric information adopted by Blanchard and Kiyotaki, cannot be obtained by resorting to the basic role of the Walrasian auctioneer.[8] Any increase in the supply of money could therefore have real effects thus making completely superfluous the need to resort to menu costs.

EXISTENCE AND STABILITY OF EQUILIBRIUM IN THE EFFICIENCY WAGE THEORY

Notwithstanding the methodological limits we have just tried to emphasize, a great amount of enthusiasm surrounds New Keynesian literature. Most of this enthusiasm appears to derive from New Keynesians' claim that their search for microfoundations to macroeconomics has already gained an important goal: that of explaining involuntary unemployment on the basis of the optimizing behaviour of both workers and firms. The principal version of this suggested explanation pivots around the existence of a specific relation between wage and work effort which leads rational firms not to accept the underbidding offers of unemployed workers.

As already emphasized in the previous section, the importance of this hypothesis evidently derives from the adherence to the idea that explaining unemployment and explaining wage rigidity are one and the same thing. In this section we try to demonstrate that the attempt to explain unemployment equilibria assuming the existence of a direct relationship between wage and labour productivity (effort) is analytically weak, independently of the degree of reasonableness of the underlying assumptions. In particular we focus our attention on the so-called 'shirking models', emphasizing the problems connected with both the existence and the stability of efficiency wage equilibria.

In the most popular of the 'shirking' models (Shapiro and Stiglitz, 1984), the existence of involuntary unemployment is explained as follows:

> Under the conventional competitive paradigm, in which all workers receive the market wage and there is no unemployment, the worst that can happen to a worker who shirks on the job is that he is fired. Since he can immediately be rehired, however, he pays no penalty for his misdemeanour. ...To induce its workers not to shirk, the firm attempts to pay more than the 'going wage'; then, if a worker is caught shirking and is fired, he will pay a penalty. If it pays one firm to raise its wage, however, it will pay all firms to raise their wages. When they all raise their wages, the incentive not to shirk again disappears. But as all firms raise their wages, their labour demand decreases, and unemployment results. With unemployment, even if all firms pay the same wages, a worker has an incentive not to shirk. For if he is fired, an individual will not immediately obtain another job.
>
> (ibid., p. 433)

Consistent with the New Keynesian approach, this analytical argument is first developed at a micro level. Each firm, on the basis of the given relationship between wage and work effort, sets the wage rate so as to minimize cost per unit of effort and goes back and forth in hiring workers until it has reached the

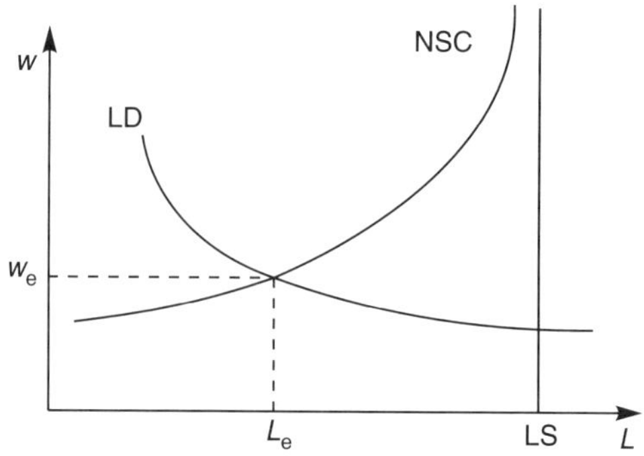

Figure 7.1

point wherein the marginal product of labour (redefined in order to take into account the role of work effort) equals this wage. The analysis is then extended to the macro level simply through aggregation of the micro functions. Equilibrium (un)employment is then determined, as shown in Figure 7.1, where the aggregate demand for labour intersects the 'no shirking constraint' which represents, for each level of aggregate employment, the wage that firms must offer in order to prevent workers from shirking.

The aggregate no shirking function is built starting from the previously mentioned assumption that a particular relation exists, *for any given level of aggregate employment*, between wage and productivity. In the New Keynesian literature there are mainly two versions of the so-called 'effort function'. The first is built upon the hypothesis that the relation between wage and work effort is discrete, with a first tract where workers supply a minimum (given) level of effort and a second tract, where the wage exceeds its *reservation* value and workers supply a higher (given) level of effort (see the B-type effort function in Figure 7.2). In the other version the function is supposed to be continuous: after a first stage where work effort increases more than proportionally to increases in the wage, there is a point beyond which the slope of the effort function decreases (see the A-type effort function in Figure 7.2). 'Unfortunately', as Stiglitz himself has admitted, 'there is insufficient empirical evidence' to prove the existence of such a wage–productivity relationship (Stiglitz, 1987, p. 36, footnote 69).

In the case of a continuous effort function the 'no shirking constraint' has to be redefined, since it now represents the wage that firms must pay in order to maximize the ratio between effort (*e*) and wage (*w*),[9] in correspondence with any possible level of aggregate employment.

It seems important to emphasize that the discrete version of the effort function can only make sense with the introduction of the highly restrictive hypothesis that the lower level of the effort function is zero. This hypothesis is used by Shapiro and Stiglitz in their 1984 model, with effort excluded from the arguments of the single-firm production function.[10] In the absence of this assumption, firms could

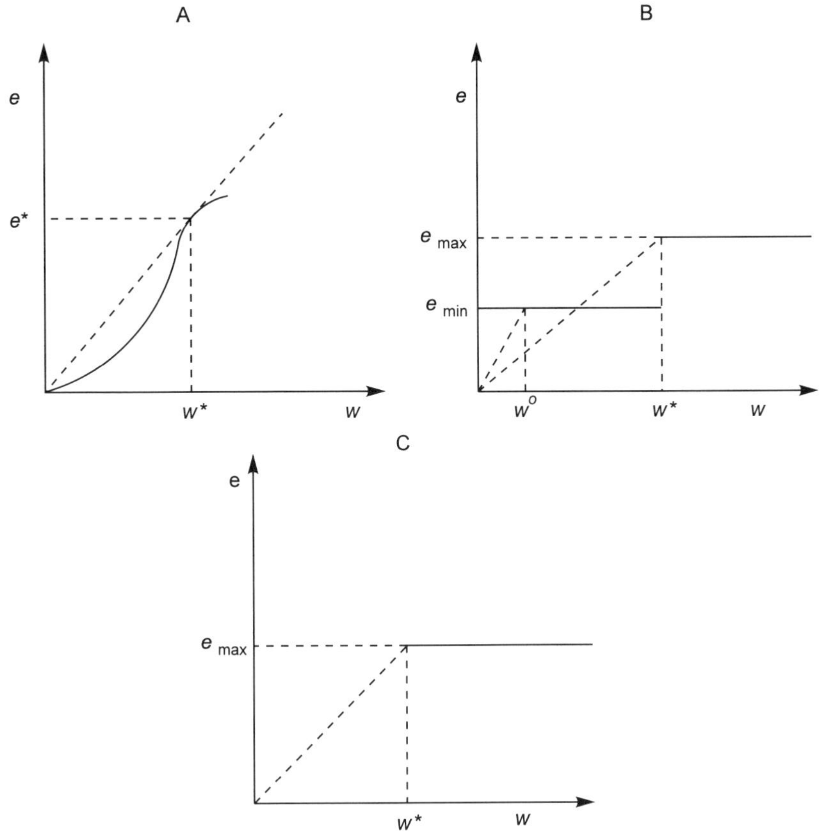

Figure 7.2

in fact increase their profits by reducing the wage level, a circumstance which is clearly incompatible with the idea that downward wage rigidity – the claimed cause of unemployment – is determined by firms' maximizing behaviour. As shown in Figure 7.2, for a B-type effort function, a reduction of the wage level from w^* to w_o would increase the ratio e/w. This cannot happen for the C-type effort function.[11] These considerations hold true also in the case of a continuous effort function. In fact if the workers' lowest effort level is greater than zero, firms would have no reasons for paying efficiency wages.[12] Thus, the same existence of a 'no shirking constraint' rests crucially upon the hypothesis that the lowest level of effort is nil.

Our claim is that the theory has so far not been able to demonstrate, for sufficiently general cases and models, either the existence of a significant macroeconomic equilibrium linked to the payment of 'efficiency wages' by firms, or its stability. And these problems, contrary to what the efficiency wage theorists maintain,[13] are significantly greater for the general case of a continuous effort function.[14]

Even adopting – as almost all New Keynesians do – a very simple production function containing labour as the sole input, the same internal logic of the theory requires that the (e) effort enters the production function of the single firm together with the labour input (L_i). The effort must, in turn, be treated as a function of the wage rate (w) and, given the size of the labour force, of the aggregate level of employment[15] (L_a). In other words the single-firm production function should be the following:

$$Y_i = f_i(L_i, e(w, L_a))$$

If e is treated as a multiplier of L_i (see e.g. Solow, 1979, p. 173), and firms are sufficiently small not to influence the aggregate level of employment L_a (that they treat therefore as given), the first-order conditions for profit maximization are

$$w = f' e(w)$$
$$L_i = f' L_i e'(w)$$

Now, in the general case of a continuous effort function, given the level of the wage rate, there is a different work effort for any level of aggregate employment (for low levels of employment the effort is greater while for high levels of employment the workers, since they can easily find another job, will consider the penalty of being fired less serious and tend to shirk more). In Figure 7.3 it is shown how, for any increase in the level of aggregate employment, shifting downward the effort function, both the level of effort and the wage rate that maximizes profit for the single firm change.

For this reason the marginal productivity function (i.e. the demand for labour of the single firm) that in this formulation includes effort as one of its arguments, is

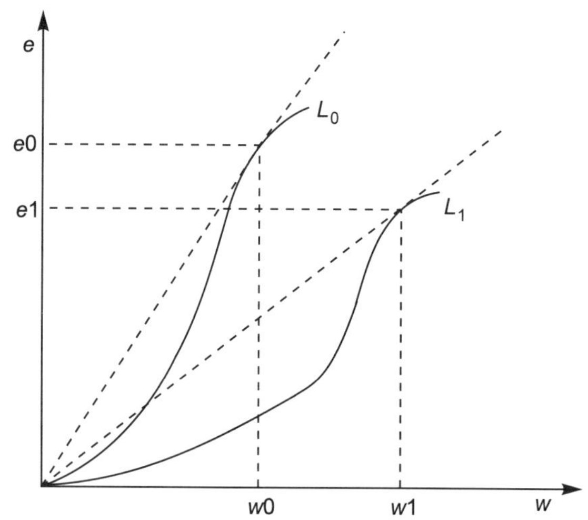

Figure 7.3

parametric to the aggregate level of employment. But the inclusion of aggregate employment as one of the arguments of the microeconomic production function has the consequence of complicating the formal description of the explicit aggregate demand curve for labour as a function of the wage rate. In the Appendix (A.3) it is shown that this relation can assume almost any form and any slope, without general regularities. It is therefore extremely difficult to identify the macroeconomic equilibrium position through the intersection of the aggregate labour demand curve and the no shirking constraint.

However, the equilibrium position may be identified in a different way. First of all, one should define a relation between aggregate labour demand (ΣL_i) and, *given labour supply* (LS), the level of *effective* employment L_a (or a relation between aggregate labour demand and the rate of unemployment). Such a relation can be derived from the first-order conditions for profit maximization of the single firm; for each firm, the maximizing procedure identifies in fact a value for labour demand and a value for the wage rate, given the actual level of employment. Under the assumption of efficient allocation of workers among the single firms, this aggregate labour demand function would be the following:

$$\text{ALD} = \max_{\{L_i\}} \Sigma_{i=1}^{N} \frac{(f_i')^{-1}[w/e(w, L_a)]}{e(w, L_a)}$$

A sufficient condition for the existence of an equilibrium level of employment is that aggregate labour demand (the desired level of employment) as a function of actual aggregate employment ($\Sigma L_i = f(L_a)$) is downward sloping or, if upward sloping, with a slope lower than 1.

In this case, the equilibrium level of employment can be identified as the point at which the sum of profit maximizing labour demand of single firms is equal to the level of employment which each firm considers as a *datum* in the maximizing procedure. In Figure 7.4 this is made to correspond to the point E where the labour demand function intersects the 45° line.

But nothing ensures that, as employment L_a rises (and workers become more likely to shirk), single firms maximize profits lowering their labour demand, which means that we may have higher labour demand for higher levels of employment (and lower rate of unemployment) with the result that the function $\Sigma L_i = f(L_a)$ is *not* downward sloping. A formal example of the possibility that such a 'perverse' microeconomic behaviour occurs is provided in the Appendix (A.2). In general, the only thing we can reasonably assume about the slope of the relation $\Sigma L_i = f(L_a)$ is that, when the economic system is close to full employment (and all workers shirk), the function will be downward sloping, as shown in Figure. 7.5. The efficiency wage theory can, in this case, prove the existence of a *close-to-full-employment* equilibrium.

Therefore, for the general case of a continuous effort function, the requirements for the existence of an equilibrium position and for its uniqueness clearly depend upon the characteristics of the effort functions and of the production functions of the single firms. We might have multiple equilibria or *close-to-full-employment equilibria.*

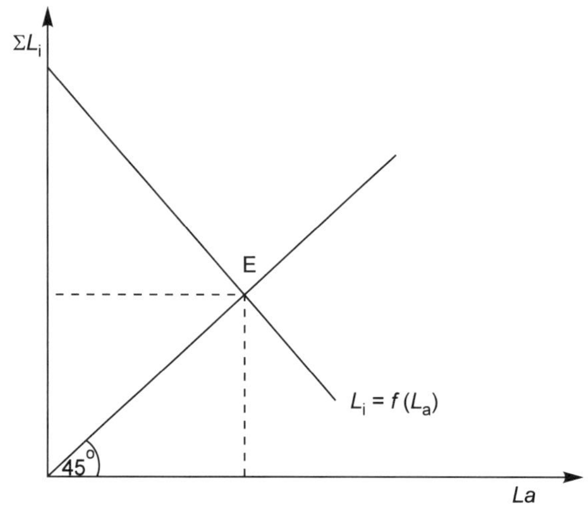

Figure 7.4

It is only in the particular case of a discrete effort function that the theory can unambiguously solve the problem of the existence and uniqueness of an unemployment equilibrium. In the presence of a discrete effort function, with the lower level of effort being zero, each firm would in fact face only one marginal productivity function: that corresponding to $e = e_{\max}$. The existence problem could thus be solved in the way suggested by the theory because the discrete form of the effort function eliminates the dependence between the labour demand function and

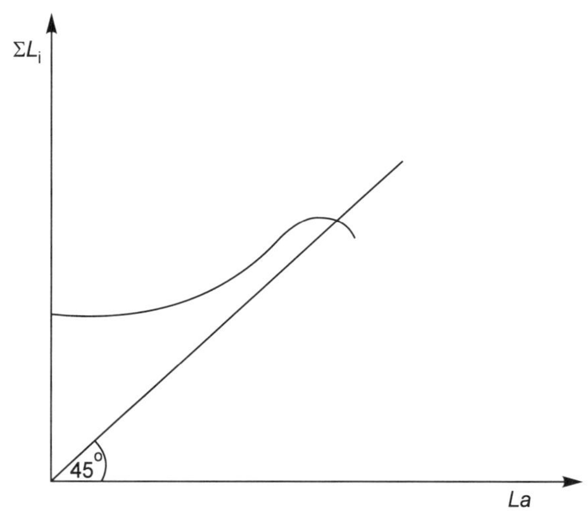

Figure 7.5

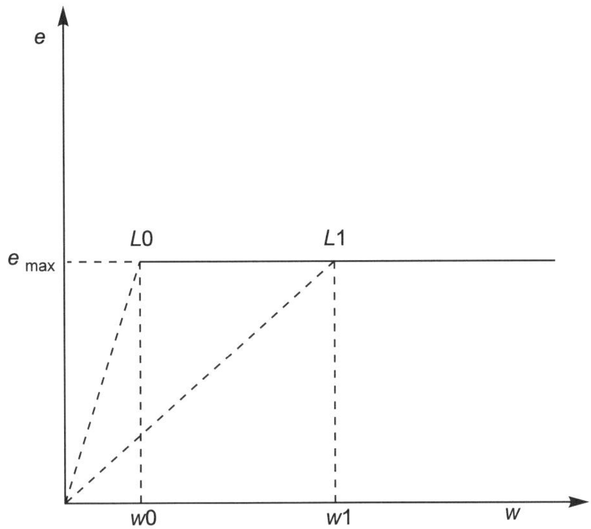

Figure 7.6

aggregate employment. Since, as is shown in Figure 7.6, any shift of the effort function in the presence of an increase in aggregate employment does alter the wage rate but *not* the level of effort, this latter can, in this case, be treated as given, and can thus be omitted as an argument of the production function. Thus, both the labour demand function of the single firm and the aggregate labour demand function tend to be well behaved (even if the corresponding equilibrium positions are not necessarily stable).

But, as we have already emphasized, this can happen only if the lower level of the effort function is zero – which, contrary both to common sense and to the internal logic of the efficiency wage theory, would imply that a minimal reduction of the wage below a crucial level drives the effort level from its maximum level to zero, determining a kind of paralysis of all the workers employed. The Appendix (A.5) shows, on the other hand, the inadequacy of the attempts to derive the (discrete) 0–1 effort function from the maximizing behaviour of agents.

The other problem that efficiency wage theory faces is that of demonstrating the stability of the macroeconomic equilibrium that it determines. In fact, even if a non-trivial macroeconomic equilibrium exists, this may be stable or unstable according to the slope of the relation $\Sigma L_{\mathrm{i}} = f(L_{\mathrm{a}})$. Assuming that this latter function is downward sloping and linear, we can write

$$\Sigma L_{\mathrm{i}(t)} = a - bL_{\mathrm{a}} \quad \text{with } a > 0 \text{ and } b > 0$$

Since $L_{\mathrm{a}} = \Sigma L_{\mathrm{i}(t-1)}$, labour demand – both at the level of the single firm and in the aggregate – at time t will depend, given labour supply, on aggregate labour

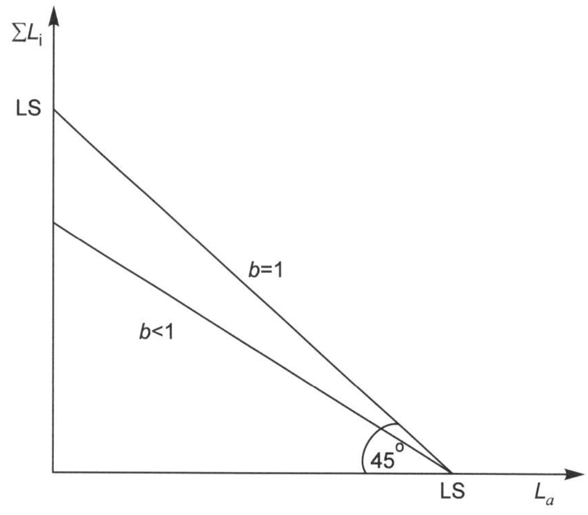

Figure 7.7

demand at time $t - 1$. Therefore, it is possible to describe the dynamics of the system through the following equation:

$$\Sigma L_{i(t)} = a - b\Sigma L_{i(t-1)}$$

the stability condition being $b < 1$.

The economic meaning of this condition can properly be understood by looking at Figure 7.7, where the observed level of employment (L_a) is measured on the horizontal axis and present labour demand (ΣL_i) on the vertical one.

The function $\Sigma Li_{(t)} = a - b\Sigma L_{i(t-1)}$, whatever its slope, will intersect the horizontal axis at a point situated between the origin and LS. In fact, one of the main assumptions of the efficiency wage theory is that at (or in the vicinity of) full employment, workers' effort becomes nil ($e = 0$). This is a necessary hypothesis in order to exclude the existence of efficiency wage full employment equilibria. Now, since effort enters the production function as a multiplier of the employment level, labour demand *must* become zero at (or in the vicinity of) full employment. Let us temporarily suppose that our function intersects the horizontal axis in correspondence with LS.[16] With reference to this function, the stability condition $b < 1$ implies therefore that the maximum level of labour demand – given by the intersection with the vertical axis – is lower than the given level of labour supply. But if this is true for the particular function intersecting the horizontal axis in correspondence with LS, it will also be true for any other possible function intersecting the horizontal axis at a point situated between the origin and LS (Figure 7.8).

This result deserves a brief comment. The maximum level of labour demand is the amount of labour force that firms want to hire when – being the observed level

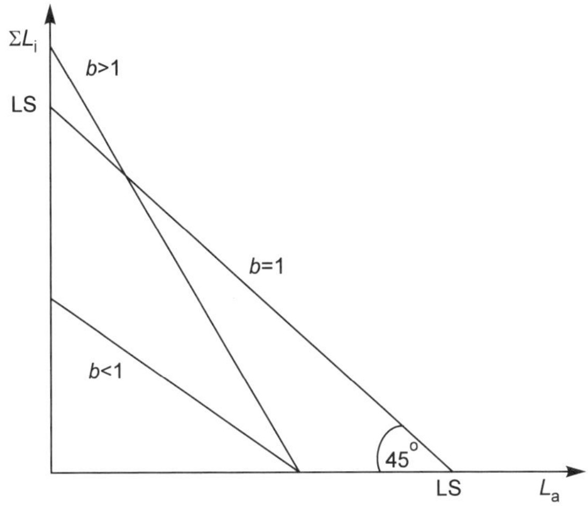

Figure 7.8

of employment zero – the ratio between the work effort and the wage rate is at its maximum. In other words, it is the level of labour demand expressed by firms when workers do not shirk at all and the wage rate is fully downward flexible. The analysis carried out here has therefore shown that if an 'efficiency wage unemployment equilibrium' exists, it will be stable only if firms would not hire the existing amount of labour force even when workers did not exhibit any propensity to shirk and the wage rate were perfectly flexible. The interesting result is that a hypothetical 'efficiency wage unemployment equilibrium' is stable only if unemployment is to be explained by referring to causes different from those highlighted by the efficiency wage theory. The Appendix (see A.4) shows that such a result, here obtained by assuming that ΣL_i is a linear function of L_a, can generally be obtained also with reference to non-linear functions.

CONCLUSION

It can be said in conclusion that any attempt to construct, along New Keynesian lines, a theoretical paradigm that has at the same time analytical rigour and internal coherence cannot ignore the following questions:

1 the inconsistency, within New Keynesian economics, between one group of models that relies on the existence of an aggregate labour demand curve, and a second group which rejects the existence of this latter notion;
2 the absence of a clear indication as to the assumptions regarding the rational behaviour of economic agents within a context where asymmetric information and imperfect competition play fundamental roles;

3 the existence of some analytical drawbacks which do not allow the determination of a meaningful unemployment equilibrium starting from the efficiency wage hypothesis.

APPENDIX BY BENEDETTO SCOPPOLA

A.1 The essential feature of the efficiency wage theory is the assumption that workers' effort is a function of the wage rate and of aggregate employment. The theory requires that, given L_a, workers' effort increases or decreases together with the wage rate. As indicated in the text, two different kinds of relationships have been proposed in the literature: the discrete and the continuous one. The aim of this appendix is to show: (a) that the intuitive results, generally obtained by the efficiency wage theory, are crucially linked to the very restrictive hypothesis of a discrete effort function; (b) that the required discrete effort function can be derived from the utility maximizing procedure only under a highly restrictive hypothesis on the workers' temporal horizon.

A.2 At a micro level, the equilibrium level of labour hired by each firm is determined on the basis of the usual conditions:

$$\frac{\partial \pi_i}{\partial L_i} = 0, \; \frac{\partial \pi_i}{\partial w} = 0, \quad \text{where } \pi_i = f_i(eL_i) - L_i w \tag{A.1}$$

and therefore

$$f_i'(eL_i) = w/e \tag{A.2}$$

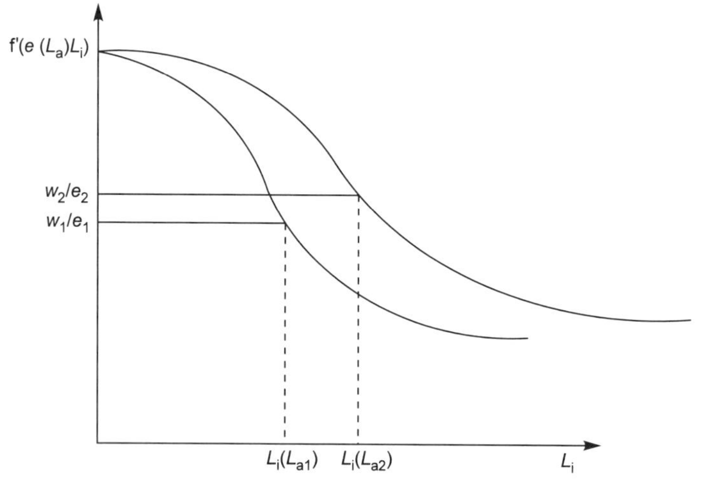

Figure A7.1

In order to study the sign of the derivative $\partial L_i / \partial L_a$, relation (A.2) can be linearized in the vicinity of its solution. In this approximation $f'(eL_i)$ is

$$f'(eL_i) = A - BeL_i \qquad A, B > 0 \tag{A.3}$$

so that

$$A - BeL_i = w/e \tag{A.2'}$$

The equilibrium level of unemployment is thus obtained, for the single firm, by solving the following equation:

$$L_i = \frac{A}{eB} - \frac{1}{B}\frac{w}{e^2} \tag{A.4}$$

This relationship cannot be ascertained a priori when workers' effort changes continuously together with the wage rate. It is for instance possible to find an effort function that generates a direct relationship between labour demand and aggregate employment: since workers' effort is a (negative) function of L_a, a rise in the employment level induces – through a decrease of e – a rise in both terms of (A.4), so that the sign of $\partial L_i / \partial L_a$ cannot be determined a priori. Figure A7.1 shows that the rightward shift of $f'(eL_i)$ due to the decrease in the value of effort can generate a positive relationship between L_a and L_i. It depicts a situation in which $f'(x) = 1/(1 + x^2)$, $w_1/e_1 = 1/9$, $e_1 = (8/5)e_2$, $w_1 = (8/9)w_2$. In these conditions, for $L_{a1} < L_{a2}, L_i(L_{a1}) = (25/32)L_i(L_{a2})$.

A.3 One of the crucial problems that New Keynesians must face is the very delicate passage from the micro to the macro level of analysis. In Shapiro and Stiglitz (1984), the aggregate marginal product – assuming the existence of a discrete effort function – is obtained through the following procedure:

$$f'(L_a) = \frac{\mathrm{d}}{\mathrm{d}L_a} \max_{\{L_i\}} \Sigma_{i=1}^{N} f_i(L_i) \tag{A.5}$$

This definition of an aggregate demand for labour, though disputable from an economic perspective, is certainly correct from a mathematical viewpoint. We shall therefore use procedure (A.5) also for the case of a continuous effort function, so that aggregate marginal productivity becomes

$$\frac{\mathrm{d}}{\mathrm{d}L_a} f(eL_a) = \frac{\mathrm{d}}{\mathrm{d}L_a} \max_{\{L_i\}} \Sigma_{i=1}^{N} f_i(e(L_a, w)L_i) \tag{A.6}$$

The determination of this function is now extremely complex precisely from a mathematical viewpoint, because of the dependence of effort on wage and on all L_i. Though the possible relative maxima of the function (A.6) might be identified, there are now no adequate algorithms for the identification of its absolute maximum when N is greater than 10. Neither it is possible to derive intuitive quantitative conclusions, since the non-linearity of (A.6) is extremely complex. As seen at a micro level, the very intricate dependence among the relevant magnitudes

– a dependence which evaporates when the effort function is supposed to be discrete – can in fact generate counter-intuitive variations of the endogenous variables.

A.4 The importance of assuming a discrete effort function can be detected also from the analysis of the equilibrium stability. In the efficiency wage theory, the local stability condition is given by the following:

$$\left|\Sigma L_i'(L_a)\right| < 1 \tag{A.7}$$

The argument developed above shows that – given the complex dependence of both L_i and L_a on the specific value of the parameters – it is impossible to detect the value of the modulus (A.7) by merely scrutinizing the structural properties of the relationships involved in the model. In other words, the equilibrium stability in the efficiency wage theory does not depend on any structural properties of the production or of the effort function but rather on the very specific value of the parameters defining them. However, something more can be said. As clarified in the text, the same logic of the efficiency wage theory requires that the following relations be satisfied:

$$\Sigma L_i(\mathrm{LS}) = 0 \tag{A.8}$$

$$\mathrm{Max}(\Sigma L_i) \geq \mathrm{LS} \tag{A.9}$$

where LS indicates the existing labour force. Even assuming that the maximum value of L_i corresponds to $L_a = 0$ – which is the most favourable case in order to get stability results – relations (A.8) and (A.9) imply that

$$\left|\int_0^{\mathrm{LS}} \left(\frac{\mathrm{d}}{\mathrm{d}L_a}\Sigma L_i(L_a)\right)\mathrm{d}L_a\right| > \mathrm{LS} \tag{A.10}$$

Inequality (A.10) implies that the integral mean of $|\Sigma L_i'(L_a)|$, i.e. its typical value, is greater than 1. In other words, unless one can identify the economic justification for (A.7), any unemployment equilibrium determined on the basis of the efficiency wage theory is generally unstable.

A.5 The argument developed above explains why it is so important for the efficiency wage theory to demonstrate that only one meaningful ($e = 1$) level of effort exists, whatever the unemployment rate happens to be. As recalled in the text (see footnote 11), Pisauro (1991) has in fact recently proposed a model in which it is shown that the utility maximization procedure induces workers to apply themselves either with a zero or with a maximum (i.e. 1) level of effort. For a worker's expected utility function (linear with respect to wage and effort), which can be written as $U = \alpha w - \beta e$, Pisauru obtains the following conditions:

$$ud[\alpha(w - b) - \beta e] + [1 - ud(1 - e)]\beta = 0 \qquad \text{with } 0 \leq e \leq 1 \tag{A.11}$$

where u is the unemployment rate, d is the probability of being caught while shirking, and b is the unemployment allowance. This result is, however, strictly dependent on the assumption that only two possible 'states' exist for the worker in consequence of his or her decision concerning the amount of work effort to deliver: either hired (H) or fired (F). This assumption presupposes that the worker's time horizon is limited to his or her possible status for the day immediately following the one in which the decision is taken. But if the worker is – at least – also concerned with the consequences that his or her decision has for his or her possible status two days later, then the possible outcomes are obviously four: HH, HF, FH, FF. In this case, by assuming $U(b, 0) = 0$, conditions (A.11) become

$$\frac{d}{de}\left[\left((1-up)^2 - U^2 p\right)\left(\alpha(w-b) - \beta e\right)\right] = 0 \tag{A.12}$$

where $p = (1-e)d$ is the probability of being fired within the time horizon. This latter expression is non-linear in e and can therefore generate complex relations between e and w implying, in any case, an explicit dependence of effort on aggregate employment, also with this oversimplified form of the utility function.

ACKNOWLEDGEMENTS

Though the planning and development of the work are the result of a common effort of the authors, the first part should be attributed to Sergio Nisticó whereas the second should be attributed to Fabio D'Orlando. An earlier Italian version of this chapter appeared in *Studi Economici* (1995, n. 57). The authors benefited from discussions with the late Giovanni Caravale, and Domenico Tosato, as well as from comments by Gary Mongiovi, Anna Maria Pirro, Roy Rotheim, Francesco Saraceno and Alessandra Tonazzi.

NOTES

1 Greenwald and Stiglitz (1988a) have referred to the various New Keynesian contributions as 'building blocks' of a new theory.

2 According to these authors, the absence of coordination of pricing decisions after a monetary shock determines in fact the existence of multiple equilibria ranked according to Paretian criteria.

3 The list of models we provide is obviously far from exhaustive. It is important to recall that the New Keynesian 'research' has produced interesting results on the effects that asymmetric information can generate on the credit market and thus on the level of investment (e.g. Stiglitz and Weiss, 1981; Bernanke and Blinder, 1988). From the viewpoint of the distinction suggested here, these models should enter the second group.

4 It is the same distinction between micro-and macroeconomics that should in fact be questioned. Any theory which aims at explaining the functioning of a complex economic system must necessarily provide a reasonable description of agents' behaviour. Nevertheless, any theory which takes for granted the possibility of investigating the single agent's behaviour, starting from an *a priori* description of how the system as a whole works, inevitably lacks interpretative power and can, at best, aim to be descriptive of individuals' behaviour. That Keynes has not neglected the need to buttress his

macroeconomics with microfoundations has been recognized by Hahn himself: 'about two thirds of the *General Theory* deals with the theory of the action of agents, their motives for saving and for holding money, their investment and speculative behaviour etc.... the fundamental postulate that agents will not persist in actions when more advantageous ones are open to them plays a central role in the Keynesian scheme' (Hahn, 1973, pp. 64–5).

5 On the subject of the similarity between the classical and the Keynesian approach see Caravale (1992C, 1994).

6 As will be shown in the following section, within the efficiency wage theory, the equilibrium level of employment is determined by assuming that each firm knows the exact relationship between wage, aggregate employment and work effort. And this, again, in a context 'dominated' by asymmetric information.

7 On this point see also Akerlof and Yellen (1985). It is moreover important to recall that Weitzman's idea, according to which increasing returns is a necessary condition for the existance of involuntary unemployment, is incompatible with all those models founded on the monopolistic competition hypothesis charaterized by an infinity of small firms.

8 Patinkin's analysis is in fact developed within a Walrasian context and without any reference to the stability question.

9 See also Phelps (1994, p. 32 and note 24).

10 This is justified by the fact that for the single firm there is only *one* significant level of effort, the higher between the two (the productive contribution of a shirker is supposed to be nil), so that effort can be considered as given.

11 In some recent formulations (e.g. Pisauro, 1991), New Keynesians have provided an attempt to derive the C-type effort function from the maximizing behaviour of workers. This is done by assuming the existence of a continuous function with reference to which workers can maximize their utility only for $e = 0$ or $e = 1$ (for a critique of this argument see A.5 in the Appendix). One of the expedients through which this result is obtained is that of resorting to a new definition of effort. According to Pisauro, in fact, effort represents for a worker 'the fraction of the fixed working time he wants to spend actually working' (1991, p. 331). This new definition clearly conflicts with that used in most of the efficiency wage models wherein the level of effort is not forced to be located in the range 0–1. In a very lucid work, Currie and Steedman (1993) have recently denied the possibility of using the notion of effort 'seriously', i.e. in a way which is meaningful for economic theory. Their objections mainly refer to the circumstance that effort is essentially multidimensional and therefore not measurable in a cardinal sense.

12 On this point see Weiss (1990, section 7.3), who argues – although in a different context – that firms have an incentive to sustain monitoring expenses only when the lowest level of effort is zero.

13 'Including effort as a continuous variable would not change the qualitative results' (Shapiro and Stiglitz, 1984, p. 435, footnote 4).

14 This might explain why a minority of efficiency wage theorists resorted to the new notion of effort indicated above (see footnote 11).

15 Stiglitz says that 'the productivity of a worker at one firm depends on the wages paid at other firms and on the unemployment rate. We wish to avoid this complication (Stiglitz, 1987, p. 8, footnote 11). In fact, in Stiglitz's (1987) model, the effort function is $e = e(w)$, and the production function is simply $Y_i = fi(L_i)$.

16 The economic meaning of this assumption is that before full employment is reached, workers will provide a level of effort compatible with a positive level of labour demand. Only in correspondence will full employment will the workers' propensity to shirk induce firms to have the desired level of employment equal to zero.

8

SOCIAL NORMS AS RATIONAL CHOICES

Murray Milgate and Cheryl B. Welch

The idea that in a given society at a given stage in its historical development, wage rates are established as much by the influence of social, cultural and institutional factors as by 'market forces' is as old as the study of economics itself. It featured prominently in the work of the classical economists and, particularly, Marx; and it was only barely submerged even after the rise to dominance of the more individualistic, contractarian approach to economic transactions associated with the marginal revolution. Thus, for example, it was very much to the fore in Marshall's treatment of wages, especially in his celebrated discussion of the so-called 'evil paradox'. The same idea was also present in Keynes's *General Theory* and, in the last decade or so, New Keynesian economics has returned to this old theme in its attempts to model the social dimension of wage contracts as being essentially the result of individual rational choices.

In law as well as in economics the model of private contract dominates the theoretical landscape and commands an ever-widening share of attention.[1] Indeed, modern law and economics inhabit a theoretical universe of private agreements which are thought to be almost exclusively the outcomes of the rational choices of individual agents. Yet both lawyers and economists have always found it necessary to account for the exceptions and complications that exist in the real universe: the apparently indiscreet transactions. In such cases the problem is to account for actions and arrangements, freely entered into by individuals, which cannot readily be reduced to distinct distillates of will, intention and rational choice. The real world is a complex mosaic of social and cultural norms that shape individuals and individual action; and the challenge for individualist theories of action has always been how to theorize this social complexity (see, for example, Elster, 1988, 1989).

One way to do so is to manipulate or expand the notion of contract itself – one can attempt both to explain and justify a social outcome by showing that it is consistent with the implicit, if not the explicit, wills of the contracting parties. This seems to be the route followed by New Keynesian writers who explore the social dimension entering into implicit contracts on labour and credit markets. In the law, the use of the notion of implied contract has a longer and more complicated history, but wherever it appears it retains the distinctive imprint of a purely will-based theory action. Tacit consent has always functioned in certain legal and political theories as a useful fiction designed to translate the perceived existence of some obligation into the language of rational choice and promise. However, although this construct has appeared both in law and in economics, the common features have been little remarked upon.

The implied contract path towards the resolution of the apparent tension between a real world of social norms and a hypothetical world of rational choices has been travelled by many individual thinkers, at many different times, and with various ends in mind. The aim of this chapter is to chart the terrain that must be covered in following such a route. To this end, it will examine three different contexts in which a notion of implied contract was forged, and within which that notion functioned to adjust a highly individualistic theory of human interaction to a richer social reality. The first two cases (tacit pacts in seventeenth-century natural law theory and quasi-contract in late nineteenth-century French political discourse) arose in the context of legal and political debate. The third (the contemporary theory of implicit labour contracts) comes from a recent literature in theoretical economics, but one with direct implications for public policy. The point, however, is not merely to recover these arguments but to clarify some of the difficulties encountered by any theoretical project that seeks to reinterpret the action of social norms in terms of rational choices. We shall attempt to show that these difficulties have a persistent character about them and that they compromise the ability of such arguments to sustain both the proposition that the resultant contractual order is enforceable, and the claim that the fundamental determining circumstance behind contractual arrangements is individualistic rational choice rather than the unmediated operation of social norms themselves.

THE NATURAL LAW THEORY OF TACIT PACTS

In the course of the seventeenth and eighteenth centuries a new jurisprudence came into being which sought to elaborate relations among individuals that were 'true' by virtue of reason alone. Natural lawyers declared their independence from theology as well as from the various existing laws of peoples. To replace these old authorities, the new jurisprudential theorists sought to design a legal architecture founded upon a set of *natural* legal principles that were alleged to be inherent in the nature of persons and entirely independent of any past historical developments and/or of any particular institutional contexts. Previous bodies of law, so their argument ran, had no compelling claim to legitimacy. At best, existing law simply furnished more or less suitable raw materials for building an entirely new structure. Of course, older sources continued to appear in these early–modern constructions, but those who forged the central doctrines of natural law worked towards a theory that would provide an ahistorical, abstract and rational account of contractual obligations.

As is well known, natural law theory exerted its greatest influence in the area of public law. The idea that society and civil government originated in a tacit pact or contract, and that one might deduce from the implicit terms of that contract answers to questions concerning political obligation and legitimacy, provided the foundations for a long series of decisive contributions to political thought.[2] However, for an analysis of the ways in which tacit pacts were deployed more generally, it is to the contributions of Samuel von Pufendorf that one should turn. In his work one encounters an analysis of the nature and significance of implied contracts in civil law rare among the natural lawyers. Pufendorf's enterprise reveals not only the source and the strength of the impulse towards the presentation of social norms as rational choices, but also the hazards of such an undertaking.

The examination of the fabric of relations constituting civil society in *De jure naturae et genitum* (1672) was highly formalized and was premised on a voluntaristic conception of social order. According to Pufendorf, those individuals who came together to form a society should be thought to have done so voluntarily and intentionally.[3] The first principle of the whole of Pufendorf's analysis was that all legitimate social relations were based exclusively upon a set of intentionally chosen obligations that were freely entered into by consenting parties: 'we presuppose at the outset that by nature all individuals have equal rights, and no one enjoys authority over another, unless it has been secured by an act of himself or of the other' (ibid., p. 853). On this line of reasoning, the ties that bound individuals and society together were nothing other than promises, especially promises as to future performance and compliance.[4] For Pufendorf, the natural bases of the contractual order and social harmony were to be sought in individual intentions and freely chosen obligations.

Although society was held to be the product of intentional agreements, the problem of how to demonstrate that this contractual order was, in fact as well as in theory, entirely the product of the unencumbered rational choices of individual agents remained. On this subject, Pufendorf was somewhat unusual among the founders of natural law jurisprudence in that he gave considerable attention to the specific question of how to determine that an obligation had been incurred by choice in the absence of explicit evidence (written or other) of such consent. Pufendorf's answer was relatively straightforward. While he agreed that consent was 'usually expressed by signs, such as speaking, writing, and nodding', he recognized that it sometimes happened that 'it is inferred, without such signs' (ibid., p. 402). Consent, that is, came in two distinct varieties: express and tacit. Courtesy of this distinction, the locus of determination of contractual obligation (for the natural lawyers) could still be analysed in concepts related directly to the nature of persons (rather than to the customary beliefs and practices of society) even in the case of otherwise anomalous real world contracts where factors other than individual will, intention and choice seemed to be at work. The next requirement was that of establishing when and how the inference of consent (or intention) could legitimately be made.

Pufendorf's answer was that everything turned upon 'the nature of the business and other circumstances' surrounding the contract (ibid., p. 402). He illustrated his meaning with a familiar example: 'sometimes the absence of signs, or silence, when viewed in certain circumstances, is equivalent to a sign of consent'. Given this premise, according to Pufendorf, in any tacit pact 'we are bound to that for which those who expressly make a covenant about such things are commonly in the habit of contracting' (1660, p. 98; see also 1673, p. 70). Customary arrangements and social norms, therefore, could be regarded as implicit rational choices. However, having rendered the external circumstances within which a contractual agreement was struck as a part of the internal intentions brought to the agreement by the contracting parties, Pufendorf recognized that an element of arbitrariness might be introduced. In an effort to limit the potential consequences of this ambiguity, he held that in the case of a tacit pact it was necessary that circumstances 'agree from every point of view in presuming consent, and that there be no probable conjecture that would lead to a different conclusion' (1672, p. 402). In this manner, Pufendorf effectively asserted that for a tacit pact to be legitimate it should be as will-based as an explicit agreement.

Considered from this perspective, tacit consent must always be interpreted carefully so as to give it no greater (but no less) force than that entailed by a clear and explicit understanding of the agreement. Should this not be done, Pufendorf argued that an 'onerous obligation' might be laid upon a person against that person's will. But the danger of delivering unjust judgements was not the only problem. Pufendorf was equally alive to the possibility that an overreliance on the idea of tacit pacts could jeopardize the contractual order of society itself, since too great a readiness to resort to the notion of an implied contract threatened to 'render pacts too slippery and uncertain' (ibid., p. 402).

Notwithstanding these difficulties, Pufendorf indicated that one should be prepared to encounter tacit agreements in many practical contexts. Although actual contracts were, for him, always the analogues of the reciprocal relations generated in a theoretical universe of individual rational actors, Pufendorf conceded that in the real world instances of tacit conditions and exceptions would be met 'on every hand' (1672, p. 403).[5] The task was to make the exceptions intelligible (and hence tractable) in terms of the degree to which they were conformable to the rule. Pufendorf's theoretical analysis of implied contracts, despite its concessions to the difficulties of mapping a theory of discrete transactions onto the difficult terrain of real relationships, stressed the importance of clear signs of intention (or presumed intention) on the part of the promisor.

Nevertheless, in his own discussions of tacit pacts the apparently stringent conditions that were supposed to be applied to the determination of the legitimate obligations embodied in tacit pacts were often allowed to lapse. In one of his very first illustrations of what was supposedly an unambiguous tacit pact, Pufendorf offered a case not just where agreement was left implicit, but where it was actually not present at all. The example was a now familiar principal–agent problem. When 'in a man's absence some business of his is done without his express orders', Pufendorf maintained that 'a tacit pact is understood, whereby the man is bound to compensate any person for the labour and expense to which he was put in managing the business to good advantage'. The basis of his claim was that 'it is presumed that, if the absentee had known about the matter, he would have expressly agreed to its dispatch' (1672, p. 403; see also 1660, pp. 97, 99 and 281).

Obviously, in this particular case, the element of intention was completely missing and Pufendorf simply forged an implied contract *ex post facto*. The presumption was that since the absent party (the principal) had benefited materially from the action of the individual who had managed the party's business affairs (the agent), one was justified in inferring that tacit consent had been given (after all, the absentee would not have intended to benefit unjustly). In fact, though this particular example is an especially transparent one, the category of tacit consent functioned consistently throughout Pufendorf's jurisprudence in precisely this fashion. Tacit acceptance was uniformly offered as grounds for translating traditional obligations or customary understandings into the language of consent.

Exemplary of this function are Pufendorf's lengthy disquisitions on the subject of the contract of marriage. Here the situation of a 'regular and consummated marriage' was held to be based on a tacit pact to engage in 'such a manner of conduct as the nature of that society requires' (1672, p. 856). Where tradition mandated that certain social relationships be attended by a certain behaviour, such behaviour became an implied part of the contract (in this case, the marriage contract). What society required, its social norms so to speak, which for the natural lawyers were supposed to be nothing more than the confusing detritus of the law of peoples, were reincarnated as rationally (albeit tacitly) chosen contractual obligations.[6]

Society was implicated even with regard to the market. According to Pufendorf, insurance, tenancy, franchising, loan and labour contracts all embodied tacit elements. The same mode of reasoning applied in the case of the marriage contract was applied to these cases to determine the legitimate obligations entailed by such arrangements. Labour contracts, for example, were regulated by tacit terms arising from what he styled the accepted demands of *humanity*. Introducing an analogy that was later to be of great theoretical moment in economics, Pufendorf compared the rules governing the hiring of labour to those which govern the buying and selling of commodities. Just as 'a purchase is completed when the price has been agreed upon, so also is hiring when the wages have been fixed' (ibid., p. 741). However, and this is what matters, Pufendorf immediately added that the labour contract may well embody tacit clauses, so that 'wages may be extended in some way and tacitly'. One such tacit extension to which he called attention was the case of full-time (as opposed to casual) employees, where labour contracts have to conform to certain socially accepted standards of fairness in the treatment of workers temporarily incapacitated by illness. 'It is only human', Pufendorf argued, that an employment contract implied an agreement neither to dismiss nor to withhold the wages of workers who fall ill.[7] In this instance it was the claims of *humanity* that mandated the extension of the labour contract to cover the payment of wages to a full-time worker who could not perform the services contracted for as a result of illness. It is worth observing that the flexibility of the notion of tacit pacts is rendered especially clear in this example by the fact that these demands of humanity apparently did not extend to contracts for part-time or casual work.

But it was not only the demands of humanity that entered implicitly into labour contracts on Pufendorf's reading of the situation. Certain customary understandings also came into play. Pufendorf also maintained that there usually exists in society some commonly accepted rate of wages, so that even a worker who 'places his services at the disposal of another before the wage has been determined' (thereby leaving the worker's pay 'to the equity of his employer') must be understood to have entered into a tacit labour contract in which 'no less shall be paid than the common wage' (1672, pp. 741–2). In this context it is clear that Pufendorf meant by the common wage that rate of wages which was generally accepted to be a fair minimum in the prevailing conditions of society; it was, for him, one of those clauses which were in 'the nature of the business and other circumstances' surrounding the labour contract.

What becomes apparent in these accounts of tacit pacts in civil life is that Pufendorf had moved far beyond an unproblematic imputation of promissory intent. The difficulties associated with his treatment of social norms as rational choices are obvious enough. To consider social obligations as having their basis in the free consent of individual agents is to privilege consent as the 'most relevant reason' for undertaking an obligation (1673, p. 70). In the case of implied consent, the standards governing what should be considered a valid implication are crucial. But it was precisely these standards that were ambiguous in Pufendorf's account. When readable signs of consent are taken to be on a par with traditional or customary expectations, as they were for Pufendorf, then one has assumed the prior existence of the very thing one set out to establish – namely, the social practices that would be entered into by a rational individual.

The tensions inherent in this position became acute when the question at issue was whether a tacit contract should be enforced. Pufendorf himself was able to avoid confronting this issue directly because of the larger religious framework of his theory. For Pufendorf, neither individual consent nor social norms sufficed as accounts of human obligation. The ultimate source of that obligation was to be found in the intentions of the 'author of the universe' (1673, p. 28). Thus, divine will functioned as the 'extrinsic principle' (1660, p. 230) underwriting the legitimacy of obligation. As Pufendorf put it:

> though these precepts [of natural law] have a clear utility, they get the force of law only upon the presuppositions that God exists and rules all things by His providence, and that He has enjoined the human race to observe as laws those dictates of reason which He has Himself promulgated by the force of the innate light.
>
> (1673, p. 36)

The problems associated with establishing a case for treating social norms as rational choices in the absence of a divine regulator are illustrated in our next case – the late nineteenth-century political controversy in France over what was known as solidarism.

THE SOLIDARIST NOTION OF QUASI-CONTRACT

The solidarist controversy focused on attempts to invoke the legal concept of quasi-contract to support the provision of government-financed welfare benefits, an argument exemplified by Léon Bourgeois in his immensely influential *Solidarité* (1896). Social provision required redistributive taxation which, argued its critics, threatened to undermine the private contractual order. However, according to Bourgeois, if there were an already existing intergenerational quasi-contractual agreement – one that obliged the present generation to ensure that the fruits of past accumulation were fairly distributed amongst themselves – redistributive taxation would not be a threat to the contractual order, but rather necessary to its support.

The solidarist notion of quasi-contract as deployed by Bourgeois was closely related to Pufendorf's conception of tacit pact.[8] However, the increasingly individualist version of contract law that had come to dominate jurisprudential thinking in the nineteenth century had led to a change in terminology. As we have seen, although in theory Pufendorf had held a narrow view of the realm in which contracts could be legitimately implied, in practice he had used the notion to cover not only situations in which consent was almost explicit, but also those cases in which agents were merely presumed to have intended what custom demanded. By the middle of the nineteenth century implied contracts of this latter kind – that is, contracts that gave legal force to customary obligations – were being called by the French civil law term quasi-contracts.[9]

The essence of quasi-contract doctrine in French law was that obligations arose not directly from the parties' agreement, but as a consequence of a beneficial act on the part of one of them. The underlying principle was that one person should not benefit at another's expense. A familiar example of a quasi-contract was the one offered by Pufendorf as an obvious example of a tacit pact; namely, the case in which a man benefits from work done to his property in his absence, and is considered to have tacitly authorized that work. The doctrine of quasi-contract brought into the foreground what Émile Durkheim called the non-contractual element in contract (Durkheim, 1893, p. 158), since it envisaged the normative rule governing the disposition of a quasi-contract case as being in some sense external or prior to the contract. Nevertheless, it insisted that a case of unjust enrichment could still be usefully conceptualized as an implied agreement in which the grounds for judgement lay in a reconstruction of the intentions of the contracting parties.

This notion of unjust enrichment embodied in Articles 1371–81 of the French Civil Code offered Bourgeois a way to combine the highly individualist assumptions of French legal and economic liberalism with a sensitivity to social justice. Bourgeois's first tactic was to express strong support for the individualist premise that contract *librement discuté et fidlement exécuté des deux parts, devient la base définitive du droit humain* (1896, p. 132). He then claimed, however, that the law governing any ongoing association could only be *une interprétation et une représentation de l'accord qui eut du s'établir préalablement entre eux s'ils avaient pu etre également et librement consultés* (ibid., pp. 132–3). According to Bourgeois, this hypothetical consensual agreement was a quasi-contract establishing legitimate terms of economic and social interaction.

Of most interest to Bourgeois's contemporaries was the question of how the existing terms of economic interaction (e.g. in the unwritten but powerful *contrats de travail* that were presumed to govern relations between employers and employees) would be affected by this new doctrine of the social quasi-contract. Here Bourgeois explicitly argued that free contracts between individuals were justifiable only in a social environment that enforced the social quasi-contract. On this line of reasoning, a correct reading of this supposedly pre-existing implicit agreement revealed a large backlog of social debts and credits that encumbered individuals in the initiation of discrete transactions. These debts were no less obligatory and no less the expression of rational choice (broadly construed) than those generated by express contracts.[10] Indeed, if such debts remained outstanding, they would jeopardize the contractual order itself. It was the role of the state to assure the fulfilment of the quasi-contract, as of all other contracts. According to Bourgeois, this was no more an encroachment on the rights of individuals than were other specifications of the limits of free contract (e.g. limitations on agreements between spouses or the non-enforcement of immoral agreements).

Clearly, Bourgeois had recognized two elements that were central to the notion of implied contract in natural law. First, he subscribed to the idea that free individual choice (and consent) alone could provide the basis of law. Second, he assumed that the notion of a socially defined equivalence of benefits provided reasonable grounds for inferring consent. The difficulty for Bourgeois was to show that shared norms about distributive justice were in fact inherent in social practice. However, instead of confronting this problem directly, he was able to side-step it by invoking solidarity – in much the same way in which the 'author of the universe' entered Pufendorf's argument.

The idea of a socially defined equivalence of benefits gained its substantive content from Bourgeois's particular interpretation of social solidarity. As he saw it, solidarity was both a factual description of the interdependence of individuals in modern market society (a fact confirmed by the findings of biology, history and sociology), and a moral demand that the anomalies of that social life – namely, that only a few reap what the many have sown – be corrected. Consent, then, turned out to be both fundamental and unnecessary. Given the commands of social solidarity, one could always infer consent.

Bourgeois's use of implied contract appears to have been designed to reassure his contemporaries that the basic elements of the welfare state (interpreted as embodying and enforcing the requirements of solidarity) posed no radical threat to the existing regime of private contracts. The contractual order could be extended to accommodate any number of social reforms. Indeed, if it were not, the basis of contract itself – that is, the belief that promises must be kept – would be weakened. At a deeper level, Bourgeois wished to preserve the view that individuals had choice and control over the social arrangements in which they were embedded, even as he redefined individuals themselves as the products of those arrangements.

Perhaps the single most prevalent adjective to be found among the numerous critiques of Bourgeois's use of the theory of quasi-contract is 'ingenious' (see, for example, Hayward, 1961, p. 28; Demogues in Fouillée *et al.*, 1916, p. 526). One set of criticisms called attention to the problems of what might be called misleading precision; that is, the transposition of a technical term with a clear meaning into an inappropriate context where that meaning is inevitably lost.

These criticisms pointed to the lack of a clear or satisfying standard to determine which elements in a contract were legitimately implied. The standard generally used in contract cases – that is, the debt a reasonable person could be presumed to have intended to shoulder – is itself ambiguous. Indeed, that standard became even more difficult to read in a social context where rapid change had unsettled traditional social practices. In such a case, the notion of quasi-contract opened up a theoretical space that could be filled by almost anything. Furthermore, even if one assumed that an intergenerational quasi-contract could be identified – implying that some group of fortunate individuals (the debtors) had already drawn more than their fair share of some common legacy, and that another group of less fortunate individuals (the creditors) were the proper recipients of that debt – it would be impossible to assess the respective charges and payments due to particular individuals. Bourgeois himself recognized that the social quasi-contract was in some sense collective. Since it was impossible to calculate each individual's indebtedness, and hence the proper tax burden which that individual had implicitly promised to shoulder, the most reasonable solution was to extend the principle of mutualization to all the major risks of social life.

Bourgeois's admission of the saliency of mutual insurance risk suggested the line of criticism that was taken up by a second group of commentators, many of whom were his allies in the solidarist movement. Their allegation was that the use of a will-based theory of contract in this particular context masked the real issues that had to be faced if social reform was to be accomplished. They argued that it was disingenuous of Bourgeois to fall back on mutuality by default:

> [w]ould it not be better simply to say: Whenever a loss is suffered either by a disaster or an accident or even by a foreseen cause like old age, the burden of it should be apportioned among several and thus lightened; or rather... every human being should be assured a certain minimum of existence.
> (Demogues in Fouillée *et al.*, 1916, p. 527; cf. Gide and Rist, 1913, p. 598)

These critics argued that contracts and quasi-contracts were based on the giving and receiving of equivalences, whereas mutual insurance was a kind of substitute for direct liability. As a result, it would be better to confront the non-contractual element directly, on this view, rather than to engage in 'ironical subterfuge' (Gide and Rist, 1913, p. 598). In particular, one had to recognize the diverse interests of classes and groups and the hard political work of finding a mutually agreed upon consensus about what solidarity required. Other critics went in a different direction and argued that it was necessary to substitute a scientific examination of social and legal norms for the subjectivist principle of contract. The functionalism of Durkheim and the radical sociological jurisprudence of Duguit – which advocated an appeal to the 'plain unvarnished fact' of solidarity – took this explicitly anti-contractual form (see, for example, Hayward, 1960).

Although the natural law theory of tacit pacts and the solidarist doctrine of the social quasi-contract emerged in quite different circumstances, it is apparent that the ambiguities have remained remarkably consistent. While they promised theoretical acuity, they often delivered practical confusion. The confusion grew as the standards governing valid implied inferences became less widely shared and more deeply contested. While few seventeenth-century minds directly bristled at Pufendorf's assumption of the tacitly acquired obligations of marriage, many nineteenth-century thinkers disputed supposedly tacitly acquired welfare obligations of living in a modern market economy. Moreover, the use of implied contract avoided a direct consideration of the social factors that impinge upon the contracting situation. The device allowed these factors to remain shadowed, marginal and peripheral. There may have been sound practical and strategic reasons for this; however, there were also costs, not least the loss of historical and institutional complexity.

THE ECONOMIC THEORY OF IMPLICIT CONTRACTS

A third context in which the idea of implied contract has come to play a decisive role is of more recent origin. The field in which it arose was one whose character differs quite dramatically from either of the cases outlined so far. It arose neither in the context of the development of political and legal philosophy nor in the heat of political debate, but in one of the most austere areas of economic analysis: the general theory of exchange. It would probably be true to say that the economic theory of implicit contracts, as it is known, has been developed in complete isolation of these other realms in which implied contract had been important in the past. Nevertheless, by attempting to represent social norms as the outcome of individual economic decision making, it is essentially an analogue of those earlier arguments. The economic theory of implicit contracts provides a particularly clear illustration of a feature noted above: the use of implied contract to model social norms in terms of rational choices in order to avoid strain on the individualist premises of the theory of contract. The economic example is clearest largely because it articulates a formal (mathematical) constrained–maximization problem where social norms are included in the agent's objective function.

The impulse to the development of the theory of implicit contracts in economics was the observed discrepancies between contractual arrangements actually struck on certain markets and those which might have been expected to emerge from a pure exchange model. Actual contracts often seemed to be drawn up where there remained possibilities for a renegotiation which would make both parties to the agreement materially better off. Theoretically speaking, this was not supposed to happen; rational agents were not supposed to make such irrational choices (see

Akerlof and Yellen, 1987). The single most famous example of this was the observation that wages might not adjust to secure full employment, and it was primarily (though not exclusively) in the area of labour contracts that most of the developments in the theory of implicit contracts took place during the last decade. When faced with the possibility that actual or express contracts could not cope with sticky wages, economists turned to the idea of reconstructing an implied contract that might account for them. In these models, the idea is that 'society' exerts a decisive influence on contractual arrangements voluntarily entered into by individual agents.

Of course, *society* had never been entirely excluded from the traditional theory of contracts in economics. Every formal account of exchange, from the Walrasian auction market model and the Edgeworth bargaining model of the late nineteenth century onwards, presupposed the existence of a well-defined and enforceable environment of property rights and to this extent had invoked society's legal codes and institutions at the start. Ask a representative economist why it is the case that the vast majority of contracts that put into effect market transactions are typically fulfilled, and the answer would probably run something like this: it is because each of the individual agents party to a contractual arrangement (an exchange relationship) has a material interest in conforming to their side of the agreement on the expectation that the other party will conform to theirs, and that each can count on recourse to a legal system to enforce property rights should that expectation be disappointed. In short, the mutual interplay of different private interests in a well-defined and enforceable environment of private property rights would be sufficient to guarantee the fulfilment of contractual obligations.[11]

There were also models in which *society* was introduced to act as an inhibition to the ability of private contracting parties to exhaust the possibilities for mutually beneficial trade. Indeed, treating society as a barrier to efficient exchange has been a favoured approach among many who sought to explain involuntary unemployment by deferring to institutional rigidities. In these imperfectionist models of unemployment, society was not implied as part of the contract; it was an obstacle to it. The point of departure of research on implicit labour contracts consists in a change in the usual economic conception of what exactly *society* is, and of how it actually stamps its authority upon freely arrived at contracts of sale and purchase.

If one takes the work of George Akerlof (1980, 1982) and Robert Solow (1979, 1980, 1990) to be representative cases, then the theory of implicit labour contracts appears to require us to go beyond these accepted ways of thinking about the *social* element in economic processes in two quite novel ways. First, it involves a reconsideration of the kind of social forces that are at work when economic agents come to contractual agreements: it is argued that factors like custom, social honour and esteem, and tradition enter the contracting process. These factors are usually summarized under the umbrella of social norms. Second, a new view of the way in which these social factors actually exert and sustain their effect in contractual relations is called into play. The authority of social norms over contractual arrangements was not so much exerted through the usual legal-rational channels of, say, the auction market of Walras, nor yet was it exercised through the more bureaucratic channels sometimes admitted by imperfectionist models of the firm (though both may be present). Instead they were modelled as entering into the objective functions which individual agents sought to maximize when entering into private contractual relations.

Like the other examples of implied contract examined above, a presumed equivalence of (socially defined) benefits exists within the confines of a choice-based agreement between employer and employed. In the previous cases, however, the ambiguities surrounding legal interpretation and enforcement forced some recognition of the independent existence of social norms. If enforcement depended on the contract having been freely willed (many lawyers argued), then some implied contracts (namely, those that did not exhibit any elements of choice) could not be enforced at all under the rubric of contract doctrine (although they might fall under some other province of the law). The economists did not directly confront the ambiguities of enforcement precisely because they interpreted implicit labour contracts as self-enforcing (see Kronman and Posner, 1979, pp. 59–64).

The question of how implicit labour contracts were sustained automatically, as it were, was answered in different ways. The sanction of social norms was exerted upon the individual contracting parties through their desire to meet ideal rather than just material interests. Implicit contracts were enforced, therefore, by individual calculations of status indicators like reputation, honour, approbation and stigma rather than exclusively by individual calculations of material gain or loss. Formally speaking, in these models of contract, social forces enter into the objective function, rather than the constraints, of the individual's problem of maximization.

It is relatively simple to summarize the concrete results of this line of research, since most of it has been conducted with an eye to explaining some of the most characteristic features of labour markets: precisely those features which the traditional model of exchange is unable to account for at all adequately. It can be (and has been) deployed to explain features like wage rigidity, involuntary unemployment, dual labour markets, labour market segmentation and discrimination. A definite example may serve to highlight the point.

The key characteristic of implicit wage contracts that needs explaining is the payment of a real wage to workers higher than that which will clear the labour market. This higher real wage (the efficiency wage as it was called) was accounted for in a number of ways – all of which bring 'society' back into the picture. One way of answering was to argue that workers had a propensity to shirk, so that firms may have to pay a premium, arising from the social character of labour, to cover themselves against the moral hazard inherent in the hiring of labour services. Another response was to argue that employment contracts were incomplete in the sense that they did not (and could not) specify productivity requirements in anything like the detail demanded by the Walrasian auction market contract; this may be caused by problems of bounded rationality, high costs of supervision and monitoring, the difficulty of actually measuring on-the-job effort, and the like. Still another rationale involved the argument that real-wage rates higher than those associated with market clearing offered employers a method of disciplining workers in that they had the effect of raising the costs of job loss (Bowles, 1985).

Efficiency wage contracts, however, were only one of many types of implicit labour contract that might be imagined. Indeed, they all fall under a general class of implicit contracts that would be drawn up in situations where the parties to a transaction have differential (asymmetric) information; that is, a situation where inside information is available to one party and not another. Another example of a labour contract with an implicit element is the risk-sharing contract. In some cases, risk-averse workers may be able to shift the risk associated with, say, an uncertain stream of future income onto the employer. For their part, workers will certainly wish to do this whenever they are imperfectly informed as to the state of demand for labour services in the future (as when future markets for labour services fail to exist, or when the economic system is subject to unpredictable fluctuations between good and bad times). For their part, employers will be willing to accept the offer of a risk shifting (or partial risk sharing) arrangement whenever the costs of monitoring, enforcement or screening are non-negligible (and, of course, as long as there is little likelihood of the firm going out of business as a result).

It is worth noticing that this example allows one to examine the question of enforcement more closely. For whether (and how) these implied contracts would be enforceable at law is uncertain. The difficulty is obvious. When times are good, a worker would be able to find higher wages elsewhere; however, if the worker breaks his or her existing (implied) contract by quitting to take a higher-paid job, is the worker liable to compensate the employer? Alternatively, when times are bad, the employer would be able to hire workers for less than the contract wage rate; if the employer breaks an existing contract by firing a worker (or lowering the worker's wage), is the employes liable to compensate the worker?

It does not require much effort to appreciate that this new invention of the economists, the implicit labour contract, turns out to be nothing more than the kind of implied labour contract Pufendorf had discussed. There the labour contract was subject to an implied agreement that the employer share the risk of the worker's falling ill by offering the worker a long-term contract of employment, in return for the worker's maximum effort when healthy. In Pufendorf's example, fluctuations between good and bad health are the analogue to fluctuations between good and bad times in the economists' models. Unfortunately, Pufendorf did not offer any suggestions about the legal liability for damage on the non-fulfilment of this implied agreement by one or other party.

On this subject, the economists have advanced beyond Pufendorf, and have come up with a number of possible solutions to this kind of conundrum. According to one line of argument, workers might sign long-term contracts which involved them posting a bond (in the form of accepting a lower wage in the initial period of the contract) which underwrites their part of the contractual arrangement, and employers are simply assumed to be reliable. Alternatively, it has been suggested that issues involving reputation might be at stake in the abrogation of implicit contracts; contract breakers might be handicapped in securing employment or recruiting labour in the future if they have a bad reputation. In fact, some combination of employee bonds and employer reputation seems at present to be the favoured method of meeting the problem of unreliability. The solution is to attempt to make the contract self-enforcing.

Whether these attempts are likely to be successful is, however, another matter. More important in the present context are the claims of these theories to be more sociologically sensitive (as Solow has put it). In one sense this is true enough – especially when the comparative case is the Walrasian auction market contract. But it is worth noticing that all existing theories of implicit labour contracts, whether of the efficiency wage or asymmetric information variety, while they often speak of workers and employers arriving at contractual arrangements, do not talk about a labour market in which organized groups of workers play an active role in wage negotiations. The whole of the argument is about individual agents, some of whom offer labour services, others of whom demand them. One might have hoped that this would have been among the first of the limitations of such models that a more sociological approach to labour contracts might have helped to overcome. This has not, so far, been the case.

CONCLUDING REMARKS

In the three cases considered in this chapter, there are a number of recurring difficulties. Although each separate project attempted to furnish an explanation of social norms in terms of implicit rational choices, in none of them was it actually possible to do so. For example, Pufendorf simply asserted that the demands of humanity provided reasonable grounds for inferring consent to a labour contract with implied insurance clauses. Bourgeois, likewise, merely assumed that the ethical imperatives arising from market interdependence provided reasonable grounds for inferring consent for redistributive policies. The economists took it for granted that, for example, reputational factors provided reasonable grounds for inferring implicit contracts on credit markets. These exercises in modelling social norms as rational choices, therefore, do not yield the degree of precision that their authors intended – moreover, they come at a cost. As Bourgeois's critics noted a century ago, they can divert attention away from those institutional, historical and political factors that are crucial to understanding or legitimizing social practices.

In one area, however, the economic theory of implicit contracts seems to involve a distinct advance over its precursors. The deficiencies of tacit pacts and quasi-contracts became obvious when the question turned to their enforcement. At this point, Pufendorf invoked the divine sanction and Bourgeois called upon *solidarité*. This unacceptable recourse to extrinsic authority is apparently avoided in the theory of implicit contracts where the rational calculation of self-interest ensured compliance with contractual obligations. But obviously, as more and more economists have begun to recognize, a heuristic assumption of pure rationality begs the question of enforcement. In this light, neither God nor solidarity, nor economic rationality, are able to bear the theoretical weight they are asked to carry.

NOTES

1 Macneil (1980, p. 1). An example is Richard Posner's notion that the law of contracts is nothing other than the legal expression of the requirements of efficient market exchange (1972; see also Kronman and Posner, 1979); another is Gary Becker's reduction of social relations to the consequences of individual constrained utility maximization (1976).

2 The foundations were laid down by Grotius in *De jure belli ac pacis* (1631) and were developed by Wolff, Althusius, Hobbes, Pufendorf and Locke. The standard treatment of these developments remains that of Gierke (1913).

3 Compare *Elementorum jurisprudentaie*: 'we call voluntary actions those actions placed within the power of man, which depend upon the will, as upon a free cause, in such wise that, without its decision setting forth from the man's actions as elicited by previous cognition of the intellect, they would not come to pass' (1660, p. 3; see also 1673, p. 19).

4 Here is how Pufendorf actually put it: 'Since promises and pacts regularly limit our liberty and lay upon us some burden in that we must now of necessity do something, the performance or omission of which lay before entirely within our own decision, no more pertinent reason can be advanced, whereby a man can be prevented from complaining hereafter of having to carry such a burden than that he agreed to it of his own accord, and sought on his own judgement what he had full power to refuse' (1672, p. 402).

5 Pufendorf's best-known application of the notion of implied contract was in the realm of public law and politics, an enterprise in which he was strongly influenced by Hobbes and Grotius and, in turn, decisively influenced Locke and Hume. This, however, is another story, and need not detain us here.

6 The fact that as a result of this manipulation social norms would themselves become enforceable under the Law of Nature is a matter of the first importance, since it was through this door that the state itself would later menacingly enter the world of private contract bearing regulations governing the conduct of private life which were, even for the early-modern natural lawyers, as much the product of ignorance and prejudice as they were of reason.

7 The full passage is as follows: 'Regarding the hiring of labour it should be observed that, if a man engages the temporary, and, as it were, transient services of a person, he does not have to pay him when some accident has prevented him from being able to furnish the services agreed upon. But if he has engaged his permanent services, it is only human, in case the latter has been incapacitated by disease or some other mischance from performing his tasks for a short time, not to take from him his position or cut off his salary, especially when there is hope that he can make for the services last by showing diligence later, or when his former good record has been such as to merit this humanity' (1672, p. 743).

8 The continuity between this line of argument and earlier discussions of implicit contract was recognized immediately by fellow solidarist Celestin Bouglé, who called Bourgeois's use of the idea of quasi-contract a means of 'developing and perfecting the art of interpreting assents wholly unexpressed, as they most often are' (Bouglé in Fouillée *et al.*, 1916, p. 526).

9 As future-oriented transactions became more important to the market economy, contract doctrine became more explicitly will-based and less accommodating to traditional mores and practices (see Atiyah, 1979, pp. 149–84).

10 Of course, it was pointed out by his critics that even if we owe a debt to our ancestors, it is one that they do not and probably would not recognize: 'the cave man cut and polished the stone for his own use and not for mine' (Malapert in Fouillée *et al.*, 1916, p. 92).

11 As Atiyah put it: 'If it is enlightened self-interest which lies at the root of these [contractual] obligations, it is because promises and contracts invite trust, involve reliance and dependence by others on the world of promises' (1979, p. 32).

9

NEW KEYNESIANS, POST KEYNESIANS AND HISTORY

John B. Davis

The New Keynesian research programme possesses a number of features which are not unattractive to Post Keynesians. New Keynesians reject policy ineffectiveness, *laissez-faire* New Classical economics, and argue that the economy can lock into underemployment equilibria. New Keynesians allow for asymmetric information, imperfect competition, adjustment costs, externalities, strategic complementarity and increasing returns, and in some instances emphasize institutions and conventions. Yet New Keynesianism also possesses features Post Keynesians are generally critical of, including the standard subjective probability framework, rational expectations, the ISLM model, an insistence on microfoundations for macroeconomics, a reliance on traditional optimizing behavioural analysis, and little interest in Keynes's own thinking. In contrast, Post Keynesians emphasize true uncertainty regarding the future, reject rational expectations, regard the ISLM model as artificial and static, call for macrofoundations for microeconomics, argue for richer accounts of individual economic behaviour, and draw often on Keynes's own thinking.

Among these differences, Post Keynesians' emphasis on true uncertainty regarding the future has been central. Thus an interesting issue is whether there is also a related and equally strong dividing line between Post Keynesians and New Keynesians regarding the influence the past and our ignorance of it has on the present. Were both uncertainty about the future and ignorance about the past to distinguish Post Keynesianism from New Keynesianism, this might then point towards important differences between the two research programmes in regard to their respective views of the nature of economic behaviour. Recently Cross (1993) has suggested that there need not be important disagreements over the influence of the past by arguing that Post Keynesians might find the concept of hysteresis amenable to their understanding of the economic process. Hysteresis concerns phenomena that display a persistence of effects beyond the occasion of their initial causes. They may be thought characteristically historical in that the presence of such effects violates the standard presumption that physical systems are reversible. Indeed Post Keynesians have long used notions that apply irreversibility characteristics. Their analysis of fixed capital investment as fundamentally illiquid treats long-lived capital assets as firm- or at best industry-specific, and thus as rarely remarketed without significant loss. Their analysis of money contracts focuses on the relation between current and future money flows and financial obligations determined by past decisions.

Katzner (1993) has replied, however, that hysteresis as specifically understood by Cross and other contributors to the literature relies on systems of periodic equations that presuppose logical time and perfect knowledge, and that an analysis of the economy in terms of true historical time understood as unidirectional and irreversible better captures a Post Keynesian understanding of an economic process in time.[1] Because 'reality is overwhelmingly complicated', our perceptions of the past 'are fraught with errors and gaps', implying that 'successive moments in historical time bring with them their own unique institutional and analytical structures' (p. 340). In effect, 'history is created period by period' (p. 343), and ignorance about the past plays directly into our uncertainty about the future. Indeed, ignorance about the past and uncertainty about the future are but two species of a knowledge about the world whose limitations rule out using subjective probability theory as an analytical device for economics.

Keynes clearly believed uncertainty about the future was central to our understanding of the economy. But how did he understand the effect of the past on the present, and did he believe that the economy moved in historical time in the sense of being created period by period? In an effort to develop the foundations for Post Keynesianism in terms of Keynes's own thinking, Kregel (1976) distinguished three alternative models used by Keynes in *The General Theory* and in his 1937 lectures in connection with differing assumptions about the nature and interaction of short-period and long-period price expectations. Dutt (1991–2) has argued, however, that only one of these three models is compatible with an account of the economy in which history might be said to matter in determining the direction and development of the economy. This chapter makes use of Dutt's path-dependency model of Keynes's thinking to produce – if not an account of an economy moving in true historical time – none the less an account in which the past can be seen to have a pattern of determinate effects on later time periods. The purpose in doing so is to begin to uncover the sorts of behavioural phenomena such an analysis implies – phenomena which would receive fuller investigation in a genuinely historical analysis of the economy. The main assumption underlying the chapter is that the most important dividing line between Post Keynesianism and New Keynesianism concerns the degrees of realism in their respective understandings of individual behaviour. New Keynesians are strongly attached to formal, rational choice models, whereas Post Keynesians' concern with time, ignorance and uncertainty requires abandonment of static optimizing behavioural analysis and attention to decision making in concrete, historical circumstances. To sharpen this point, then, the chapter builds onto Dutt's path-dependency analysis of Keynes's thinking a Post Keynesian account of individual economic behaviour in terms of recent findings from the psychological literature on economic behaviour critical of rationality theory.

In the first section below, Dutt's discussion of Kregel's three models in Keynes is briefly reviewed to isolate the properties of Keynes's shifting equilibrium model that favour an account of the economy as path-dependent. In the section second, recent experimental evidence on the psychology of individual decision making consistent with there being a role for history in the economy is briefly summarized. In the third section, I supply an interpretation of Keynes's thinking in relation to this recent evidence about decision making that makes use of his own emphasis on the role conventions play in the economy. The final section draws conclusions about the heuristics of Keynes's models and the differences between New Keynesianism and Post Keynesianism.

STATIC, STATIONARY AND SHIFTING EQUILIBRIUM MODELS

Kregel calls the model in which individuals' long-period price expectations, E, are constant and short-period price expectations e are realized Keynes's static model, the model in which E is constant but e may be disappointed and changing Keynes's stationary model, and the model in which E is shifting and e may be disappointed Keynes's shifting equilibrium model. Only in the last, as the idea of shifting equilibrium suggests, are e and E interdependent. The static model appears only in Keynes's 1937 lectures, where it can be argued that in response to his critics and possible misunderstanding Keynes simplified his arguments from *The General Theory* to hammer home the single point that 'the theory of effective demand is substantially the same if we assume that short-period expectations are always fulfilled' (Keynes, 1973, p. 181). This suggests that he found the stationary model tactically inopportune, since obviously he knew short-period expectations were regularly disappointed, and thus that the static and stationary models were together a conceptualization alternative to the shifting equilibrium model. It also seems fair to say that Keynes principally used the stationary/static model when he thought a simplified exposition of his underemployment analysis required temporarily putting aside interdependence between e and E. The shifting equilibrium model described how the economy moved from one underemployment equilibrium to another, and might consequently only be appreciated once economists were disabused of their Say's Law commitments.

Does the shifting equilibrium model capture the idea of an economy in historical time? Dutt argues that how seriously we take the equilibrium method generally in Keynes's thinking depends upon the relative weight placed on two different purposes for which the method can be used: 'to examine some qualitative property of the equilibrium position, and... to attach some real-world significance to the precise position of that equilibrium' (1991–2, pp. 218–19). Keynes's main purpose clearly – given that reigning classical theory presupposed the equilibrium method – was to show that unemployment equilibria were possible, and, thus, to exhibit this particular qualitative property of equilibria obtained. From the perspective of this goal, 'Issues regarding the path-dependence of equilibrium, and the role of history, were no concern of his: wherever the economy ended up, it was possible for it to end with unemployed labor' (ibid., p. 219). But, Dutt adds, this focus is compatible with also arguing that the economy was path-dependent, nor would doing so undermine Keynes's main goal in qualitative analysis.[2] And that Keynes also developed the shifting equilibrium model in *The General Theory* gives good reason to think this other goal was important to him also.

It is reasonable to ask, then, how the shifting equilibrium model may be thought to approximate an analysis of the economy in historical time. Suppose first, Dutt suggests, that the interdependence between e and E in the model arises from assuming that disappointed short-period expectations[3] reasonably cause firms to alter their long-period expectations, so that $E = E(e)$ and $E' > 0$, as firms extrapolate the near future into the distant future. This results in three possibilities.[4] First, a unique stable equilibrium may indeed exist (provided short-period expectations adjust adaptively), should we assume that the relationship between E and e reflects only current expectations. Here history does not matter. Second, the short-period equilibrium may also be unstable (when investment is highly responsive to changes in long-period expectations, and long-period expectations are highly responsive to changes in short-period expectations). Here equilibrium does not matter. Third, under certain circumstances pertaining to the relationship between e and the price of output, there may also be multiple equilibria, where whether stable short-period equilibria are achieved depends upon the economy's starting-point. Here history matters.

Can the first case, then, be said to be Keynes's? Dutt's analysis is meant to show that a necessary condition for the economy to possess a unique stable equilibrium not dependent upon the economy's starting point and independent of the economy's dynamic path is that current levels of E depend on current levels of e. But clearly it is not very plausible to say that current disappointed short-period price expectations alone determine current long-period price expectations. Firms undoubtedly also consider past realized and unrealized short-period expectations in formulating long-period expectations, and accordingly Dutt recommends that E be thought also to depend upon lagged values of e. Thus suppose that $E_t = S^T k_{t-i} e_{t-i}$, the k_j are weights and T is the length of the firm's memory. Then the final equilibrium is path-dependent in that the final level of E will depend upon the path by which e adjusts, and history matters in determining the position of the economy in equilibrium. Dutt notes that this path-dependence depends upon the asymmetry in his analysis between how expectations are formed when short-period expectations are realized and how they are formed when they are not. He interprets this to mean that memory plays a role for firms when short-period expectations are disappointed, but has no role when they are realized (because then e and E cease to be interdependent). More specifically, firms remember their mistakes, and act to change what they regard as mistakes, but see no reason to change what they are doing when their expectations are fulfilled.

This is surely a reasonable thing to say about the psychology of decision making in firms and indeed with respect to human behaviour generally. But whether we should regard Keynes's shifting equilibrium model as one that makes history matter in this way, and indeed whether Post Keynesians should give weight to Keynes's shifting equilibrium model or develop alternative modes of historical analysis requires further argument. I address the first of these issues in the next two sections of this chapter by, first, looking at some recent experimental evidence concerning the psychology of individual decision making to see what general sorts of phenomena might underlie a memory that emphasizes mistakes and errors, and by, second, then turning to an account of Keynes's thinking about conventions in the economy that draws on similar considerations. Comment on the latter issue of how Post Keynesians should look upon the shifting equilibrium model in addressing the nature of time is reserved for the concluding section.

THE PLACE OF ERROR IN MEMORY: RECENT EVIDENCE FROM EMPIRICAL PSYCHOLOGY

Here I only attempt to draw attention to a small portion of the empirical literature from psychologists that has attracted the interest of economists increasingly sceptical in recent years of the adequacy of the traditional axiomatization of rational choice. Of course economists have had doubts of this sort since the early work of Simon (1957) on bounded rationality and Allais' (1952) thought experiments (see Allais and Hagen, 1979) challenging the independence axiom of expected utility theory, but it has only been in the last decade and a half that confidence in the a priori deductive method of explaining choice seems to have begun to be seriously shaken (e.g. Sugden, 1991). Three phenomena are described here: loss aversion, preference reversals, and time-inconsistent preferences. In each case, I argue that the phenomenon in question might contribute to an account of individual behaviour in which a memory of mistakes has a role in influencing expectations of the future.

Loss aversion

Kahneman and Tversky (1984) have drawn attention to an asymmetry in ascriptions of value they term loss aversion, whereby individuals feel that the disutility involved in giving up an object exceeds the utility associated with acquiring it. Loss aversion may be understood to imply that individuals' evaluation of risky outcomes tends to reflect a status quo bias, so that there may well be important irreversibilities in our preferences. Recall that the standard theory of rational choice assumes that indifference curves are reversible in the sense that an individual regarding two bundles of goods as equally valuable should be indifferent between having one and trading it for the other and having the second and trading it for the first. Having a status quo bias or being loss averse means that this may often not be the case, and that in certain circumstances indifference curves may even cross one another (cf. Knetsch, 1990). Individuals faced with objects of equal value in their own view thus tend to prefer those objects that they already possess, even when this violation of the transitivity axiom implies that they may be irrational in the specific sense of being a potential money pump.[5]

That preferences may often be irreversible clearly raises serious questions about the adequacy and generality of the standard theory of rational choice that assumes individuals possess stable and unchanging preference orders. Tversky and Kahneman (1991) have thus developed an alternative preference theory that explains how indifference curves may be indexed to reference levels that count as status quo factors for individuals. One advantage of such an approach is that it improves on rational choice models ignoring individuals' status quo bias that generally predict 'greater instability than is observed in the world' (Samuelson and Zeckhauser, 1988). Another advantage of their approach is that its emphasis upon irreversibilities in individuals' evaluation of risky outcomes serves to place important emphasis upon how choice may be embedded in historical time as opposed to logical time. That individuals tend to exhibit status quo bias might be understood to reflect their concern with an uncertain future (in regard to both states of nature and the qualities of goods), and thus count as an effective demonstration of the idea that the conditions needed to apply subjective probability theory to the world do not always hold.

What is the implication of loss aversion and status quo bias for Keynes's shifting equilibrium model interpreted as a path-dependent analysis? On the argument that we disproportionately remember our mistakes, fulfilled short-period expectations might be regarded as choices that involve no departure from the status quo and no mistakes, i.e. as status-quo-preserving choices. In contrast, when short-period expectations are not realized, they might be seen as mistakes about which the firm felt a special aversion. On this view, one should not confuse mistakes associated with loss aversion with business or personal losses *per se*, since clearly some of a firm's mistakes may be associated with expectations that are, as it were, overfulfilled, as when a firm's price and sales are better than expected. From the perspective of how short-period expectations influence long-period expectations, that the former are under-or over-fulfilled would always have some impact on the latter. Loss aversion, then, is more a matter of how a relatively settled state of affairs, as manifest in a set of short-period expectations, is disturbed, either unfavourably or favourably. From the point of view of human psychology, individuals are thus more comfortable with modest or no change whatsoever in their environment when faced with the task of evaluating risky future prospects.

Preference reversals

One of the best-known psychological results that challenges standard rational choice theory concerns preference reversals. First demonstrated by Lichtenstein and Slovic (1971, 1973), and then replicated by many others, preference reversals occur when individuals are asked, first, to choose between two gambles of nearly the same expected value (one with a high chance of winning a small prize and one a low chance of winning a large prize), and, second, to price each of those gambles. Most subjects choose the high-chance–small-prize gamble, but then put a higher price on the low-chance–high-prize gamble, thus exhibiting what has come to be known as preference reversal. Interestingly, Grether and Plott designed a set of experiments explicitly meant 'to discredit the psychologists' work as applied to economics' (1979, p. 623), but found themselves unable to do so. They concluded that 'no optimisation principles of any sort lie behind the simplest of human choices and that the uniformities in human choice behaviour which lie behind market behaviour may result from principles which are of a completely different sort than generally accepted' (ibid.).

Subsequent research has focused on explaining the various possible causes of preference reversals. Some have thus supposed that preference reversals involved intransitive preferences, and proposed non-transitive preference choice models to address the problem (e.g. Loomes and Sudgen, 1983). Other researchers questioned the formulation of payoff schemes in such a manner as to test the independence axiom of expected utility theory (e.g. Karni and Safra, 1987). Finally, a third set of researchers tested procedure invariance or whether alternative ways of presenting a choice always give rise to the same ordering (Slovic *et al.*, 1990). The latter argued that intransitivities and payoff schemes explained only a relatively small share of preference reversals, while a failure of procedure invariance accounts for a large portion of preference reversals. They also argued that procedure invariance breakdowns could be seen to be related to the compatibility of stimulus and response for experimental subjects involved in decisions involving both choice and pricing, reasoning that individuals grasp some stimuli more readily than others.

How is this research relevant to Keynes and the issue of path-dependency? The failure of procedure invariance implies that different ways of presenting a choice to individuals change the way in which they order the options before them. In the view of Slovic *et al.* (ibid.), it suggests that individuals may not have stable and unchanging preferences which are elicited in one situation after another, and that preference is (at least in part) context dependent. Such a state of affairs would be just what one would expect if the economic process occurred in historical rather logical time. Indeed it would be consistent with Katzner's view that 'history is created period by period', when there are 'steady alterations in the epistemic statuses and decision opportunities of individuals as they learn of and experience new things' (1993, p. 343). It would also be consistent with memory of mistakes possessing an important role in choice if mistakes in short-period expectations were to transform the opportunities firms faced. If unrealized expectations, as contrasted to realized ones, were to alter 'the epistemic statuses and decision opportunities of individuals', then firms might exhibit preference reversals and the economy then behave in a path-dependent manner.

Time-inconsistent preferences

Another well-established anomaly from the perspective of rational choice theory is the phenomenon of time-inconsistent preferences associated with intertemporal choice. It has long been recognized that individuals may well exhibit negative, declining and variable time discount rates, as opposed to the constant rates that standard theory predicts. Strotz (1955) thus demonstrated that dynamic inconsistencies in behaviour of the sort involving discount rates that decline over time imply that individuals consume more in the future than their earlier plans had permitted. Elster (1979) argued that individuals who revise their earlier consumption plans gone awry with the passage of time ought to be said to reflect a second-best rationality. A number of researchers have looked upon intertemporal choice as a manifestation of internal conflict between an individual's multiple selves, bringing up Arrow-type difficulties for intrapersonal as compared to interpersonal collective choice (Thaler and Shefrin, 1981; Schelling, 1984).

Psychologists have termed any tendency to favour the present over the future myopia. Its extent can depend upon a variety of factors including how choices are framed for individuals and whether they look upon future benefits or costs with favour or dread. In connection with the framing idea, it has been shown that individuals react differently to relative money amount differences and absolute money amount differences (Lowenstein and Prelec, 1989). Benzion *et al.* (1989) have shown that individuals discount time differently according to how far off a gain or loss lies in the future. Lowenstein (1987) showed that the maximum payments individuals would make to obtain or avoid various future outcomes also varied according to the perceived pleasantness or unpleasantness of the outcome. More generally, individuals appear to react differently to the prospects of gains as compared to losses in the future. These and other similar results suggest intertemporal choice involves additional complications to our understanding of complexities of choice at a point in time.

Intertemporal choice inconsistencies, however, are especially relevant to an investigation of how history might matter in the economy. If individuals systematically mis-estimate gains and losses at different points in the future, and often then find themselves in a position of wanting to revise their past choices, then they not only make mistakes regularly, but just as regularly make adjustments in their situations to accommodate those mistakes. Long-period expectations on this view would be sensitive to lagged values of short-period expectations in that firms would likely come to recognize general patterns of short-period expectation failure. Specifically, if errors regarding future values are a persistent feature of decision making, firms would be unable to correct for their future mistakes in advance, and would find it their best – or more accurately second-best – strategy to put themselves in a position regularly to discover and adjust to past mistakes. The economy would then be path-dependent in the sense that in each period decision makers would find themselves in the position of having to discover new phenomena that could not previously have been anticipated.

KEYNES AND CONVENTION

Might Keynes have allowed that such psychological phenomena as loss aversion, preference reversals, and time-inconsistent preferences may play a role in the development of the economy over time? Though traditional choice-theoretic reasoning underlies parts of *The General Theory*, Keynes also drew attention to the animal spirits of entrepreneurs as that 'spontaneous urge to action rather than inaction' (1973a, p. 161), and thus clearly did not believe that individuals always behaved as constrained maximizers. In addition, many of Keynes's other writings on history and policy, such as *The Economic Consequences of the Peace*, demonstrate insight into the psychological complexities of character and personality, and it thus seems not unrealistic to suppose that Keynes developed his understanding of the behaviour of entrepreneurs and speculators alongside his understanding of politicians, Treasury officials and artists. In any event, here I put aside what Keynes might himself have thought, and suppose that there is enough in the overall framework of *The General Theory* to allow that a history of mistakes made in forming short-period expectations possesses a role in determining long-period expectations. On this analysis, Keynes's shifting equilibrium model can be understood to treat the economy as if it were path-dependent, and to do so on account of the sorts of psychological characteristics of individual decision making that have been the subject of recent interest in the empirical literature on rational choice.

To flesh out this argument I turn to a subject on which Keynes appears to have been most alive to a richer account of behaviour and individual reasoning: that is, his thinking about the role of conventions in the economy, specifically in connection with firms' investment decisions. My strategy is to look at how Keynes thought conventions acted as a framework for individual decision making that might have enabled individuals to adjust to the sorts of psychological anomalies discussed above. We know that Keynes thought that individuals relied upon conventions when uncertainty about the future and presumably ignorance about the past limit rationality. But just how do conventions play this role in this decision making? More to the point, what specific difficulties in decision making do the special characteristics Keynes attributed to conventions permit individuals to address? On the argument here, since psychological anomalies of the sort described in the recent literature arise specifically in atomistic reasoning contexts, it is the atomistic nature of rational choice reasoning that conventions may be said to address and counter-balance. Conventions thus assist individual decision making by providing an interactionist framework for choice in comparison with what atomistic rational choice theory assumes.

First, then, how did Keynes understand conventions? I have argued elsewhere (Davis, 1994) that Keynes's philosophical development led him to take conventions to be (dynamic) structures of interdependent individual expectations.[6] Conventions, that is, are not habits of mind, rules of thumb, or customary practices that an individual might elect to consult, but rather modes of interaction between individuals all forming judgements on related matters. This comes out most clearly in Keynes's treatment of investment in *The General Theory*, in which the convention 'that the existing state of affairs will continue indefinitely, except in so far as we have specific reason to expect a change' (1973a, p. 156) is analysed in terms of the interplay between average expectation and individual expectation regarding the value of any given investment. Average expectation is redetermined daily as individual investors bid and offer equity issues at various prices. Individual expectations adjust daily in response to the changing average expectation of the market recorded as end-of-the-day values. Thus the 'existing state of affairs' regarding any set of investment prospects 'will continue indefinitely' as long as the average expectation regarding those investments remains relatively settled; that is, until a large enough number of individual investors 'have specific reason to expect a change' in the value of those investments.

This interaction that conventions tend to structure between individuals, in Keynes's treatment of both investment and money markets, has been recognized by many readers of *The General Theory*. Less often emphasized, however, has been what makes the interaction Keynes describes an interaction in which individuals are also interdependent with one another in the very process of decision making. To see this difference, we may make a distinction between an individual reacting to the choices others make, as, say, reflected in market outcomes, and an individual reacting to the thinking others are thought to employ in making their choices. Keynes emphasizes that when individual investors try to outguess the market or 'outwit the crowd' (p. 155) they actually try to anticipate the thinking of other investors. They are not content, that is, to act only on the basis of how others actually invest, but also attempt to construe how others reach their conclusions about how, when and why to invest, in order then to be in a position to form an 'opinion of what average opinion expects average opinion to be' (p. 156).[7]

The sort of reasoning that an attention to the thinking of others requires differs in one important respect from what is typically assumed about the reasoning process of economic agents. Whereas traditional rational choice analysis supposes individuals only make use of their own preferences, to form judgements about the thinking of others one needs to be able to see things from their point of view, or attempt to grasp the nature of their preferences. One needs, in effect, to place oneself in the shoes of one's competitors. Reasoning of this sort may be termed analogical in that it involves individuals working out their own thoughts by using the thinking of other individuals they suppose to be like themselves and in similar circumstances as reference points. It represents a significant departure from traditional atomistic decision making in which inference from tastes and circumstances to choice is assumed to be strictly autonomous, Robinson Crusoe style, in that it allows individuals may determine or 'complete' their own preferences by imagining those of others. Of course in Keynes's view, investors and speculators were not a collection of independent Robinson Crusoes, since when the opinions of the crowd mattered more than the underlying essentials of an investment, individual investors were likely to cobble together patterns of inference for themselves out of what appeared to be successful intuitions and insights on the part of others. The passing of the age of enterprise with the separation of ownership and management thus produced a new form of reasoning in the speculative practices of modern investment markets, and this gave conventions as structures of interdependent decision making a central role in the operation of the economy.

Generally, then, the reason why one would wish to think conventions were important in economies with significant uncertainty about the future and ignorance about the past is straightforward. When rationality is limited in these ways, one obvious and available means of attempting to enhance one's decision-making capacity is to survey and make use of the reasoning of others who are similarly constrained. Keynes's treatment of time and uncertainty can thus be said to presuppose the proposition that atomistic individual rationality is not just bounded but also inadequate as an account of the interdependent decision-making process in which individuals actually engage. But how does this general conclusion apply to the psychological phenomena above that have been of recent interest in the literature on choice anomalies? I have already suggested that loss aversion, preference reversals, and time-inconsistent preferences could be associated with circumstances in which individuals' long-period expectations are influenced by their mistakes in forming short-period expectations. What remains to be done is to say how these sorts of phenomena might play a role in Keynes's shifting equilibrium model by saying how these problems in atomistic individual rationality were the sorts of problems Keynes thought conventions addressed. More specifically, what remains to be done is to show that loss inversion, preference reversals and time-inconsistent preferences produce in individuals a recourse to the sort of analogical thinking that conventions as structures of truly interdependent expectations make possible.

Loss aversion and conventions

In the case of loss aversion, we saw that individuals tend to exhibit a status quo bias in their evaluation of risky prospects, and that this implied the existence of important irreversibilities in taste and intransitive preferences. Tversky and Kahneman (1991) built upon this evidence in developing an alternative preference theory in which indifference curves are indexed to reference levels that constitute status quo factors for individuals. If we interpret this in terms of how a history of mistakes regarding short-period expectations influences the formation of long-period expectations, then the economy may be said to be path dependent in part because of the phenomenon of loss aversion. If we now add to this account Keynes's thinking about conventions as structures of interdependent expectations, it can be argued that the reference levels Tversky and Kahneman conceptualize correspond to average expectations regarding firm pricing success and investment values across markets. Investors form their individual expectations with the most recent evidence from the market in mind. Their uncertainty about the future impels them to investigate whether past short-period expectations have been fulfilled, and to incorporate this information in forming their long-period expectations. They do this by considering others' views about short-period performance and the prospects for various investments. Individual expectations are then interdependent and dependent upon a complex system of reference points comprising measures of different market's average performance and individuals' various assessments of that average performance. If we take the formation of long-period expectations to reflect attention to unfulfilled short-period expectations in this way, Keynes's understanding of conventions as structures of interdependence can be thought to make the loss aversion and status quo bias analysis of Kahneman and Tversky a part of the story of an economy's path dependency.

Preference reversals and conventions

We saw that preference reversals arise when individuals prefer one of a pair of risky gambles, but place a higher price on the other. We also saw that though one set of researchers has attributed preference reversals to intransitive preferences and another has attributed them to problems in the formulation of payoff schemes (and expected utility theory's independence axiom), a case can be made for saying that most preference reversals derive from breakdowns in procedure invariance, where at issue is the compatibility for individuals of stimulus and possible response. For Slovic *et al.* (1990), this opens up the possibility that, contrary to traditional rationality theory, preferences may not be stable and unchanging, but rather are often formed in specific contexts. Such a view would be consistent with what Keynes's suggestions regarding analogical reasoning and conventions would allow about how individuals constitute their own reasoning processes. When speculators borrow inferences and thinking from rivals and colleagues, their preferences are indirectly influenced by other's preferences, so that, to the extent that individuals have their own preferences, interdependent judgement guarantees that those preferences are always in a state of development. Then, as Katzner says, history could be thought to develop 'period-by-period', in that steady alteration in the terms on which interdependent individuals reason about their current and past experience would transform the opportunities they faced in an uncertain future.

Time-inconsistent preferences and conventions

Time-inconsistent preferences are associated with perverse discount rates and the phenomenon of individuals revising their consumption plans as the future becomes the present. The myopia psychologists see this reflecting is often interpreted to be the product of various cognitive framing effects, where, for example, individuals tend to assess future prospects differently according to whether they look upon them with favour or dread. An interesting contribution to this literature on the part of economists concerns multiple selves analysis. They argue that just as there are a variety of interpersonal collective choice problems, so there may also be said to be a variety of parallel intrapersonal collective choice problems in which the single individual is seen to possess multiple utility functions. Such an analysis, it seems, is not much removed from what Keynes believes to be involved in conventions as structures of interdependent judgement. Thus to the extent that investors try to anticipate 'what average opinion expects average opinion to be' (1973a, p. 156), they effectively acquire multiple selves whose opinions compete with one another in such a manner that the voice that periodically emerges as uppermost for the individual investor is often enough later seen as ill-advised and myopic. Certainly time-inconsistent preferences and perverse discount rates are no stranger to speculation. Long-period expectation formation here too, then, might be said to be the product of past patterns of unfulfilled short-period expectations.

CONCLUDING REMARKS

Keynes has generally been understood to have placed considerable emphasis upon demonstrating that an economy in equilibrium could have unemployment. Indeed his attention to the static model version of his theory in his post-*General Theory* writings is commonly taken as a tactic for communicating with readers strongly wedded to equilibrium thinking. This hardly implies, however, that he thought the economy was not path-dependent or that history did not matter to the development of the economy. Indeed, a case can be made for just such a view based on Dutt's interpretation of Keynes's shifting equilibrium model. It should be noted, then, that the discussion here is not meant to imply that, given a longer life, Keynes would have built upon an interaction between short-period and long-period expectations in the manner of this chapter to utilize the sort of recent psychological evidence regarding individual behaviour the chapter surveys. It is rather meant to show, first, that Keynes's understanding of conventions as structures of interdependent expectations reflects an understanding of human decision making that draws on themes similar in nature to those in recent empirical research in psychology, and, second, that this shared view of human decision making permits an account of the economy operating in historical time. From this perspective, it is suggested that Keynes's views about interactive decision making combined with recent empirical research in psychology provide foundations for a Post Keynesian account of individual economic behaviour in real time that is significantly different to that which New Keynesianism allows.

This last point deserves comment. Arguably one important reason why traditional, ISLM Keynesians have been unable to respond effectively to the New Classicals' attack on Keynesian thinking in recent years is that they accepted the neoclassical claim that macroeconomic thinking needs to be erected on a microfoundations base of atomistic rational choice theory. New Keynesian thinking in this respect represents not a return to Keynes, but rather an effort to supplement traditional Keynesian theory with rational expectations–rational choice foundations that are complicated by information asymmetries, strategic complementarity, imperfect competition, etc. Keynes, we might say, anticipated this kind of New Keynesian innovation with his own emphasis upon the limitations in human decision making and individuals' consequent recourse to conventional behaviour. Post Keynesians recognize this distinctive element in Keynes's views when they emphasize the importance of uncertainty about the future. The recommendation of this chapter is that Post Keynesians should further supplement this insight with an account of ignorance about the past and in terms of a general view of decision making in historical time.

ACKNOWLEDGEMENTS

The author is indebted without implication to Amitava Duff, Tracy Mott, Steve Pressman, Roy Rotheim, Jochen Runde, and two anonymous readers for comments on an earlier version of this chapter.

NOTES

1 The debate originated in Davidson's assertion that 'hysteresis does not deal with the impact of those societal historical changes which create a true uncertainty environment for many economic decisions' (1991, p. 133). Davidson (1993) is a response to Cross's argument that hysteretic processes are non-ergodic.
2 Though it does rule out that technocratic fine-tuning of the economy by fiscal and monetary policy means is possible.
3 The analysis of disappointed short-period expectations is put in all-or-nothing terms to simplify the discussion. As one (anonymous) reader to the chapter pointed out, expectations normally comprehend a range of possible outcomes.
4 See Dutt (1991–2) for exposition of the model on which the following depends.
5 Were an individual's preferences intransitive ($a > b > c > a$) and the individual willing to pay some amount to exchange a less preferred for a more preferred good, others could trade with this individual until 'pumping out' all of the individual's money or wealth.
6 See Littleboy (1990) for a general discussion of Keynes on convention.
7 Keynes allows that this sort of higher-order 'second' guessing may occur in many markets.

10

ELEMENTS OF CONFLICT IN UK WAGE DETERMINATION

Philip Arestis and Iris Biefang-Frisancho Mariscal

INTRODUCTION

Wage determination is the outcome of a decentralized bargaining process where distributional conflict arises over relative income shares (Rowthorn, 1977). Conflict, however, does not only arise between workers and capitalists: there is, furthermore, the influence of wage relativities on wage formation (Keynes, 1936, and more recently Skott, 1991) which can play an important role in explaining wage stickiness. Wage efficiency theories as well as hysteresis models (Shapiro and Stiglitz, 1984; Lindbeck and Snower, 1986; Blanchard and Summers, 1987) may also be embedded into this framework as complementary theories, providing further reasons why wages do not fall to clear the market. These theories are compatible with the framework proposed in this chapter but our approach differs from most other contributions in two areas: we emphasize the importance of wage relativities and the existence of conflict over the functional distribution of income. Clearly, there are differences between the Post Keynesian 'real wage resistance' hypothesis, the very Keynesian 'wage relativities' hypothesis and the more labour-market-oriented model of 'wage efficiency' and 'hysteresis', which adopt a New Keynesian perspective. This chapter, however, demonstrates that so long as conflict elements are the focus of the analysis, the three theories can sit comfortably in a model which is validated by the UK experience.

This chapter comprises five sections: the first is the introductory section; the second section is concerned with the investigation of the constituent theories which are ultimately combined in a general model. The sections that follow are concerned with the empirical aspects of the model. The third section looks at the steady-state properties of our wage model, the fourth section will provide an application to the dynamic counterpart of the model, and the fifth section will summarize and conclude the chapter.

THE THEORETICAL MODEL

The model put forward in this section draws on the four theoretical propositions mentioned above: on the notion of an aspiration gap, that of wage relativities, on aspects of the 'wage efficiency' hypothesis, and on hysteresis elements. We begin with conflict considerations.

Conflict and the aspiration gap

This section deals with the conflict over relative income shares in the private sector (Rowthorn, 1977)[1]. The mechanism may be described as follows: on a firm-by-firm basis workers negotiate wage increases. Assuming that in the wage settlement allowance is made for future inflation, the negotiated wage will provide workers with a certain real take-home pay. In addition, if inflation is anticipated and productivity is constant, it also provides them with a negotiated share of private sector income. Capitalists who receive a residual negotiated profit share (r^n) will, after the wage settlement, set prices according to their target profit share (r^*). We have now two potentially different profit shares, one negotiated with regard to a certain expected rate of inflation, the other which capitalists seek to achieve through their pricing policy. If the negotiated and the target profit share do not match, conflict will arise as capitalist pricing policy is inconsistent with what was negotiated in the bargaining process so that workers' actual wage falls short of the negotiated wage share. The degree of conflict is measured by the aspiration gap ($r^* - r^{\mathrm{n}}$). Social, economic and political factors (z), as well as demand, determine capitalists' and workers' market power and thus the aspiration gap. Demand, which acts as a regulator of conflict, imposes on the side of the union restrictions on wage claims and on the side of the firm restrictions in price increases. Assuming that there is a close correlation between conditions in the product market and the labour market, unemployment (u) may be a good indicator of demand conditions in both markets.

This analysis suggests that if workers try to make up for disappointed wage aspirations, a modified version of the Rowthorn model may be summarized as in (1) below, where $r^* - r^{\mathrm{n}}$ influences now nominal wages instead of prices as in the original Rowthorn (1977) model:

$$W_{t+1} = P^{\mathrm{e}} h(r^* - r^{\mathrm{n}}, u, z) \tag{1}$$

where the variables are as defined above, and P^{e} is expected price inflation. A positive aspiration gap implies that workers' share of private sector income falls below the negotiated share so that conflict arises ($r'^* > 0$, $r'^{\mathrm{n}} < 0$), where the prime denotes first partial derivative. Unions are the more successful in their wage claim, the lower the unemployment rate is ($u_1 < 0$) and the more favourable economic and ideological factors are ($z_1 > 0$).

Keynes's wage relativities

Conflict between different groups within the same broad income category can also have an impact on wage determination. Keynes (1936) emphasized that workers resisted money-wage cuts not so much because they feared a cut in their absolute real wage, but more because they feared a decline in their relative position in the wage structure. The implication of this explanation is that if the general wage level is expected to rise, then each group of workers will demand wage increases so as to maintain their relative position in the wage hierarchy. It is also postulated that an increase in unemployment may reduce workers' wage demands. At the aggregate level the argument can be formalized as

$$W = f(u, W^e) \tag{2}$$

with $u_1 < 0$ and $W^e_1 > 0$, where W^e is the expected average wage level. Wage expectations will not always be fulfilled, but in the long run the restriction $W = W^e$ is assumed.

Efficiency wage elements

Unions can only be successful in their wage claims if firms are willing to meet the unions' demands. Efficiency wage theories try to give an answer to why it is profitable for the firm even in times of excess supply of labour not to change the prevailing wage structure. Efficiency wage models suggest that the cost of labour is simultaneously determined by the real wage payment and workers' effort. Firms then seek to minimize the cost of effective labour, balancing the direct cost of a wage payment against its positive effect on effort (Bowles and Boyer, 1988). If firms ignore the effect of real wages on labour productivity, this may increase firms' labour cost through a reduction in labour effort, increased labour turnover and ultimately through industrial action.

The worker's wage demand in the efficiency wage framework is an increasing function of the cost of job loss which itself is determined by the relative attractiveness of opportunities workers have inside and outside the firm, that is to say, the real wage the representative firm offers (W_i/P), the real wage paid by other firms (W_j/P), the real income from unemployment (W_u/P) and the rate of unemployment (u). Conventionally, the effort function is determined by each worker's utility of leisure, consumption and effort. Contrary to the conventional approach, the effort function here is influenced by workers' and employers' actions both individually and collectively through unions, employers' associations and the state. These collective interactions create the environment in which workers react to different wage offers with strikes or other forms of industrial action, depending on their relative strength *vis-à-vis* these institutions (Rowthorn, 1977; Arestis, 1986).

Efficiency wage theories assume that firms can set real wages. In fact, wages are negotiated and wage settlements determine nominal wages so that allowance for price expectations is made. As neither firms nor workers have complete information about wage differentials (W_j/P), they are replaced by expected average real wages (W^e/P^e). The aggregate wage function is then

$$W_{t+1} = P^e_{t+1}\, g(u, W^e_{u,t+1}/P^e_{t+1}, W^e_{t+1}/P^e_{t+1}, z) \tag{3}$$

An increase in real benefits $\left((W_u/P)_1 > 0\right)$ and/or a reduction in unemployment ($u_1 < 0$) reduce workers' cost of dismissal. In order to maintain a 'normal' level of effort, which secures firms' target profit, firms may be inclined to accept higher wage demands.

Up to this stage, all theories have emphasized the role that unemployment plays in containing wage demands. The existence of unemployment discourages workers' militancy and restrains excessive wage demands. Each group of workers attempts to restore wage relativities which it regards as fair, considering price inflation and wage movements in other groups. Without unemployment, conflict over relative income shares will cause inflation. Furthermore, high unemployment reduces the probability of a worker finding an alternative job in the case of dismissal. A worker will avoid shirking, increase work effort and increase productivity in order to secure his or her job. The implications are that unemployment prevents a process of accelerating wage inflation.

Hysteresis effects

We turn our attention next to the dynamics of the unemployment function which introduces the notion of hysteresis in the analysis. Following Nickell (1987), we assume that the unemployment function is concave as at high unemployment rates additional job seekers have little downward impact on wage determination. The dynamics of unemployment introduce hysteresis through (a) the duration of unemployment and (b) membership dynamics. Duration theories stress the negative effects of the duration of unemployment on human capital and subsequent effective labour supply (Hargreaves-Heap, 1980; Clark and Summers, 1982). There are mainly three candidates which contribute to the explanation of duration effects: deterioration of skills, changes in motivation and/or search behaviour, and the perception of firms of such differences between long-term and short-term unemployed (Blanchard and Diamond, 1990). Initially high unemployment decreases wages, but gradually its effect declines. Consequently, in the short run a large increase in unemployment exerts a large pressure on wages, while persistent high unemployment rates mitigate this effect (Nickell, 1990). Insider–outsider theories relate wages more to the demand conditions facing the employed worker than to 'outsider' pressure exerted by the unemployed. The basic idea here is that insiders only care about the currently employed and that they can set wages so as to preserve their employment, because they have some degree of monopoly power (Lindbeck and Snower, 1986). If we define as insiders those who are employed or recently unemployed and as outsiders those who have been unemployed for a long time, we may combine elements of both theories. These considerations lead to a specification of wage determination where wage inflation depends inversely on current unemployment and recent changes in unemployment, or, alternatively, in explicitly introducing elements of duration and membership theories. With reference to the former approach, the effect of unemployment on wages may be specified as (Layard *et al.* 1991)

$$W = l(\dot{u}_t, u_t) \tag{4}$$

with $\dot{u}_t = u_t - u_{t-1}$.

The combined model

We may now combine wage aspiration effects, the relative wage hypothesis, efficiency wage theory and hysteresis effects in one general model to arrive at equation (5):

$$W_{t+1} = P^{\mathrm{e}}_{t+1}\; k(u_t, \dot{u}_t, W^{\mathrm{e}}_{u,t+1}/P^{\mathrm{e}}_{t+1}, W^{\mathrm{e}}_{t+1}/P^{\mathrm{e}}_{t+1}, r^{\mathrm{e}}_{t+1}, r^{\mathrm{n}}_{t}, x_t) \tag{5}$$

where the target profit share r^* is replaced by the expected profit share r^{e}_{t+1} and the z variable by strikes or other forms of industrial action (x). We also define a simple profit function as follows.[2] If we assume that the rate of profit is proportional to the profit share (r), then we may write (Skott, 1991)

$$r = \frac{PQ - WL}{PQ} = \frac{PQ}{PQ} - \frac{W}{P}\frac{L}{Q} = 1 - \frac{W}{P}\frac{1}{Y} \tag{6}$$

where Q stands for output, L for employed labour and Y for productivity.

Substituting (6) into (5) and assuming that k in (5) is additively separable and log–linear, we may write

$$\begin{aligned} w_{t+1} =& p^{\mathrm{e}}_{t+1} + \alpha_1(w^{\mathrm{e}}_{u,\,t+1} - p^{\mathrm{e}}_{t+1}) + \alpha_2(w^{\mathrm{e}}_{t+1} - p^{\mathrm{e}}_{t+1}) + \alpha_3(p^{\mathrm{e}}_{t+1} + Y^{e}_{t+1} - w^{\mathrm{e}}_{t+1}) \\ & - \alpha_4(p_t + y_t - w_t) + \alpha_5 x_t - \alpha_6 u_t - \alpha_7 \dot{u}_t + \varepsilon_t \end{aligned} \tag{7}$$

where lower-case letters stand for the logarithm of the relevant variable and ε_t is a disturbance term. Equation (7) may be written as (Arestis and Skott, 1993)

$$\begin{aligned} w_{t+1} - w_t =& (1 - \alpha_1 - \alpha_2 + \alpha_3)(p^{\mathrm{e}}_{t+1} - p_t) + \alpha_1(w^{\mathrm{e}}_{u,\,t+1} - w_{u,\,t}) \\ & + (\alpha_2 - \alpha_3)(w^{\mathrm{e}}_{t+1} - w_t) + \alpha_3(y^{\mathrm{e}}_{t+1} - y_t) + (\alpha_2 - 1)(w_t - p_t) \\ & + \alpha_1(w_{u,t} - p_t) + (\alpha_3 - \alpha_4)(p_t + y_t - w_t) + \alpha_5 x_t \\ & - \alpha_6 u_t - \alpha_7 \dot{u}_t + \varepsilon_t \end{aligned} \tag{8}$$

Approaches to modelling expectations vary from rational expectations models over the construction of expected data from survey information to general autoregressive distributed lag models. Here we assume that current and recent inflation rates have been a good guide to inflation rates in the near future. The following expectational hypothesis is adopted (ibid.):

$$\begin{aligned} &\dot{w}^{\mathrm{e}}_t = \dot{w}_{t-1} + \sum_{i=0}^{\infty} \lambda_i \dot{w}_{t-1-i}, \quad \dot{w}^{\mathrm{e}}_t = w^{\mathrm{e}}_{t+1} - w_t, \quad \dot{w}_{t-1} = w_t - w_{t-1} \\ &\dot{p}^{\mathrm{e}}_t = \dot{p}_{t-1} + \sum_{i=0}^{\infty} \mu_i \dot{p}_{t-1-i}, \quad \dot{p}^{\mathrm{e}}_t = p^{\mathrm{e}}_{t+1} - p_t, \quad \dot{p}_{t-1} = p_t - p_{t-1} \\ &\dot{w}^{\mathrm{e}}_{u,\,t} = \dot{w}_{u,\,t-1} + \sum_{i=0}^{\infty} v_i \dot{w}_{u,\,t-1-i}, \quad \dot{w}^{\mathrm{e}}_{u,\,t} = w^{\mathrm{e}}_{t+1} - w_t, \quad \dot{w}_{u,\,t-1} = w_{u,\,t} - w_{u,\,t-1} \end{aligned} \tag{9}$$

$$\dot{y}_t^e = \dot{y}_{t-1} + \sum_{i=0}^{\infty} \rho_i \dot{y}_{t-1-i}, \quad \dot{y}_t^e = y_{t+1}^e - y_t, \quad \dot{y}_{t-1} = y_t - y_{t-1}$$

Substituting (9) into (8) yields:

$$\begin{aligned} \dot{w}_t - \dot{w}_{t-1} = &(\alpha_2 - \alpha_3 + \alpha_4 - 1)(w_t - p_t) + (\alpha_2 - \alpha_3 - 1)(\dot{w}_{t-1} - \dot{p}_{t-1}) \\ &+ \alpha_1(w_{u,t} - p_t) + \alpha_1(\dot{w}_{u,t-1} - \dot{p}_{t-1}) + (\alpha_3 - \alpha_4) y_t + \alpha_3 \dot{y}_{t-1} \\ &+ \alpha_5 x_t - \alpha_6 u_t - \alpha_7 \dot{u}_t + (1 - \alpha_1 - \alpha_2 + \alpha_3)\Sigma\lambda_i \dot{p}_{t-1-i} \\ &+ \alpha_1 \Sigma v_i \dot{w}_{u,t-1-i} + (\alpha_2 - \alpha_3)\Sigma\mu_i \dot{w}_{t-1-i} + \alpha_3 \Sigma\rho_i \dot{y}_{t-1-i} + \varepsilon_t \end{aligned} \qquad (10)$$

The relationship in (10) can be described by saying that: nominal wage acceleration depends on real wages, productivity, unemployment, real benefits, the expected changes in these variables and a strike variable. Though this specification appears not to differ very much from other major studies (e.g. Layard *et al.* 1991), the idea behind this specification is very different and is summarized in what follows. Conflict in the private sector determines the distribution of income. Trade unions may wish to shift distribution in their favour by fighting more forcefully for higher wages at the cost of higher unanticipated inflation as firms react by increasing prices in order to maintain their income share. Thus, wage militancy leads to a faster rate of inflation. Demand affects the market power of both sides. When labour is scarce, workers obtain bigger wage increases, the rate of inflation increases and workers' share of private sector income rises. A similar argument holds for the firm too. When demand conditions in the product market are favourable, the firm's target share rises, resulting in a faster rate of inflation. However, wage determination is concerned not only with conflict between workers and capitalists, but conflict also arises in a more disaggregated level between different groups of workers who, regarding the established system of wage relativities as fair, are reluctant to accept any changes which might violate their relative position in the wage structure (Hicks, 1975). The expected average wage is a benchmark below which it is difficult to force wages. Employers, who do not wish to upset the established system of differentials, meet unions demands. Costs of lowering wages, as suggested by the efficiency wage theory discussed above, prevent firms from cutting wages simply because of unemployment. This effect operates through unemployment which prevents a wage explosion as it limits excessive wage demands. It moderates class conflict, conflict between workers and, on an individual basis, makes it more difficult for a worker to shirk. Changes in unemployment mitigate downward pressure on wages because of insider and duration effects, as discussed earlier.

THE STEADY-STATE WAGE MODEL

Most economic variables are non-stationary and the identification of cointegrating combinations of variables allows valuable information concerning the long-run behaviour between such non-stationary variables to be embedded in stationary econometric models, through an error correction term. Engle and Granger (1987) propose a two-step procedure under which a cointegrating vector is estimated first. A dynamic relationship is estimated subject to that steady state. In this section we utilize the Johansen methodology to estimate long-run wage determination (Johansen, 1988). Subsequently, a dynamic model will be determined on the basis of the results obtained in the long-run relationship.

The data is seasonally adjusted and the estimation period is from 1968Q1 to 1989Q2. We derive from equation (10) the long run as follows. In equilibrium $\dot{w}, \dot{y}, \dot{p}, \dot{w}_u, \dot{u}$ are assumed stationary and we may write: $\dot{w} = \dot{y} = \dot{p} = \dot{w}_u = \dot{u} = 0$, so that the long-run relationship may be described as

$$\sigma(w - p) = \alpha_1(w_u - p) + (\alpha_3 - \alpha_4)y + \alpha_5 x - \alpha_6 u \quad \text{with } \sigma = -(\alpha_2 - \alpha_3 + \alpha_4 - 1) \tag{11a}$$

During the sample period, average working hours changed. A change in hours worked will affect the measured wage if wages and salaries do not move enough to offset this effect, so that frequently the dependent variable in the UK is average hourly wages. Furthermore, as overtime hours are paid at a different rate from basic hours, changes in working hours will mainly occur in the overtime component and the weighting pattern of basic and overtime pay will vary with the number of hours worked (Hall and Henry, 1987). It follows that the elasticity for average hours worked may be greater than 1 in absolute terms. Equation (11a) may then be changed by adjusting both sides of the equation by average hours worked which then yields

$$\sigma(w - p - a) = \alpha_1(w_u - p) + (\alpha_3 - \alpha_4)y + \alpha_5 x - \alpha_6 u - \alpha_7 a \quad \text{with } \sigma = -(\alpha_2 - \alpha_3 + \alpha_4 - 1) \tag{11b}$$

where the dependent variable is real average hourly earnings,[3] a stands for average hours worked, u is the unemployment rate, x is the number of strikes[4] and $(w_u - p)$ stands for real benefits. All variables are in logarithms and wages and benefits are deflated by the retail price index.

A preliminary to the testing of a cointegrating relationship is to determine the order of integration of the variables in question. Table 10.1 provides the results of the unit root tests.

The tests show that all variables in question are integrated of order 1, which allows us to proceed with Johansen's cointegration tests. However, before applying the Johansen procedure, we should test whether the unrestricted VAR model is a congruent representation of the data (Johansen and Juselius, 1990). The maximum likelihood procedure requires approximate normality of the residuals, though the robustness of the procedure when this assumption is violated is not yet known (ibid., 1990), although substantial deviations from normality may be problematic. A fourth-order unrestricted VAR model is estimated. The initial tests showed that for all equations the residuals were not normally distributed and the residuals were serially autocorrelated in most of the equations. The non-normal skewness and kurtosis in the residuals is probably due to outliers.

Table 10.1 Unit root test

Variable	DF_c	DF_t	ADF_c	ADF_t	*I*
$(w-p-a)$	−1.24	−2.55	−1.52	−2.85	
$(\dot{w}-\dot{p}-a)$	−10.47	−10.47	−4.37	−4.40	1
a	−2.78	−3.28	−1.73	−1.68	
$\dot{a}$	−12.48	−12.47	−4.37	−4.43	1
(w_u-p)	−4.02	−6.44	−2.27	−2.89	
$(\dot{w}_u-\dot{p})$	−13.14	−13.08	−5.72	−5.83	1
x	−1.75	−3.17	−1.12	−3.28	
$\dot{x}$	−11.58	−11.57	−4.50	−4.58	1
u	−2.64	+0.17	−1.13	−1.57	
$\dot{u}$	−3.07	−3.27	−3.32	−3.50	1
y	−0.48	−1.94	−0.44	−2.03	
$\dot{y}$	−10.50	−10.43	−3.63	−3.61	1
Cr. value (a=0.05)	−2.89	−3.46	−2.89	−3.46	

DF_c Dickey–Fuller test including a constant
DF_t Dickey–Fuller test including a constant and a trend
ADF_c Augmented Dickey–Fuller test including a constant
ADF_t Augmented Dickey–Fuller test including a constant and a trend
The lag length is 4

We have attempted to capture the outliers by dummies which can afford sensible economic interpretation. The following dummies were introduced: *D*75.1 with the value 1 in 1975(1) and zero elsewhere, which captures the sharp rise in earnings in that quarter (Clements and Mizon, 1991). In 1979(2) there was a sharp rise in productivity, which may be explained by the beginning of the Thatcher era. The equation for average hours needed a number of dummies as follows. The effects of the three-day week restrictions and the change in government in March 1974 (ibid.) are captured by a dummy which has the value 1 in 1974(1) and −1 in 1974(2). At the beginning of 1972, the confidence of companies was reduced, which partly showed in low stocks and in reduced average working hours. In the second quarter, however, average hours worked increased significantly, making up for low stocks. In 1980(4), the trough of the recession was reached, which led to a sharp rise in unemployment and a significant decline in the number of hours worked. After a fall in output after 1979, industrial output levelled out in the third quarter of 1981, leading to an increase in working time.

The mis-specification results of the unrestricted VAR are presented in Table 10.2. The notation is as follows: *s* is the standard deviation of the equation, SK denotes skewness, EK excess kurtosis, $\chi^2(2)$ is the Jarcque–Bera test for normality with the critical value $\chi^2(2) = 5.99$, AR(16) is the Lagrange multiplier test for autocorrelation of order 16 with the critical value of 26.30 at 5% significance level.

There is no evidence of any remaining non-normalities for all equations. However, the Lagrange multiplier test statistics show autocorrelation in the unemployment and the strike equation, which may suggest a more complex dynamic structure (ibid.). On the whole, the results are satisfactory.

Table 10.2 Mis-specification test for the unrestricted VAR

	s	SK	EK	$\chi^2(2)$	$AR(16)$
$(\dot{w} - \dot{p} - a)$	0.009	−0.32	0.47	2.29	23.05
$\dot{y}$	0.006	−0.41	0.36	2.94	6.25
$\dot{u}$	0.024	−0.21	0.46	1.38	32.91
$\dot{a}$	0.004	−0.29	0.17	1.33	23.50
$\dot{x}$	0.141	−0.17	0.12	0.49	28.95
$(\dot{w}_u - \dot{p})$	0.031	0.18	0.27	0.70	13.93

We may now proceed to analyse the long-run relationship amongst the key variables, using Johansens's cointegration tests. The deterministic part of the model implies the above-mentioned dummies and a linear trend which is significant with a $\chi^2(1) = 10.14$.

First, we present the cointegrating tests, the maximum eigenvalue test and the trace test:

Maximum eigenvalue test

H_0	H_1	*Actual*	*(0.95)*	*(0.90)*
$r = 0$	$r = 1$	59.98	39.37	36.76
$r \leq 1$	$r = 2$	49.78	33.46	30.90
$r \leq 2$	$r = 3$	20.31	27.07	24.73
$r \leq 3$	$r = 4$	11.73	20.97	18.60
$r \leq 4$	$r = 5$	7.54	14.07	12.07
$r \leq 5$	$r = 6$	1.17	3.76	2.69

The hypothesis that there are one or two cointegrating vectors is not rejected at the 5 per cent significance level. The results of the trace test are as follows:

Trace test

H_0	H_1	*Actual*	*(0.95)*	*(0.90)*
$r = 0$	$r \geq 1$	150.50	94.15	89.48
$r \leq 1$	$r \geq 2$	90.53	68.52	64.84
$r \leq 2$	$r \geq 3$	40.74	47.21	43.95
$r \leq 3$	$r \geq 4$	20.43	29.68	26.79
$r \leq 4$	$r \geq 5$	8.71	15.41	13.33
$r \leq 5$	$r = 6$	1.17	3.76	2.69

and confirm those of the maximum eigenvalue test. The estimation results are as follows:

Cointegrating vectors (in rows)

$(w - p - \mathrm{a})$	y	u	a	$(w_u - p)$	x
−1.00	0.99	−0.15	−1.60	0.36	0.04
0.68	−1.00	−0.17	−0.06	1.56	−0.09

Loadings (in rows)

0.37	−0.21	0.04	−0.07	−0.61	−1.88
−0.11	−0.07	−0.08	0.00	−0.15	0.89

The two cointegrating vectors need to be identified using economic theory. It has been argued that the identification of economical relationships in the space spanned by these two vectors is problematic (Alogoskoufis and Smith, 1991). Johansen and Juselius (1992) suggest testing as a device to find out whether any specific structural relationship can be identified. We tested the two cointegrating vectors for the validity of the assumption of proportionality between productivity and real wages and the null hypothesis was not rejected by the likelihood ratio statistic with $\chi^2(2) = 0.48$ and a significance level $a = 0.79$. This result is quite plausible in an economy, where conflict arises over relative income shares so that in the long run unions are not prepared to accept wage increases below labour productivity growth.

The loadings matrix may also help to identify structural relationships (ibid.). The loadings of the first (second) row can be understood as the weights with which real earnings (productivity) enter the six equations of the system. The sizes and signs of the estimated weights seem to indicate that the wage vector, though correctly signed, is not important for the unemployment function, but most important for the benefit and strike equations. The coefficients of the second row may suggest that the second eigenvector is most important for the strike equation and to a minor degree for benefit and wage determination. Productivity, though correctly signed, appears to have little influence on the unemployment function. However, formal testing would be needed to make these statements more precise. A promising way forward has recently been suggested by Pesaran and Shin (1994), which does not rely on homogeneous restrictions as in Johansen and Juselius (1992), and in what follows this is the approach we adopt.

The Pesaran–Shin approach relies heavily on imposing non-homogeneous restrictions on the two cointegrating vectors and with the help of an appropriate χ^2-statistic the restrictions are tested for their validity. The first of the two cointegrating vectors describes wage formation in the long run as suggested by our theoretical model and is validated by the Pesaran–Shin procedure. We normalized the second vector with regard to unemployment and imposed null restricions on strikes, average hours worked and real earnings. The following long-run relationships could be derived:[5]

$(w - p - a)$	y	u	a	$(w_u - p)$	x
−1.00	1.00	−0.13	−1.51	0.25	0.04
0.00	−2.10	−1.00	0.00	5.91	0.00

where we have imposed two overidentifying restrictions on the cointegrating vectors. All the restrictions are valid with a $\chi^2(2)$ statistic of 2.52 and a significance level $a = 0.28$. The first cointegrating vector has hardly changed and confirms the theoretical priors. The second vector describes unemployment determined by real benefits and productivity. Both variables are correctly signed. High unemployment compensation may cause the unemployed to be less willing to accept jobs and may also induce those in employment to quit unattractive jobs.[6] Increased labour productivity reduces labour costs and may in the long run reduce unemployment. Though unemployment determines real wages, there is no feedback from real wages to unemployment, as already indicated by the loadings. Theoretically, the role of wages is ambiguous with regard to unemployment as, on the one hand, they provide purchasing power and stimulate demand, and on the other hand, they mean higher costs of production and may dampen economic activity. Whether aggregate demand or aggregate supply effects are more relevant in an economy depends to some degree on the market conditions. If, in a closed economy, capitalists are very strong in the product market, they may be able to compensate higher labour costs (almost) fully through higher prices. The effect on output and unemployment may then be minimal, as indicated by our empirical result. The system was re-estimated, but this time the coefficient on real earnings was not restricted to zero. However, the previous null restriction could not be rejected.[7]

With the two cointegrating vectors having been identified as a real wage and an unemployment relationship, there is still the question of the origins of the latter. It is plausible that the origins of the unemployment vector can be deduced from the model put forward in this chapter to explain real wages. More precisely it emanates from the conflict between insiders and outsiders as described in the hysteresis models discussed above. The underlying idea is that insiders have the power to increase wages and secure their employment with little or no consideration of the conditions in the labour market. Thus, increases in unemployment benefits may raise the reservation wage and make the unemployed less competitive. In view of this, insiders may try to increase wages with unemployment persisting or even increasing.[8] The effect of increases in productivity on unemployment is not so clear cut in this model, but can be justified on the following grounds. Insiders may be able to absorb small positive output shocks, emanating from increases in productivity, in higher wages and increased effort without any effect on unemployment. However, more significant and lasting positive shocks must decrease unemployment in the longer run as the given stock of the employed can only rely on increasing productivity in a limited time frame.

THE DYNAMIC COUNTERPART OF THE WAGE MODEL

In the second step of the estimation procedure, the lagged residuals ($\hat{u}$) may be employed as the error correction term in an overparameterized model. The underlying model for the empirical specification of the dynamic model is equation (10).

The dynamic specification was derived by estimating a general model which included all variables with a lag length up to 5. Variables which were insignificant were sequentially excluded. The simplifying procedure applied was suggested by Hendry (1979) and leads to the OLS estimation shown below, where the error correction term results from the first cointegrating vector:

$$\begin{aligned}(\dot{w}_t - \dot{w}_{t-1}) = {} & \underset{(2.51)}{0.204} + \underset{(2.40)}{0.051}D75.1 + \underset{(1.47)}{0.055}(\dot{w}_{\mathrm{u}} - \dot{p})_{t-1} + \underset{(2.35)}{0.425}\dot{y}_{t-1} \\ & + \underset{(3.39)}{0.646}\dot{y}_{t-4} - \underset{(3.28)}{0.172}\dot{u}_{t-1} + \underset{(2.93)}{0.167}\dot{u}_{t-2} - \underset{(4.31)}{0.151}\dot{u}_{t-5} \\ & - \underset{(2.50)}{0.063}(\hat{u})_{t-3} - \underset{(9.48)}{0.881}(\dot{w} - \dot{p})_{t-1} - \underset{(2.68)}{0.493}\dot{a}_{t-4} \end{aligned} \qquad (12)$$

and $R^2 = 0.77$, $e = 0.0146$, DW $= 2.31$, AR$(5, 67) = 2.04$, HET$(1, 80) = 3.04$, RESET$(1, 71) = 2.47$, NORM$(2) = 1.09$

The t-values are in brackets and the other diagnostics have the following meaning: e is the standard error of the equation; DW is the Durbin–Watson statistic; AR$(q, T-q-k)$ is the qth-order LM test for residual autocorrelation with T observations and k regressors; HET$(q, T-q-k)$ is the qth-order LM test for heteroscedasticity quadratic in the regressors; RESET$(q, T-q-k)$ is Ramsey's functional form mis-specification test and NORM(2) is the χ^2 Jarque–Bera test for normality.

The equation is satisfactory with regard to the coefficients which are consistent with the theoretical expectations as discussed above and which are significant. Changes in real wages and changes in productivity influence wage acceleration strongly. The overall effect of changes in unemployment is negative, supporting the ideas of hysteresis models. Though the coefficient of the error correction term indicates slow adjustment towards equilibrium, it is, however, significant. The diagnostic tests as reported above clearly indicate that the model is satisfactory especially in view of the fact that none of the diagnostics is significant at the 5 per cent level. Furthermore, the forecasting ability of the model as shown in the two graphs in the Appendix is satisfactory. The Chow test of predictive failure is insignificant for a period of five years, with $F(20, 51) = 0.28$, and also for a period of ten years, with $F(40, 31) = 0.57$.[9]

If we compare the performance of our model with other studies, we find considerable support for our results. To begin with, a number of empirical studies on wage determination consider elements that are present in our model. On a disaggregate level, there is some empirical evidence for efficiency wage effects as wage differentials increase output with an elasticity of nearly 1 (Wadhwani and Wall, 1990). The same study also suggests that a rise in unemployment increases productivity. On an aggregate level, positive effects of a benefit variable are found by Layard and Nickell (1986) while Hall and Henry (1987) report a wrongly signed and insignificant coefficient. Empirically sound effects are usually found with productivity effects (sometimes hourly adjusted) and hysteresis effects (Nickell, 1987). There is plentiful evidence on a firm-specific level as well as in aggregate wage equations for the UK and a number of European countries (Layard *et al.* 1991). Unions' influence on wage settlements has been examined in a variety of studies and it frequently proved difficult to attribute wage changes to union activity with any degree of certainty (ibid.). Nevertheless, there is some evidence that wage pressure rose noticeably since 1969. Newell and Symons (1985) used a wage explosion dummy in order to capture a period of unprecedented conflict in the OECD and found that there was a marked increase in wage pressure in a number of countries. Grubb (1986) also uses dummy variables to capture wage explosion but also introduces alternative specifications of the wage equation, including a measure of strike activity as an indicator of increased militancy.

These elements all perform satisfactorily in our model and thus support the theoretical priors. In fact, in a recent study we re-estimated Hall's 1989 model, where the long-run behaviour of his and a similar model to ours were examined at some length (Arestis and Biefang-Frisancho Mariscal, 1994). The result was that both models were quite robust and similar in the variables they had in common. We have also shown in the same study that there are some additional significant income distributional and wage efficiency effects, a result which is strengthened and supported by the findings of the current chapter.

However, there are some important aspects which distinguish our model empirically from other UK wage studies. Our empirical evaluation employs Johansen's cointegration tests and we know of only very few UK wage studies which apply the same method (Hall, 1989; Clements and Mizon, 1991). More important, though, the problem of identification of structural relationships in the case of more than one cointegrating vector is usually solved by rather arbitrarily finding linear combinations in the cointegration space, which are then understood as economic valid relationships. The validity of these relationships is never tested, though the importance of testing is well acknowledged. By contrast, we tested for the validity of the imposed restrictions in the identified structural relationships employing a new technique as mentioned above, which produced a real earnings and an unemployment relationship. A further result is that there is no feedback from real wages to unemployment, which of course is of considerable importance for policy analysis.

SUMMARY AND CONCLUSION

The issues raised in this chapter may be summarized as follows. A general theoretical wage model was developed. This model is based on conflict over relative income shares amongst workers and capitalists along with elements from different but complementary theories, these being wage relativities, wage efficiency and hysteresis theories.

The model was estimated and tested with regard to its long-run and dynamic properties. In a first step an unrestricted VAR model, interrelating real average earnings, productivity, real benefits, average hours worked, unemployment and strike activity, was estimated and tested. This system formed the basis for further reductions through which a structural wage equation was derived.

Commencing with an analysis of the integration properties of the relevant data, the cointegrating vectors were estimated using Johansens's (1988) FIML method. Two cointegrating vectors were established, one of which corresponds to a long-run wage function with proportionality between productivity and real wages. The other vector describes an unemployment function determined by productivity and unemployment compensation. Likelihood ratio tests confirmed the validity of the imposed restrictions on both vectors.

On the basis of this information an error correction structural model was developed. Wage acceleration appeared to be substantially influenced by changes in productivity, in average hours worked, in real wages and in unemployment, as well as by the gap between negotiated and target real wages. Furthermore, a long-run relationship for unemployment could be determined.

APPENDIX

All the data is taken from the NIESR except for the following variables: the number of strikes and average hours worked in manufacturing, which come from the *Employment Gazette*; they are seasonally adjusted UK data for 1966Q1 to 1989Q2.

x_t	$x_t - x_t - 1$
u	log of the ratio of unemployment, i.e. unemp/(unemp + emp)
emp	employees in employment
unemp	unemployment
y	productivity = (output GDP)/emp
ws	gross wages and salaries
w	ws/(emp. a)
a	index of weekly average hours worked per operative in manufacturing industries
x	number of strikes
w_u	unemployment benefits

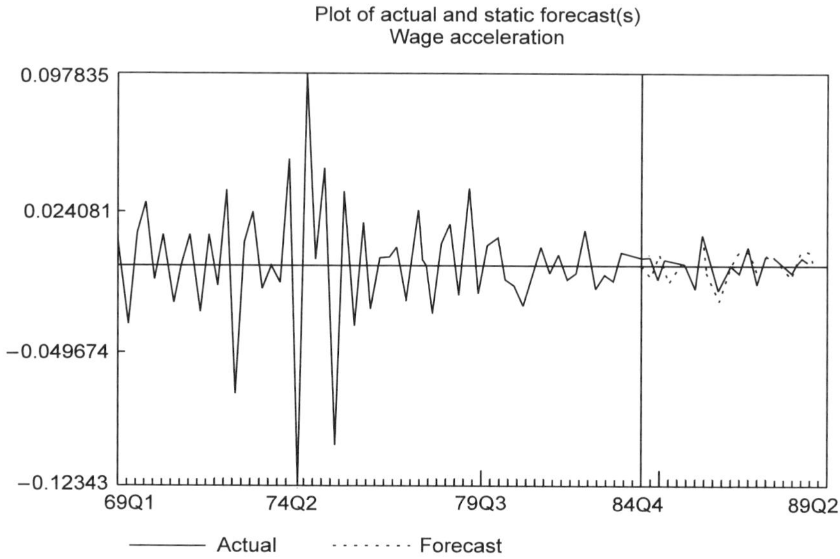

Figure A10.1

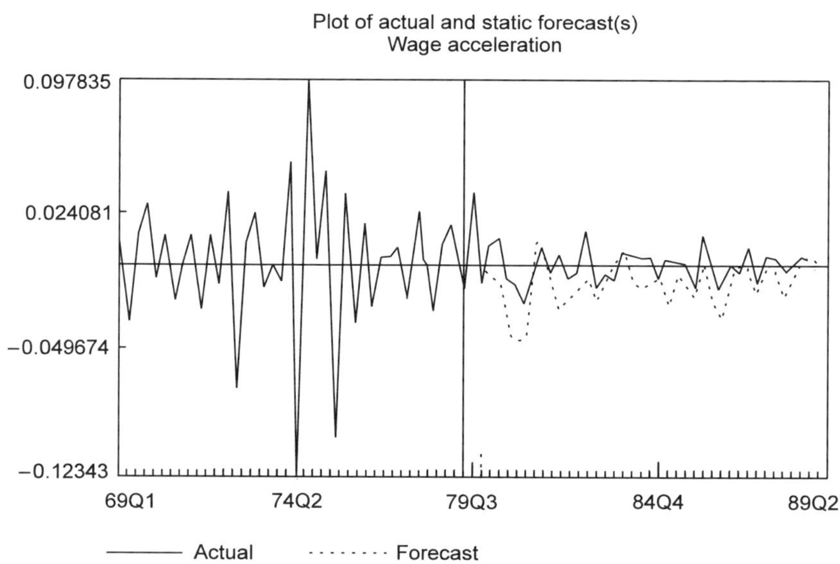

Figure A10.2

NOTES

1 The discussion is constrained to the private sector, only. A future version of the model would be extended to include the foreign sector and the public sector.

2 Carruth and Oswald (1987) found that profit considerations are theoretically and empirically important in wage determination and criticized therefore the Layard and Nickell model as being misspecified.

3 The dependent variable is constructed as follows: $w_s/(emp.\ a)$ with w_s as gross wages and salaries, *emp* as the number of employees and a as an index of average weekly hours worked per operative. The dependent variable is the hourly average wage.

4 This variable does not capture all aspects of union power, as strikes are only one means of a union to express its power. Other variables as, for example, union membership (Minford, 1983) or a mark-up on trade union wages (Layard and Nickell, 1985) – and for a critical comment on this variable see Hall and Henry (1987) – do not represent all aspects of union power. Furthermore, the data for these variables is only annually available, while our model is estimated with quarterly data.

5 We are very grateful to Bahram Pesaran for his help in the identification of these vectors.

6 Atkinson and Micklewright (1991) modify this general view with respect to different labour market conditions.

7 The results are as follows:

$(w-p-a)$	y	u	a	(w_u-p)	x
−1.00	1.00	−0.14	−1.53	0.29	0.04
0.62	−2.40	−1.00	0.00	6.14	0.00

with $\chi^2(1) = 2.31$ ($a = 0.13$) which compares with $\chi^2(2) = 2.52$ ($a = 0.28$) of the more parsimonious system as described in the text.

8 An increase in unemployment is possible as the recently employed are *not* insiders so that they do not enjoy job security.

9 The graphs for the cusum and cusumsq functions, not reported here but obtainable from the authors on request, are satisfactory with regard to the usual criteria.

Part III

MONEY, CREDIT RATIONING AND ASYMMETRIC INFORMATION

Part III

MONEY, CREDIT RATIONING AND ASYMMETRIC INFORMATION

This part of the book, on 'Money, Credit Rationing and Asymmetric Information', contains five chapters each directed to the role of money and finance in New and Post Keynesian models.

New Keynesian writers tend to follow two paths of reasoning, although with a fair degree of overlap. In its narrowest incarnation, New Keynesian theory focuses on the circumstances underlying some market, in this case a credit market, which prevents an efficient allocation of loanable funds between savers and investors. The primary reason given for these misallocations is the existence of asymmetries in information which lead to a relative stickiness in real interest rates. Money in these narrowly defined models must take on the role of an exogenously given stock; otherwise the possibility of an endogenous money stock reduces the relevancy of any relationship between savings, investment and the rate of interest – we move out of a loanable funds theory of the rate of interest into a Keynesian world where liquidity preference becomes the decisive factor in explaining the behaviour of individuals and financial institutions.

In the less narrow models of asymmetric information and credit rationing, New Keynesians – especially Stiglitz and Greenwald – have begun to downplay the importance of sticky prices in the overall model. Inefficiencies in capital markets may now find their source in credit rationing behaviour on the part of lending institutions. Such attempts at realism, over the last decade, have led these New Keynesian writers into two conflicting positions, however. On the one hand, their continued reliance on the notion of an aggregate capital market has restricted any richness that might emerge from their appeal to realism. On the other hand, such movements towards realism, and away from the limiting, closed, deductive, market-based New Keynesian conclusions of the narrow model, have pushed them onto an irrevocable path towards a Post Keynesian perspective where income, output and employment are liable to change in the aggregate. To the extent that the New Keynesian research programme falls back into the safe confines of the narrow market-based model, the project begun by Stiglitz and Greenwald will bear little fruit. To the extent that they reject the supply and demand framework of an aggregate capital market, the assumption that lending and borrowing decisions are based on calculable probabilities of the yield on capital assets, and the assumption of an exogenous stock of money, we can expect a meeting of the New and Post Keynesian minds, something that clearly will be advantageous to the discipline at large.

In the opening chapter of this section, 'Menu Costs and the Nature of Money', Malcolm Sawyer first reviews the New Keynesian use of menu costs to explain fluctuations in economic activity in the face of nominal demand shocks. He argues that whilst there are undoubtedly costs of price adjustment, there are also costs of output adjustment, and it is not clear that firms would always willingly incur the output adjustment costs rather than price adjustment costs. The major argument of this chapter is that the New Keynesian explanation of fluctuations in economic activity is based on the assumption of exogenous money, whereas in an industrialized economy money is endogenously created within the private sector, and that the explanation of fluctuations would not survive a change of assumptions from exogenous to endogenous money. Shifts in nominal demand are modelled as akin to changes in the money stock, and hence if the analysis based on changes in the money stock is invalid then so is the analysis of nominal shocks. It is thus concluded that the New Keynesian analysis of economic fluctuations, based on menu costs and exogenous money, is not applicable to a modern industrialized economy.

The question of endogenous money is also at the heart of the difference between a Post Keynesian theory of money and credit and the New Keynesian theory of credit rationing. In her contribution to this volume, 'Knowledge, Information and Credit Creation', Sheila Dow contends that New Keynesian theory treats information on risk as knowable, limiting rationing to a deviation from some *correct* notion of credit total. The Post Keynesian theory regards knowledge as uncertain, i.e. not knowable in principle; credit creation is then based on risk assessment by banks (and firms) under conditions of uncertainty which vary over the cycle. Furthermore, while New Keynesians focus only on bank assets, Post Keynesians see banks as distinctive also on the liability side, allowing a blending of demand for money theory and endogenous money theory.

The next two chapters consider the role of asymmetric information with regard to the New Keynesian theory of credit rationing focused specifically at the nature of the principal–agent problem. In the first, 'The Role of Asymmetric Information', Dorene Isenberg argues that the similarities that do exist between the New and Post Keynesians are superficial, at best. Their mutual interest in financial institutions and financial regulatory structures and their acknowledgement that these financial institutions do affect the level of production in the economy are generated from very different theoretical foundations. Isenberg's concern is with the methodological underpinnings of each of the two theories, akin to the issues considered by Sheila Dow in the previous chapter. Like Dow, Isenberg sees the pivotal difference between the two theories to be the knowability of the particular types of information involved. In asymmetric information theory knowledge is assumed to exist and to be known. This dichotomy allows the asymmetric information theorists to construct a world in which risk defines the structure of existing and known information while strategic game playing is responsible for the maldistribution of that information. This view stands in contrast to the Post Keynesian reliance upon Keynesian uncertainty to argue that the maldistributed or missing information of the asymmetric information school is actually unknown and unknowable. The chapter directs these fundamental differences back into each theory's view of money, financial institutions, regulatory structure and intervention, and financial crisis in order to emphasize how these essential differences are manifested at the level of institutions.

Then, Gary Dymski in his chapter 'Disembodied Risk or the Social Construction of Creditworthiness?', continues this methodological critique of the asymmetric information microfoundation of New Keynesian economics. He argues that the asocial and axiomatic treatment of risk in New Keynesian models of the credit market trivializes principal–agent relations. What he calls for is a richer microfoundational treatment which recognizes that the *rules* of principal–agent games are moulded, in many cases, by principals' exercise of power over time. When the power imbalance is too large, structural determinants heavily outweigh strategic interactions in deciding any such game's outcome.

No Post Keynesian critique would be complete without some mention of the extent to which New Keynesian economics is seen in light of the writings of Michal Kalecki. In 'A Kaleckian View of New Keynesian Macroeconomics', Tracy Mott illustrates how New Keynesian explanations of unemployment by nominal and real price and wage rigidities are compared and contrasted with Michal Kalecki's explanations based on income distributional factors. New Keynesian stories about limits on firms' access to credit and equity finance show a greater similarity with Kalecki's arguments for recursive fluctuations in investment spending and profits. The New Keynesian limits on access to capital are derived from informational imperfections, however, while Kalecki's are based on the systemic reproduction of inequalities in income and wealth. And, from a Kaleckian perspective, the idea of establishing nominal price rigidities inherent in the New Keynesian model is beside the point.

Kalecki's macroeconomics does rely on a real rigidity, the inflexibility of price–cost mark-ups, to ensure that real wages do not rise to increase consumption spending to offset a drop in investment spending. The volatility of investment spending is what primarily causes changes in aggregate demand and therefore in employment for Kalecki. Investment spending in turn is determined by the interactions among investment, profits and capacity. The effect of profits on investment is due to Kalecki's 'principle of increasing risk', the idea that investment is limited by access to own, or unencumbered, funds in the form of retained profits. Mott uses this argument of Kalecki's to assess the theories of credit and equity rationing put forth by Joseph Stiglitz, Bruce Greenwald and others.

The key question in Mott's mind is whether or not the macroeconomic phenomena which we seek to understand, such as unemployment or inflation, can be best understood by reference to individual optimization in the presence of informational imperfections or by determinations at the level of the system as a whole.

In other words, can macroeconomic phenomena be considered in terms of imperfections in an otherwise smoothly functioning aggregate capital market, or should we be looking at a more traditional, but more open, Keynesian framework, based on a theory of effective demand, in order to consider such macroeconomic questions?

11

MENU COSTS AND THE NATURE OF MONEY

Malcolm Sawyer

INTRODUCTION

This chapter begins by outlining the New Keynesian treatment of menu costs with particular reference to the use of such costs in providing an explanation for fluctuations in economic activity in the face of nominal demand shocks. It is argued that whilst there are undoubtedly costs of price adjustment, there are also costs of output adjustment, and it is not clear that firms would always willingly incur the output adjustment costs rather than price adjustment costs. The second and major argument of this chapter is that the New Keynesian explanation of fluctuations in economic activity is based on the assumption of exogenous money, whereas in an industrialized economy money is endogenously created within the private sector, and that the explanation of fluctuations would not survive a change of assumptions from exogenous to endogenous money. Shifts in nominal demand are modelled as akin to changes in the money stock, and hence if the analysis based on changes in the money stock is invalid then so is the analysis of nominal shocks.

NOMINAL RIGIDITIES AND MENU COSTS

New Keynesian macroeconomics has two main elements of significance for this chapter. The first is the idea that there are nominal rigidities, whereby prices change only slowly, particularly in the face of changes in demand because of adjustment costs under the general heading of menu costs. These adjustment costs have been long recognized (as well as the small gains to changing price when the elasticity of demand and the average variable costs facing a firm are perceived to be approximately constant).[1] There is much evidence on the pricing side that prices are relatively insensitive to demand (whether the level of or changes in).[2] The new element has been to argue that a small effect such as menu costs can have large effects on the level of economic activity.

> Thus, if failure of the classical dichotomy is important to fluctuations in aggregate activity, it must be that nominal frictions that appear small at the level of individual households and firms – like the fact that prices are posted

> in nominal units, or that obtaining accurate information about the aggregate price level involves a cost – somehow have a large effect on the macro economy. It is this insight, due to Mankiw (1985) and Akerlof and Yellen (1985), that has led to the recent progress in understanding the microeconomic foundations of the real impact of aggregate demand disturbances.
>
> (Romer, 1993)

The failure of the Classical Dichotomy because of the stickiness of prices is central to New Keynesian economics (cf. Mankiw and Romer, 1991a, p. 2).

Menu costs are only one part of the factors tending to limit price changes, and consideration also has to be given to the size of profits foregone if the price change is not made.[3] For a profit maximizing firm, price equals $[e/(e-1)]$.MC where e is the elasticity of demand and MC marginal cost (with allowance made for the perceived interdependence amongst firms in an oligopolistic situation). A shift in the demand curve facing the firm only leads to a change in price if there are consequent changes in the elasticity of demand or in marginal cost (and it is possible that a downward shift in the demand curve may be associated with a fall in the elasticity of demand, thereby raising price; see Harrod, 1936). With small changes in the elasticity of demand and marginal costs following a shift in nominal demand, the losses from not changing price are small and may be outweighed by the administration costs. In the limiting case where marginal costs and the elasticity of demand are constant, prices would clearly be constant in the face of demand changes: this corresponds to what is often labelled, incorrectly in our view, the fix price case, and clearly does not need to invoke menu costs to explain a lack of price movement in the face of demand changes. In contrast, a shift in the level of marginal costs through a rise in input prices has (roughly) a one-for-one effect on the profit maximizing price and a failure to adjust prices to a cost change could involve substantial losses.

The significance of the price stickiness which is seen to result from menu costs arises from the consequent effects of shocks in nominal aggregate demand on the level of economic activity. A nominal shock is translated into a real shock since prices are sluggish to adjust: hence a negative nominal shock becomes a negative real shock leading to a lower level of economic activity. In so far as menu costs are lump sum costs (i.e. is making and implementing a decision on a price change is costly but the costs do not depend on the scale of the price change) then they lose their significance in an inflationary world. When prices are rising rapidly, then any particular firm will be changing its prices frequently anyway; thus the impact of nominal shocks would be smaller under conditions of rapid inflation than under zero or low inflation:

> [I]f the classical dichotomy is to fail, it must be that marginal cost does not fall sharply in response to a demand-driven output contraction, or that marginal revenue does [*sic*] fall sharply, or some combination of the two. At a more general level, the incentive to change price in response to a change in economy-wide output can be expressed as a function of two factors: the

impact of the change on the firm's profit-maximising real price, and the cost to the firm of a given departure of its real price from the profit-maximising level.

(Romer, 1993, p. 11)

In effect the argument is that the gains from the price being at the profit maximizing level, as compared with its present level, following a demand shock may be small and hence in the face of adjustment and menu costs it may not be worthwhile to change price. Whilst prices are not being adjusted, the level of output is being adjusted in response to a change in demand. Suppose a profit maximizing firm is initially producing Q_0 at a price of P_0, and nominal demand falls such that the new profit maximizing position (ignoring any adjustment costs) would entail a price P_2 with output of Q_2; but adjustment costs mean that the price remains unchanged and output falls to Q_1. Whilst the constant price case obviously does not incur menu costs, it does involve greater output adjustment costs than if the price were adjusted since the change in output would be larger. Ramsey (1991) finds that for a range of industries marginal costs of production are declining and also that for some of the industries there are significant costs of adjustment of output, leading to the bunching of output changes rather than production smoothing.

In the comparative static case, the comparison to be made would be between the adjustment costs of moving from Q_0, P_0 to Q_1, P_0 or to Q_2, P_2. Obviously unless the relative magnitudes are known, then nothing can be said as to whether the constant price option would be taken. Further, if each enterprise takes the price adjustment option with the expectation that other enterprises will follow suit at some stage, it may well find it worthwhile to cumulate stocks rather than reduce output, awaiting a general lowering of prices and increase in the level of real demand.

However, the comparative static analysis is constraining in this context. Firms face a demand which is continuously fluctuating on a combination of random and non-random bases. The firms' response to a demand shock may initially depend on whether that shock is compatible with the random variations in demand which firms face or whether it clearly signals a move to a quite different level of demand. Further, if firms are continuously reviewing their price and output decisions, then some, at least, of the menu costs of price change will be incurred anyway.

Enterprises may decide to allow output to vary little with sales fluctuating in the face of varying aggregate demand through variations in stock, and that would mean that there may be relatively little immediate variation in output and employment in response to a variation in demand. Thus the argument that variations in demand lead to variations in output requires not only that enterprises do not find it profitable to adjust prices but also that the variations are not met by inventory adjustment. Other discussions of price stability would suggest that some, at least, of the movement in demand is absorbed by stock changes (e.g. Hay and Morris, 1991, pp. 185–9).

MENU COSTS AND THE NATURE OF MONEY

The menu-cost approach strongly suggests that fluctuations in the levels of employment and output in the economy will be caused by fluctuations in nominal demand (especially arising from the stock of money) which are not fully and/or immediately offset by price changes so that there are fluctuations in the level of real demand. Thus variations in the money stock have real effects through price stickiness and money is not always neutral. Much of macroeconomic analysis outside of the Post Keynesian tradition draws heavily on some form of the Classical Dichotomy whereby there is a separation between the monetary and real sides of the economy. New Keynesian macroeconomists, amongst others, see monetary changes as having some short-run effects on output before prices fully adjust, but preserve the Classical Dichotomy in the longer term (where some form of long-period equilibrium is assumed to exist). The separation of the monetary and the real sides of the economy also tends to involve a separation between demand and supply sides, and to involve a supply side which is unaffected by events on the demand side of the economy (in particular it presumes the absence of any hysteresis effects).

The source of nominal shocks is generally modelled as an exogenous change in the stock of money with the discussion focusing on whether or not the Classical Dichotomy holds (e.g. Romer, 1993). However, Ball *et al.* (1991) argue that 'we can interpret M [stock of money] as simply a shift term in the aggregate demand equation. Thus . . . the results in recent papers concern the effects of any shock to aggregate demand, not just changes in the money stock' (footnote 7, p. 7). Shocks such as a change in investment behaviour or in consumer expenditure would be seen as real ones. However, note that Ball *et al.* (1991) argue that

> if we interpret M in the aggregate demand equation . . . as simply a shift term . . . real disturbances that shift demand affect output through the same channels as changes in money. . . . Thus nominal rigidities, while not the only explanation for the effects of real demand, are perhaps the most appealing. (p. 17)

In a similar vein, Ball and Romer (1990) say that 'to make nominal disturbances possible, we introduce money' (p. 185) and that 'we assume below that fluctuations in aggregate demand *arise from* fluctuations in money' (footnote. 4, p. 185, emphasis added).

The nature of money assumed in this type of analysis is essentially exogenous government-controlled money. The exogeneity of money means that it is possible to think in terms of changes in the money stock generated outside of the (private market) economy. With government-created money, shocks to the private sector are viewed as in some considerable degree caused by government. As indicated below, exogenous government money is of limited relevance in industrialized economies. Further, the New Keynesian analysis of nominal shocks is undertaken for an economy with only exogenous government money, but intended to apply to an economy in which there is endogenous money created through the banking system.[4] Hence, it is argued that the analysis of the impact of a change in the stock of money is flawed (when applied to an industrialized economy): as other nominal shocks are analysed by analogy with the money change case those other analyses would also appear to be flawed.[5] The causes of changes in exogenous money clearly lie outside of the model, and here in particular outside of the private sector, and would be seen as arising through government action (or perhaps related to the foreign sector). The argument pursued here is that the assumption of exogenous money, rather than endogenous money, is not just an innocuous simplifying one but provides a misleading analysis.

Some leading New Keynesians have described the central proposition of Keynesian economics as '[a]ccording to the Keynesian view, fluctuations in output arise largely from fluctuations in nominal aggregate demand. These fluctuations have real effects because nominal wages and prices are rigid' (Ball, *et al.*, 1991, p. 1). But as Tobin (1993, p. 47) notes that 'Keynes would have been appalled to see his cycle model' described in this manner and that '[i]n Keynesian business cycle theory, the shocks generating fluctuations are generally shifts in *real* aggregate demand for goods and services, notably in capital investment'.

The assumption of the exogeneity of money, rather than its endogeneity, can be seen from the following quotation. 'Suppose that agents set prices believing that *M* [stock of money] will equal one (a normalisation).... After prices are set, there is an unanticipated shock to *M*' (Ball and Romer, 1990, p. 186). If money is created by government, then it is possible for that government to create money without the prior knowledge of the public, giving rise to an unanticipated shock. But with endogenous money created within the private sector, then at least those who are party to the creation of money will know in advance of its creation. The bank granting the loan and the individual or firm taking out the loan know of its existence and the consequent increase in the stock of money. Thus it is no longer possible to talk in general terms of unanticipated shocks but rather it becomes necessary to specify unanticipated for whom.

It would be widely acknowledged that a substantial element of the stock of money in an industrialized economy is credit money in the form of the liabilities of the (private) banking system. How substantial that element is depends on the precise definition of the stock of money adopted but even for a relatively narrow definition such as M2 the proportion is relatively high (e.g. in the UK it is around 95 per cent). The prevailing orthodoxy in macroeconomics would portray the relationship between the stock of money M (however defined) and the monetary base B in terms of the money or credit multiplier m, i.e. $M = mB$. Control over the monetary base is seen to provide control over the stock of money with the money multiplier being treated as constant. In contrast, Post Keynesians (and others)[6] have doubted the ability of the monetary authorities to control the monetary base, have questioned the constancy of the money multiplier and have focused on the role of the demand for and the supply of loans in the process of the creation of money. There are continuing debates within Post Keynesian economics on the precise nature of endogenous money[7] but these debates are not central to the argument here. It is sufficient here to acknowledge that the bulk of money in an industrialized economy is credit bank money created within, and by decision makers in, the private sector.

If the stock of money is exogenous (for the private sector), then a thought experiment of what would happen if the stock of money were changed is a relevant one to undertake. It is that type of analysis which is usually undertaken, whether in the IS/LM framework, New Classical macroeconomics, or New Keynesian macroeconomics. But when the stock of money is endogenous, then such a thought experiment makes little sense in that the stock of money evolves in response to private sector (and other) behaviour. The thought experiment often presented in the New Keynesian macroeconomics literature whereby the stock of money is varied (implicitly by the government) is an extraordinarily limited one for no one would see the appropriate definition of money in a developed economy as consisting of that which is issued by government or central bank (i.e. base money or M0).[8] Hence, at a minimum, it is necessary to consider how an initial change in the monetary base is translated into a change in the stock of the more broadly defined money.

We now consider in turn two cases. First where broad money is a multiple of base money, with the former largely created by the banking system and the latter controlled by the government or central bank with consideration of the process through which money is created. The second case is that of money being wholly created within the private sector through the granting of bank credit.

In the first case, the stock of money is directly related to base money via the credit multiplier where the latter is taken to be constant.[9] A change in base money has to be translated into a larger absolute change in broad(er) money through part of it being deposited with banks, and then lent on by the banks to the non-banking private sector. There has to be a willingness of the banks to make loans and more significantly for the non-bank public to take out the loans. The process by which the broader concept of money expands is well known, involving banks accepting deposits and being willing to grant loans and the public willing to make deposits with the banking system and wishing to take out loans from that system. But loans are granted and accepted for some purpose, usually linked to expenditure plans (whether to finance a real increase in consumer expenditure, investment or to cover higher prices). The point here is that if an increase in base money (constituting the nominal shock) is to be translated into a corresponding proportionate increase in the stock of money, more broadly defined, then the private sector has to be prepared to grant and take out loans and to increase expenditure. Thus the route by which the stock of money expands necessarily involves expenditure decisions, and unless there are decisions to take out loans the stock of money does not expand proportionately to the increase in base money.

In the second case, when the stock of money is created within the private sector then two features of the determinants of the stock of money are particularly relevant here.[10] First, the evolution of the stock of money is dependent on the planned spending decisions of the non-bank private sector. Thus, it is not shocks to the monetary stock which generate movements in nominal demand, but rather decisions by the non-bank private sector to vary their nominal demand (whether corresponding to variations in prices or in real level of demand) which lead to changes in the monetary stock. Hence, there are not externally imposed shocks in the stock of money for with endogenous credit money someone, somewhere, in the private sector has to make the decision to increase nominal demand, and thereby the stock of money: in general, an increase in the stock of money will require a bank to wish to extend a loan and an individual to be willing to take out the loan.

Second, the non-bank private sector not only helps to create money when it takes out loans from the banking system but it destroys money by the repayment of loans (cf. Kaldor and Trevithick, 1981). Then, even if it is possible to think of a random shock to the stock of money[11] (coming from, say, changes in the regulation of the banking system), any increase in the stock of money only remains in existence provided that the non-bank private sector is willing to hold it. If people are not willing to hold the money, then repayment of outstanding loans will extinguish some of the stock of money (there may, of course, be some delay before the 'excess' money is disposed of in this way). Thus at least part of the adjustment of the economy to a variation in the stock of money may take the form of extinguishing the money rather than through movements in price. In the limiting case, an initial increase in the stock of money (say, through the granting of further bank loans) for which there is no corresponding demand (to hold) will be extinguished and hence there is no final increase in the stock of money. As a number of authors have pointed out (e.g. Arestis, 1996b; Howells, 1995), the money created through the loans process will only ultimately remain in existence if people are prepared to hold that money. If not, then loans will be repaid and the stock of money diminished. The analysis of a shock to the money supply assumes that the money created remains in existence, but in the endogenous money situation this would only be the case if there are people willing to hold the money rather than repay any outstanding loans.

When the nominal shock comes about through the actions of some private sector economic agents, it may be expected that the effect of the change in the monetary stock depends on the precise set of actions which led to the shock. We briefly consider three. The first is where prices and costs are rising, and as a consequence enterprises (and others) are seeking further loans from the banks to cover the resulting higher expenditures. But note that price inflexibility is not the issue, for prices are assumed to be rising and thereby stimulating an increase in the money supply. The second is where enterprises are seeking to increase real expenditure (notably investment) in which case the apparent nominal shock (increase in loans and thereby in the stock of money) is a real demand shock. As Keynes (1937) and many others have pointed out, the expansion of expenditure requires financing by the granting of credit and where this is undertaken by banks there is an initial corresponding increase in the money stock. In these two cases, the expansion of the stock of money arises in response to economic events rather than be the cause of them. The third is where banks become more willing to lend, e.g. change criteria for credit worthiness, or through changes in the regulations governing banks. This is perhaps the closest to a nominal shock, but it still requires that the non-bank private sector is willing to accept loans which it may do presumably for reasons of increasing expenditure.

A thought experiment in which the money stock changes (in a manner reminiscent of Friedman's infamous "helicopter money", Friedman, 1969, p. 4) is rather uninteresting for, in an industrialized economy, money is largely credit money created within the private sector. But the new Keynesian analysis of monetary shocks and fluctuations in economic activity is dependent on the assumption of exogenous government-created money. The dependence of new Keynesian economics on an exogenous money supply is well illustrated by the following

> An economist can be a monetarist by believing that fluctuations in the money supply are the primary source of fluctuations in aggregate demand and a new Keynesian by believing that microeconomic imperfections lead to macroeconomic rigidities. Indeed... much of new Keynesian economics could also be called new monetarist economics.
>
> (Mankiw and Romer, 1991, p. 3)

CONCLUSIONS

In this chapter, we have first argued that the menu-cost approach to price stickiness focuses on the costs of price adjustment in a comparative static framework, overlooking the costs of output adjustment and the fluctuating nature of demand. However, the major part of the chapter concerns the use of menu costs to explain economic fluctuations. Our central claim is that this analysis rests on the assumption of government-created 'outside' money as the only form of money, whereas most money in an industrialized economy is 'inside' money created by the banking system. We have then argued that the New Keynesian analysis does not carry over from the exogenous money case to the endogenous one. Since the latter is relevant for industrialized economies the New Keynesian analysis in respect of economic fluctuations is not relevant for such economies.

ACKNOWLEDGEMENTS

I am grateful to Philip Arestis, Bill Gerrard, Geoff Harcourt, Man-Seop Park, Roy Rotheim and Nina Shapiro for comments on the first draft. The usual disclaimer applies.

NOTES

1 See, for example, Sawyer (1985, ch. 9).
2 See, for example, Sawyer (1983).

3 'Thus the profit loss from non adjustment [of price] is second order – that is, proportional to the square of (P*–P) [profit maximizing price minus actual price]. As long as the predetermined price is close to the profit-maximising price, the cost of price rigidity to the firm is small' (Ball *et al.*, 1991, p. 6). Romer (1993) notes that 'this argument... rests on a confusion of the two uses of the term "small". What is needed to provide a microeconomic basis for the view that aggregate demand movements are important to macroeconomic fluctuations is a demonstration that frictions that are "small" *in the sense of empirically plausible barriers to nominal price flexibility* are enough to keep prices from adjusting fully in response to aggregate demand movements of the size typically observed in cyclical fluctuations. The fact that the necessary frictions are "small" in the sense of being second order in the size of the aggregate demand movements is simply irrelevant to that issue' (footnote. 4, p. 10). See also Ball and Romer (1990).

4 I would argue that endogenous credit money characterizes industrialized economies: this is not to say that exogenous money was ever a good characterization of the nature of money even in non-industrialized economies, but rather that my concern in this chapter is with industrialized economies.

5 Whilst the line of criticism being developed in the text relates to the New Keynesian macroeconomics, it could also be applied to New Classical macroeconomics where the notion of 'surprises' in the money supply is also seen to generate business cycles. It is difficult to perceive of the private sector being surprised by changes in the stock of money if it is that sector which is responsible for those very changes. Thus, the New Classical macroeconomics is firmly rooted in exogenous money, for without such there is little meaning given to 'surprises': at a minimum when money is created within the private sector it does not come as a surprise to those creating and those receiving the loans.

6 For example, Goodhart (1994) argues that 'virtually every monetary economist believes that the CB [Central Bank] *can* control the monetary base, and, subject to errors in predicting the monetary multiplier, the broader monetary aggregates as well. [However,] almost all those who have worked in a CB believe that this view is totally mistaken' (p. 1424).

7 For reviews of the debate see Arestis (1992, ch. 8) Moore (1988), Palley (1991), Pollin (1991), Howells (1995), Lavoie (1992, ch. 4) But all would adhere to the essential endogeneity of money.

8 There are arguments to the effect that the government or central bank does not exercise effective control over M0, many of which we would accept. But since that is not central to our argument here we leave the point to one side.

9 If the shock came through a shock to the money multiplier or through banks being less than fully loaned up, the economy would effectively be in the second case considered in the text where the stock of money changes for reasons which are internal to the private sector.

10 The particular feature of endogenous money here is that it is entirely created within the private sector. The argument in the text does not rely on an extreme horizontalist position (as adopted by Moore, 1988).

11 Random with respect to the variables of the model under investigation. It may not be random in other respects for, as the example in the text illustrates, there may be identifiable reasons for the change in the stock of money.

12

KNOWLEDGE, INFORMATION AND CREDIT CREATION

Sheila Dow

INTRODUCTION

Post Keynesian monetary theory is associated with the view that the money supply is generated endogenously by the private sector through the process of credit creation. At the same time, a literature has been building up within orthodox economics, under the umbrella of New Keynesian economics, which appears to adopt a similar position. Indeed Fazzari (1992) and Fazzari and Variato (1994) have argued that there is here an 'opportunity for convergence':

> There is reason to hope that the intersection of post-Keynesian interests and real-world empirical observation with the analytical and empirical tools developed primarily in mainstream neoclassical analysis can lead to important new insights into how the macroeconomy behaves. Both schools of thought have much to gain by taking the work of each other seriously.
>
> (Fazzari, 1992, p. 129)

Certainly there would appear on the face of it to be much in common between New Keynesian and Post Keynesian 'interests'. According to the leading New Keynesians Greenwald and Stiglitz (1993a, p. 1), all Keynesians agree on the possibility of persistent unemployment, the significance of the business cycle other than as a result of real shocks, and the real significance of money. In addition, there is in the literature the suggestion that essential features of Keynes (uncertainty in terms of belief, liquidity preference in the face of uncertainty) have been operationalized within the New Keynesian framework (see Jones and Ostroy, 1984).

The purpose of this chapter is to assess the extent of overlap between the New Keynesian and Post Keyensian theories of money and credit. The chapter is offered in the spirit of taking New Keynesian credit theory seriously; there is indeed much scope for mutual learning among Post Keynesians and New Keynesians. Nevertheless, the argument is developed here that there are fundamental differences between the two approaches.[1] If the foundations of Post Keynesian theory were taken seriously by New Keynesians, it is not clear how useful their analytical and empirical tools would be. The differences between the two approaches stem ultimately from the difference between information as the basis of decision making, as in New Keynesian economics, and knowledge, as in Post Keynesian economics. This difference has profound consequences, not only for the supply of and demand for credit, but also for the demand for money. While New Keynesian economics offers a sophisticated analysis of one aspect of credit creation, that aspect is too narrow to address the full role of credit portrayed by Post Keynesian analysis; nor does it provide a satisfactory monetary theory.

In the next section, an account is offered of the New Keynesian analysis of credit creation. The difference between knowledge and information is then explored, as a prelude to explaining the different nature of Post Keynesian analysis of credit creation.

NEW KEYNESIAN THEORY OF CREDIT CREATION

The New Keynesian theory of finance and investment falls squarely within the New Keynesian paradigm as defined by Mankiw and Romer (1991a, p. 2); it posits that fluctuations in nominal variables influence fluctuations in real variables; it further posits the central role of imperfect information in understanding economic fluctuations; in particular, *contra* real business cycle theory, business fluctuations may have financial origins. As with other schools of thought, there are significant differences within New Keynesianism; in setting out an account of New Keynesian theory here, the focus will be on those contributions which seem to have most in common with Post Keynesianism.

At the macro level, New Keynesian theory is similar to monetarism in arguing that business fluctuations are seen as having financial elements. But, unlike monetarism, the New Keynesian approach rejects a focus on the demand for money on the grounds that it has been rendered redundant by financial innovation. Rather, the focus is on credit, of which money is a by-product. Empirical work is adduced which shows the relationship between macroeconomic aggregates and credit as being more stable than the relationship with money (see Blinder and Stiglitz, 1983), and implications are drawn for understanding business fluctuations and for the conduct of monetary policy. The emphasis has thus been shifted from the liability side of the banks' balance sheet to the asset side.

As with other New Keynesian theories, the key lies in microfoundations. The importance of credit is seen as stemming from imperfect substitution between different sources of finance, which in turn are generally seen as stemming from different information sets. The theory is thus explicitly counterposed to the Modigliani–Miller theorem, which posits perfect substitutability between sources of finance. In particular, firms may have a preference for internal finance because of the risk premium attached to all bank loans in the absence of information on the risk attached to individual loans. Further, financial intermediaries may ration credit. Both factors may inhibit output growth. By suggesting that bank finance is not perfectly substitutable for equity or internal finance, New Keynesian credit theory also sets itself up against the New Monetary economics, which sees banks as having no intrinsically special role; the New Keynesian rationale for that special role refers to banks' comparative advantage in information collection. Indeed, information is the key concept in New Keynesian credit theory: 'The essence of the credit creation process is the gathering and transmission of information' (Bernanke, 1993, p. 51).

The particular importance of information in the context of bank credit stems from two features. First, there is the heterogeneity of the product in terms of the creditworthiness of borrowers; Akerlof's (1970) analysis of the used-car market is often referenced as a formative influence. The second feature is the asymmetric nature of the debt contract: either the bank earns the return contracted with the borrower, or the borrower defaults. The essence of the New Keynesian account is generally put as that borrowers have more information on their default risk than do lenders. The literature addresses a range of other factors: risk aversion; differences in risk aversion between borrowers and lenders; monitoring costs; symmetric but incomplete information; etc. – in terms of what constitutes a sufficient condition for credit rationing. Asymmetry of information between borrowers and lenders on borrowers' default risk is presented most commonly as the essence of the particular significance of banks *vis-à-vis* alternative sources of credit. It is also the feature singled out by Fazzari (1992), as being the only logically acceptable reason for credit rationing. Meza and Webb (1992), however, argue that the asymmetries involved in debt contracts are sufficient to generate credit rationing as an equilibrium outcome with symmetric information (providing a justification for models which assume both credit rationing and perfect foresight, such as Blinder, 1987); we shall bear this in mind in the later discussion of the information concept. But information asymmetry persists as the rationale for separate banking institutions.

Rationing is defined as the refusal of credit where identical borrowers have already been granted credit, or else the refusal of credit to a particular class of borrower (e.g. small firms). The normal market mechanism to eliminate excess demand is a rise in price. But, according to Stiglitz and Weiss's (1981) seminal augment, banks choose instead to ration credit because raising the interest rate would reduce their expected profits in the absence of full information on individual default risk. Higher expected returns are assumed to be associated with higher risk, and therefore the demand for credit which would remain effective at higher interest rates would represent higher default risk for the bank (the adverse selection argument). In addition, borrowers are concerned with return so that a rise in interest charge encourages borrowers to adopt higher-risk projects. Banks on the other hand are concerned with an absence of default; the interests of borrower and lender are not symmetric, and there is a moral hazard issue involved in the behaviour of borrowers when interest rates rise.

The decision to keep interest rates below what would appear to be the market clearing rate is thus an equilibrium one; the conventional market diagram cannot deal with the fact that banks do not know the default risk by which to discount expected returns. As Bernanke puts it:

> [T]he market for credit is suffused with imperfect and asymmetric information. So, in the credit market – as in Akerlof's used-car market – decentralised, arm's-length transactions based only on price (or the interest rate, in this case) are unlikely to work. Instead, in order to clear the credit market, "price" (that is, the interest rate or expected yield) may have to be supplemented by a variety of other institutional mechanisms to overcome the problems of imperfect information.
>
> (1993, p. 52)

The diagrammatic framework suggested by Stiglitz and Weiss (1981) to substitute for the conventional market diagram is as shown in Figure 12.1.

The demand for loans (presumed to be based on full knowledge of default risk), L^D, is a negative function of the interest charged by banks, *r*. The supply of loans, L^S, is defined with respect to ρ, the expected return to the bank (taking account of default risk). The relationship between expected return and the interest rate becomes negative at high interest rates because of moral hazard and adverse selection. The credit supply curve with respect to the interest rate thus also becomes negative at high interest rates. Credit market equilibrium, shown here at the maximum expected return, results in credit rationing by the amount *Z*. The market clearing interest rate would not yield the maximum return.

Finally, there is the possibility of an excess supply of credit which banks do not eliminate by a reduction in interest rates. The argument is that, if one bank were to

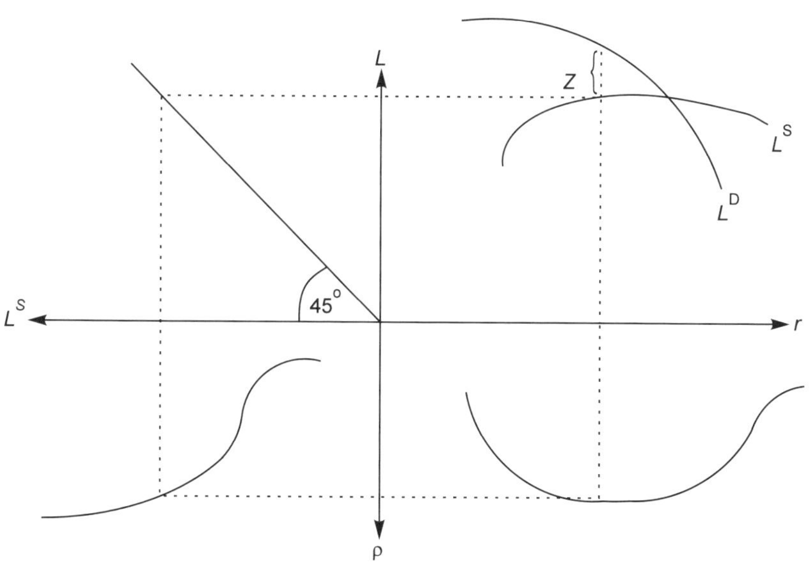

Figure 12.1 Determinaion of credit market equilibrium (Stiglitz and Weiss)

reduce rates, other banks would match the reduction for creditworthy borrowers but not for high-risk borrowers; the first bank would reduce expected profits by attracting high-risk borrowers. The overall picture is thus one of interest rate rigidity together with either unsatisfied demand for credit or excess capacity to create credit.

These and related microeconomic results are not always translated into macroeconomic terms. Indeed there is a marked difference in perception as to the prevalence of rationing: Stiglitz and Weiss (1981), for example, suggest that it 'may occur', not that it always occurs, whereas others imply that rationing is an endemic feature of bank behaviour. The implications drawn for monetary policy are that it acts through shifting the banks' credit supply curve, and thus the availability of credit. Since bank credit is an imperfect substitute for other sources of finance, changes in availability will cause changes in investment expenditure and thus real activity. Aside from monetary policy, the macroeconomic expression of credit rationing appears to arise from changing dependence on bank credit relative to other forms of finance. Thus Fazzari (1992) argues that the cyclical role of bank credit arises from the cyclical pattern of retained earnings; in a downturn, as profitability is reduced, firms rely more heavily on bank credit and thus are more likely to be constrained by credit rationing. Further, debt deflation can increase firms' vulnerability to changing conditions in external finance and can deplete banks' capital base and thus capacity to create credit; at the same time, as in 1990–1, the debt overhang can weaken the demand for credit (see Bernanke, 1993). Greenwald *et al.* (1984) suggest that increasing uncertainty in a recession can increase the incidence of credit rationing.

Several features of this endogenous credit theory should be noted before we proceed further. First, to the extent that they are on the short side of the market, it is the banks which determine the volume of credit, not the borrowers. Here is an important difference from the horizontalist version of the Post Keynesian endogenous money theory, which shows credit as being demand determined. In fact the New Keynesian focus on the role of banks in this sense is closer to Keynes's own theory (see Dow, 1997). However, there is an endogenous money theory within Post Keynesian economics which allows banks a significant role in the determination of credit (see Cottrell, 1994). But this theory also draws on Keynes's theory of liquidity preference; where a demand for money function is explicit in New Keynesian theory, it is only a transactions demand for money (see e.g. Blinder, 1987).

Second, New Keynesian theory persists in the mainstream view of money in terms of loanable funds. Citing Bernanke:

> 'By *credit creation process* I mean the process by which, in exchange for paper claims, the savings of specific individuals or firms are made available for the use of other individuals or firms (for example, to make capital investment or simply to consume).
>
> (1993, p. 50)

Further:

> Many economists have suggested that banks and similar institutions play a particularly central role in credit markets because of their expertise in conveying the savings of relatively uninformed depositors to uses . . . that are information-intensive and particularly hard to evaluate . . . . Among factors that have been cited are economies of specialisation (lending officers can gain expertise in a particular industry, for example), economies of scale (it is cheaper for a bank to evaluate a loan than for many small savers to do so independently), and economies of scope (it is efficient to provide lending services in conjunction with other financial services).
>
> (ibid., p. 53)

Thus the discussion of credit rationing is couched in terms of spare capacity to extend credit, with the implicit notion of a ceiling to that capacity. This differs markedly from the Post Keynesian view of endogenous credit creation as being subject only to influence by the authorities, not control, and of credit as being a potential initiator of income, and thus savings, generation.

Third, while the New Keynesian theory refers to a volume of credit creation which is insufficient for full employment, there is no scope for excessive credit creation. Where there have been marked expansions of credit, as in the 1970s, this is understood as reflecting the best information available at the time, so that there is no sense in which it could be regarded as excessive.

Finally, it is not uncontroversial to assert that borrowers have better information than lenders. The discussion of the virtues of the German banking system has rested not insignificantly on the argument that banks provide good advice: banks are after all in a better position to understand systemic risk than their customers. Certainly Cable (1985) has argued that it was the banks' acquisition of internal information by having directors on borrowers' boards which circumvented the asymmetric information problem. But still there seems to be not inconsiderable scope for discussing the implications of *different information*, rather than the full information/no information split represented by many New Keynesian models.

THE INFORMATION–KNOWLEDGE DISTINCTION

Because information is so central to the New Keynesian argument, it is important to understand exactly what is meant by it, and by the New Keynesian use of the related terms of risk and uncertainty. The term 'information' is used to refer to a data set which is, in principle, knowable. Risk is quantifiable on the basis of frequency distributions. Risk is often captured in this literature by the more sophisticated measure of mean preserving spreads, rather than the more traditional measures of variance and covariance (see Rothschild and Stiglitz (1970) for the original statement of mean preserving spreads in the context of New Keynesian economics; see Newbery and Stiglitz (1981) for a good explanation of the measure). But either measure requires a frequency distribution for its calculation. The term 'uncertainty' is either used interchangeably with 'risk' (see, for example, Greenwald and Stiglitz, 1993b), or used to refer to reducible risk (see Rothschild and Stiglitz, 1970; Bernanke, 1993; Jones and Ostroy, 1984); the term 'risk' then refers to irreducible risk. Risk is reducible if it refers to information which will be forthcoming in due course. Uncertainty is then measured by the mean preserving spread of beliefs as to the content of forthcoming information. Uncertainty therefore, just like risk, refers to a data set which is in principle knowable (at least eventually), where the relevant variables are known in advance. The subject of uncertainty, once it becomes known, feeds into the frequency distributions which generate measures of irreducible risk.

As far as borrowers are concerned, it is assumed that there is full information on past activities, costs and markets; borrowers are therefore seen as being in a position to estimate the risk to them of taking on a bank loan, where risk is estimated from a frequency distribution. Borrowers' risk is seen as important, particularly given the judgement that firms are risk averse. Greenwald and Stiglitz thus suggest that firm decision making be analysed in terms of portfolio theory:

> Production itself is risky; it takes time and there are no future markets for the sale of goods. Firms are often uncertain about the consequences of their actions . . . and their uncertainty grows with the size of the change. In general, firms know more about the status quo than about what things might be like if they changed their actions. The risk averse nature of firms under . . . conditions of [instrument] uncertainty is the basis of the "portfolio theory" of the firm, in which firms simultaneously choose all of their actions . . . taking into account the risk (covariances as well as variances) and expected returns with each "portfolio" of decisions.
>
> (1993b, p. 28)

But in formalizing the relationship between borrower and lender, borrowers are generally treated as having perfect knowledge. In terms of the Stiglitz and Weiss diagram, therefore, the loan demand schedule is based on full information on risk and return. Borrowers' risk is thus not seen as an issue of much importance in the New Keynesian literature.

The issue of risk assumes importance for lenders, in contrast, because of limitations on their information on borrowers, and thus on their capacity to estimate risk. Lenders do not have full information on borrowers. Thus risk assessment is regarded as being subjective:

> Since a borrower's classification determines the interest rate charged, the efficiency of credit allocation in the economy is dependent on the accuracy of the classification system. With our decentralised system of banking, competition among suppliers of credit works to eliminate systematic misclassifications . . . . However, owing to the intrinsically subjective nature of

> risk evaluations and judgements, competition in the market for loans is not likely to be as "perfect" as competition in the market, say, for chairs.
> (Jaffee and Stiglitz, 1990, p. 843)

Nevertheless, lenders are presumed to have information on aggregations of borrowers, allowing conclusions to be reached about the risk–return tradeoff. Thus, lenders are depicted in the Stiglitz and Weiss diagram as being able to stimate the mean return on loans for different interest rates, generating a U-shaped relationship. However, dualistically, lenders are depicted as being unable to calculate risk for any one borrower owing to imperfect information.

This use of the information concept can be contrasted with the notion of knowledge as it is used in a range of literatures (such as Post Keynesian, Institutionalist and neo-Austrian). The term 'knowledge' refers more to processes than to facts; information on facts is thus a subset of knowledge. The knowledge–information distinction is thus parallel to the distinction between 'knowing how' and 'knowing that'. This distinction has profound implications for credit market analysis.

First, the range of potential knowledge is not known in advance (or even in retrospect). The clearest statement of this is Shackle's (1972) argument that firms' investment projects are crucial experiments; there is in general no relevant frequency distribution on which to estimate risk. More generally, institutional evolution and human creativity mean that the future is not like the past in ways which cannot possibly be predicted. Keynes's (1973e) *Treatise on Probability* builds on the argument that the range of knowledge which can be captured by frequency distributions is small; most knowledge is subject to uncertainty in the sense of unquantifiable risk. Keynes classified knowledge as being direct (based on pure logic and/or direct experience) and indirect (based on theorizing, referring to direct knowledge as evidence). In the absence in general of quantitative probability distributions, qualitative probability is based on judgement as to the relevant theoretical structure, and as to the relevance of evidence; these judgements rely at least partly on convention. In the case of lenders' risk assessment of borrowers, conventions are employed as to factors increasing risk; these conventions may change from time to time, and will generally involve a categorization of borrowers. Action on the part of borrowers was described by Keynes as stemming from the upsurge of animal spirits (given the absence of certain expectations of project returns, or even of their frequency distribution). Where borrowers go against convention in their risk assessment, as may occur in the early stages of an upswing in the cycle, this also may be seen as the exercise of animal spirits.

Knowledge therefore requires knowledge of structural relationships in order for judgements to be made as to what is and what is not relevant information. Since full knowledge of structural relationships is not in general attainable, decision makers must assess how much ignorance they are prepared to recognize and also to accept (see Dow, 1995). As Runde (1990) has pointed out, additional information may reveal more ignorance than was previously recognized, thus increasing rather than reducing uncertainty. (Interestingly, Jones and Ostroy (1984), make a parallel point within their information framework.) Action, in this case the granting of a loan, requires an acceptance of irreducible ignorance whose scope may increase the more evidence is gathered.

More fundamentally, Farmer (1995) pointed out the dangers of thinking in terms of imperfect information-knowledge, or in terms of informational-knowledge limitations, since such thinking entails the view that full information or full knowledge is in principle attainable. She argued that it was essential to the social nature of knowledge that there was no such state as full knowledge which we could use as a benchmark. Applied to the context of the credit market, this argument suggests that it is in the nature of the banks' and borrowers' risk assessment processes that a strong element of judgement be employed. This is not the result of borrowers intentionally concealing information in an opportunistic manner, but rather the nature of the process of knowledge acquisition in an uncertain world. Borrowers themselves are similarly subject to uncertainty. Since borrowers and lenders have different knowledge, which may indeed be incommensurate, they will generally arrive at different risk assessments. What a borrower might interpret as credit rationing may be seen by the lender as ineffective credit demand due to excessive risk.

Credit rationing is generally understood as the refusal of credit at the going interest rate where there are identical borrowers who have been granted credit. But the notion of identicality implies that the risk profile of borrowers is knowable. If the risk profile is not knowable, identical borrowers cannot be identified at any point in time. Further, in historical time, changing knowledge may change risk assessments, leading to some borrowers being judged to be uncreditworthy. Similarly, as banks change their risk assessment with respect to existing loans and also investments, their willingness to lend may change, leading to some being refused credit. More generally, this analysis of credit creation implies that the total volume of credit, as well as its distribution, are the outcome of banks' assessment of risk with respect to the total portfolio as well as individual loan applicants. As Minsky, on whose work Post Keynesian credit theory draws most heavily, puts it:

> The decision makers are at once rational agents and maximizers, but they know that their well-being rests upon the performance of markets that are subject to both evolution and breakdowns. Furthermore, they know that they do not have the gift of perfect foresight. For economics the appropriate question is, How do rational agents behave in an irrational world, that is, a world they do not fully understand? Rational agents know that they might not know.
>
> (Minsky, 1993, p. 79)

The notion of rationing in Post Keynesian theory takes on a different light from New Keynesian theory. There is no longer a maximum credit total (presumably determined by the monetary authorities) against which credit rationing can be measured as a shortfall. In Post Keynesian credit theory the credit total is the outcome of the banks' state of knowledge. This total may be either excessive or inadequate by some criterion such as the needs of the productive sector. It may well be that it is possible to identify at a particular time a fringe of unsatisfied borrowers. But the credit total cannot be judged excessive or inadequate relative to any 'correct' total; the notion of a correct total requires the capacity to assess risk objectively. As Minsky has pointed out:

> While asymmetric or private information is a pervasive fact of life and of decision making in historical time, it is not necessary to non-neutrality, for even if information were symmetric and no private information existed, the prices of capital assets and current output would be determined in quite different markets and the dominant proximate determinants of the two would differ.
>
> (ibid.)

Minsky's (1975) diagram (see Figure 12.2) of the firm's financing decision (as expressed in Dow and Earl, 1982, ch. 11) is helpful in seeing the significance for credit theory of using the concept of knowledge rather than information.

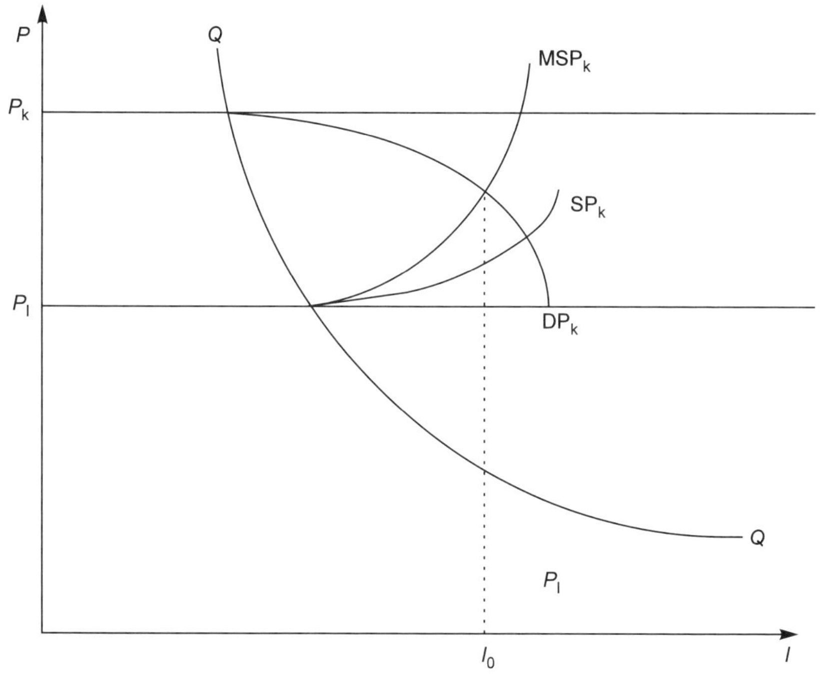

Figure 12.2 Determinaion of afirmm's external finance (Minsky)

The demand for external finance is determined by three factors. First, P_K is the expected value of the capital to be purchased. Demand for credit is initially perfectly elastic at this value, as long as P_K exceeds P_I, the purchase price of the capital. But beyond a certain level of borrowing, the demand for credit becomes increasingly elastic, the distance from P_K measuring borrower's risk, i.e. the risk perceived by the borrower of going illiquid by incurring debt. The supply of credit is similarly perfectly elastic at P_I, but then becomes inelastic by an amount measuring lender's risk. The actual amount borrowed is then determined by the intersection of the demand curve and the marginal supply price of capital curve, less the amount of internal finance allowed by retained earnings, *QQ*. The size of loan may therefore vary with changes in profitability, and thus retained earnings, and also with changes in the purchase price of capital. Less predictably, the size of the loan may change with a change in expected value, P_K, a change in borrower's risk and/or a change in lender's risk. These will change with changing knowledge on the part of borrowers or lenders, including knowledge which either increases or reduces confidence.

A New Keynesian would interpret the diagram very differently. Borrowers know their own risk, and also the value of the project within a probability distribution. Risk and the probability distribution are connected in a deterministic way (by variance, mean preserving spread, or whatever). But the lender has no information on risk with respect to an individual borrower. There are two possibilities. For some firms, the supply of credit would be perfectly elastic at the interest rate which maximizes return (including default risk) for the class of borrowers to which the firm belongs. For other firms, the supply curve would be non-existent; these are the rationed borrowers. The level of credit to the firm varies, then, with a change in that set interest rate, and in the objective conditions which determine the return on the project, or with the (unexplained) position of the firm relative to the rationing cut-off. The rich analysis of knowledge base which is the essence of Minsky's theory of a firm's investment finance, and the foundation of his theory of the cycle, is quite absent from the New Keynesian analysis.

Finally, Post Keynesian credit theory is closely related to the theory of liquidity preference, which is likewise based on the notion of knowledge rather than information. Uncertainty, the relative absence of certain knowledge, explains liquidity preference (see Runde, 1994). Liquidity preference in turn is relevant to banks and firms as much as to depositors. Thus an upsurge in confidence associated with a fall in liquidity preference reduces borrower's perceived risk and lender's perceived risk, while also increasing banks' willingness to expand their direct lending and firms' willingness to go illiquid and invest in capital projects. Thus is created the paradox of liquidity (see Dow, 1994, pp. 146–52) whereby the supply of deposits, as the counterpart of credit, is greatest when liquidity preference is lowest, and lowest when liquidity preference is highest. New Keynesian theory does not seek to explain the demand for deposits. Implicitly, deposits are seen as being passively absorbed in transactions demand as credit, and thus activity, increase. Post Keynesian monetary theory in contrast suggests downward pressure on interest rates during an upturn and upward pressure during a downturn, as a result of the paradox of liquidity. This in turn fuels the pro-cyclical movement of credit creation which in turn fuels the cycle itself. The analysis of the cycle rests on the foundations of the Post Keynesian theory of knowledge and how it impinges on economic behaviour.

CONCLUSION

It is centrally important for credit theory, and its implications, whether the micro-foundations are couched in terms of information or knowledge. First, the two approaches suggest a different analysis of aggregate credit. The New Keynesian approach refers only to a shortfall from some notional aggregate, determined presumably by the monetary authorities. When the authorities raise interest rates, the consequence may be significant rationing which inhibits economic activity. In contrast, the Post Keynesian theory suggests that the credit total is determined to a significant extent by the banking system, in conjunction with borrowers. The volume of credit reflects the state of knowledge among borrowers and among lenders, which in turn is the product of the evidence, theoretical knowledge, conventions and animal spirits of each. This total may entail a fringe of unsatisfied borrowers, i.e. rationing, whether or not this is perceived as such by the banks. But it may also entail credit creation in excess of the needs of the productive sector. There is no objective (certain) benchmark by which to identify a *correct*, volume of credit.

Where credit rationing is the product solely of asymmetric information, there is the possibility, in principle at least, that credit rationing could be eliminated, or at least reduced. This has application, for example, to the case of European monetary integration; here one of the explicit goals is to improve information, reducing the scope of local monopoly, thus increasing the availability of credit. But where the total and distribution of credit are the product of knowledge sets, there is no corresponding reason why credit availability should be increased. Indeed availability may be decreased for some classes of borrowers if the outcome of monetary integration is concentration in the banking sector which increases remoteness from small, local borrowers (as opposed to multinational borrowers whose head offices are located close to banking centres). (See Dow, 1997b.)

Finally, the issue of information versus knowledge is relevant to the desirability of different types of banking system. The increasing liquidity needs of banks have encouraged a move away from direct lending and towards off-balance-sheet activities, even among German banks. In terms of information, it is not so clear why banks should have a comparative advantage over non-bank financial intermediaries, or if they do that they can expect to maintain that comparative advantage. In terms of knowledge, in contrast, it is not so much a matter of knowing facts as of knowing processes; this cannot be acquired easily. It is more readily acquired through relationship banking, which is being squeezed out by competitive pressures. More generally, knowledge acquisition is a feature of corporatist styles of economic system, like Germany and Japan, where mutual knowledge is routinely acquired by borrowers, lenders and government (and potentially by the work force). Keynes's theory of knowledge points to the limited scope for certain knowledge. But it also points to ways of increasing knowledge by a variety of (normally) incommensurate means, all of which increase the capacity for risk assessment as well as the capacity to recognize where risk assessment is virtually impossible, and thus a decision to lend can only be justified by animal spirits.

ACKNOWLEDGEMENTS

This chapter has benefited from helpful comments and suggestions provided by the Post Keynesian Economics Study Group and by the Economics Departmental Workshop at the University of Stirling.

NOTES

1 This argument is developed in a rather different way with respect to New Keynesian credit theory by Dymski, (1994a), and with respect to the Modigliani–Miller theory by Glickman (1994).

13

POST AND NEW KEYNESIANS

The role of asymmetric information and uncertainty in the construction of financial institutions and policy

Dorene Isenberg

Recent writings (Fazzari, 1992; Fazzari and Variato, 1994; Delli Gatti and Gallegatti, 1992; Delli Gatti *et al.* 1994) have linked the New Keynesian asymmetric information theorists with the Post Keynesians. From a more general perspective, both Post and New Keynesians are linked by their claims to a Keynesian theoretical framework and outcome. Within these two schools of economic thought that bear the same last name there are many similarities – the absence of complete information, importance of financial institutions, persistence of credit rationing, non-neutrality of money, and necessity of governmental intervention. So, the question arises: are these points of overlap significant or superficial? This chapter joins a growing body of work in arguing that the underlying assumptions, behavioural motivations and, therefore, view of the economy that drives New Keynesian theory are fundamentally different from the Post Keynesians'.[1]

This analysis of the relationship of the New Keynesians to the Post Keynesians restricts itself to that subgroup of theorists relying on asymmetric information in the credit markets. This subgroup is like all of the other subgroups – menu costs, efficiency wages and contracts. It removes a restriction from the perfectly competitive neoclassical model, perfect information, so that the theoretical result, an underemployment equilibrium level of production, will deviate from the traditional full employment result. For the asymmetric information New Keynesians, missing information produces an underemployment equilibrium and a theoretical rationale for financial intermediation and governmental intervention: they increase economic efficiency. These results sound Post Keynesian, but this chapter will indicate why one of the two approaches is a pretender to the Keynesian name. In fact, by many of their own accounts New Keynesians are theoretically more closely allied with the Monetarists than with the Post Keynesians.

Overall, this chapter will analyse the underlying methodologies of the two Keynesians in order to show their dissimilarities. The first section briefly describes the theoretical approach of the asymmetric information New Keynesians (hereafter referred to as the asymmetricians). The second section begins the comparison of the Post and New Keynesian economic analyses by looking at their methodologies. The third section continues the methodological analysis by comparing the two schools' approaches to money, liquidity and stability, which leads to the following section's exploration of the differences in the economic role of financial intermediation that emerge because of their different methodologies. The final section compares the Post and New Keynesian views of the role of governmental intervention.

ASYMMETRIC INFORMATION NEW KEYNESIANS

While most asymmetricians cite Akerlof's (1970) 'lemons' article as their foundation, it appears that Stiglitz and Weiss (1981) pioneered its formulation in credit market terms. The methodological format is the traditional neoclassical aggregate demand and aggregate supply equilibrium analysis, but with a twist: information is perceived to be imperfect. The imperfection, described as a principal–agent problem, means that lenders (principals) only have public information and borrowers (agents) have both public and private information. These informational disparities take various forms: the lender's inadequate knowledge of a project's riskiness; the lender and borrower having different pieces of knowledge about the project which leads to each having different probability distributions of the project's outcomes.[2] Since lenders have less information than borrowers, they are put in the position of possibly making loans of higher than average risk if the interest rate is allowed to determine the level of lending. This pool of loans of higher than average risk is the first part of the problem that lenders face: adverse selection.

Once a loan is extended, lenders face the other part of the problem, i.e. moral hazard. Given the information disparity, the borrower has an incentive to seek his or her own personal gain at the lender's cost. Mishkin (1991) offers this example, 'the borrower has incentives to cheat by misallocating funds for his own personal use, either through embezzlement or by spending on perquisites which do not lead to increased profits' (p. 72). The combination of adverse selection and moral hazard produces a financial sector, which, left to market principles, will achieve a less than perfect outcome. The outcomes from these credit imperfections are varied and dependent on the imperfection's source; they include: credit rationing, high interest rates for borrowers and low profits for lenders, and financial crises as an equilibrium outcome. In general, the result is a less than full employment equilibrium level of production (Stiglitz and Weiss, 1981; Myers and Majluf, 1984; Mishkin, 1991; Mankiw, 1986).

Asymmetricians' imperfect information is unique; it differs from both adaptive expectations and Post Keynesian views of imperfect information.[3] The asymmetricians posit a world in which all information is knowable, but 'agents specialise in particular economic activities and their informational advantages are specific to their circumstances' (Fazzari and Variato, 1994, p. 361). Information is known, but it is dispersed throughout the economy among various agents according to their particular economic role. So, each agent only knows a part of the total 'knowable' information and is not inclined to share his or her knowledge.

Since information is exchanged only when agents are willing to divulge it, financial markets must be characterized as missing information or incomplete. This structure of information leads asymmetricians to argue that free market solutions are not optimal. Decision making left to markets results in a loan mix with a level of higher than average risk which leads to a less than optimal level of profits. Instead, they argue that intermediated credit markets provide greater efficiency and stability. Financial intermediaries screen potential borrowers, determine their creditworthiness, and monitor them once a loan has been extended. Choosing borrowers as a result of screening and credit checking processes supplants the interest rate as the credit allocation mechanism and acts to keep the actual risk level of the loan mix at the average level. Using financial intermediaries, however, does not necessarily produce a level of lending commensurate with full employment. Banks are firms; and in response to their risky environment, they will ration credit producing a less than full employment level of production (Stiglitz, 1992).

Since the economy does not automatically reach a full employment production level, asymmetricians argue that proper governmental intervention is economically advantageous. The form that intervention takes varies depending on the focal point of the imperfect information in the credit producing process. Mishkin (1991), Stiglitz (1992), Mankiw (1986), and Diamond and Dybvig (1983) propose using the lender of last resort role of the Federal Reserve to break the credit reduction reaction by banks that propels a downturn into a recession and turns a bank run into a financial crisis. Diamond and Dybvig also show how governmentally sponsored deposit insurance can achieve optimal risk sharing between depositors and bank owners so that bank runs can be avoided. Mankiw, along with indicating the Fed's role, emphasizes the problem of risk born by the private sector when it enters into a debt contract. He argues that the government must *remove* this risk by providing a guarantee.[4] In this way social welfare will be enhanced.

In sum, the asymmetricians' incomplete market separates them from the adaptive expectations model by constructing an economy that produces an equilibrium underemployment level of output. This difference, however, is the only significant difference between these two schools of thought. The asymmetricians alter one assumption, but continue to rely on the rest of the adaptive expectations methodology. In fact, Davidson (1994b) argues that the asymmetricians' minor change to imperfect information is only *ad hocery*, for in the longer run the economy achieves its full employment equilibrium level of production. Imperfection, therefore, is only an epiphenomenon.

The succeeding sections present an argument showing that the Post and New Keynesians are not kin. Their differences begin with their methodologies which form the building blocks of their theories. The result is theories that are superficially similar and fundamentally in disagreement.

METHODOLGICAL UNDERPINNINGS

Time

The asymmetricians emphasize the short run. They work in a framework that produces an equilibrium solution based upon a competitive market, but the achieved result is not a price taking equilibrium. As Stiglitz and Weiss (1981, p. 395) put it: banks compete, but the equilibrium interest rates achieved would lead to greater bank profits if the rates were reduced. This tension leads the bank to ration credit, and enhance profits, rather than charge the market price. While the operation of the bank or market in the short run is highlighted, ultimately, it is attached to a longer-run analysis. Bernanke (1983b) when investigating liquidity constraints in financial institutions during the Great Depression defines his research as following the line of investigation begun by Friedman and Schwartz (1963). Mishkin also situates his work in this line of thought. He explains that his analysis of financial crises is complementary to that of the monetarists and indicates that it 'supplies a transmission mechanism for a decline in the money supply to lead to a decline in aggregate economic activity' (1991, p. 75). In such a classical or New Classical framework, the short run is merely a moment on the path to the long-run equilibrium which ultimately dominates it. This long-run framework leads to problems for a short-run analysis defined in terms of the behaviours of financial institutions, for the long-run equilibrium demands certainty, reversible time and an ahistorical economy.

The Post Keynesians, unlike these New Keynesians, take Joan Robinson's approach: time matters, so history is important. Davidson describes the difference between the equilibrium approach with its emphasis on being at the end point versus the historical approach which emphasizes the process, the path that leads to an end point at some future point in time (1978, pp. 25–6). Arestis expands on this aspect of the methodological approach when he states that a Post Keynesian study of an economic system focuses on 'three essential characteristics . . . the second [of which] is the existence of *irreversible time* where production takes time and economic agents enter into commitments well before outcomes can be predicted' (1988, pp. 41–2). This view argues against the reversibility of time inherent in the neoclassical approach. It also leads to economic theory that emphasizes more than just prices and quantities in markets. The economic institutions, the contracts struck, the innovations, the type of credit money, the distribution of assets and liabilities, and the power relationships among the institutions and economic actors are important because they produce the resulting economy. The Post Keynesian methodology underscores the time-bound and institutional nature of a market-driven monetary production economy, instead of foregrounding the static equilibrium end point which is the New Keynesians' organizing principle.

The unknown: risk vs. uncertainity

These two different methodologies also operate with fundamentally different conceptions of what can be known about the future. In New Keynesian methodology, the unknown refers only to the outcome of an event for which the probability distribution is known, not to the asymmetric distribution of information about the probability distribution underlying that event.[5] New Keynesians use probability theory's concept of risk to describe their decision-making process in the face of the unknown. Alternatively, Post Keynesians draw upon Keynes's concept of uncertainty.

Keynesian uncertainty differs from probability in that it corresponds to a situation of unknowability. Lawson details the differences between both subjectivist and objectivist probability theories and Keynesian uncertainty. He notes that '[Keynes] associates uncertainty not with probabilistic knowledge, but with the *absence* of probabilistic knowledge. Uncertainty corresponds to a situation in which probabilities are *not* numerically determinate – or even comparable, in terms of more or less, with other probability relations' (Lawson, 1988, p. 48). Definitionally, probability theory and Keynesian uncertainty do not have a point of overlap.

Davidson also argues that risk, as manifested in probability theory, both objective and subjective, operates with a different view of history and the future than is encapsulated in uncertainty.[6] For objective probability to be able to capture the unknown conceptually, the economic environment must be ergodic. Effectively this means that 'probability distributions regarding historical phenomena have existed, but also that the same probabilities which determined past outcomes will continue to govern future events' (1991, p. 132). While the conditions that would have to exist for such a view to hold true are extremely limited, if they did, then the future is not unknown and would instead be described by risk. In such a case, economic agents are acting with a knowledge of the future that not only is inclusive of all possible events, but that also includes the probability distribution function of their occurrences. This conception of the unknown runs counter to that embodied in Keynesian uncertainty.

Rather than rely upon objective probability theory, Stiglitz and Weiss forged their theory on subjective probabilities (1981 p. 395). Davidson, following Savage's (1954) vision of subjectivity, argues that this requires 'a preference ordering which is both timeless and complete over the set of all conceivable outcomes' (1991, p. 135). While he also notes that preference orderings may not be generated for events that are unique episodes and that, since the expected utility orderings rely on having evaluated the consequences of all possible cases, the question of how one knows when all cases have been exhausted is necessary, but remains without an answer. Davidson believes that Savage realizes that for a 'large world' of cases this exhaustive evaluation is impossible, so Savage limits the applicability of subjective probability to 'small world' states. The result is a very limited set in which subjective probability theory approximates uncertainty. An analysis of the interation of an economy's financial and productive sectors would exceed the parameters of this 'small world' state. Davidson notes that with such a limitation subjective probability must be considered a special case, not a general theory (ibid., p. 136).

Asymmetric information and uncertainity

The concept of asymmetric information builds on the primary notion that all information is *knowable* and has an objective or a subjective probability distribution function. Once information is available, *knowable*, and has a distribution function, then it can be asymmetrically distributed, divided into private and public knowledge. It is this skewed distribution of information linked to its probability distribution that leads to a financial structure that matters.

While this is the dominant view for many asymmetricians, Fazzari and Variato (1994) ostensibly take another approach, one that attempts to make a methodological connection between the Post and New Keynesians. They posit that asymmetric information can be separated from its relationship to risk and then be seen as the fundamental element in producing a financial structure that matters.[7] Their objective in this delinking is to show the inherent linkage between Keynesian uncertainty and asymmetrical information. They cast their argument in two domains: (a) a world with symmetric information (all agents have the same information) which is interpreted differently by different agents prior to undertaking action; and (b) a world with asymmetric information which is also interpreted differently by different agents prior to their action. In both domains it is the agents' differing interpretation of the same or different facts (it does not matter), that Fazzari and Variato define as uncertainty. While the first scenario is 'empirically vacuous' in their opinion, the second one, they insist, links asymmetrical information and uncertainty: 'Fundamental uncertainty, by necessitating interpretation in advance of action, *implies* the existence of asymmetric information in any real-world context' (ibid., p. 364). In order to make this linkage, Fazzari and Variato have to move outside of probability theory and view the decision making process only at its surface. They shift the focus of the argument away from the fundamentals, whether information necessary to the decision-making process is knowable, to the subordinate notion that differing interpretations of information that is known lie at the heart of the methodology. In Keynesian uncertainty such a discussion is superfluous, for it fails to reckon with the core concept of knowability.

Even at the level of the real world, Fazzari and Variato's analysis is misguided. Earlier in their article they define asymmetrical information as that which is unknown because 'agents specialise in particular economic activities and their informational advantages are specific to their circumstances.... It would be a great surprise if *everyone* "knew" exactly the same thing. When different agents know different things, information is asymmetric' (ibid., p. 360). This view of information indicates that while all agents do not have the same knowledge, the knowledge that is desired does exist. The problem lies in the skewness of its distribution. At a later point in the article, they point out that 'it will not be in agents' interest, in general, to reveal all the information they have' (ibid., p. 364). In this statement, their argument takes a decidedly strategic twist in terms of informational flows, and this twist underlines the difference between asymmetric information and uncertainty. For asymmetricians knowledge exists, and it is part of the game not to reveal what is known. Under Keynesian uncertainty, the information *does not exist.* As Davidson puts it,

> the decision maker believes that during the lapse of calendar time between the moment of choice and the date(s) of payoff, unforeseeable changes can occur. In other words, the decision maker believes that reliable information regarding future prospects *does not exist* today.
>
> (1994a, p. 89, emphasis added)

So far, this investigation has argued that there is a fundamental incompatibility that exists between the Post and New Keynesians at the methodological level. In the next section I argue that the methodological role played by uncertainty motivates the use of money and the financial institutions, which were created specifically for its flow. The role of uncertainty is also the key element in evaluating the alleged similarities that exist between the Post Keynesian and asymmetric financial structures.

FINANCIAL STRUCTURE: POST AND NEW KEYNESIAN

Uncertainty, money, and monetary contracts

Post Keynesians, like the New Keynesians, are interested in producing theory that describes and explains the operations of a real world monetary economy. It is one of the primary reasons that the financial structure, which results from the uncertainty that permeates the capitalist economy, is a major topic of Post Keynesian discussion.[8]

The logic of this analysis begins with Keynesian uncertainty forming the foundation for money's role as a store of value. Given the unknowability of the future, not all people in the economy will desire to use all of their income to purchase consumption or investment goods or financial assets. Also, because their expectations of future outcomes may not be realized, people hold money. Money, while not interest bearing, carries a liquidity premium, which is valuable in a world where expectations may not be realized. Money as a store of wealth retains its value through time. It is this characteristic of perfect liquidity that makes money desirable to hold when the expectations of investment failure outweigh those of success.

Just as uncertainty leads to holding money because of its liquidity, it also leads to writing contracts that are denominated in money terms. Davidson explains this relationship:

> Modern society has developed the institution of legally enforceable forward money contracts to permit the contracting parties to possess a measure of control over future performance and cash flows, even in the face of ignorance regarding future real economic conditions. All legal contractual agreements among parties are enforceable solely by monetary payments under the civil law.... The organisation of production and exchange transactions on a

> money-contractual basis permits the seller and the buyer to maintain control over future cash flows in an otherwise unpredictable future.
>
> (1994a, pp. 99–100)

This uncertainty of future outcomes infuses the capitalist monetary economy and provokes the creation of institutions in an attempt to exert control over those outcomes. Money and contracts are two of these institutions; financial intermediaries develop out of the need for, use and characteristics of money and monetary contracts. In the Post Keynesian discourse about money and its institutions, a number of voices are engaged in what is not always a harmonious conversation. Regardless of how raucous the discussion may get, at its centre is the linkage between uncertainty and the institutions that emerge in the financial structure of a dynamic monetary production economy.

Financial institutions

Banks serve a variety of functions which are primarily aimed at reducing uncertainty and enhancing liquidity.[9] The first of these is serving as the clearing house for debits and credits. Bank debt is private debt, but when it is regulated by the monetary authority, it attains the role of money. In its role as money it is 'used in settlement of the overlapping myriad of other private contracts [which] immensely increases the efficiency of the monetary system' (Davidson, 1994a, p. 104). So, at its most basic level, banking institutions and their regulators promote greater efficiency because they effect the orderly clearing of private debits and credits. This orderliness also enhances the liquidity of the economic system. By maintaining the orderliness of the channels through which money flows, financial institutions also reduce the uncertainty that arises from chaos.

Second, financial intermediaries provide liquidity in another, more direct form to the economy. Banks create credit money.[10] Wray (1988, 1992) takes the act of money creation and shows its dual nature: meeting demand for money and creating the money supply. This credit money creation process is carried out by meeting the demand for money which is satisfied by the expansion of bank liabilities.[11] In this way, it is the demand for credit money that creates its supply: the money supply is endogenous.

Banks respond to the demand for loans because they are profit oriented; borrowers are demanding credit because they have expectations that their project will be profitable. The successful loans are paid off because the borrowers' expectations about their projects' returns were realized. In this way the demand for money, the money creation process and the supply of money are functions of profit expectations. The realization of these profit expectations validates the banks' assets and promotes the continued expansion of credit which may lead to extended economic expansions (Wray, 1988; Minsky, 1986). When expectations are not realized, the value of the banks' assets is reduced which may lead to a decline in lending and extended economic contractions. Under some of the most usual of circumstances, these fulfilled and unfulfilled expectations lead to financial instability.[12]

Third, the previous points imply this final one: Post Keynesians view the bank as a firm.[13] Minsky discusses the business of banking noting that the bank's fundamental activity is 'guaranteeing that some party is creditworthy' (1986, p. 228). The bank is in the business of extending credit; its financial product is a loan.[14] Since it wants to make a profit by engaging successfully in lending activities, it is necessary to screen loan applicants and monitor borrowers.

The bank gathers information on potential borrowers because it is profit-oriented and its product is purchased over time. Wray (1992) agrees with Stiglitz and Weiss (1981) that price ratios provide an inadequate level of information on which to base a loan. He points out that a bank monitors and screens its loans: it uses rules of thumb to ration credit. Some of the rules of thumb come from regulators, such as the proportion of bank equity that can be lent to one borrower; others come from secondary markets, such as total debt payment to income ratios of the loan applicant; and still others are self-imposed so as to protect their balance sheets. Since credit demand may actually be stimulated by increasing price ratios (adverse selection and moral hazard), the bank must seek other procedures for allocating credit. Credit rationing is the bank's response to the tension that results from pressures induced by credit demand, lender's and borrower's risks, and liquidity preference (Wray, 1992, pp. 305–6).

The previous description highlights the obvious point of operational overlap in the Post and New Keynesian views of banks: they screen and monitor borrowers. Why banks behave in this manner and what kinds of undesirable consequences result if they do not are answered differently by each school of thought.

The asymmetricians, as we have already seen, situate bank behaviour in (a) the existence of private and public information and (b) the strategic use of private information to defraud lenders. The Post Keynesians cite the pervasiveness of uncertainty in a market economy which leads to the social construction of legal and financial institutions to shift or contain as much of the uncertainty as is possible.

Because the asymmetricians believe that all information is knowable and merely being withheld in order to enhance personal gain, financial intermediaries grow out of the lenders' need to capture as much of the existent knowledge as is possible as they attempt to make profit-enhancing and lender-protecting decisions. Whereas in the classical school of thought, the interest rate would provide sufficient information to lenders concerning the riskiness and expected profitability of a potential borrower's project, in an asymmetric information approach, the skewed distribution of information precludes the interest rate playing this role. In fact, the interest rate is tainted by the missing information, so sole reliance upon it as an informational source produces a loan portfolio with risk characteristics higher than desired. The latter result is achieved because borrowers behave in an opportunistic manner. They withhold information that indicates the true probability of their projects' returns which is lower than the probability-as-information that they provide to the lender. So, in contrast to the usual reliance upon markets for price and quantity determinations, the asymmetricians argue for the efficiency enhancing role played by financial intermediaries as they screen loan applicants and monitor loans.

Post Keynesians' fundamental disagreement with the knowability of certain types of information sets them apart from the New Keynesian argument for financial intermediation. While they, too, acknowledge the missing information in the market interaction, they believe that this information is unattainable because it does not exist. Probabilities of returns cannot be constructed and neither can the riskiness of loans be determined. 'Guesses' have to be made.[15]

The information is missing, and hence the market which is supposed to provide such information is missing. Kregel (1980) notes that in classical theory the interest rate is supposed to equilibrate the desires of underconsumers – savers – with investors – borrowers. Unfortunately, all that saving does is give a signal of current non-consumption; therefore there is 'no information for the market to signal' (ibid., p. 37). As a result of uncertainty, the economy fails to reach full employment, not because uncertainty leads to perverse buyer behaviour, but because there is *no market* capable of linking future consumption decisions to present expenditure decisions if the former do not exist when the latter must be undertaken (ibid., p. 38). Without market-provided information on which to base lending decisions, the financial intermediary fills the void. However, this occurs not by providing the unprovidable, but by gathering as much information as is available and then using its 'expertise' to analyse it.

While the Post Keynesians and the asymmetricians have fundamentally different theoretical foundations for financial intermediation, they both agree that the financial sector does affect the level of economic activity through its extension of credit. This impact on the production sector, whether it is expansionary or contractionary, provides the rationale in both schools of thought for financial regulation where the central bank is the primary regulatory agent.

The role of regulation

For the asymmetricians, problems arising from asymmetric information produce increased opportunities for financial crises leading to reduced economic activity. Mishkin (1991) summarizes the work of others as to the mechanisms that induce a reduction in credit flows to profitable borrowers: reduction in value of collateral resulting from inflation; increase in borrowers' debt burdens because of deflation; and decrease in lending activity as a response to increased fears of bankruptcy. He also points out that there are periods when financial institutions respond to increased fears of their own bankruptcy by becoming risk-lovers. This change in behaviour leads to increased lending to high-risk borrowers who have high-risk projects with big payoffs.

Both Stiglitz (1992) and Mishkin (1991) look to the central bank, the monetary authority and primary regulator of financial institutions, as the most capable agent for addressing these problems arising from asymmetric information. While asymmetricians argue that financial institutions in and of themselves produce a more efficient and usually less risky financial sector, they acknowledge that they may engage in risk-loving behaviour when faced with deep recessions or bankruptcy. To stem such activity, Stiglitz promotes the notion of *effective* banking regulation. Mishkin follows up by arguing that the Federal Reserve in its role as bank regulator has the capability of curbing this behaviour when it acts as lender of last resort. He cites the minimal disruption in the commercial paper market after the bankruptcy of Penn Central Railroad and the failure to enter a recession after the stock market crash of 1987 as examples of the Federal Reserve's ability to prevent the development of serious asymmetric information problems in the credit markets (ibid. p. 104).

Stiglitz (1992) also includes the Federal Reserve's use of monetary policy as another conduit for restricting the economic impact of financial crises. For some crises, he argues, the problem lies in maintaining the amount of credit that is available to borrowers without altering the terms, so he emphasizes the use of reserve requirements and open market operations to make that credit readily available. The policy he promotes is a reduction in reserve requirements and the purchase of Treasury Bills. By reducing reserve requirements more credit becomes available to borrowers without altering the lending rate. Buying Treasury Bills induces a drop in their interest rate thereby making loans a more desirable asset. When promoting these policies, Stiglitz acknowledges that if a bank is strongly risk-averse, then even these easy-money policies may not overcome its fear of bankruptcy costs. Ultimately, he posits, it is the restrictions and incentives that inhibit a financial institution acting in a risk-loving manner which are built into the regulatory structure and the central bank's lender of last resort role that stand between the financial crisis's eruption and a recession.

For Post Keynesians, the financial institution is a profit-oriented financial firm that is attempting to enhance its competitive position through lending activities, portfolio management, and innovative products and processes. Problems arise, however, because the product these institutions produce is money: the perfectly liquid asset which is demanded as a store of value against uncertainty and a means by which to actualize or expand economic activity. While, as Davidson argues, financial institutions produce greater efficiency by promoting orderliness, it is also the case that they induce greater instability in the economy. The move towards greater instability grows out of the profit-motivated behaviour which results in increased risk taking. This risk taking has been seen in lending decisions which resulted in the leveraged buy-out débâcles and speculative and Ponzi debt positions in the 1980s. It can also be seen in the proliferation of new products, such as derivatives, which promise big problems for the 1990s (Minsky, 1986; Wolfson, 1994).

The Post Keynesian view of regulation grows out of this conflicted role played by financial institutions. The Federal Reserve, as regulator and overseer of monetary policy, acknowledges their dichotomized operation and adjusts its operations so as to promote financial practices that foster growth without putting the financial system at risk. Minsky captures this dichotomy when he notes that

> any prescription for the behaviour of the Federal Reserve must be tempered by the recognition of its obligation – implied in its role as lender of last resort – to ensure that the financial system as a whole functions in a normal, or a nondisruptive, way.... it [the Federal Reserve] must be concerned with and guide the growth and evolution of financial practices in periods of tranquillity as well as when circumstance forces it to intervene.
>
> (1986, p. 39)

Like the asymmetricians, the Post Keynesians perceive the Federal Reserve as the proper regulatory authority to oversee the operation of the financial system. The Federal Reserve's role as lender of last resort is, for Post Keynesians also, the most important of its roles. In contrast to the asymmetricians, however, Post Keynesians see the problems raised by financial institutions not as a principal–agent problem, but as a systemic one. Financial firms, like the economic system in which they are players, act in a dynamic and innovative manner which leads to new levels and modes of instability and, then, to repeated regulatory interventions.

The repetitive nature of these interventions reflects the dynamic, innovative nature of market-driven financial and non-financial institutions. When the Federal Reserve intervenes as lender of last resort it usually corrects the problem by providing liquidity or absorbing potential losses. However, this refinancing and socialization of potential losses imposes costs as well as benefits on the economy, for it affects the behaviour of the economy after the lender of last resort operations have been carried out. Historically, episodes of severe financial instability have lead to controversy about the structure of financial institutions and have often triggered institutional changes (ibid., pp. 39–40). So, the intervention does not just put an end to the financial disruption as the asymmetricians note. The Federal Reserve's provision of liquidity leads to the possibility of an ensuing inflationary economic environment which it will then have to attack with monetary policy, and its assessment of systemic fragility may lead to new regulations, and so, a new institutional environment.

For the Post Keynesians, the regulatory agent is an integral part of the financial/economic system. The need for it arises from the Keynesian uncertainty that pervades the economic environment in which profit-oriented lenders must make lending decisions. These financial firms produce a more fragile financial sector as they initiate innovative methods for meeting credit demand; they also cry for help when the fragility threatens their existence. Because this succession of events is a repetitious cycle which produces varying levels of economic distress, a regulator dedicated to overseeing the needs of the financial sector is imperative if the ongoing credit needs of the production sector are to be met successfully. For the Post Keynesians, the effective regulator keeps the economy functioning and re-establishes the foundation on which the next wave of financial innovations will commence.

CONCLUSION

The genealogical search for the roots common to these two Keynesian schools of thought has concluded that they do not exist. While the Post and New Keynesians have points of overlap in the role of financial institutions in their theorizing, exploration of the overlap shows it to be no more than a superficial likeness. Their theories arise from different methodologies, rely on different perceptions of the nature of the economic system, and work from a different view of the impact of the primary regulator, the Federal Reserve. The search has drawn to a close and the question left to answer now is: who named the New Keynesians, Keynesian?

ACKNOWLEDGEMENTS

The thoughtful comments of the editor, Roy Rotheim, and Gary Dymski were very helpful in the final shaping of these ideas. The problems that remain are all mine.

NOTES

1 Some of the more salient arguments are found in Davidson (1994a, 1994b), Dymski (1993, 1994 a and b, this volume) and Heise (1992).

2 This list is not exhaustive, but merely indicative. The differing opinions as to the importance of such a list can be seen in the following two statements. 'The results [from each author's research] often depend greatly on the particular information asymmetries posed between borrowers and lenders' (Gertler, 1988, p. 570). 'Though we, and others, have related these capital market imperfections to costly and imperfect information and transaction costs, it is our belief that the source of the imperfection is not so important as its nature and consequence' (Stiglitz, 1992, p. 278). The second section will explore this division more thoroughly.

3 In the adaptive expectations model, as in the asymmetric information one, there is a group that has perfect information and one that does not. Over time, however, the uninformed group 'learns' and acquires the necessary information so that a long-run full employment equilibrium level of output is produced. This learning process is absent in the New Keynesians' analysis, for their problem of imperfect information resides in the different economic roles of the two groups. In both of these approaches to informational imperfections, the pertinent knowledge is knowable. This ability to know is a major point of contrast with the Post Keynesian approach which will be discussed below.

4 The government does not have the capability, literally, to remove risk. All that it can do is structure a contract so that risk is redistributed. Instead of the private sector bearing all of the risk of a debt default, the imposition of a governmental guarantee will shift the risk so that the government bears some or all of it. In Dymski and Isenberg (1994) we discuss risk shifting versus risk removal in the context of housing finance contracts.

5 Asymmetric information is a concept at the secondary level in the methodological construct of the New Keynesians. Their primary assumptions describe the economic environment and decision-making processes. This role of the asymmetrical distribution of information in the New Keynesian methodology will be discussed in the following subsection.

6 Among the New Classical theorists, the Rational Expectationists utilize objective probability theory and the Monetarists or Adaptive Expectationists draw upon subjective probability theory in their methodological structures. For the most part, New Keynesians rely upon subjective probability theory, like the Monetarists.

7 Dymski (1994) in arguing against Fazzari (1992) shows that uncertainty, not asymmetric information, is fundamental to understanding why financial structure matters. While highly critical of the asymmetricians' use of risk in their analysis, Dymski finds that the distributional problems of information in credit markets are an important attribute in explanations of discrimination. He, however, turns the asymmetricians' causality on its head by arguing that the inherent conflict in credit relations gives rise to asymmetric information (personal correspondence, June 1995). See his chapter in this volume.

8 This uncertainty–finance relationship forms the foundation for much of Post Keynesian macroeconomic thinking. Some of the seminal works in this area include: Davidson (1978), Kregel (1980), Minsky (1975, 1982, 1986) and Moore (1988).

9 While I have chosen banks as the representative financial institution, this analysis remains valid for other depository institutions.

10 While liquidity is an attribute of an asset, the most liquid assets are considered to be money (Wray, 1992; Dymski, 1988). In the Post Keynesian discourse this is a non-controversial definition.

11 Wray uses a liability management approach to credit creation, so purchased liabilities become the reserves which support the credit money expansion and defy the bounds of liquidity constraints.

12 Minsky's financial fragility hypothesis, which results from the interaction of unrealized expectations with a financial structure dominated by speculative and Ponzi-financed firms, is the systemic response to uncertainty, profit seeking and aggressive growth strategies (Minsky, 1975, 1982, 1986).

13 The discussion on behavioural characteristics of a Post Keynesian bank is rich. Dymski (1988) leads the way with a thoroughly fashioned model of banking. This article fostered a large response with the criticism focusing on its use of subjective probabilities and asymmetrical information, and its inadequate focus on credit creation and liquidity enhancement (Wray, 1989; Heise, 1992; van Ees and Garretsen, 1993b). In subsequent articles, Dymski (1989, 1994a, 1994b) responded by showing that uncertainty is foundational to his banking model. He still argues, however, that asymmetric information in an atheoretical form exists and plays an important role in a bank's lending decision making. Therefore, banks enact procedures to reduce the information gap that arises from uncertainty and asymmetric information.

14 Loans are not the only profit-making activities in which banks are engaged. However, while fees for services have become important since the 1980s, lending is still the primary income generating activity for commercial banks.

15 There is a wide a array of structures and processes of decision making in Post Keynesian theory. G. L. S. Shackle's work emphasizes the unknowability of the future, whereas Peter Earl (1990) and Geoffrey Hodgson (1988) create non-neoclassical versions of the bounded rationality approach.

14

DISEMBODIED RISK OR THE SOCIAL CONSTRUCTION OF CREDITWORTHINESS?

Gary A. Dymski

INTRODUCTION

In the 1970s, New Classical economists criticized the then dominant Neo-Keynesian macroeconomic model for lacking a consistent behavioural basis. They asserted that aggregate outcomes should result from microfoundations, and offered models based on a single *representative agent* maximizing utility over a multi-period lifespan. New Keynesian economists accepted the need for microfoundations, but challenged the adequacy of the single-agent approach. Instead they developed models describing a representative market exchange between a principal, who controls scarce resources such as credit or jobs, and an agent, who needs access to these resources.

The two leading figures in this early 1980s modelling counter-offensive, George Akerlof and Joseph Stiglitz, suggested very different paths for characterizing principal–agent encounters in factor markets. Akerlof's essays showed how many market decisions and processes are embedded in dense social and psychological contexts, sometimes with results that are inexplicable in strictly economic terms. Stiglitz, by contrast, favoured an axiomatic approach emphasizing the defining formal aspects of this scenario – the asymmetric distribution of information between incentive-incompatible principal and agent, together with an exogenous source of risk.[1] While Akerlof's models earned praise for their originality and scope, Stiglitz' approach has become the standard for the New Keynesian microfoundations. In effect, Stiglitz' 'thin' characterization of risk, agent motivations and institutional context won out over Akerlof's 'thick' characterization.

As a result, New Keynesian models treat agents as simple entities, and the risks they take on as axiomatic and presocial: any agent's creditworthiness or potential productivity is either an accident of history (he or she is a 'bad type') or the agent's own fault (he or she is prone to bad behaviour). This minimalist approach has facilitated the application of relatively standardized principal–agent models to a wide variety of economic problems. The New Keynesians' asymmetric information approach thus seems an apt vehicle for demonstrating how, contrary to the New Classicists' Walrasian perspective, institutions and market structure 'matter'.

This chapter disagrees.[2] It argues that the favoured 'thin' approach to behavioural foundations, while analytically tractable, is neither a sufficient nor a logically consistent framework for capturing principal–agent interrelations set in real economic time. The importance of principal–agent relations *per se* is not challenged – indeed, relations of this sort seem pervasive in capitalist societies with unequally distributed wealth. Nor are the relative merits of the principal–agent and (New Classical) single-agent microfoundation in question.[3] This chapter focuses instead on the problems stemming from New Keynesian models' 'thin' treatment of the principal–agent scenario.

The idea that risk is disembodied and orthogonal to market outcomes leads theorists to ignore the path-dependence and, consequently, the unstable dynamic trajectories, often associated with principal–agent interactions. The stylized characterization of principal and agent ignores the fact that agents are often complexly constituted – with the consequence that neither the preferences nor the objectives of 'agent' or 'principal' may be clear, unitary or stable. Further, the implications of unequal power between principals and agents are not fully appreciated in the New Keynesian microfoundations.

Path-dependence, agent complexity and power imbalances, in turn, imply that the outcomes of principal–agent relations may be due more to structural factors that have accumulated over time than to the character of market transactions at any point in time. The 'rules' of principal–agent games are created endogenously by a long history of interaction moulded, in many cases, by principals' exercise of power. This history creates agents' creditworthiness, and hence their 'riskiness' for principals. Agents, in turn, are often complexly constituted, not simple; and they are often embedded in thick social relations which determine their behaviour in markets. Thus the 'economic problem' encompasses not simply the occasional strategic encounters of principals and agents, but their construction of the circumstances of rationing and deprivation in the first place.

New Keynesians conceptualize principal–agent move-and-countermove sequences as the heart of any microfoundation. But this game-theoretic dimension may not be as important as structural factors determined by prior interactions in determining who gets what. New Keynesians' taut, ahistorical rendering of agents and risk leads them to underestimate structural factors and overlook the intractability of much principal–agent conflict. Strategic interactions may be less important than structural determinants when agents are complexly constituted or constrained, or when principal–agent power imbalances are too large. This overemphasis on strategic aspects of principal–agent scenarios leads New Keynesians astray when they assess whether policy activism can enhance economic welfare.

In sum, the 'thin' treatment of risk maximizes New Keynesians' contact with the New Classical framework, but comes at a high cost in terms of their models' historical relevance, institutional specificity and even conceptual consistency. After presenting the central arguments, this chapter shows how asymmetric information models based on disembodied risk have made incomplete and possibly misleading diagnoses of three contemporary credit market crises: the LDC debt crisis, the US bank-insolvency crisis and banks' racial 'redlining'.

ASYMMETRIC INFORMATION AS A NEW KEYNESIAN MICROFOUNDATION

What makes asymmetric information so essential a component of New Keynesian economics in the first place? The New Classical macroeconomics dethroned the neoclassical synthesis model by exposing its inconsistent microfoundations: specifically, its failure to explain why 'rational' agents would have lagged, not 'rational' expectations, and why they would agree to the rigid prices which led to this model's Keynesian conclusions. Rational agents could best look after their interests with flexible prices, leaving no role for welfare improving policy activism. The initial responses to the New Classical economics (e.g. Fischer, 1977; Taylor, 1980) showed how coordination failures would result from long-term contracts, which generated wage–price stickiness, even when agents held rational expectations. However, these initial models were unsatisfactory responses, because 'the existence of such contracts is never explained from microeconomic principles' (Mankiw, 1990, p. 1656): truly rational agents would not enter into contracts that could result in such large welfare losses.

New Keynesian economics emerged as a self-conscious enterprise in response to this critique; Gordon defines New Keynesian economics as 'research within the Keynesian tradition that attempts to build the microeconomic foundations of wage and price stickiness' (1990, p. 1115).[4] Since models positing price rigidity as a primitive did not pass muster, the New Keynesians burrowed deeper into microfoundational explanations of rigidity. They found that asymmetric information models could account for optimally rigid prices in equilibrium. The gain in rigour was not without cost: asymmetric information models are difficult to solve, and so are often presented in overly simplified, partial equilibrium contexts.[5]

In purely logical terms, asymmetric information is compatible with a Keynesian or 'post' Walrasian context because it implies the existence of one or more missing markets. That is, some agents cannot buy or sell a commodity to which they would assign a positive value if it existed.[6] Adding even one missing market to a model which has at most one determinate equilibrium given complete markets has a profound effect: that same model will now have infinite possible equilibria.[7] This *ex ante* indeterminacy of equilibrium creates a role for activist policy. It also transforms the role of theory: the theorist's central problem is no longer to demonstrate one inevitable equilibrium, but instead to explain why one equilibrium might arise, and not another.

Two prototypical models

The introduction noted that Stiglitz' approach to asymmetric information modelling has been favoured within New Keynesian theory over that of (for example) George

Akerlof. We now summarize the analytical elements of models of this sort, using a credit market example.[8] The model centres on a principal, who controls credit, and agents, who seek access to credit. The scenario is partial equilibrium in character.[9]

Principal and agents are incentive incompatible in that one's (utility) gain is the other's (utility) loss. Incentive incompability arises because of two conditions: the agent would like either to take more risk or to work less hard than the principal wants; and the lender/borrower contract confers asymmetric rewards – the lender can at best be repaid its loan with interest, but the borrower wins hugely if the loan project receives a higher than anticipated draw.

There are two prototypical confrontations between principal and agent. First, suppose the lender faces a borrower pool whose members are of two types – 'good' (capable) and 'bad' (undependable). The two types are indistinguishable *ex ante*. Suppose initially that more borrowers want credit than the lender can provide (at that interest rate). The principal would like to differentiate between good and bad borrowers, and lend only to the good. Normally, this would be readily accomplished by raising prices and driving out tepid buyers. But this is not feasible when three assumptions are granted: (a) lenders cannot readily distinguish good borrowers from bad ones owing to missing and costly information; (b) lenders and borrowers have incompatible goals; (c) good borrowers are more likely than bad borrowers to withdraw from the pool as the interest rate is increased. Because of assumption (b), the scenario is a zero-sum game (i.e. the lender's gain is the borrower's loss, and vice versa), and borrowers cannot credibly inform lenders of whether they are good or bad. The lender's action depends, in turn, on whether potential borrowers have any way to signal their capability. If they cannot, lenders settle for a pooling equilibrium with excess loan demand at the prevailing interest rate, choosing their borrowers randomly from their applicant pool. If borrowers can signal their capability, lenders may be able to construct separating equilibria that divide borrowers according to their creditworthiness scores.

The second prototypical confrontation between principal and agent arises when loan contracts leave borrowers with some flexibility in how they will use the funds they receive. By assumption, borrowers can choose among projects with different degrees of riskiness. Borrowers' expected gain increases as projects become more 'risky' (have larger variance), but lenders' expected default costs fall as projects become less 'risky'. In effect, lenders and borrowers face asymmetric rewards and losses: lenders' gain is capped at the contractual loan rate, but borrowers' loss is no more than whatever collateral they pledge. So again incentive incompatibility plagues principal–agent relations. Rationing need not arise here in equilibrium; instead, lenders may force borrowers into less risky projects by imposing conditions such as higher collateral, contingent loan renewal and performance covenants.

Treatments of risk in some New Keynesian models

Some selected examples drawn from New Keynesian microfoundational models will allow a deeper enquiry into their character. The four credit-market papers included in the two-volume collection edited by Mankiw and Romer offer as good a sample as any.[10] The first of these papers is the path-breaking 1981 article by Stiglitz and Weiss. These authors provide this characterization (in Mankiw and Romer, 1991a, pp. 250–251):

> We assume that the bank has identified a group of projects. For each project *q* there is a probability distribution of gross returns *R*…
>
> Different firms have different probability distributions of returns…the bank cannot ascertain the riskiness of a project. For simplicity, we write the distribution of returns as *F*(*R*,*q*) and…assume that greater *q* corresponds to greater risk in the sense of mean preserving spreads…
>
> If the individual borrows the amount *B* and the interest rate is $\hat{r}$, then we say the individual defaults on his loan if the return *R* plus the collateral *C* is insufficient to pay back the promised amount, i.e. if:
>
> $$C + R \leq B(1 + \hat{r})$$

The next paper pertains to subsidies in credit markets. Mankiw first acknowledges his debt to Stiglitz and Weiss. He then describes his aim of developing a model that is 'general', illustrated by a 'specific credit market' (in ibid., p. 278). He writes:

> This section presents a simple model of a market for loans to a particular group of students. To the banks,..the students are indistinguishable. The students, though, differ by the expected return on their education and by their probability of repaying the loan. Each student knows his own expected return and repayment probability, even though they are not observable by the banks or by the government.
>
> Each potential student is considering investing in some human capital, say, a college degree. The project is discrete, has unit cost, and has expected future payment *R*. The other characteristic of each student is the probability *P* that he will repay the loan. The values of *R* and *P* vary across students. Each student knows his own *R* and *P*, but these characteristics are not observable by banks. These two characteristics are distributed throughout the population with the density function *f*(*P*,*R*), which is public knowledge.
>
> The model takes each student's parameters *P* and *R* as primitive. One could construct a more complete model in which the student's default behaviour is endogenous. For example, one could model the students as having varying degrees of honesty; certain students get greater disutility from dishonest acts.
>
> (ibid., pp. 279–80)

The third paper, by Bernanke, argues that credit markets helped to propagate cyclical downturns in the Great Depression period. Bernanke first notes that governments and large corporations buy and sell securities on exchanges. He then describes the credit markets in which asymmetric information prevails:

> banks specialise in making loans to small, idiosyncratic borrowers whose liabilities are too few in number to be publicly traded. (Here is where the complete-markets assumption is dropped.)
>
> The small borrowers to whom the banks lend will be taken, for simplicity, to be of two extreme types, "good" and "bad." Good borrowers desire loans in order to undertake individual-specific investment projects. These projects generate a random return from a distribution whose mean will be assumed always to exceed the social opportunity cost of investment. If this risk is nonsystematic, lending to good borrowers is socially desirable. Bad borrowers try to look like good borrowers, but in fact they have no "project." Bad borrowers are assumed to squander any loan received in profligate consumption than to default. Loans to bad borrowers are socially undesirable.
>
> In this model the real service performed by the banking system is the differentiation between good and bad borrowers... Banks presumably choose operating procedures that minimise the [cost of credit intermediation]. This is done by developing expertise at evaluating potential borrowers, establishing long-term relationships with customers, and offering loan conditions that encourage potential borrowers to self-select in a favourable way.
>
> (ibid., p. 302)

Disembodied risk as a primitive

Several things are notable about the scenarios in each of these papers. All describe the character of risk in a very circumscribed and abbreviated manner. Borrowers' 'projects' and their 'riskiness' are described skeletally, in largely abstract statistical terms. Projects are pre-identified and freely available to agents. Risk, and the projects generating risk, arise naturally. In Mankiw's phrase, risk is taken as a primitive – that is, as axiomatic.

The explanation for this peculiar treatment of risk lies in the analytical challenge to which New Keynesians are responding. In introducing their edited volumes, Mankiw and Romer describe this challenge as follows:

> Th[e] Keynesian consensus in macroeconomics faltered in the 1970s with the birth of the new classical macroeconomics. The new classical macroeconomists argued that Keynesian economics was theoretically inadequate, that macroeconomics must be built on a firm microeconomic foundation.
>
> (1991b, p. 1)

The New Classical macroeconomics is, of course, an equilibrium paradigm which deviates only minimally and strategically from the rigorous complete market, pre-coordinated setting of the Walrasian general equilibrium. So if New Keynesian models are to generate results whose ramifications for New Classical economists are clear, the austere, institution-free environment of the Walrasian general equilibrium must be both their point of departure and their point of final reference. As

Roger Farmer (1993) has recently put it, 'the future of macroeconomics is as a branch of applied general equilibrium theory'.

In effect, New Keynesian asymmetric information models can be seen as adding several assumptions to those underlying Walrasian general equilibrium:

- unequal endowments of factors (productive assets and labour supply);
- incentive incompatibility, i.e. a zero-sum aspect of exchanges in factor markets;
- a missing factor market due to an informational advantage by whichever agents have lesser lending or hiring capacity;
- price setting by those who hire or lend in factor markets;
- unforced participation in, and equal access to, factor markets by sellers and buyers;
- identical, independently distributed (i.i.d.) probabilistic risk – the existence of economic processes with indeterminate *ex ante* outcomes, which are drawn from a fixed event space whose parameters are independent of the model.

DISEMBODIED RISK AND THE NEW KEYNESIAN ECONOMICS

New Keynesian microfoundational models deviate from the Walrasian reference system as little as possible. Indeed, New Keynesian equilibria are sometimes characterized in terms of 'second-best', where 'first-best' equals the competitive, full information market equilibrium. Further deviations from the Walrasian assumption set, apart from those set out in the second section, are not only unnecessary: they would make it more difficult to tell which deviation from Walrasian assumptions had caused which non-Walrasian effect (rationing, unemployment, etc.).

So while not Walrasian, New Keynesian models retain the flavour of atomistic interaction. Principals are not responsible for agents' circumstances – they have no power over them prior to exchange; no bonds inherited from the past, whether of exploitation or loyalty, pulling agents to principals. But do the assumptions set out above permit a reasonable characterization of the relations of 'principal' and 'agent'?

The first four assumptions set out above are relatively innocuous: they generate a modelling situation in which principals and agents will gain from market exchanges of factor services, principals can set prices, and market exchanges are problematic. But the fifth and sixth assumptions are not so innocent. The assumptions of voluntary exchange and of i.i.d. – that is, as disembodied and abstract – risk are, first and foremost, analytical conveniences that both motivate game-theoretic interactions and ensure the generality of results. But beyond this, the acceptance of these assumptions, as in the New Keynesian microfoundations, implicitly accepts several unacknowledged maintained hypotheses about the economy in the society. These include:

MH1 *Social orthogonality*. Forces and processes external to the economy exert no systematic effects on the model's outcomes; that is, the model's 'economic' processes are orthogonal to all 'non-economic' processes involving the agents in the model.

MH2 *'Thin' power imbalances.* Both principals and agents exercise some control over the terms of their participation in any principal–agent game. One party may have more power – in the sense of exit options – than another; but the game is voluntary in that both parties can choose, at a minimum, whether or not to participate.

MH3 *Dynamic independence.* Prior outcomes of the principal–agent process do not systematically alter the initial conditions in subsequent repetitions of this process.

Further, the assertion that a given principal–agent model can be viewed as a microfoundation for a macroeconomic result – and that policy implications can be based on the results generated by this model – depends on an additional maintained hypothesis:

MH4 *Absence of spillovers from excluded markets.* Markets excluded from the model have no effects that spill over onto outcomes in the markets included within the model.

These unacknowledged maintained hypotheses are not presented as axiomatic further additions to the assumptions listed in the second section; indeed, they are interrelated, not independent. They are instead presented here to highlight some of the social and economic relations that are ignored in the New Keynesian microfoundations. Considered singly and together, these maintained hypotheses have numerous analytical ramifications.

SIMPLE AGENTS WITH SINGLE, STABLE OBJECTIVE FUNCTIONS

The asocial setting of 'principal' and 'agent' of the Stiglitz approach favoured in New Keynesian microfoundations clearly requires MH1. Indeed, MH1 must hold if we are even to use the Walrasian general equilibrium as an analytical reference point. Because of MH1, all 'agents' in economic settings are understood as unitary entities with clearly specified goals – even if they are composites, such as large corporations or borrower countries.

THE CENTRALITY OF STRATEGIC INTERACTION AND CHOICE

MH2 guarantees that strategic considerations and not to structural parameters are at least the proximate determinants of modelled outcomes. Regardless of whatever other risks principals and agents are exposed to in other arenas of their lives, the risks they take on voluntarily within the context of New Keynesian principal–agent interactions are what count. For example, the agent's period-to-period survival between plays of the game is taken for granted; it is not the economically interesting part of that agent's life.

MH2 also clearly implies the centrality of strategic choice in principal–agent interactions. The principal has power in so far as he or she controls a resource that the agent needs; but the agent retains some options, and is not effectively powerless. Remaining in or withdrawing from an applicant pool is a choice. So too is the decision about how hard to work, or whether to borrow funds for excessively risky projects. Power conditioned by history is set aside. To see this last point, note that New Keynesian theorists use the commonplace assumption that the principal, endowed with disproportionate resources (capital), sets prices for agents. But they do not consider that this power (price-setting plus possession of scarce resources) also entails the ability to define the relationship – to mold the rules of the game. That is, they do not examine how the principal–agent game arises: nature – or prior social relations?

TEMPORAL NEUTRALITY AND REPLICABILITY

MH3 allows the formulation of the logical construct of New Keynesian models as one-shot static games, in which principals and agents are free to engage at will in any period. No connections within the model connect outcomes in one period with *ex ante* positions in the next. But if such connections were drawn, the positions – and hence the relative power – of winners and losers would alter notably after just several plays. The logical consistency of New Keynesian models depends, however, on not drawing such connections. The very notion that agents draw outcomes from stable (i.i.d.) probability distributions assumes there is no connection for any agent between previous outcomes and future ones. The entire process is replicable, for every agent who plays, and prior outcomes are of equal use to every agent in (constructing probability distributions of returns and) calculating their own odds. That is, social interactions are repetitions of prior experiments.

If we also relax MH4, and allow for spillover effects – that is, increasing returns of any sort – then the idea of temporal neutrality is not just an oversimplification, but an impossibility. As Arthur (1994) has shown, external effects necessarily imply path dependence over time. So an evolutionary approach, which takes account of winners and losers and their altered odds in subsequent plays, is the only logically consistent one.

UNDEPENDABLE AGENTS

These maintained hypotheses also lead to the myth of the cheating-prone agent. Much of the moral-hazard-based New Keynesian models assert not just that agents can choose among projects with different degrees of risk, but that agents will, unless checked, systematically try to cheat principals by opting for riskier projects. In effect, borrowers are essentially con artists. This assumes the disconnectedness of agent and project. But for agents to be undependable in this sense, there must be no relationship between an agent's *ex post* outcome in one period and the agent's *ex ante* position in the next period. Agents have no history, and their pasts leave no trace – so they are free to do whatever they wish, without consequence, in the present period. That is, they are free to cheat. Again, however, once dynamic interconnections between periods are recognized, along with path dependence, then cheating is no longer so costless and so easy. Indeed, the more important ties might be those that bind an agent to continued involvement with his or her assets in the future, regardless of current-period outcomes.

STATEGIC INTERACTION VERSUS STRUCTURAL DETERMINATION

Social interactions involve two analytically distinct components: structural determinants and strategic elements. The New Keynesian approach (especially because of MH2) elevates strategic elements: indeed, strategic elements – the situation as 'game' – define the action of the model. But which aspect of the situation dominates depends on the differential power of the two parties. The more differential the power, the less relevant are the strategic elements in determining the outcome of the interaction, and the more important are the structural elements. Then asymmetric information may be irrelevant, and signalling immaterial. Figure 14.1 depicts the tension between structural determinants and strategic elements in principal–agent relationships. It suggests that the effect of the degree of power

Structural determinants	**vs.**	**Strategic elements**
Power imbalance (one party has no recourse)	⇔	Distributed power (both parties have exit options)
	as amplified or dampened by:	
'Inherited' resource inequality	⇔	Resources equitably spread
Principal possesses monoploy market power	⇔	Principal must compete with others for agents
Volatility in expectations; future viewed as uncertain	⇔	Stable expectations; future viewed as benign
Implications:		**Implications:**
P/A relations entail force, dictated terms		P/A relations are open, with move/countermove indeterminacy
Bargaining unimportant; signalling unlikely; markets are fragile		Bargaining determines gain-sharing; signalling common; markets are robust

Figure 14.1 Structural determination vs. strategic elements in principal–agent relationships

imbalance can be amplified or weakened by several other factors: the degree of resource inequality; the degree of the principal's monopoly power; and the volatility of expectations.

Characterizations of market processes may go seriously awry when they do not allow for the left-hand side of Figure 14.1. In particular, the wrong inferences may be drawn about agent motivations. An agent in a situation whose structural determinants are dominant will not necessarily play the game with the same enthusiasm or verve as when structural determinants are more neutral. So, for example, whether this agent signals his or her value – by getting an education or training – depends on whether there is any likelihood that this signal will lift the dead hand of the other determinants from a pre-written path. There will appear to be self-fulfilling prophesies for those who are stuck – those who do not signal, get no jobs – even though the causality runs the other way (or is two-way).

The social construction of creditworthiness

When the idea of risk as a pre-given datum is set aside, we instead embrace the idea that it is socially constructed. This means that market opportunities themselves are endogenous and socially constructed at any point in time.

Agents are at a disadvantage in seeking out market opportunities because they must find principals who will supply the scarce resource in question (jobs, credit). Any agent's search for resources can be split into three phases: first, will any principal make the market; second, on what terms will market transactions occur; and third, what is the likelihood of success from any project the agent might undertake? There is clearly feedback from the third to the first phase. There is also a zero phase: should the agent even seek out a principal?

The agent's individual circumstances – that is, wealth, income, expected income and degree of social isolation – affect his or her decision to search or signal, and the terms of any market relations the agent enters. That is, these circumstances are socially conditioned and dynamically dependent. And interlinked market outcomes (giving rise to spillovers, in violation of MH4) affect the agent's likelihood of success. The more socially isolated the prospective agent, the poorer, and the less the access to other market opportunities, the more unlikely the agent is even to initiate the process.

Once initiated, the character of market relations into which an agent enters is determined to a large extent by the relative power of principal and agent, and by the presence or absence of spillover effects. Figure 14.2 summarizes the alternatives. Power in this figure is measured by the presence of equally good alternatives – that is, by whether an agent has an exit option. When the agent has exit options and spillovers are small, there is substantial scope for signalling and for bargaining on equal terms by principals and agents. Excessive gains or losses will be avoided through arbitrage operations. When spillovers enter this picture, the character of outcomes depends on an additional factor – the strategic interaction of the principals. Here is the Mecca for strategic interaction, i.e. for games without

What is the character of market relations for different configurations of power and spillovers?		**Are spillovers from credit decisions present?**	
		No	Yes
Does the agent have a non-punitive exit option?	Yes	Bargaining, signalling on equal terms for P & A; gains or losses bid away by arbitrage (1,1)	Strategic interaction of principals determines P & A gains/losses; alternative principals fill in market holes (1,2)
	No	Agents must accept terms incorporating rent-payments to principals; little or no strategic aspect to market exchange (2,1)	No market ralations, or extremely exploitative exchange at expense of agents (2,2)

Figure 14.2 Power, spillovers and the character of market relations

predetermined equilibria. Agents' ability to signal and attract other resource owners means that all markets are made.

Quite different outcomes occur when the agent lacks an exit option. In the absence of spillovers, the agent must accept disadvantageous contractual terms which transfer surplus to the principal. Strategic interaction is relatively unimportant, for the agent lacks any wiggle-room; either the agent takes the principal's deal as offered, or the deal is off. When spillovers exist, the situation is worse. Either the market will not be made, or it will be made at exploitative terms benefiting colluding principals at the expense of the agent.

These circumstances all create a pool of potential borrowers in particular geographic areas, each with particular creditworthiness quotients; and these circumstances determine whether a market in credit will exist, and what type of market it will be.

ASYMMETRIC INFORMATION MODELS OF SOME FINANCIAL CRISES

To this point we have argued that New Keynesian models trivialize risk by conceptualizing it as disembodied and asocial; and models with disembodied risk ignore dynamic dependence and structural determinants, invariably making strategic interaction (the playing of the game by simple, disconnected agents) the centrepiece of any economic problem. But how badly off the mark is the New Keynesian characterization of risk?

It is difficult to answer this question precisely because of the abstract characterization of risk in New Keynesian models. The Stiglitz–Weiss model excerpted in the second section does not inform us who the putative borrowers and lenders are. Presumably they are small businesses, as in Bernanke's model. It is not at all clear that small businesses, as borrowers, are well captured by the disembodied treatment of risk. Does a small business owner really choose disinterestedly from a set of projects with different degrees of variance – periodically switching from one to another? Is that owner really in any position to cheat by slacking off? Will the owner take a 'riskier' course of action when one making survival more likely is available? Are the options in any one period independent of success or failure in previous periods? Undoubtedly, perverse cases exist, but is there any reason to think that cheating and slacking are systematic?

Mankiw's model contains more detail. Indeed, his model of student loans encompasses the case of a financial crisis or, as he puts it, collapse. He argues that when the fundamentals – collateral, inherent risk of borrowers' projects, and so on – become sufficiently poor, the credit supply and demand curves will no longer intersect, and thus the credit market will collapse. This begs the question: why? Mankiw does not address the issue. He describes the scenario thus: 'In this case there is no equilibrium in which loans are made. At any interest rate the pool of students who seek loans is too risky to give the banks their required return. I call this a "collapsed" credit market' (1991b, pp. 282). He does not describe what forces might cause this gap to open up. The message is, if inherent risks are large enough, markets will not exist. This is perhaps the extreme case of a representation of disembodied risk: a market appears or disappears, leaving no trace that affects the model's dynamics, its initial conditions or its equilibrium. If there is no strategic interaction, there is no economic interaction.

Another way to check the validity of the New Keynesian characterization of risk is to take a hard second look at asymmetric information models of credit market crises. We look, very briefly, at three situations in which credit markets have malfunctioned: the insolvency crisis of US banks and thrifts; the less developed country (LDC) debt crisis; and the problem of racial redlining in the cities. In each case, asymmetric information models that follow Stiglitz's – not Akerlof's – approach have been proposed to explain these crises.[11] A review of these explanations finds remarkable uniformity: in each case, these models accentuate the strategic interaction of borrower and lender, ignore power imbalances, oversimplify agents and their motives, overestimate the importance of cheating motives by borrowers. As a result, the policy prescriptions suggested in each case are overly narrow and insufficiently bold.

Deposit insurance and bank insolvency

During the 1980s a third of the savings and loan associations in the United States disappeared through insolvency, government seizure and merger. A massive bailout financed by taxpayers was necessary. Just as legislation handling this thrift crisis was taking effect, the commercial banking industry appeared on the brink of collective insolvency, as well.[12]

An asymmetric information explanation of this crisis was proposed: deposit insurance distorted incentives in the principal–agent relations binding together bank depositors, owners and borrowers, and led thrifts and banks to make too many risky loans. In the presence of deposit insurance, depositors become indifferent about their banks' credit risks; but bank owners seek out risky borrowers at higher interest rates. Bank owners' expected return from lending to risky borrowers exceeds that from lending to safer borrowers; and bank depositors force owners to exercise no due diligence. So eliminate deposit insurance and you eliminate the source of bank insolvency.

Ironically, a different asymmetric information model justified deposit insurance. Diamond and Dybvig (1983) showed that deposit insurance would eliminate the possibility of sunspot bank runs. This paper was, however, quickly followed by others, Postlewaite and Vives (1987) and Williamson (1988), showing that bank runs could be interpreted as equilibrium (welfare-enhancing) phenomena.

The use of asymmetric information models on either side of the debate over deposit insurance offers eloquent testimony of the plasticity of principal–agent models. But the telling point about this explanation of bank/thrift insolvency was its incompleteness and its overemphasis on strategic interaction: if deposit insurance was the culprit, why did not the banking system not fail in, say, 1937? Or 1953? And framing the principal–agent interaction of depositors, owners and borrowers was the regulatory and macroeconomic environment. There were clearly many other factors involved in the 1980s' episodes: competitive pressures on banks and thrifts in the wake of financial innovation, internationalization and computerization; regulatory forbearance; political interference; and so on. However, none of these factors were built into the theoretical account of the behavioural (microeconomic) roots of these episodes.

So the asymmetric information theories of bank insolvency have overemphasized strategic interaction and the costs of undependable agents (in this case, crooked or risk-prone thrift and bank managers), to the exclusion of any attention to the structural determinants of these crises, and of the historically specific path that led to systemic insolvency. The interaction of political and economic outcomes is acknowledged only partially – through an indictment of the political tampering of Congress and President in regulators' efforts to rein in the worst instances of moral hazard. Meanwhile, other aspects of political/economic interaction – including the idea that the US banking system has been underwritten by public subsidies and carried out public purposes since at least the the Depression – are ignored.

If MH1–MH3 are not so readily invoked, other features of the bank insolvency situation are more easily seen. For example, thrifts' and banks' situation is not orthogonal to social developments, and in particular to the regulatory climate; nor is their situation immune to spillovers from outcomes elsewhere in financial markets. Further, the terms of the borrower/lender game depend on the regulatory regime and on the evolving macroeconomic environment.

The microfoundations of the LDC debt crisis

Why did loans flow from banks in developed countries to borrowers in developing countries? And why have these loans been so difficult to repay? Answers rooted in the asymmetric information approach have been suggested to both questions.[13] We have already summarized the asymmetric information model of why risky loans to LDCs were made.[14]

Asymmetric information has also been used to explain why the LDC debt crisis (of non-payment) broke out. The 'enforceability' model, advanced in Eaton and Gersovitz (1981) and Eaton *et al.* (1986), relies on neither lender irrationality nor credit market segmentation. These authors argue that debt repudiation may be rational for borrowers of cross-border debt because contract laws do not extend across national boundaries. The borrower country, conceptualized as a unitary agent, compares the relative utility of default and no-default states over its planning horizon; as a rational agent, it defaults when the utility from default is larger. To ensure incentive compatibility, the lender must create a penalty for non-payment, P, whose present value exceeds the principal lent, L – that is, P must be such that $L < P(1 + r)$, where r is the loan rate. In this perspective, LDC borrower nations' net worth invariably exceeds their debt burdens; the repayment crisis arose because lenders lacked the leverage to enforce their contractual terms. The debt 'crisis', in short, results from a principal–agent problem rooted in agent (borrower) unwillingness to honour debt obligations. The solution to the debt crisis is straightforward – make it more costly not to repay.

As with asymmetric information models of bank insolvency, the 'enforceability' model illuminates some aspects of the LDC debt crisis, but obscures others. As above, we can ask why, if these microeconomic problems are the key to scenario, did the debt crisis not arise in 1979? The outbreak of the debt crisis in 1982 surely reflected specific historic circumstances which were not present in an earlier year. The determinants of the debt crisis evidently included world macroeconomic conditions (see, for example, Kreuger, 1987), and the corrosive competitive pressures on money-centre banks from the mid-1970s onward. Some authors have argued that the debt crisis is attributable to overlending – either because of 'disaster myopia' (Guttentag and Herring, 1984), or because of segmentation in world capital markets, which has made LDCs at best a residual outlet for overseas bank lending (see Darity, 1985).

A microfoundational rejoinder might be that only the enforceability model rests on consistently rational behaviour, and thus it alone is defensible methodologically. But why is it any more defensible to grant the universal rationality and foresightedness of the borrower countries? Why is it less plausible to postulate 'loan pushing' than to imagine that recalcitrant borrowers' net worth can be stripped away from them? And we again see the overreliance on strategic interaction. Can it really be imagined that higher repayment penalties would have averted the crisis? Was the weight of the structural determinants not too great?

Another implicit problem in this characterization is the overly simple depiction of the 'agents' in this principal–agent game. The 'borrowers' were not unitary agents with complete control over their collateral (national wealth); instead, they were autonomous firms, state enterprises and political executives – with different objectives and time horizons. Even when the declaration of crisis centralized responsibility for repayment in each borrower country's executive office, the executive's scope of action was constrained by local and overseas investors, the local electorate and working class, and by representatives of international agencies. The economy of explanation afforded by imagining a unitary borrower precludes any attention to the evolving roles of these various 'sub-agents' in determining each country's moves in this game.

This analysis goes further awry – inappropriately invoking MH2 – in that it ignores the important role of power imbalances between the LDC borrowers and the lenders. Ultimately the crisis was resolved through performance compacts brokered by international monetary authorities and overseen by lender nations' central banks; in effect, the lenders relied on the *ex post* enhancement of the punishment for non-compliance, while the borrowers did what they could to walk a line between internal social crisis and external political/economic retribution and isolation. As the continuing saga of Mexico demonstrates, simple policy prescriptions may lead to unintended consequences when power imbalances are great, the macroeconomic and financial market environment shifts over time, and borrower 'agents' have multiple goals and constraints.

Credit rationing and bank redlining

The past fifteen years have seen an ongoing debate among economists and practitioners over whether banks practise racial redlining in their lending behaviour – that is, whether banks are more likely to deny loan applications for minority neighbourhoods than for white neighbourhoods, all else being equal. Stiglitz and Weiss' 1981 paper offers a microfoundational explanation of – or rather justification for – bank redlining.[15] These authors assume that risk is greater on loan 'projects' in minority neighbourhoods than in white neighbourhoods, and that the borrower pool is characterized by adverse selection. Lenders want to discourage borrowers from taking on overly risky loan projects. The possibility they fear is that borrowers will use their loans to invest in projects in the riskier minority neighbourhood. Banks can solve this problem by getting borrowers to pre-commit to using their loan funds for projects in one or the other neighbourhood. Then banks maximize profits by lending in the white neighbourhood and avoiding the riskier minority neighbourhood.

As in the other two cases, this characterization obscures much more than it reveals. Perhaps the most striking problem with the Stiglitz–Weiss explanation is its violation of the basic facts of the case. For one thing, loan commitments to households or small businesses never give borrowers the choice of neighbourhood implied in this explanation. For another, can we really take seriously the argument that innumerable white borrowers would, if they could, take on more risks than lenders want by purchasing homes and businesses in minority communities? The price paid in positing MH1 is revealed starkly – it leads Stiglitz and Weiss to make an argument that constitutes sociological nonsense.

The other glaring shortcoming of the Stiglitz–Weiss explanation is its inattention to the causes of the greater riskiness of the minority neighbourhood. This greater riskiness is simply posited as parametric. This inattention is puzzling. It would seem important to identify what economic features of the minority neighbourhood were responsible for its greater riskiness, and whether these features interacted with any elements incorporated explicitly into the model. That is, MH4 should not be granted so easily. If these differential economic features were identified, then a natural follow-on question would be whether the gap between neighbourhoods is widening over time. That is, is MH3 appropriate in this instance?

Elsewhere, I have argued (see Dymski, 1995) that race effects in credit markets, such as redlining and discrimination, may well arise because MH3 and MH4 do not hold. If minorities face labour market discrimination, they may be subjected to 'rational discrimination' and/or redlining in the credit market. And if urban loans have spillover benefits, the creditworthiness of loans in any neighbourhood depends in part on lenders' behaviour – that is, on the outcome of strategic interaction between banks. In this case, as in the previous two, the direction of causation runs from the social to the individual level. Again MH1–MH4 can only be viewed as an inadequate basis for modelling these social dynamics. A 'thicker' approach is needed.

CONCLUSIONS

The interpretation of asymmetric information in an economic model depends on how the modeller interprets risk. In the New Keynesian economics, risk is interpreted 'thinly' as an abstract, naturally occurring parameter. This approach carries with it the maintained hypotheses which are labelled MH1–MH4 above. We have argued that these maintained hypotheses result in models that strain credulity. Compensating for this is just one advantage, though a considerable one. Precisely because of MH1–MH4, the question that immediately frames analysis is: 'How can I interpret your model and results relative to those derived from a Walrasian general equilibrium?' If the argument of this chapter is granted, and risk and creditworthiness are understood as socially constructed, this immediate dialogue with the Walrasian reference point is not possible. The question framing analysis is: 'Is your depiction of the situation consistent with the institutional background, and is it well-enough specified that I understand your meaning?'

The New Keynesians' rationale for their models' 'thin' approach to risk is their interest in deriving results which have some claim to generality. In principle, general models should be capable of shedding light on policy choices. In practice, this case is hard to sustain. One might look again at the contradictory interpretations of Williamson (1994) and Calomiris *et al.* (1994) concerning whether government intervention can improve credit market outcomes. Both sets of authors use asymmetric information models; but Williamson uses models with information (costly state verification) and adverse selection, whereas Calomiris *et al.* use a model with moral hazard. But even if both papers imposed the same sort of informational problem, agreement would be unlikely; in models with infinite possible equilibria (see the second section), equilibria depend on parameterization, and on assumptions about agent beliefs, conjectures and endowments.

The very fact that these two papers use such widely disparate types of asymmetric information models indicates a problem of another sort: that is, these models are not firmly grounded by the institutional 'setup' of the problem at hand. Attention focuses on strategic elements of the problem; institutional conditions simply inform one's choice of initial conditions, and these are chosen at the convenience of the modeller.

Is New Keynesian economics any longer 'Keynesian'?

Indeed, precisely because so many New Keynesian microfoundational models seek generality by hewing closely to Walras, they may no longer deserve to be termed Keynesian. To see this, consider how a grounding in Walrasian general equilibrium transforms the policy implications of '(New) Keynesian' economics.

New Keynesians' interest centres on how small deviations from general equilibrium lead to non-optimal rationing equilibria. To paraphrase Keynes out of context, only a few information problems keep us out of the classical world.[16]

New Keynesian economists delight in showing the potentially large implications that follow from small deviations from perfect competition. In asymmetric information models with 'thinly' constructed risk, the small deviations that occupy the theorist all have to do with the character of principal–agent interactions in any period. That is, the theoretical focus is on the interlocking strategies of principal and agent in a zero-sum game. This is indeed a strange terrain for models calling themselves 'Keynesian'. For there is no core, microlevel justification for government intervention.[17] Indeed, Mankiw and Romer write, in the essay quoted above:

> new Keynesian economists do not necessarily believe that active government policy is desirable. Because the theories . . emphasise market imperfections, they usually imply that the unfettered market reaches inefficient equilibria.

> Thus these models show that government intervention can potentially improve the allocation of resources.
>
> (Mankiw and Romer 1991, p. 3)

But it may not.[18] Coordination failure – whose amelioration is ostensibly the point of government intervention – is inherent in these equilibrium rationing outcomes; so is ongoing government intervention into market processes not justified to overcome the ill economic effects of credit (and job) rationing? Jaffee and Stiglitz write:

> When credit is allocated poorly, poor investment projects are undertaken, and the nation's resources are squandered. Credit markets . . may not function well . . in allocating credit. The special nature of credit markets is most evident in the case of credit rationing, where borrowers are denied credit even though they are willing to pay the market interest rate (or more), while apparently similar borrowers do obtain credit.
>
> (1990, p. 839)

But as Stephen Williamson notes (1994, p. 524), these authors stop short of suggesting that the 'special nature of credit markets' justifies government intervention. Williamson himself shows that under microfoundational assumptions referred to above as New Keynesian, no role for allocation improving government credit programmes arises.[19]

Gordon (1990) observes that a theme which can unify (old Neo-)Keynesian and New Keynesian economics is their shared concentration on coordination failures as a common feature of macroeconomic outcomes. Cooper and John (1988) show that coordination failures in New Keynesian models derive from problems in recognizing and capturing external effects – that is, from the demonstration of strategic complementarity.

Unfortunately, coordination failure is often hard to find in many 'New Keynesian' microfoundational models, including those examined above. Ironically – given the importance of the Walrasian general equilibrium as a conceptual backdrop – the problem is these models' partial equilibrium approach, which disallows any attention to coordination failure. As we have seen, the theorist is typically examining just one market, and doing it from the perspective of asocial, disembodied risk. This trivialization of risk allows New Keynesian economics to imagine that macroeconomic results arise in seamless processes that convert (individual-level) primitives into (social) aggregate results. But the 'thin' treatment of risk, combined with the methodological interest in emphasizing minimal deviations from the Walrasian reference point, give too much away. All the strategic complementarities and historical determinants that Cooper and John see as crucial for the Keynesian character of the framework become embedded in an innocuous risk term, whose asocial characterization is contrary to the idea of strategic complementarity.

The kind of spillovers Cooper and John envision in a 'Keynesian' New Keynesian model can be envisioned if the structureless, representative–market approach taken to date is replaced by the richer social and institutional approach advocated here. In general, multifaceted problems like those discussed above can be sketched out in models that appreciate their complexity, and resist the temptation to reduce a history of path-dependent evolution to a single behavioural regularity. The social can be isolated from the individual only at the risk of the real world relevance of the analysis. If the Keynesian character of microfoundational analysis is not to be sacrificed on the altar of Walrasian rigour, then microfoundational models must allow for risk that is not thin, but instead is historically informed, institutionally nuanced and structurally determined – that is, 'thick' and, hence, more 'real'.

ACKNOWLEDGEMENTS

The author is indebted to participants in seminars of the Post Keynesian Study Group and the University of Denver, and especially to Jim Crotty and Ilene Grabel, for constructive comments on an earlier version of this chapter. Remaining errors are the author's responsibility.

NOTES

1 Akerlof's principal essays are collected in a 1984a volume. Perhaps the best-known illustration of his perspective is the idea that employers 'overpay' employees in some industries because this leads employees to reciprocate this 'gift' by working harder than their contract calls for (or could call for, in some cases). Stiglitz' main papers are Stiglitz and Weiss (1981) and Stiglitz (1987); these are discussed below.

2 Davidson's comment (1994a) on Williamson (1994), published when this chapter was in draft form, makes arguments similar to some of those developed here.

3 Other methodological critiques of the New Keynesian economics have been made by Post Keynesians. In particular, Davidson (1991) and Dymski (1994a, 1994b), among others, have argued that if uncertainty is fundamental (Keynesian), not merely risky in a statistical sense, the standard asymmetric information models cannot be coherently formulated.

4 Mankiw's definition is almost identical: 'Much of this research can be viewed as attempting to resurrect the consensus view, with some modifications, by providing a cogent theoretical foundation of hard-headed microeconomic reasoning.' (1990, p. 1655). The key assumption of the 'consensus view' is 'the short-run sluggishness of wages and prices' (p. 1654).

5 The partial equilibrium setting is problematic in conceptualizing coordination failure. As Gordon (1990) points out, this raises the question of whether this work is Keynesian. We discuss this question below.

6 For example, a financial market trader may be unable to make contracts to cover certain future contingencies; or an employer may not be able to contract separately for the labour of those who work hard and those who do not.

7 See Magill and Quinzii (1994).

8 Theoretical New Keynesian models incorporating credit market effects are Greenwald and Stiglitz (1990) and Blinder (1987). Fazzari (1993) provides empirical evidence of interest-rate stickiness.

9 The partial equilibrium character of New Keynesian models is often implicit: for example, a 'general equilibrium' describing credit markets may be presented, while labour or product markets are not explicitly modelled. This partial equilibrium approach is problematic because it precludes any attention to coordination failure. As Gordon (1990) points

out, this raises the question of whether this framework is 'Keynesian', an issue to which we return in the concluding section of this chapter.

10 The Mankiw–Romer volumes contain four papers. One of these, by Blinder and Bernanke, places its discussion in the context of asymmetric information models of the credit market; however, the reference is only fleeting, and asymmetric information *per se* plays no role therein.

11 The models described in this section have not been characterized as 'New Keynesian', but all these models deploy the Stiglitz–Weiss apparatus and conform with New Keynesian microfoundational methods. In any event, the boundaries of New Keynesian models are drawn imprecisely – for example, is the burgeoning labour market literature on the minimum wage and employment (see Card and Krueger, 1995) 'New Keynesian'?

12 These events are summarized, and others literatures are cited, in Barth, *et al.* (1992). These authors also summarize the moral hazard model of bank insolvency discussed here.

13 The literature on models of the LDC debt crisis is reviewed in Eaton and Taylor (1986). The arguments made in this subsection follow Dymski and Pastor (1990a, 1990b).

14 Many discussions of deposit insurance routinely single out LDC debt as an example of an overly risky loan type; see, for example, Barth *et al.* (1992). A paper that links deposit insurance with LDC loans is Penati and Protopapadakis (1986).

15 Unlike the other two cases reviewed in this section, there is no consensus among economists that bank redlining in US cities constitutes a problem, much less a crisis. See, for example, Lacker (1995). However, the economic modelling of this phenomenon aptly illustrates the arguments made in this chapter. Dymski (1995) reviews the theoretical literature on race effects in credit markets, and suggests some alternative ideas for why profit maximizing banks might practise discrimination and/or redlining.

16 Farmer, quoted earlier, goes on to argue that 'All the models in this book begin with a version of the general equilibrium economy described by Debreu…, but..departures from the assumption that markets are 'perfect'… [while] relatively minor can have major consequences for both the positive and normative implications of the theory' (1993, p. 1).

17 The New Keynesian models of wage and price rigidity were initially attractive precisely because they demonstrated that periodic government intervention (stabilization policy) was welfare improving. When rational expectations is accepted, macrostabilization can no longer permanently alter the levels of macroeconomic variables; instead, it can dampen the variance of business cycle fluctuations. See, for example, Ball *et al.* (1991) and DeLong and Summers (1986).

18 The operative word in the Mankiw and Romer quote is 'usually'. Certainly the papers in the Mankiw–Romer volumes are not of one mind on policy interventions and economic welfare. On one hand, Bernanke's paper (cited above) reaches the sort of New Keynesian policy conclusions set out in footnote 11. He argues that 'institutions that work well in normal times may break down in tough times' (1991, p. 320); hence, government stabilization policies aimed at preventing tough times are welfare improving. On the other hand, the Shapiro–Stiglitz paper (in Mankiw and Romer 1991a) finds that the competitive equilibrium will have too much employment.

19 In the same conference, Calomiris *et al.* (1994) used a different asymmetric information model to show that while direct government intervention may not be warranted, the development of specialized lending institutions capable of overcoming informational problems may be. A reader familiar with these authors' work might object that Williamson is not a New Keynesian, whereas arguably Calomiris is. But this does not make Williamson's comments irrelevant. The terrain of debate is formed by different informational characteristics about the credit market, and Williamson's assumptions are as valid as those of, say, Bernanke or Stiglitz.

15

A KALECKIAN VIEW OF NEW KEYNESIAN MACROECONOMICS

Tracy Mott

Recent developments in macroeconomics have sought to revive *Keynesian* explanations for fluctuations in output and employment by demonstrating that they represent responses of rational, maximizing individuals to economic shocks. This *new* Keynesianism thus attempts to overcome the criticism that Keynesian macroeconomics lacks adequate *microfoundations*. This chapter seeks to compare and contrast the New Keynesian economics with the work of Michal Kalecki. There are, I believe, some significant similarities between at least the resultant of Kalecki's ideas on the financing of investment and some New Keynesian work on capital markets, though the foundations of each come from different sources and their implications I think go beyond what the New Keynesians realize. Kalecki's theory will also help us evaluate and critique other aspects of New Keynesian economics.

THE NEW KEYNESIAN ECONOMICS

The body of thought described here as New Keynesianism arose most directly as a response to the *New Classical* macroeconomics, with its appeal to the equilibrium method and its critique of the *ad hoc* nature of Keynesian models without microfoundations based on optimizing behaviour. There was some earlier work called New Keynesian, associated with such economists as Robert Clower, Axel Leijonhufvud and Jean-Paul Benassy. This way of thinking put forth the proposition that Keynesian economics was *disequilibrium dynamics*.

Old Keynesianism was said to be the hypothesis of sticky money wages, since in the full *neoclassical synthesis* of the ISLM model with *Keynes* and *Pigou* effects the only way to have an *underemployment equilibrium* was if money wages would not fall in response to unemployment. The Clower *et al.* New Keynesians proposed rather that in an economy without an *auctioneer* quantities should move in response to a demand shock faster than prices. This thus came to be known as *non-Walrasian* economics and finally, ironically, as the *fixed price* analysis.[1]

The *newer* New Keynesianism argues rather for the *equilibrium* approach to macroeconomics. This means that it accepts the New Classical challenge to remove *ad hoc* elements from macroeconomics by deriving its Keynesian results from maximizing behaviour and avoiding any appeal to free adjustment parameters. It has in common with the earlier New Keynesianism an emphasis on imperfections in the availability of information, but it eschews the disequilibrium methodology, seeing unemployment, for example, as an equilibrium phenomenon.

New Keynesian explanations for unemployment rely then for the most part on *imperfections* within a neoclassical framework. One way by which the New Keynesian theory has been characterized is to say that it requires some combination of nominal rigidities and real rigidities.[2] First, the theory needs some sort of nominal price rigidity to block neoclassical market clearing outcomes.[3] These are found in what are often called *menu costs*, or menu changing costs, from the idea of the cost of printing new price lists. Since the actual cost of reprinting a restaurant menu could be quite small these days, the theory really must rely on the type of customer attachments which economists like Arthur Okun (1981) have emphasized.

To make it optimal, however, for, say, monopolistically competitive firms (which have some price setting power in the neoclassical paradigm) to refrain due to menu-changing costs from changing prices when demand shifts, firms cannot be losing too much in real profits. If the profits lost exceed the menu-changing costs, price rigidity is not optimal behaviour. The losses from not changing prices are seen largely to be a matter of the elasticity of demand for a firm's products, the behaviour of a firm's rivals, and the elasticity of marginal cost. The lower the elasticity of demand, the less threatening the response from rivals, or the lower the elasticity of marginal cost, the lower will be the losses to any firm from not changing its price when demand shifts.

There are obviously dependencies among these, since, for example, elasticity of demand is affected by the behaviour of rivals as well as being a matter of product differentiation, and the behaviour of rivals has to do with product differentiation and the elasticity of marginal cost, among other strategic considerations. The dynamics of price changing have been analysed as a matter of time-dependent and state-dependent rules affected by these considerations.

The elasticity of marginal cost of course is determined by technology and by the elasticity of labour supply. It is not far-fetched to assume a linear technology, but the assumption of a flat labour supply curve does strain credulity and would be particularly embarrassing for the New Keynesians, since they have used the studies supporting a low intertemporal substitutability of labour for leisure as an argument against the New Classical macroeconomics' dependence upon such a condition.

The theory thus needs some other argument establishing real wage rigidity to ensure that the nominal rigidities are able to maintain equilibrium unemployment. And, there is no shortage of stories of such *real* rigidities, from implicit contract theory to insider–outsider issues to the efficiency wage hypothesis, among others.[4]

Implicit contract theory lowers the variation of the real wage across states of the economy with an insurance contract in which risk-neutral firms insure risk-averse workers who pay by giving up higher wages when productivity is high for protection against lower wages when productivity is low. The efficiency wage theory posits labour productivity to be an increasing function of the real wage, as higher real wages increase the quality of job applicants, make the cost of being fired if caught shirking higher, reduce costly turnover, or some combination of these and other stories. This makes the profit function flat in the neighbourhood of the existing real wage, thus mitigating any losses from keeping prices sticky due to, for example, menu costs, when demand for output falls.

Real wage cuts due to money-wage cuts are thought perhaps to prevent a decrease in employment on their own, and such money-wage cuts would also increase the profitability of cutting prices to maintain sales. These are ruled out, however, by, for example, the implicit contract or the loss in productivity that real wage cuts bring under the efficiency wage hypothesis. Thus we have the real rigidity necessary to support the existence of nominal rigidities.[5]

One might ask, though: why all the fuss about nominal rigidities in the first place? We see some appeal to the need to prevent *market clearing outcomes*. Market clearing will prevent equilibrium unemployment from occurring in the long run under wealth effects of the type of the Pigou effect, wherein deflation increases aggregate demand without limit, and in the short run under *rational expectations* when it is rational to expect the long-run workings of the Pigou effect.

There is, however, a literature, beginning with Kalecki (1944), but anticipated by Irving Fisher (1933), and summarized by James Tobin (1980), which argues for the irrelevance of such wealth effects, which work through changes in the real value of nominal outside money. Indeed, the effect will work in reverse if debtors have a higher propensity to spend than creditors, which is quite plausible and was Fisher's point. It is thus not clear that the absence of nominal rigidities prevents equilibrium unemployment.[6] We cannot then say that the presence of nominal rigidities, however plausible their existence may be, is necessary to establish equilibrium unemployment.

KALECKI'S THEORY[7]

In Kalecki, there is a real rigidity which maintains equilibrium unemployment when aggregate demand decreases and wealth effects according to the Pigou perspective are inoperative or even perverse. This is price–cost mark-up rigidity.[8] If mark-ups were properly flexible, i.e. falling sufficiently with aggregate demand, real wages would rise and consumption spending would increase when investment falls. Mark-up rigidity prevents such an occurrence and so ensures that the fall in demand causes a fall in output and employment.

The contrast here with the New Keynesian story, apart from the irrelevance of nominal rigidities, comes from Kalecki's emphasis on the role of income distribution in macroeconomic analysis. With the postulate of a much higher propensity to consume out of wage-income, than profit-income, Kalecki's models, like Nicholas Kaldor's (1956) model, require real rigidities to prevent the *rise* rather than the fall of real wages to cause unemployment when investment spending decreases.

In the New Keynesian literature the cause of changes in aggregate demand is often a change in the quantity of nominal money. This fits with the idea that the New Keynesian problem is how to defeat wealth effects. In Kalecki, however, the source of aggregate demand changes is found in endogenous fluctuations in investment spending.[9] When investment decreases, aggregate demand decreases, and employment and profits decrease. The attempt to protect profits by maintaining or even raising mark-ups preserves or worsens the employment and profits decline. The nature of competition, however, is such as to discourage individual firms from cutting mark-ups as long as they believe that their rivals will follow.

The matter of the existence of sufficient 'imperfections' in competition is itself not justified but simply assumed in New Keynesian models. Kalecki makes some remarks about the implausibility of perfect competition, but it is really the work of Josef Steindl (1976 [1952]) that provides the grounds for the particular type of competition to which Kalecki appeals. Steindl's argument has to do with cost differentials across firms. If lower-cost firms can price below their rivals' costs, it is in their interest to cut prices and so mark-ups when demand declines or even while demand is increasing. Once cost differentials become small among firms, however, as normally happens with the emergence of oligopoly, or *maturity*, in an industry, price or margin cutting competition is no longer desirable.

The type of oligopolistic competition discerned by Steindl will also cause stagnation in investment spending, as it leads to the emergence of undesired excess capacity. Mark-up rigidity thus ensures that interactions among investment, profits and productive capacity will cause business cycles. Increases in investment increase profits and capacity. The increase in profits encourages more investment by making it easier to finance investment, but the increase in capacity tends to retard the profitability of more investment. The mathematics of how this process can generate cycles is well known.

The role of profits in this process comes from Kalecki's (1937; 1971 [1954], ch. 9) *principle of increasing risk*. Retained profits provide the primary source of finance for investment, Kalecki says, because of the increased riskiness to the capital position of a firm as indebtedness increases. Issuing new shares is not a viable alternative owing to the dilution of the existing ownership it brings.

THE NEW KEYNESIANS ON CAPITAL MARKETS

Work under the heading of New Keynesian macroeconomics dealing with finance and investment has mostly been done by Joseph Stiglitz in partnership with Bruce Greenwald or Andrew Weiss or both. Stiglitz and Weiss (1981) argue that lenders ration credit at below market clearing interest rates to firms owing to asymmetric information. Since lenders cannot perfectly monitor borrowers, they fear adverse selection. Allowing the borrowing rate to clear the market would discourage safer borrowers with lower risk and so lower return projects from applying, leaving the lenders with a pool of applicants with riskier projects.

Greenwald *et al.* (1984) claim similarly that new equity issuance is limited by incentive and signalling effects favouring debt over equity issue. This again rests on asymmetric information between the owners of finance and firms which need finance. Debt is said to give the providers of finance more control owing to the costs of bankruptcy, the fixed commitment of the debt payments, and the ability of debt to be withdrawn more easily. Equity issuance also is said to send a negative signal about the prospects of a firm. Since debt issuance is preferred by financiers to equity issuance, firms which do issue equity are taken to be more risky. Thus new equity can normally only be issued at a lower price than that for which outstanding equity is trading, lowering the value of the outstanding shares.

Greenwald and Stiglitz (1988c) thus argue that movements in interest rates following changes in money supply or demand are both diminished and made less relevant to investment. Since firms cannot easily turn to equity finance to get around a debt limit, they must be heavily reliant upon financing generated internally through profits. And, in response to a negative shock to the economy, the cost of capital rises. For Greenwald and Stiglitz, this explains why investment is pro-cyclical and why there are multiplier responses to changes in investment. This also leads them to say that firms might optimally raise mark-ups in a recession, since they should be willing to trade profits tomorrow lost from higher prices for profits today gained from higher mark-ups. Finally, they recognize that falling prices will worsen a recession by increasing the burden of debt.

KALECKI VS THE NEW KEYNESIANS

Greenwald and Stiglitz's version of New Keynesian economics thus shows some similarities with some of Kalecki's economics. We might well say that this branch of New Keynesianism gives microfoundations based ultimately on informational imperfections, which Kalecki did not bother to furnish, showing why rational, utility maximizing individuals would behave so as to give Kaleckian macroeconomic results. Stiglitz *et al.* thus supply arguments, not explicitly stated in Kalecki, to support the capital market imperfections necessary to show, for example, why the opportunities for capital owners to diversify away the idiosyncratic illiquidity risk of any particular investment cannot overcome the limits on that investment given by the availability of internal finance or why there is an increasing cost of new share issues to firms.

In this view, Kalecki was the partially perceptive ancestor, formulating Keynes's insights perhaps on a better basis than Keynes himself, but also failing to break through to the ultimate foundation for these views in imperfect information. It is also proper to call the school 'New Keynesian' rather than 'New Kaleckian', since the kind of unemployment problems attempted to be explained are associated mainly with the name of Keynes.

The major failing of Kalecki then is the old one of simply writing macroeconomic models without providing adequate microfoundations – the charge hurled at all Keynesian macroeconomics until the recent work. But why did Kalecki come closer than others to seeing the microeconomic points on which the Stiglitz *et al.* New Keynesianism now rests? In the 1954 revision of Kalecki's original article on the principle of increasing risk Kalecki (1971 [1954], p. 109) writes,

> The limitation of the size of the firm by the availability of entrepreneurial capital goes to the very heart of the capitalist system. Many economists assume, at least in their abstract theories, a state of business democracy where anybody endowed with entrepreneurial ability can obtain capital for starting a business venture. This picture of the activities of the "pure" entrepreneur is, to put it mildly, unrealistic. The most important prerequisite for becoming an entrepreneur is the *ownership* of capital.

From the Kaleckian perspective this is an unstated but required point of and for much of the New Keynesian work on the capital and labour markets. The reproduction of capital in the hands of a limited number of capitalists and of labour as having little or nothing to sell but its labour power must take place for there to be real rigidities in the labour market and imperfections in the capital market.

Though, according to the argument of this chapter, the efficiency wage hypothesis does not explain unemployment, it may have relevance to the explanation of real wage determination. To the extent that workers have an independent accumulation of capital, however, they should be immune to efficiency wage considerations. Higher pay may not motivate them to work harder, quit less often, and so on. If they are less dependent upon employment for their living, they should also be less sensitive to changes in their pay, though of course it is possible that the opposite phenomenon of greater demands for pay and greater resistance to pay cuts could occur. The point is, though, that it is only people with independent means who can make such action regarding their labour supply a matter of choice. Indeed, to ensure that efficiency wage considerations cannot be overcome by having workers post a bond, it is normally assumed in such models that the workers cannot save.[10]

Similarly, if every actual or would-be entrepreneur were well-endowed with own capital, finance constraints of the type that Greenwald, Stiglitz and Weiss establish would not be binding.[11] Finance, or liquidity, constraints, which play such an important role in New Keynesian capital market theory, are fundamentally wealth constraints.[12]

Stiglitz *et al.* seek to base these phenomena ultimately on informational imperfections, but the type of principal–agent problems and other informational imperfections we have in capitalism have also to do with the social conditions of ownership of capital. Limited and asymmetric information are just the other side of the coin of wealth distributional divisions. When agglomerations of finance are not in the hands of workers and firms, investment is governed by retained profits.[13]

Wealth need not be divided unequally to have these problems, but then there must simply be a low level of wealth in the society, at least relative to the size of *efficient* projects, or wealth must not be in the hands of those undertaking the projects (the class of entrepreneurs). The insight of the Ricardian branch of the Old Classical economics was to see in some way that wealth had to be in the hands of a certain social class to generate economic growth. The insight of *underconsumptionism*, associated with T. R. Malthus, J. A. Hobson, and to some extent Karl Marx, and revived to a degree by Kalecki and Keynes, was that too unequal a distribution would impede growth by providing too little effective demand. In this way distribution and ownership were held to determine most fundamentally macroeconomic outcomes.

This way of looking at macroeconomics emphasizes *macro* foundations.[14] The logic of the reproduction of the economic *system* outweighs or even determines the actions of individuals. Kalecki's portrayal of the macroeconomy combines the systematic reproduction of the income distribution with the problem of *realizing* the profits desired from capital investment.

The key discovery, or rediscovery, of Stiglitz *et al.* then is not the argument for equilibrium credit and equity rationing due to asymmetric information but the realization of the importance of bankruptcy costs. Indeed, in Greenwald and Stiglitz (1988b, 1993b), it is solely equity rationing due to bankruptcy costs which generates their results. They motivate this in terms of informational matters – financial distress sends a signal that management *may* be bad. I would suggest that the fixity, or illiquidity, of productive capital is rather what makes financial distress costly. The capital which becomes redundant in the competitive struggle is that which cannot meet its liquid obligations and not necessarily that which is productively inferior.[15] That capital which cannot meet its liquid obligations is that which is overleveraged and/or has insufficient cash flow. The fixed nature of such a firm's productive capital prevents it from moving into a different market. This is why investment spending is volatile and normally insufficient to provide full employment.[16]

Greenwald and Stiglitz (1987, 1988c) imply that their work is an alternative to neoclassical ways of thinking. One should be clear, though, about what one means by the term *neoclassical*. If it means economics based on rational maximizing behaviour, then the New Keynesian theory is neoclassical. But if rational maximizing behaviour just means that everyone does the best they can with what they have, then we are all neoclassicals. Greenwald and Stiglitz seem rather to identify non-neoclassical analysis with market imperfections.

From the Marxian–Kaleckian perspective,[17] however, these are not imperfections. The economy is not seen as the equivalent of a *swap meet*,[18] in which the economic problem is the allocation of actual and potential resources among competing uses given exogenous preferences and the initial distribution of endowments, so that any interference with this process of allocation is an *imperfection*.

In a swap meet participants can be indifferent to sources of finance and preservation of the value of their capital and labour. Once one is dependent for one's livelihood on the swaps, though, these matters do become of concern. Trading also then becomes a vehicle for the extension of the division of labour and the growth of the wealth of nations. The accumulation and reproduction of capital which follows produces and reproduces wealth, and it also creates barriers in the form of effective demand and income distributional problems to the production of wealth which do not permit individual rationality to exploit all the gains from trade.[19] From the Marxian–Kaleckian perspective, the New Keynesian theory is both dependent upon and pointing the way to this vision of the economy.

KALECKI, THE NEW KEYNESIANS AND 'KEYNESIAN' ECONOMICS

In any event, Kalecki's principle of increasing risk and Greenwald and Stiglitz' ideas should be seen to revolutionize Keynes's theory of liquidity preference. Rather than giving the idea that liquidity preference has merely to do with agents' exogenously determined preferences to hold 'money' vs bonds or even short-term vs long-term securities, however, Kalecki's formulation tells us that it comes from the way our economic system works and that it applies to *every* investment decision. The central 'Keynesian' concern for the level of aggregate effective demand then is also a matter of liquidity preference so understood. How willing investors, physical *and* financial, are to become illiquid is what determines the level of output and employment. Investment 'mistakes' cannot be liquidated and reconstructed without new sources of finance. Neither can they be hedged or insured against beyond a low limit, because the risk that would need to be shed is not idiosyncratic. A falling tide may not run all boats aground, but those still left floating cannot pull many of the others off the shoals. It takes wealth to generate more wealth.

In an economy with a great deal of productive capacity already in existence, 'printing money' and giving it to those who will spend it will alleviate this problem somewhat because it will allow the wealth that exists to begin to work. Just making money available in the form of bank reserves, however, will not help as much because of the problem of getting lenders willing to lend when balance sheets and profitability are weak.[20]

These ideas, whether spawned by Kalecki on the basis of an interpretation of the inner logic of capitalism or by the New Keynesians on the basis of informational imperfections, furnish very important supports for a 'Keynesian' view of the macroeconomy. Some *Post* Keynesians, however, find the Stiglitz *et al.* results irrelevant or inappropriate to the ideas of Keynes because they assume a knowable probability distribution rather than the *true uncertainty* of which Keynes (and Frank Knight) spoke.[21]

I see no problem in accepting both informational asymmetries and true uncertainty as part of the economic environment. This chapter wants to argue that it is still rather the logic of the capital accumulation process and of the reproduction of the distribution of income and wealth that is of fundamental significance. Informational incompleteness would exist but would be handled differently presumably under other social arrangements.

In any event, it seems to me that there is nothing about the condition of true uncertainty which makes the Stiglitz *et al.* results *wrong*.[22] Furthermore, though true uncertainty undoubtedly has some effect on investment behaviour, as Keynes (1936, chs. 11 and 12) proposed, there is also much more that we can say about the determination of investment, and so it seems to me that the ideas about the determinants of investment which follow from either Kalecki or Stiglitz *et al.* make a significant contribution to the 'Keynesian' theory of investment. Similar contributions to this theory have been made by Hyman Minsky (1975, 1986).[23]

The question of the ultimate determinants of these Keynesian features of the economic landscape at its deepest level of course is the question of whether it is correct to ground economic analysis on the rational maximizing individual or on a conception which asks how the economy as a whole constitutes itself. In the latter case the whole cannot be conceived of as merely the sum of its parts.

The issue of 'microfoundations' favours the first of these alternatives. Yet if social interactions produce outcomes which alter the behaviour of individuals, the 'macrofoundations' are equally or more important. In neoclassical economics determinations at the level of the system act as constraints (e.g. the structure of property rights or other 'rules of the game'). If the constraints, however, are endogenously determined as a result of how individual actions add up in the aggregate, then we have macro-level effects that can override or determine individual behaviour. The idea that aggregate determinations can override individual choice was certainly one of Keynes's significant emphases, for example, in the 'paradox of thrift', wherein increased desire to save actually decreases saving, or in Keynes's (1936, ch. 2) theory of the labour market, in which it is shown that there is no way that the workers can achieve a real wage equal to the marginal disutility of their labour through the money-wage bargain.[24]

The New Keynesian perspective follows the neoclassical view by seeing macroeconomic results to come fundamentally from limits on the availability of information – a constraint ultimately given by the nature of human limitations and the given rules of the game and so an exogenous one. The Kaleckian perspective derives its macroeconomics rather from limits on the access to wealth, arising from the systematic reproduction of a 'social formation', to use the Marxian term. This constraint is taken to be endogenously created in history by the logic of capitalist production and reproduction. It is interesting to note a case in which economists starting from each of these two alternative positions have created a remarkably similar macroeconomics.

By starting from maximizing individuals with limited information, the New Keynesians derive 'Kaleckian' results. The challenge to this raised by Kalecki's own work is that if the argumentation is pressed to its necessary underpinnings, it becomes apparent that the results are less determined by individual agents facing 'imperfections' than by the logic of a system of economic arrangements.

ACKNOWLEDGEMENTS

This research was supported in part by a fellowship from the Jerome Levy Economics Institute. I would also like to thank Steve Fazzari, Julio López, Philip Arestis, Gary Dymski, Jeff Pliskin, Randall Bausor, David Levine, Randy Wray and participants in a seminar at the University of Denver for very helpful comments and suggestions regarding the ideas presented here, without implicating anyone in my opinions and conclusions.

NOTES

1 Robert Barro and Herschel Grossman (1976) and Edmond Malinvaud (1980) provide good examples of what this point of view came to be.
2 Much of the succeeding discussion follows Olivier Blanchard and Stanley Fischer (1989, ch. 8). The nominal/real rigidity characterization will not neatly encompass every idea passing under the heading 'New Keynesian'. For example, the work on multiple equilibria and coordination failures does not fit into those categories.
3 Emphasizing price rigidity rather than money-wage rigidity is another distinction between New Keynesian macroeconomics and the older neoclassical Keynesianism. See Gregory Mankiw (1987).
4 What immediately follows here can be found in Joseph Stiglitz (1986) and in several other places. Note particularly Janet Yellen (1984) on efficiency wages.
5 Price–cost mark-up rigidity can also do the trick. See, for example, Blanchard and Fischer (1989, pp. 465–9).
6 Greenwald and Stiglitz (1993a) make similar points concerning the reliance of this strand of New Keynesianism on price rigidities and the problems with this.
7 A collection of Kalecki's most important papers is Kalecki (1971 [1954]), which contains his ideas presented here not otherwise referenced.
8 Note 5 cites the use of mark-up rigidity by New Keynesians in their real rigidity to support the nominal rigidity story.
9 There is New Keynesian work which demonstrates endogenous cycles. See, for example, Michael Woodford (1988) and the papers in Jean-Michel Grandmont (1987).
10 See, for example, Stiglitz (1986).
11 David Evans and Boyan Jovanovic (1989) find empirically that liquidity constraints tend to exclude people with insufficient own wealth from becoming entrepreneurs. They associate this idea with Frank Knight's (1921) argument that risk bearing is an essential aspect of entrepreneurship, but it conforms also and perhaps even more closely to Kalecki's principle of increasing risk.
12 See also the literature on the excess sensitivity of consumption to current income due to liquidity constraints, e.g. Glenn Hubbard and Kenneth Judd (1986). It is precisely the households which are not wealthy that cannot consume on the basis of expected lifetime income.
13 This is corroborated empirically in Steven Fazzari and Tracy Mott (1986–7) and Fazzari *et al.* (1988).
14 Cf. G. C. Harcourt (1985, p. 136).
15 The bankruptcy laws in the United States do allow firms to continue to produce in bankruptcy. This does not normally, however, make it advantageous for a firm to declare bankruptcy other than as a last resort to attempt to survive.
16 See David Levine (1977) for an interpretation of the resolution of the debate between Malthus and Ricardo over the possibility of a 'general glut' as having to do with the appreciation of the fixity of capital.
17 The term 'accumulation theory' has been suggested by Carol Heim (1986) to refer to the emphases we find in Marx and the Old Classical economists that connect with the issues raised by Kalecki and Keynes.
18 Hyman Minsky (1986) calls it a 'village fair' perspective.
19 Cf. Marx (1967 [1894], vol. III, p. 250): 'The *real barrier* of capitalist production is *capital itself*.'

20 See also Greenwald and Stiglitz (1988b, 1988c). This is the 'revised view of monetary policy' which Greenwald and Stiglitz (1987) identify as one of the 'major ingredients' of New Keynesianism. Ben Bernanke and Mark Gertler (1990) argue that the usual policy actions in the face of such financial fragility (e.g. loan guarantees, lender of last resort provisions of liquidity, debtor bailouts, etc.) can be interpreted as transfers that support or increase the net worth of borrowers or lenders. Stiglitz (1992) presents a model of risk averse-banks which cut their lending in recessions for fear of impairing their own net worth. Monetary policy can only restimulate the economy then if it lowers rates on competing instruments (e.g. Treasury Bills) enough to make lending to business seem more profitable. This will be quite hard to do if business and bank balance sheets are weak (unless the banks are so in danger that they have nothing more to fear).

21 I heard this from participants in a seminar presentation of this chapter at the University of Denver.

22 Gary Dymski (1994a) has indeed argued that under such true uncertainty credit rationing is rational behaviour even in the absence of asymmetric information.

23 For Kalecki's initial critique of Keynes's theory of investment, see Ferdinando Targetti and Bogulslawa Kinda-Hass (1982). Keynes's theory of investment may serve much better as a theory of the behaviour of financial (portfolio) investment in the stock market. Uncertainty undoubtedly does have a significant effect on the behaviour of physical investment, but the existence of a climate of uncertainty may simply reinforce the determinants identified by Kalecki.

24 The view that Keynes's economics is based on a conception that the economy is more an organic (in which the whole is not just the sum of its parts) than an atomic entity (proposed, for example, by E. G. Winslow (1989), and others cited there) has been challenged by John Davis (1989). This controversy, it seems to me, reflects a real tension in Keynes's work on just this point, which tension is also reflected in the contrast between the New Keynesian and Kaleckian viewpoints. The older, Clower *et al.* New Keynesians (e.g. Clower, 1965) and the newer New Keynesian literature on coordination failures (e.g. Cooper and John, 1988) also raise issues of macro-type constraints.

Part IV

POST WALRASIAN MACROECONOMICS

Part IV

NEW WALRASIAN AND STRONG NEW KEYNESIAN MACROECONOMICS

As the title of this volume suggests, there is not a single Post Keynesian alternative to New Keynesian economics. The authors of this volume have their separate influences which allow them to be critical of New Keynesian economics, to one degree or another, but in many cases in their own unique way. Such perspectives are explored in the current part.

The first chapter, 'Beyond New Keynesian Economics: Towards a Post Walrasian Macroeconomics', by David Colander, summarizes some issues in a meaningful analysis of macroeconomic issues, and discusses how alternative approaches to macroeconomics deal with these issues. It presents an alternative classification system of approaches to macroeconomics that goes beyond the traditional Keynesian/Classical classification. Specifically, it argues that the New Keynesian terminology is more confusing than helpful, and proposes in its stead a Walrasian/Post Walrasian classification.

Walrasian macroeconomics includes all macroeconomic work that accepts the existence of a unique aggregate equilibrium towards which the aggregate economy is tending. Walrasian macroeconomics includes most Classical and Neo-Keynesian work. Post Walrasian macroeconomics does not accept the existence of a unique equilibrium. Instead it argues that a coordination variable should be included within a modified aggregate production function. The work of Clower, Leijonhufvud, Rosser and Colander falls within this category, as does the work of some New Keynesians (such as Cooper and John) and the work of all Post Keynesians.

Then, J. Barkley Rosser, Jr. in his 'Complex Dynamics in New Keynesian and Post Keynesian Models' examines various Keynesian models, Old, New and Post, for their applicability within the complex dynamics framework which can be seen as consistent with the Post Walrasian framework explored by Colander. Rosser argues that non-linear complex dynamics of various kinds can provide the basis for endogenously generating fundamental Keynesian uncertainty without explicit axiomatization. Models most consistent with this framework include the Strong New Keynesian ones and several non-linear Post Keynesian ones. Here he finds that hysteresis and financial fragility models are seen as being consistent with both New and Post Keynesian as well as non-linear Post Walrasian perspectives.

Less convinced about the compelling potential of Post Walrasian economics to provide that sought-after meeting of the minds between New and Post Keynesians is Colin Rogers. In his chapter, 'Post Keynesian and Strong New Keynesian Macroeconomics: Compatible Bedfellows?', Rogers summarizes and evaluates developments in that branch of New Keynesian economics which deals with sunspot equilibria, self-fulfilling prophecies and endogenous business cycles – the so-called Strong New Keynesian (SNK) economics. It is argued that these developments do raise issues of central importance for Post Keynesians as the concept of bootstrap equilibria is central to Keynes's principle of effective demand. All Keynes's equilibria are monetary, bootstrap equilibria, Rogers contends. However, he is less persuaded of the possibility that Post Keynesians should adopt the language of Arrow and Debreu as claimed by some exponents of SNK economics.

16

BEYOND NEW KEYNESIAN ECONOMICS

Towards a Post Walrasian macroeconomics

David Colander

In the early 1990s in a two-volume edited book (Mankiw and Romer, 1991a) and in two survey articles (Gordon, 1990; Mankiw, 1990), the economics profession has seen the popularization of a new school of Keynesian macroeconomics. Now it is becoming commonplace to say that there is New Keynesian economics, to go along with Post Keynesian economics (no hyphen), Post-Keynesian economics (with hyphen), Neo-Keynesian economics (sometimes with a hyphen, sometimes not), and, of course, just plain Keynesian economics.

While the development of a New Keynesian terminology was inevitable after the New Classical terminology came into being – for every classical variation there exists a Keynesian counterpart – it is not so clear that the new classification system adds much to our understanding. There are now so many dimensions of Keynesian and Classical thought that the nomenclature is becoming more confusing than helpful. Most economists I talk to, even Greg Mankiw who edited the book that popularized the term, are tired of the infinite variations on the Keynesian/classical theme.[1] I agree. But the fact that the Keynesian/classical variations have played out does not resolve the problem of how one explains to non-specialists the variations in approaches to macroeconomics that exist.

REQUIREMENTS FOR USING NEW TERMINOLOGY

As an historian of recent economic thought and as a textbook author, I look upon nomenclature issues as issues of serious concern. I see my job as trying to make sense of what economists are doing, putting their work into perspective, and providing a summary of high-level work that students and other economists who do not specialize in the field will find helpful. The development of new classifications is a natural way to achieve these goals.

Any classification scheme that will be helpful to students and non-specialists requires significant simplification and squeezing of ideas into cubbyholes into which they do not quite fit. So I am sympathetic to the problems of classifying schools of thought, and recognize that any classification system will be less than perfect. It was in attempting to simplify some recent developments in macro thinking for students that I first started to use the term, New Keynesian.[2]

In considering the development of any terminology it is helpful to start with the question: what set of characteristics should a body of thought have to warrant its own name? In my work I have developed the following criteria: (a) the use of the name should help organize thinking about the issues to which it refers and it should do so in a way that is understandable to the non-specialist; (b) it should seem natural and intuitive to most practitioners and acceptable to those thus classified.[3] If the name does not meet these two criteria it will simply clutter the terminological landscape; if it does, then the name can serve a useful purpose: it can complete a picture, and make not only the new work clear, but, like the final piece of a puzzle, also make the previous work clearer. Otherwise the classification will confuse, not clarify. Just as a piece of a puzzle in the wrong place will obscure a picture rather than complete it, so, too, will a loosely used term.

THE PROBLEM WITH THE NEW KEYNESIAN TERMINOLOGY

It is because it does not meet the above criteria that people are disparaging of the New Keynesian terminology. Using the above criteria, if the term New Keynesian is to be helpful, it must be easily distinguishable from other classifications of Keynesianism and from Classical thought. Since these other classifications are vague, this is a difficult goal to meet. The standard use of the term, New Keynesian, which is based in large part on Mankiw and Romer's definition, does not meet this goal.

To see the problems the vagueness creates consider Mankiw and Romer's definition. They define New Keynesian economics in relation to two questions about a macroeconomic theory:

1 Does the theory violate the classical dichotomy?
2 Does the theory assume that real market imperfections in the economy are crucial for understanding economic fluctuations?

(Mankiw and Romer, 1991a, vol. 1, p. 2)

They respond to these questions by writing: 'Among the prominent approaches to macroeconomics, New Keynesian economics is alone in answering both questions in the affirmative' (vol. 1, p. 2). This response is problematic. All Keynesians would answer both those questions affirmatively and thus would be classified as New Keynesians by Mankiw and Romer.

Later in their discussion Mankiw and Romer accept that 'many older macroeconomic theories rejected the classical dichotomy', so it seems that it is the second part of the definition that Mankiw and Romer believe separates New Keynesians from other types of Keynesians. But that second part is not defining; what Keynesian would argue, if he or she is judging markets relative to a unique equilibrium Walrasian system, that he or she is not assuming real market imperfections, and that those market imperfections are not crucial to understanding economic fluctuations? The distinguishing characteristics among subgroups of Keynesians are not in whether market imperfections are crucial; the distinguishing characteristics are in how those imperfections enter in and what they are.

Mankiw and Romer (1991, p.2, emphasis added) provide little support for their definition; in the one line of justification they do give to the second characteristic they concede that '[Keynesians] usually *did not emphasize* real imperfections as a key part of the story. For example, most of the Keynesian economists of the 1970s imposed wage and price rigidities on otherwise Walrasian economics.'

Gordon (1990) gives a good, clear perspective and overview of the work Mankiw and Romer call New Keynesian. But he does not ask the terminological question: does this set of work deserve to be called by a separate name? He essentially accepts the use of the Mankiw and Romer terminology. Gordon's short discussion of the definition of the term, New Keynesian, states that it is 'research within the Keynesian tradition that attempts to build the microeconomic foundations of wage and price stickiness'. Since work on microfoundations has been ongoing since the late 1960s, particularly with the Phelps volume (1969), this places the origins of New Keynesian economics prior to New Classical economics. But that is not the case; as Gordon states immediately following that quotation, and as he reiterates in a footnote, New Keynesian work is a reaction to New Classical work.[4]

Gordon's excellent survey of the literature that Mankiw and Romer call New Keynesian is critical of much of it. For example, he writes, 'Much existing new-Keynesian theorizing is riddled with inconsistencies as a result of its neglect of constraints and spillovers' (p. 1138). His critical discussion of how that work fits together calls Mankiw and Romer's use of the term into question; work that is inconsistent, and that is incompatible with other work, should not be classified under the same name as the work with which it is said to be inconsistent and incompatible.

In summary the problem with the term, New Keynesian, is that it includes a wide variety of disparate work under the term 'New Keynesian' and provides little insight about what is revolutionary about the work.

CLASSIFYING THE DIFFERENT COMPONENTS OF NEW KEYNESIAN LITERATURE

Despite the problems with the terminology most people use the New Keynesian classification because they find much original work in the papers which Mankiw and Romer classify as New Keynesian. The problem is not its originality; it is its disparity. The work includes within it subgroups of work so broad and disparate as to require at least three different classifications, one of which is not even Keynesian.

STIGLITZIAN ECOMONICS

For example, the partial equilibrium work of Stiglitz (Stiglitz and Weiss, 1981), and Akerlof (1970), and others on the informational content of prices is definitely new and exciting work. In it prices have multiple functions; besides equating supply and demand, they also provide information to individuals. This information role of prices means that they do not necessarily equate supply and demand, at least in the traditional sense. For example, say an unemployed worker offers to work for half the going wage. If firms interpret that offer as meaning he or she is a low-quality worker, they may still not hire him or her. When that happens strategies change and there can be no presumption that the market equilibrates at a no involuntary unemployment equilibrium.

Siglitz's work has much relevance to providing a microfoundation to Keynesianism far down the road, but this work's importance is far greater than that. Accepting the Stiglitz argument does no less than change one's conception of what is meant by a partial equilibrium supply–demand equilibrium; it deserves its own classification which conveys the breath of its import. New Keynesian is far too confining. It might be called Stiglitzian, Akerlofian, or even Akerlitzian (Stiglofian?), but if the classification terminology is to be helpful, it should not be limited to a Keynesian macroeconomic term.

In this aspect of their work neither Stiglitz nor Akerlof claim to be writing in a Keynesian tradition; they are, instead, providing a theory about how equilibrium unemployment could come about in a single market. They are providing a partial equilibrium explanation of unemployment that is fundamentally different than the Keynesian attempt to provide a general theory of the aggregate economy that would lead to an under full employment equilibrium. In many ways Stiglitz' work fits much better in the Classical Pigovian tradition of unemployment that Keynes was providing an alternative to, than it does in a Keynesian tradition. Classifying Stiglitz's informational work as New Keynesian misleads people as to its origins and connections and does not help people understand the revolutionary aspect of that work. The same holds for Phelps' new macroeconomic synthesis in *Structural Slumps* (1994). His equilibrium explanations for a moving steady-state natural rate equilibrium are far more characteristic of Pigou's structural analysis than of Keynes's demand deficiency analysis.

NEW NEO-KEYNESIAN ECONOMICS

A second theme of the work that has been called New Keynesian does fall under the broad Keynesian label as that label has been used. This includes the work of Mankiw (1985) and others on costly price adjustment, the work of Fischer (1977) and Taylor (1979) and others on slow wage and price adjustment, and the work of Hall (1986), Hart (1982), and others on imperfect competition. This work is definitely in a Neo-Keynesian tradition, but it is not clear that it is a dramatic enough departure from earlier work to warrant the 'new' prefix. Keynesian economists have long been worried about these issues of microfoundation of macroeconomics; they may not have modelled it quite as formally as these authors, but the themes have long been there.

One could argue that since the more recent work uses a different methodology than previous work, and structures the questions it poses slightly differently, and more systematically attempts to provide a microfoundation to the Neo-Keynesian ISLM model, that it might warrant a subclassification of its own. If that is true, a far better classification would be New Neo-Keynesian to distinguish it from Old Neo-Keynesian.

The reason it should be called New Neo-Keynesian, if it is to have a separate classification, is that it is traditional Keynesian work that provides a foundation for the Neo-Keynesian model; it is evolutionary within the Neo-Keynesian tradition, not revolutionary. Indeed, most of the authors of this work have the traditional Neo-Keynesian model in the back of their minds. Mankiw actually states as much; he writes, 'this [New Keynesian] research can be viewed as attempting to put textbook Keynesian analysis on a firmer microeconomic foundation' (Mankiw, 1990, p. 1648). Let me be clear: I am not advocating the term, New Neo-Keynesian; since I don't think the term New Keynesian meets an appropriate 'new terminology criteria' I do not support subdivisions of that terminology. I point it out only to show how difficult it is to classify work meaningfully while using this New Keynesian terminology.

EXTRA-MARKET COORDINATION PROBLEMS

A third theme in the work that has been classified as New Keynesian involves extra-market coordination failures, and spillover effects among markets. This work accepts the Keynesian notion that the competitive market will not necessarily lead to a Pareto-optimal result and explores why. In this work the macroeconomic problem is analysed as a strategic game-theoretic problem with multiple solutions and dynamic spillovers from one market to another become the central focus of economic analysis. Work that fits in here that Mankiw includes as New Keynesian includes work by Cooper and John (1988) and John Bryant (1983).

It was to separate out this work from other work that I argued about the definition of New Keynesian economics. I tried to limit the term, New Keynesian, to this work. I had little success. One problem with my alternative definition which focused on extra-market coordination failures was that some practitioners were not happy with it. Post Keynesians objected to a new term which I argued included them, but also included me, Robert Clower and Axel Leijonhufvud. Their objections were reasonable since Post Keynesian work had prior claim to many of the views that I ascribed to New Keynesian work. If 'new' included most of 'post', how could it be new? A second problem was that this coordination failure economics had little to say in the way of policy, and the term Keynesian usually conjured up significant visions of policy.

I did have some success and I am pleased to see that Paul Davidson (1994b) notes that Michael Parkin, who was cited by Gordon as the originator of the term, has now agreed with me that if the term New Keynesian is to be used, it should be limited to this coordination work. None the less, I hereby concede the definitional battle for New Keynesian economics. Mankiw's broad, almost meaningless, definition is what people have in their minds when they think of New Keynesian economics, and it is not going to change. Given this reality I have come to the conclusion that the term, Keynesian, has too much baggage with it to be useful in classifying any new work. It is more than fully subdivided. Thus, it is time to come up with a new division of approaches to macroeconomics.

AN ALTERNATIVE CLASSIFICATION SCHEME FOR DISTINGUISHING APPROACHES TO MACROECONOMIC THEORIZING

The new classification system of macroeconomics that I propose is between *Walrasian macroeconomics* in its various forms, and what I call *non-Walrasian macroeconomics*. The former includes all macroeconomic work that accepts the existence of a unique aggregate equilibrium towards which the aggregate economy is tending.[5] Since most existing Classical and Neo-Keynesian work accepts the existence of a unique aggregate equilibrium this term includes much of what is currently called neoclassical economics, Neo-Keynesian economics and what I above called New Neo-Keynesian economics.

Non-Walrasian macroeconomics does not accept the existence of a unique equilibrium for the aggregate economy. It approaches macroeconomics from a fundamentally different perspective than does Walrasian macroeconomics, and analyses it under the presumption that there are multiple equilibria. The existence of multiple equilibria makes an enormous difference for macroeconomic theorizing. Specifically, assuming equilibria is no longer the equivalent to assuming optimality. Moreover, the entire modelling strategy changes since simple calculus is no longer relevant. It leads on to an analysis of strategic complementarities in which there are multiple paths the aggregate economy can follow depending on which of a set of reasonable strategies individuals choose.

Notice that non-Walrasian macroeconomics overlaps with one part of New Keynesian macroeconomics – with the work that sees the requirement for extra-market coordinating mechanisms. It is an enormously broad division and will be broken up in numerous ways as researchers follow different strategies in trying to come to grips with the problems of conceptualizing within this non-Walrasian framework. For example, in my work (Colander, 1996) I have tried to deal with the complexities by additional assumptions and have given this approach the name Post Walrasian macroeconomics. The additional assumptions I propose are:

1 Not only does the economy exhibit multiple equilibrium, it also exhibits complex dynamics. An economy with complex dynamics cannot meaningfully be analysed

within a comparative state model that assumes the aggregate equilibria are unaffected by the dynamic adjustment process.

2 I further conjecture that the aggregate economy is so complex that general equilibrium rational decision making is impossible. I do not give up rationality – I simply give up global rationality as being beyond the capabilities of individuals. For Post Walrasians rationality is bounded rationality.

3 The above two conjectures would likely mean that the economy would exhibit chaotic results. What prevents those chaotic results is a third conjecture – that the reason the aggregate economy is relatively stable is the existence of multilayered institutions – conventions, legal and social, that impose restrictions in individual actions – which limit individual actions within ranges. These institutions impose the stability that exists in the system and reduce the complexity of decision making for individuals. Thus, institutions play a central role in Post Walrasian macroeconomics; one cannot analyse an institutionless world. Markets coordinate individual actions within institutions; to understand that coordination, one must understand how the institutions work.

Exploring the implications of these three assumptions in a multiple equilibrium world is an enormous task, but, when done, will likely lead to a new view of the way the economy works that differs significantly from current mainstream approaches. It has much more connection with economists currently working out of the mainstream. For example, this Post Walrasian approach is a broad approach which I believe is big enough to include myself, Robert Clower, Axel Leijonhufvud, many, if not all Post Keynesians, as well as many Marxists and Austrians.

The litmus test for whether work is Post Walrasian is its approach to the microeconomic foundations of macroeconomics. Walrasian macroeconomics is searching for some unique microfoundation as an explanation for market failure. This allows it to move from an analysis of a representative individual to the aggregate economy. From a Post Walrasian perspective, such a representative individual approach does not make sense. Post Walrasian macroeconomics denies the existence of a non-contextual microfoundation and hence of a unique representative individual. It argues essentially that the macro economy is sufficiently complex and decisions sufficiently strategic that determining a rational approach to macro decisions that fits a Walrasian general equilibrium framework is impossible for the actors in the economy. Instead, 'Post Walrasian rational' individuals must make decisions within a macro context; they exhibit bounded rationality, not global rationality. and the aggregate economy must be modelled accordingly.

I would include a variety of disparate work within the Post Walrasian label. I would include the work of John Bryant (1983), Cooper and John (1988), Costas Azariadis (1981), Cass and Shell (1983), Leijonhufvud (1993), Colander and Koford (1985), Garretsen (1991), van Ees (1991), Farmer (1993) and Rosser (1991). Brian Arthur's (1994) and the Santa Fe Institute's work also tie in closely with this approach.

Notice the enormous disparity of this work when considered along traditional Keynesian/Classical lines. Clower cringes when called a Keynesian; Davidson cringes if he is called anything but a Keynesian; Bryant is working in a New Classical tradition and is highly technical; Leijonhufvud is working in a historical Keynesian tradition. Cass and Shell and Farmer are highly technical general equilibrium theorists discussing why sunspot equilibria are likely; van Ees and Garretson are working in a European Malinvaudesque Keynesian tradition; and who knows what tradition I am working in?

Despite these differences, from this diverse work comes a fundamentally different vision of the macroeconomic problem as compared to the Walrasian vision. The difference concerns the uniqueness of the equilibrium towards which the economy will gravitate, and the nature of the market's solution to the coordination problem. In a Walrasian tradition markets are assumed somehow to exist, and somehow to cause the economy to gravitate to a unique equilibrium. The Keynesian version of Walrasian macroeconomics allows for temporary deviations from that equilibrium solution of that combination of markets, while the Classical version sees the economy always on that equilibrium, but otherwise the Walrasian Classical and Keynesian approaches are the same.

The Post Walrasian approach to macroeconomics does not take markets as given. Markets are built up by individuals as a method of coordinating individuals' actions. Thus, markets involve institutions created by people, and the analysis of economic problems must include an analysis of the constraints those institutions impose on the individual decision makers.

The difference between Walrasian and Post Walrasian macroeconomics can be demonstrated in their alternative formal specification of the aggregate production functions. Walrasian work models the aggregate production function either implicitly or explicitly as stable and unique. By that I mean it assumes that the production function is relatively stable and that there is a specific amount of aggregate output forthcoming for every specific amount of capital and labour. Its canonical production function is

$$x = f(K, L)$$

Shifts in aggregate production due to coordination failures of non-market variables are afterthoughts.

In Post Walrasian work, the aggregate production function must be modelled differently to allow direct consideration of alternative levels of output due to non-market coordination failures and multiple equilibria. The production function must allow the same amount of capital and labour to be associated with different levels of output. It must allow for shifts in aggregate output due to demand spillover effects, externalities, coordination failures, or whatever. One way to include such effects in the aggregate production function is to specify it as follows:

$$x = f(K, L, C)$$

where C stands for the degree of non-market coordination in the economy

Post Walrasian macroeconomics focuses on the analysis of the *C* variable. Coordination is a very general term, so let me give an example of what I mean. Say people expect low demand – they produce little based on that expectation, and thus the expectation of low demand becomes self-fulfilling. Output decreases because people expected low output. In the Walrasian production function, for that result to be formally explained one must show the reason firms wanted to hire fewer workers – that is, the real wage is too high. One is then led to search for an explanation of why the wage rate is held too high to explain a decrease in aggregate output.

Using the Post Walrasian production function, a decrease in aggregate output can have many explanations which have nothing to do with the real wage. For example, the decrease could be explained as an expectations coordination failure that the market does not resolve. In the Post Walrasian approach there is no presumption that some abstract market will lead to an ideal result; the market itself is endogenous, as are expectations, and a broad array of activities may accur. When there is poor coordination of expectations, factor productivity, and aggregate output, can fall even with no change in inputs or technology.

With multiple aggregate equilibria, depending on how the causes of unemployment interact with expectations and other coordinating variables, unemployment equilibria may be preferable to full employment equilibria. For example, maintaining full employment in the market economy would require a highly flexible wage and price level. That flexibility could cause other serious coordinating failures which would lower output so much that less, not more, output is forthcoming. Thus, in the Post Walrasian specification of the aggregate production function wage inflexibility could be a good thing, rather than a bad thing.

The coordination specification of the production function is broad, and many different interpretations are possible. It is simply a construct that allows for a broader range of argumentation than does the Walrasian production function. In the Post Walrasian approach one does not need to rely on microfoundation problems to explain undesirable aggregate results. What one needs is a macrofoundation for microeconomics – and that macrofoundation determines the degree of coordination in the economy.

IS AN ANALYTIC POST WALRASIAN MODEL POSSIBLE?

The above broad conceptualizations are the easy part of the analysis. In many ways, those broad conceptualizations are too easy since the multiple equilibria framework can be consistent with just about any result. For Post Walrasian economics to be meaningful, it must say something more than 'anything goes'. Most economists, quite correctly, demand more than broad conceptualizations, and, to be honest, Post Walrasian economics has not delivered anything more as yet. This failure has led many economists, who accept that the problems of multiple equilibria exist, none the less to make a leap of faith: that assuming those problems away to make the macro model tractable will not do too great an injustice to their analysis. They will make this leap of faith based on tractability, not intuition.

People who work in the Post Walrasian tradition are not willing to make that leap of faith. But that does not mean that they accept the 'anything goes' model. Instead they try to understand small aspects of the aggregate dynamic adjustment process, and see potential problems that can arise. They are willing to content themselves with a much smaller domain for theory in understanding the macro economy than are economists working in a Walrasian tradition.

Accepting the full complexity of the economy most likely means that no analytic solution to the macro question of how markets interact will be reachable. At best, what one can hope for from a theory that accepts the complexity of the aggregate economy is that it provides some insight into the directional implications of observed shocks – how the economy might deviate from the direction it might like to go. Compared to the broad goals of the Walrasian strands of macroeconomics, these Post Walrasian hopes for what one might get out of macro theory are limited; such reduced hopes are the costs of taking the complexities of the aggregate economy seriously.

The above work and vision of the economy which I have described as Post Walrasian is a vision that turns New Classical economics on its head. It sees Walrasian economics as a special, and not especially interesting, subclass of Post Walrasian economics, one which assumes a unique aggregate equilibrium and therefore eliminates the need for an explicit analysis of the macrofoundations of microeconomics. Its general equilibrium foundations are in Marshall, not Walras.[6] Post Walrasian economics does not assume a single equilibrium and hence has at its foundation a macrofoundation to microeconomics to set the context for micro analysis. Precisely what that macrofoundation will be has yet to be determined; the work is still in its infancy, but the recognition of the need for it ties the Post Walrasian work together. The focus of Post Walrasian policy analysis is not the choices made by people, given institutions; the focus of policy analysis is the choices presented to people by institutions, and a consideration of how changing institutions will change those choices, and thereby change the aggregate equilibrium.

WAS KEYNES A POST WALRASIAN?

I make no formal claims that Keynes was a Post Walrasian. Keynes said many things, and can be interpreted in different ways, and I do not want to get into any debate about what Keynes really meant. I'd lose, and I don't care that I'd lose. What I do claim is that thinking of the Keynesian arguments within a Post Walrasian framework opens up new avenues of discussion between different views that the Walrasian approach closes off. That is precisely why the Post Walrasian approach needs to be distinguished from the Walrasian approach.

CONCLUDING COMMENT

Classification is fundamentally important. But it is primarily for students to learn about different approaches. As ideas change, as certain approaches pan out, and others do not, the nature of approaches changes, and when that happens, the classifications can become albatrosses around people's necks. Fights ensue about who is what, and whether one approach or another belongs in a certain classification. Researchers close their minds to alternative approaches simply because it does not fit their classification.

Just as I believe the economy is path-dependent, so too do I believe that classifications are path-dependent; they evolve over time, and the useful classifications used in one time period become the blinders of another. For a number of years now I have become convinced that the term 'neoclassical' is no longer relevant. The interesting and dynamic mainstream economists that I talk to, and there are many of them, are working on issues that do not fit what non-mainstream economists mean when they say 'neoclassical'. Non-mainstream economists use the term neoclassical as a catch-all for what they do not like. That is the worst type of use of a classification. I've also become disenchanted with any classification that has the term 'Keynesian' in it, and, yes, that includes New, Neo, Post, post-, New Neo-, and non. There's too much baggage associated with the terminology and debates become centred around the baggage rather than around the issues.

In my view there are many interesting issues which are totally underexplored, and various groups are beginning to explore them. I'm tempted to say that we are entering the Post Classical era – an era in which the enormous restrictions on thinking that characterized the neoclassical era have been removed – and there has been a collateral reduction in heterodox approaches. There are significant rents to be lost in that reduction, but there are, simultaneously, enormous gains to be made in our understanding of the economy.

NOTES

1 In a personal letter to me Mankiw wrote that he felt the Keynesian distinction was no longer useful.
2 Michael Parkin, I, and perhaps others, started using the term New Keynesian in the mid-1980s to describe the Keynesian response to New Classicals. I started using the term (Colander, 1986; Colander and Koford 1985) to classify the work of those economists who were trying to provide an answer to New Classicals.
3 I am thankful to Michael Parkin for suggesting this second criterion.
4 Gordon states that 'the adjective, "New Keynesian", nicely juxtaposes this body of research with its arch-opposite, the new-classical approach' (1990, p. 1115).
5 Just as the term Keynesian can mean many things, so too can the term Walrasian. I am using it to mean the unique equilibrium system in which an auctioneer sets the price and no trading is done at disequilibrium prices even though the system is always in disequilibrium. Donald Walker (1994) points out that while this view of Walras follows from the forth edition of the *Elements*, the version most English speaking economists are familiar with, since that was the version translated, in earlier versions there was a different, more meaningful system – one which is closer to what I am calling Post Walrasian. Walker calls this earlier version the 'mature Walras' and attributes the later version to Walras's intellectual decline that began in the mid-1890s. Thus, in some ways, what I am calling Post Walrasian, and which elsewhere (Colander, 1995) I associate with Marshall, could in some ways be called 'mature Walrasian'.
6 For a discussion of the Marshallian general equilibrium approach, see Colander (1995).

17

COMPLEX DYNAMICS IN NEW KEYNESIAN AND POST KEYNESIAN ECONOMICS

J. Barkley Rosser, Jr.

> We have all of us become used to finding ourselves sometimes on one side of the moon and sometimes on the other, without knowing what route or journey connects them, related apparently, after the fashion of our waking and dreaming lives.
>
> (John Maynard Keynes, 1936, p. 292)

INTRODUCTION

Much debate has arisen recently regarding the relationship between New Keynesian and Post Keynesian economics. At one extreme is the view that they are utterly incompatible, that New Keynesian economics is merely a redone version of New Classical economics and thus a vile travesty of Keynesian economics in any form.[1] At another are those who argue that they are mutually compatible and reinforcing. A problem with this discussion is that there are multiple varieties of both approaches[2] and those taking each position argue in terms of specific brands of each that are seen to support respectively either mutual incompatibility or compatibility.

There is no easy way around this. In this chapter there will be an effort to consider a wide, if not comprehensive, range of both schools.[3] The method of comparison will be to consider how the various schools fit in with the broader approach of complex non-linear dynamics. It has been argued (Rosser, 1990, 1996a, 1996b) that complex and especially chaotic dynamics are consistent with broadly Keynesian-type implications for economic analysis. Thus, this method of comparison allows for a potential bridging among schools.

Clearly this method involves defining what is meant by 'complex dynamics'. As with the varieties of Keynesianism, so there are varieties of complex dynamics. We shall provide a definition sufficiently broad to encompass most views of the phenomenon. Even so, it would be a mistake to underestimate the 'complexity' of the problem of complex dynamics and this chapter perforce will barely scratch the surface of this topic.[4]

The basic thesis of this chapter can be summarized as follows. Complex dynamics are those which are erratic in some sense owing to endogenous causes and thus seriously lacking in predictability. Such dynamics can arise in many, although not all, New Keynesian models, especially those that might be characterized as *Post Walrasian*.[5] This lack of predictability can be seen as a basis for the important Post Keynesian concept of fundamental uncertainty.[6] Thus, New Keynesian models which can generate such outcomes are compatible with those Post Keynesian models consistent with fundamental uncertainty. Some models are widely viewed as being both New and Post Keynesian, notably hysteresis and financial fragility. However, other approaches appear to be less compatible with each other, notably the 'menu-cost' and related New Keynesian models[7] as well as the (fundamentalist) 'Keynes–Post Keynesianism' of Davidson.

This chapter will first present a quick review of varieties of complex dynamics. Then it will briefly discuss Old (Neo-)Keynesian economics. After this will come a presentation of the schools of New Keynesian economics with a discussion of how consistent they are with complex dynamics. This will be followed by a similar discussion of Post Keynesian schools and some approaches claimed by both New and Post Keynesians. The 'generality' of competing approaches will be considered before final conclusions are presented.

VARIETIES OF COMPLEX DYNAMICS[8]

Eschewing a precise mathematical definition, a dynamical system can be described as 'complex' if it is non-linear[9] and can be characterized by possessing at least one of the following features: (a) discontinuities in state variables over time, (b) sensitive dependence on initial conditions, or (c) aperiodic ('erratic') fluctuation patterns. Most importantly the feature occurring above must arise *endogenously* from within the dynamical system itself rather than being the result of an exogenous influence such as a series of random shocks as in New Classical real business cycle models. This gives the systems in question a Keynesian character. A shortlist of kinds of complex dynamics with applications in economics includes catastrophe theory, chaos theory, interacting particle systems, strange attractors, fractal basin boundaries, and evolutionary synergetics.

Catastrophe theory, due principally to Rene Thom (1972), provides an explanation of discontinuities in structure and dynamic paths. Now often derided after a period of great faddishness,[10] it has been applied in macroeconomics by Varian (1979) to a model of Kaldor (1940) and by Fischer and Jammernegg (1986).

Chaos theory, drawing on the work of Lorenz (1963) and Li and Yorke (1975) among others, depends on the idea of sensitive dependence on initial conditions (SDIC): that a small change in the value of a parameter or a starting value and a system will behave dramatically differently. This is known as the 'butterfly effect' for Lorenz's idea that a butterfly flapping its wings in China could cause a hurricane in the United States. This SDIC is seen as fundamentally destructive of the possibility of forming rational expectations in a noisy environment (Rosser,

1996a, 1996b), especially because chaotic dynamics can arise even in models with rational expectations (Benhabib and Day, 1982; Grandmont, 1985). They thus can be seen as a source of fundamental Keynesian uncertainty.[11] Chaotic dynamics also exhibit endogenously generated aperiodicity.

Models of interacting particle systems draw on statistical mechanics theory (Kac, 1968) in which there are critical thresholds in the interaction of entities which can lead to discontinuous changes in the outcomes of their activities.[12] These models can represent coordinaton failure in multiple equilibria situations very well. Brock (1993) applies this idea to various economic situations and Rosser and Rosser (1994) apply it to economic collapse in transitional economies.

An attractor is the set towards which a dynamical system asymptotically tends if it is inside the basin boundary of the attractor. An attractor will be *strange* if it possesses a non-integer dimensionality known as *fractal dimensionality* (Mandelbrot, 1983). It has often been thought that chaotic dynamics and strange attractors coincide, but this is not true in general, although there are many models in which both do occur. Lorenz (1992) has developed a model based on the Kaldor (1940) model with a strange attractor but without chaotic dynamics.

Even though a dynamical system may be non-chaotic and possess non-strange attractors, if it has multiple attractors they may be separated by basin boundaries which themselves possess a fractal dimensionality. Lorenz (1993b) has noted that in such cases a trajectory can remain in a saddle zone for a long time appearing to track one basin and then suddenly jumping into another basin. Isomaki and Kantola (1995) develop such a model for ecological–economic dynamics and Thompson (1992) provides a more complete discussion of possible dynamics in such systems.

Evolutionary synergetics was developed by Haken (1977) and his associates in Stuttgart (Weidlich and Haag, 1983)[13] and is closely related to the Brussels School models (Prigogine and Stengers, 1984; Allen, 1994). These models emphasize out-of-equilibrium phase transitions in non-linear dynamical systems which can generate systemic evolution in a punctuated form.

The positive non-linear complementarities involved invite comparison with the path dependence models (Arthur, 1988) with their multiple equilibria arising from positive feedbacks. In synergetics models slow variables 'slave' fast variables with critical evolutionary phase transitions arising when fast variables destabilize to become controlling slow variables, the 'revolt of the slaved variables'. Long-wave dynamics applications of something similar to this have been considered by Goodwin (1986) and Rosser and Rosser (1994).

VARIETIES OF KEYNESIAN ECONOMICS

Old (Neo-) Keynesian Economics

Old Keynesian models used to be called Neo-Keynesian models and are based on the ISLM model developed in the late 1930s by John Hicks (1937) and Alvin Hansen (1938).[14] Although long criticized as internally inconsistent and not truly

Keynesian (Leijonhufvud, 1968), as well as '*ad hoc*' by New Classicals, this model remains the workhorse core of most macroeconometric forecasting models. It persists as the most widely taught and believed in of all Keynesian models, despite decades of abuse and repudiation.[15]

Its original version and most of its successors are strictly linear with a unique and stable equilibrium. Although dynamic derivations have sometimes exhibited unstable dynamics, as in the 'razor's edge' phenomenon, these have generally been non-complex. If sufficient non-linearities are introduced into an ISLM model, it can generate complex dynamics, in particular chaotic dynamics.

Day and Shafer (1985) present a fix price model with consumption a positive function of income and a negative one of interest rates as is money demand. The variation from the usual ISLM comes with specifying investment as non-linear and non-monotonic in income, becoming negative at high levels of income, as well as possessing the standard negative relationship with interest rates. With a sufficiently non-linear income–investment function ergodic chaotic dynamics can happen (Day and Shafer, 1987).[16]

New Keynesian Economics

Weak New Keynesian models

GENERAL FOUNDATION

New Classicals criticized the Old Keynesian ISLM model for the allegedly *ad hoc* nature of its assumptions regarding expectations (Lucas, 1972). They developed models with continuous Walrasian market clearing with rational expectations as a microfoundation that implied the impossibility of involuntary unemployment, arguably the core Keynesian idea. The theoretical triumph of such models in the 1970s led to declarations of the death of Keynesian economics. Such declarations triggered a response.

The initial response came in what Rosser (1990) calls 'Weak New Keynesian' models. They assume a weakened version of rational expectations and then derive the possibility of involuntary unemployment as a result. Usually they involve deriving some stickiness of wages or prices or investment from the near rational expectations assumption.

The core concept is that of *information asymmetry* as the foundation of the deviation from perfectly rational expectations, ultimately derived from the work of Akerlof (1971). In a canonical result, Akerlof and Yellen (1985) ask, 'can small deviations from rationality make significant differences to economic equilibria?' and answer, 'yes'. Generally these models have been linear without involving complex dynamics, although in principle they could.

MENU COSTS

The best known, if not the most theoretically and empirically satisfying, of New Keynesian models is that of menu costs (Mankiw, 1985; Akerlof and Yellen, 1985).

Asymmetric information and a variety of costs are invoked as explanations for an unwillingness of firms to change prices frequently. This becomes the 'small deviation' from perfect rationality that triggers large output swings.

Of course any nominal price stickiness can trigger declines in real output in response to declines in aggregate demand, at least temporarily. That these are merely temporary results has drawn criticism from Post Keynesian critics (Davidson, 1994b). Other problems arise from symmetry questions, questions of why the analysis does not apply equally to output decisions, weaknesses of the model when long time horizons are considered, and a failure to explain differential price variability across sectors (Gordon, 1990). Closely related to the menu-cost approach are models emphasizing rule-of-thumb pricing behaviours arising from search costs (Okun, 1981) and models of staggered price contracts (Blanchard, 1983).[17]

INVISIBLE HANDSHAKES AND EFFICIENCY WAGES

Although nominal wage stickiness does not have to cause nominal price stickiness, it can do so. Thus theories of nominal wage stickiness have also been part of the Weak New Keynesian canon. These have drawn on either asymmetric information and search costs (Okun, 1981) or asymmetries of risk aversion between employers and employees (Baily, 1974).[18]

The more recent development has been the efficiency wage theory (Shapiro and Stiglitz, 1984) that sees the quality of the labour force in a firm as endogenous to the wage rate. This can lead to high and sticky wages.[19]

Post Keynesian critics of these models, such as Davidson (1994b), emphasize that although Keynes allowed for wage and price stickiness through much of *The General Theory*, he ultimately sought an explanation for involuntary unemployment that did not depend on that assumption and relaxed it in chapter 19.

PRINCIPAL–AGENT PROBLEMS AND FINANCIAL ISSUES

Asymmetric information problems in financial markets lead to problems of either credit availability or inappropriate levels of investment. The key is that asymmetric information lies at the heart of the principal–agent problem which is pervasive in financial markets.

In particular, risk-averse banks will ration credit to customers they deem the most reliable rather than simply provide credit to whomever at the going rate of interest (Stiglitz and Weiss, 1981). This can lead to a sub-optimal amount of lending and thus of investment with unemployment resulting.[20]

Closely related to this are models focusing on risk-averse firm behaviour as a function of the financial structure of the firm (Greenwald and Stiglitz, 1986). Given risk aversion, changes in demand affect asset positions and lead to cutbacks in investment. Inventory adjustments actually exacerbate the fluctuations rather than performing a smoothing function (Blinder and Maccini, 1991).

Strong New Keynesian Economics

GENERAL FOUNDATION

In contrast to the Weak New Keynesian models, Strong New Keynesian models go all the way in introducing full rational expectations to generate results. This has generated criticism (Davidson, 1992, 1994b; Mirowski, 1990; Carrier, 1993) that this violates the fundamental uncertainty Keynesian concept, hence making these models 'unKeynesian'. But, in their non-linear forms these assumptions lead to complex dynamics, thus using the rational expectations assumption to show the unlikeliness of rational expectations actually obtaining in the real world.

Another problem is that many observers do not consider these models to be 'New Keynesian', but rather something else, 'Post Walrasian' (Romer, 1993). Nevertheless, many of these models are viewed as part of the New Keynesian canon, especially those involving coordination failure (Clower, 1965; Leijonhufvud, 1973; Cooper and John, 1988).

PERFECT FORESIGHT CHAOS AND MULTIPLE EQUILIBRIA

The canonical Strong New Keynesian model is that of Benhabib and Day (1982) with perfect foresight and overlapping generations (OLG). In each time period t let there be two generations (y, o) with endowments (w_y, w_o). At $t = 0$, the old possess fiat money eequal to M. Prices and consumption by the generations in t are given by $p(t), c_y(t), c_o(t)$. The young maximize utility subject to an intertemporal budget constraint,

$$p(t)c_y(t) + p(t+1)c_o(t+1) = p(t+1)w_o \tag{1}$$

which yields an intergenerational offer curve on their part. The old face in $t = 1$ the constraint

$$p(1)c_o(1) = p(1)w_o + M \tag{2}$$

which combines with (1), the young's utility maximization and a Ricardian intertemporal production possibilities frontier,

$$R = [(c_y, c_o) \colon cy + c_o = w_y + w_o] \tag{3}$$

to solve for a sequence of efficient perfect foresight price and consumption equilibria levels. For each initial condition there is a different equilibrium, thus allowing for multiple equilibria.

Crucial to the dynamics is the offer curve, O. Its non-linearity is determined by constrained intertemporal marginal rates of substitution, endowment levels and rates of population growth. There exists a critical level of non-linearity of O for which these perfect foresight dynamics are chaotic.[21] Such a case is depicted in Figure 17.1.[22] Although this is an essentially neoclassical type of model, we note

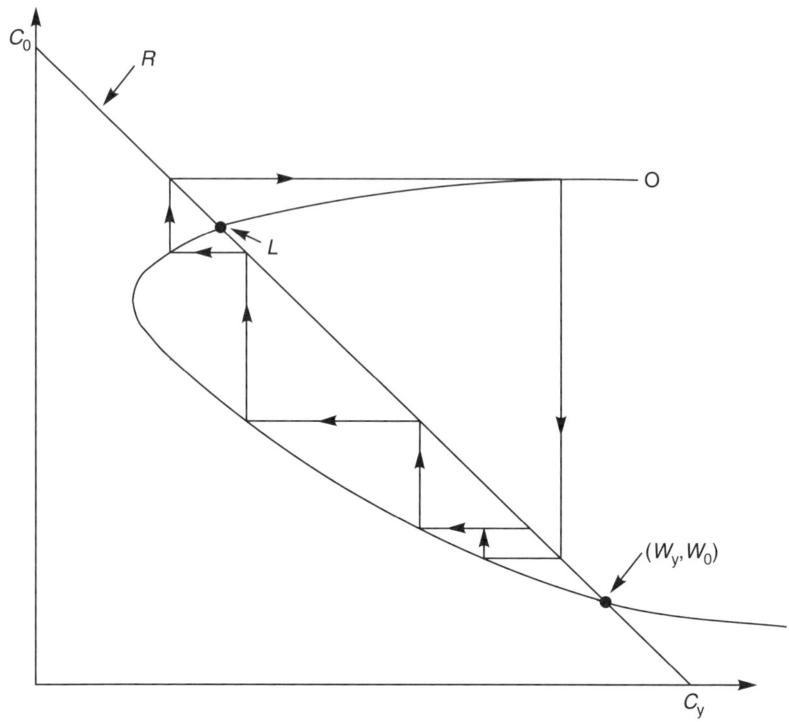

Figure 17.1

the damage to the possibility of forming rational expectations that is implied by such a model. This model provided the foundation for the Grandmont (1985) model of chaotic real monetary balance dynamics with perfect foresight.

SUNSPOTS AND SELF-FULFILLING PROPHECIES

A concept that enters these models is self-fulfilling prophecies or sunspot equilibria. The latter idea, initially formalized by Shell (1977), suggests that agents might be driven by their belief that other agents believe in some 'extrinsic' variable (sunspots, the Sibyl of Cumae's prophecies) to act together to bring about a self-fulfilling prophetic equilibrium outcome. Different beliefs will bring about different outcomes and thus such models also imply multiple equilibria.

Although this can explain rational price bubbles, sunspot models involve real economic decision making, especially real capital investment. This links with Keynes's idea of 'animal spirits' driving investment and his theory of long-run expectations in chapter 12 of *The General Theory*. That idea is a fundamental inspiration to the sunspot theorists.

Azariadis and Guesnerie (1986) show possible cyclical behaviour in such models. More generally this behaviour can be chaotic or otherwise complex (Guesnerie and Woodford, 1992).

VARIETIES OF COORDINATION FAILURE

Multiple self-fulfilling sunspot equilibria can generate coordination failure. Although not posed in terms of non-linear dynamics models, Clower (1965) and Leijonhufvud (1973) posed the problem of coordination failure as a central Keynesian issue, with Howitt (1985) and Cooper and John (1988) updating the idea.[23] Again the issue is agents trying to act on the basis of the behaviour of other agents. Cooper and John posit a non-linearity in the optimal output response of the representative firm to the levels of output of other firms due to external complementarities. This generates multiple equilibria which are welfare ranked.

But coordination failure goes beyond output or investment decisions of firms as they try to figure out what each other are going to do – the *expectations coordination* problem. There is the question of *learning coordination* as well: if expectations are not coordinated can they become so through learning processes? Models in which learning converges on rational expectations steady-state golden rule paths have been developed with simple rules such as least-squares learning (Marcet and Sargent, 1989).[24] But, in general, learning processes can converge on cycles or sunspot equilibria or even involve chaotic dynamics (Guesnerie and Woodford, 1992; Grandmont, 1994).[25]

Thus, the general outcome of Strong New Keynesian models is that they readily generate complex dynamics with multiple equilibria. This undermines New Classical outcomes and provides a potential foundation for Keynesian fundamental uncertainty.[26]

Post Keynesian Economics

General foundations

Compared to the above three schools of thought, there is greater diversity of approach among Post Keynesians, with many offshoots which we shall not consider such as the Sraffian-neo-Ricardian strand. It has been suggested that the label Post Keynesian is really a broad cover for *any* heterodox approach.[27] However, we shall limit ourselves to models that are closer in spirit to Keynes himself or his immediate followers.

Given the great diversity of Post Keynesian approaches, there is no single answer as to how Post Keynesian economics relates to complex dynamics. Whereas we argue that Weak New Keynesianism is generally linear and non-complex while Strong New Keynesianism is generally non-linear and complex, with Post Keynesian models it depends and varies broadly, although most Post Keynesian approaches are amenable to complex dynamics.

However, despite this diversity the idea of fundamental uncertainty has been widely identified as central to Post Keynesian theory, even though not all self-identified Post Keynesians focus on it. It was important to Keynes even before he was writing economics (Rotheim, 1988). Debates over the relationship between New Keynesian and Post Keynesian models from the perspective of complex dynamics revolve substantially around this issue.

Keynes–Post Keynesian[28]

This is the approach of Davidson (1994b) and some others (Moore, 1988; Wray, 1990),[29] that a proper Post Keynesian economics must be the economics of Keynes himself. As mentioned in note 3, Blaug (1994) argues that there are several possible different models that have been teased out of *The General Theory* alone. The approach mentioned by him that Davidson particularly fits is that which focuses on chapter 17 of *The General Theory* which emphasizes the imperfect substitutability of money for other goods and its effects on real output.

Davidson sees the failure of the ergodic axiom as key to explaining fundamental uncertainty which in turn drives the demand for money for contractual purposes. He draws the line against Strong New Keynesian theories by arguing that one does not need non-linear dynamics for the possibility of non-ergodicity and hence fundamental uncertainty. One can derive a fully Keynesian model with a strictly linear static model and he is correct on this point.[30]

Although one can find non-linearities in *The General Theory*, such as in the *de facto* aggregate supply curve in chapter 21 and even hints of the possibility of multiple equilibria on p. 191 in his discussion of Ricardo's view of interest, most of Keynes' own theorizing is in largely linear models which, assuming a given state of agents' expectations, will generate a single equilibrium. Consideration of the different sets of expectations and the interactions of actors in generating those expectations underlies the multiple sunspot equilibria approach.

Imperfect Competition Models

Just as imperfect competition plays a role in some Weak New Keynesian models, so various schools of Post Keynesian economics rely upon it. Most important is the Kalecki 'degree of monopoly' approach (Kalecki, 1939–40, 1954). Kalecki saw it as explaining income distribution and basically did not use it to discuss issues such as multiple equilibria or complex dynamics.

However, the controversies surrounding his work have focused importantly on the question of multiple equilibria. Thus Basile and Salvadori (1984–5) present a proof of the uniqueness of prices in a Kaleckian system, whose generality has been challenged on grounds of inconsistencies within Kalecki's model over time (Kriesler, 1987) and on grounds that under more general conditions Kalecki's model generates multiple equilibria (Carson, 1994). This has not led to modelling with complex dynamics, despite some of Kalecki's (1935) other work leading that way.

An alternative is Kaldor's (1986) disequilibrium model. Key is his insistence on the ubiquity of increasing returns in industry. This leads to monopoly power models but also to models of non-linear and complex dynamics (Day, 1993).

Class struggle models

Close to a Marxist approach are 'class struggle' models of various sorts. The most important of these is the model of Goodwin (1967) based on predator–prey cycle dynamics. Pohjola (1981) showed that a non-linear version of this model could generate chaotic dynamics, a topic Goodwin (1990) pursued further himself .

Somewhat different is a Ricardian model, due to Bhaduri and Harris (1987), of the transition to a classical steady state in a fixed land model with a maximum marginal product of labour. Dynamics depend on the ratio of the maximum marginal product of labour to the wage rate which they identify as 'the rate of exploitation at primitive accumulation'. If this is sufficiently great then chaotic dynamics can occur.

Non-linear investment functions

A broad group of models, arguably closer to Old Keynesian models in spirit, impose non-linear investment functions of one sort or another.[31] Most of these initially appeared in the period of Keynes or shortly thereafter, but only later were understood to be capable of generating chaotic or other complex dynamics. The Kaldor (1940) model was first shown by Dana and Malgrange (1984) to be capable of producing chaotic dynamics.

Others in this category include the non-linear multiplier–accelerator model of Samuelson (1939) which Gabisch (1984) showed could generate chaotic dynamics, non-ergodically so (Nusse and Hommes, 1990), and the Hicks (1950) trade cycle model shown to be possibly chaotic by Blatt (1983).

Evolutionary models

At the border of Keynesian modelling is the array of models calling themselves 'evolutionary'. We are interested in those with a non-linear dynamics foundation and some connection to a Keynesian approach. Examples are the long-wave model of Goodwin (1986) with Schumpeterian elements and the long-wave entrainment model of Mosekilde *et al.* (1993).

A model exhibiting even longer-wave dynamics with chaotic interludes is Day and Walter (1989). It models epochs of given demoeconomic–infrastructure combinations, with erratic shorter-term dynamics within large-scale phase transition jumps from one epoch to another.

Since none of these rely on information asymmetries they are not New Keynesian, but rather more in the Post Keynesian category, if peripherally. As noted in the discussion of evolutionary synergetics there are many possibilities open for this approach. New models emerge taking these approaches, many not identifiably Keynesian in any clear way, although some are.

CAN THE TWAIN MEET?

Hysteresis Models

Finally we have a set of models that have been identified as both New Keynesian and Post Keynesian by various observers. One of these is the hysteresis approach, clearly drawing on non-linear underpinnings.[32] Sharing elements in common with the path dependence approach, the fundamental idea is that the economy is influenced by its history of past shocks (Elster, 1976; Cross, 1987).[33] Thus, to the extent that there is a 'natural rate of unemployment', it is endogenous to past rates of unemployment.

Cross (1993) argues that hysteresis models are non-ergodic and therefore consistent with Post Keynesian economics. Davidson (1993) questions this, labelling hysteresis a 'New Keynesian' model and arguing that it is not truly Keynesian (or presumably Post Keynesian) because it depends on exogenous 'real' shocks, although those could be demand shocks endogenously generated, at least in some models. Another issue involves whether hysteresis is 'permanent' or merely 'persistent'.

In any case it would appear that there is good reason to view these models as lying in the intersection between New and Post Keynesian economics. They are clearly consistent with non-linear dynamics, even if they have not been used to generate dramatic forms of complex dynamics.

Financial fragility models

Finally we come to models of financial fragility which have also been variously labelled as both New Keynesian (Delli Gatti *et al.* 1993)[34] and as Post Keynesian (Delli Gatti and Gardini, 1990),[35] even by the same authors. The father of such models was Minsky (1972, 1982) who emphasized waves of overconfidence and crashes in the financial system as driving forces. He saw his approach as Keynesian, which is reasonable given the discussion of irrational stock market dynamics appearing in *The General Theory*, especially in chapter 12.

Several of the above involve non-linear and even chaotic dynamics, especially Delli Gatti *et al.* (1993) and Keen (1995). It is known that liquidity constraints can underlie complex dynamics of various sorts (Woodford, 1989). These are present in Minsky-type financial fragility models. Minsky's own writings suggest discontinuous financial crashes. Such models can be viewed as both New Keynesian in that they reflect information asymmetry problems and Post Keynesian in that they can reflect Post Keynesian fundamental uncertainty. Both explanations are reinforced in non-linear dynamics versions which imply complex dynamics. More than anywhere else we see in this model the common elements of the various complex dynamics Keynesian approaches.

THE QUESTION OF GENERALITY

A central feature of the debates over New Keynesian and Post Keynesian economics has been which is the more 'general' approach. Thus Davidson (1994b, 1995) argues that his version of 'Keynes–Post Keynesianism' is more general because it involves a minimum number of axioms. He obtains core Keynesian results with a linear unique equilibrium model and thus claims that this is more general than approaches relying upon non-linear dynamics and their associated complexity phenomena. There is something to this argument.

But things are not so simple. One of his axioms is that of non-ergodicity. Certainly Keynes basically accepted fundamental uncertainty, but it is less than clear that he would go as far as Davidson on this. Focusing on some chapters of *The General Theory* one can get a model of underemployment without any resort to non-ergodicity, e.g. in the Old Keynesian models drawing largely from chapters 3 and 10.

Indeed, one may have fundamental uncertainty *without* non-ergodicity, as in models displaying chaotic dynamics. This may even be 'effectively ontological' rather than merely epistemological if combined with noise or with fractal basin boundaries. Here we come to the crux of the issue: *non-linear and complex dynamics provide a clear foundation for fundamental uncertainty that embraces cases not covered by non-ergodicity*. Furthermore, non-linearity is mathematically the general case of which linearity is the special case. Empirically there is almost no reason to believe that the world is linear.

Thus, the issue of which approach is more general – the non-linear Strong New Keynesian or the linear Keynes–Post Keynesian – remains unresolved. Each applies in areas where the other does not. We can conclude that Strong New Keynesian approaches are consonant with most Post Keynesian approaches in both generating complex dynamics. In this regard the Weak New Keynesian models are seen as not overlapping with the others as much and not able to produce fundamental uncertainty either.

CONCLUSIONS

Non-linear models can generate a variety of complex dynamics, including catastrophic discontinuities, chaotic sensitive dependence on initial conditions. Strange attractors generating erratic trajectories, fractal basin boundaries with sudden leaps from one basin of attraction to another, and evolutionary synergetics models in which 'slave variable revolts' can lead to an entirely different dynamical pattern. All of these possibilities undermine the ability of agents to form rational expectations and thus endogenously generate Keynesian fundamental uncertainty without the need to axiomatize it explicitly .

We reviewed Old Keynesian ISLM models, Weak New Keynesian models dependent on asymmetric information, Strong New Keynesian models that use rational expectations assumptions to generate results that undermine rational expectations, a variety of Post Keynesian models from linear ones to non-linear evolutionary ones, and models such as of hysteresis and financial fragility which can be viewed as both New and Post Keynesian. Those New Keynesian and Post Keynesian approaches which readily produce non-linear complex dynamics models are more consistent with each other. This suggests a division between the Weak New Keynesian models which have little non-linearity to them and most Post Keynesian approaches.

Finally we conclude that Strong New Keynesian and linear Post Keynesian models compete with each other in their generality as sources of basic Keynesian fundamental uncertainty. The former generate it endogenously from complex dynamics in non-linear models, the latter derive it from the axiom of non-ergodicity. The former can generate uncertainty even with ergodicity whereas the latter do so with linearity.

ACKNOWLEDGEMENTS

This chapter arose out of a series of discussions on the pkt (Post Keynesian thought) Internet network, especially involving Paul Davidson. I wish to acknowledge the participants in that discussion. Also, the ideas in this chapter were presented in preliminary form to the Post Keynesian Study Group in London, chaired by Philip Arestis and Victoria Chick, and to the Department of Economics at the University of Pisa, comments from the participants in those sessions also being useful. An earlier version entitled 'A Complex Systems Dynamics Perspective on New Keynesian and Post Keynesian Economics' was presented at the Eastern Economic Association meetings in New York in March 1995, and I appreciate comments by Ric Holt and others at that meeting as well. In addition, I wish to acknowledge either comments or receipt of useful materials from Peter Allen, William A. Brock, Jean-Paul Chavas, Carl Chiarella, David Colander, Rod Cross, Richard H. Day, W. Davis Dechert, Hans van Ees, Harry Garretsen, Roger Guesnerie, Cars Hommes, Heikki Isomaki, Ted Jaditz, Steve Keen, Blake LeBaron, Hans-Walter Lorenz, William F. Mitchell, Tonu Puu, Roy Rotheim, Neri Salvadori, Willi Semmler, John D. Sterman, Wolfgang Weidlich and Wei-Bin Zhang. None of the above is responsible for any errors or misinterpretations contained herein.

NOTES

1 A Strong supporter of this view is Davidson (1992, 1994b, 1995) who asks, 'Where's the Keynesian beef in New Keynesian economics?' (1992, p. 449) and declares in referring to New Keynesian economics that, 'Although a rose by any other name is still a (sweet smelling) rose, it does not follow that calling the foul smelling fruit of the gingko tree a rose will make it smell any better for policy making purposes' (ibid., p. 456).

2 This connects with the problem of multiple varieties of Keynesianism. Thus Blaug (1994) identifies different schools as focusing on different chapters of *The General Theory*: a wage and price stickiness approach focused on chapter 19, an elasticity pessimism approach focused on chapters 3 and 10, an irrational expectations and persistent dynamic

disequilibria approach focused on chapter 12, a denial of gross substitutability between money and other assets approach focused on chapter 17, and an intertemporal coordination failures approach 'rationally reconstructed' from a discarded introduction printed in volume XXIX of *The Collected Works of John Maynard Keynes* (Keynes, 1979) and arguably from his 'The End of Laissez-Faire' (1926).

3 Surveys of New Keynesian economics include Gordon (1990), Mankiw and Romer (1991) and van Ees and Garretsen (1993). A survey of Post Keynesian economics is Arestis and Chick (1992).

4 Varieties of economic applications can be found in Barnett, *et al.* (1989), Rosser (1991), Lorenz (1993a), Puu (1993) and Day and Chen (1993).

5 In contrast with 'Post Keynesians' who tend to admire and extend the work of Keynes, 'Post Walrasians' tend to criticize the main body of Walras's work. However, Rosser (1996a, 1996b) argues that certain arguments of Walras are consistent with a complex dynamics perspective, thus making him the 'first Post Walrasian'.

6 Davidson (1995) argues that complex dynamics only generate epistemological uncertainty whereas true Keynesian uncertainty is ontological. This chapter will argue that complex dynamics effectively elide this distinction.

7 Colander (1992b) argues that these are not really 'New Keynesian' but 'New neo-Keynesian'.

8 For a more complete discussion see Rosser (1991, ch. 2).

9 Not all non-linear dynamical systems generate complex dynamics, e.g. simple unconstrained exponential growth.

10 The first application of catastrophe theory in economics was to stock market crashes by Zeeman (1974). In their general criticism of catastrophe theory Zahler and Sussman (1977) attacked this model because it allowed 'chartist' investors lacking rational expectations. This critique now looks ridiculous but most observers only remember the critique and not how ridiculous was much of its basis. For a more balanced view see Arnold (1986).

11 Davidson (1995) disputes this arguing that chaotic uncertainty is merely 'epistemological', owing merely to computational difficulties, rather than 'ontological', truly fundamental Keynesian uncertainty. It can be argued that, especially when combined with fractal basin boundaries as in Brock and Hommes (1995), chaotic dynamics can generate 'effective ontological uncertainty'.

12 A competing theory is that of self-organized criticality or 'sandpile' models (Bak *et al.*, 1993). However, such models depend fundamentally on exogenous shocks to a system with constant internal structure with the accumulation of internal effects generating a skewed distribution of final outcomes even with a normal distribution of shocks.

13 See Zhang (1991) for a discussion of economics applications.

14 Hence ISLM is known as the 'Hicks–Hansen synthesis' and in conjunction with an assumption of well-behaved micro markets as promulgated by Paul Samuelson, as the 'neoclassical synthesis'.

15 For a defence of it see Tobin (1993). On the announcement of his Nobel Prize, Robert Lucas declared 'There is still no alternative to the orthodox Keynesian model' (*Washington Post*, 11 October 1995, p. B1).

16 Other models dating from the period of Keynes with non-linear investment functions can generate chaotic dynamics, like the Kaldor (1940) trade cycle model. We label all these as 'Post Keynesian' although many are not far from the non-linear ISLM model.

17 An assumption underlying all these models is that of monopolistically competitive market structures which are price flexible without the introduction of these various frictions. New Classicals thus reject these models as depending on this 'special case' assumption, noting that more generally allowing oligopoly or pure monopoly leads to price stickiness.

18 A variation on these models is the 'insider–outsider' model (Lindbeck and Snower, 1988a). This model can be associated with the hysteresis model discussed below.

19 A more traditional explanation of sticky wages is labour unions, but New Classicals merely sneer at this as an 'imperfection' to be wiped away.

20 This theory is related to the financial fragility model discussed below.

21 Crucial to proving this is the existence of three-period cycles which are sufficient for chaotic dynamics under the appropriate conditions according to the Li–Yorke (1975) theorem.

22 Such models have been criticized by New Classicals because of their OLG nature, implying that optimization is not over an infinite time horizon. A variety of models with infinite time horizon optimization have been developed (Boldrin and Montrucchio, 1986; Deneckere and Pelikan, 1986).

23 Colander (1994a) poses this as the problem of the macrofoundation of micro economics.

24 Under the influence of complex dynamics, Sargent (1993, p. 28) has 'retreated from rational expectations'.

25 A variation is to have a conflict between different expectational schemes based on information costs with this conflict generating chaotic dynamics (Brock and Hommes, 1995).

26 Some are optimistic that government can pin down expectations by using fiscal policies (Grandmont, 1985; Evans and Honkapohja, 1993) or indicative planning (Guesnerie, 1993).

27 Thus many Marxists, institutionalists and even Austrians consider themselves to be Post Keynesians to some degree.

28 This term is due to Davidson (1994b) although some might label it 'fundamentalist Keynesian'.

29 Although recently on the pkt net (1995) Moore has supported the view that non-linear complex dynamics can underlie Keynesian uncertainty.

30 Actually his model contains non-linearities in his aggregate supply curve. But, they are not sufficiently great to generate multiple equilibria.

31 The Day and Shafer (1985) non-linear variation on the ISLM model can generate chaotic dynamics, as noted above.

32 Although it can arise in linear models under certain circumstances (Setterfield, 1993). Hysteresis can arise in catastrophe-theoretic models.

33 Arestis and Skott (1993) find empirical support for its applicability to the UK economy. Hysteresis and persistence are not strictly identical (Mitchell, 1993).

34 See also Taylor and O'Connell (1985), Bernanke and Gertler (1991) and Cooper and Ejarque (1995).

35 See also Foley (1987), Semmler and Sieveking (1993) and Keen (1995).

18

POST KEYNESIAN AND STRONG NEW KEYNESIAN MACROECONOMICS

Compatible bedfellows?

Colin Rogers

INTRODUCTION

This chapter deals with what Rosser (1990) calls Strong New Keynesian (SNK) economics. Strong New Keynesian economics is distinguished from the majority of New Keynesian contributions surveyed in the Mankiw and Romer (1991a) volumes by the fact that it is not concerned with the provision of micro-foundations to account for real and/or nominal rigidities.[1] The latter theories are considered to be Neo-Keynesian or even classical. Describing some New Keynesian contributions as 'classical' is perhaps most apt in view of Mankiw's (1991a) acknowledgement that the term Keynesian seems to have outlived its usefulness (see Garretsen, 1991, p. 54). By contrast SNK macroeconomists seek to take on New Classical macroeconomics on its own terms. As Rosser (1990, p. 207) puts it, SNK economics 'goes all the way in adopting the assumptions of the new classical school, all the better to undermine the critics of Keynesianism in its many forms'.

The objective of the chapter is to assess SNK economics critically both on its own terms and from the perspective of Post Keynesian macroeconomics. The latter perspective is of particular relevance in view of the claim by many exponents of SNK economics that their models capture important elements of Keynes's *General Theory*.

The second section of the chapter outlines some of the key features of SNK economics as presented, for example, by Blanchard and Fischer (1989), Azariadis (1993) or Farmer (1993). Simple models are applied to illustrate the concepts of indeterminateness, multiple equilibria, sunspots, 'bootstraps' or self-fulfilling prophecy equilibria which exponents of SNK economics interpret as properties of the *General Theory*.

The third section presents a critical evaluation of SNK theory both on its own terms and from the perspective of Post Keynesian macroeconomics. The chapter concludes with an assessment of the view, due to Colander (1992c) and van Ees and Garretsen (1992) that there is scope for some form of synthesis between SNK and Post Keynesian economics.

STRONG NEW KEYNESIAN MACROECONOMICS

To set the scene it is useful to sketch some features of the intellectual environment in which SNK economics flourishes. It is well known that New Keynesian macroeconomic is a reaction to the claim by New Classical macroeconomists that Keynesian macroeconomic models were *ad hoc* because many of the postulated functional relationships did not possess sound microeconomic foundations. By sound microeconomic foundations exponents of New Classical macroeconomics (NCM) meant the Walrasian general equilibrium structure represented by the Arrow–Debreu system. As Farmer (1993, p. 171) explains, NCM amounted to 'the wholesale adoption of the Arrow–Debreu program as the research agenda for macroeconomics'. In all important respects this is what was meant by the claim that Keynesian economics lacked microeconomic foundations – there was no obvious connection between aggregate Keynesian macroeconomic theory and the Arrow–Debreu system. Many older Keynesians actually think that this is sensible, e.g. Tobin (1980) and Solow (1986), and in any event the microeconomic foundations of *The General Theory* are to be found in Marshall, not Walras.

Despite the obvious nature of Keynes's Marshallian pedigree the younger generation of macro theorists interested in Keynesian ideas have embraced the Arrow–Debreu system as the language of the research agenda for modern macroeconomics. Azariadis (1993, pp. xi–v) outlines the view that the younger generation of macroeconomists have evolved a new paradigm and a new language in which they communicate their findings. Key insight of the new paradigm is that macroeconomics is about human interactions over time and consequently the new language is based on the theory of dynamical systems. The mathematics rests on the theory of linear and non-linear differential or difference equations.[2] The 'new' paradigm with its dynamic perspective is intended to replace the static perspective of the IS–LM or AD–AS models. Azariadis also interprets the neoclassical growth model and the overlapping generations model (OLG) as distinct dialects within a broad language that he calls neoclassical growth theory – at the core of which lies the Arrow–Debreu system.

Farmer (1993, p. 234), echoing Azariadis, argues that general equilibrium theory provides a common language with which competing schools in macroeconomics can converse and he suggests 'that a "Keynesian" sacrifices very little by choosing to accept the battleground of equilibrium as laid out by new classical economists in the 1970s. What he or she gains is a coherent framework within which to develop a theory of policy'. Blanchard and Fischer (1989) tacitly adopt the same position when they endorse the optimal growth and OLG models as the workhorses of modern macroeconomics.

In short, SNK theorists propose to take on the NCM by making some apparently minor extensions of the Arrow–Debreu system so as to generate major changes in the conclusions. Farmer (1993, p. 1) explains that all of the models he discusses begin with a version of an equilibrium economy described by Debreu;

> but most of the interesting features of macroeconomics require departures from the assumption that markets are perfect [i.e. the assumptions underlying the Arrow–Debreu model hold]. I will argue that departures that seem relatively minor have major consequences for both the positive and normative implications of the theory.

(See Blanchard and Fischer (1989, p. xii) for a similar view). In this respect the overlapping generations model holds most appeal for SNK macroeconomists because it readily generates results that look suspiciously like many of the points raised by Keynes in *The General Theory*. For example, the so-called sunspot or self-fulfilling prophecy equilibria are thought to be 'very close to Keynes's world of beauty contests and bootstraps' (Burnell, 1989, p. 409) or to capture what Keynes meant by the term 'animal spirits', fluctuations in which generate the business cycle (Farmer, 1993, p. 171; Grandmont, 1989). In view of this association the remainder of this section will consider some of these properties of the OLG model.

A simple OLG framework

Any assessment of the OLG framework will quickly conclude that there are a multitude of possible specifications all with somewhat different properties. The general OLG framework differs from the Arrow–Debreu economy by assuming an infinite number of commodities and an infinite number of agents. This specification is regarded as an idealization which provides insight into the behaviour of models with a large but finite number of commodities. For a summary of these issues see Kehoe (1989). SNK macroeconomists have, however, applied small and/or simplified versions of the more general OLG specification and these models may have special properties that do not hold in a more general specification. Nevertheless, these relatively simple models can be used to demonstrate the general properties of non-optimality and indeterminateness of equilibria that are of interest to SNK theorists.

The general properties of the OLG structure are by now well known so here we will briefly sketch a simple version of the model.[3] Complexity will be introduced only if necessary to illustrate a particular point. We begin with the simple case of a constant population and two generations: the young and the old.[4] Each period, indexed by t, n individuals are born and each individual lives for two periods, indexed by $1 =$ young and $2 =$ old. Each individual has a utility function that depends on the consumption of the only commodity when young, and likewise when old, which individuals attempt to maximize. That is,

$$u(c_{1t},\ c_{2t}) \tag{1}$$

Each individual receives an endowment of the perishable commodity each period and can transfer purchasing power between periods only by exchanging some of the commodity for a durable asset called money. As the old die at the end of the second period they wish to consume as much as possible in period 2 and to that end wish to trade their entire stock of the durable commodity to the young generation in exchange for the consumption good. The budget constraints facing an individual that lives two periods are therefore

$$c_{1t} = e_1 - M/p_t \quad \text{and} \quad c_{2t} = e_2 + M/p_{t+1} \tag{2}$$

where e = endowment of perishable consumption good received each period; M = the durable commodity 'money' and p_i = price of the perishable consumption good in period $i = t, t+1, \ldots$

The young save by converting some initial endowment into the durable commodity called money, M. When old the durable commodity is converted back into the perishable consumption commodity. Assuming, for the sake of simplicity, that all individuals have identical endowments and utility functions the model can be represented in terms of the familiar diagram of intertemporal choice found in any undergraduate text (see Hoover, 1988, Figure 6.1). The analysis of intergenerational trade can now be represented in a number of ways to illustrate properties of the OLG structure that are of interest to SNK macroeconomists.[5]

Following Hargreaves-Heap (1992) it is a simple matter to illustrate that this OLG structure has an infinite number of rational expectations equilibria. Intergenerational trade involves the exchange of the consumption commodity for money by the young and the converse for the old. An equilibrium in period t determines a price for the consumption good in terms of money, p_t, such that, given the nominal quantity of money, M, and the expected price of the consumption good in the next period, p_{t+1}, the total nominal money stock changes hands from old to young. This situation is illustrated in Figure 18.1 which is based on Hargreaves-Heap (ibid., p. 91).

The curve labelled D represents the demand for money balances by the young based on the expectation of next period's price p^e_{t+1}. The curve labelled M represents the total supply of nominal money balances which the old generation is holding but which it must trade with the young to maximize its utility in period 2. The price of the consumption commodity in period t adjusts to reconcile the trades between the two generations so that the demand for the commodity by the old equals the supply of the commodity by the young.

Now, as is well known, and Hargreaves-Heap demonstrates very clearly, there are an infinite number of rational expectations equilibria in this model. Inspection of Figure 18.1 suggests immediately that the equilibrium price in period t, p'_t, depends on the price expected in period $t + 1$. Any price in period t can be an equilibrium price by suitable selection of p^e_{t+1} and the same argument applies in general given the recursive structure of the model. Any price expectation for $t + 1$ can be converted into a rational expectations equilibrium (= perfect foresight in this non-stochastic model) by suitable adjustment of p^e_{t+2} and so on. Hence there are an infinite continuum of price vectors $(p_t, p_{t+1}, p_{t+2}, \ldots)$ which are competitive equilibrium solutions to the model.

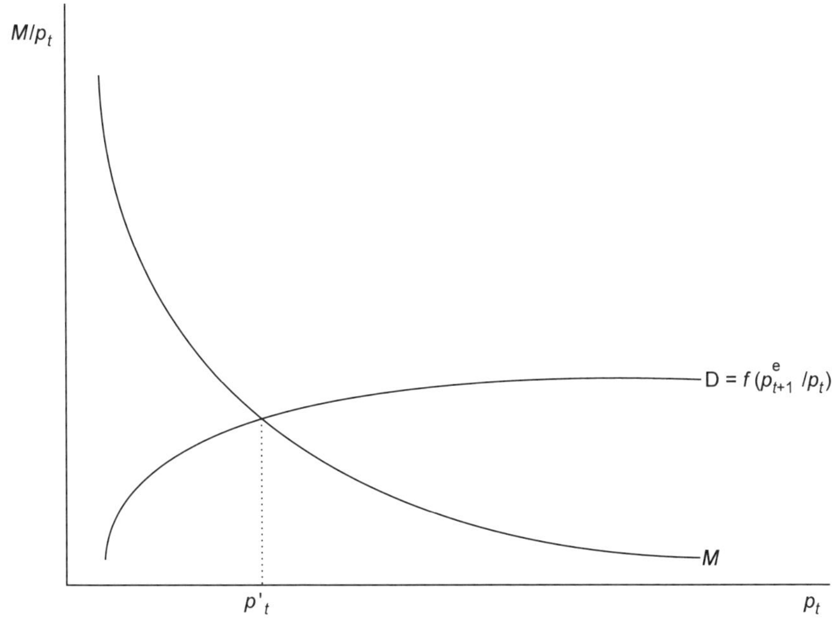

Figure 18.1 Multiple equilibria exist when P^{e}_{t+1} is a free coordinating variable

The same setup can obviously be applied to demonstrate that agents' expectations determine the equilibrium outcome (Hargreaves-Heap, 1992). In these cases expectations are self-fulfilling in the sense that if agents believe that the world has monetarist properties than a change to the nominal money stock produces a monetarist result. Alternatively, if agents believe that the world is Keynesian then Keynesian outcomes result. These two possible outcomes are illustrated in Figure 18.2 for the case of an increase in the nominal money supply from M to M'.

Agents who have Keynesian expectations about how the world works do not expect prices to rise when they perceive an increase in the nominal money stock, so their offer curve shifts to pass through point K. Conversely, agents with monetarist and New Classical views expect prices to rise and these expectations are self-fulfilling as the offer curve shifts to pass through the point marked NCM.

Hargreaves-Heap (ibid., p. 94) goes on to outline how the analysis sketched above offers a SNK interpretation of Keynes's notion of 'animal spirits' and their role in the determination of equilibrium:

> Suppose there is a surge of optimism about the future which translates into the belief that prices will be lower in future than had previously been expected. The offer curve will shift [up in Figure 18.1] and for a given money supply we will observe a fall in current prices as well as an increase in

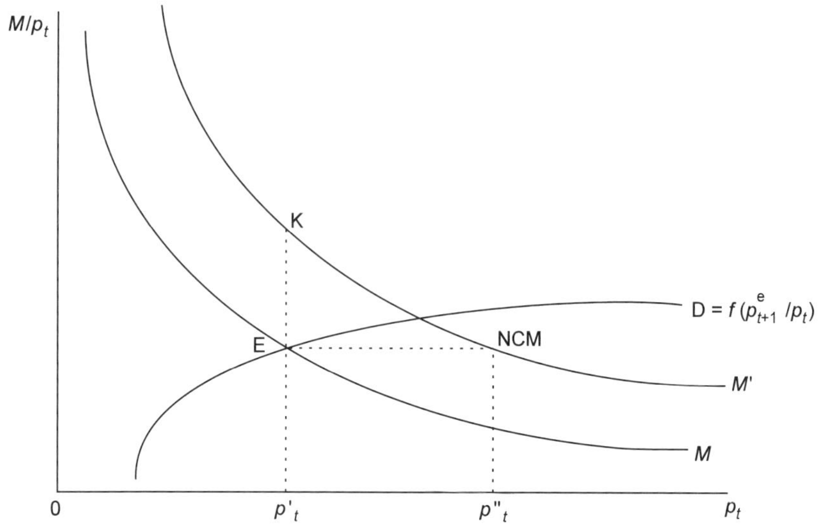

Figure 18.2 Self-fulfilling expectations or bootstrap equilibria

current offers....'Animal spirits' is, of course, a kind of free-floating equilibrium selection device. The point of introducing it is simply to show that it is possible to make sense of the claim that 'animal spirits' drive the economy. (Broadly speaking, this is one of the claims of Keynes and it makes perfect sense in this model.)

Grandmont (1989, pp. 279, 288) and Farmer (1993, p. 143) offer similar interpretations.

Sunspots, bubbles and self-fulfilling prophecies

The concept of sunspot equilibria arises quite naturally in the context of the simple OLG model. As Burnell (1989, p. 394) explains, 'a "sunspot" is to be thought of as a state of nature that does not affect the real parameters of the model; its sole impact is upon the beliefs held by agents concerning prices in the next period'. In situations where asset market prices are determined solely by expectations of what prices will be tomorrow – and they are in turn determined by what prices are expected to be the day after tomorrow and so on – then price expectations rather than fundamentals can determine prices. Examples of such markets are stock markets, foreign exchange markets or markets in which supply is fixed or in which price is unrelated to marginal cost.

In the model sketched above price expectations are a free-floating coordinating variable so any rational agent will recognize that the price tomorrow will depend on the actions of other agents tomorrow. As Burnell (ibid.) puts it:

> The potential then exists for a rational agent to believe that certain events will affect the price of the asset simply because (he believes) other agents believe these events matter. In this way, a theory of price formation can be thought of as a social convention that may have no 'intrinsic' economic justification – the theory justifies itself (see Keynes 1936, pp. 152–8).

In the previous example, if an agent observes that NCM is the dominant view of the world then it is rational to expect the NCM outcome even if the particular agent does not believe the NCM analysis to be true. Because equilibria can be self-fulfilling prophecies it is essential to know what other agents believe even if that has nothing to do with the real parameters of the model.

Given the openness and consequent multiplicity of equilibria that exist in the OLG framework it lends itself to the existence of so-called sunspot equilibria. All that needs to be assumed is that rational agents believe that other agents believe some arbitrary events will have consequences for some future market outcome and will act on this belief.[6] Burnell (1989, p. 394) gives as an example of a sunspot the belief that if the President of the United States rides a horse tomorrow all other agents in the foreign exchange market will be more optimistic about the US dollar relative to the UK pound the day after tomorrow. Thus the interesting point to note about sunspot equilibria is that the events on which agents base their rational beliefs may be entirely arbitrary. The theory has nothing to say about the basis of rational belief. It simply demonstrates that, in principle, when faced with the case of a free-floating coordinating variable, equilibrium is indeterminate unless a basis for the rational belief of agents can be established. It is for this reason that Farmer (1993, p. 183) argues:

> In models where there are multiple rational expectations equilibria, we should think of the belief function as a primitive construct that tells us how agents predict the future. The rational expectations assumption, in this class of models, is a consistency principle that restricts the class of belief functions that are admissible to the modeller, and it plays the same role in models with multiple equilibria that the assumption of transitivity plays in the theory of rational choice.

In a similar vein Kehoe (1989, p. 392) calls for a serious theory of expectations formation to eliminate the indeterminacy revealed by OLG models.

Further insight into these properties of the OLG model is obtained by recasting the offer or aggregate demand curve in $(M/p_t,\ M/p_{t+1})$ space. This statement of the model follows in straightforward fashion from the property that equilibrium in each period requires the 'money' market to clear. All points along the D curve in Figure 18.3 represent temporary equilibria. Imposing a 45° line indicates that two of these equilibria are stationary in the sense that if attained they replicate themselves indefinitely.[7] The stationary equilibrium at the origin is the autarky or no intergenerational trade equilibrium. The stationary equilibrium labelled GR is the golden rule equilibrium and is so called because it can be shown to maximize

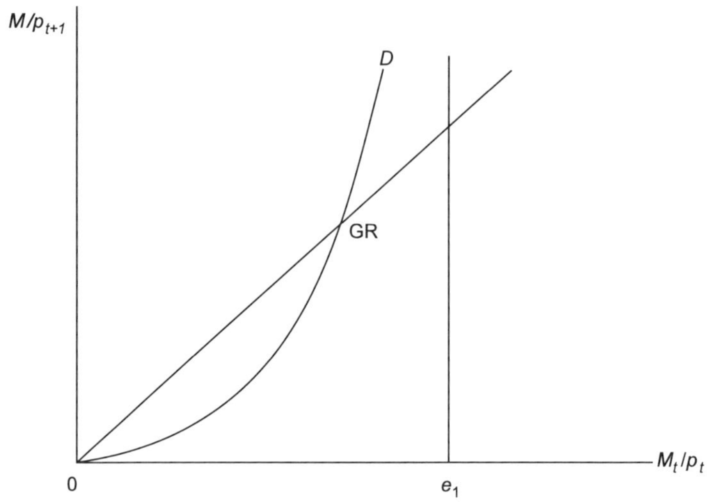

Figure 18.3 The offer curve for a simple OLG model in $(M/P_t, M/P_{t+1})$ space

steady-state per capita consumption. The autarky solution is obviously a non-monetary equilibrium while the golden rule equilibrium implies a positive value for money and is described as a monetary equilibrium. In this case money is used to facilitate intergenerational trade and the golden rule equilibrium Pareto-dominates the autarky or non-monetary equilibrium. The monetary equilibrium in this model has some interesting properties.

First, it is now recognized that money serves only as a means of transferring consumption between periods and has value only because it is expected to have value. This expectation can be maintained because of the assumption of an infinite time horizon. If a finite time horizon is imposed then money has zero value at that date, say T. Hence money would not be accepted in trade at time $T - 1$ and by the same argument it would not be accepted at time $T - 2$ and so on, so its value would be zero to begin with (Azariadis, 1993, pp. 357–8). This property of the OLG model first drew comment from Lerner (1959) who described the role of money in Samuelson's (1958) version of the model as a 'chain letter swindle' which would collapse if ever a young generation reneged on the deal to accept some intrinsically worthless asset from the old. More recently Tirole (1985) has described money as a 'bubble' in the sense that money has value only because it is expected to have value.

Second, the existence of a monetary equilibrium in the OLG model is entirely fortuitous. A monetary equilibrium exists only if the aggregate excess demand or offer curve cuts the 45° line from below as in Figure 18.3. But there is no reason why this should be the case. Many plausible combinations of endowments and utility functions yield no monetary equilibrium solution (Hoover, 1988, pp. 120–3;

Azariadis, 1993, ch. 24, Figure 24.1(c)). There are fundamental matters of principle here which we will take up in the next section.

Third, the monetary equilibrium illustrated in Figure 18.3 is unstable. This is best seen by writing the continuous set of temporary equilibria described by the offer curve D in the form of a non-linear difference equation. Following Farmer (1993, pp. 110–11), the set of competitive equilibria can be represented by a difference equation in relative prices:[8]

$$\frac{p_{t-1}}{p_t} f(p_{t-1}/p_t) - f(p_t/p_{t+1}) = 0 \tag{3}$$

The two stationary equilibria illustrated in Figure 18.3 satisfy expression (3). In the autarky case $f(.) = 0$ while in the golden rule equilibrium (3) collapses to $f(1) - f(1) = 0$. Writing relative prices as $\pi = p_{t+1}/p_t$ expression (3) can then be written as

$$(1/\pi) f(1/\pi) - f(1/\pi) = 0 \tag{4}$$

which shows that the autarky equilibrium occurs when $\pi \rightarrow \infty$ so that $f(\cdot) \rightarrow 0$. This situation is often described as a competitive equilibrium which is 'supported' by an infinite price level (Azariadis, 1993, p. 365). Presumably what this shows is that as inflation accelerates the model economy abandons money and reverts to the Pareto-inferior autarky equilibrium.

This means, moreover, that the monetary equilibrium in Figure 18.3 is unstable in the sense that any disturbance will produce either accelerating inflation and a return to autarky, or deflation which ceases when the young trade their entire period 1 endowment for money (see Hoover (1988, ch. 6) for a clear exposition). For example, at point X in Figure 18.4 (chosen arbitrarily), agents expect prices to be higher in period $t + 1$, which means they also expect real money balances will be lower. Hence the incentive for the young generation to trade goods for money is weakened and the process accelerates over generations as expectations of inflation are confirmed (under the perfect foresight assumption expectations are never disappointed in this model) and the model converges on autarky. A similar, but bounded, deflationary process begins at any point above the golden rule (GR) equilibrium.[9]

The instability of the monetary equilibrium arises because the substitution effect of intertemporal relative price changes outweighs the income effect. If income effects dominate then the offer curve may be backward-bending in the region of the 45° degree line producing a locally stable monetary equilibrium. This case is illustrated in Figure 18.5. Starting from point X in Figure 18.5 the inflationary expectations (rather than deflationary expectations as they would be in an unstable case) lead to the monetary equilibrium at GR. Similarly, from point Y deflationary expectations lead to the monetary equilibrium so the golden rule equilibrium is stable in this case. The existence of a stable case means that the multiplicity of equilibria generated by the rational expectations hypothesis cannot be discounted as explosive and hence non-observable paths.

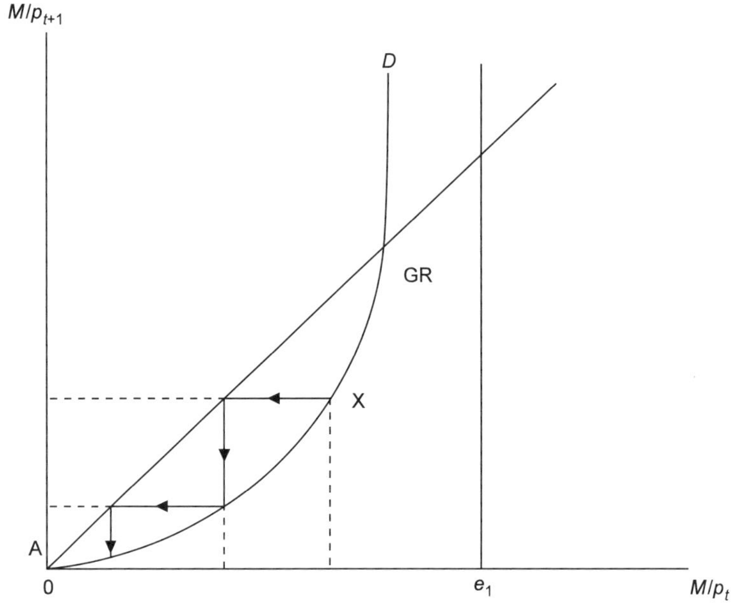

Figure 18.4 Unstable monetary equilibrium

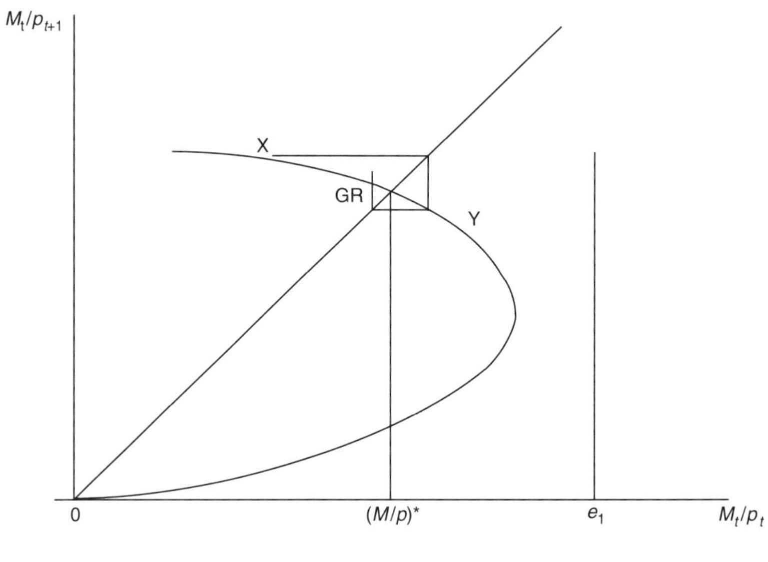

Figure 18.5 Stable monetary equilibrium

What has captured the attention on SNK economists, however, is the fact that the stable case opens up the possibility of expectations-driven cycles. Cyclical behaviour arises in the model in particular cases of the backward bending offer curve. One such example is illustrated in Figure 18.6 which is adapted from Hargreaves-Heap (1992, Figure 5.7). In this case it must be assumed that agents have a particular version of what Farmer (1993) calls the belief function as it is this which drives the cycle because the belief function acts as the coordinating device underlying rational expectations (= perfect foresight in this case) (Grandmont, 1989, p. 282).[10] For example, the belief function underlying Figure 18.6 assumes that when agents have real money balances M/p_2 they expect prices to be such that real money balances are M/p_3 in the next period. This belief function then produces the expectations-driven cycle illustrated in Figure 18.6. Without the belief function there is no reason to rule out a return to autarky. In this sense cycles in OLG models are entirely arbitrary: the belief functions on which they rest are arbitrary.

The fact that the OLG model can easily be adapted to produce cycles also opens up the door to the generation of chaotic cycles (Grandmont, 1985, 1989; Rosser, 1990). A model capable of generating a three-point cycle is capable of generating cycles of any period as well as an 'uncountably infinite set of possible aperiodic cycles' (Rosser, 1990, p. 275). Hargreaves-Heap (1992, p. 98) concludes that these possibilities provide an alternative explanation of the business cycle as an endogenous property of the multitude of rational expectations equilibria that exist.

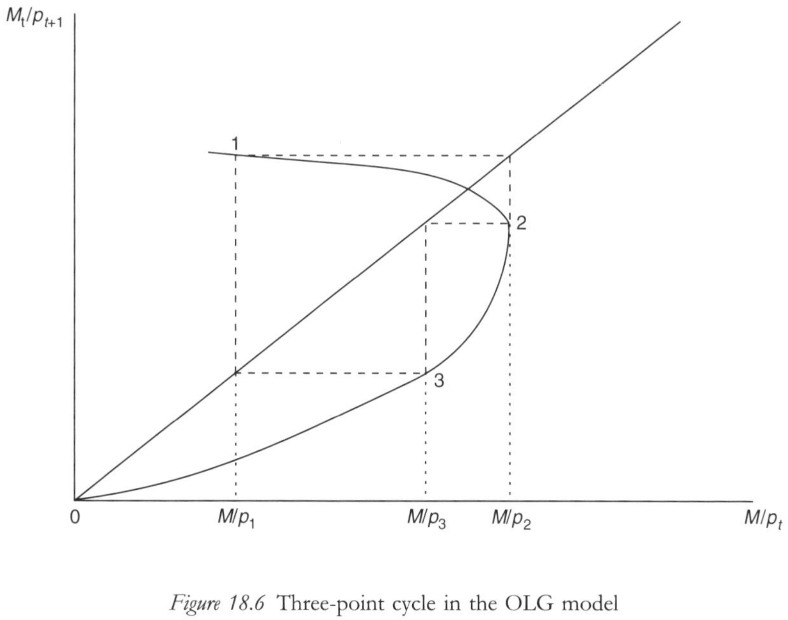

Figure 18.6 Three-point cycle in the OLG model

CRITICAL EVALUATION OF SNK ECONOMICS

There are a number of obvious limitations to the SNK analysis. First, from the perspective of monetary theory the obvious limitation of the SNK version of Keynesian indeterminacy resides in the properties of the OLG model and its Arrow–Debreu foundations. As is now known only too well the Arrow–Debreu model is fundamentally non-monetary. Money cannot be given an essential role in the model even when some of the assumptions are weakened to produce an imperfect capital market. This point was demonstrated initially by Hahn (1965, 1984) and the issue is comprehensively surveyed by Hoover (1988, ch. 6) who concludes that:

> Simple overlapping generations models give money a role but not an indispensable role: consumption patterns are Pareto inferior without money, but consumption nonetheless can continue in its absence. They [OLG models] are an inadequate foundation for monetary theory.
>
> (Hoover, 1988, p. 122)

From the perspective of Post Keynesian economics the fact that SNK models are inherently non-monetary immediately rules them out as a suitable framework for the assessment of Keynes's monetary analysis in *The General Theory*. However, some exponents of SNK economics acknowledge that the OLG framework does not capture all the dimensions of Keynes's analysis. In particular, Garretsen (1991, p. 115) concedes that the OLG framework is, at present, non-monetary. He goes on to suggest that because the fundamental indeterminacy in Keynes is associated with the existence of money the OLG results are nothing more than a proxy for the analysis of *The General Theory* (ibid., p. 135).

Second, the treatment of expectations and/or rational belief functions in the OLG context deals with the question of indeterminacy in an arbitrary way. As outlined above, the belief functions are entirely arbitrary and the analysis provides no way of establishing how particular belief functions come to be established and acted on. The latter is no easy task because once it is known that agents cannot forecast accurately even if they know the fundamentals, but must also know how other agents envisage the future, the question of strategic behaviour and infinite regress (expectations of higher and higher order) arises. Consequently, as Hahn (1989, p. 3) puts it, 'until some progress is made here, the project of constructing a theory of the economy with strategically acting agents cannot proceed with any confidence'. (See also Blanchard and Fischer, 1989, p. 260.)

Third, it should be obvious that SNK OLG models are incapable of dealing with involuntary unemployment. They are no more capable of dealing with this than was Patinkin's (1965) analysis in chapter 13. The logical implication of the analytical framework is, as Lucas (1972) concluded, that involuntary unemployment is not defined in these models. Models in the Arrow–Debreu tradition deal with the question of the efficient allocation of given endowments – they can account for unemployed resources only as a consequence of real relative price rigidity. SNK

OLG models that embrace the Arrow–Debreu framework have the same property and although it may be possible to Pareto-rank equilibria, this ranking has nothing whatsoever to do with Keynes's claim regarding the existence of an unemployment equilibrium.[11] Combined with the non-monetary nature of OLG models this aspect of the SNK embrace of the Arrow–Debreu research programme would have fatal consequences for Keynesians.

Fourth, the indeterminacy and multiplicity of stable equilibria thrown up by the SNK OLG model is treated as a theoretical curiosum by some Keynesian economists. For example, Blanchard and Fischer (1989) reject the relevance of the 'sunspots' and indeterminacy analysis on the grounds that it involves implausibly large income effects:[12]

> Thus, for the time being, though we find the phenomena analysed in this chapter [bubbles, sunspots] both interesting and disturbing, we are willing to proceed on the working assumption that the conditions needed to generate stable multiplicities of equilibria are not met in practice.
>
> (p. 261)

Despite these limitations the conclusions concerning indeterminacy and multiplicity of equilibria are seen by some SNK macroeconomists, quite rightly in my view, as more consistent with Keynes's intentions in *The General Theory*. More consistent, that is, than are the traditional Keynesian concerns with rigid prices and/or wages. This perspective is adopted by Garretsen (1991) who argues that the SNK OLG literature, although only a proxy for Keynes, nevertheless raises questions of fundamental importance to Post Keynesians. A similar view is expressed by Grandmont (1989, p. 289) with respect to Keynes's treatment of uncertainty. That said, the question remains: what is the positive contribution of SNK economics to an understanding of Keynes's analysis? To answer this question it is necessary to outline briefly some of the main analytical properties of Post Keynesian analysis.

SOME PROPERTIES OF POST KEYNESIAN ANALYSIS

Several interdependent properties of Post Keynesian analysis are relevant for our purposes here. First, Post Keynesian macroeconomics follows Keynes in basing macroeconomic analysis on the monetary theory of production. The monetary theory of production in turn reflects the belief that important characteristics of the labour and capital markets of classical theory are simply false or at best special cases of historical interest.

In particular the classical analysis of the labour market in which employment is determined by auction for real shares of output was emphatically rejected by Keynes (1936, ch. 2) and Post Keynesians (see Chick (1983) for a comprehensive discussion). Although the real wage may be equated with the marginal product of labour in equilibrium, Post Keynesians reject the interpretation of the marginal product of labour curve as the demand for labour function in an auction market

(Davidson, 1994b). In a Post Keynesian entrepreneur economy entrepreneurs determine employment (Torr, 1980).

From the perspective of an entrepreneur economy the role of money takes on added significance because the money rate of interest may constrain the profitable activities of entrepreneurs. Hence the importance of the liquidity preference theory of the rate of interest to Post Keynesian macroeconomics.

Liquidity preference theory encapsulates two important dimensions of Post Keynesian analysis: (a) the existence of money and money (not real) contracts; (b) the existence of irreducible uncertainty. These two features are of fundamental importance because they take over the role performed by the classical capital market. The classical capital market, or loanable funds theory of the rate of interest, provides a mechanism which is sufficient to generate automatic full employment in the long run and validate Say's Law even in an entrepreneur economy. If a classical capital market exists the natural rate of interest ensures that the money rate of interest coincides with the natural rate in long-run equilibrium producing what Keynes called a neutral money economy (Rogers, 1997b).[13] The existence of money is therefore not sufficient to generate Post Keynesian results – although it is necessary.

The existence of money takes on added significance once the classical loanable funds theory is abandoned – as it must be (ibid.). The absence of a classical capital market contributes to the existence of irreducible uncertainty which in turn leads to two important characteristics: (a) the existence of irreducible uncertainty imposes a liquidity premium on money which is not subject to the laws of returns; and (b) the absence of a classical capital market leaves the determination of the rate of interest hanging by its own bootstraps as Hicks and Robertson claimed. In other words the Post Keynesian model of an entrepreneur economy is underdetermined without some explanation for the rate of interest. Liquidity preference theory provides the framework for that explanation. Of particular importance is the analysis of rational behaviour in the face of irreducible uncertainty and the role that conventions play in guiding rational behaviour in the face of uncertainty.

Post Keynesians follow Keynes and treat expectations and not probability as the fundamental concept in *The General Theory*. As O'Donnell explains:

> expectation is the key concept of the GT, not probability. Keynes's approach to behaviour under uncertainty was expectational, but neither purely probabilistic nor purely non-probabilistic. He accepted probabilities when they were available, and irreducible uncertainty when they were not: and even when probabilities were available, there was no guarantee of their numericality.
>
> (1990, p. 265)

Rational agents in Keynes's world face the entire spectrum of uncertainty: from cases where probabilities are quantifiable and known (a minority of cases) to situations where there is simply no objective basis whatsoever on which to base a rational decision. In the latter situations, where rationality has reached its limits, then arbitrary procedures, hunches, or in Keynes's terms, 'animal spirits', dictate the outcome. But to class behaviour in the absence of numerical probabilities as irrational is unwarranted:

> if informationally deprived but nevertheless rational agents have nothing to fall back upon except the strategies of weak rationality, then expectations so formed contain an element of rationality and are entitled to the membership of the extended family of rational expectations.
>
> (O'Donnell, 1990, p. 265; see also Darity and Horn, 1993)

The strategies that rational agents fall back on are, of course, not entirely arbitrary. They arise in a social and historical context and liquidity preference theory is empty without that context (Lawlor, 1994). That is where history comes in. Of particular significance is the role of induction and the reliance on conventions that are adopted by a majority of agents. In the face of irreducible uncertainty Keynes claimed that: '[w]e tend, therefore, to substitute for the knowledge which is unattainable certain conventions.... This is how we act in practice' (CW XIV, p. 214, quoted by Carabelli, 1988, p. 224). Once generally accepted, conventions have their own inertia and are difficult to change unilaterally (even though they may be fragile); cooperation and coordination are often required to amend a convention (Wärnneryd, 1990).

The existence of conventions is central to Post Keynesian analysis of a monetary–entrepreneur economy because the model is underdetermined without the introduction of some belief function to account for behaviour in the financial system in general and with respect to the rate of interest in particular. In *The General Theory* conventions play a coordinating role which underpins the stability of the system. Without this degree of stability economic analysis would be impossible. As with all his work Keynes attempts to outline the limits of economic theory by highlighting the fact that a monetary–entrepreneur economy is not the deterministic system envisioned by all (old and new) classical economists.

Money in Post Keynesian analysis is, consequently, an integral part of the theoretical structure in the sense that all equilibria are monetary and the analysis cannot be dichotomized into real and monetary subsets (Rogers, 1989, 1997b; Rogers and Rymes, 1994).[14] In turn the conventions in financial markets underpin the explanation of the normal rate of interest in the context of the theory of liquidity preference. In *The General Theory* Keynes identified views about the 'normal' rate of interest as an historically relevant convention dictating the behaviour of interest rates. As Keynes (1936, p. 204) put it, under those circumstances the rate of interest may then fluctuate for decades about a level that is too high for full employment especially if rational agents believe (wrongly) that the 'normal' rate of interest is determined by real market forces rather than by liquidity preference and arbitrary conventions. In a monetary–entrepreneur economy operating in an environment of irreducible uncertainty the 'bootstraps' label is an accurate description of Keynes's theory.[15] Hence, in Post Keynesian monetary analysis all equilibria are monetary and all are *self-fulfilling expectations equilibria.*

This point needs stressing because the Post Keynesian literature has yet to come to terms with the general version of the principle of effective demand.[16] At present the consensus interpretation of the principle of effective demand, as outlined by Amadeo (1989) for example, is presented as the notion that it is changes in output that equate saving and investment rather than changes in the rate of interest as claimed by classical theory. This is an accurate description of Keynes's and Post Keynesian analysis, yet it misses a crucial point. What determines the equilibrium towards which this adjustment is taking place? Unfortunately Post Keynesians generally do not have an answer if they are constrained to the consensus version of the principle of effective demand. Perhaps some are content to leave the matter there – the Post Keynesian model is underdetermined and that is that. But Keynes went further and Post Keynesians can benefit from developments in SNK economics to strengthen their position.

To see this consider first the general statement of Say's Law. Following Chick (1983) the general version of Say's Law is the simple statement that no limit to the profitable expansion of output is encountered until full employment is achieved. The essence of Keynes's principle of effective demand is that the rate of interest may set a limit to the profitable expansion of output before full employment is reached. Say's Law then fails in the monetary–entrepreneur economy of Post Keynesian macroeconomics. As explained above, retaining the loanable funds theory – the classical theory of the natural and market rates of interest – is sufficient to negate this result even in an entrepreneur economy. That is, the classical theory of the rate of interest validates Say's Law even in an entrepreneur economy because the natural rate of interest is consistent with full employment and acts as an attractor for the market rate of interest in long-period equilibrium. There is then no limit to the profitable expansion of output in an economy in which the classical loanable funds theory applies (Rogers, 1997b).

The liquidity preference theory of the rate of interest is, therefore, a central element in the principle of effective demand, and the principle of effective demand in turn replaces Say's Law as the determinant of employment in a monetary–entrepreneur economy. In contradistinction to Say's Law, the principle of effective demand states that a limit to the profitable expansion of output may occur before full employment has been achieved. This is an almost inevitable outcome in a *laissez-faire* monetary–entrepreneur economy because the money rate of interest is not driven by automatic market forces to the natural rate as claimed by all classical economists, old and new (and some Keynesians too!). The essence of Keynes's rejection of classical theory is his rejection of the classical theory of the rate of interest as espoused by Wicksell, or Robertson (Rogers, 1989, 1997b). A monetary–entrepreneur economy does indeed offer efficiency gains over barter but it implies also that the liquidity properties of money and conventions in financial markets may act on the money rate of interest in such a way that unemployment results. This may happen because there is no mechanism in a monetary–entrepreneur economy without a classical capital market that will automatically adjust the money rate of interest to the optimum rate consistent with full employment.[17]

What then can the SNK approach contribute to Post Keynesian analysis? At a general level it should be apparent that SNK analysis demonstrates that the concept of a self-fulfilling expectations equilibrium, which lies at the heart of Keynes's principle of effective demand, is not the absurd notion that Hicks and Robertson implied with their 'bootstraps' description. A monetary–entrepreneur economy without a classical capital market is underdetermined without the introduction of some explanation of the rational belief functions underlying existing conventions in financial markets. As noted earlier, Farmer (1993, p. 183) is making a similar point, but in a rather sterile context, when he argues that rational belief functions should be treated as part of the primitives along with tastes, endowments and technology. In this endeavour Post Keynesians should be better placed than their classical colleagues, most of whom are still wedded to a narrower model of rational behaviour based on a probabilistic interpretation of uncertainty. As Runde (1994) demonstrates, these approaches miss important dimensions of the concept of liquidity preference and hence the principle of effective demand.

CONCLUDING REMARKS

Despite its obvious limitations as a result of its close association with the Arrow–Debreu system SNK economics does raise an issue of central importance to Post Keynesian macroeconomics. As the previous section attempted to make clear the concept of 'bootstraps' or self-fulfilling expectations equilibria are central to Keynes's analysis. Post Keynesians can draw on the development of these ideas by SNK macroeconomists to reinforce their own analysis. This is the perspective adopted by Colander (1992c) and Garretsen (1991). Van Ees and Garretsen (1992, p. 473) summarize this position in the following terms: 'In our view the Keynesian content of New Keynesian economics and the similarity with Post-Keynesian theory are enlarged if the theoretical implications of multiple equilibria or self-fulfilling expectations, for example, are taken into account'.

From the perspective adopted in this chapter this view has merit subject to the proviso that the Arrow–Debreu framework is abandoned. Arrow–Debreu is but a narrow, rather uninteresting, special case remote from the Post Keynesian analytical scheme. This means, of course, rejecting the call by Farmer and Azariadis for the adoption of the Arrow–Debreu framework as the common language of macroeconomics. Other aspects of the Colander–Garretsen–van Ees position also imply this rejection and point to a return to the traditional view that macroeconomics is not simply the aggregation of micro markets.[18] The importance of strategic behaviour undermines the view that the behaviour of the aggregate economy can be understood from an individualistic perspective. This is an issue which lies at the heart of the Arrow–Debreu framework (Kirman, 1989).

Colander *et al.* also stress the fact that Keynes and Post Keynesians identify the inability of a monetary economy to adjust automatically to full employment, even in the long run, as the defining characteristic of Keynesian economics. They refer to this property under the generic title of the 'co-ordination problem', e.g. Garretsen

(1991), and point to the indeterminacy that is implicit in Keynes's scheme and the role that conventions play in resolving that indeterminacy. All of this Post Keynesians can and should accept. It does not mean that they need to speak a dialect of Arrow-Debreu. What SNK economics has done is open up a Pandora's box which should force economists of a classical persuasion to take Keynes seriously once more.

NOTES

1 Elements of Strong New Keynesian economics are covered by Mankiw and Romer (1991) under the heading of 'co-ordination failures'.

2 Azariadis (1993, p. xii) expresses the view that if current trends continue younger macroeconomists will need to learn a lot of dynamical mathematics early in their careers.

3 Hoover (1988, ch. 6) provides an accessible and comprehensive discussion of the OLG structure.

4 The assumption that agents live for only two periods is not restrictive because a model in which agents live for an infinite number of periods can easily be converted into a two-period case (Kehoe, 1989, p. 379). However, the fact that agents are born sequentially does mean that they cannot participate in insurance markets that close before they are born. This feature, called incomplete participation, is necessary for the generation of sunspot equilibria in the Cass and Shell (1983) analysis. See also Farmer (1993, ch. 9).

5 For the moment it is simply assumed that the configuration of utility functions and endowments is such that intergenerational trade occurs.

6 For accessible but more formal demonstrations of the existence of sunspot equilibria see Hargreaves-Heap (1992, pp. 98–9) or Farmer (1993, ch. 9).

7 Given M, if $M/p_i = M/p_{t+1}$ then $p_t = p_{t+1}$ and the interest factor $R_t = p_t/p_{t+1} = 1$. Hence, from the fact that the interest factor is also defined as $R_t = 1 + r$ where $r =$ the real rate of interest, the real rate of interest is zero in monetary equilibrium with zero population growth.

8 The element $f(.)$ is the agent's excess demand function and by applying the market clearing assumption and the fact that rational agents are on their lifetime budget constraints expression (3) follows. (See e.g. Farmer, 1993, pp. 110–11 or Hoover, 1988, ch. 5.)

9 The equilibria in this model are said to be indeterminate because each equilibrium is arbitrarily close (in a mathematical sense) to its neighbours. Thus both the stationary and non-stationary equilibria in this model are indeterminate (Farmer, 1993, pp. 59, 113).

10 Grandmont (1989, p. 282) states that deterministic cycles are driven by expectations that vary periodically. Rosser (1990, p. 274, n. 10) suggests that SNK models produce business cycles by 'shocking' expectations in sunspot equilibria while RBC models produce cycles by shocking technology.

11 I regard this as a claim about long-period equilibrium (Rogers, 1989, 1997b) but many Post Keynesians treat *The General Theory* as the analysis of short-period equilibrium, which reduces it to a theory of the business cycle only.

12 However, they do note that increasing returns to scale in production can produce similar results.

13 Barens's (1990) analysis of Keynes's taxonomy of economies is flawed as a result of this too narrow version of Say's Law.

14 In a recent survey of Post Keynesian monetary theory Cottrell (1994, p. 590) described this feature in the following terms: 'For Post-Keynesians, it is the very existence of money that is non neutral, rather than simply variations in its quantity'.

15 For a complete discussion of the importance of the rate of interest in Keynes's analysis see Rogers (1989, 1997b).

16 Some Post Keynesians follow Keynes's attack on Say's Law too closely and consequently fail to develop a general version of the principle of effective demand. For example, Davidson (1994b), following Keynes, interprets Say's Law to mean that aggregate demand, *D*, and aggregate supply, *Z*, coincide for their entire length. Although coincidence of *D* and *Z* curves is sufficient to generate Say's Law it is not necessary. This means also that a propensity to spend of less than 1 is not sufficient to refute Say's Law as some Post Keynesians imply. The refutation of Say's Law in a monetary–entrepreneur economy occurs when the classical loanable funds theory is abandoned and replaced by liquidity preference theory. Then the normal rate of interest may set a limit to the profitable expansion of output (Rogers, 1997b).

17 The fact that the schedule of the marginal efficiency of capital is downward sloping is not sufficient to ensure that the money rate of interest adjusts to the optimum level (Rogers, 1997b).

18 Colander (1992c) stresses this point in terms of the somewhat awkward phrase 'the macroeconomic foundations for macroeconomics'.

Part V

PUBLIC POLICY

Part V

PUBLIC POLICY

This last part of the book includes chapters by authors who chose to write on the subject of public policy. What most New and Post Keynesians share is a view that some forms of public policy are legitimate devices for smoothing the inimical effects of business cycle fluctuations and for promoting sanguine conditions for long-term growth, despite their clearly divergent theoretical bases for such policies. In this way the New Keynesian perspective may be permitted to wear just a bit of the designation Keynesian. It distinguishes them from the real business cycle New Classical theorists who, while also grounding their paradigmatic lenses in market phenomena, adhere to a non-interventionist approach to any form of public policy. Still, New Keynesians would be cautious about embracing the types of policies specifically proposed in this part of the book. Finally, the reader should note that the chapters below are by no means exhaustive of the myriad recommendations Post Keynesians make for effective policies to achieve the goals listed above.

In the first chapter, the late Giovanni Caravale addresses a policy unique to Post Keynesians: incomes policies. The chapter, 'On a Recent Change in the Nation of Incomes Policy', argues that the cultural climate predominant in the field of economic theory in the last two decades inevitably influenced the conception of economic policy and in particular the notion of incomes policy. In its original meaning incomes policies were seen as the set of measures designed to make the growth of income and employment compatible with price stability through the strict connection between real wages and labour productivity.

Caravale considers a new conception of incomes policies which has come to be established in recent years – a manoeuvre to curb nominal and real wages aimed at fostering employment – finding its ultimate foundation in the assumption of an inverse relation between wages and employment, which is an essential component part of New Keynesian economics. He criticizes the view according to which wage moderation is the essential tool for the support of employment, and concludes that such moderation – important as it may be for the control of inflation – is not a sufficient condition for the defence of employment.

Then Basil J. Moore, in his 'Money and Interest Rates in a Monetary Theory of Production', illustrates how equilibrium analysis can be abandoned and replaced by sequence analysis to provide increased understanding, although not prediction, of central macroeconomic phenomena. The nihilistic analytical implications of taking historical time and non-ergodicity seriously have been widely exaggerated. Production takes time, and real world firms must pay for their productive factors before they receive their output receipts. They do this by borrowing from banks for their working capital needs. Loans are demand determined, since borrowers have previously been authorized credit commitments based on bank loan officers' estimates of their credit-worthiness. In the process credit money is created – loans make deposits. These newly created deposits are always retained in the banking system by economic units, and may be represented as an increase in convenience lending. When they are received by debtor units in the circular flow of transactions they may be used to repay outstanding bank loans, in which case the money supply is extinguished.

Based on this framework, Moore outlines a new monetary transmission mechanism enumerating the various channels by which exogenous changes in interest rates initiated by the monetary authorities impact on consumption and investment expenditure. The main conclusions of this framework reveal that: (a) the goal of business firms is always to end up with more wealth than they started with; (b) capitalist economies are ordinarily demand- and not supply-constrained; (c) monetary change is fundamentally non-neutral; (d) there is no 'natural' rate of interest or of unemployment; (e) interest rates are exogenous, and are the government's chief policy instrument to raise or lower aggregate demand; (f) newly created money finances increases in aggregate demand; (g) an increase in investment spending always generates its own saving; (h) an interest-inelastic demand for investment is a social virtue rather than a social evil; (i) in the presence of an effective incomes policy cheap credit is the optimal monetary policy, leading as Keynes stated to the euthanasia of the rentier class.

Finally, Herbert Gintis, in his chapter entitled 'Macroeconomic Policy for the Long Haul', presents what is the most far-reaching proposal for an alternative policy in this part of the book. Gintis asserts that market and state are complementary rather than alternative policy instruments, since all successful economies have both strong market institutions and strong public sectors. The question is not whether to promote market competition but how best to do so, and not whether the state should intervene, but where and how.

Relying on some of the same methodology espoused by Isenberg and Dymski, he develops a *dual agency* model of state/market interaction, in which both state and market contribute to the attainment of economic objectives, but both also involve severe agency problems. To implement a policy, agency theory suggests, the policy maker is a principal who must not only select a set of instructions that, if followed by the agents, will achieve the policy objective in a cost-effective manner, but also supply the proper incentives ensuring that agents find it in their interest to behave as prescribed by the policy. A policy implementation is incentive-compatible if it includes rewards, penalties, and a structure of accountability (i.e. a monitoring system) that ensure that agents responsible for implementing the policy will implement the policy maker's objectives.

The dual agency perspective holds that economies are successful to the extent that they develop political and economic institutions that adjudicate the interests of major economic actors in a manner consistent with the key agency problems of the state and private economy.

19

ON A RECENT CHANGE IN THE NOTION OF INCOMES POLICY

Giovanni Caravale

MACROECONOMIC THEORY AND ECONOMIC POLICY

Even though in some respects it can legitimately be said, in the words of Beaud and Dostaler (1993, p. 149), that 'Keynesianism is a nebulous space crossed by currents and undercurrents ... [in which] economists with very differing theoretical or political views have been able ... to find that with which to feed or support their theories', it is undeniable that the figure and work of J. M. Keynes should be placed centre stage of what has been called *the golden age of interventionism.* In the struggle with opposing views, the Keynesian concept appeared at a certain phase of the recent history of the Western world, as the triumphal winner both in the field of economic theory and in that of institutions and politics. In the former this triumph was symbolized, for many, by the post-mortem recognition paid to Keynes by his fiercest Cambridge critic, A. C. Pigou.[1] From the latter viewpoint one can cite by way of example the commitment to maintain a high and stable level of employment included in the UK government's *Budget judgement* since the early 1940s; the *Employment Act* approved by the US Congress in 1946; the inclusion of the Keynesian principles in the 1946 French Constitution, in the United Nations' Charter, in the 1957 Treaty of Rome; and the explicit references to the Keynesian concept in the programmes drawn up by President Kennedy's economic advisers.[2]

Yet, the liberalism of the neoclassical tradition, which appeared decisively defeated, had far from disappeared; it survived, and even developed, in the shadow of Keynesianism.[3] For a complex series of reasons the last two decades have been marked by a radical transformation of the situation with a change in the cultural climate which brought with it the *crisis of Keynesianism.* Although these reasons should be analysed in much more detail, some elements can be indicated as important. Among these are: the progressive exhaustion of the enthusiasm deriving from the impestuous process of growth in the post-war period; the simultaneous manifestation of complex problems (first and foremost the joint presence of inflation and unemployment) for which the analyses inspired by Keynes's theories appeared inadequate; the increasingly obvious crisis, and subsequent collapse, of the so-called *real socialism* economies – often crudely considered as a direct expression of the failure of the role of the state in the economy in general; the phenomenon which can be called *the tragedy of praxis* – that is, the concrete manner in which (especially in Italy) the state intervened in the economy and in which the logic of public intervention was hampered and overturned by logics, personal or party, of a completely different nature; the *conquest of power* in the United States and Europe by political forces that were intransigently liberalist in inspiration.[4] The outcome is a revival of pre-Keynesian liberalism: *laissez-faire* is once again back on the agenda, to an extent that would have been unthinkable up to twenty years ago; and an attitude (illustrated, for example, by the adage common in the 1980s in the United States 'there are no Keynesians under the age of 40') of intolerance towards anything that might appear related to the macroeconomics and economic policies of Keynes is becoming increasingly widespread.[5]

In reality, the renewed predominance of the traditional approach has come about through the restatement in apparently new forms (ranging from the Walrasian-type neoclassical synthesis, Friedman's monetarism, the so-called New Classical macroeconomics based on the idea of rational expectations, to the recent *New Keynesian economics*[6]) of old, pre-Keynesian theories, and through the opposition of these latter theories to the *heretic* ones (Post Keynesian; Marxist-inspired neo-Ricardian; or classical- and Keynesian-inspired non-neoclassical), positions which, in a complex feedback process, came gradually to be modelled also with reference to the *new* forms assumed by the theories inspired by neoclassicism. The debate around these positions has thus ended up by representing, albeit in a new form, some *old* differences: that between the opposing visions of the working of contemporary capitalist systems (Beaud and Dostaler, 1993; Dow, 1989, Milgate, 1988), and that between differing notions of equilibrium in economic theory (Caravale, 1992a, 1992b).

The most strident contrast concerned the notion of economic policy, with stances that, for the sake of brevity, we shall classify into four groups: (a) the categorical denial of the role of economic policy, typical of the most radical liberism such as that of the New Classical macroeconomics;[7] (b) the mechanical conception of the role of economic policy, which is implicit for example in the identification of the sole intervention admissible in the so-called *automatic rule*, suggested by Friedman's monetarism to ensure price stability;[8] (c) the *subsidiary notion* of this role, linked to the *imperfectionist* vision of the working of the economy that characterizes the neoclassical synthesis and most of the New Keynesian economics (optimum equilibrium is possible in theory but in practice it is hindered by a series of imperfections that should be countered by a series of measures aiming at the re-establishment of the *natural* conditions of optimality); (d) the more complex and demanding *Keynesian-type* notion which is based on the assumption that the system, if left to itself, tends to move towards an equilibrium that is not an optimum, either from the viewpoint of the use of available resources, or from that of social justice. This notion implies that the state bears significant responsibilities (in the field of monetary, fiscal and social policies) that should manifest themselves in the form of measures aiming to make good the *structural* shortcomings of the system (in terms of effective demand, distributive equilibrium, control of price levels, equality of starting conditions, and of social protection) that go well beyond the definition and defence of a framework within which the market forces could and should freely express themselves. Unfortunately, the contents of this notion cannot be defined a priori once and for all, thus creating, in the words of Joan Robinson, 'the uncomfortable situation of having to think for ourselves' (Robinson, 1962, p. 98).[9]

INCOMES POLICY IN ITS ORIGINAL MEANING

The notion of incomes policy in its original meaning should be placed in this latter conception of economic policy – the one which has been labelled above as *Keynesian-type* (where the addition of any specification, such as *neo* or *new*, would be both misleading and redundant). This notion could be defined as the set of policy measures aiming to establish the conditions which could ensure that the growth of income and employment be made compatible with price stability through the close pegging of real wages to the evolution of labour productivity.

This definition contains a series of elements whose nature appeared in the past to be clear enough to be commonly accepted but have become unclear and confused as a consequence of some recent developments in economic theory. The recall of such nature – although pedantic – may thus be of some use. Some aspects appear particularly relevant.

1 The first aspect which should be emphasized is that the growth in income *and* employment is, in this context, simply a hypothetical circumstance whose presence would pose the question of compatibility with price stability. Nothing is said about how, in the context of this definition of incomes policy, it could be possible to guarantee that such growth is actually realized – spontaneously, automatically or otherwise. No act of faith is necessarily made either as regards the capability of spontaneous market forces to bring about such a result outside the framework of incomes policy or as regards the possibility that the outcome of growth will be automatically produced by the fulfilment of the conditions defining this latter policy. In other words, even the existence of a general agreement of social parties on the strict respect of the *incomes policy rules* would not have as a necessary outcome the growth in income and employment. Such growth should find its sources elsewhere.
2 Other relevant aspects relate to the implicit reference points of the whole theoretical construction. The first of these is represented by the interpretation of inflation known as *cost inflation*. This idea, whose origin can be traced back to Keynes's attack on the quantity theory of money,[10] identifies the origin of the inflationary process not in the excess of demand over global supply, but rather in *excessive* increases of production costs, and in particular labour costs. According to this interpretation – whereas, in conditions of perfect competition, firms are not able to set the prices of their goods, so that if relative increases in salaries are greater than relative increases in the average labour productivity, the profit rate

will suffer a reduction – when the market structure is non-competitive firms are able to influence prices, so that their reaction to a possible imbalance between percentage variations in wages and percentage variations in productivity is, in fact, represented by an increase in prices in defence of the previously obtained profit margin: the inflationary phenomenon would therefore be provoked by an *excessive* variation of one of the components of the production costs.

3 The other reference point is represented by the definition of the conditions for *dynamic equilibrium* or *balanced* growth of an economic system. These conditions occur when, in the presence of positive growth rates both in the labour force and in labour productivity, the fundamental variables (income, consumption, investments) increase at a rate equivalent to the sum of the above-mentioned rates. Money wages increase at the rate of the increase in labour productivity, and real wages – given the stability of prices – follow the same trend in time as that of money wages. The profit rate, and the distribution of income between wages and profits, remain constant. If the available labour force is assumed to be totally employed at the outset, balanced growth implies that the condition of full employment is maintained throughout.

The joint consideration of these reference points implies that in a context characterized by non-competitive market conditions, the abandonment of *laws* of balanced growth (especially for what concerns wages) would generate inflationary pressures in defence of the previous distributive order.

SOME LIMITATIONS OF THE ORIGINAL SCHEME OF REFERENCE

The abstract character of the above indicated conditions – well rendered by the expression *golden age* used to depict this ideal type of economic growth – relates, on the one hand, to the implicit reference to a closed economic system, and on the other to the fact that the ideal conditions of growth are derived from the analysis of *aggregate* growth models. While the limitations connected with the assumption of a closed economic system may be overcome at a successive stage of the analysis in terms of qualifications of the results that may be arrived at, those emerging from the implicit assumptions of aggregate growth models cannot be avoided.

Real economic systems – it is fairly obvious – as opposed to these latter theoretical models of economic growth are always made of a plurality of sectors where labour productivity does not increase at the same rate. In those sectors where productivity increases rapidly, equivalent increases in wages (without variations in prices and profit rate) would be possible. This would not be the case for other sectors where productivity increases are smaller or nil. The outcome, also from the trade unions' viewpoint, would be disruptive. Under these circumstances, the reference point for the evolution of wages could no longer be represented by the increases in productivity actually realized in each productive sector, but rather by the average productivity growth in the whole system. Wages could thus increase at the same pace everywhere, while prices should increase in the sectors where the wages rate of growth has exceeded that of productivity, and diminish where the opposite is true. In principle the average price level could thus remain constant and the rate of profit could be uniform throughout. However, given the prevalent non-competitive structure of markets, one can assume that while there will be an increase in prices of goods supplied from areas where productivity increases at a rate below the average (in order to maintain constant profit rates with increases in wages), it is unlikely, if not impossible, to see a decrease in the prices of those goods supplied by sectors in which productivity has increased above the average. Not even the labour unions' acceptance of the incomes policy rules of behaviour would thus be sufficient to guarantee monetary stability. Industries that are technologically highly efficient (those having monopolistic powers who operate in sectors characterized by high productivity rates) would register an increase in their profit margin which would presumably be used to reinforce their position in the markets, and the incomes policy scheme of reference would appear as intended to reduce real wages – which would hardly be accepted by the labour unions.

With reference to the theory of growth models, another difficulty in applying incomes policies can be briefly recalled. The only two categories of income normally considered in aggregate growth models and in the study of incomes policy are profits and wages. In reality, however, incomes of a different nature than profits and wages are also distributed: on the one hand those which, notwithstanding the many difficulties in classification and qualification, may be referred to as *inefficiency rents* (the main aspects of this phenomenon being found in areas such as construction and housing, in commerce, in phenomena linked to inefficiencies of the fiscal apparatus, and in the structure of the State's and public corporations' budgets); on the other hand, the incomes accruing to the whole group of workers in the great and variegated public administration sector. Several problems arise here both for what concerns the contrast of and defence from inefficiency rents, and for what regards the identifications of reasonable patterns of development of wages and salaries of those who supply services in the public administration sector. This latter problem appears to be particularly delicate in view of the fact that the measurement of the level and growth of productivity in this latter sector lacks any conceptually definite point of reference.

One further obstacle should be mentioned. Incomes policy in its original conception pivots around the idea of maintaining constant the distributive *status quo*. Since there exists no criterion whatsoever for the *a priori* definition of the *rightness* or *equity* of any distributive set up between social groups, and since one of the trade unions' *raison d'être* has traditionally been that of changing this latter set up through increases in the income share attributed to labour, it is unlikely that the trade unions could explicitly accept the incomes policy rules as a *permanent* objective of their conduct. In this perspective the presence of non-competitive features allowing enterprises to transfer on price cost increases in defence of their profit rate can be easily indicated as a cause of inflation on exactly the same footing as increases in wages. It must be said, however, that these latter difficulties to accept the ultimate philosophical foundation of incomes policy is accompanied by the necessity, increasingly felt by the trade unions, to face realistically and pragmatically two types of questions: (a) the consequences that – apart from the identification of the causes of the inflationary pressures – would arise on prices, on the workers' purchasing power and on the general outlook of the economy, from an excess in the wage increases over productivity growth; (b) the effects that a permanent or long-term reduction in the profit rate can have on the pace of the accumulation process and hence on the growth rate of income and employment.

The mere indication of the above-mentioned limitations – to which other weaknesses could be added – makes it quite clear that, even if incomes policy can be viewed as a useful (though rather abstract in character) scheme of reference for policy choices, it is by no means a magic formula for the solution of the main economic problems of actual systems.

INCOMES POLICY AND KEYNES'S THEORETICAL FRAMEWORK

There is no direct and necessary connection between Keynes's theory and the idea of incomes policy in this original meaning of a coordinated set of measures aimed at reconciling the growth of income and employment with price stability, through the control of *all* incomes.[11]

It can be argued, however, that Keynes himself, in the years following the publication of the *General Theory*, addressing with ever increasing anxiety the problem of controlling inflation, thought of hypotheses of this type. In his letter of 31 December 1943 to Professor F. Graham of Princeton University on possible instruments for controlling inflationary pressures, Keynes – in rejecting the idea that the creation of severe depressionary conditions was the only possible instrument for controlling price levels – observed:

> How much otherwise avoidable unemployment do you propose to bring about in order to keep the Trade Unions in order? Do you think it will be politically possible when they understand what you are up to? My own preliminary view is that other, more reasonable, less punitive, means must be found.
>
> (Keynes, 1973c, p. 36).

It is highly likely that by 'more reasonable, less punitive, means' Keynes refers to policies aiming at the consensus of the social parties and advocates the adoption of such policies in the place of the measures – or inactions – capable of creating depressive conditions in order to cure inflationary pressures. Keynes did not supply any detailed indication as to the specific content of these *means*, but the guess may perhaps be legitimate that he had in mind the creation of a climate of mutual trust in which the labour unions could obtain – in exchange for wage moderation and for the abandonment of the defence of merely corporative interests – a series of adequate counter-concessions. In this perspective one can for instance think of the government's commitment to fight what have been called above the *inefficiency rents* (with specific reference to the lack of equity in the tax system); to improve the efficiency of the public administration and of its social services – education, health, transportation – which would have a beneficial effect on the level of real wages; and to increase the participation of trade unions in the definition of the basic strategic choices of economic policy, especially for those concerning the labour market. While attempts of this type fit well in the traditional notion of incomes policy, and in the connected Keynesian-type vision of economic policy, the same would not be true with the new notion of incomes policy, which is mainly based, as will become clear, on the existence of some kind of inverse relationship between the level of wages and the level of employment, which leaves little room for the search of an active role of economic policy in defence of the level of employment.

SOME RADICAL CHANGES IN APPROACH

The cultural climate that has come into being in the past two decades has produced some profound changes in the meaning attributed to the expression *incomes policy* and hence to the context in which it is considered legitimate to use this expression. It is important to emphasize that these changes – instead of trying to cope with the above-mentioned difficulties and limitations of the incomes policy's scheme of reference – mark a radical departure with respect to this latter's original meaning. The most significant example of this is the diffusion of the notion of incomes policy as 'a manoeuvre to curb nominal and real wages and aimed at fostering employment'.[12] This notion embraces two incorrect implications: (a) on the one hand it implies an overlap between the notions of incomes policy, income support and employment policies, and inflation control policies, and hence in practice between incomes policy and economic policy *tout court*; (b) on the other, the legitimization of the increasingly common decision, of considering as an essential pillar of economic analysis the assumption of an inverse relation between the real wages and employment – the very relation whose denial represents the theoretical core of Keynes's analysis. This choice, it should be emphasized, is in fact the clearest proof that the new notion of incomes policy does not represent a formal change in a idea whose substance remains unchanged, but is instead the definition of a fundamentally different notion, characterized by a drastic change in objectives and in the instruments indicated.

On the specific ground of economic theory, this notion appears reflected in the rapid diffusion of the approach that goes under the name of New Keynesian Economics: in effect the central body of this new formulation – which according to some (Lawlor, 1993; Nisticò *et al.*, 1994) is neither new nor Keynesian – tends to attribute to wage rigidities (as was emphasized above) a fundamental role in explaining the phenomenon of unemployment. In this respect it is important to recall that the point of reference for evaluating *Keynesian loyalty* is chapter 19 of *The*

General Theory in which Keynes argues in detail his rejection of the assumption that a generalized reduction of wages will necessarily lead to an increase in employment. The argument based on an aggregate demand curve for labour was theoretically invalid, Keynes showed, vitiating the idea that it is wage inflexibility that is the source of long-term unemployment.[13]

The new cultural climate that has come into being is reflected in documents of institutional bodies. By way of example one can mention the report of Italy's CNEL (National Council of Economics and Labour) of July 1993,[14] which ironically maintains that the traditional vision of incomes policy – the vision (it is important to recall) whose essential point of reference is represented by the conditions defined by the Harrod–Domar growth model, and implies that real wages increase at the same rate as the economy's average productivity – is a static vision and thus differs from the new concept whose dynamic and propulsive nature is linked to the recognition (claimed to be new) that income is 'influenced in its evolution by the method of redistribution adopted' (CNEL, 1993, p. 1).

A CONCRETE EXAMPLE – ITALY'S JULY 1993 PROTOCOL

The *new* cultural climate reflects itself also in some recent evaluations of the agreement on labour costs which was signed by the Italian government, trade unions and employers' organizations in July 1993. This agreement opens with a section on 'incomes and employment policies' which, in view of its importance, deserves some comment.

The July 1993 Protocol is in effect an ambitious and complex attempt to define a procedural framework and set of rules for a solidarity pact, stipulated in the context of an exceptional economic and political situation, and implying an unequal distribution of the price to be paid by the interested parties.[15] The most important elements of the agreement with regard to the issue discussed here are the abolition of the wage indexation mechanism (known as the wage escalator clause) and the establishment of two levels of wage bargaining (one at national level for each sector, the other at the level of the single company). The first of these two levels is charged with recouping the loss of purchasing power of wages in the period preceding the renewal of the contract (made necessary by the *foreseeable* difference between the 'planned' inflation targets – estimated by the parties during the pay talks – and the actual rate of inflation) and with redistributing the aggregate increases in productivity (D'Antona, 1993, p. 420). The agreement envisages two-year contracts with renewals 'coherent with the planned inflation rates taken as a common objective'. In the event of a delay (of more than three months) in renewing the contract, from the fourth month onwards the workers concerned are entitled to a provisional supplement of 30 per cent of the planned inflation rate (applied to the contractual minimum pay); this percentage increases to 50 per cent if the contract is not renewed within six months.

The second *stage* of wage bargaining, the one that is to take place at single-company level every four years, is charged with distributing the company's productivity margins via special participation schemes such as productivity schemes or bonuses linked to company profitability (ibid.).

Behind the complexity of the set of tools established, the economic importance of the Protocol is that the trade unions have signed an agreement that assigns to wages the most important role in the task of slowing down the inflationary process – presumably in the hope that, in a situation of serious unemployment and hence of scarce bargaining power, wage increases moderation would have, as counterpart, a rapid effect in expanding levels of production and employment supported also by a series of appropriate economic policy measures. The trade unions' hopes have, in fact, found only limited response, at least in the successive eighteen months: the signing of the agreement was followed neither by direct (*automatic*) effects of employment expansion (a result which would appear to support Keynes's analysis in chapter 19 of *The General Theory*), nor by an incisive and coherent policy in support of the economy. As regards this second aspect, it must be noted that the existence of constraints of varying nature (all well known to the trade unions) – principally the level of public debt – helps to explain the difficulties of implementing expansionary policies in the absence of structural reforms in our economic system.[16]

The July 1993 agreement, which should be interpreted as indicating the trade unions' recognition of Italy's serious economic situation and their solidarity with the unemployed, has been seen by many, in a typically pre-Keynesian theoretical perspective of the relation between wages and unemployment, as a decisive step in the creation of new job opportunities through the control of wages. Although the expression incomes policy has been employed to indicate the framework within which the Protocol should be placed, the vision upon which this latter has been founded is profoundly different from the spirit that inspired the original notion of incomes policy.

In fact the July 1993 agreement certainly has a great relevance in the context of Italy's policy for the control of inflationary pressures, but cannot be entrusted with the task – the defence of the level of employment – for which it represents a necessary prerequisite but not a sufficient condition. This latter task – especially in a context characterized by marked geographical differences among productive areas and by the unresolved conundrums of technological unemployment – requires much more.

SUMMARY AND CONCLUSION

The present chapter argues that the cultural climate predominant in the field of economic theory in the last two decades – which brought with it the *crisis of Keynesianism*, and of which New Keynesian economics represents a relevant expression – inevitably influenced the conception of economic policy and in particular the notion of incomes policy.

In its original meaning this latter was seen as the set of measures designed to make the growth of income and employment compatible with price stability through the strict connection between real wages and labour productivity, a conception – it is argued – that seems close to Keynes's own preference for 'more reasonable, less punitive, means [with respect to the creation of severe depressive conditions]' as the crucial instrument for the control of inflationary pressures.

The *new* conception of incomes policy which has come to be established in recent years – a manoeuvre to curb nominal and real wages aimed at fostering employment – finds its ultimate foundation in the assumption of an inverse relation between wages and employment, which is an essential component part of New Keynesian economics.

The chapter criticizes the view according to which wage moderation is the essential tool for the support of employment, and concludes that such moderation – though important for the control of inflation – is not a sufficient condition for the defence of employment. This requires the adoption of active and imaginative measures, whose content and implications remain to be carefully investigated.

NOTES

1 Joan Robinson's vivid recollection of the episode is worth citing. 'He had retired and Keynes was dead, but he asked to be allowed to give two lectures to the undergraduates, to make reparation to Keynes for his unfair review [of *The General Theory*]. For the young men, to whom I suppose the *General Theory* is just another of those classics that you hope your tutor will not notice that you have not read, it was rather mystifying; for those who had lived through the old battles it was a moving and noble scene' (1962, p. 80). It should be noted, however, that Pigou's 'recognition' of Keynes embraces many of the ambiguities that fuelled the debate on *The General Theory* in subsequent years (Pigou, 1950).

2 'None of this', notes N. Kaldor 'would have occurred without the appearance of Keynes's *General Theory* – since "maintaining full employment" would not have occurred to economists and politicians as a feasible policy objective' (1983, p. 3).

3 Beaud and Dostaler perceptively note that some economists of neoclassical background and inspiration who had apparently become Keynesians contributed *from within* to a *deconstruction* of Keynesianism much the same as Keynes had done with his attack *from within* the neoclassical fortress (1993, p. 150).

4 The point is particularly delicate since it touches upon the complex relationship between the evolution of economic theory and the social and political context in which this evolution takes place (on this point see Keynes, 1973a, pp. 383–4; Pigou, 1939, p. 22; Caravale, 1992, pp. 38–9; Sawhill, 1995). It seems certain, however, that the *values* prevailing in the social and political context do have an important influence in shaping nature and aspects of the research programmes in the field of economic theory and policy.

5 See Jossa (1994).

6 The critical evaluation of this approach constitutes the main objective of the present collection of papers. The inclusion of New Keynesian economics in the above list seems to be justified by the emphasis it lays on wage rigidities as the ultimate cause of unemployment.

7 This denial echoes the old prescription, laid down by Bentham in 1793, that 'the general rule is that nothing ought to be done or attempted by government; the motto or watch word of government . . . ought to be – Be quiet. . . . The request which agriculture, manufacturers, and commerce present to governments is as modest and

reasonable as that which Diogenes made to Alexander: Stand out of my sunshine' (Bentham, 1793, p. 279).

8 This rule consists, as is known, in removing control of variations in money supply from the discretion of the monetary and political authorities and imposing, possibly also through changes in the constitution, that the growth rate of the quantity of money be brought closely into line with the long-term growth rate of GNP.

9 See also Caravale (1991).

10 Keynes (1973a, p. 309).

11 See Lecaillon (1965) and Papi (1967).

12 For example, Roncaglia (1986).

13 It has been said that 'the bastardized version of Keynes's economics peddled by the New Keynesians... currently violate the trade description act' (Thirlwall, 1995, p. 1672).

14 CNEL (1993).

15 See D'Antona (1993).

16 From this viewpoint a relevant turning point has been marked in 1995 by the government's economic measures that for the first time produced the result of an inversion in the evolution of the relationship between public debt and gross national product.

20

MONEY AND INTEREST RATES IN A MONETARY THEORY OF PRODUCTION

Basil J. Moore

INTRODUCTION: COMPLEXITY AND ITS CONSEQUENCES

Economic behaviour occurs in the real world, where historical time, ignorance, uncertainty, transactions costs and money play a central role in shaping and constraining rational action. More than half a century ago John Maynard Keynes presented a 'Monetary Theory of Production' (Keynes, 1933a) as a first sketch of what eventually became *The General Theory of Employment, Interest and Money*. Keynes there strongly rejected the idea of a barter economy as the basis for macroeconomic modelling. He contrasted it with

> an economy in which money plays a part of its own and effects motives and decisions and is, in short, one of the operative factors in the situation, so that the course of events cannot be predicted, either in the long period or the short, without a knowledge of the behaviour of money between the first state and the last. It is this which we ought to mean when we speak of a *monetary economy*.
>
> (ibid., pp. 408–9)[1]

Real world economies proceed in historical time. The world is non-ergodic, since time and space distributions differ. Fundamental (ontological) uncertainty cannot be expressed in terms of known quantitative probability distributions (Davidson, 1995; Rotheim, 1995b). Economic agents, no matter how hard they try, have only bounded rationality (Davidson, 1991).

In the face of near complete ignorance about the future, people are uncertain what to do. They make mistakes, and they know that they will make mistakes. As new information is received, their expectations of future states of the world change continuously. One implication is that they will attempt to correct their past errors. Another is that they will attempt to keep their options open, and so will desire liquidity.

Understanding macroeconomic phenomena means taking seriously the complexity posed by historical time. Postulating perfect certainty on the grounds of analytical tractability leads to serious errors of how real world economies behave.

One main difficulty in taking this step is its apparent devastating nihilistic consequences (Hahn, 1983). Modelling time seriously means the adoption of sequence (dynamic) analysis (Loasby, 1976). Time periods must be defined, and all variables must be dated. Many economic processes are subject to increasing returns, so that multiple equilibria, lock-in, hysteresis and path-dependence all occur (Arthur, 1994). No closed form solution exists for non-linear, complex adaptive systems (Waldrop, 1992). General equilibrium theory, and even the possibility of doing tractable economic theory, appear to be completely undermined.[2] Modelling appears to run into an analytical brick wall, as agents' behaviour depends on their expectations of future events. Unfortunately economists have no general theory of expectations formation (Hahn, 1983).

It is, I believe, in large part these dire indeterministic consequences, the direct logical implications of the Post Keynesian vision, that have deterred many macro theorists from climbing onto the Post Keynesian bandwagon. If we accept that the real world macro economy is non-ergodic, we have to give up at the outset any hope of being able to model formally any general equilibrium outcome, or to predict with quantitative precision its future position based on evidence from its past (see Lawson, 1994).

The possibility of economists ever being able to make exact probabilistic forecasts of the future is quite simply impossible. Economists can never do more than make qualitative statements about potential tendencies and stylized facts. They are able to predict only what can happen in consequence of certain hypothetical events, not what will happen (Shackle, 1980). This should, however, surprise no serious social scientist. Knowledge of the future behaviour of real world economies in all their manifold complexity is obviously unattainable.

Chaos theory has demonstrated how deterministic systems of simple non-linear equations yield astonishingly complex and chaotic results, which have no closed form solution (Gleick, 1987). Suppose that the economic universe is like the meteorological one, so that social behaviour must be modelled by non-linear relationships.[3] The property of extreme dependence on initial conditions implies that mere humans can never hope to go from observation of the world to prediction of its future states. To do this our measurements would all have to be impossibly (infinitely) exact (Kellert, 1993). We must simply accept this inability to predict the future as a fact of life, attributable to the disorderly nature of our universe (Dupre, 1994).

General equilibrium macroeconomic models, built up from reductionist *choice-theoretic microeconomic foundations*, and specified independently from their particular historical and institutional context, necessarily fall. The world is too complex to permit maximizing behaviour. We are confined to bounded rationality, and to simple rules of thumb for our guides.

The properties of complex adaptive systems are greater than the sum of their parts (Waldrop, 1992). Models designed to explicate open system behaviour can still be built, but not from reductionist microfoundations (Kellert, 1993). This abandonment of reductionism is in fact extremely liberating, and an occasion for

Post Keynesian rejoicing. The continuous neoclassical refrain that Keynesian macroeconomics has no rigorous 'choice-theoretic microeconomic foundations' may at last be shown to be a misplaced reductionist vestige.

Depending on the particular set of agents' expectations that are assumed, formal macroeconomic theory is consistent with almost any outcome. Since expectations are continuously changing, real world forecasters have no choice but to look elsewhere. This is in fact already happening. Practitioners are increasingly turning to pure statisticians to extract the maximum information contained in any particular economic time series, independent of any formal economic theory.

Macroeconomic behaviour cannot be usefully modelled as the simultaneous solution of a set of Walrasian general equilibrium equations, where all exchanges occur instantaneously, all coordination problems are resolved by assuming perfect and complete markets, and all agents are omnisciently rational. In this vision of what is in effect a perfect barter economy, money can have no role. All real world coordination, liquidity and transaction costs functions of money have been assumed away, so that money is left with only a residual *numeraire* role.

There appears at last to be increasing consensus in the profession that the timeless perfect barter paradigm must be rejected (Hicks, 1991). The Walrasian general equilibrium model, the mode of thought on which the vast majority of economists all over the world have been brought up, must be totally abandoned, *even as a point of reference*, for analysing macroeconomic phenomena (Heise, 1992).

The big buzzing, blooming confusion around us is in its full complexity impenetrable. We have different ways of interpreting it, and of theorizing about how it is constituted. Each may have validity on its own terms (Mirowski, 1990). The same reality looks fundamentally different, depending on one's perspective. Is the glass half full, or half empty? Is light a particle, or a wave? Is unemployment voluntary, or involuntary? Is it both? (See Dupre, 1994.)

Ultimately, any theory is built on a vision – the perspective by which reality is interpreted. That vision guides us in choosing assumptions and interpreting results. Vision allows us to make the leap of faith necessary to believe that our theory is more than a set of tautological relations. Revolutions in a discipline occur through changes in these visions. In macroeconomics it appears that such a change is currently underway.

This chapter attempts to demonstrate that the nihilistic implications of taking time and non-ergodicity seriously have been greatly exaggerated. Macroeconomic modelling and analysis can still survive, but on a different, non-reductionist level. *Sequence analysis* must replace general equilibrium analysis in macroeconomics. The modelling goal must be the increased understanding, not the precise prediction, of economic phenomena.

M–C–M'

Firms' production and investment expenditures are driven by expectations of future returns. As Keynes declared, following Marx, 'it [the firm] has no object in the world except to end up with more money than it started with' (Keynes, 1933b, p. 89).

Most markets are imperfectly competitive. Firms with market power are necessarily price-setters. Because firms cannot predict their future demand, they cannot calculate their marginal revenue. As a result it is impossible for them to calculate the price and output where marginal revenue will equal marginal costs. In the absence of perfect information, profit maximization is unattainable.

In consequence, real world firms can only follow simplified rules of thumb. They administer their prices as a mark-up over their average variable costs, in an attempt to realize some target profit rate. So long as their demand expectations are fulfilled, their sales proceeds will be sufficient to cover all their variable and fixed cost commitments, and generate their profit targets.

A firm has two ways in which to end up with more money than it started with. It can purchase labour, raw materials and illiquid capital goods with borrowed money, in the expectation of selling a sufficient quantity of the goods produced, and so realizing money quasi-rents over the life of the project in excess of the carrying costs of its debt obligations. Alternatively, it can purchase financial assets, and receive the yield directly in money. Since financial assets are claims against other issuing units, investment in financial assets is a form of saving, and does not add to effective demand for currently produced goods and services.

A FRAMEWORK FOR SEQUENCE ANALYSIS

In a monetary economy operating in calendar time, all transactions have to be performed within some particular time period, either by payment of money now (spot), or by deferred (forward) payment. Let us try to develop a framework for sequence analysis (Messori and Tamborini; Graziani, 1989; Davidson, 1994b).

Consider an economy in one discrete period in historical time, out of a succession of such periods. Let us make the following stylized assumptions:

1 All markets are open only for a finite time in each period.
2 All transactions for finance, credit, previously existing assets and factor services are open at the *beginning* of each period.
3 All transactions for producible and non-producible goods and services are open at the *end* of each period.
4 Agents are classified conventionally according to functions: labour consumption (households), production (firms), credit (banks), finance (non-bank financial intermediaries) and finally the government and its agent, the central bank.
5 The sequence economy uses a single generally accepted currency as the instrument of account. This is issued and vouchsafed as legal tender by the central bank. Banks ensure the general acceptability of their deposits in exchange by maintaining their convertibility into legal tender on demand. By offering security and record keeping services, deposits dominate currency for most large transactions.

6 Markets are organized in such a way that all transactions are settled by legal tender, bank deposits, or by issuing liabilities. In the last case the settlement of a transaction between two parties requires that the purchaser initiates a debt relationship with a bank (credit) or a non-bank (finance).

7 Central to the sequence economy is the lack of complete futures markets. The absence of markets for all possible future contingencies, unlike an Arrow–Debreu economy, forces agents to transact under non-insurable uncertainty.

8 In making sequential decisions, agents discover that their available resources are binding with respect to some allocations, since most assets are heterogeneous and illiquid. This leads them to adopt precautionary behaviour, and in particular to demand liquidity. Money is the only asset that yields instant liquidity services. The availability of credit reduces, but does not eliminate, agents' precautionary demand for money.

9 Markets are imperfectly competitive. Firms possess market power, defined as the ability to set the prices of the goods they sell.

10 To remove the complications introduced by inflation, a social contract will be assumed to exist between labour, business and government. An explicit incomes policy is in place: firms and workers agree that average increases in the wage bill will not exceed average labour productivity increases. As a result, although relative prices will change with differential productivity growth, on average unit labour costs and prices will remain constant. Changes in nominal and real output are therefore identical.[4]

Let t^0 refer to the beginning and t^1 refer to the end of the chosen accounting period. The markets for credit, finance and production services open at t^0, when agents make their overall plans for their net financial allocations (NFAs). Production takes place over the period until the markets for goods opens at t^1, when agents realize their net real allocations (NRAs).[5] The length of the period is determined by the time requirement of the production–sales process.[6]

The key point in the time profile of firms' transactions is that their factor purchases must be made *before* their product sales. Firms pay their wage and materials bills at t^0, while they must wait for their sales receipts until t^1.

Consequently, in every production–sales period, firms are required to raise an amount of working capital equal to their wage and materials bills, which are non-contingent and in money terms. They do this either by internal finance (retained earnings), or by external finance (selling short-term liabilities in the credit or financial markets). Since future markets do not exist, contingent forward contracts for goods cannot be sold in advance, unlike in an Arrow–Debreu world.

An important difference immediately emerges between those units whose receipts chronologically run ahead of disbursements (surplus units), and those whose disbursements run ahead of receipts (deficit units). The former lend money as a form of disbursement. The latter must borrow money to finance their current expenditures.

All agents face the constraint that planned NFAs at t^0 must be consistent with real NRA's at t^1. While financial constraints operate universally, their *modus operandi* is very different for surplus and deficit spending units. For surplus units (households), with receipts preceding disbursements, their financial constraint at t^0 is given by their income flow, their stock of money and wealth balances, and their unutilized credit allocations. This sum constrains the amount they can allocate to consumption and real asset accumulation.

For deficit units (firms), with receipts lagging behind disbursements, they must plan negative NFAs (net increases in debt), by increasing their liabilities at t^0, in anticipation of their future receipts from the sale of goods at t^1. If their receipts are not as anticipated, they may be unable to meet their financial commitments. In this case they must sell other assets, raise additional loans, or declare bankruptcy. For this reason they hold liquid assets, and/or seek guaranteed lines of credit. Their ability to go into debt is their chief financial constraint.

With regard to real investment expenditures, firms are in a similiar position but over a multiperiod horizon. They must pay for new investment goods at t^1 in the current period, while sales revenue will be generated only over future periods. In consequence firms must issue longer-term liabilities, equal to the value of planned net investment in excess of retained earnings at t^0. Households sell labour services at t^0 and buy consumption goods at t^1.[7] Households as a group have financial surpluses. In most economies, for historical/institutional/policy reasons, finance and credit are available primarily for business investment spending. In contrast, in the United States credit and finance to households for housing and consumer durables play a major role. As a result, in the United States a subset of households also plans deficit NRAs over a multiperiod horizon.[8]

SEQUENCE ANALYSIS OF FINANCIAL FLOWS

There are two basic constraining financial factors in a credit money economy. The first is agents' opening balance sheet position of assets and liabilities at t^0. This is inherited from the past, and applies to both households and firms. The second is the quantity and terms of the debt which agents are able to issue in order to finance planned spending in excess of money balances and current money receipts. This latter constraint applies only to deficit units.

Capital markets perform the task of enabling and coordinating the surplus and deficit flows of agents in an economy, by increasing (credit) or redistributing (finance) the existing stock of money balances. The credit market increases or reduces the money stock. Banks buy or sell non-marketable and marketable securities in exchange for *newly-credited* deposits. The financial market redistributes the existing money stock between surplus and deficit units. Non-bank financial firms buy or sell marketable and non-marketable securities in exchange for *previously existing* deposits.

The *ex ante* plans of diverse agents are brought into consistency in nominal terms through the economy's stock-flow matrix. Total assets are necessarily equal to total liabilities. Flows (net changes in assets and liabilities) sum to zero by construction. System constraints hold continuously in a bookkeeping sense. Disbursements for any one sector are receipts to another. Aggregate expenditures are necessarily equal to aggregate incomes.

Nevertheless these system constraints are not binding at the micro level. So long as economic agents have *unutilized* credit commitments, their expenditures are not limited to their existing incomes and money balances. Deficit spending can be financed by *newly-created* credit.

The sequential approach highlights how in a money economy all agents operate under a financial constraint. This constraint is more binding on firms than on households, in so far as they are perpetual debtor units, because of the timing of their cash outflows and inflows.

Firms plan deficit NFAs on the expectation of future receipts being greater than debt commitments. Debt contracts of households and smaller firms are ordinarily non-marketable. This is because of the heterogeneous nature of their uncertain repayment prospects, incomplete and asymmetric information between lender and borrower, and lenders' risk aversion (Stiglitz and Weiss, 1987).

With regard to the demand for money it is important to distinguish clearly:

1 The credit demand for deposits to spend. This represents a flow demand by prospective credit-worthy deficit spending units. It is equal to the quantity of newly created loans or securities issued over the period by debtor units in exchange for newly created (credit) or previously existing (finance) deposits.
2 The portfolio demand for money to hold. This represents a stock demand by all wealth owning spending units. It is equal to the total stock of currency and deposits held in the economy at any point in time.[9]

THE OPERATION OF CREDIT AND FINANCIAL MARKETS

The asset side of banks' balance sheets consists of non-marketable claims (loans) and marketable claims (securities) on borrowers' expected future earnings. Banks bear lenders' risk, and charge a premium for doing so to cover anticipated bad debts on loans. The liability side consists of deposits that can be liquidated on demand or notice, have a guaranteed nominal value in terms of legal tender, and in addition to liquidity services-in-kind pay an administered interest rate. Transactions deposits are quasi-perfect cash substitutes. They dominate cash for most larger transactions because of their safety from theft and recordkeeping services.

Banks diversify their loan assets among different firms, industries and geographic areas. They also benefit from scale and scope economies in collecting information and monitoring borrowers, which are available to non-bank financial intermediaries to a lesser extent. As a result banks are able to endow their liabilities with near perfect liquidity, which makes them generally acceptable in settlement of debt.

Each bank stands ready to convert its deposits on demand or call into legal tender. Interbank debts must be repaid immediately in legal tender at t^0. When agents lend fiat money (legal tender) to a bank, and receive credit money (bank deposits) in exchange, they do not perceptibly alter their liquidity position. Because of the close substitutability between cash and deposits, and the dominance of deposits over cash for many transactions, agents typically do not even regard holding deposits as an act of lending to the bank, even though the lending of fiat money is the essence of the deposit transaction.

By accepting and crediting deposits from other banks at par, banks become the payment managers of the economy. Through the purchase of non-marketable or marketable debt contracts in exchange for newlycreated deposits, banks supply credit to firms and households.

The central bank holds the monopoly rights to the creation of legal tender. It supplies legal tender to banks (non-borrowed reserves) by the purchase of marketable securities in the open market, as well as by directly lending (rediscounting selected short-term instruments) to the banks (borrowed reserves). The central bank administers the supply price of reserves (in the United States the federal funds rate, in the UK the bank rate) which determines the level of short-term wholesale interest rates, as its key instrument of monetary policy.

Each bank is aware that the amount of deposits it creates depends on the amount of credit it grants to its firm and household customers. All newly created deposits flow initially into its own balance sheet. But a large proportion flows immediately into the balance sheet of other banks, and hence turns into losses at clearing. Concurrently it receives inflows of deposits created by other banks.

Given the interest rates paid on deposits, and depositor preferences among banks, a bank's net position at clearing will depend on the rate of expansion of its loan portfolio relative to that of other banks. If all banks expand their loans at the same rate, so long as the central bank maintains its interest rate target no bank need lose reserves at clearing.

Liquidity management, the sale of their own marketable instruments (CDs) at their initiative, enables banks which are net debtors at clearing to borrow the funds required from surplus banks. As a result banks are less constrained to follow the lending policy and experience of other banks, and may if they choose pursue a more autonomous lending policy.

Increases in a bank's administered lending rates may lead to adverse selection effects and increased moral hazard, because of the informational asymmetry between a bank and its borrowers, thus raising the probabilities of loan default. As a result increases in the rate charged on loans can turn into a decrease in these same rates' net of expected default probabilities (Stiglitz and Weiss, 1987).

In consequence banks choose to ration credit by non-price means. They do this by imposing overdraft limits on all individual borrowers, based on the bank's estimate of the borrowers' ability to repay (credit, collateral and character, the banks '3 Cs'). Bank borrowers typically do not utilize their credit commitments to the full. In most countries unutilized commitments are roughly equal in magnitude to total loans granted, and serve as a precautionary provision for future financial contingencies.[10]

Information asymmetries can lead to negative signalling effects. If a firm wishes to issue new bonds or equities, this signals to potential non-bank financial lenders that it has been negatively screened in credit markets. The resulting underpricing of new bond or equity issues embodies a substantial 'lemons' premium, to overcome financial market lender risk aversion. This ordinarily makes the issue of marketable securities too costly for all but the largest and most solvent firms (Stiglitz, 1988).

Banks perform two very different functions. First, by standing ready to transfer and clear bank deposits among each other, as a by-product of creating the liquidity and general transactions acceptability of their deposits in exchange, banks manage the economy's payments system. Second, by purchasing non-marketable securities (IOUs) from debtor units in exchange for newlycreated deposits, banks monetize the debts of deficit-spending units, thereby increasing the money stock (Moore, 1988, Part 1).

Deposits are supplied to deficit-spending borrowers in exchange for securities in credit markets and financial markets. The distinction between the credit and financial channels of the supply of deposits to borrowers is central to understanding the complex relation between changes in the money supply and changes in economic activity.

The financial and credit markets play quite distinct roles in the economy. The financial market transfers *previously-existing* deposits from surplus spending units to deficit spending units, in exchange for newly-issued and previously-existing marketable securities. Insofar as current deficit spending units are financed by current surplus spending units, the effect is to redistribute current income from planned surplus spenders to planned deficit spenders. As a result aggregate demand is not directly affected by the process of finance, although there may be indirect effects related to changes in velocity.

In contrast the credit market grants *newly-created* deposits to bank borrowers in exchange for newly created non-marketable IOUs (loans) or previously existing marketable IOUs (securities). In the process banks increase or decrease the existing stock of money. Newly created deposits are always accepted, i.e. demanded, in exchange for goods and services. It is immaterial how long individual units choose to hold deposits before spending them. Deposits in the aggregate continue to be held until the loans that created them are repaid, or sold to non-bank intermediaries.

Economic units who allow their deposits to grow during the period are increasing their lending of legal tender money to the banking system. As a result they are surplus spenders in that period. Nevertheless, from a motivational point of view, they are merely 'convenience lenders' to the banking system. They suffer no reduction in liquidity and make no abstention from consumption spending, or from non-monetary financial asset accumulation (saving), or from real asset accumulation (investment), for any longer than convenience dictates.

Depositors are not volitional but *convenience* lenders and *convenience* surplus spenders. They demand no pecuniary reward for such convenience lending. Whether they are also *convenience savers* depends solely on whether the deficit spending was for real investment goods. If the deficit spending was for the purchase of financial assets, whether it represents 'convenience saving' depends on whether the security was newly issued, and whether it financed an increase in investment or consumption expenditures. The process of bank monetization of non-marketable debt (IOUs) in the credit market generates the growth in money supply and system liquidity which finances increases in effective demand (Moore, 1988, Part 2; 1995).

The ability of economic, units to issue debt and deficit spend for real or financial resources is constrained by lender perception of their creditworthiness (credit commitments). New issues of liabilities by those deficit spending units who pass lenders' tests of creditworthiness are allocated to volitional or convenience surplus spending units in credit and financial markets.

In financial markets, purchases of non-bank secondary securities represent volitional saving by surplus spending units. If these securities financed deficit spending to purchase consumption goods, the economy's saving falls. In credit markets "purchases" of deposits represent *convenience lending*. They are driven by and equal to the borrowing of deficit units.

INTEREST RATES AND MONETARY POLICY

As Keynes recognized, the level of aggregate demand may remain for long periods well below the economy's aggregate full employment output capacity. Cumulative increases in the level of aggregate demand depend on the amount of credit-financed deficit spending undertaken by economic agents. This depends directly on their expectations of future returns, and indirectly on the behaviour of the central bank.

Central banks administer the level of short-term rates exogenously as their key monetary policy instrument. In pursuit of their macroeconomic stabilization goals, price stability, full employment and rapid growth, central banks vary interest rates pro-cyclically, depending on their policy reaction function.

In every period the central bank continuously maintains short-term interest rates at some particular targeted level. This target may change within periods, depending on central bank policy. Any positive net demand for legal tender at clearing by the banking system is automatically supplied by the central bank, in the process of interest rate targeting, owing to its central role of residual supplier of system liquidity.

The process of bank arbitrage, as banks attempt to borrow and lend at the lowest and highest rate possible, results in interest rate equality for all marketable securities with identical perceived risk and maturity. As a result short-term market rates respond immediately to changes in bank rate.

Portfolio managers seek to equalize expected holding period returns among securities of different maturities but equivalent risk. Nominal long-term interest rates are determined by a time arbitrage process, as financial market participants attempt to keep expected holding period returns equal across maturities. The level of long-term rates is thus governed by the current level of short-term rates set by the central bank, and the financial markets' current expectations of the future level of rates the central bank will set over the life of the asset.

If short-term and long-term assets were perfect substitutes, market expectations would be the end of the story of the yield curve. However, short- and long-term securities differ with regard to expected income and capital risk. As a result a possibly varying liquidity and term premium may be required by wealth owners, in payment for exchanging short-term securities into less liquid, more uncertain and longer-maturity interest bearing securities.

Interest rates do not adjust to *equilibrate* the supply and demand for *funds*. Short-term rates are simply directly determined by the central bank. Long-term rates are determined by market expectations of future rates through the above arbitrage procedure. Interest rates similarly do not adjust to achieve equality of saving and investment. The supply of funds to creditworthy deficit spenders is always horizontal up to their credit limit. Bank lending rates are set at a relatively stable mark-up over the level of short-term wholesale rates set by the central bank.

There is thus a kind of *Say's Law of Money* operating: the demand for credit money creates its own supply. Increases in the stock of credit money are always demanded. Bank borrowers are never savings-constrained.

Endogenous market forces do not operate to push output and income towards any *equilibrium* level, nor to grow at any *natural* rate. The plans of economic agents are not coordinated by changes in interest rates to lead to any general equilibrium outcome. In a non-ergodic world agents' expectations are always heterogeneous. Plans never completely materialize as outcomes, and agents' expectations are never universally realized. There is no *natural* rate of interest, or *natural* rate of unemployment.

Higher interest rates result in lower deficit spending on investment, lower business profits, lower saving, bank lending, monetary creation and a resultant lower aggregate demand for goods and services. Conversely, lower interest rates produce higher deficit spending on investment, higher profits, higher saving, bank lending, monetary creation and a resultant higher level of aggregate demand.

Firms are perpetually in a debtor position, because of the time sequence that their cash outflows for productive factors always precede their cash inflows from sales. Non-financial firms are made better off by reductions in interest rates, since the present value of their future receipts, and so their net worth, rises. Similarly non-financial firms are made worse off by interest rate increases, since the present value of their net worth falls.[11]

Even though the production–sales lag is chronologically relatively short, firms remain perpetually in a debtor position. The level of interest rates thus has an extremely important effect on firms' market valuation, profitability and behaviour. A higher level of interest rates reduces the net worth of business units, and in the process depresses investment spending and the level of aggregate demand. The converse occurs when interest rates fall.

These effects of changes in interest rates occur through four distinct channels:

1 Given the expected returns on investment projects, the higher the level of interest rates, the fewer the investment projects that will be taken up. The higher the level of interest rates, the less attractive will borrowing to acquire productive factors appear, and the more attractive will be direct financial investment. It follows that the lower will be the level of investment spending, aggregate demand, income, output and employment.

2 Given the profits on past investments, the higher the level of interest rates, the higher will be the proportion of quasi-rents that must be paid out as interest on existing debt obligations. As a result the smaller will be the level of net profits, and the lower the flow of retained earnings available to finance new investment projects. In consequence of their poorer financial position, the lower will be the amount of credit that firms can expect to borrow from bank and non-bank lenders. If mark-ups are raised in response in an attempt to restore profit prospects, the rise in output prices will reduce sales volume, and possibly sales revenue, depending on the elasticity of demand faced by the firm.

3 The level of real and financial asset prices, as the capitalized present value of their expected future net earnings, is inversely related to the discount rate used to discount future expected income streams. Higher interest rates reduce the net market value of firms' real and financial assets, householders' net worth, lenders' credit commitments, and so households' and firms' consumption and investment expenditures.

If tangible assets have been pledged to collateralize debts, as in the case of mortgages, issuers may find themselves with negative net worth as market values fall with rising interest rates. If this becomes sufficiently large, it will induce debtors to walk away from their debt obligations. This erodes the net worth of the financial institutions that had extended the loans, and may drive them into bankruptcy (Stiglitz and Weiss, 1987).

4 The rate of return required on investment projects is related to the level of interest rates set by the central bank. Rather than interest rates being determined by the real rate of return on capital, as neoclassical economics has it, the direction of causality is reversed. The real rate of return on capital is not a technological given. The level of interest rates determines how far firms will be willing to move down their marginal efficiency of investment schedules. A higher interest rate regime will raise the required return on real assets, and conversely a lower interest rate regime will reduce the required return on capital.

SAVING AND INVESTMENT

Actual saving is necessarily always identical to actual investment, at all levels of income and at all levels of interest rates. An increase in investment spending necessarily creates the increase in saving required to finance it. This may be shown as follows: an increase in investment must be financed either by an increase in internal finance (saving) or by an increase in debt or equity issue. The acquisition of any such security (lending) must be associated either with an increase in volitional saving (finance) or an increase in non-volitional lending and saving (credit). In the latter case, the money supply and aggregate demand also increase. An increase in bank lending, if it finances an increase in investment spending, also generates an increase in convenience saving.

Assume that planned investment spending is given for the current period, and that economic units wish to increase their volitional saving out of their given income. This implies a reduction in their current consumption spending. *Ceteris paribus* aggregate demand must decrease in the current period. By assumption this has no effect on planned investment spending in the current period. The fall in sales will result in an increase in unintended inventory accumulation, and so produce an identical change in unplanned investment. As a result both saving and investment will temporarily rise.

But in the next period planned investment will fall, in order to restore inventories to their desired levels. As a result a current increase in planned saving, independent of increases in planned investment, by depressing the level of aggregate demand will depress future planned investment. This is of course Keynes's paradox of thrift. Increases in planned saving do not result in increases in planned investment. They rather depress aggregate demand, and so the level of economic output, income and investment.

Interest rates do not adjust to equilibrate planned saving and investment. Short-term rates are simply set by the monetary authority. They rise or fall only if the central bank initiates an increase or reduction in bank rate, and so the general level of short-term rates. How interest rates respond to divergencies of actual from targeted stabilization goals depends solely on the central bank's policy reaction function.

The above account does not depend on any underlying notion of an aggregate production function. The concept of the marginal efficiency of capital (investment) underlying the Keynesian theory of investment demand is widely believed to be based on the concept of diminishing marginal productivity of capital (e.g. Garegnani, 1983).

This is a complete misunderstanding of the Keynesian concept of estimated future yields on investment projects. The downward sloping investment demand curve has nothing to do with decreasing marginal physical productivity of capital. It follows simply and directly from the existence of heterogeneous assets.

So long as different investments have different expected returns, projects can always be ranked in order of expected return (Davidson, 1984). Investment expectations are not primarily about technology, but about the responses of other investors. As in Keynes's beauty contest example, expectations are often formed in a third degree, 'where we devote our intelligence to anticipating what average opinion expects average opinion to be' (Keynes, 1936, p. 156).

THE MONETARY TRANSMISSION MECHANISM

When all firms are price-setters, the aggregate supply curve becomes horizontal (Moore, 1988, Part 2). The price level is a relatively stable mark-up of normal average variable costs. In the present case, when as a result of an assumed incomes policy in place unit labour costs are maintained unchanged, the aggregate supply curve becomes horizontal. There is no tendency for prices to rise with increases in aggregate demand. Output and income are entirely demand determined.

With endogenous money, the aggregate demand curve becomes vertical. There is then no Pigou or Keynes effect (Moore, 1988, Part 2). Credit demand, bank loans and the supply of credit money respond endogenously to working capital needs, and vary directly with the level of costs and incomes. In every period income and output are demand determined. They are simply at the point where aggregate demand currently intersects the (horizontal) aggregate supply curve. The concepts of macroeconomic "equilibrium" and "disequilibrium" have no analytic meaning or significance.[12]

Given business expectations of future returns, investment spending and aggregate demand rise or fall with reductions or increases in the level of short-term rates set by the central bank. The central bank adjusts interest rates pro-cyclically, as expectations change over the cycle, in carrying out its stabilization goals.[13] Apart from the central bank's reaction function, there are no endogenous market forces operating to keep the system at full employment. Unemployment and excess capacity can persist indefinitely.

If the responsiveness of aggregate demand to unit changes in short-term interest rates is slight, large movements in the level of interest rates will be required to induce substantial shifts in aggregate demand. The level of interest rates must then be varied by central banks in a more sharply pro-cyclic pattern, in the attempt to reach their stabilization objectives.

Low interest elasticities of investment and consumption spending have traditionally been invariably regarded as a negative characteristic, since the economy is then less responsive to monetary policy. This is mistaken. A low interest elasticity of investment spending should rather be viewed as a positive property of an economy. If the interest elasticity of investment demand is sufficiently low, and prices remain constant, nominal interest rates can be reduced towards the economy's real growth rate. As a result the market value of household wealth can be increased without limit.

In carrying out its stabilization objectives, the central bank has the ability to reduce the level of short-term rates to any positive level. Assuming an incomes policy is in place, so that reproducible goods prices remain stable, as the level of nominal interest rates falls, asset prices rise, as does the total value of real and financial assets. The net worth of the economy can be increased indefinitely. However, the economy's long-term expected real growth rate provides a floor below which long-term real interest rates should not be reduced, or a rational bubble in asset prices may be created.[14]

It is true that wealth increases caused solely by reductions in the discount rate do not represent an increase in the economy's real physical assets or total productive capacity. They are based solely on financial conventions. As a result such wealth increases are sometimes viewed as illusionary. However, increases in wealth values, even if due solely to falls in the discount rate, represent increased purchasing power. Just as any other wealth form, they entitle the owner to increased command over real goods and services. Even though the measurement and valuation of wealth depends on social conventions, wealth owners are unambiguously made better off by reductions in interest rates and the accompanying increases in wealth values.

CONCLUSIONS

1 The goal of business firms is simply to end up each period with more wealth than they started with. By administering the level of nominal interest rates, the central bank is able to influence directly business expenditure for illiquid but socially productive real investment, and so the rate of growth of aggregate demand, income, output and employment.
2 Real world economies are typically demand- and not supply-constrained. Except in times of war, they operate well inside their full employment production possibility frontiers. The essence of Keynes's vision was that in developed monetary economies the behaviour of income and output is determined by aggregate demand, and not by aggregate supply considerations as the classical vision maintains. In a non-ergodic world, macroeconomics is about coordination and realization, not scarcity.
3 Monetary change is profoundly non-neutral. The rate of growth of the supply of credit money determines the rate of growth of aggregate demand, and so the rate of growth of aggregate income, output and employment. An increase in investment spending *ceteris paribus* always creates the saving necessary to finance it. In sharp contrast increases in planned saving *ceteris paribus* reduce aggregate demand, and so the level of investment, income and output.
4 There is no unique general equilibrium position towards which the system is tending, and no *natural* rate of unemployment or interest. The notion of general equilibrium is simply inapplicable to non-ergodic real world economies. Economic agents are always willing to accept additional money in exchange, without any change in tastes or prices. The money market can literally never be in equilibrium. Unless expectations are frozen, general equilibrium cannot exist, even as a conceptual event.
5 The level of interest rates is the key policy instrument by which governments are able to manage the level of aggregate demand. By lowering or raising the level of interest rates, governments make incurring additional debt and real assets and production for profit more or less attractive.[15]
6 The level of interest rates does not adjust to equilibrate planned saving and investment, or aggregate supply and aggregate demand. Providing the social contract remains intact, and average wage growth does not exceed average labour productivity growth, the aggregate supply curve will remain horizontal. Supply considerations determine the level of costs and prices. The position of the (vertical) aggregate demand curve determines the total volume of aggregate

income and output. The monetary transmission mechanism is extremely simple and transparent: newly created money finances increases in both aggregate demand and aggregate supply.

7 An increase in investment spending *ceteris paribus* generates its own saving. In contrast an increase in saving *ceteris paribus* discourages rather than induces additional investment. High saving is desirable only to the extent it permits the central bank to decide on a lower interest rate regime.

8 An interest-inelastic demand for investment goods is a social virtue rather than a social vice. By lowering the level of interest rates consistent with full employment aggregate demand, an interest-inelastic investment demand enables central banks to maintain a regime of lower interest rates, and a higher level of wealth, than would otherwise be the case.

9 The returns expected on real assets are governed by the returns available on financial assets, rather than the other way round. Governments, as the largest debtors, are the primary beneficiaries of a low interest rate regime. But all agents benefit in their role as debtor. Creditors on the other hand are made worse off by lower rates.

10 A lower level of interest rates would lead to a reduction in the share of income accruing to property, and so to a lower level of income inequality. This may with time lead eventually to Keynes's ultimate goal, the *euthanasia* of the rentier class. But, before we feel sorry for money capitalists, remember: it will be a painless death. In the euthanasia process all wealth values, and the ratio of wealth to income, will rise indefinitely.

NOTES

1 My main critique of this passage would be that it does not go far enough. Monetary change is not merely 'one of the operative factors'. It is the key operative factor in explaining income change.

2 In a credit money economy a position of general equilibrium, whether defined as a position of balance, or as a position where all markets clear, cannot even exist as a conceptual event (Moore, 1988).

3 We have no reason to believe that it is not. Linearity in our models is simply postulated on the grounds of mathematical tractability.

4 The unsuccessful experience of virtually all large countries that have attempted incomes policies has led many economists to regard any such assumption about incomes policies as an adventure in wishful thinking. They should be reminded that several smaller, more homogeneous Asian economies, in particular the city-state of Singapore, have been able to achieve extremely low inflation and unemployment rates simultaneously (below 1 per cent), combined with extremely high real growth rates (above 7 per cent), over long periods of time. Such performance is quite literally incredible for any large country. Small is beautiful. The failure of incomes policies in the Western world is due to political and social rather than economic factors.

5 The production–sales period will differ among individual industries, and even among firms in the same industry. For simplicity the length of the subperiods over which the different markets are open is left undefined. The key point is simply their temporal ordering.

6 Except in an agricultural economy the periods will not be synchronized over time, but rather distributed randomly. In real world economies production–sales periods are overlapping among firms.

7 The wage period for households is different from, and ordinarily shorter than, the production–sales period for firms. If, as is customarily the case, wages are paid at the end of the wage period, wages become a forward rather than a spot contract (Davidson, 1994b). This serves to reduce firms' demand for working capital.

8 In this case consumption expenditure (dissaving) is financed by deficit spending, and saving is reduced by a like amount. This is the major reason why the US savings rate is so low, in comparison to countries where deficit spending is confined primarily to the finance of investment expenditure. In the latter case deficit spending finances both additional investment and additional saving.

9 In Robertson's (1940) colorful terminology, we must distinguish money 'on the wing' (the demand for money to spend), and money 'sitting' (the demand for money to hold).

10 Despite the low average rate of utilization of credit commitments in all overdraft economies (about 50 per cent), many smaller borrowers are credit constrained. Smaller borrowers have poorer repayment prospects than larger borrowers. As a result they are granted smaller or even zero credit allocations, and constitute Keynes's 'fringe of unsatisfied borrowers'.

11 Similarly all firms in their role as net debtors are made better off by inflation. Whenever the central bank fails to adjust the level of nominal rates to keep the real interest rate invariant to the inflation rate, inflation will raise sales receipts by a greater proportion than the rise in interest costs, and firms will enjoy capital gains on assets and debts.

12 This is consistent with the empirical evidence that time series of income, and velocity output appear to be empirically characterized by unit roots.

13 As a result empirical estimates of the interest elasticity of investment demand are likely to be biased downwards.

14 The present value of a perpetuity P, with an initial annual income of X, growing at the constant rate g and discounted at the constant rate r, is given by $P = X/(r - g)$.

If the long-term rate of discount (r) falls below the growth rate (g), a rational bubble will be created. The value of the expression becomes infinite as r approaches g. Prices of perpetuities can then rise without limit and still not exceed their intrinsic value.

Land is such a perpetuity, and land rents are frequently expected to grow broadly in line with total income. In the late 1980s such a bubble in land values developed in Japan, and spread to stock prices.

The cause was that to encourage net capital inflows, in the face of its huge current account surplus, the Bank of Japan had reduced short-term interest rates to below 0.5 per cent. In the process long-term interest rates had fallen to 2.5 per cent. Since the real growth rate of GDP was about 5 per cent, this set the stage for a rational bubble.

15 Interestingly, the general level of interest rates is not something which most democratically elected governments regard themselves as competent to decide. As a result this decision is typically delegated to the central bank. Frequently steps are taken to provide the central bank with autonomy, so as to shield it from political pressures.

The fear appears to be that governments and politicians cannot be trusted not to give in to popular pressure, and to keep interest rates at a sufficiently high level to keep excess demand inflation at bay. This is not the case in a country like Singapore, where an effective incomes policy is in place, In Singapore the central bank is directly responsible to the government.

21

MACROECONOMIC POLICY FOR THE LONG HAUL

Herbert Gintis

INTRODUCTION

Macroeconomic policy for the bulk of the twentieth century was based on three assumptions that no longer obtain (if they ever did). These are:

1 short-run focus: the basic macroeconomic problem is to stabilize the economy over the business cycle and promote full employment in the short run;
2 capital/labour conflict: the basic distributional problem is the division of income between capital and labour;
3 commodity conception of welfare: economic welfare is a function of per capita real income.

By contrast, the assumptions relevant to the state of affairs today and for the foreseeable future are:

1 long-run focus: the basic macroeconomic problem is to promote long-run, egalitarian, environmentally sustainable growth in welfare;
2 intralabour conflict: the basic distributional problem is equity in the size distribution of labour income, and justice in the division of income by region, race, gender, ethnicity and nation;
3 social conception of welfare: economic welfare depends on real income, personal development, healthy community and ecological integrity.

Because of this shift in the focus of macroeconomic problems, recent decades have been cruel to traditional macroeconomic policy of both right and left. The left has suffered the demise of state socialism, which failed to deliver the goods in terms of long-run growth. It has also seen the decline of social democracy, and the weakening of unions with the corresponding political disintegration of workers' movements, both victims in the shift of distributional emphasis from capital/labour to intralabour conflict. Finally, the repeated failure of socialist development strategies in the Third World, based as they were on simple class theories of distributional conflict, has helped discredit any alternative to capitalism as a credible form of economic organization.

The right has suffered because the economies that have prospered in terms of long-term growth have not followed free market policies. The strongest economic performers over the past few decades, including Germany and the newly emerging Asian economic powers, have consistently eschewed the right's clarion call of *laissez-faire* in favour of systematic state intervention on behalf of strengthening the competitive capacities of growth industries. Conservatives have been politically successful in recent years using a 'free market' political philosophy, but it is difficult to interpret this as more than a rhetorical flourish reinforcing a call for the reversal of the widely recognized excesses of bureaucratic welfare statism.

As a result of the shift in macroeconomic priorities sketched above, the opposition of state and market, an opposition that fuelled much twentieth-century macroeconomic policy conflict, will not survive the twentieth century. Market and state, quite simply, are *complementary* rather than *alternative* policy instruments. All successful economies have both strong market institutions and strong public sectors. This fact alone, not to mention an impressive body of economic theory supporting the importance of a competitive market system but its inability to function properly in the absence of state intervention, must convince the impartial observer of a simple fact: the question is not *whether* to promote market competition but how best to do so, and not *whether* the state should intervene, but where and how.

Conservative economic policy will remain popular as long as there are gains to be made in debureaucratizing the welfare state. But we may confidently expect the public's infatuation with conservatism to wane as it becomes clear that a policy of *laissez-faire* is unable to solve contemporary macroeconomic problems. The political fortunes of the left will wax accordingly, if only because the public has nowhere else to turn. But what does the left have to offer – beyond, of course, criticism of *laissez-faire* and capitalist greed? Not much. Keynesian policy, with its emphasis on short-run job creation, is virtually irrelevant in an era where the real economic problems concern long-run, egalitarian, environmentally sustainable, economic growth. Moreover, as I shall argue, neither Nordic social democracy, nor a suitably liberalized version of the Asian interventionist model, is likely to transplant successfully to the United States, Europe or the developing countries.

This chapter explores an alternative conception of progressive economic policy.[1] This conception relegates Keynesian demand management to the relatively minor position in dealing with short-term economic fluctuations, and stresses the need for institutional innovation to deal with problems of long-term environmentally sustainable growth. Moreover, whereas state interventionist models, be they of the Nordic or Asian variety, rely on the *discretionary judgement* of a few powerful groups in state and economy to correct market inefficiency and inequity, I will stress the state as the source *of new rules of the game* that, along with markets, provide a context for the interaction of private agents in a manner conducive to egalitarian and economically efficient social goals.

I will rely on a *dual agency* model of state–market interaction. Roughly speaking, an *agency problem* exists when one economic actor, the *principal*, engages one or more other actors, the *agents*, to undertake certain tasks on the principal's behalf, but where it is difficult for the principal to monitor the agents' behaviour and to contract for and enforce specific performance standards. In the dual agency perspective, both state and market contribute to the attainment of economic objectives, but both also involve severe agency problems.

To implement a policy, agency theory suggests, the policy maker is a principal who must not only select a set of instructions that, if followed by the agents, will achieve the policy objective in a cost-effective manner, but also supply the proper incentives ensuring that agents find it in their interest to behave as prescribed by the policy. A policy implementation is *incentive-compatible* if it includes rewards, penalties and a structure of accountability (i.e. a monitoring system) that ensure that agents responsible for implementing the policy will implement the policy maker's objectives. From an agency-theoretic perspective, then, the principal is the public (or a democratically constituted majority thereof), the agents are state managers, elected public officials and private firms, and the central challenge to policy formulation is to achieve policy objectives through a cost-effective and incentive-compatible mix of policy instruments in the public and private sectors.

The characteristic prejudices of conservative policy flow, I shall argue, from its recognition of agency problems in the state but not in the economy. This selective application of agency theory leads to the conservative policy view of the state as a hopeless morass and the economy as a well-oiled and perfectly calibrated machine, a view from which exclusive reliance upon the market ineluctably follows.

Keynesianism, by contrast, has traditionally ignored agency problems. New Keynesian theory, a recent development in economic theory seeking to defend Keynesian economics from its New Classical detractors, uses agency-theoretic analysis to provide microfoundations for traditional Keynesian concepts, especially in the area of labour and capital markets. But New Keynesian economics does not provide a structural analysis of the determinants of long-term full employment and economic growth, and it does not address the problem of inducing state actors to make decisions on behalf of the working, consuming and voting public.

The dual agency perspective holds that economies are successful to the extent that they develop political and economic institutions that adjudicate the interests of major economic actors in a manner consistent with the key agency problems of state and private economy.

I suggest three principles of macroeconomic policy flowing from agency-theoretic considerations. The first is reliance on a *public infrastructure/private initiative* conception of long-term economic growth, in which the major role of the state is the financing of investment in social and environmental infrastructure, as well as the promotion of rules ensuring competition, democratic accountability and egalitarian asset distribution in the private sector. This contrasts with the right's contempt for social infrastructure and economic equality, and the left's prejudice against relying heavily on market competition and an independent private sector.

Long-term growth requires a commitment to the development of human, social and environmental resources, and hence to egalitarian social policy, broadly defined. Yet egalitarian programmes, to a greater extent than deemed necessary in the high-growth years following World War II, must be incentive-compatible, in the sense of rewarding only productive economic activity.

Hence the second principle is *asset-based redistribution*, in which egalitarian social policy takes the form of redistributing private assets to the asset poor (e.g. promoting human capital formation, home ownership, community ownership of natural resources, democratically controlled, worker-owned enterprises, and extensive estate taxation) rather than attempting to extend its traditional price, quantity and income instruments (minimum wage, rent control, highly progressive income taxation, international protectionism). The concept of asset-based redistribution flows naturally from an agency-theoretic view of the economy, in that asset redistribution avoids the incentive incompatibilities that arise when implementing redistributive goals involves separating residual claimant status (ownership) and decision-making authority (control).

The third principle is reliance on *incentive-compatible discretionary policy* in which decision makers are subject to incentive-compatible systems of reward and accountability, in place of the unconstrained discretionary policy characteristic of Keynesian and social democratic approaches. The principle of incentive-compatibility in discretionary policy suggests that public services, such as education, health, day care and communication, be provided in a context of competition and performance incentives broadly characteristic of the private sector, and, except in special circumstances, by the private sector itself. Incentive-compatible discretionary policy avoids the problem of mandating that a certain policy be implemented without ensuring that the conditions for its implementation, in terms of the carrots and sticks facing decision makers, exist and are in place. It also locates the source of bureaucratic inefficiency in improper incentive systems and focuses on the transformation of incentive systems in improving the institutional response of public agencies.

Economies develop durable, sophisticated and historically specific institutional forms to resolve the disputes and coordinate the actions of economic agents. The dual agency perspective suggests that a major role of such institutions is the effective resolution of agency problems in state and economy. *Chronic economic problems generally reflect a structural failure in these resolution mechanisms*, rather than the simple mismanagement of macroeconomic policy, as Keynesians of all varieties are predisposed to maintain. Macroeconomic policy thus involves a strong element of *institutional innovation*. Rule-based economic policy, which holds that the government should primarily institute and enforce the long-term rules that empower and constrain economic actors rather than intervening to affect short-run economic outcomes, is motivated in part by the necessity of thinking more clearly about the development of new *rules of the game* rather than new or increasingly empowered *corporate decision making bodies* for public policy.

These policy prescriptions contrast sharply with the approaches favoured by many opponents of conservative and Neo-Keynesian policies: the Nordic social democratic and the Asian corporatist models, which rely on the formally institutionalized power and discretionary intervention of powerful groups (government, labour, industrial capital and/or financial capital) to set major macroeconomic policy variables. Why might a 'rules of the game' approach be preferred to such discretionary systems?

Questions of agency aside, discretion is favoured over rules when purposeful deliberation can produce higher-quality decisions than the rote application of pre-given criteria, because decision criteria are sufficiently complex that valid categorical standards cannot be explicitly formulated. However, policy makers act to achieve their own objectives, subject to the incentives and constraints placed upon them. Thus we should prefer discretion to rules only if such reliable incentives and constraints can be established and enforced.

On general grounds of democratic accountability, where feasible, rules should be preferred to discretion. A rule-based system demands relatively simple incentive systems to ensure its proper operation – general rules of responsibility and criteria of malfeasance tend to suffice. A discretionary system, by contrast, imposes two burdens on the public. The public must be mobilized not only to choose delegated decision makers (e.g. through periodic elections), but also to establish incentives to which such delegates are to be subject. Only if such incentives are well defined (e.g. legislators' pay or tenure is a specific function of the behaviour of economic indicators) is discretion likely to produce publicly desired outcomes.

While a discretionary policy system benefits the groups who control the incentives, it is difficult to develop appropriate incentives for decision makers through a democratic process. Where incentives are weakly defined, special interest groups can impose their own incentives upon decision makers. As Mancur Olson has stressed, such groups tend to be effective in direct proportion to the wealth they control and inversely proportional to their size (Olson, 1975). They are, in short, the elites of political and economic life. Discretionary decision makers of course remain accountable to the public by virtue of the threat of removal from office, but this threat is often weak in face of the influence of such special interests.

Since discretionary economic policy tends to benefit the powerful, it is likely to benefit the public only when the powerful view their own success as predicated on the well-being of society as a whole. One condition under which this would occur is where the public has homogeneous preferences regarding social policy, creating a degree of public agreement that cannot be ignored by public sector decision makers. A second condition involves social elites so powerful that they behave as residual claimants on society, in a context where economic growth opportunities render a smaller part of a growing pie more attractive than a larger part of a stagnant pie. If a significant degree of economic equality fosters rapid economic growth, and I will argue that this is indeed the case, then modernizing elites can use their discretionary power to further the public good.

Both of these conditions are more likely to obtain *the more homogeneous are ethnic, racial and regional groups*. The success of discretionary policies in the corporatist intervention systems of Northern Europe and Asia depends on their extreme degree of social homogeneity in racial, ethnic, cultural and religious terms, and the extent to which they have a relatively small number of hegemonic economic groups. Where such homogeneity is lacking, the development of centralized corporatist institutions that internalize the diverse needs and interests of the public are not likely to occur. In its place arise the corrupt, particularist, predatory governments that are the rule rather than the exception in corporatist intervention systems around the world.

The social democratic model, for instance, has always depended on a unified and hegemonic organization of labour that would be unsustainable and politically infeasible in less culturally homogeneous societies. Moreover, while in the past it was virtually axiomatic that the political base of the left lay in the organization of producers, labour is now, and probably will continue in the future to be, both internally fragmented and only one of several complementary and equally important bases of support for progressive social change, others pursuing the struggle for citizens' rights, community power and environmental integrity, as well as gender, racial, ethnic and national equality (Bowles and Gintis, 1986). Since the political bases of a progressive economic policy are socially or structurally heterogeneous and have diverse interests, and since they tend not to have direct power in the economy, it is likely that a progressive model of corporatist intervention would empower a coalition consisting of an aristocracy of capital and labour that would act more or less the way ruling groups do in the corrupt right-corporatist systems.

This state of affairs is true of the United States, Europe and much of the Third World, where labour is but one of several basic social groups having an independent and at times conflicting interests in progressive macroeconomic policy. Social democratic corporatism is, according to this reasoning, a successful but historically non-generalizable phenomenon. The notion of importing the social democratic model to the rest of the world, then, or copying the conservative interventionist strategies of Asian capitalism with 'labour' as opposed to 'capital' in control, may then be infeasible and undesirable.

CONSERVATIVE MACROECONOMIC THEORY

The conservative policy consensus of the past two decades, encouraged by electoral successes in Europe and the United States, developed in major research universities, and implemented by international lending agencies around the globe, holds that government is the obstacle, not the facilitator, of economic growth, while increased economic equality and democratic accountability are achievable, if at all, only as a by-product of free market competition.

Since intervention in product, financial and labour markets is ineffective, conservative policy makers argue, deregulation and privatization provide potent opportunities for increasing allocational efficiency and restoring productivity growth. Similarly, according to this view, government support of labour and collective bargaining have retarded innovation and raised the rate of unemployment, and should be replaced by measures to foster a 'non-collusive' labour market environment.

There is indeed evidence that conservatives have identified certain key weaknesses of the Keynesian model. The shift in the 1980s to tighter fiscal and monetary policies, and the slowdown in the rate of increase of social spending, contributed to the dramatic reduction in inflation rates and helped to restore profitability in virtually all advanced capitalist countries. In several countries that adopted conservative policies, notably the United Kingdom and New Zealand, during the 1980s dramatic increases in productivity growth also occurred. At the same time, these policies did not generate productivity growth in many other countries.

Moreover, even where these policies were successful, they came at the expense of increases in inequality. For the OECD as a whole, for example, there was a 1.2 per cent increase in the share of the top 20 per cent of the income distribution between the late 1970s and the middle 1980s. In countries where conservative policies were most thoroughly implemented the shift to inequality was even greater: there was a 2 per cent increase in the United States and a 3 per cent increase in the United Kingdom, in the share of the top 20 per cent. In addition, there are reasons to believe that the increases in productivity associated with conservative policies in several countries are not sustainable in the long run, both because they took the form of eliminating antiquated firms rather than promoting new technologies, and because they represent short-run gains ignoring social infrastructure and the environment. Finally, the long-run record of *laissez-faire* policies is not promising. Over the period 1950–90, for example, those among the advanced capitalist countries that pursued the most extreme *laissez-faire* policies tended to have the lowest rates of productivity increases and GDP growth rates.

The weakness of conservative policy is its exaggeration of agency problems in the state, while treating market exchange as an ideal Walrasian system. Three key positions follow from this bias. First, it considers egalitarian policies as inefficient and growth inhibiting. Second, it views the public sector as a drain on investment funds, discouraging private initiative. Third, it argues that since the capitalist economy has an automatic tendency towards full employment, interventionist measures to improve labour market performance are unnecessary.

A considerable body of evidence contradicts these propositions. Concerning the link between inequality and economic performance, international comparative data exhibits no inverse relationship between social indicators of economic equality and rates of growth of output or productivity. Indeed, even the assertion that progressive governments and strong labour organization harm economic performance is not empirically supported.[2]

Finally, the conservative argument that a competitive market system has an automatic tendency to full employment has also not stood up to the empirical evidence (Blinder, 1988; Murphy and Topel, 1987).

NEW KEYNESIAN MACROECONOMICS

Disenchantment with conservative policies is likely to lead to a reassertion of Keynesianism. Indeed, the conceptual and empirical foundations for such a reassertion are already visible (see, for instance, Mankiw and Romer, 1991a). As Alan Blinder has written:

> The ascendancy of new classicism in academia was . . . a triumph of *a priori* theorising over empiricism, of intellectual aesthetics over observation and, in some measure, of conservative ideology over liberalism macroeconomics is already in the midst of another revolution which amounts to a return to Keynesianism – but with a much more rigorous theoretical flavour.
>
> (1988, p. 278)

This confidence, I believe, is unjustified: New Keynesians capably defend their turf in the realm of short-term demand management, but have abandoned their claim to possessing a compelling long-run approach to macroeconomic policy. Yet it is precisely in this area that most pressing macroeconomic problems lie, including growth rates, average rates of factor utilization, and the distribution of income and wealth.

An important example of this 'retreat to the short run' is the abandonment by New Keynesians of the traditional Keynesian notion that proper macroeconomic policy can achieve full employment. In the era after World War II this notion took the form of assuming a stable tradeoff between inflation and unemployment. The inflationary experience of the 1970s decisively discredited this assumption. There is at present no serious critique of the New Classical 'natural rate hypothesis' (Lucas and Sargent, 1978), which holds that approaching zero unemployment necessarily entails runaway inflation, and the 'nature rate of unemployment' towards which an economy should tend, is that at which price stability is assured.

New Keynesians appear to believe that abandoning the commitment to achieving full employment is a minor concession. Blinder characteristically asserts:

> Since about 1972, a Phillips curve that is vertical in the long run has been an integral part of Keynesian economics. So the natural rate hypothesis played essentially no role in the intellectual ferment of the 1972–1985 period.
>
> (1988, p. 281)

It would indeed suffice to know that traditional Keynesian demand management can keep an economy near its natural rate, were this rate really 'natural'. But in view of the fact that the 'natural' rate varies widely across time and space (Bowles, *et al.*, 1990), the Keynesian concession amounts to a serious retreat.[3]

Moreover, there are compelling reasons for believing that the inflation–unemployment tradeoff is not a technical problem, but rather reflects the precise way an economic system resolves the conflict over distributional shares among industrial capital, finance capital and labour.[4]

THE SOCIAL DEMOCRATIC MODEL

It might be argued that Neo-Keynesian short-run macro policy and the apparently successful Northern European social democratic model of long-run growth together form a cogent progressive policy alternative. This argument is strengthened by the Lange–Garrett (1985) analysis demonstrating the general viability of a combination of progressive government and centralized labour organization. Moreover, the successful economic performance of the European countries conforming to the social democratic model is evident (Bowles *et al.*, 1990).

However, for reasons suggested above this model may not be generalizable. Indeed, social democracy appears to be declining even in the countries where it has been historically most successful. Thus even such sympathetic social scientists as Moene and Wallerstein (1991) report that '[T]he social democratic model of industrial relations... has completely disappeared in Sweden.' The bargaining environment has become decentralized, the dynamics of wage inflation now approximate that of the more traditional advanced capitalist economies, and even the last social democratic government announced its intention to use a policy of monetary austerity to discipline the labour market.

This decline in social democracy is probably due to the infeasibility of centralized economic coordination intervention in a heterogeneous, multicentred economic context (Moene and Wallerstein, 1991). The unity of the labour movement in social democratic countries has been based on a degree of ethnic and social class homogeneity that is breaking down under the pressure of increasing labour force differentiation and expanded international labour migration. Perhaps more important, the integration of the Nordic countries in the European Community, with its multiculturalism, heterogeneous labour and capital organizations, and multiplicity of local centres of economic power, precludes the corporatist planning that is key to social democratic success. The notion that social policy can be implemented by representatives of the major interest groups sitting down at a table and 'working it out' is increasingly unrealistic and untenable. A rule of law must replace a rule of persons.

It is important, then, to explore new avenues for progressive economic policy. The 'dual agency' approach to economic policy captures the valid insights of older approaches, while avoiding some of their more obvious shortcomings.

THE AGENCY-THEORETIC MODEL OF INDIVIDUAL ACTION

The central character of the agency model of individual action flows from dropping what I term the *integrity principle*: the assumption of traditional social theory (economics included) that among the constraints on individual behaviour is the *obligation to keep promises, honour agreements and conform to accepted social norms*. By contrast, agency theory models agents as treating laws, agreements and social norms as obstacles to and tools for the achievement of their personal (not necessarily selfish) goals. Possessing proper *personal values* is not sufficient; we expect agents to fulfil their roles only when they are exposed to proper *social incentives*. Thus where the integrity principle assumes that information is passed among agents according to moral and scientific conceptions of veracity and truth, in fact agents tend to pass information to one another best to achieve their personal goals subject of course to whatever constraints are imposed by society and their own ethical standards.

If this description of the integrity principle seems to set up a straw man, consider the traditional theory of socialist planning. In the state socialist economy, planners are expected to act in the public interest, managers are expected to innovate and produce efficiently, and workers are expected to do their best on behalf of the enterprise and in the larger interest of society.

When asked, planners are supposed to reveal their actions and intentions to government authority, managers are supposed to divulge the true conditions of production and opportunities for innovation, and workers are supposed to reveal both the actions they have taken and the personal goals which motivate their choices. Were the integrity principle correct, and in the presence of the proper system of laws, regulations and internal checks and balances, this might be sufficient to ensure the accountability of economic agents. But it is not.

PUBLIC AGENCY, THE STATE AND ECONOMIC POLICY

We may analyse the state as a principal–agent problem in which the public is the principal and state officials are the agents responsible for implementing collective established objectives. Since the public cannot write contracts dictating precisely their proper behaviour, public servants must be exposed to incentives that elicit this behaviour. The central incentive in such cases is *contingent renewal*: holders of political and administrative office are given high salaries and perks, with the threat of their withdrawal in case they do not 'deliver the goods'.[5] As conservative policy analysis has traditionally stressed, this incentive mechanism is in many key cases insufficient to ensure compliance with the public mandate.

Contingent renewal in the public sector, however is relatively ineffective because it is difficult to measure the quality of the public servants' behaviour, and to ensure that they remain subject to incentives compatible with the execution of their duties. The first of these difficulties is common to all situations in which the agent's behaviour cannot be assessed by the agent's *inputs* (e.g. hours worked, energy expended, ulcers contracted) but only by the agent's *outputs* (number of widgets produced, level of nuclear safety achieved). Where an objective standard for and acceptable level of output is not available, which will generally be the case, the most effective way to assess an agent's output is often to subject several agents to the same incentives under conditions preventing collusion among the agents, using the results to reward their relative performance and set the standard for future performance. In short, *contingent renewal in the public sector is ineffective when the state holds a monopolistic position in the production of the relevant goods and services.*[6] As a result the electoral success of public officials depends only weakly on their performance, administrators are sheltered from all but the most egregious performance-related dismissal, and public enterprises normally face 'soft budget constraints' (Kornai, 1986).

The second reason for the difficulty in instituting efficient incentives is that particular groups with an especially strong stake in the public agent's decisions have an interest in constituting alternative incentives to influence the public agent's behaviour (e.g. electoral contributions, promise of lucrative private sector employment, bribes and threats). Moreover, in general only small and influential groups (such as organized business and labour lobbies) are likely to have the long-term interest and means to impose such alternative incentives (Olson, 1975). The rent-seeking behaviour of such special interest groups then tends to replace socially desirable mechanisms with others that favour whatever groups currently have access to positions of political power. Hence government failure, like market failure, is the rule rather than the exception.

AGENCY AND POWER IN THE MARKET ECONOMY

Traditional economics assumes that market exchanges consist of legally enforceable contracts. Where writing such a contract is impossible or excessively costly, an agency problem exists, in which the *de facto* terms of an exchange result in part from endogenous claim enforcement: the parties to the exchange themselves adopt sanctions, surveillance and other strategic enforcement activities to improve their exchange position. I term such a transaction a *contested exchange*.[7]

The two most important contested exchanges involve labour, in which a wage is exchanged for a promise to work faithfully on behalf of the enterprise, and capital, in which funds today are exchanged for the promise of repaying a larger amount in the future. Since the worker's promise cannot generally be enforced by the state or other third party, it must be enforced by whatever system of control the enterprise may devise. Similarly, since the promise to repay can be enforced only for fully collateralized loans (and not at all for equity transactions), the lender must devise incentive mechanisms and forms of private enforcement that induce borrowers to act in a manner consistent with the lender's interests.

The dual agency approach provides insights into the political economy of macroeconomic policy that escape the more traditional classical and Keynesian approaches. Most important, it supports the interpretation of liberal Keynesian policy as fundamentally supportive of labour, both by its commitment to maintaining a low unemployment rate and to providing high levels of social and unemployment insurance (Bowles and Gintis, 1982, 1986).[8]

Moreover, it argues that the 'missing variable' underlying the wage elasticity of unemployment is the cost of job loss, and thus explains the shift of the Phillips curve over time and across countries in terms of differences in the institutional conditions affecting the cost of job loss (Bowles *et al.*, 1990). It thus explains the ability of Nordic social democracy to achieve very low unemployment rates: centralized wage policies and non-dismissal-based labour discipline institutions detach the cost of job loss from labour productivity and wage inflation (Green and Weisskopf, 1990).

Keynesian theory, while affirming the failures of competitive markets, has not integrated an endogenous enforcement analysis of labour and capital markets into its framework. This accounts for its unwillingness to recognize its *parti pris* in the political economy of contemporary capitalism, and hence its underestimation of the structural impediments to the deployment of Keynesian policy, as well as its excessive faith in the ability of the government, with little structural innovation, to produce full employment through demand management, and to generate an acceptable rate of growth of income and productivity.

ASSET-BASED REDISTRIBUTION

Asset-based redistributions conform to an important agency principle: where the contribution of one party to a market exchange is difficult to monitor, residual claimancy and control should *ceteris paribus* reside with this party. Where the transaction involves the exchange of an easy-to-monitor claim (e.g. money) for a difficult-to-monitor service (e.g. labour or entrepreneurial initiative) the party supplying the latter service should, on efficiency grounds, be the residual claimant. On these grounds, there is a prima facie case for individuals to own and control their human capital, for families to own and control their homes, and for workers to own and control the firms in which they are employed.

In traditional economic models, no such presumption exists. According to the famous fundamental theorem of welfare economics, any attainable distribution of welfare can be achieved by an initial lump sum redistribution of assets, followed by competitive exchange. The problem with the fundamental theorem is that the lump sum redistribution of *ownership* rights in a productive asset (raw materials inputs, physical and human capital, talent) has strong implications for the assignment of *control* rights in this factor. I shall give several examples.

The skill and talents of a worker can be easily assigned to another person. But why in this situation, given the contested nature of the labour market, why should the worker, who directly *controls* this skill and talent, actually work?[9] The asset-based approach suggests in this case that redistribution costs can be reduced by stressing an egalitarian distribution of human capital through a public commitment to universal education, training, and basic health and nutrition. This conclusion is of course not controversial, although its agency-theoretic basis is normally not stressed.

The difficulty of separating ownership and control in housing assets is considerably less severe, but still significant. The exchange between landlord and tenant is a contested exchange because the obligation of the tenant to maintain and improve the capital value of the asset cannot be contractually specified. In particular, improvements by tenants, both through individual and community initiative, benefit the landlord, and hence are not generally undertaken. Traditional public programmes promoting affordable housing, which have stressed rent control, subsidies to the construction of low-rental housing, and public housing, thus tend to have high costs of implementation and generally unsatisfactory results. The asset-based redistribution approach suggests that the asset rather than its service be redistributed; reliance on such traditional public programmes would be reduced in favour of providing widespread financial opportunities for home ownership.

A final example is financial assets, especially claims on the profits of enterprise. The efficiency of a Walrasian economy is independent of the distribution of these claims, since competition forces firms to maximize profits, factors of production (including physical capital) are rented at a competitive rate, and the expected value of the residual is zero. In real market economies, by contrast, the contested character of credit markets implies that the link between residual claimancy and control of the firm cannot be arbitrarily ruptured. Indeed, firms in capitalist economies are generally controlled by agents with residual claims to the profits of the enterprise (through ownership or managerial incentives) or who hold their positions only with the approval of owners and creditors.

Agency problems are thus at the root of the difficulty in redistributing financial assets. When ownership is transferred away from agents who monitor and control the enterprise, control must also be relocated or the mechanisms that induce firms to produce and invest efficiently will become inoperative. The communist regimes in the former Soviet Union and Eastern Europe foundered on this issue, failing to institute efficient non-capitalist forms of enterprise control. But the issue is no less valid when applied to the taxation of wealth in the capitalist countries: high tax rates on wealth are incentive incompatible with control of investment and production.

The most natural solution from the asset-based redistribution perspective is to link the redistribution of wealth to a redistribution of control of the enterprise to workers. The worker-controlled enterprise is attractive on grounds of democratic accountability: as a contested exchange, the employment relationship involves the exercise of power; hence its governance ought to be accountable to its membership. Of course, no more than in the capitalist case can the ownership and control of democratic firms be arbitrarily ruptured. Thus a prerequisite for the democratic firm's efficient operation is that its membership enjoy significant residual claimancy status: worker control requires a significant degree of worker ownership. Indeed, a key attraction of workplace democracy is its capacity to coordinate a redistribution of economic power and a redistribution of wealth in a potentially incentive-compatible manner (Bowles and Gintis, 1993).

Whereas the previous examples of asset-based redistribution clearly accord with the principle of locating residual claimancy with the difficult-to-monitor service, the case of the democratic firm is more problematic. It is true that labour services in the enterprise are typically more difficult to monitor than other inputs. The capitalist firm, which allocates residual claimancy to the most easily monitored input of all (financial capital), is thus *ceteris paribus* inferior to a firm in which residual claimancy is allocated to those who participate directly in the firm's production and investment activities.

The efficiency gains associated with the democratic firm arise from a correct social accounting of the costs of regulating the intensity of labour and consequently an optimal mix of monitoring costs and wage incentives, an increased effectiveness of monitoring due to the incentive for workers to report private information on the activities of their fellow workers, and improved incentive compatibility concerning the intensity of labour (ibid.). There is evidence that such efficiency gains exist (e.g. Weitzman and Kruse, 1990). In response to the argument that such firms, were they efficient, would emerge autonomously in a competitive capitalist framework, I note that contested exchange models of capital markets attribute the bias against democratic firms to wealth constraints faced by workers and the difficulty of passive investors controlling the behaviour of democratic majorities (Gintis, 1989b).

The general presumption in favour of the efficiency of the democratic firm does not extend, however, to one key area of enterprise performance: optimal risk taking. While it is socially optimal that firms act risk neutrally, economic agents tend to be risk-averse, and more so the larger the portion of their wealth involved in a particular project. Capitalist firms mitigate this problem by being controlled by wealthy and hence relatively less risk-averse agents, and by being financed through relatively risk-neutral institutions, such as stock markets, that induce firms to innovate and take risks.

In a purely worker-owned democratic firm, members are neither wealthy nor compelled by outside interests to take risks. They can thus be expected to engage in a socially sub-optimal level of risk taking and innovation.[10] Indeed, since workers earn employment rents, they incur additional costs of failure (the loss of job rents) not imposed on their capitalist counterparts, thus inducing even more risk-averse behaviour on democratic firms (Gintis, 1989a). It follows that the optimal ownership structure of the democratic firm, taking account of the tendency of external ownership to promote innovation and risk taking, and of worker ownership to promote productive efficiency, involves a balance of internal and external residual claimancy and control.

NOTES

1 The arguments in this chapter are adapted from Epstein and Gintis (1995).
2 Lange and Garrett (1985) and Persson and Tabellini (1991) find that inequality and GDP growth are *inversely* related.
3 Keynesians have carefully documented the tendency for the long-run natural rate to differ across countries and to have strong structural elements (Blanchard and Summers, 1986). But there is no Keynesian policy corresponding to this appreciation.
4 For theoretical and empirical treatments along these lines, see Bowles and Gintis (1982) and Epstein (1991).
5 Other enforcement mechanisms have been tried sporadically (e.g. executing, or tar and feathering, unpopular politicians and their families), but these have been found ineffective or otherwise undesirable.
6 Of course, when public organizations are compelled to compete with private counterparts, accountability can be secured through contingent renewal (e.g. the coexistence of private and public hospitals).
7 The term is from Bowles and Gintis (1990).
8 For additional support, see Haveman (1978), Sachs (1980) and Schultze (1981).
9 The taxation of worker earnings is, of course, a partial redistribution of ownership rights, and implies similar redistribution costs at sufficiently high tax rates.
10 Of course there is no presumption that the level of risk taking in capitalist firms is optimal. Managerial control can lead to insufficient risk taking, and bank finance can entail excessive risk taking.

BIBLIOGRAPHY

Aftalion, A. (1913) *Les Crises Periodiques De Surproduction*, 2 vols, Paris: Riviere.

Akerlof, G. (1970) 'The Market for Lemons: Quality Uncertainty and the Market Mechanism', *Quarterly Journal of Economics*, 84 (August), pp. 488–500.

—— (1971) 'The Market for "Lemons": Qualitative Uncertainty and the Marhet Mechanism', *Quarterly Journal of Economics*, 84, 448–50.

—— (1980) 'A Theory of Social Custom, of which Unemployment may be One Consequence', *Quarterly Journal of Economics*, 94 (June), pp. 749–75.

—— (1982) 'Labor Contracts as Partial Gift Exchange', *Quarterly Journal of Economics*, 97 (November), pp. 543–69.

—— (1984a) *An Economic Theorist's Book of Tales*, Cambridge: Cambridge University Press.

—— (1984b) 'Gift Exchange and Efficiency Wage Theory: Four Views', *American Economic Review*, Papers and Proceedings, 74 (May), pp. 79–83.

—— (1985a) 'Can Small Deviations from Rationality Make Significant Differences to Economic Equilibria?', *American Economic Review*, September, pp. 708–21.

Akerlof, G. and Yellen, J. L. (1985) 'A Near Rational Model of Business Cycle, with Wages and Price Inertia', *Quarterly Journal of Economics*, 100, pp. 823–38.

—— —— (eds) (1986) 'Introduction', *Efficiency Wage Models of the Labor Market*, New York: Cambridge University Press, pp. 1–21.

—— —— (1987) 'Rational Models of Irrational Behavior', *American Economic Review, Papers and Proceedings*, 77 (May), pp. 137–42.

Alchian, A. and Demsetz, H. (1972) 'Production, Information Costs, and Economic Organization', *American Economic Review*, December, pp. 777–95.

Allais, M. and Hagen, O. (eds) (1979) 'The Foundations of a Positive Theory of Choice Involving Risk and a Criticism of the Postulates and Axioms of the American School', *Expected Utility Hypotheses and the Allais Paradox*, Dordrecht: Reidel.

Allen, P. M. (1994) 'Evolutionary Complex Systems: Models of Technology Change', in L. Leydesdorff and P. Van den Besselaar (eds) *Evolutionary Economics and Chaos Theory: New Directions in Technology Studies*, New York: St Martin's Press, pp. 1–17.

Alogoskoufis, G. and Smith, R. (1991) 'On Error-Correction Models Specification, Interpretation, Estimation', *Journal of Economic Surveys*, pp. 1–32.

Altman, M. (1992) 'Business Cycle Volatility in Developed Market Economies, 1870–1986: Revisions and Conclusions', *Eastern Economic Journal*, 18(3), pp. 259–75.

Amadeo, E. J. (1989) *Keynes's Principle of Effective Demand*, Aldershot: Edward Elgar.

Arestis, P. (1986) 'Wages and Prices in the UK', *Journal of Post Keynesian Economics*, pp. 339–58.

—— (ed.) (1988) 'Post-Keynesian Theory of Money, Credit and Finance', *Post-Keynesian Monetary Economics: New Approaches to Financial Modelling*, Aldershot: Edward Elgar, pp. 41–71.

—— (1992) *The Post-Keynesian Approach to Economics*, Aldershot: Edward Elgar.

—— (1996a) 'Post Keynesian Economics: Towards Coherence', *Cambridge Journal of Economics*, January, pp. 111–35.

—— (1996b) *Money, Pricing, Distribution and Economic Integration*, London: Macmillan.

Arestis, P. and Biefang-Frisancho Mariscal, I. (1994) 'Wage Determination in the UK: Further Empirical Results Using Cointegration', *Applied Economics*, pp. 417–27.

Arestis, P. and Chick, V. (eds) (1992) *Recent Developments in Post-Keynesian Economics*, Aldershot: Edward Elgar.

Arestis, P. and Skott, P. (1993) 'Conflict, Wage Determination, and Hysteresis in U.K. Wage Determination', *Journal of Post Keynesian Economics*, 15, pp. 365–86.

Argyrous, G. (1991) 'Investment, Demand and Technological Change: Transformational Growth and the State in America During World War II', Ph.D. Dissertation, New School for Social Research, New York.

Arnold, V. I. (1986) *Catastrophe Theory*, 2nd edn, Berlin: Springer-Verlag.

Arrow, K. S. and Hahn, F. R. (1971) *General Competitive Analysis*, San Francisco: Holden-Day.

Arthur, B. (1988) 'Self-Reinforcing Mechanisms in Economics', in P. W. Anderson, K. J. Arrow and D. Pines (eds) *The Economy as an Evolving Complex System*, Redwood City, CA: Addison-Wesley, pp. 9–32.

—— (1994) *Increasing Returns and Path Dependence in the Economy*, Ann Arbor: Michigan University Press.

Atiyah, P. S. (1979) *The Rise and Fall of Freedom of Contract*, Oxford: Clarendon Press.

Atkinson, A. B. and Micklewright, J. (1991) 'Unemployment Compensation and Labour Market Transitions: A Critical Review', *Journal of Economic Literature*, pp. 1679–1727.

Azariadis, C. (1975) 'Implicit Contracts and Underemployment Equilibria', *Journal of Political Economy*, 83, pp. 1183–1202.

—— (1981) 'Self Fulfilling Prophecies', *Journal of Economic Theory*, 25, pp. 380–96.

—— (1993) *Intertemporal Macroeconomics*, Oxford: Blackwell.

Azariadis, C. and Guesnerie, R. (1986) 'Sunspots and Cycles', *Review of Economic Studies*, 53, pp. 725–36.

Azariadis, C. and Stigltiz, J. E. (1983) 'Implicit Contracts and Fixed-Price Equilibria', *Quarterly Journal of Economics*, 98, pp. 1–22.

Baily, M. N. (1974) 'Wages and Unemployment Under Uncertain Demand', *Review of Economic Studies*, 41, pp. 37–50.

Bak, P., Chen, K., Scheinkman, J. and Woodford, M. (1993) 'Aggregate Fluctuations from Independent Sectoral Shocks: Self-Organized Criticality in a Model of Production and Inventory Dynamics', *Ricerche Economiche*, 47, pp. 3–30.

Balke, N. S. and Gordon, R. J. (1989), 'The Estimation of Prewar National Product: Methodology and New Evidence', *Journal of Political Economy*, 97, pp. 38–92.

Ball, L. (1991) 'Sticky Prices as Coordination Failure', *American Economic Review*, June.

Ball, L. and Mankiw, N. G. (1994) 'Asymmetric Price Adjustment and Economic Fluctuations', *Economic Journal*, March, pp. 247–61.

Ball, L. and Romer, D. (1989) 'Are Prices Too Sticky?', *Quarterly Journal of Economics*, August, pp. 507–24.

—— —— (1990) 'Real Rigidities and the Non-Neutrality of Money', *Review of Economic Studies*, vol. 59.

—— —— and Romer, D. (1991) 'Sticky Prices as Coordination Failure', *American Economic Review*, June.

Ball, L., Mankiw, G. and Romer, D. (1991) 'The New Keynesian Economics and the Output-Inflation Trade-Off', in Gregory Mankiw and David Romer (eds) *New Keynesian Economics*, vol. I, Cambridge, MA: MIT Press, pp. 147–211.

Balls, E. (1994) 'No More Jobs for the Boys', in J. Michie and J. Grieve Smoth (eds) *Unemployment in Europe*, London: Academic Press.

Baran, P. and Sweezy, P. (1966) *Monopoly Capital*, New York: Monthly Review Press.

Barens, I. (1990) 'The Rise and Fall of the "Entrepreneur Economy": Some Remarks on Keynes's Taxonomy of Economies', in D. Moggridge (ed.) *Perspectives on the History of Economic Thought*, vol. IV, Aldershot: Edward Elgar.

Barnett, W. A., Geweke, J. and Shell, K. (1989) *Economic Complexity: Chaos, Sunspots, Bubbles and Nonlinearity*, New York: Cambridge University Press.

Barro, R. and Grossman, H. (1976) *Money, Employment, and Inflation*, Cambridge: Cambridge University Press.

Barth, J., Brumbaugh, D. and Litan, R. (1992) *The Future of American Banking*, Armonk, NY: Sharpe.

Basile, L. and Salvadori, N. (1984–5) 'Kalecki's Pricing Theory', *Journal of Post Keynesian Economics*, Winter, pp. 249–62.

Beatson, M. (1995a) 'Progress Towards a More Flexible Labour Market', *Employment Gazette*, February.

—— (1995b) 'Labour Market Flexibility', *Employment Department Research Series*, no. 48, April.

Beaud, M. and Dostaler, G. (1993) *La Pensée Economique depuis Keynes*, Paris: Editions du Seuil.

Becker, G. S. (1976) *The Economic Approach to Human Behavior*, Chicago: University of Chicago Press.

Benhabib, J. and Day, R. H. (1982) 'Characterization of Erratic Dynamics in the Overlapping Generations Model', *Journal of Economic Dynamics and Control*, 4, pp. 37–55.

Bentham, J. (1793) *A Manual of Political Economy*, in Bowring (ed.) *Works of J. Bentham.*

Benzion, U., Rapoport, A., and Yagil, J. (1989) 'Discount Rates Inferred from Decisions: An Experimental Study', *Management Science*, 35, pp. 270–84.

Bernanke, B. S. (1983a) 'Irreversibility, Uncertainty and Cyclical Investment', *Quarterly Journal of Economics*, 98, pp. 85–106.

—— (1983b) 'Nonmonetary Effects of the Financial Crisis in the Propagation of the Great Depression', *American Economic Review*, 73(3), pp. 257–76.

—— (1991) 'Nonmonetary Effects of the Financial Crisis in the Propagation of the Great Depression', in Gregory Mankiw and David Romer (eds), *New Keyensian Economics*, vol. II, Cambridge, MA: MIT Press, pp. 293–322.

—— (1993) 'Credit in the Macroeconomy', *Federal Reserve Bank of New York Quarterly Review*, 18, pp. 50–70.

Bernanke, B.S. and Blinder A.S. (1988) 'Credit, Money, and Aggregate Demand', *American Economic Review*, 78, pp. 435–9, reprinted in Romer and Mankiw (1991), vol II, pp 325–35.

—— and Gertler, M. (1990) 'Financial Fragility and Economic Performance', *Quarterly Journal of Economics*, 105, pp. 87–114.

Bertolila, S and Dolado, J. J. (1994) 'Labour flexibility and wages lessons from Spain', *Economic Policy*, no. 18, pp. 53–85.

Bhaduri, A. and Harris, D. J. (1987) 'The Complex Dynamics of the Simple Ricardian System', *Quarterly Journal of Economics*, 102, pp. 893–901.

Blanchard, O. J. (1983) 'Price Asynchronization and Price Level Inertia', in R. Dornbusch and M. H. Simonsen (eds) *Inflation, Debt, and Indexation*, Cambridge, MA: MIT Press, pp. 3–24.

—— (1990) 'Why Does Money Affect Output? A Survey', in B. M. Friedman and F. Hahn (eds) *Handbook of Monetary Economics*, vol. 2, Amsterdam: Elsevier, pp. 779–835.

Blanchard, O.J. and Diamond, P. (1990) 'Unemployment and Hysteresis', *Pamphlet of the Employment Institute.*

Blanchard, O.J. and Fischer, S. (1989) *Lectures on Macroeconomics*, Cambridge, MA: MIT Press.

Blanchard, O.J. and Kiyotaki, N. (1987) 'Monopolistic Competition and the Effect on Aggregate Demand', in *American Economic Review*, 77, pp. 647–66.

Blanchard, O.J. and Summers, L. (1986) 'Hysteresis and the European Unemployment Problem', in S. Fischer (ed.) *NBER Macroeconomics Annual 1*, Cambridge: MIT Press, pp. 15–77.

—— —— (1987) 'Hysteresis in Unemployment', *European Economic Review*, pp. 288–95.

Blatt, J. M. (1983) *Dynamic Economic Systems: A Post-Keynesian Approach*, Armonk, NY: Sharpe.

Blaug, M. (1994) 'Recent Biographies of Keynes', *Journal of Economic Literature*, 32, 1204–15.

Blinder, A. (1987) 'Credit Rationing and Effective Supply Failures', *Economic Journal*, 97 (June), pp. 327–52.

—— (1988) 'The Fall and Rise of Keynesian Economics', *Economic Record* , December, pp. 278–94.

—— (1989) *Microeconomics Under Debate*, Ann Arbor: University of Michigan Press.

—— (1991) 'Why Are Prices Sticky? Preliminary Results from an Interview Study', *American Economic Review*, May, pp. 89–96.

Blinder, A. and Maccini, L. J. (1991) 'Taking Stock: A Critical' Assessment of Recent Research on Inventories', *Journal of Economic Perspectives*, Winter, pp. 73–96.

Blinder, A. and Stiglitz, J. (1983) 'Money, Credit Constraints and Economic Activity', *American Economic Review, Papers and Proceedings*, 73, pp. 297–302.

Blinder, A. and Woodford, M. (1990) 'Equilibrium Models Displaying Endogenous Fluctuations and Chaos: A Survey', *Journal of Monetary Economics*, 25, pp. 189–222.

Block, T. (1997) 'Prices vs. Output Adjustments: A Study of the Changing Nature of the Business Cycle in Germany, 1871–1909', in E. J. Nell *et al.* (eds) *Transformational Growth and the Business Cycle*, London: Routledge.

Blöndel, S. and Pearson, M. (1995) 'Unemployment and Other Non-employment Benefits', *Oxford Review of Economic Policy*, vol. 11.

Bloomfield, A. I. (1959) *Monetary Policy Under the International Gold Standard: 1880–1914*, New York: Federal Reserve Bank of New York.

Boldrin, M. and Montrucchio, L. (1986) 'On the Indeterminacy of Capital Accumulation Paths', *Journal of Economic Theory*, 40, pp. 26–39.

Bourgeois, L. (1896) *Solidarité*, Paris: Armand Colin, 3rd edn 1902.

Bourgeois, L. and Croiset, A. (eds) (1907) *Essai d'une Philosophie de la Solidarité: Conférences et Discussions*, 2nd edn, Paris: Félix Alcan.

Bowles, S. (1985) 'The Production Process in a Competitive Economy: Walrasian, Neo-Hobbesian, and Marxian Models', *American Economic Review*, 75 (March), pp. 16–36.

Bowles, S. and Boyer, R. (1988) 'Labour Discipline and Aggregate Demand: A Macroeconomic Model', *American Economic Review*, May, pp. 395–400.

Bowles, S. and Gintis, H. (1982) 'The Crisis of Liberal Democratic Capitalism', *Politics and Society*, 11, pp. 51–93.

—— —— (1986) *Democracy and Capitalism: Property, Community, and the Contradictions of Modern Social Thought*, New York: Basic Books.

—— —— (1990) 'Contested Exchange: New Microfoundations of the Political Economy of Capitalism', *Politics and Society*, 18, pp. 165–222.

—— —— (1993) 'The Democratic Firm: An Agency-Theoretic Evaluation', in Samuel Bowles, Herbert Gintis and Bo Gustafsson (eds) *Democracy and Markets: Participation, Accountability, and Efficiency*, Cambridge: Cambridge University Press.

Bowles, S., Gordon, D. and Weisskopf, T. (1990) *After the Waste Land: A Democratic Economics for the Year 2000*, Armonk, NY: Sharpe.

Brock, W. A. (1993) 'Pathways to Randomness in the Economy: Emergent Nonlinearity and Chaos in Economics and Finance', *Estudios Economicos*, 8, 3–55.

Brock, W.A. and Hommes, C. H. (1995) 'Rational Routes to Randomness', *SSRI Working Paper*, no. 9506, University of Wisconsin–Madison.

Brown-Collier, E. K. and Collier, B. E. (1995) 'What Keynes Really Said About Deficit Spending', *Journal of Post Keynesian Economics*, vol. 17.

Bryant, J. (1983) 'A Simple Rational-Expectations Keynes-Type Model', *Quarterly Journal of Economics*, vol. 98.

Bryant, R. C. (1988) *Empirical Macroeconomics for Interdependent Economies*, Washington, DC: Brookings Institute.

Burnell, S. (1989) 'Sunspots', in F. H. Hahn (ed.) *The Economics of Missing Markets, Information and Games*, Oxford: Clarendon Press.

Cable, J. (1985) 'Capital Market Information and Industrial Performance', *Economic Journal*, 95 (March), pp. 118–32.

Calomiris, C., Kahn, C. and Longofer, S. (1994) 'Housing-Finance Intervention and Private Incentives: Helping Minorities and the Poor', *Journal of Money, Credit, and Banking*, 26, Part 2, pp. 634–74.

Canova, F. (1991) *Detrending and Business Cycle Facts*, Badia Fiesolana: European University Institute.

Caplin, A. S. and Spulber, D. (1987) 'Menu Costs and the Neutrality of Money', *Quarterly Journal of Economics*, November, pp. 703–25.

Carabelli, A. (1988) *On Keynes's Method*, New York: St Martins Press.

Caravale, G. (1982) 'Redditi – Politica dei', in *Enciclopedia Italiana*, Appendice IV.

—— (1991) 'Le prospettive per l'occupazione in Europa dopo il 1992', *Rivista di Politica Economica*, maggio.

—— (1992a) 'The Notion of Equilibrium in Economic Theorizing', in *Atlantic Economic Journal*, 20(1), March.

—— (1992b) 'Alcune Considerazioni sulla nozione di Equilibrio nella Teoria Economica', *Studi Economici*, no. 47.

—— (1992c) 'Keynes and the Concept of Equilibrium', in M. Sebastiani (ed.) *The Notion of Equilibrium in Keynesian Economics*, London, Macmillan.

—— (1994) 'Prices and Quantities: Walras, Sraffa and Beyond', in *Studi Economici*, no. 52.

Card, D. and Krueger, A. (1995) *The New Economics of the Minimum Wage*, Princeton, NJ: Princeton University Press.

Carrier, D. (1993) 'Will Chaos Kill the Auctioneer?', *Review of Political Economy*, 5, pp. 299–320.

Carus-Wilson, F. M. (1952) 'The Woollen Industry', *Cambridge Economic History of Europe*.

—— (1954a) 'An Industrial Revolution of the Thirteenth Century', *European Economic History*.

—— (1954b) 'Evidences of Industrial Growth on Some Fifteenth Century Manors', *European Economic History*.

Carruth, A. and Oswald, A. (1987) 'Wage Inflexibility in Britain', *Oxford Bulletin of Economics and Statistics*, pp. 59–78.

Carson, J. (1994) 'Existence and Uniqueness of Solutions to Kalecki's Pricing Equations', *Journal of Post Keynesian Economics*, 16, pp. 411–34.

Cass, D. and Shell, K. (1983) 'Do Sunspots Matter?', *Journal of Political Economy*, 91, pp. 193–227.

Champernowne, David (1963) 'Expectations and the Links Between the Economic Future and the Present', in R. Lekachman (ed.) *Keynes' General Theory: Reports of Three Decades*, London: Macmillan.

Chandler, A. D. Jr., (1977) *The Visible Hand: The Managerial Revolution in American Business*, Cambridge, MA: Belknap Press of Harvard.

—— (1990) *Scale and Scope: The Dynamics of Industrial Capitalism*, Cambridge, MA: Belknap Press of Harvard.

Chick, V. (1983) *Macroeconomics After Keynes*, Oxford: Philip Allan.

—— (1995) 'Is There a Case for Post Keynesian Economics?', *Scottish Journal of Political Economy*, February, pp. 20–36.

Clark, K. B. and Summers, L. H. (1982) 'Labour Force Participation: Timing and Persistence', *Review of Economic Studies*, 69, pp. 825–44.

Clements, M. P. and Mizon, G. E. (1991) 'Empirical Analysis of Macroeconomic Time Series', *European Economic Review*, pp. 887–932.

Clower, R. (1965) 'The Keynesian Counterrevolution: A Theoretical Appraisal', in F. H. Hahn and F. P. R. Brechling (eds) *The Theory of Interest Rates*, London: Macmillan.

CNEL (Consiglio Nazionale dell Economia e del Lavoro) (1993) *La Politica dei Redditi tra Impegni del Governo e Concertazione con le parti Sociali*, Roma.

Coase, R. (1988) *The Firm, the Market and the Law*, Chicago: University of Chicago Press.
Colander, D. (1986) *Macroeconomics*, Glenview, IL: Scott Foresman.
——(1992a) 'A Real Theory of Inflation', *American Economic Review*, May.
——(1992b) 'The New, the Neo and the New Neo', *Methodus*, 4, pp. 166–70.
——(1992c) 'New Keynesian Economics in Perspective', *Eastern Economic Journal*, Fall, pp. 438–48.
——(1994a) 'The Macrofoundations of Microeconomics', *Eastern Economic Journal*, 19, 447–58.
——(1994b) 'Economists, Institutions and Change', in Mario Rizzo (ed.) *Advances in Austrian Economics*, Greenmile, CT: JAI Press.
——(1995) 'Marshallian General Equilibrium', *Eastern Economic Journal*, Fall.
——(1996) (ed.) *Beyond Microfoundations: Post Walrasian Macroeconomics*, Cambridge: Cambridge University Press.
Colander, D. and Koford, K. (1985) 'Externalities and Macroeconomic Policy', in Shlomo Maital and Irwin Kipnowski (eds) *Macroeconomic Conflict and Social Institutions*, Boston: Ballinger.
Cooper, R. and Ejarque, J. (1995) 'Financial Intermediation and the Great Depression: A Multiple Equilibrium Interpretation', *NBER Working Paper*, no. 5130.
Cooper, R. and John, A. (1988) 'Coordinating Coordination Failures in Keynesian Models', *Quarterly Journal of Economics*, August, pp. 441–63. Reprinted in Mankiw and Romer (1991), vol. II, pp. 3–24.
Cottrell, A. (1994) 'Post-Keynesian Monetary Economics', *Cambridge Journal of Economics*, 18, pp. 587–605.
Coutts, K., Godley, W. and Nordhaus, W. (1978) *Industrial Pricing in the United Kingdom*, Cambridge: Cambridge University Press.
Cross, R. (1987) 'Hysteresis and Instability in the Natural Rate of Unemployment', *Scandinavian Journal of Economics*, 89, pp. 71–89.
——(1993) 'Hysteresis and Post Keynesian Economics', *Journal of Post Keynesian Economics*, 15, pp. 305–8.
Currie, M. and Steedman, I. (1993) 'Taking Effort Seriously', *Metroeconomica*, 44, pp. 134–45.
Dana, R. A. and Malgrange, P. (1984) 'The Dynamics of a Discrete Version of Growth Model', in J. P. Ancot (ed) *Analysing the Structure of Econometric Models*, Boston: Martinus Nijhoff, pp. 115–42.
D'Antoma, M. (1993) 'Il protocollo sul costo del lavoro e l''autunno freddo' dell'occupazione', *Rivista Italiana di Diritto del Lavoro*, Parte I.
Darity, W. (1985) 'Loan Pushing: Doctrine and Theory', *International Finance Discussion Paper*, Board of Governors of the Federal Reserve, Washington, DC.
Darity, W. and Horn, B. L. (1993) 'Rational Expectations, Rational Belief and Keynes's General Theory', in W. J. Samuels and J. Biddle (eds) *Research in the History of Economic Thought and Methodology*, 11, pp. 14–47.
Davidson, P. (1967) 'A Keynesian View of Patinkin's Theory of Employment', *Economic Journal*, vol. 77, pp. 559–78.
——(1978) *Money and the Real World*, 2nd edn, New York: John Wiley.
——(1984) 'Reviving Keynes' Revolution', *Journal of Post Keynesian Economics*, 6, pp. 561–75.
——(1987) 'The Aggregate Supply Function', *The New Palgrave*, London, Macmillan.
——(1991) 'Is Probability Theory Relevant for Uncertainty?: A Post Keynesian Perspective', *Journal of Economic Perspectives*, 5, pp. 129–43.
——(1992) 'Would Keynes be a New Keynesian?', *Eastern Economic Journal*, 18, pp. 449–64.
Davidson, P. (1993) 'The Elephant and the Butterfly: or Hysteresis and Post Keynesian Economics', *Journal of Post Keynesian Economics*,15, pp. 309–22.
——(1994a) 'Comment on "Do Informational Frictions Justify Federal Credit Programs"?', *Journal of Money, Credit, and Banking*, 26), Part 2, pp. 545–51.
——(1994b) *Post Keynesian Macroeconomic Theory*, Aldershot: Edward Elgar.

—— (1994c) 'The Concepts of Uncertainty and an External Economic Reality in Economic Theory', *Mimeo.*

—— (1995) 'Reality and Economic Theory', *Journal of Post Keynesian Economics*, Summer.

—— (1998) 'Setting the Record Straight', this volume.

Davis, J. (1989) 'Keynes on Atomism and Organicism', *Economic Journal*, 99, pp. 1159–72.

—— (1994) *Keynes's Philosophical Development*, Cambridge: Cambridge University Press.

Day, R. H. (1993) Nonlinear Dynamics and Evolutionary Economics, in R. H. Day and P. Chen (eds), *Nonlinear Dynamics and Evolutionary Economics*, Oxford: Oxford University Press, pp. 18–41.

—— (1994) *Complex Economic Dynamics*, vol. I, Cambridge, MA: MIT Press.

Day, R. H., and Ping Chen (eds) (1993) *Nonlinear Dynamics and Evolutionary Economics*, Oxford: Oxford University Press.

Day, R. H. and Shafer, W. (1985) 'Keynesian Chaos', *Journal of Macroeconomics*, 7, pp. 277–95.

—— —— (1987) 'Ergodic fluctuations in deterministic economic models', *Journal of Economic Behavior and Organization*, 8, pp. 339–61.

Day, R. H. and Walter, J. L. (1989) 'Economic Growth in the Very Long Run: On the Multiple Phase Interaction of Population, Technology, and Social Infrastructure', in W. A. Barnett, J. Geweke, and K. Shell (eds) *Economic Complexity: Chaos, Supports, Bubbles and Nonlinearity*, New York: Cambridge Universty Press, pp. 23–289.

Day, R. H. and Wayne, S. (1985) 'Keynesian Chaos', *Journal of Macroeconomics*, 7, pp. 277–95.

—— —— and Wayne, S. (1987) 'Ergodic fluctuations in deterministic economic models', *Journal of Economic Behavior and Organization*, 8, pp. 339–61.

Deleplace, G. and Nell, E. J. (eds) (1996) *Money in Motion: The Circulation and Post Keynesian Approaches*, London: Macmillan.

Delli Gatti, D. and Gallegatti, M. (1990) 'Financial Instability, Income Distribution, and the Stock Market', *Journal of Post Keynesian Economics*, 12, pp. 356–74.

—— —— (1992) 'Imperfect Information, Corporate Finance, Debt Commitments and Business Fluctuations', in S. Fazzari and D. Papadimitriou (eds) *Financial Conditions and Macroeconomic Performance: Essays in Honor of Hyman P. Minsky*, Armonk, NY: Sharpe, pp. 133–60.

Delli Gatti, D., Gallegati, M. and Gardini, L. (1993) 'Investment Confidence, Corporate Debt and Income Fluctuations', *Journal of Economic Behavior and Organization*, 22, pp. 161–188.

—— —— —— (1994) 'Complex Dynamics in a Simple Macroeconomic Model with Financing Constraints', in G. Dymski and R. Pollin (eds) *New Perspectives in Monetary Macroeconomics: Explorations in the Tradition of Hyman P. Minsky*, Ann Arbor: University of Michigan Press, pp. 51–76.

DeLong, B. and Summers, L. H. (1986) 'Is Increased Price Flexibility Stabilizing?', *American Economic Review*, 76, pp. 1031–44.

—— —— (1988) 'How Does Macroeconomic Policy Affect Output?', *Brookings Papers on Economic Activity*, no. 2, pp. 433–80.

Deneckere, R. and Pelikan, S. (1986) 'Competitive Chaos', *Journal of Economic Theory*, 40, pp. 13–25.

Diamond, D. and Dybvig, P. (1983) 'Bank Runs, Deposit Insurance, and Liquidity', *Journal of Political Economy*, 91, pp. 401–19.

Diener, M. and Poston, T. (1984) 'The Perfect Delay Convention, or the Revolt of the Slaved Variables', in H. Haken (ed.) *Chaos and Order in Nature*, 2nd edn, Berlin: Springer-Verlag, pp. 249–68.

Dobb, M. (1929) 'A Skeptical View of the Theory of Wages', *Economic Journal*, December.

Doeringer, P. and Piore, M. (1973) *Internal Labour Markets*, Lexington, MA: Heath.

Dow, S. (1989) *Macroeconomic Thought*, London: Macmillan.

—— (1991) 'The Post Keynesian School', in D. Mair and A. G. Miller (eds) *A Modern Guide to Economic Thought*, Aldershot: Elgar, pp. 176–206.

—— (1994) *Money and the Economic Process*, Aldershot: Edward Elgar.

—— (1995) 'Uncertainty about Uncertainty', in S. C. Dow and J. Hillard (eds) *Keynes, Knowledge and Uncertainty*, Aldershot: Edward Elgar.

—— (1997a) 'Keynes and Endogenous Money', in G. C. Harcourt and P. Riach (eds) *The Second Edition of the General Theory*, London: Routledge.

—— (1997b) 'Financial Structure and the Economic Performance of Peripheral Economies: The Case of Europe', in S. Hill and B. Morgan (eds) *Inward Investment, Business Finance and Regional Development*, London: Macmillan.

Dow, S. and Earl, P. E. (1982) *Money Matters*, Oxford: Martin Robertson.

Duesenberry, J. (1958) *Business Cycles and Economic Growth*, New York: McGraw-Hill.

Dunlop, J. G. (1938) 'The Movement of Real and Money Wage Rates', *Economic Journal*, September.

Dupre, J. (1994) *The Disorder of Things*, Cambridge, MA: Harvard University Press.

Durkheim, É. (1893) *De la Division du Travail Social*, trans. by W. D. Halls, New York: Free Press, 1984.

Dutt, A. (1991–2) 'Expectation and Equilibrium: Implications for Keynes, the Neo-Keynesians, Keynesians, and the Post Keynesians', *Journal of Post Keynesian Economics*, 14, pp. 205–24.

Dymski, G. (1988) 'A Keynesian Theory of Bank Behavior', *Journal of Post Keynesian Economics*, 10(4), pp. 499–526.

—— (1989) 'Keynesian Versus Credit Theories of Money and Banking: A Reply to Wray', *Journal of Post Keynesian Economics*, 12, pp. 157–63.

—— (1993) 'Keynesian Uncertainty and Asymmetric Information: Complementarity or Contradictory?', *Journal of Post Keynesian Economics*, 16(1), pp. 49–54.

—— (1994a) 'Asymmetric Information, Uncertainty, and Financial Structure: "New" versus "Post-" Keynesian Microfoundations', in G. Dymski and R. Pollin (eds) *New Perspectives in Monetary Macroeconomics: Explorations in the Tradition of Hyman P. Minsky*, Ann Arbor: University of Michigan Press.

—— (1994b) 'Fundamental Uncertainty, Asymmetric Information, and Financial Structure: "Post" Versus "New" Keynesian Microfoundations', in Gary Dymski and Robert Pollin (eds) *New Directions in Monetary Macroeconomics: Essays in the Tradition of Hyman P. Minsky* Ann Arbor: University of Michigan Press, pp. 77–103.

—— (1995) 'The Microfoundations of Bank Redlining and Discrimination: An Exploratory Model', *Review of Black Political Economy*, Winter, pp. 37–74.

Dymski, G. and Isenberg, D. (1994) 'Housing Finance in the Age of Globalization: From Social Housing to Life-Cycle Risk', presented at Economics Policy Institute, Conference on International Aspects of Financial Policy, 24–25 June, Washington, DC.

Dymski, G. and Pastor, M., Jr. (1990a) 'Misleading Signals, Bank Lending, and the Latin American Debt Crisis', *International Trade Journal*, 6, pp. 151–91.

—— —— (1990b) 'Debt Crisis and Class Conflict in Latin America', *Review of Radical Political Economics*, 22, Spring, pp. 155–78.

Earl, P. (1990) *Monetary Scenarios: A Modern Approach to Financial Systems*, Aldershot: Edward Elgar.

Eaton, J. and Gersovitz, M. (1981) 'Debt with Potential Repudiation: A Theoretical and Empirical Analysis', *Review of Economic Studies*, vol. 48, pp. 289–309.

Eaton, J. and Taylor, L. (1986) 'Developing Country Finance and Debt', *Journal of Development Economics*, 22, pp. 209–65.

Eaton, J., Gersovitz, M. and Stiglitz, J. (1986) 'The Pure Theory Country Risk', *European Economic Review*, 30, pp. 481–513.

ECE (1992) *Economic Survey of Europe in 1990–1991*, United Nations publications, Sales No. E.92.II. E.1.

Ees, H. van (1991) *Macroeconomic Fluctuations and Individual Behaviour*, London: Edward Elgar.

Ees, H. van and Garretsen, H. (1992) 'On the Contributions of New Keynesian Economics', *Eastern Economic Journal*, 18, pp. 465–77.

—— —— (1993a) 'How to Derive Keynesian Results from First Principles', *De Economist*, 141, pp. 323–52.

—— —— (1993b) 'Financial Markets and the Complementarity of Asymmetric Information and Fundamental Uncertainty', *Journal of Post Keynesian Economics*, 6, pp. 37–48.

Eichengreen, B. (1985) *The Gold Standard in Theory and History*, New York: Methuen.

Eichner, A. S. (1976) *The Megacorp and Oligopoly*, Cambridge: Cambridge University Press.

—— (1987) *The Macrodynamics of Advanced Market Economics*, Armonk, NY: M. E. Sharpe.

Elster, J. (1976) 'A Note on Hysteresis in the Social Sciences', *Synthese*, 33, pp. 371–91.

—— (1979) *Ulysses and the Sirens*, Cambridge: Cambridge University Press.

—— (1988) 'Economic Order and Social Norms', *Journal of Institutional and Theoretical Economics*, 144, April, pp. 357–66.

—— (1989) 'Social Norms and Economic Theory', *Journal of Economic Perspectives*, 3, Fall, pp. 99–117.

Engle, R. F. and Granger, C. W. J. (1987) 'Co-integration and Error Correction: Representation, Estimation and Testing', *Econometrica*, 50, pp. 251–76.

Epstein, G. A. (1991) 'Profit Squeeze, Rentier Squeeze, and Macroeconomic Policy under Fixed and Flexible Exchange Rates', in *Economies et Societies*, 8, November–December, pp. 219–57.

Epstein, G. A. and Gintis, H. (1995) 'Macroeconomic Policies for Sustainable Growth', in G. A. Epstein and H. Gintis (eds) *Macroeconomic Policy After the Conservative Era: Research on Investment, Savings, and Finance*, Cambridge: Cambridge University Press.

Evans, D. and Honkapohja, S. (1993) 'Learning and Economic Fluctuations: Using Fiscal Policy to Steer Expectations', *European Economic Review*, 7, pp. 595–602.

Evans, D. and Jovanović, B. (1989) 'An Estimated Model of Entrepreneurial Choice Under Liquidity Constraints', *Journal of Political Economy*, 97, pp. 808–27.

Evans, M. K. (1969) *Macroeconomic Activity*, New York: Harper & Row.

Fair, R. (1984) *Specification, Estimation, and Analysis of Macroeconomic Models*, Cambridge: Cambridge University Press.

Farmer, M. (1995) 'Knowledgeability, Actors and Uncertain Worlds', in S. C. Dow and J. Hillard (eds) *Keynes, Knowledge and Uncertainty*, Aldershot: Edward Elgar.

Farmer, R. (1993) *The Macroeconomics of Self-fulfilling Prophecies*, Cambridge, MA: MIT Press.

Fazzari, S. M. (1992) 'Keynesian Theories of Investment: Neo-, Post-, and New', in S. M. Fazzari and D. Papadimitriou (eds) *Financial Conditions and Macroeconomic Performance*, Armonk, NY: Sharpe.

—— (1993) 'Monetary Policy, Financial Structure, and Investment', in Gary Dymski, Gerald Epstein and Robert Pollin (eds) *Transforming the U. S. Financial System: Equity and Effeciency for the 21st Century* Armonk, NY: Sharpe, pp. 35–64.

Fazzari, S. M. and Mott, T. (1986–7) The Investment Theories of Kalecki and Keynes: An Empirical Study of Firm Data, 1970–1982, *Journal of Post Keynesian Economics*, 9, pp. 171–87.

Fazzari, S. M. and Variato, A. M. (1994) 'Asymmetric Information and Keynesian Theories of Investment', *Journal of Post Keynesian Economics*, 16, pp. 351–70.

Fazzari, S. M., Hubbard, G. and Petersen, B. (1988) 'Financing Constraints and Corporate Investment', *Brookings Papers on Economic Activity*, 1, pp. 141–206.

Fischer, E. O. and Jammernegg, W. (1986) 'Empirical Investigation of a Catastrophe Theory Extension of the Phillips Curve', *Review of Economics and Statistics*, 68, pp. 9–17.

Fischer, S. (1977) 'Long-Term Contracts, Rational Expectations, and the Optimal Money Supply Rule', *Journal of Political Economy*, 85, pp. 191–205.

Fisher, I. (1933) 'The Debt-deflation Theory of Great Depressions', *Econometrica*, 1, pp. 337–57.

Flemming, J. S. (1973) 'The Consumption Function When Capital Markets are Imperfect: the Permanent Income Hypothesis Revisited', *Oxford Economic Papers*, July.

Foley, D. (1987) 'Liquidity-Profit Rate Cycles in a Capitalist Economy', *Journal of Economic Behavior and Organization*, 8, pp. 363–77.

Fouillée, A. (1884) *La Propriété Sociale et la Démocratie*, Paris: Hachette.

Fouillée, A. Charmont, L., Duguit, L. and Demogue, R. (1916) *French Legal Philosophy*, trans. J. Chamberlain and E. F. Scott, Boston: Boston Book Company (reprinted by Rothman Reprints, 1968).

Friedman, M. (1969) *The Optimum Quantity of Money and Other Essays*, London: Macmillan.

Friedman, M. and Schwartz, A. (1963) *A Monetary History of the United States*, Princeton, NJ: Princeton University Press.

Gabisch, G. (1984) 'Nonlinear Models of Business Cycle Theory', in G. Hammer and D. Pallaschke (eds) *Selected Topics in Operations Research and Mathematical Economics*, Berlin: Springer-Verlag, pp. 205–22.

Galbraith, James K. (1994) 'Keynes, Einstein, and Scientific Revolution', *The American Prospect*, Winter.

Gallman, R. E. (1966) 'Gross National Product in the United States, 1834–1909', *Studies in Income and Wealth*, vol. 30.

Garegnani, P. (1976) 'On a Change in the Notion of Equilibrium in Recent Work on Capital Theory', in M. Brown *et al.* (eds) *Essays in Modern Capital Theory*, Amsterdam: North-Holland.

—— (1978) *Il Capitale Nelle Teorie Della Distribuzione*, Milano: Giuffre.

—— (1983) 'Notes on Consumption, Investment, and Effective Demand', in J. Eatwell and M. Milgate (eds) *Keynes' Economics and the Theory of Value and Distribution*, London, Duckworth, pp. 21–71.

Garretsen, H. (1991) *Keynes, Coordination and Beyond: The Development of Macroeconomic and Monetary Theory since 1945*, Aldershot: Edward Elgar.

Gerrard, B. (1994) 'Beyond Rational Expectations: A Constructive Interpretation of Keynes's Analysis of Behaviour Under Uncertainty', *Economic Journal*, March, pp. 327–37.

—— (1995) 'Keynes, the Keynesians and the Classic: A Suggested Interpretation', *Economic Journal*, March, pp. 445–58.

Gertler, M. (1988) 'Financial Structure and Aggregate Economic Activity: An Overview', *Journal of Money, Credit, and Banking*, 20, Part 2, pp. 559–88.

Gide, C. (1890) 'L'École nouvelle', *Quatre Écoles d'Économie Sociale*, March.

Gide, C. and Rist, C. (1913) *A History of Economic Doctrines*, trans. R. Richards, New York: Heath.

Gierke, O. (1913) *Natural Law and the Theory of Society: 1500–1800*, trans. Ernest Barker, 1934. Reprinted, Boston: Beacon Press, 1960.

Gintis, H. (1989a) 'Financial Markets and the Political Structure of the Enterprise', *Journal of Economic Behavior and Organization*, 1, pp. 311–22.

—— (1989b) 'The Principle of External Accountability in Financial Markets', in Masahiko Aoki, Bo Gustafsson and Oliver Williamson (eds) *The Firm as a Nexus of Treaties*, New York: Russell Sage.

Gleick, J. (1987) *Chaos*.

Glickman, M. (1994) 'The Concept of Information, Intractable Uncertainty and the Current State of Efficient Markets' Theory: A Post Keynesian View', *Journal of Post Keynesian Economics*, 16, pp. 325–50.

Goodhart, C. A. E. (1994) 'What Should Central Banks Do? What Should Be Their Macroeconomic Objectives and Operations?', *Economic Journal*, 104, pp. 1424–36.

Goodwin, R. M. (1967) 'A Growth Cycle', in C. H. Feinstein (ed.), *Socialism, Capitalism, and Economic Growth*, Cambridge: Cambridge University Press, pp. 54–8.

Goodwin, R. M. (1986) 'The Economy as an Evolutionary Pulsator', *Journal of Economic Behavior and Organization*, 7, pp. 341–9.

—— (1990) *Chaotic Economic Dynamics*, Oxford: Oxford University Press.

Gordon, R. J. (1986) *The American Business Cycle: Continuity and Change*, Chicago: National Bureau of Economic Research.
——(1990) 'What is New-Keynesian Economics?', *Journal of Economic Literature*, 28, pp. 1115–71.
Grandmont, J. M. (1985) 'On Endogenous Competitive Business Cycles', *Econometrica*, 53, pp. 995–1045.
——(1987) (ed.) *Nonlinear Economic Dynamics*, Orlando, FL: Academic Press.
——(1989) 'Keynesian Issues and Economic Theory', *Scandanavian Journal of Economics*, 91, pp. 265–93.
——(1994) 'Expectations Formation and Stability of Large Socioeconomic Systems', *CEPREMAP Working Paper*, no. 9424.
Gray, J. A. (1976) 'Wage Indexation: A Macroeconomic Approach', *Journal of Monetary Economics*, April.
Graziani, A. (1989) 'The Theory of the Monetary Circuit', *Thames Papers in Political Economy*, Spring.
Green, F. and Weisskopf, T. (1990) 'The Worker Discipline Effect: A Disaggregative Analysis', *Review of Economics and Statistics*, 72, pp. 241–9.
Greenwald, B. (1989) 'Toward a Theory of Rigidities', *American Economic Review*, May.
Greenwald, B. and Stiglitz, J. E. (1986) 'Externalities in Economies with Imperfect Information in Incomplete Markets', *Quarterly Journal of Economics*, 101, pp. 229–64.
————(1987) 'Keynesian, New Keynesian, and New Classical Economics', *Oxford Economic Papers*, 39, pp. 119–33.
————(1988a) 'Examining Alternative Macroeconomic Theories', *Brooking Papers on Economic Activity* no. 1, pp. 207–60.
————(1988b) 'Imperfect Information, Finance Constraints, and Business Fluctuations', in Meir Kohn and Sho-Chieh Tsiang (eds) *Finance Constraints, Expectations, and Macroeconomics*, Oxford: Clarendon Press, pp. 103–40.
————(1988c) 'Money, Imperfect Information, and Economic Fluctuations', in Mier Kohn and Sho-Chieh Tsiang (eds) *Finance Constraints Expectations, and Macroeconomics*, Oxford: Clarendon Press, pp. 141–65.
————(1990) 'Macroeconomic Models with Equity and Credit Rationing', in Glenn Hubbard (ed.) *Asymmetric Information, Corporate Finance, and Investment*, Chicago: University of Chicago, Press, pp. 15–42.
————(1993a) 'New and Old Keynesians', *Journal of Economic Perspectives*, 7, pp. 22–44.
————(1993b) 'Financial Market Imperfections and Business Cycles', *Quarterly Journal of Economics*, 108, pp. 77–114.
Greenwald, B., Stiglitz, J. E. and Weiss, A. (1984) 'Informational Imperfections in the Capital Market and Macroeconomic Fluctuations', *American Economic Review, Papers and Proceedings*, 74, pp. 194–9.
Gregg, P. and Wadsworth, J. (1995) 'A Short History of Labour Turnover, Job Tenure, and Job Security, 1975–93', *Oxford Review of Economic Policy*, vol. 11.
Grether, D. and Plott, C. (1979) 'Economic Theory of Choice and the Preference Reversal Phenomenon', *American Economic Review*, 75, pp. 623–38.
Grossman, S. J. and Stiglitz, J. E. (1980) 'On the Impossibility of Informationally Efficient Markets', *American Economic Review*, 70, June.
Grotius, H. (1631) *De jure belli ac pacis, libri tres*, trans. W. Kelsey, Oxford: Clarendon Press, 1925.
Grubb, D. (1986) 'Topics in the OECD Philips Curve', *Economic Journal*, 96, pp. 55–79.
Guesnerie, R. (1993) 'Successes and failures in coordinating expectations', *European Economic Review*, 37, pp. 243–68.
Guesnerie, R. and Woodford, M. (1992) 'Endogenous Fluctuations', in J. J. Laffont (ed.) *Advances in Economic Theory: Sixth World Congress*, volume II, Cambridge: Cambridge University Press, pp. 289–412.

Guttentag, J. and Herring, R. (1984) 'Commercial Bank Lending to Less Developed Countries: From Overlending to Underlending to Structural Reform', *Brookings Discussion Papers in International Economics*, 16, Washington, DC: Brookings Institution.

Hahn, F. H. (1965) 'On Some Problems of Proving the Existence of Equilibrium in a Monetary Economy', in F. H. Hahn and F. P. R. Brechling (eds) *The Theory of Interest Rates*, London: Macmillan.

——(1973) *On the Notion of Equilibrium in Economics*, London: Cambridge, University Press.

——(1977) 'Keynesian Economics and General Equilibrium Theory', in G. C. Harcourt (ed.) *Microfoundations of Macroeconomics*, London, Macmillan.

——(1983) *Money and Inflation*, Cambridge, MA: MIT Press.

——(1984) 'On the Foundations of Monetary Theory', *Equilibrium and Macroeconomics*, Oxford: Blackwell.

——(1989) 'Introduction', in F. H. Hahn (ed.) *The Economics of Missing Markets, Information and Games*, Oxford: Clarendon Press.

Haken, H. (1977) 'Synergetics', *Nonequilibrium Phase Transitions and Social Measurement*, Berlin: Springer-Verlag.

Halevi, J., Laibman, D. and Nell, E. J. (eds) (1992) *Beyond the Steady State*, London: Macmillan.

Hall, R. (1986) 'Market Structure and Macroeconomic Fluctuations', *Brookings Papers on Economic Activity*, no. 2, pp. 285–322.

Hall, S. G. and Henry, S. G. B. (1987) 'Wage Models', *National Institute Economic Review*, pp. 70–5.

Hall, S.G., Walsh, M. and Yates, T. (1996) 'How Do UK Companies Set Prices?', *Bank of England Quarterly Bulletin*, May, pp. 180–92.

Hansen, A. H. (1938) *Full Recovery or Stagnation*, New York: Norton.

——(1949) *Monetary Theory and Fiscal Policy*, New York: McGraw-Hill.

Harcourt, G. C. (1985) 'Post-Keynesianism: Quite Wrong and/or Nothing New?', in Philip Arestis and Thanos Skouras (eds) *Post Keynesian Economic Theory*, Adershot: Edward Elgar, pp. 125–45.

Harcourt, G. C. and Hamouda, O. F. (1988) 'Post Keynesianism: From Criticism to Coherence?', *Bulletin of Economic Research*, January, pp. 1–33. Reprinted in Sardoni, C. (ed.) (1992) *On Political Economists and Modern Political Economy: Selected Essays of G. C. Harcourt*, London: Routledge, pp. 209–32.

Hargreaves-Heap, S. P. (1980) 'Choosing the Wrong Natural Rate: Accelerating Inflation or Decelerating Unemployment and Growth', *Economic Journal*, 90, pp. 611–20.

——(1992) *The New Keynesian Economics: Time, Belief and Social Interdependence*, Aldershot: Edward Elgar.

Hargreaves-Heap, S. P. and Varoufakis, Y. (1995) *Game Theory: A Critical Introduction*, London: Routledge.

Harrod, R. F. (1936) 'Imperfect competition and the trade cycle', *Review of Economics and Statistics*, 18 (May), pp. 84–8.

——(1951) *The Life of John Maynard Keynes*, London, Macmillan.

Hart, O. (1982) 'A Model of Imperfect Competition with Keynesian Features', *Quarterly Journal of Economics*, February, pp. 109–38.

Haveman, R. H. (1978) 'Unemployment in Western Europe and the United States', *American Economic Review*, 68(2), pp. 44–50.

Hay, D. A. and Morris, D. J. (1991) *Industrial Economics and Organization*, Oxford: Oxford University Press.

Hayward, J. E. S. (1959) 'Solidarity: The Social History of an Idea in Nineteenth-century France', *International Review of Social History*, 4, pp. 261–84.

——(1960) 'Solidarist Syndicalism: Durkheim and Duguit', *International Review of Social History*, 5, Part I: pp. 17–36, Part II: pp. 185–202.

Hayward, J. E. S. (1961) 'The Official Social Philosophy of the French Third Republic: Léon Bourgeois and Solidarism', *International Review of Social History*, 6, pp. 19–48.

Heim, C. (1986) 'External Spheres and the Theory of Capitalist Development', *Social Concept*, 3, pp. 3–34.
Heise, A. (1992) 'Commercial Banks in Macroeconomic Theory', *Journal of Post Keynesian Economics*, 14, pp. 285–96.
Hendry, D. F. (1979) 'Predictive Failure and Econometric Modelling in Macroeconomics: The Transactions Demand for Money', in P. Omerod, (ed.) *Economic Modelling*, London : Heineman.
Herman, E. S. (1981) *Corporate Control, Corporate Power*, Cambridge: Cambridge University Press.
Hicks, J. R. (1937) 'Mr. Keynes and the "Classics": A Suggested Interpretation', *Econometrica*, 5, pp. 147–59.
—— (1950) *A Contribution to the Theory of the Trade Cycle*, Oxford: Oxford University Press.
—— (1975) *The Crisis in Keynesian Economics*, Oxford: Basil Blackwell.
—— (1989) *A Market Theory of Money*, London: Macmillan.
Hodgson, G. (1988) *Economics and Institutions*, Philadelphia: University of Pennsylvania Press.
Hoffman, W. G. (1965) *British Industry 1700–1950*, Oxford: Basil Blackwell.
Hollis, M. (1995) *Philosophy of Social Sciences*, Cambridge: Cambridge University Press.
Hoover, K. (1988) *The New Classical Macroeconomics*, Oxford: Blackwell.
—— (1990) *The Element of Social Scientific Thinking*, New York: St Martin's Press.
Howell, D. (1993) 'Stages of Technical Advance, Industrial Segmentation and Employment', in E. J. Nell (ed.) *Economics and Worldly Philosophy*, London: Macmillan.
Howells, P. (1995) 'Endogenous money', *International Papers in Political Economy*, 2(2).
Howitt, P. (1985) 'Transactions Costs in the Theory of Unemployment', *American Economic Review*, 75, pp. 88–100.
Hubbard, G. and Judd, K. (1986) 'Liquidity Constraints, Fiscal Policy, and Consumption', *Brookings Papers on Economic Activity*, 1, pp. 1–59.
Ingrao, B. and Israel, G. (1990) *The Invisible Hand: Economic Equilibrium in the History of Science*, Cambridge, MA: MIT Press.
Isaac, A. (1993) 'Is There a Natural Rate?', *Journal of Post Keynesian Economics*, vol. 15.
—— (1994) 'Fiscal policy and the natural rate', in A. K. Dutt (ed.) *New Directions in Analytical Political Economy*, Aldershot: Edward Elgar.
Isomaki, H. and Kantola, S. P. (1995) 'Bifurcations and Chaos in an Environmental Macroeconomic System', *Mimeo*, Helsinki University of Technology and University of Turku.
Jaffee, D. and Stiglitz, J. E. (1990) 'Credit Rationing' in Benjamin Friedman and Frank Hahn (eds) *Handbook of Monetary Economics*, Amsterdam: North Holland.
Jenkinson, T. (1987) 'The Natural Rate of Unemployment: Does It Exist?', *Oxford Review of Economic Policy*, vol. 3
Johansen, S. (1988) 'Statistical Analysis of Cointegrating Vectors', *Journal of Economic and Dynamic Control*, pp. 231–54.
Johansen, S. and Juselius, K. (1990) 'Maximum Likelihood Esimation and Inference on Cointegration – with Application to the Demand for Money', *Oxford Bulletin of Economics and Statistics*, 52, pp. 169–210.
—— —— (1992) 'Testing Structural Hypotheses in a Multivariate Cointegration Analysis of the PPP and the UID for the UK', *Journal of Econometrics*, 75, pp. 211–44.
Jones, R. A. and Ostroy, J. M. (1984) 'Flexibility and Uncertainty', *Review of Economic Studies*, 1, pp. 13–32.
Jossa, B. (1994) *Il Neoliberismo: Teoria e Politica Economica*, Milano: Franco Angeli.
Kac, M. (1968) 'Mathematical Mechanisms of Phase Transitions', in M. Chretien, E. Gross and S. Dreser (eds) *Statistical Physics: Phase Transitions and Superfluidity*, vol. 1, Brandeis University Summer Institute in Theoretical Physics, 1966, pp. 241–305.
Kahn, R. (1984) *The Making of Keynes' General Theory*, Cambridge: Cambridge University Press.
Kahneman, D. and Tversky, A. (1984) 'Choices, Values and Frames', *American Psychologist*, 39, pp. 341–50.

Kaldor, N. (1940) 'A Model of the Trade Cycle', *Economic Journal* 50, pp. 78–92.
—— (1956) 'Alternative Theories of Distribution', *Review of Economic Studies*, 23, pp. 94–100.
—— (1983) 'Keynesian Economics After Fifty Years', in D. Worswick and J. Trevithick (eds) *Keynes and the Modern World*, Cambridge: Cambridge University Press.
—— (1985) *Economics without Equilibrium*, Armonk, M. E. Sharpe.
—— (1986) *Nonequilibrium Economics*, New Haven, CT: Yale University Press.
Kaldor, N. and Trevithick, J. (1981) 'A Keynesian Perspective on Money', *Lloyds Bank Review*, 139, Spring.
Kalecki, M. (1935) 'A Macrodynamic Theory of Business Cycles', *Econometrica*, 3, pp. 327–44.
—— (1937) 'The Principle of Increasing Risk', *Economica*, 4 (new series), pp. 440–7.
—— (1944) 'Prof. Pigou on "The Classical Stationary State". A Comment', *Economic Journal*, 54, pp. 131–2.
—— (1954) *Theory of Economic Dynamics*, London: George Allen & Unwin.
—— (1971[1954]) *Selected Essays on the Dynamics of the Capitalist Economy, 1933–1970*, Cambridge: Cambridge University Press.
Karni, E. and Safra, Z. (1987) 'Preference Reversal and Observability of Preferences by Experimental Methods', *Econometrica*, 55, pp. 675–85.
Katz, L. F. (1986) 'Efficiency Wage Theories: A Partial Evaluation', in S. Fischer (ed.) *NBER Macroeconomics Annual*, vol. 1, Cambridge, MA: MIT Press.
Katzner (1993) 'Some Notes on the Role of History and the Definition of Hysteresis and Related Concepts in Economic Analysis', *Journal of Post Keynesian Economics*, pp. 323–46.
Keen, S. (1995) 'Finance and Economic Breakdown: Modeling Minsky's "Financial Instability Hypothesis"', *Journal of Post Keynesian Economics*, 17, pp. 607–35.
Kehoe, T. (1989) 'Intertemporal General Equilibrium Theory', in F. H. Hahn (ed.) *The Economics of Missing Markets, Information and Games*, Oxford: Clarendon Press.
Kellert, S. (1993) *In the Wake of Chaos*, Chicago, University of Chicago Press.
Kerr, C. (1954) 'The Balkanization of Labor Markets', in E. Wright Bakke (ed.) *Labor Mobility and Economic Opportunity*, Cambridge, MA: MIT Press.
Keynes (1921) *A Treatise on Probability*, reprinted as *The Collected Writings of J. M. Keynes* (hereafter CW), vol. VIII, London: Macmillan, 1973.
—— (1923) *A Tract on Monetary Reform*, CW IV, London: Macmillan, 1971.
—— (1926) 'The End of Laissez-Faire', in *Essays in Persuasion* CW IX, London: Macmillan, 1972.
—— (1930) *A Treatise on Money, 2 vols.* CW V and VI, London: Macmillan, 1971.
—— (1933a) 'A Monetary Theory of Production', in Keynes (1973b).
—— (1933b) 'The Characteristics of an Entrepreneur Economy', in Keynes (1979).
—— (1936) *The General Theory of Employment, Interest and Money*, London: Harcourt, Brace & World; reprinted as Keynes (1973a).
—— (1937a) 'The General Theory of Employment,' *Economic Journal*, reprinted in Keynes (1973c).
—— (1937) 'Alternative Theories of the Rate of Interest', *Economic Journal*, June, reprinted in Keynes (1973c).
—— (1939) 'Relative Movements of Real Wages and Output,' *Economics Journal*, reprinted in Keynes (1973a), pp. 394–412.
—— (1940) 'How to Pay for the War,' in CW IX (1972).
—— (1973a) *The General Theory of Employment, Interest, and Money*, CW VII, London: Macmillan.
—— (1973b) *The General Theory and After: Preparation*, CW, CW XIII, London: Macmillan.
—— (1973c) *The General Theory and After: Defence and Development*, CW XIV, Lndon: Macmillan.
—— (1973d) *Activities: 1941–46, Shaping the Post War-World, Bretton Woods*, CW XXVI, London: Macmillan.
—— (1979) *The General Theory and After: A Supplement*, CW XXIX, London.

Keynes (1980) *Activities: 1940–1946, Shaping the Post-War World, Employment*, CW XXVII, London: Macmillan.
—— (1980) *The Collected Writings of J. M. Keynes*, vol. XXVII London: Macmillan.
Kindleberger, C. P. (1978) *Manias, Panics and Crashes*, New York: Basic Books.
Kirman, A. (1989) 'The Intrinsic Limits of Modern Economic Theory: The Emperor has no Clothes', *Economic Journal*, 99 (Supplement), pp. 126–39.
Klein, and Kosobud, (1952) 'The Great Ratios of Economics', *Quarterly Journal of Economics*.
Kohn, M. and Tsiang, S. C. (1988) *Finance Constraints, Expectations, and Macroeconomics*, Oxford: Oxford University Press.
Knetsch, J. (1990) *Derived Indifference Curves*.
Knight, F. (1921) *Risk, Uncertainty, and Profit*, New York: Houghton Mifflin.
Kornai, J. (1986) 'The Soft Budget Constraint', *Kyklos*, 39, pp. 3–30.
Kregel, J. A. (1976) 'Economic Methodology in the Face of Uncertainty', *Economic Journal*, June, pp. 209–25.
—— (1980) 'Markets and Institutions as Features of a Capitalist Production System', *Journal of Post Keynesian Economics*, 2, pp. 32–48.
—— (1998) 'Keynes and the New Keynesians on Market Competition', this volume.
Kreuger, A. (1987) 'Origins of the Developing Countries' Debt Crisis: 1970 to 1982', *Journal of Development Economics*, 27, pp. 165–87.
Kriesler, P. (1987) *Kalecki's Microanalysis*, Cambridge: Cambridge University Press.
Kronman, A. T. and Posner, R. A. (1979) *The Economics of Contract Law*, Boston: Little, Brown.
Kucera, D. (1997) 'Transformational Growth in Japan', in E. J. Nell *et al.* (eds) *Transformational Growth and the Business Cycle*, London: Routledge.
Kurz (1991) 'Technological Change, Growth and Distribution: A Steady-state Approach to Unsteady Growth on Kaldorian Lines', in E. J. Nell and W. Semmler (eds) *Nicholas Kaldor and Mainstream Economics*, London: Macmillan.
Kuznets, S. (1961) *Capital in the American Economy: Its Formation and Financing*, New York: National Bureau of Economic Research.
Lacker, J. (1995) 'Neighborhoods and Banking', *Federal Reserve Bank of Richmond Economic Quarterly*, 8(2), pp. 13–38.
Lange, P. and Garrett, G. (1985) 'The Politics of Growth: Strategic Interaction and Economic Performance in the Advanced Industrial Democracies, 1974–1980', *Journal of Politics*, 47, pp. 792–827.
Lavoie, M. (1992) *Foundations of Post-Keynesian Economic Analysis*, Aldershot: Edward Elgar.
Lawlor, M. S. (1993) 'Keynes, Cambridge and The New Keynesian Economics', in W. Darity, (ed.) *Labor Economics: Problems in Analyzing Labor Markets*, Philadelphia: Kluwer.
—— (1994) 'The Own-rates Framework as an Interpretation of The General Theory: A Suggestion for Complicating the Keynesian Theory of Money', in J. B. Davis (ed.) *The State of Interpretation of Keynes*, Dordrecht: Kluwer.
Lawson, T. (1985) 'Uncertainty and Economic Analysis', *Economic Journal*, December, pp. 909–27.
—— (1988) 'Probability and Uncertainty in EconomicAnalysis', *Journal of Post Keynesian Economics*, 11, pp. 38–65.
—— (1991) 'Rationality in Economics', in Rod O'Donnell (ed.) *Keynes and Rationality*, London: Macmillan.
—— (1994) 'The Nature of Post Keynesianism and its Links to Other Traditions', *Journal of Post Keynesian Economics*, Summer, pp. 503–38.
—— (1995) 'A Realist Perspective on Economics', *Journal of Economic Methodology*, vol. 2.
Layard, R. and Nickell, S. (1985) 'Unemployment in Britain', *Economica*, 53, pp. S121–69.
Layard, R., Nickell, S. and Jackman, R. (1991) *Unemployment: Macroeconomic Performance and the Labour Market*, Oxford: Oxford University Press.

Lecaillon, P. (1965) 'La Politique des Revenues', *Congres des Economistes de Langue Française*, Paris.

Leijonhufvud, A. (1968) *On Keynesian Economics and the Economics of Keynes*, Oxford.

—— (1973) 'Effective Demand Failures', *Swedish Journal of Economics*, 75, pp. 27–58.

—— (1974) 'Keynes's Employment Function', *History of Political Economy*, vol. 6.

—— (1981) *Information and Coordination: Essays in Macroeconomic Theory*, New York: Oxford University Press.

—— (1993) 'Towards a Not-Too-Rational Macroeconomics', *Southern Economic Journal*, vol. 6.

Leontief, W. (1931) *The Structure of the American Economy 1919–1939: An Empirical Application of Equilibrium Analysis*, 2nd edn, White Plains, NY: IASP.

Lerner, A. P. (1959) 'Consumption-loan Interest and Money', *Journal of Political Economy*, LXVII, pp. 512–18.

Lerner, A. P. and Colander, D. (1981) *MAP: A Market Anti Inflation Plan*, New York: Harcourt Brace Jovanovich.

Lever, W. F. (1979) 'Industry and Labour Markets in Great Britain', in F. Hamilton and G. Linge (eds) *Spatial Analysis, Industry and the Industrial Environment*, Chichester: John Wiley.

Levine, D. P. (1977) *Contributions to the Critique of Economic Theory*, London: Routledge & Kegan Paul.

Li, T. Y. and Yorke, J. A. (1975) 'Period 3 Implies Chaos', *American Mathematical Monthly*, 82, pp. 985–92.

Lindbeck, A. (1992) 'Macroeconomic Theory and the Labor Market', *European Economic Review*, 36, pp. 209–35.

—— (1993) *Unemployment and Macroeconomics*, Cambridge, MA: MIT Press.

Lindbeck, A. and Snower, D. J. (1986a) 'Wage Setting, Unemployment and Insider Outsider Relations', *American Economic Review*, 76, pp. 235–39.

—— —— (1986b) 'Wage Rigidity, Union Activity and Unemployment', in W. Bekerman (ed.) *Wage Rigidity and Unemployment*, Baltimore, MD: The Johns Hopkins University Press, pp. 97–125.

—— —— (1988a) *The Insider–Outsider Theory of Employment and Unemployment*, Cambridge, MA: MIT Press.

—— —— (1988b) 'Cooperation, Harrassment, and Involuntary Unemployment: An Insider-Outsider Approach', in *American Economic Review*, 78, pp. 167–218.

Lichtenstein, S. and Slovic, P. (1971) 'Reversals of Preference between Bids and Choices in Gambling Decisions', *Journal of Experimental Psychology*, 89, pp. pp. 46–55.

—— —— (1973) 'Response-induced Reversals of Preference in Gambling: An Extended Replication in Las Vegas', *Journal of Experimental Psychology*, 101, pp. 16–20.

Littleboy, B. (1990) *On Interpreting Keynes: A Study in Reconciliation*, London: Routledge.

Loasby, B. (1976) *Choice, Complexity and Ignorance*, London: Cambridge University Press.

Lombard, M. (1995) 'A Re-examination of the Reasons for the Failure of Keynesian Expansionary Policies in France, 1981–1983', *Cambridge Journal of Economics*, 19, pp. 359–72.

Loomes, G. and Sugden, R. (1983) 'A Rationale for Preference Reversal', *American Economic Review*, 73, pp. 428–32.

Lorenz, E. N. (1963) 'Deterministic Non-Periodic Flow', *Journal of Atmospheric Sciences*, 20, pp. 130–41.

Lorenz, H. W. (1992) 'Multiple Attractors, Complex Basin Boundaries, and Transient Motion in Deterministic Economic Systems', in G. Feichtinger (ed.) *Dynamic Economic Models and Optimal Control*, Amsterdam: North-Holland, pp. 411–30.

—— (1993a) *Nonlinear Dynamical Economics and Chaotic Motion*, 2nd edn, Berlin: Springer-Verlag.

—— (1993b) 'Complex Transient Motion in Continuous-Time Economic Models', in P. Nijkamp and A. Reggiani (eds) *Nonlinear Evolution of Spatial Economic Systems*, Berlin: Springer-Verlag, pp. 112–37.

Lovering, J. (1990) 'A Perfunctory Sort of Post-Fordism: Economic Restructuring and Labour Market Segmentation in Britain in the 1980s', *Work, Employment Society*, May (Special Issue).

Lowe, P. (1970) *The Study of Production*, London: Macmillan.

Lowenstein, G. (1987) 'Anticipation and Valuation of Delayed Consumption', *Economic Journal*, 97, pp. 666–84.

Lowenstein, G. and Prelec, D. (1989) *Anomalies in Intertemporal Choice: Evidence and Interpretation*, Chicogo: Graduate School of Business, University of Chicago.

Lucas, R. E., Jr. (1972) 'Expectations and the Neutrality of Money', *Journal of Economic Theory*, 4, pp. 103–24.

Lucas, R. E. and Sargent, T. (1978) 'After Keynesian Macroeconomics', in *After the Phillips Curve: Persistence of High Inflation and High Unemployment*, Conference Series 19, Federal Reserve Bank of Boston.

—— —— (1981) *Rational Expectations and Econometric Practices*, Minneapolis: University of Minnesota Press.

McDonald I. M. and Solow R. M. (1981) 'Wage Bargaining and Employment', *American Economic Review*, 71, pp. 896–908.

Macneil, I. R. (1980) *The New Social Contract: An Inquiry Into Modern Contractual Relations*, New Haven, CT: Yale University Press.

Maddison, Angus (1982) *Phases of Capitalist Development*, New York: Oxford University Press.

—— (1984) 'Origins and Impact of the Welfare State', Banca Nazional del Lavoro, pp. 55–87.

—— (1991) *Dynamic Forces in Capitalist Development: A Long Run Comparative View*, New York: Oxford University Press.

Magill, M. and Quinzii, M. (1994) *The Theory of Incomplete Markets*, Vol. I. Cambridge, MA: MIT Press.

Malinvaud, E. (1980) *Profitability and Unemployment*, Cambridge: Cambridge University Press.

Mandelbrot, B. B. (1983) *The Fractal Geometry of Nature*, 2 edn, San Francisco: Freeman.

Mankiw, G. N. (1985) 'Small Menu Costs and Large Business Cycles: A Macroeconomic Model of Monopoly', *Quarterly Journal of Economics*, 100, pp. 529–37.

—— (1986) 'The Allocation of Credit and Financial Collapse', *Quarterly Journal of Economics*, 101 (August), pp. 455–70.

—— (1987) 'The New Keynesian Microfoundations: Comment', *NBER Macroeconomics Annual*, pp. 105–10.

—— (1990) 'A Quick Refresher Course in Macroeconomics', *Journal of Economic Literature*, vol. 28.

—— (1991a) 'The Reincarnation of Keynesian Economics', Paper presented at the September 1991 Meeting of The European Economic Association, Cambridge, England.

—— (1991b) 'The Allocation of Credit and Financial Collapse', in Gregory Mankiw.

—— (1992) 'The Reincarnation of Keynesian Economics', *European Economic Review*, vol. 36.

—— (1993) 'Symposium on Keynesian Economics Today', *Journal of Economic Perspectives*, Winter.

—— (1994) *Macroeconomics*, 2nd edn, New York: Worth:

—— and Romer, D. (1991) *New Kenesian Economics*, 2 vols. Cambridge: MIT Press.

Manning, A. (1992) 'Multiple equilibria in the British labour market: some empirical evidence', *European Economic Review*, vol. 36.

Mansfield, E. (1978) *Monopoly Power and Economic Performance*, New York: Norton.

Marcet, A. and Sargent, T. J. (1989) 'Convergence of Least Squares Learning Mechanisms in Self-Referential Linear Stochastic Models', *Journal of Economic Theory*, 48, pp. 337–68.

Marshall, A. (1961) *Principles of Economics*, ed. C. W. Guillebaud, 9th (Variorum) edn, London: Macmillan.

Marx, K. (1967[1894]) *Capital*, vol. III, Frederick Engels, (ed.) New York: International.

Matthews, R. C. O. (1959) *The Trade Cycle*, Cambridge: Cambridge University Press.

Messori, M. and Tamborini, R. 'Money, Credit and Finance in a Sequence Economy: Foundations of a Macroeconomic Model', Discussion Paper 20, Departmento di Scienze Economiche, Universata di Roma.

de Meza, D. and Webb, D. (1992) 'Efficient Credit Rationing', *European Economic Review*, 36, pp. 1277–90.

Michie, J. (1987) *Wages in the Business Cycle*, London: Francis Pinter.

Michl, T. (1992) 'Why is the Rate of Profit Still So Low?', in D. Papadimitriou (ed.) *Profits, Deficits and Imtabilisly*, London: Macmillan, pp. 40–59.

Milgate, M. (1977) 'Keynes on the Classical Theory of Interest', *Cambridge Journal of Economics*, 1, September.

—— (1988) 'Controversies in the Theory of Employment', *Contributions to Political Economy*, vol. 7.

Mill, J. S. (1844) *Principles of Political Economy*, New York: Appleton.

Minford, P. C. (1983) 'Labour Market Equilibrium in an Open Market Economy', *Oxford Economic Papers*, 35 (Supplement), pp. 207–44.

Minsky, H. P. (1972) 'Financial Instability Revisited: The Economics of Disaster', *Reappraisal of the Federal Reserve Discount Mechanism*, 3, pp. pp. 97–136.

—— (1975) *John Maynard Keynes*, London: Macmillan.

—— (1982) *Can It Happen Again?*, New York: Sharpe.

—— (1986) *Stabilizing an Unstable Economy*, New Haven, CT: Yale University Press.

—— (1993) 'On the Non-Neutrality of Money', *Federal Reserve Bank of New York Quarterly Review*, 18, pp. 77–82.

Mirowski, P. (1990) 'From Mandelbrot to Chaos in Economic Theory', *Southern Economic Journal*, 57, pp. 289–307.

Mishkin, F. S. (1981). 'The Real Interest Rate: An Empirical Investigation', *Carnegie–Rochester Conference Series on Public Policy*, vol. 15, pp. 151–200.

—— (1992) *Money, Banking and Financial Markets*, 3rd edn, New York: Harper Collins.

—— (1991) 'Asymmetric Information and Financial Crises: A Historical Perspective', in R. G. Hubbard (ed.) *Financial Markets and Financial Crises*, Chicago: University of Chicago Press, pp. 69–108.

Mitchell, W. F. (1993) 'Testing for Unit Roots and Persistence in OECD Unemployment Rates', *Applied Economics*, 25, pp. 1489–1501.

Modigliani, F. (1944) 'Liquidity Preference and the Theory of Interest and Money', *Econometrica*, pp. 45–88.

Moene, K. O. and Wallerstein, M. (1991) 'What's Wrong with Social Democracy?', Department of Economics, University of Oslo, May.

Moore, B. (1988) *Horizontalists and Verticalists: The Macroeconomics of Credit Money*, New York: Cambridge University Press.

—— (1995) 'Monetary Change and Aggregate Demand Growth', *Mimeo.*

Mosekilde, E., Larsen, E. R., Sterman, J. D. and Thomsen, J. S. (1993) 'Mode Locking and Nonlinear Entrainment of Macroeconomic Cycles', in R. H. Day and P. Chen (eds) *Non-linear Dynamics and Evolutionary Economics*, Oxford: Oxford University Press, pp. 58–83.

Murphy, K. M. and Topel, R. H. (1987) 'The Evolution of Unemployment in the United States: 1968–1985', *National Bureau of Economic Research Macroeconomics Annual.*

Myers, S. C. and Majluf, N. S. (1984) 'Corporate Financing and Investment Decisions When Firms Have Information that Investors Do Not Have', *Journal of Financial Economics* 13, June, pp. 187–221.

Nätti, J. (1993) 'Temporary Employment in the Nordic Countries: A Trap or a Bridge?', *Employment and Society*, vol. 7.

Nell, E. J. (1976) 'An Alternative Presentation of Lowe's Basic Model', A. Lowe (ed.) *The Path of Economic Growth*, Cambridge: Cambridge University Press, pp. 289–329.

—— (1988) *Prosperity and Public Spending*, Boston: Unwin Hyman.

—— (1992) *Transformational Growth and Effective Demand*, London: Macmillan.

—— (1993) 'Transformational Growth and Learning: Developing Craft Technology into Scientific Mass Production', in R. Thomson (ed.) *Learning and Technical Change*, London: Macmillan.

Nell, E. J. (1993a) *Economics and Worldly Philosophy*, London: Macmillan.

—— (1994) 'Minsky, Keynes and Sraffa: Investment and the Long Period', in G. Dymski and R. Pollin (eds) *New Perspectives in Monetary Macroeconomics: Explorations in the Tradition of Hyman P. Minsky*, Ann Arbor: University of Michigan Press.

—— (1996a) 'Transformational Growth and the Long-Period Method', *Review of Political Economy*, 8(4), October.

Nell, E. J. (1996b). *Making Sense of a Changing Economy*, London: Routledge.

—— (1997a) *Keynes After Sraffa: The General Theory of Transformational Growth*, Cambridge University Press.

Nell, E. J. and Phillips, T. F. (1995) 'Transformational Growth and the Business Cycle', *Eastern Economic Journal*, 21(2), pp. 125–42.

Nell, E. J. and Semmler W. (eds) (1991) *Nicholas Kaldor and Mainstream Economics*, London: Macmillan.

Nell, E. J. (1997a) *The General Theory of Transformational Growth: Keynes After Sraffa*, Cambridge: Cambridge University Press.

Nell, E. J. *et al.* (eds) (1997b) *Transformational Growth and the Business Cycle*, London: Routledge.

Newbery, D. and Stiglitz, J. E. (1981) *The Theory of Commodity Price Stabilization: A Study in the Economics of Risk,* Oxford: Oxford University Press.

Newell, A. and Symons, J. S. V. (1985) 'Wages and Unemployment in OECD Countries', *London School of Economics Centre for Labour Economics, Discussion Paper*, no. 219.

Nickell, S. (1987) 'Why is Wage Inflation in Britain so High?', *Oxford Bulletin of Economics and Statistics*, 49, pp. 103–128.

—— (1990a) 'Unemployment: A Survey', *Economica*, 57, pp. 391–439.

—— (1990b) 'Inflation and the UK Labour Market', *Oxford Review of Economic Policy*, 6, 4, pp. 26–35.

Nickell, S. and Andrews, M. (1983) 'Unions, Real Wages and Employment in Britain 1951–79', *Oxford Economic Papers*, 35, Supplement, pp. 183–206.

Nield, A. (1980) 'A Symptomatic Dispute? Notes on the Relation Between Marxian Theory and Historical Practice in Britain', *Social Research*, Autumn.

Nistico, S., D'Orlando, F. and Pirro, A. M. (1994) 'Some Questions for the New Keynesians', Paper Presented at the Annual Meeting of the Atlantic Economic Society, Atene, Marzo.

Nurkse, (1944) *Problems of Capital Formation in Underdeveloped Countries*, Oxford: Oxford University Press.

Nusse, H. E. and Hommes, C. H. (1990) 'Resolution of Chaos with Application to a Modified Samuelson Model', *Journal of Economic Dynamics and Control*, 14, pp. 1–19.

Ochoa, E. (1984) 'Labor Values and Prices of Production: An Interindustry Study of the U.S. Economy, 1947–72', Ph.D. Dissertation, New School for Social Research, New York.

—— (1986) 'Is Reswitching Empirically Relevant? US Wage–Profit Rate Frontiers 1947–1972', *Economic Forum*, XVI, pp. 45–67.

O'Donnell, R. A. (1988) *Keynes: Philosophy, Economics and Politics*, London: Macmillan.

—— (1990) 'An Overview of Probability, Expectations, Uncertainty and Rationality in Keynes's Conceptual Framework', *Review of Political Economy*, 2, pp. 253–66.

OECD (1994a) Employment Outlook, 1994.

—— (1994b) Economic Outlook, no. 58 (December 1994).

OECD Survey, 1986, Paris.

Okun, A. (1981) *Prices and Quantities*, Washington, DC: Brookings Institution.

Olson, M. (1975) *The Logic of Collective Action*, Cambridge, MA: Harvard University Press.

Olson, M. and Colander, D. (1984) 'Coalitions and Macroeconomics', in David Colander (ed.) *Neoclassical Political Economy*, Boston: Ballinger.

Osiatinski, J. (1990) *Collected Works of Michael Kalecki, Volume 1, Capitalism, Business Cycles, and Full Employment*, Oxford: Clarendon Press.

Osterman, P. (1992) 'Internal Labor Markets in a Changing Environment: Models and Evidence', in D. Lewin, O. S. Mitchell and P. D. Sherer (eds) *Research Frontiers in Industrial Relations and Human Resources*, Madison, WI: IRRA.

Palley, T. (1991) 'The Endogenous Money Supply: Consensus and Disagreement', *Journal of Post Keynesian Economics*, vol. 13.

Panico, C. (1987) 'The Evolution of Keynes's Thought on the Rate of Interest', *Contributions to Political Economy*, 6, 53–71.

Papadimitriou, D. (ed.) (1992) *Profits, Deficits and Instability*, London: Macmillan.

Papi, G. U. (1967) *Dizionario di Economia*, Torino: UTET.

Pasinetti, L. (1960) 'A Mathematical Formulation of the Ricardian System', *Review of Economic Studies*, 27, pp. 78–98.

—— (1977) *Lectures on the Theory of Production*, New York: Columbia University Press.

Pasinetti, L. (1981) *Structural Change and Economic Growth: A Theoretical Essay on the Dynamics of the Wealth of Nations*, Cambridge: Cambridge University Press.

Patinkin D. (1956) *Money, Interest and Prices*, Evanston, IL: Row Peterson.

—— (1965) *Money, Interest and Prices*, second edition, New York: Harper and Row.

Pedersen, J. and Pedersen, O. (1938) *An Analysis of Price Behaviour*, London: Humphrey Milford and Oxford University Press.

Penati, A. and Protopapadakis, A. (1986) 'Implicit Deposit Insurance and Banks', *Portfolio Choices: A Positive Theory of International 'Overexposure'*, Mimeo, Wharton School.

Penrose, E. (1954) *A Theory of the Growth of the Firm*, Oxford: Basil Blackwell.

—— (1974) *The Large International Firm*, Oxford: Oxford University Press.

Perez, C. (1983) 'Structural Change and Assimilation of New Technologies in Economic Social Systems', *Futures*, October, pp. 357–75.

—— (1985) 'Microelectronics, Long Waves and World Structural Change: New Perspectives for Developing Economies', *World Development*, 13(3), pp. 441–63.

Persson, T. and Tabellini, G. (1991) 'Is Inequality Harmful for Growth? Theory and Evidence', *National Bureau of Economic Research Working Paper*, no. 3599.

Pesaran, M. H. and Shin, Y. (1994) 'Identification of and Testing for Cointegrating Relations with General Non-homogeneous Restrictions', Department of Applied Economics, University of Cambridge, Mimeo.

Phelps, E. (1969) *Microeconomic Foundations of Employment and Inflation*, New York: Norton.

—— (1994) *Structural Slumps*, Boston: Harvard University Press.

Phelps Brown, H. and Hopkins, S. (1981) *A Perspective of Wages and Prices*, London: Methuen.

Pigou, A. C. (1929) *Industrial Fluctuations*, 2nd edn, London: Macmillan (reprinted New York: Augustus Kelley, 1967)

—— (1939) 'Presidential Address', *Economic Journal*, June.

—— (1944) *Employment and Equilibrium*, London: Macmillan.

—— (1950) *Keynes' General Theory – A Retrospective View*, London: Macmillan London. Traduzione Italiana in *Keynes: Riletture e Rievocazioni*, a cura di Federico Caffè, Einaudi, 1983.

Pisauro, G. (1991) 'The Effect of Taxes on Labour in Efficiency Wages Models', *Journal of Public Economics*, 46, pp. 329–45.

Pohjola, M. T. (1981) 'Stable, Cyclic and Chaotic Growth: The Dynamics of a Discrete Time Version of Goodwin's Growth Cycle', *Zeitschrift für Nationalokonomie*, 41, pp. 27–38.

Pollin, R. (1991) 'Two Theories of Money Supply Endogeniety: Some Empirical Evidence', *Journal of Post Keynesian Economics*, vol. 13.

Posner, R. A. (1972) *Economic Analysis of the Law*, Boston: Little, Brown.

—— (1990) *The Problems of Jurisprudence*, Cambridge, MA: Harvard University Press.

Postlewaite, A. and Vives, X. (1987) 'Bank Runs as an Equilibrium Phenomenon', *Journal of Political Economy*, 95, pp. 485–91.

Prigogine, I. and Stengers, I. (1984) *Order out of Chaos*, New York: Bantam.

Pufendorf, S. von. (1660) *Elementorum Jurisprudentiae Universalis*, Libri Duo. Translated from the edition of 1672 by William Abbott Oldfather. Oxford: Clarendon Press, 1931.

Pufendorf, S. von. (1672) *De Jure Naturae et Genitum*, Libri Octo. Translated from the edition of 1688 by C. H. Oldfather and W. A. Oldfather. Oxford: Oxford University Press, 1934.
—— (1673) *De Officio Hominis et Civis Juxta Legem Naturalem*, Libri Duo. Translated by Michael Silverthorne and edited by James Tully. Cambridge: Cambridge University Press, 1991.
Puu, T. (1993) *Nonlinear Economic Dynamics*, 3 edn, Berlin: Springer-Verlag.
Ramsey, V. (1991) 'Nonconvex costs and the behaviour of inventories', *Journal of Political Economy*, vol. 99.
Richardson, G. B. (1959) 'Equilibrium, Expectations and Information', *Economic Journal*, June.
—— (1960) *Information and Investment*, Oxford: Oxford University Press.
Robertson, D. (1940) 'Mr. Keynes and the Rate of Interest', *D. Robertson, Essays in Monetary Theory*, London: Staples.
Robinson, E. A. G. (1931) *The Structure of Competitive Industry*, Cambridge: Cambridge University Press.
Robinson, J. (1962) *Economic Philosophy*, Chicago: Adline.
—— (1965) 'The General Theory After Twenty-Five Years', in *Collected Economic Papers*, vol. III, Oxford: Basil Blackwell.
—— (1966) *Ideologie e Scienza Economica*, Firenze: Sansoni.
—— (1973) 'The Second Crisis in Economic Theory', in *Collected Economic Papers*, vol. IV, Oxford: Basil Blackwell.
Rogers, C. (1989) 'Money, Interest and Capital', *A Study in the Foundations of Monetary Theory*, Cambridge: Cambridge University Press.
—— (1995a) 'The General Theory: Existence of a Long-period Monetary Equilibrium', in G. C. H. Harcourt and P. Riach (eds) *The General Theory 2*, London: Routledge.
—— (1997b) 'Post Keynesian Monetary Theory and the Principle of Effective Demand', in A. J. Cohen and J. Smithin (eds) *Money, Financial Institutions and Macroeconomics*, Dordrecht: Kluwer.
Rogers, C. and Rymes, T. K. (1994) 'Keynes's Monetary Theory of Value and Modern Banking', in G. C. H. Harcourt and P. Riach (eds) *The General Theory 2*, London: Routledge.
Romer, C. (1986) 'New Estimates of Prewar Gross National Product and Unemployment', *Journal of Economic History*, 46(2), pp. 341–52.
—— (1987) 'New Work on Business Cycles in Historical Perspective: A Review of Theories and Evidence', *Journal of Economic Literature*,
—— (1989) 'The Prewar Business Cycle Reconsidered: New Estimates of Gross National Product, 1869–1908', *Journal of Political Economy*, 97(1), pp. 1–37.
Romer, D. (1993) 'The New Keynesian Synthesis', *Journal of Economic Perspectives,* 7, pp. 5–22.
Roncaglia, A. (1986) 'Le Politiche dei Redditi', *Banca Popolare dell'Etruria.*
—— (1988) *The Neo-Ricardian Approach and the Distribution of Income*, Lancaster: Kluwer.
Rosser, B. (1990) *Chaos Theory and The New Keynesian Economics*, The Manchester School, pp. pp. 265–91.
—— (1991) *From Catastrophe to Chaos: A General Theory of Economic Discontinuities*, Boston: Kluwer.
—— (1995a) 'Chaos Theory and Rationality in Economics', in E. Elliott and J. D. Kiel (eds) *Chaos Theory in the Social Sciences*, Ann Arbor: University of Michigan Press,
—— (1995b) 'Chaos Theory and Post-Walrasian Macroeconomics', in D. Colander (ed.) *Beyond the Microfoundations of Macro: Post-Walrasian Macroeconomics*, Cambridge: Cambridge University Press.
Rosser, B. and Rosser, M. V. (1994) 'Long Wave Chaos and Systemic Economic Transformation', *World Futures*, 39, pp. 197–207.
Rotheim, R. J. (1981) 'Keynes's Monetary Theory of Value (1933)', *Journal of Keynesian Economics*, Summer.
—— (1988) 'Keynes and the Language of Probability and Uncertainty', *Journal of Post Keynesian Economics*, Fall.

—— (1989) 'Organicism and the Role of the Individual in Keynes's Thought', *Journal of Post Keynesian Economics*, pp. 316–26.

—— (1991) 'Marx, Keynes and the Monetary Theory of Production', in G. Caravale (ed.) *Marx and Modern Economic Analysis*, vol. II, Aldershot: Elgar.

—— (1992) 'Interdependence and the Cambridge Economic Tradition', in B. Gerrald, and J. Hillard (eds) *The Philosophy and Economics of J. M. Keynes*, Aldershot: Edward Edgar.

—— (1993) 'On Butterflies' Wings and Hurricanes: A Post Keynesian Critique of New Keynesian Economics', Paper presented to the Post Keynesian Study Group, University College London.

—— (1995) 'Keynes on Uncertainty and Individual Behaviour in the Theory of Effective Demand', in S. Dow and John Hillard (eds) *Keynes, Knowledge and Uncertainty*, Aldershot: Edward Edgar pp. 161–76.

—— (1997) 'New Keynesian Economics', in T. Cate, D. Colander and G. Harcourt (eds) *Encyclopedia of Keynesian Economics*, Aldershot: Elgar.

—— (1998) 'Keynes and the Marginal Productivity Theory of Distribution,' *Journal of Post-Keynesian Economics* (forthcoming).

Rothschild, M. and Stiglitz, J. (1970) 'Increasing Risk I: A Definition', *Journal of Economic Theory*, 2, pp. 225–43.

Rowthorn, R. E. (1977) 'Conflict, Inflation and Money', *Cambridge Journal of Economics*, September, pp. 215–23.

—— (1982) 'Demand, Real Wages, and Economic Growth', *Studi Economici*, 18, pp. 2–53.

Runde, J. (1990) 'Keynesian Uncertainty and the Weight of Arguments', *Economics and Philosophy*, 6, pp. 275–92.

—— (1994) 'Keynesian Uncertainty and Liquidity Preference', *Cambridge Journal of Economics*, 18(2).

Sachs, J. (1980) 'The Changing Cyclical Behavior of Wages and Prices: 1890–1976', *American Economic Review*, 70(1), pp. 78–90.

Salop, S. (1979) 'A Model of the Natural Rate of Unemployment', *American Economic Review*, 69, pp. 117–25.

Samuelson, P. A. (1939) 'A Synthesis of the Principle of Acceleration and the Multiplier', *Journal of Political Economy*, 47, pp. 786–97.

—— (1958) 'An Exact Consumption-loan Model of Interest with or without the Social Contrivance of Money', *The Journal of Political Economy*, LXVI, pp. 467–82.

—— (1969) 'Classical and Neoclassical Theory', in R. W. Clower (ed.) *Monetary Theory*, London: Penguin.

Samuelson, P. and Zeckhauser, R. (1988) 'Status Quo Bias in Decision Making', *Journal of Risk and Uncertainty*, 1, pp. 7–59.

Sardoni, C. (1992) 'Market Forms and Effective Demand: Keynesian Results with Perfect Competition', *Review of Political Economy*, 4, pp. 1–25.

Sargent, T. J. (1993) *Bounded Rationality in Macroeconomics*, Oxford: Clarendon Press.

Savage, L. (1954) *The Foundation of Statistics*, New York: John Wiley.

Savage, M., Dickens, P. and Pielding, T. (1988) 'Some Social and Political Implications of the Contemporary Fragmentation of the Service Class in Britain', *International Journal of Urban and Regional Research*, 12, pp. 455–75.

Sawhill, I. W. (1995) 'Distinguished Lecture on Economics in Government: The Economists vs. Madmen in Authority', *Journal of Economic Perspectives*, 9, Summer.

Sawyer, M. (1982) 'Collective Bargaining, Oligopoly and Macro Economics', *Oxford Economic Papers*, vol. 34.

—— (1983) *Business Pricing and Inflation*, London: Macmillan.

—— (1985) *Economics of Industries and Firms*, London: Routledge.

—— (1992) 'The Nature and Role of the Market', *Social Concept*, 6(2). (A slightly revised version appeared in C. Pitelis (ed.) (1993) *Transaction costs, markets and hierarchies*, Oxford: Blackwell.)

—— (1995) *Unemployment, Imperfect Competition and Macroeconomics*, Aldershot: Edward Elgar.
Sayers, R. (1957) *Central Banking After Bagehot*, Oxford: Oxford University Press.
Schefold, B. (1980) 'The General Theory for a Totalitarian State? A Note on Keynes's Preface to the German Edition of 1936', *Cambridge Journal of Economics*, 4, pp. 175–6.
Schelling, T. (1984) 'Self-command in Practice, in Policy, and in a Theory of Rational Choice', *American Economic Review*, 7, pp. 1–11.
Semmler, W. and Franke, R. (1989) 'Debt-Financing of Firms: Stability and Cycles in a Dynamical Macro Model', in W. Semmler (ed.) *Financial Dynamics and Business Cycles*, Armonk, NY: M. E. Sharpe.
—— —— (1996) 'The Financial-Real Interaction, and Investment in the Business Cycle: Theories and Empirical Evidence', in G. Deleplace and E. J. Nell (eds) *Money in Motion: The Circulation and Post Keynesian Approaches*, London: Macmillan.
Semmler, W. and Sieveking, M. (1993) 'Nonlinear Liquidity Growth Dynamics with Corridor-stability', *Journal of Economic Behavior and Organization*, 22, pp. 189–208.
Setterfield, M. (1993) 'Towards a Long-run Theory of Effective Demand: Modeling Macroeconomic Systems with Hysteresis', *Journal of Post Keynesian Economics*, 15, pp. 347–64.
Setterfield, M., Gordon, D. V. and Osberg, L. (1992) 'Searching for a Will o' Wisp: An Empirical Study of the NAIRU in Canada', *European Economic Review*, vol. 36.
Shackle, G. L. S.(1972) *Epistemics and Economics*, Cambridge: Cambridge University Press.
—— (1974) *Keynesian Kaleidics*, Edinburgh: Edinburgh University Press.
—— (1980) *Uncertainty in Economics*, Cambridge: Cambridge University Press.
Shapiro, C. and Stiglitz, J. (1984) 'Equilibrium Unemployment as a Worker Discipline Device', *American Economic Review*, 74, pp. 433–44.
Sheffrin (1989) *The Making of Economic Policy*, Oxford: Basil Blackwell.
Shell, K. (1977) 'Monnaie et Allocation Intertemporale', CNRS Seminaire d'Econometrique Roy-Malinvaud, Mimeo, Paris.
Shleifer, A. (1986) 'Implementation Cycles', *Journal of Political Economy*, 94, pp. 1163–90.
Simon, H. (1957) *Models of Man: Social and Rational*, New York: John Wiley.
Skott, P. (1991) 'Efficiency Wages, Mark-up Pricing and Effective Demand', in J. Michie (ed.) *The Economics of Restructuring and Intervention*, Alderhot: Edward Elgar.
Slovic, P., Griffin, D. and Tversky, A. (1990) 'Compatibility Effects in Judgment and Choice', in R. Hogarth (ed.) *Insights in Decision Making: Theory and Applications*, Chicago: University of Chicago Press.
Smith, A. (1762–3 and 1766) 'Lectures on Jurisprudence', ed. R. L. Meek, D. D. Raphael and P. G. Stein, vol. five of the Glasgow edition of *The Works and Correspondence of Adam Smith*, Oxford: Oxford University Press.
Snyder, C. (1924) 'New Measures in the Equation of Exchange', *American Economic Review*, December, pp. 698–705.
Société Chrétienne Suisse d'Économie Sociale (1890) *Quatre Écoles d'Économie Sociale*, Paris: Fischbacher.
Solomou, S. (1986) 'Non-Balanced Growth and Kondratief Wages in the World Economy, 1850–1913', *Journal of Economic History*, March, pp. 165–9.
Solow, R. M. (1979) 'Another Possible Source of Wage Stickiness', *Journal of Macroeconomics*, 1, pp. 79–82.
—— (1980) 'On Theories of Unemployment', *American Economic Review*, 70 (March), pp. 1–11.
—— (1986) 'What is a Nice Girl Like You Doing in a Place Like This? Macroeconomics After 50 Years', *Eastern Economic Journal*, XII, pp. 191–8.
—— (1990) *The Labour Market as a Social Institution*, Oxford: Basil Blackwell.
Sraffa, P. (1925) *Sulle relazioni fra costo e quantita prodotta.*
—— (1926) 'The Laws of Return Under Competitive Conditions', *Economic Journal*, 36, pp. 535–60.
—— (1960) *The Production of Commodities by means of Commodities*, Cambridge: Cambridge University Press.

Steindl, J. (1976 [1952]) *Maturity and Stagnation in American Capitalism*, New York: Monthly Review Press.

Stiglitz, J. (1985) 'Credit Markets and the Control of Capital', *Journal of Money, Credit and Banking*, May.

—— (1986) 'Theories of Wage Rigidity', , in James Butkiewicz, Kenneth Koford and Jeffrey Miller (eds) *Keynes's Economic Legacy* New York: Praeger.

—— (1987) 'The Causes and the Consequences of the Dependence of Quality on Price', *Journal of Economic Literature*, 25, pp. 1–48.

—— (1992) 'Capital Markets and Economic Fluctuations in Capitalist Economies', *European Economic Review*, 36, pp. 269–306.

Stiglitz, J. and Weiss, M. (1981) 'Credit Rationing with Markets with Imperfect Competition', *American Economic Review*, 71, pp. 22–44

—— —— (1987) 'Macroeconomic Equilibrium and Credit Rationing', *NBER Working Paper*, no. 2164.

Strotz, R. (1955) 'Myopia and Inconsistency in Dynamic Utility Maximization', *Review of Economic Studies*, 23, pp. 165–80.

Sugden, R. (1991) 'Rational Choice: A Survey of Contributions from Economics and Philosophy', *Economic Journal*, 101, pp. 751–85.

Sylos-Labini, P. (1989) 'Changing Character of the so-called Business Cycle', *Atlantic Economic Journal.*

—— (1993) 'Long-Run Changes in the Wage and Price Mechanisms and the Processes of Growth', in Baranzini and Harcourt (eds) *The Dynamics of the Wealth of Nations*, London: Macmillan.

Targetti, F. and Kinda-Hass, B. (1982) 'Kalecki's Review of Keynes's General Theory', *Australian Economic Papers*, 21, pp. 244–60.

Tarshis, I. (1938) 'Real Wages in the United States and Great Britain', *The Canadian Journal of Economics*, August.

Taylor, J. (1979) 'Staggered Wage Setting in a Macro Model', *American Economic Review*, May, pp. 108–13.

—— (1980) 'Aggregate Dynamics and Staggered Contracts', *Journal of Political Economy,* 88, pp. 1–23.

Taylor, L. and O'Connell, S. A. (1985) 'A Minsky Crisis', *Quarterly Journal of Economics,* 100, pp. 875–85.

Thaler, R. and Shefrin, H. (1981) 'An Economic Theory of Self-Control', *Journal of Political Economy*, 89, pp. 392–410.

Thirlwall, A. P. (1995) 'Review of P. Davidson's *Post Keynesian Macroeconomic Theory*', *Economic Journal*, November, pp. 1671–2.

Thom, R. (1972) *Stabilité Structurelle et Morphogenese*, Reading, MA: Benjamin.

Thompson, J. M. T. (1992) 'Global Unpredictability in Nonlinear Dynamics: Capture, Dispersal and the Indeterminate Bifurcations', *Physica*, D58, pp. 260–72.

Thomson, R. (ed.) (1993) *Learning and Technical Change*, London: Macmillan.

Tirole, J. (1985) 'Asset Bubbles and Overlapping Generations', *Econometrica*, LIII, pp. 1499–1528.

Tobin, J. (1974) 'Friedman's Theoretical Framework', in R. J. Gordon (ed.) *Milton Friedman's Monetary Framework*, Chicago: University of Chicago Press.

—— (1980) 'Real Balance Effects Reconsidered', *Asset Accumulation and Economic Activity*, Chicago: Chicago University Press.

—— (1983) *Macroeconomics: Prices and Quantities*, Oxford: Basil Blackwell.

—— (1992) 'An Old Keynesian Counterattacks', *Eastern Economic Journal*, vol. 18.

—— (1993) 'Price Flexibility and Output Stability: An Old Keynesian View', *Journal of Economic Perspectives*, vol. 7.

Torr, C. (1980) 'The Distinction Between an Entrepreneur Economy and a Co-operative Economy', *South African Journal of Economics*, 48(4), pp. 429–34.

Tversky, A. and Kahneman, D. (1991) 'Loss Aversion and Riskless Choice: A Reference Dependent Model', *Quarterly Journal of Economics*, vol. 106.

Tylecote, A. (1991) *The Long Wave in the World*, London: Routledge.

UNCTAD (1995) *Trade and Development Report*, 1995, New York and Geneva: UN.

Urquhart, M. C. (1986) 'New Estimates of Gross National Product, Canada, 1870–1926: Some Implications for Canadian Development', in S. L. Engerman and R. F. Gallman (eds) *Long-Term Factors in American Economic Growth*, NBER Studies in Income and Wealth, vol. 51, Chicago: University of Chicago Press.

Varian, Hal R. (1979) 'A Catastrophe Theory and the Business Cycle', *Economic Inquiry*, 17, pp. 14–28.

Wadhwani, S. B. and Wall, M. (1990) 'A Direct Test of the Efficiency Wage Model Using UK Micro-Data', *London School of Economics Centre for Labour Economics, Working Paper*, no. 1022.

Waldrop, M. (1992) *Complexity: The Emerging Science at the Edge of Order and Chaos*, New York, Touchstone.

Walker, D. (1994) 'The Structure of Walras's Consumer Commodities Model in the Mature Phase of His Thought', *Revue Economique*, March.

Walras, L. (1936) *Études d'Économie Politique Appliquée*, Edition définitive, Paris: Pichon & Durand-Auzias.

Wärnneryd, K. (1990) 'Legal Restrictions and Monetary Evolution', *Journal of Economic Behavior and Organization*, 13, pp. 117–24.

Weidlich, W. and Haag, G. (1983) *Concepts and Models of a Quantitative Sociology: The Dynamics of Interaction Populations*, Berlin: Springer-Verlag.

Weintraub, S. (1958) *An Approach to the Theory of Income Distribution*, Philadelphia: Chilton.

—— (1978) 'The Missing Theory of Money Wages', *Journal of Post-Keynesian Economics*, 1, pp. 59–79.

Weiss, A. (1980) 'Job Queues and Layoffs in Labor Markets with Flexible Wages', *American Economic Review*, 80, pp. 96–117.

—— (1990) *Efficiency Wages: Models of Unemployment, Layoffs, and Wage Dispersion*, Princeton, NJ: Princeton University Press.

Weitzman, M. L. (1982) 'Increasing Returns and the Foundation of Unemployment Theory', *Economic Journal*, 92, pp. 787–804.

Weitzman, M. L. and Kruse, D. (1990) 'Profit Sharing and Productivity', in A. Blinder (ed.) *Paying for Productivity*, Washington, DC: Brookings Institute, pp. 95–141.

Wells, Paul (1973) 'Review of Davidson: *Money and the Real World*', *Journal of Economic Literature*, December, pp. 1387–8.

Williamson, O. (1985) *The Economic Institutions of Capitalism*, New York: Free Press.

Williamson, S. D. (1988) 'Liquidity Preference and Aggregate Instability', in M. Kohn and S. C. Tsiang (eds) *Finance Constraints, Expectation and Macroeconomics*, Oxford: Oxford University Press, pp. 229–61.

—— (1989) *Imperfect Financial Intermediation and Complex Dynamics*, in W. A. Barnett, J. Geweke and K. Shell (eds) *Economic Complexity: Chaos, Sunsports, Bubbles and Nonlinearity*, New York: Cambridge University Press, pp. 309–34.

Williamson, O. E. (1980) 'The Organization of Work: A Comparative Institutional Assessment', *Journal of Economic Behavior and Organization*, pp. 5–38.

—— (1994) 'Do Informational Frictions Justify Federal Credit Programs?', *Journal of Money, Credit, and Banking*, 26(3), Part 2: August, pp. 523–44.

Winslow, E. G. (1989) 'Organic Interdependence, Uncertainty, and Economic Analysis', *Economic Journal*, 99, pp. 1173–82.

Wolfson, M. (1994) *Financial Crises: Understanding the Postwar Experience*, Armonk, NY: M. E. Sharpe.

Wood, A. (1976) *A Theory of Profits*, Cambridge: Cambridge University Press.

Woodford, M. (1988) 'Expectations, Finance, and Aggregate Instability', in Meir Kohn and Sho-Chieh Tsiang (eds) *Finance Constraints, Expectations, and Macroeconomics*, Oxford: Clarendon Press, pp. 103–40.

—— (1989) 'Imperfect Financial Intermediation and Complex Dynamics', in W. A. Barnett (eds) *Economic Complescity: Chaos, Sunsports, Bubbles and Nonlinearity*, New York: Cambridge University Press, pp. 309–34.

Worswick, D. (1985) 'Jobs for All?', *Economic Journal*, vol. 95.

Wray, L. R. (1988) 'Profit Expectations and the Investment-Savings Relation', *Journal of Post Keynesian Economics*, 11, pp. 131–47.

—— (1989) 'A Keynesian Theory of Banking: A Comment on Dymski', *Journal of Post Keynesian Economics,* 12, pp. 152–6.

—— (1990) *Money and Credit in Capitalist Economies: The Endogenous Money Approach*, Aldershot: Edward Elgar.

—— —— (1992) 'Commercial Banks, the Central Bank, and Endogenous Money', *Journal of Post Keynesian Economics* 14(3), pp. 297–310.

Yellen, J. (1984) 'Efficiency Wage Models of Unemployment', *American Economic Review, Papers and Proceedings,* 74, pp. 200–5.

Zahler, R. and Sussman, H. (1977) 'Claims and Accomplishments of Applied Catastrophe Theory', *Nature*, 269, pp. 759–63.

Zarnowitz, V. (1985) 'Recent Work on Business Cycles in Historical Perspective: A Review of Theories and Evidence', *Journal of Economic Literature*, June, pp. 523–80.

Zeeman, C. E. (1974) 'On the Unstable Behavior of the Stock Exchanges', *Journal of Mathematical Economics,* 1, pp. 39–44.

Zhang, W. (1991) *Synergetic Economics: Time and Change in Nonlinear Economics*, Berlin: Springer-Verlag.

INDEX

note: numbers in bold indicate where entry is discussed at length.

aggregate production functions 284
Akerlof, G. 46, 107, 163, 216, 228, 241, 260
Amadeo, E. 318
Arestis, P. 230
Arthur, B. 283, 290
aspiration gap **183**
Azariadis, C. 304

Ball, L. 65, 208
Barens, I. 320
bastard Keynesianism 42
Becker, G. 167
Bentham, J. 337
Bernanke, B. 215–18, 230, 245–46
Blanchard, O. 31–32, 66, 69, 138, 271, 304, 315
Blaug, M. 300–301
Blinder, A. 6, 69
Bourgeois, L. **159**

Calomiris, C. 258, 261
capital stock adjustment principle 71–2.
Caravale, G. 151
catastrophe theory 289
Champernowne, D. 63
chaos theory 289, 340
classical axioms 30
classical dichotomy 3–5, 53, 59, 68, 69, 128, 208
Clower, R. 132
Coase, R. 13, **43**
Colander, D. 120, 321
competition; perfect 129; imperfect 23–4, 129
Cooper, R. 64, 132, 259
coordination problems 64–7, 259, 281–2
Cottrell, A. 320
credit markets **201**
credit rationing and bank redlining 256–7
critical realism 69
Cross, R. 168

Davidson, P. 2, 67, 96, 181, 229–34, 237, 260, 299, 300, 301, 321, 355
Davis, J. 176
degree of competition 12, **15**, **39**, 58, 67
deposit insurance and bank insolvency, 254–5
distribution 104, 108, 367–9
Dobb, M. 70
Duesenberry, J. 95
Durkheim, E. 159
Dutt, A. 169–71, 181
Dymski, G. 239–40, 261

Earl, P. 240
Ees, H. 120
efficiency wages 103, 119, 122–5, **148**, 184–5; and aggregate demand 129–32
Einstein's general theory of relativity 15
Elster, J. 175
endogenous money 6, 21–2, 78–80, **201**, **205**, **214**, **339**
ergodic hypothesis 36
Evans, M. 95
exogenous money 6, **208**

Fair, R. 95
Farmer, M. 222
Farmer, R. 247, 261, 304, 319
Fazzari, S. 214–18, 232
Fischer, S. 271, 304, 315

Fisher, I. 13, **39**, 264
Friedman, M. 212; monetary rule 329
fundamental uncertainty 5, 29, 67, 90, 96, 202–3, **214**, **225**, **241**, **269**, 316

Galbraith, J. K. 15
Garrettsen, H. 120
general equilibrium, Walrasian; 287, 341; Marshallian, 287
Gerrard, B. 2
Gibson's paradox 76, 82
gold standard 75–6
Goodhart, C. 213
Gordon, R. 259, 279
Greenwald, B. 50, 55, 57, 70, 151, 201, 214, 220, 265–8
gross substitution, axiom of 23, 30–1

Hahn, F. 19, 51, 151
Hargreaves-Heap, S. 307–8, 313
Heim, C. 271
Hicks, J. 41, 95
Hodgson, G. 240
Hoover, K. 320
hysteresis **168**, **185**, 298

ignoratio elenchi 20, 60, 63, 136
imperfections, aggregate supply 18, 22; labour market **121**
implicit contracts **162**
incomes policies 325, **328**
inflation; cost 330
insider–outsider models 119, 302
interest rate policy **339**
interest rate rigidity 13, **201**
Isaac, A. 128
Isenberg, D. 239
ISLM model 41, 62, 168, 180, 210, 262, 290, 301

John, A. 64, 132, 259

Kahneman, D. 172–3, 178
Kaldor, N. 72, 93, 264, 337
Kaldor's law 72, 78
Kalecki, M. 203, **262**
Keynes John Maynard 286; Keynes effect 21, 41, 352; conventional behaviour 63, **175**, 317; critique of aggregate capital market 61; *Economic Consequences of the Peace* 176; essential properties of money 22–23, 30–31, 36, 62, 318; finance motive 211; *General Theory Of Employment, Interest, And Money* ix, 1, 11, 15, 17, 21, 25, 27, 58, 70, 153, 171, 299, 305, 314, 317, 334–5, 336; *How To Pay For The War* 16; monetary theory of production 4–5, 58, 62–4, 68, 339; on David Ricardo 25–26; on wages and employment 58–61, **106**; path dependency 174; real wage economy 59; response to Dunlop and Tarshis 22; shifting equilibrium model **170**; theory of effective demand 14, **15**, 68, 102, **106**, 318; *Treatise On Probability* 221
Kiyotaki, N. 66, 138
Kregel, J. A. 169–70, 236

Lawson, T. 1, 231
Layard, R. 126
LDC Debt Crisis, 255–6
Leijonhufvud, A. 23, 25
Levine, D. 271
Lindbeck, A. 107, 132
liquidity preference 201, 316–17
Littleboy, B. 181
Lorenz, H. 289–90
Lucas, R. 301, 314

Majewski, R. 94
Mankiw, N. G. 52, 56, 106, 245–6, 253, 260, 261, 277–9
Marshall, A. 21, 23, 70, 86
Marx, K. 271, 341–2
Matthews, R. 95
menu costs 53, 56, 70, 202, **205**, 263
methodological individualism 5, 13, 52, 54, 59, 62, 69, 70
Milgate, M. 68, 70
Minsky, H. 222–3, 238, 240, 270, 271, 298
Mishkin, F. 228, 236–7
Modigliani, F. 41
Moss, L. 69
multiplier/accelerator process 83–84, 95

natural law theory of tacit pacts **154**
neo-Keynesian economics 11, 280–81
neo-Ricardian economics 90–1
neoclassical synthesis 49, 106
neutral money, axiom of 30–31
new classical macroeconomics 11, 26, 45, 51, 62, 88–9, 120, 213, 230, 239, 241–3, 246, 262–3, 304–5, 325, 329
new deal policies 39–40
new Keynesian economics, defined 2–4, **51**, 87–8; strong NKE 13, 52, 275, 293–5,

new Keynesian economics (*contd.*)
303; weak NKE 14, 291–2; not Keynesian ix, 129, 325; Keynes-type questions (Keynesian Features) 49, 54–5, 64; labour market theory **39**, 55–6, **116**, **134**
new school for social research 94
non-accelerating inflation rate of unemployment (nairu) 4, 101–2, **118**, 126–8, 353
non-accelerating wage inflation rate of unemployment (nawru) 126–7
non-ergodicity 29, 326, 339

O'Donnell, R. 316–17
Okun's law 78, 92
old Keynesians **24**
orthodoxy, restrictive assumptions **15**

Patinkin, D. 23, 152, 314
Pesaran, H. 191–2
Pigou effect 41, 264, 352
Pigou, A. C. 13, 86, 101, 107, 328
positivism 13
Posner, R. 167
post Keynesian economics, defined 4–6, 89–90 230; see *incomes policies*; defined 5–7; theory of money and credit, 202, **214**; public policy 6, 35, **71**, **323**
post Keynesian study group 1, 6, 300
post Walrasian macroeconomics 243, **275**, **288**
price and quantity adjustments 81–6
price flexibility **71**
principal-agent models **241**, 326–7, **356**
Pufendorf, S. **155**

rational choice **153**
rational expectations 120
Richardson, G. B. 13, **42**
Robertson, D. 26,
Robinson, J. **41**, 230, 330, 337
Romer, C. 91–92
Romer, D. 65, 106, 205–6, 246, 261, 277–9
Rosser, B. 13, 52, 303
Rowthorn model **183**

Samuelson, P. 36
Sante Fe Institute 283
Sardoni, C. 70
Sawyer, M. 133
Say's law 27, 122, 120, 320, 349
Schefold, B. 35
Scoppola, B. **148**
self-fulfilling prophecies 294–5, 308–9
sensible expectations 30
sequence analysis 326
Shackle, G. 221, 240
Shapiro 139–40, 152
Smith, A. 87
social democracy 363–64
solidarist notion of quasi-contract **159**
Solow, R. 163, 166
speeds of adjustment of price and quantity 12, **15**
spillover effects 3, 14, 52, 65–6, 259–60
Sraffa, P. 70, 90
Steindl, J. 265
sticky prices **205**
Stiglitz, J. 50, 55, 57, 70, 139–40, 151–2, 201, 214–21, 228, 236, 241–2, 244, 248, 265–71, 280
strategic complementarities 3, 14, 52, 65
stylized facts **71**
sunspot theories 294–5, 308–9

technological change 85
Thom, R. 289–90
Tobin, J. 12, **15**, 52, 209, 264
Tversky, A. 172–73, 178

unemployment equilibrium (involuntary unemployment), Keynes 22–5, 34, 36, 63, 67, **106**, 348, and the price mechanism **39**; new Keyensian 46, 54, **55**
unemployment, fordist 123; shirking 125–6, 139,
unemployment, historical experience **121**

Variato, A. 232

wage determination, conflict in **182**
wage rigidity **106**, **118**
Walker, D. 287
Weiss, A. 152, 216–18, 228, 265
Weitzman, M. 135–7
Wells, P. 2
Williamson, S. 258–9, 261
Wray, L. 234–5

Yellen, J. 107